Jesus of Nazareth

Jesus of Nazareth

JÜRGEN BECKER

Translated by
James E. Crouch

WALTER DE GRUYTER
NEW YORK · BERLIN

About the Author

Jürgen Becker is Professor of the New Testament at the Christian Albrecht University of Kiel, Germany.

Library of Congress Cataloging-in-Publication Data
Becker, Jürgen, 1934–
   [Jesus von Nazaret. English]
   Jesus of Nazareth / Jürgen Becker ; translated by James E. Crouch
     p. cm.
   Includes bibliographical references and index.
   ISBN 3-11-015773-X (cloth).—ISBN 3-11-015772-1 (pbk. ; alk. paper)
   1. Jesus Christ—Biography.   I. Title.
   BT301.2.B35413   1998
   232.9′01—dc21
   [B]   97-48488
                                              CIP

Manufactured in the United States of America

10 9 8 7 6 5 4 3 2 1

Contents

Preface

There is no denying, even if I wished to do so, that the portrayal of Jesus that I offer in these pages has grown out of my activity as a university professor. In its methodology, its design, and its claims it is part of a world that has left its imprint on every page of the book. Yet, throughout the work I have tried to move beyond the narrow limits of academic scholarship and to build bridges to those who, although they have had no previous contact with formal theology, are looking for a picture of Jesus that is open to the modern understanding of historical truth without regarding the traditional faith of the church as obsolete.

Thus I am hoping that readers who are working toward, or have already earned, a theological degree will find the book both interesting and profitable and that my arguments will contribute to their own inner dialogue with the tradition of Jesus. At the same time, I have written for a wider circle of readers in the hope that they will derive pleasure from the book and will come to an understanding of the proclamation of Jesus that will open up to them texts that often are stubborn and unyielding.

To that end I have avoided in this book all purely philological arguments and words in ancient languages. I have simplified the technical discussion, limiting it to essential explanations, in order to focus attention on the major themes of the tradition of Jesus.

I also have attempted to make this study different from those books that systematically ignore the qualities in Jesus that are alien to the modern mind. These qualities, so foreign to our age, are quite understandable within the context of Early Judaism, and for that reason I talk about Early Judaism more in this book than is the case in many other books about Jesus.

Any attempt to offer a comprehensive portrayal of Jesus inevitably faces the difficulty of holding in tension two competing processes. One must analyze the individual traditions within the gospels while aiming at the same time for a synthesis, a presentation of the major themes of the preaching of Jesus. It seems to me that, in the tension between analysis and synthesis, the analytical side is always short-changed. For this reason in the following pages I have chosen to give the readers my reconstructions of the oldest extant textual traditions, in translation, followed by a section in small print in which I offer the analytical details that seem important to me. I hope that in this way I have made it possible for the readers both to understand my conclusions and to follow my arguments leading to those conclusions. Those who wish to do so can skip the fine print in order to follow the main line of argument. It should be understandable even without the sections in fine print.

This work, unlike my monograph on the Apostle Paul, offers at the beginning of each section a selection of the special, technical literature. At the end of the book I add a bibliography listing more general publications. Thus it should be possible for those persons who have access to a professional library to follow the general scholarly dialogue. Of course, one should be able to understand my own portrayal of Jesus without consulting other works. I have used footnotes infrequently in order to force myself to offer a presentation that is self-contained.

There is so much literature still being produced on Jesus that it can overwhelm an author who wants as much as possible not to overlook anything of importance. That I have been able to maintain creative joy in my own work has been due not least of all to W. G. Kümmel's reviews of the literature in: *Vierzig Jahre Jesusforschung (1950–1990)*, second edition, 1994, which make accessible an almost unmanageable wealth of diffuse material. From the remaining literature I would like to mention two books on Jesus that I have consulted regularly: the studies from the Catholic colleagues H. Merklein and J. Gnilka. I am delighted that in these conversations the ecumenical-exegetical dialogue can be conducted in such a congenial way. Finally, I owe a special word of professional gratitude to the authors in E. Kautsch's collected sources and in the series JSHRZ. I consulted their translations throughout this work, and in most cases I used them without specific notations.

I mention with sincere thanks those persons in the Institut für Neutestamentliche Wissenschaft und Judaistik who have stood by me in word and deed during the production of the book. Among them is Privatdozent Dr. U. Mell, who was always ready to give professional advice and to help with complicated computer questions. Mr. Chr. Franke proofread tirelessly in all stages of the manuscript's production. Later Mr. M. Schümers joined the project and performed a valuable service in putting together the index. Initially Mrs. R. Gerlich, then, with the bulk of the work, Mrs. M. Lorenzen, put into the computer the material that originated on my desk. Finally, I thank Dr. H. von Bassi for seeing the work through publication so smoothly.

Kiel, July 15, 1995
Jürgen Becker

1
Methodology

Becker, J. "Das Johannesevangelium im Streit der Methoden (1980–1984)," in: idem, *Annäherungen*, 204–81.

Berger, K. *Einführung in die Formgeschichtey*. Tübingen: Franke, 1987.

———. *Formgeschichte des Neuen Testaments.*

———. "Hellenistische Gattungen im Neuen Testament," in: *ANRW*. Berlin/New York: de Gruyter, 1984, II 25.2, 1031–1432, 1831–1885.

Birdsall, J. N. "The Continuing Enigma of Josephus' Testimony about Jesus," *BJRL* 67 (1985) 609–22.

Boring, M. E. "The Historical-Critical Method's 'Criteria of Authenticity': The Beatitudes in Q and Thomas as a Test Case," in: *The Historical Jesus and the Rejected Gospels.* C. W. Hedrick, ed. *Semeia* 44. Atlanta: Scholars Press, 1988, 9–44.

Bornkamm, G. "Evangelien, formgeschichtlich/synoptische," *Religion in Geschichte und Gegenwart.* Volume II. 3d ed. Tübingen: J.C.B. Mohr (Paul Siebeck), 1958, 749–66.

Breytenbach, C. "Das Problem des übergangs von mündlicher zu schriftlicher überlieferung," *Neotest* 20 (1986) 47–58.

Bultmann, R. *History.*

Conzelmann, H. and A. Lindemann. *Interpreting the New Testament: An Introduction to the Principles and Methods of New Testament Exegesis.* Peabody, MA: Hendrickson, 1988.

Dahl, N. A. *Jesus the Christ: The Historical Origins of Christological Doctrine.* Minneapolis: Fortress, 1991.

Dibelius, M. *From Tradition to Gospel.* New York: Scribners, 1935.

Egger, W. *How to Read the New Testament: An Introduction to Linguistic and Historical-Critical Methodology.* Peabody, MA: Hendrickson, 1996.

Ernst, J. *Anfänge der Christologie.* SBS 57. Stuttgart: KBW, 1972.

Farmer, W. R. *The Synoptic Problem. A Critical Analysis.* New York: Macmillan, 1964.

Feldman, L. H. *Josephus and Modern Scholarship 1937–1980.* Berlin/New York: de Gruyter, 1984, 680–84, 957–58.

Feneberg, R. and W. Feneberg. *Das Leben Jesu im Evangelium.* QD 88. Freiburg/Basel/Vienna: Herder, 1980.

Gerhardsson, B. *Memory and Manuscript.* ASNU 22. Uppsala: Almquist & Wiksells, 1961.

———. "Der Weg der Evangelientradition," in: *Das Evangelium und die Evangelien.* P. Stuhlmacher, ed. WUNT 28. Tübingen: J.C.B. Mohr (Paul Siebeck), 1983, 79–102.

Gnilka, J. "Das theologische Problem der Rückfrage nach Jesus," in: *Anfänge der Christologie.* Festschrift F. Hahn. C. Breytenbach and H. Paulsen, eds. Göttingen: Vandenhoeck & Ruprecht, 1991, 13–24.

Güttgemanns, E. *Candid Questions Concerning Gospel Form Criticism.* PThMS 26. Pitts-
    burgh: Pickwick, 1979.
Hahn, F. (ed.) *Der Erzähler des Evangeliums.* SBS 118/9. Stuttgart: KBW, 1985.
———. (ed.) *Zur Formgeschichte des Evangeliums.* Darmstadt: Wissenschaftliche
    Buchgesellschaft, 1985.
———. "Methodologische überlegungen zur Rückfrage nach Jesus," in: *Rückfrage nach
    Jesus.* K. Kertelge, ed. QD 63. Freiburg/Basel/Vienna: Herder, 1974, 11–77.
Jeremias, J. "Characteristics of the *ipsissima vox Jesu*," in: idem, *Prayers*, 108–15.
Kelber, W. H. "Die Anfangsprozesse der Verschriftlichung im Frühchristentum," in:
    ANRW. Berlin/New York: de Gruyter, 1992, II 26.1, 3–62.
———. *The Oral and the Written Gospel.* Philadelphia: Fortress, 1983.
Kingsbury, J. D. *Matthew as Story.* 2d ed. Philadelphia: Fortress, 1988.
Koch, D.-A. *Die Bedeutung der Wundererzählungen für die Christologie des Mark-
    usevangeliums.* BZNW 42. Berlin/New York: de Gruyter, 1975.
Kümmel, W. G., P. Feine, and J. Behm. *Introduction.*
Lehmann, M. *Synoptische Quellenanalyse und die Frage nach dem historischen Jesus.*
    BZNW 38. Berlin/New York: de Gruyter, 1970.
Lentzen-Deis, F. "Kriterien für die historische Beurteilung der Jesusüberlieferung in den
    Evangelien," in: *Rückfrage nach Jesus.* K. Kertelge, ed. QD 63. Freiburg/
    Basel/Vienna: Herder, 1974, 78–117.
Merkel, H. "Die Gottesherrschaft in der Verkündigung Jesu," in: *Königsherrschaft Gottes
    und himmlischer Kult im Judentum, im Urchristentum und in der hellenistischen
    Welt.* M. Hengel and A. M. Schwemer, eds. WUNT 55. Tübingen: J.C.B. Mohr (Paul
    Siebeck), 1991, 119–61.
Mussner, F. "Methodologie der Frage nach dem historischen Jesus," in: *Rückfrage nach
    Jesus.* K. Kertelge, ed. QD 63. Freiburg/Basel/Vienna: Herder, 1974, 118–47.
Nielsen, H. K. "Kriterien zur Bestimmung authentischer Jesusworte," *SNTU* 4 (1979) 5–26.
Ong, W. J. *Orality and Literacy.* New York/London: Methuen, 1983.
Pesch, R. *Jesu ureigene Taten? Ein Beitrag zur Wunderfrage.* QD 52. Freiburg/
    Basel/Vienna: Herder, 1970, 135–58.
Pokorný, P. "Zur Entstehung der Evangelien," *NTS* 32 (1986) 393–403.
Polkow, D. "Method and Criteria for Historical Jesus Research," *Society of Biblical
    Literature Seminar Papers* 26 (1987) 336–56.
Riesenfeld, H. *The Gospel Tradition and Its Beginnings.* London: Mowbray, 1957.
Riesner, R. *Jesus als Lehrer.* WUNT, Second Series 7. 3d ed. Tübingen: J.C.B. Mohr (Paul
    Siebeck), 1988.
———. "Der Ursprung der Jesus—Überlieferung," *ThZ* 38 (1982) 493–513.
Roloff, J. *Kerygma.*
Sanders, E. P. *The Question of Uniqueness in the Teaching of Jesus.* London: University of
    London Press, 1990.
Sauer, J. *Rückkehr und Vollendung des Heils,* Theorie und Forschung 133, 1991, 79–94.
Schmithals, W. *Das Evangelium nach Markus.* ÖTK 2/1; 2/2. 2d ed. Gütersloh: Mohn;
    Würzburg: Echter Verlag, 1986.
Schürmann, H. "Die vorösterlichen Anfänge der Logientradition," in: idem, *Traditions-
    geschichtliche Untersuchungen zu den synoptischen Evangelien.* Düsseldorf: Patmos,
    1968, 39–65.

Schwarz, G. *"Und Jesus sprach."* BWANT 118. 2d ed. Stuttgart: Kohlhammer, 1987.
Sellin, G. "'Gattung' und 'Sitz im Leben' auf dem Hintergrund der Problematik von Mündlichkeit und Schriftlichkeit synoptischer Erzählungen," *EvT* 50 (1990) 311–31.
Stein, R. H. "The 'Criteria' for Authenticity," in: *Gospel Perspectives* Volume I. R. France and D. Wenham, eds. Sheffield: JSOT, 1980, 225–63.
Strecker, G. "The Historical and Theological Problem of the Jesus Question," *TJT* 6 (1990) 201–23.
———. (ed.) *Minor Agreements*. GTA 50. Göttingen: Vandenhoeck & Ruprecht, 1993.
Tannehill, R. C. "Types and Functions of Apophthegms in the Synoptic Gospels," in: *ANRW*. Berlin/New York: de Gruyter, 1984, II 25.2, 1792–1829.
Teeple, H. C. "The Oral Tradition That Never Existed," *JBL* 89 (1970) 56–68.
Theissen, G. *Gospels in Context*.
Walker, W. O. "The Quest for the Historical Jesus. A Discussion of Methodology," *ATR* 51 (1969) 38–56.

Important questions are at issue in the modern discussion about historical truth: the question of methodology in our use of the sources, the basic philosophical question about our understanding of history or the nature of history, and the question of the human person itself as a historical being. With its essentially historical dimension theology cannot avoid this discussion, because the truth that it represents originated in the bright light of history and continues to be a historical truth. For theology, therefore, the question of historical truth is a fundamental problem—a problem that it must deal with for the sake of its own truth claims.

One of the more sensitive problem areas in this discussion, which is a continuing effect of the European Enlightenment, is the search for the historical Jesus of Nazareth, a search that began with the so-called Life-of-Jesus research in the eighteenth and nineteenth centuries as a primarily Protestant, middle-European phenomenon. This Life-of-Jesus research is, on the one hand, a good example of the way Christianity has approached its own historical origins in light of the challenges posed by modernity's historical understanding. That is to say, it shows how Christianity found the courage to create distance between itself and its normative beginnings and did not simply accept its present reality as self-evident. Instead, it used the insights derived from the new inquiry into its origins to begin a critical dialogue about itself.

This same Life-of-Jesus research became, on the other hand, a devastating example of how quickly the historical quest for Jesus was co-opted by modern ideals and options.[1] In the hands of an interpreter, texts are rather defenseless creatures. When gospel texts, separated from their traditional liturgical use, were exposed to the interpretive power of historical reasoning, the attack on them initially was unrestrained, often naive, and too seldom sensitive. That interpreters must exert some self-control and must pay special attention to the foreign and unique dimensions of the text before using it for their own purposes was a lesson that we first had to learn and that continually we must learn anew.

Under different conditions this classical Life-of-Jesus research has continued in a search for Jesus of Nazareth in the present century that has stimulated, precisely in this area, an international and ecumenical expansion of the inquiry. Indeed, we now have a solidly established Jewish engagement with the figure of Jesus and even the beginnings of a Muslim discussion of the issue. Along with this welcome expansion of interest in Jesus, there has come an unexpected increase in our knowledge of Early Judaism, i.e., of that period of time in Jewish history in which Jesus was active. Of course, the discussion about methodology has continued as well, but unfortunately we have here a divided market. A lively dialogue is going on in professional circles about questions of methodology while at the same time the public is overwhelmed by many books about Jesus that give free reign to undisciplined fantasy and that come close to surpassing the agony of the old Life-of-Jesus research.

How is this international dialogue to proceed? It should be clear that for the sake of its own truth Christianity must continue its historical-critical examination of its origins. Instead of dropping out of the discussion about historical thinking, we must continue what was positive in the old Life-of-Jesus research under the conditions given by the current discussion. That positive element, namely the distance we have achieved from our own origins, is fruitful precisely for the ecumenical and interreligious dialogue. It now is possible for us to recognize our own historically conditioned situation and thus to be less stubborn in insisting on our own point of view. This hard-won distance forces us to be modest when we press our arguments, knowing that in the final analysis we just might be wrong.

Even the negative features of the old and new Life-of-Jesus literature teach us a valuable lesson. Historical thinking does not manipulate sources or lapse into a euphoric never-never land by accident. In books about Jesus it happens as a rule in three stages. First, Jesus is divorced from the earliest traditions about him in Primitive Christianity. This separation is so thorough that it leaves an almost unbridgeable gulf between Jesus and the post-Easter churches, imputing to them changes in the Jesus tradition that cannot be verified in the texts. Indeed, frequently one does not even appeal to the witnesses for verification. The Jesus who is separated from any effect on subsequent events is then subtly stripped, albeit with quietly effective persistence, of everything that is not up-to-date or that does not agree with one's own intended interpretation. After this process of subtraction, one gathers what is left of the Jesus material into a portrait of Jesus that accomplishes precisely what one had wanted all along.

To see through such behavior is to learn to avoid it. We must especially keep in mind the tension between Jesus' proclamation and activity on the one hand and the creative reformulating of this tradition by the post-Easter churches on the other. Those who minimize or even deny the continuity in this complex process of action and reception end up with an artificially isolated Jesus, and at the same time they are forced to rewrite radically the history of Primitive Christianity. Easter's new beginning makes operative again in a special way the experience of

God that Jesus mediated with his person and his activity. This point of continuity is both theologically and historically of crucial importance, for such a comprehensive perspective created the conditions in which the churches after his death appropriated the individual traditions about Jesus.[2] Writing a book about Jesus, therefore, requires that we not only offer a comprehensive picture of Jesus that is well-grounded, but at the very least also outline how we understand the history of Primitive Christianity with Jesus as its beginning point. Naturally we must include this larger context in the interreligious and interconfessional conversation.

Now the complexity created by the special ways the early churches appropriated and reinterpreted the activity of Jesus not only tempts us to separate quickly and completely the quest of the historical Jesus from what followed him; it also can lead to the claim that we are able to sketch only a theological history of Primitive Christianity, not a historical picture of Jesus. If such an assertion were true, the search for a picture of Jesus using historical-critical tools would of necessity end in failure. From at least five points of view, illustrated in the following paragraphs, objections have been raised, sometimes individually, sometimes collectively, to justify the claim that a historical Jesus is beyond our reach.

Among the already classic justifications is a double-edged assertion: (1) Since it is no longer possible to understand how the post-Easter churches radically appropriated the Jesus material, the attempt to reconstruct the proclamation of Jesus can lead only to assumptions that are strongly hypothetical and that therefore can no longer command a consensus. (2) Since the faith of the church was grounded in the post-Easter kerygma and took its bearings from the risen Lord, theologically we are justified when we dispense with the quest for a picture of the historical Jesus.[3] Thus we should not be surprised, it is claimed, if the historical Jesus has disappeared unretrievably from the historian's view; indeed, theologically we can get along quite well without him.

One can see just how far the post-Easter reshaping of the Jesus tradition was able to go by comparing the Fourth Gospel with the other three or by comparing Matthew's Sermon on the Mount and Luke's Sermon on the Plain (Matt 5–7; Luke 6:20–49). It is clear, therefore, that the Jesus tradition was changed as it was passed on. At the same time we can often observe an astonishing consistency in the transmission of the tradition, so that a relatively broad consensus has emerged about a nucleus of synoptic material that can be attributed to Jesus and about some common features for a comprehensive understanding of the proclamation of Jesus. Among them is talk about the imminence of the Kingdom of God, which clearly was typical of Jesus. We can describe this central element of the proclamation of Jesus with some precision, and that in turn enables us to understand other statements of Jesus.

Jesus also remains, in spite of the total process of transmission, a concrete person. No one will deny, e.g., that Jesus died, that he performed miracles, and that he engaged in table-fellowship. Naturally there are within this consensus still variations in the details of the picture of Jesus. Such variety is only natural, given history's complexity and the finite visual and interpretative abilities of every person who tries to explain history. Yet one cannot cite this diversity as a major objection against producing an image of Jesus of Nazareth, for the breadth of diversity is limited and is not a matter of arbitrary whim. Furthermore, we must weigh rather than count the various interpretations of Jesus. We can dismiss many of them easily as arbitrary and false, and in the case of the serious interpretations we may, indeed we must, determine how hypothetical are the individual claims that make up each picture of Jesus.

Furthermore, those who want to abandon Jesus to history's obscurity must not only justify their decision in light of the Jesus traditions themselves, but must above all bring to the discussion their total understanding of Primitive Christianity. There is also an excessive confidence in the creative abilities of the post-Easter churches—a confidence born of the view that asking what happened before Easter is a theological fall-from-grace.

Nor is it the case that, as one occasionally reads, the gospels were not interested in history, and for that reason alone it is not possible to push back to Jesus. When the gospels define the time of Jesus as Christianity's normative primeval-time, they demonstrate their interest in the historical Jesus and show that they are not simply wanting to write a commentary on the post-Easter confessions of faith. Their alleged lack of historical interest simply cannot be used as an argument against looking for historically useful material in them.

Another objection against a search for Jesus comes from exegetes who are indebted to the discipline of literary criticism.[4] In one way or another they regard the gospels as autonomous formations, claiming that the creative process led to something so totally new that an analytical inquiry into what lies behind the literature is methodologically off limits.

While we owe a great deal to the discipline of literary criticism for its insights into the synchronic web of the narrative, we must resist the effort to absolutize the synchronic dimension, for even the surface of the gospel texts forces us to illuminate the diachronic background. By comparing analytically the parable of the banquet in Matt 22:1–14 and Luke 14:16–24, for example, not only can we better understand the way each gospel understands the parable; we can also push beyond them to an earlier form of the parable that is coherent in structure and content and at the same time has its own authority.[5] We could give numerous other examples.

There are, moreover, other phenomena. Mark frequently refers summarily to Jesus' teaching (1:14–15, 21–22, 38–39; 2:2, 13; 4:1–2, 33, etc.). Yet he clearly does so under the assumption that the church in essence knows this teaching. Papias, according to Eusebius, *Hist. eccl.* 3.39.4, still remembers that, "reports obtained from books . . . cannot have the same value as the living . . . oral testimony." Thus both the authors and the readers have in common a social memory with which one of them creates a new literary product and with which the others read and compare. From their background in Early Judaism, the people were accustomed to creating and reading that way. To illustrate with but one example: The author of *The Testaments of the Twelve Patriarchs* worked with a knowledge of the Genesis stories about the sons of Jacob and with many oral, especially wisdom, traditions. The readers of the resulting work came to their task with a knowledge of the Genesis narratives similar to that which the author brought to his work. When we ignore diachronic questions, we end up with unhistorical abstractions, and we ignore the authors and their recipients as real people. Only a combination of synchronic and diachronic questions does justice to this reality.

This literary and structuralist limitation on the text has led, in the third place, to a new way of thinking about the transition from oral to written tradition. It begins with the claim that oral tradition obviously is more fluid than is a tradition that is fixed in written form and then questions whether the fluid nature of loosely related material allows us, with the help of pregospel oral tradition, to determine with any precision what goes back to Jesus.[6]

Now it is true that for many reasons it is impossible to reconstruct an exact quotation from Jesus. Nor should we use literary creativity any longer as a model for creativity in the oral stage of the tradition. There is more room for narrative creativity in the oral phase of the tradition. Again we are not justified, however, in posing an unbridgeable gulf between the two phases. The relation, e.g., between the structure and the intended message of a form such as the parable, which Jesus clearly liked to use, was so strong that it limited the possible variety of meanings.[7] Thus in the act of oral repetition two factors were at work at the same time: the creative formulation in the present and the resistance to change in what was already there. As a result the synoptic tradition yields a rather broad picture: One time the will to reformulate can assert itself aggressively; the next time a saying resists change and is preserved in multiple attestations that are almost identical. Recognizing the customarily fluid nature of oral tradition, therefore, does not in and of itself a priori prevent the analytical reconstruction of the proclamation of Jesus. What it does do is warn us in our individual analysis not to underestimate how complex is the process of passing on a tradition.

The fragmentary nature of the tradition is often claimed as a fourth obstacle to the study of Jesus. It is asserted that, while the material may enable us to recognize individual tendencies, it does not permit us to draw up a comprehensive picture of Jesus without constructs that are simply too vague. Our interpretative evaluation of this material of necessity overemphasizes what is recognizable while it has no way of weighing what has been lost.

Now it is true that a comparison of the Gospel of Mark with the sayings source (i.e., the material that Matthew and Luke have in common beyond Mark's material and that they found already compiled), shows how in both sources there were rugged processes of selection at work, but it is not only Mark to whom material is available; Matthew and Luke at the same time offer material, each with a different process of selection. Moreover, it can scarcely be denied that in the synoptic area it is likely that the continuing process of collecting material was more dominant than was the suppression or subsequent restriction of traditional material. The passion narrative, for example, expands much more than it shrinks through sporadic abbreviation of the material.[8] Matthew and Luke are considerably more extensive than Mark, even though Matthew, e.g., shortens miracle stories and Luke avoids doublets.

Such examples clearly illustrate that in general in the synoptic tradition accumulating material takes precedence over eliminating or abbreviating material, although it is clear that the latter does happen.[9] The only way to proceed is to construct as precisely as possible a comprehensive picture from what is available to us, recognizing that material has been lost. Fortunately it is often the case that the traditions were formed in such a way that a whole Jesus was captured in an individual unit. We build a comprehensive picture of Jesus not simply by adding fragments from the synoptic gospels; these fragments themselves imply at the very least a comprehensive picture and thus provide conditions for a framework, a sense of direction, and relevant materials for a comprehensive picture. Thus a comprehensive picture of Jesus will be not so much a jigsaw puzzle that has been pieced together as a synthesis of folios, each of which is a self-contained picture and which together have been mounted on a wall.

Finally, and in the fifth place, we should by no means minimize the fact that Jesus spoke in the West Aramaic dialect, while we have the gospel tradition in Greek. This reality poses two related problems: We have no way of determining how reliably the translation was made from Aramaic to Greek. A language is not merely a phonetic medium of exchange; it also represents a culture. Languages are not interchangeable tools. One's mother tongue is, rather, an integral part of the development of the self and of the way one gives expression to life. Admittedly, the transition from Aramaic into Greek in the Primitive Christian tradition was relatively smooth, since the people doing the translating probably were bilingual Christians whose mother tongue was Aramaic. It is likely that they continued to live and think in Aramaic rather than in Greek, as is evidenced by the frequent examples of Semitizing Greek in the synoptic tradition. Yet this linguistic transition is another reason why traditional material can be traced back to Jesus only by analogy and not literally. While on occasion it might be helpful to translate from Greek back into the Semitic thought world, there is simply no way we can authenticate a literal reconstruction of Aramaic sentences of Jesus.[10] Semitisms in our present Greek text often are capable of other explanations and, even when it can be established with some certainty that they are Semitisms, they lead initially only to the Aramaic-speaking Jewish Christian church and not directly to Jesus. Another side to these arguments is that texts are not necessarily foreign to Jesus simply because they appear in good Koine Greek or, e.g., bear a markedly Lukan style. Such stylistic observations are clues, but they cannot by themselves justify the conclusion that the intention of a statement does not go back to Jesus.

Whether it is at all possible to conduct a search for Jesus is a question that has led again and again to an evaluation of the sources. Yet the sources themselves pose a further problem for us: Anything of substance that we know about Jesus comes to us only through Christian witnesses. There are no statements in the rabbinic tradition that can stand up against historical criticism,[11] and the passage from the Jewish historian Flavius Josephus, the famous *Testimonium Flavianum* (*Ant.* 18.63–64), that describes Jesus as a foundling is probably a Christian interpolation.[12] Even if we were to conjecture that the fragment is only partially a Christian revision, it still would be of no historical value for us.[13] Josephus does mention elsewhere (*Ant.* 20.200), in his report about the death of James the brother of Jesus, that he was "a brother of the Jesus" who is also called *Christ*. Even here, however, there are doubts about the authenticity of the reference to Jesus.

The Romans are somewhat more helpful. Tacitus (*Ann.* 15.44) and Suetonius (*Claud.* 25) are aware of first-generation, urban Roman Christians who appeal to Christ. Such sources are of interest for the history of early Christianity, but we gain nothing from them for a portrayal of Jesus. The same is true of Pliny (*Ep.* 10.96), who reports on the situation of the Christians in Bithynia at the beginning of the second century. In general we can say that non-Christian witnesses about the Christian churches (and thus by implication brief references to Jesus) first appear when conflicts break out between the Roman authorities and the churches.

Nor are the Christian sources all of equal importance. We must distinguish among the three synoptic gospels (i.e., Matthew, Mark, and Luke); the Gospel of John; the individual sayings of Jesus that, beginning with Paul, we find quoted here and there in Christian sources; and the other gospels, among which the Coptic-Gnostic Gospel of Thomas plays a special role.[14] All told, the discussion of these sources, apart from the four gospels in the New Testament canon, has led to the conclusion that at most, in an occasional individual case, they might help us bring some greater precision to our exegesis of the synoptic gospels. On the whole, however, we get no significant help from this material for a presentation of the proclamation of Jesus.[15]

The Fourth Gospel also occupies a special position. While it offers some help with a few biographical-historical questions, because of its christological stance it contributes nothing to an understanding of the message of Jesus. The image of a Jesus who claims to be sent by the Father differs in type and content so much from the Synoptics that we are forced to choose between presenting Jesus in synoptic terms or offering a Johannine Jesus. Faced with that alternative we must go with the Synoptics, for the Johannine christology, which leaves its mark on every detail of the Fourth Gospel, most certainly represents a late form of Primitive Christian theology. All of which is to say that our Christian sources, for all practical purposes, are limited to Matthew, Mark, and Luke.

Of course, these three synoptic gospels are not independent witnesses that we can use arbitrarily or even play off against each other, as is done all too often in popular literature about Jesus. They are bound together in a literary relationship for which the Two-Source Theory is still the best explanation.[16] The following sketch illustrates the theory.

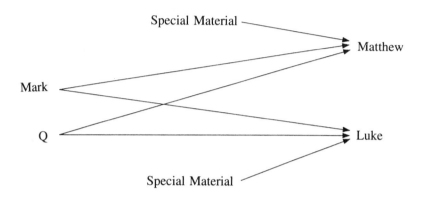

As this sketch shows, Mark is the oldest gospel. Matthew and Luke both base their work on Mark's gospel by following Mark's outline in their own presentation. In addition, independently of each other Mark's two coreporters make use of a collection of words of Jesus, namely the sayings source (Q), along with special material from their own churches. For the major gospels of Matthew and Luke we must assume, therefore, two independent sources, Mark and Q. It is likely, however, that the problem is even more complicated—that Matthew and Luke use not the canonical Gospel of Mark but slightly differing copies of that gospel. It is also probably the case that Matthew and Luke have slightly differing versions of the sayings source.[17] Yet these possibilities, even if they are all true, do not weaken the basic usefulness of the Two-Source Theory.

While it is true that this well-established hypothesis cannot answer all of the questions that the Synoptics raise, it is also true that the competing theories create more problems than they are able to solve.[18] The following presentation presupposes, therefore, the Two-Source Theory.

Almost as important is the recognition that the framework of the story of Jesus, as it was portrayed by Mark and taken over by his coreporters, is essentially the work of the earliest evangelist himself.[19] Apart from this Markan framework we have only individually transmitted units, small collections, and the passion narrative with its expanded narrative fabric. What we are really dealing with, therefore, is only the proclamation of Jesus along with a few nonrecurring (e.g., baptism, death) or typical (e.g., table-fellowship, miracles) biographical details. Given the nature of the sources, a biography of Jesus is out of the question. This judgment is true even with regard to the infancy narratives in Matt

1–2 and Luke 1–2, which independently of each other expand on their Markan source. These narratives, which serve as introductions to the story of Jesus, cannot be harmonized with each other. Indeed, their core affirmations also are at variance with other statements of Primitive Christianity (cf. §2).

Now in order to submit our analysis of the tradition lying behind the gospels to some sort of control, we must first of all come to an understanding about the forces that were at work in the process of receiving and transforming the synoptic material before it achieved its present literary form. Naturally we are not able to see all of the formative influences, but the following five consistently effective formative events certainly are the most typical.

At the head of the list is the recognition that the experience of and reflection on Easter meant that people appropriated the person and activity of Jesus by means of a direct christological interpretation. That Jesus claimed no christological titles for himself is clear not only from an analysis of the synoptic materials; examining the immediate post-Easter situation also leads to the conclusion that attributing christological meaning to the person of Jesus is the theological work of the post-Easter church.[20] Those people only obscure the situation, therefore, who describe the activity of Jesus in a general sense as messianic, in an attempt to drown out the christological discordance between the cross and the resurrection with a muted, albeit christological melody.

As soon as the post-Easter church is born, the synoptic tradition begins to be subjected to the pressures of the church's interests. In the narrative world, for example, the disciples now represent the church. The church's internal organization (Matt 18:15–20), its missionary activity (Mark 4:14–20 as an allegorical interpretation of Mark 4:3–8), the warning to individual members of the church (Luke 16:8–13 as an interpretation of Luke 18:2–7) all leave their mark on the tradition. The second and third generations continue the process. The normalization of Christian life, e.g., leads to the Sermon on the Mount (Matt 5–7) as the Matthean church's pattern for living.

Of course, the tension between Jewish and Gentile Christianity that threatened to tear apart the first Christian generation also left its traces in the texts (clear examples are Mark 13:10 and Matt 28:19). A related and currently controversial problem is the issue of Jesus' own continuity with and criticism of the Torah. It is only natural that this crucial difference between Jewish and Gentile Christianity would have influenced the tradition about Jesus. Compositions such as Matt 5:17–48 and Mark 2:1–3:6 originate against this background. Indeed, since the post-Easter churches' avowed reason for accepting the Jesus material is to consolidate their position, it is natural that they would reveal that position by the way they reformulate traditions on this theme.

It is clear that the attitude toward time and history changes during the course of Primitive Christianity. Jesus maintained that the end-time began with him (cf. §4.2.2). A later age looked back on his time as the primeval period of Christianity, which, although temporally in the past, was normative for all time. Since all of the gospels regard the time of Jesus that way, they shape their portrayal of it from a Christian perspective so that it is connected to an Israelite prehistory of promise, which then was fulfilled in Jesus. One thinks, by way of example, of Matthew's formula quotations.

The gospels also closely relate the time of the fathers, i.e., the first generation of Primitive Christianity, to the time of Jesus. Their purpose in so doing is to present an almost seamless continuity between Jesus and the apostles after Easter. Jesus can thus predict his death and resurrection (cf., e.g., Mark 8:31–32 parr.; 9:31–32 parr.; 10:32–34 parr.), ordain the disciples as apostles, or grant Peter special importance in the church (Matt 10:1–4; 16:17–19). Thus the gospels repress the element of surprise that originally was part of Easter, and they gloss over the distinctions between pre-Easter discipleship and post-Easter community as Church.

By the time the gospels were written, Christianity had long since given up its belief that the end was near. To be sure, the evangelists' generation still understood itself to be living in a general sense at the end of history, but it was aware of a lengthening of the time until the end. Since the time of Jesus was the primeval time of all Christian history, it was necessary that Jesus make specific statements about the delay of the end and about what would happen after he appeared. Thus Jesus becomes the announcer of the Christian history that was to begin after his death; indeed he reports about world history in general (e.g., Mark 13; Matt 24–25).

Once we have caught a vision of the Jesus material in the process of being appropriated and passed on, we most likely will no longer be able to explain the synoptic tradition simply as the literal transmission of that material. It appears, rather, as a changing, living history. We may regret that, because of the nature of our sources, we must live with a great deal of uncertainty in our analytical reconstruction of the oldest Jesus material. Often the difficulties are insurmountable. We may not argue, however, for the reliability of the tradition by claiming that the disciples of Jesus constituted a school in which the pupils memorized his sayings—that is, by removing the post-Easter transmission of the Jesus material from the dialectic of tradition and reinterpretation. There is simply no basis in the texts for that kind of argument.[21]

Those who hold such a point of view reveal the weakness of their position when, in a flanking move, they postulate that the burden of proof for the authenticity of a tradition lies not with the tradition but with those who question its reliability.[22] Such a requirement naturally inoculates a tradition against criticism and prejudices the decision in favor of the claim of reliability. We can grant serious consideration to a line of argument, however, only when it bases its judgment about a tradition on an analysis of the material itself. Premature judgments about the question of authenticity are not in order;[23] valid is only the tedious process of evaluating all observations and then, as a final result, assessing the results. Those who begin their study prejudiced in favor of one or the other assumption naturally as a rule will reach conclusions that confirm their prejudice. Such a concocted result has little to do with a line of reasoning that is worth discussing.

How then can we construct such a line of reasoning? Synoptic scholarship is working on criteria for judging the authenticity of traditional material, although the scope, the relative value, and the sequence of such criteria are still matters of controversy. In the present state of affairs we must suspend all individual linguistic and form-critical criteria. Jesus' designation of God as *abba* or his custom of beginning a sentence with "Amen, I say to you . . . "—two phenomena that most frequently are mentioned in this context—do not represent valid criteria. Nor can we use the form of the parable or the frequent appearance of parallelisms that, although formally symmetrical, differ in their specific contents (a phenomenon that stands out in the synoptic material).[24] Even if we grant that these phenomena go back to Jesus, we cannot exclude the possibility that the church itself further cultivated these ways of speaking and of forming the material. Observations about vocabulary and form are appropriate only at the end of our analysis; they cannot serve as criteria.

It is different, of course, with criteria that, rather than focusing on details, establish a line of reasoning that one can follow. A discussion of such criteria is not only meaningful; it is necessary, because it helps us compare individual methods of analytical thinking.[25] It also helps us present consistent and lucid arguments that are not subject to arbitrary change. What we are talking about here is methodological consistency.

The first and fundamental criterion of this kind for the analysis of an individual tradition is the criterion of dissimilarity.[26] It is justifiably the most generally accepted criterion; indeed, some use it exclusively. It claims a tradition as authentic Jesus material when its content is unique in two contexts, Early Judaism and Primitive Christianity, and thus can lay claim to originality in both areas. The criterion is weakened when one does not apply it consistently—that is to say, when one applies it rigorously when comparing Jesus to the later church but only timidly when comparing him to Early Judaism.

The criterion also self-destructs when the demand for originality is so unrealistic that the only thing left of Jesus is a solipsistic phantom. It should go without saying that we can use this criterion only when we understand that every person is part of a historical nexus and that the individuality of Jesus that we seek to discover occurred only within the culture of Early Judaism and thus must be understood today in that context. It is also true, of course, that the early church also lives in continuity with Jesus.

We are not saying, therefore, that Jesus is to be understood primarily as a nomad in world history, which in the final analysis would be to understand him unhistorically. To use the criterion of dissimilarity is, rather, to elevate to the center of the discussion of authenticity that which is especially and unmistakably characteristic of him in order to begin with the best possible basis for a more comprehensive understanding of Jesus. The criticism that this criterion has at-tracted,[27] when examined by the light of day, speaks only to its misuse as the only criterion rather than to its use to secure a beginning nucleus of material. The criterion is by far without peer when we understand that its goal is to find an unmistakable nucleus of Jesus material that is at one and the same time an expression of his Jewish context and an antecedent that stands in continuity with Primitive Christianity.[28]

Thus what we are saying, albeit cautiously, is that the criterion of dissimilarity is a beginning criterion for the task at hand. Were we to stop there, doubtless we would omit much from the proclamation of Jesus that belongs to it. Once we have used this criterion to determine authentic core traditions, however, we must go further. The originality that results from the criterion of dissimilarity is never absolute; it is always found in larger contexts, which in every detail claim originality in at least some aspect. Now each individual saying presupposes a world in which it lives and from which it comes to expression. Other material, while lacking a distinctiveness that is immediately noticeable, may nevertheless be part of the same world. This sharing of worlds is the basic aspect of the principle known as the criterion of coherence, and the more clearly the new material can become part of the fabric of the authentic material, the easier it is to use this criterion with confidence. It is especially helpful in this regard when material appears more than once. In that case the phenomenon is often cited separately as the criterion of multiple attestation.

In any case, the principle of coherence enables us to outline both qualitatively and quantitatively a comprehensive view of the proclamation of Jesus. This outline then for its part should agree both with the way Jesus lived his life and as much as possible with his destiny as one who was executed as a criminal. Thus the principle of coherence applies both to the activity of Jesus in word and deed and to his fate. Of course, as with every other historical person, we must allow for a certain amount of tension. We may demand unambiguous consistency in the field of logic, but not with historical persons. A too-smoothly constructed total view of Jesus is in danger of being historically one-dimensional. Still, we must explain the tensions within a total picture of Jesus and consider whether they could not better be explained as resulting from the process of receiving and passing on the material.

This last observation calls attention to another criterion that may help confirm our judgments, even if it does not by itself create new analytical possibilities. The criterion of dissimilarity and the criterion of coherence direct attention from the present level of the texts back to Jesus. What we also need, however, is the re-verse proof that reasons from Jesus to the present text. Assuming, e.g., that the beatitudes of Luke 6:20–21 par. belong to the proclamation of Jesus, we should be able to understand from precisely this beginning the entire history of the synoptic beatitudes. This line of reasoning, so familiar to text critics (that text has the best claim to originality from which all others can be explained as variants), could well be used in the diachronic exegesis of the Synoptics more than is commonly acknowledged. That is to say, if it is true not only that the textual fabric of the literary surface of the gospels is a new creation out of traditional material, but also that the same is true for every stage in the diachronic process of the tradition, then we must explain, as much as possible, the creative impulse in each individual case. It would be difficult to exaggerate how much we could gain on behalf of the proclamation of Jesus—i.e., how much better would be the quality of our reasoning—if we could thus make transparent the history of a single tradition.[29]

Now in the following presentation we cannot always use all of these criteria for each synoptic text that we discuss. We will, of course, not simply lay out the criteria here at the beginning and then present the proclamation of Jesus thematically, but the desire to lay out a repeatable line of reasoning for each decision is limited by the need to produce a book that is readable and not too long. I hope to have achieved a reasonable compromise by offering in most cases, the first time they appear, the important texts in translation in their probable earliest form, followed by an excursus in smaller print, which summarizes the reasons for the decisions implied by the translated text. In addition, in discussing an individual theme of the proclamation of Jesus I will begin the relevant section with the critical minimum established by means of the criterion of dissimilarity, and then I will expand the material with further evidence.

I will also offer the translation in verse, because in a traditional culture the aphorism, with its formal qualities that make it easily grasped, is typical of prophets, philosophers, and priests. Corresponding to this external form is the content with its epigrammatic sayings, terse ideas, and graffitilike style (cf. Eccl 12:9, 11). A final quality of the aphorism is the immediacy with which it engages the listener. One gets to the point quickly without worrying about a balanced presentation. One does not simply address the hearers intellectually; one confronts them existentially. One offers mnemonic aids with material that is gripping, irritating, scandalous, and often presented in doublets.[30]

There is an increasingly positive attitude today about the trustworthiness of the synoptic tradition, especially when compared with the early days of Form Criticism. This change is due in part to the fact that today we recognize two false judgments that earlier fed historical skepticism:[31] the assumption that only ideally formed, simple traditions can be original, and an exaggerated view of the creative power of the church to which everything was attributed at the slightest suspicion that something might not be authentic. While it is true that we needed to move beyond the earlier skepticism, today's more positive attitude unfortunately reveals a wholesale assertion within a general milieu, which for historical scholarship simply is not adequate. Therefore, we conclude this section on methodology by emphasizing again that we must submit both general skepticism and general trust to trial by fire and that we can do that only in the analysis of each individual tradition.

NOTES

1. Cf. the classic work on this phenomenon, Schweitzer, A., *Quest*.

2. We are indebted to E. Schillebeeckx for having recognized again in a systematic way the connection between Jesus of Nazareth and his continuing effect. J. Gnilka (*Jesus*, 26) has recently confirmed this basic insight.

3. More recent representatives of this position, e.g., are W. Schmithals, *Markus*, and G. Strecker, "Problem," both of whom in their approach go back to R. Bultmann. L. Schottroff offers a sociohistorical variation of this approach in L. Schottroff and W. Stegemann, *Jesus*, 5–6.

4. A recent example of this direction is J. D. Kingsbury, *Matthew*.

5. For other examples cf. J. Becker, "Streit."

6. Cf. E. Güttgemanns, *Questions*; W. J. Ong, *Orality*; C. Breytenbach, "Problem"; G. Sellin, "Gattung"; W. H. Kelber, "Anfangsprozesse."

7. Cf., e.g., W. Harnisch, *Gleichniserzählungen*. One can see the same relationship in other forms, whereby the basic principle is: Whenever a statement captures something that is noteworthy, unusual, unexpected, or pithy (cf., e.g., the hyperboles in Mark 9:43–48 parr., 10:25 parr., the announcement of the imminence of the Kingdom of God in Luke 11:20, or the blessing of the poor in Luke 6:20–21 par.), there is likely to be little change in the tradition. The opposite is also true: Statements that appear as part of the normal world of the bearers of the tradition are less likely to make an impact on their memory and thus are more likely to be changed.

8. Cf. W. Reinbold, *Bericht*, 75–76.

9. Such a phenomenon is not surprising in light of observations from analogous traditions. See, e.g., H. Donner, *Aufsätze*, 279–85.

10. G. Schwarz's translation of the words of Jesus back into Aramaic leads in part to completely new constructions, postulated with all the certainty of apodictic pronouncements, but methodologically it stands on such precarious ground that it offers little help.

11. Cf. J. Maier, *Jesus*.

12. Cf. E. Schürer, *History*, I 428-441; L. H. Feldman, *Josephus*, 680-691; J. P. Meier, *Jew*, I 56-88; W. Reinbold, *Bericht*, 297-300.

13. One of the recent attempts to divide the text of Josephus into Christian additions and a Jewish remnant is that of J. H. Charlesworth, *Jesus within Judaism*, 90–102. Charlesworth eliminates what makes sense only from a Christian point of view without considering the syntactic fabric of the text. This methodologically questionable approach leads at best to a few bits of information about Jesus that also appear in the gospels. When W. Reinbold claims to find even more reliable historical reports in the pre-Christian version of Josephus, he overinterprets the text (*Bericht*, 300). J. N. Birdsall is justifiably more cautious.

14. Cf. W. Schneemelcher, *Apocrypha*, Vol. 1.

15. J. D. Crossan differs, granting much more significance to the nonsynoptic Jesus material than is justified (*Jesus*, 427–50).

16. Cf. W. G. Kümmel, *Introduction*, §5.

17. Cf. most recently G. Strecker, *Agreements*.

18. Among the more recent attempts to explain the synoptic relationships without recourse to the Two-Source Theory, cf. W. R. Farmer, *Problem*, and W. Schmithals, *Markus*.

19. Cf. K. L. Schmidt, *Rahmen*. In this regard the abiding contribution of Dibelius and Bultmann, the classical representatives of Form Criticism, is clear.

20. Cf. J. Becker, *Epoche*, §§2.2–2.3.

21. Contra B. Gerhardsson, *Memory* and R. Riesner, "Ursprung."

22. Thus, e.g., P. Stuhlmacher, *Theologie*, 44–46.

23. Thus, e.g., J. Sauer, *Rückkehr*, 81–84.

24. Manson was the first to describe this phenomenon (*The Teaching of Jesus* [Cambridge: Cambridge University Press, 1931] 54–56). Recently M. Reiser has argued for it as a criterion (*Gerichtspredigt*, 194–96).

25. Cf. the summaries of this debate offered by W. O. Walker, "Quest"; F. Hahn, "Überlegungen," 32–37; F. Lentzen-Deis, "Kriterien," 78–117; M. E. Boring, "Criteria"; J. Sauer, *Rückkehr*, 79–94.

26. This criterion is also known as the criterion of distinctiveness. [The usual German term, which the author uses in the original, is *Differenzkriterium*. Tr.]

27. H. Merklein has recently produced a brief summary of the discussion (*Gottesherrschaft*, 132–35).

28. It is important to recognize that the designation *unmistakable* is a purely historical judgment, just as all human beings as individuals are unmistakable, and especially as great persons have distinguishing characteristics. We must reject even the hint of a christologically tinted use of such terms as *uniqueness* or *singularity*. In a historical presentation of Jesus it would justify the charge of a false apologetic, and it would saddle christological reflection with hopeless problems.

29. Naturally this kind of reverse test is not to be understood mechanically as a second part of the analysis. It can, of course, be integrated into the use of the other two criteria.

30. Cf. W. H. Kelber, "Anfangsprozesse."

31. R. Bultmann's *Tradition*, one of the classical works of Form Criticism, serves as a prime example of such skepticism.

2

Biographical Matters

Alt, A. "Die Stätten des Wirkens Jesu in Galiläa," in: idem, *Kleine Schriften zur Geschichte des Volkes Israel*. Volume 2. Munich: Beck'sche Verlagsbuchhandlung, 1953, 436–55.

Anderson, J. N. D. *Jesus Christ. The Witness of History*. Downers Grove, IL: InterVarsity, 1985.

Blinzler, J. *Trial*, 101–8.

Braunert, H. "Der römische Provinzzensus und der Schätzungsbericht des Lukasevangeliums," *Historia* 6 (1957) 192–214.

Conzelmann, H. "Jesus Christus."

Dinkler, E. "Petrus," in: *Religion in Geschichte und Gegenwart*. Volume 5. 3rd ed. Tübingen: J.C.B. Mohr (Paul Siebeck), 1961, 247–49.

Dockx, S. *Chronologies néotestamentaires et Vie de l'Eglise primitive*. Paris/Gembloux: Duculot, 1976.

Finegan, J. *Handbook of Biblical Chronology*. Princeton, NJ: Princeton University Press, 1964.

Galling, K. (ed.) *Textbuch zur Geschichte Israels*. 3rd ed. Tübingen: J.C.B. Mohr (Paul Siebeck), 1979.

Hoehner, H. W. *Chronological Aspects of the Life of Christ*. 5th ed. Grand Rapids, MI: Zondervan, 1981.

Instinti, H.-V. *Das Jahr der Geburt Christi*. Munich: Kösel, 1957.

Jeremias, J. *Eucharistic Words*, 36–41.

Kee, H. C. "The Transformation of the Synagogue after 70 CE: Its Import for Early Christianity," *NTS* 36 (1990) 1–24.

Klauck, H.-J. *Judas—Ein Jünger des Herrn*. Freiburg: Herder, 1987.

Kuhn, H.-W. and R. Ariv. "The Bethsaida Excavations," in: *The Future of Early Christianity: Essays in Honor of H. Koester*. B. A. Pearson et al., eds. Minneapolis: Fortress, 1991, 77–106.

Ogg, G. *The Chronology of the Public Ministry of Jesus*. Cambridge: Cambridge University Press, 1940.

Pesch, R. "Petros," in: *EWNT* Volume 3. 2nd ed. (1992) 193–201.

Schmahl, G. *Die Zwölf im Markusevangelium*. TThSt 30. Trier: Paulinus, 1974.

Schneemelcher, W. *Das Urchristentum*. Urban TB 336. Stuttgart: Kohlhammer, 1981, 43–53.

Schwarz, G. *Jesus und Judas*. Stuttgart: Kohlhammer, 1987.

Strobel, A. "Der Termin des Todes Jesu," *ZNW* 51 (1960) 69–101.

———. *Ursprung und Geschichte des frühchristlichen Osterkalenders*. Berlin: Akademie, 1977, 70–121.

Trilling, W. "Zur Entstehung des Zwölferkreises," in: *Die Kirche des Anfangs*. Festschrift
    H. Schürmann. R. Schnackenburg et al., eds. Freiburg: Herder, 1978, 201–22.
Vogler, W. *Judas Iskarioth*. ThA 42. 2nd ed. Berlin: Evangelische Verlagsanstalt, 1985.
Wells, G. A. *The Historical Evidence for Jesus*. Buffalo, NY: Prometheus, 1982.

Historians who insist on a cautious approach to the biographical details of the life
of Jesus—even those who do not regard themselves as agnostic historians—are
able to offer only the shabbiest of fare. While the scant biographical information
passed on to us by Primitive Christianity occasionally tempts people to expand
this meager menu by citing allegedly unobserved clues in the sources or even by
appealing to astronomy, until now all such attempts have been short-lived. Nor
do clever constructs and optimistic affirmations offer an acceptable way of satis-
fying the understandable desire for more information about Jesus. The nature of
our sources simply places limitations on our knowledge of Jesus, and those who
have refused to accept these limitations have always, like Icarus of old, flirted
with disaster. It is not a hypercritical attitude but rather the sober evaluation of
the sources that forces us to admit that there is little that we can know about the
life of Jesus.

We should not be tempted, as is sometimes done, to blame our ignorance
simply on missing sources as if, were we to discover new texts, we could shed
more light into this darkness. Nor is our limited biographical information due
simply to the kerygmatic nature of the gospels, although that the concerns of
preaching are a factor is clear even to those who do not believe that the early
Christian kerygma prevented Primitive Christianity from having an interest in
history. The restriction on our knowledge is rooted primarily in Antiquity's
general historical attitude. It is only in the modern age, since the classical and
romantic periods, that we have begun to understand people developmentally.
That is to say, in order to understand historical figures as personalities we put
them in social, political, and cultural contexts; we probe their most basic inner
attitudes to discover motives and goals that drive their development; and we try
to discover how their predecessors and contemporaries influenced them.

Antiquity had no interest in this kind of developmental approach. Here the
historian was interested primarily in the subject's public role and activity and
what that person might mean for the polis or for philosophy or for discoveries
that might benefit humanity. If it served those ends one might also speak of the
person's background (if, e.g., of noble ancestry) or training at the hands of a
famous teacher. Or one might describe the person in question as self-disciplined
or quick-tempered. A biography from a developmental point of view, however,
was simply foreign to the ancient mind. Any attempt to fill the gaps in our
knowledge of Jesus by trying to discover his development, his emotions, his
experience, or his character with the claim that one can recognize such things
lying behind the synoptic texts, will end up with biographical fantasy.

Another factor that kept Jesus or one of his followers or family members or contemporaries from collecting written material for a biography of Jesus in the way that one would ordinarily expect for a public figure was that they all lived, as we have seen in §1, in a traditional, nonliterary culture. There are no records about Jesus in a village registry of Nazareth (or Capernaum). No one preserved an itinerary, such as may have been available to Luke for Paul's journeys. Nor did his hearers preserve in transcriptions of his speeches what seemed to them to be important; all synoptic addresses are later compositions. What struck people as noteworthy about Jesus was preserved, rather, as specially formed sayings in rhythmic language, in apophthegmatic units (in which a special figure offers an authoritative saying, which is framed as a solution to a problem that has been posed), and in narrative material about him (e.g., miracle stories). That is to say, information about and from Jesus in the oldest layer of the material is shaped in an episodic, conventional way that has no interest in biographic continuity. Even the sequence of the pericopes in Mark is a contribution of the first evangelist himself. We might note by way of comparison that often our knowledge of pre-Socratic or other figures from Antiquity is dependent on this traditional way of preserving information.

When we compare what we know today about other persons from the ancient world who lived in traditional cultures we are amazed at how much we do know about Jesus. We know much less about other historically important persons from Antiquity. Indeed, we know less about immediate contemporaries of Jesus such as Annas, Caiphas, Pilate, John the Baptist, Peter, James (the brother of Jesus), or even the mother of Jesus.

Thus our limited information about Jesus in no way justifies the claim that Primitive Christianity relegated him to history's darkness. Given the limitations posed by Antiquity's attitude, there is ample evidence to the contrary. The origins of the formation of early Christian confessions (e.g., Rom 1:3b–4; 1 Cor 15:3b–4; Gal 4:4) as well as the beginnings of the synoptic tradition (e.g., Mark 6:1–6; 14–15) preserve specific biographical information, admittedly from a particular point of view. Are the table-fellowships in Galilean villages, miracles, conflicts about the Sabbath, etc. not glimpses of the public activity of Jesus with a biographical interest?

Our discussion of the sources in §1 focused on the public figure of the adult Jesus and his importance for the gospels and for the formation of the earliest confessions. Yet there are the infancy narratives in Matt 1–2 and Luke 1–2.[1] Do they not offer concrete biographical information? At first glance the answer is yes, but on further reflection the answer must be no. These two efforts to describe at least something of the life of Jesus before his public appearance are incompatible with each other. They pursue different interests and goals, and they preserve in the style of popular piety themes and motifs that in Antiquity also appear in stories about other persons. Thus they have little historical value. This judgment is especially true of the statements about the ancestry and birth of Jesus. The two divergent genealogies (Matt 1:1–17; Luke 3:23–38) are more than likely the result of scribal work done by comparing various Septuagint texts. A special element in both infancy cycles is the reference to Bethlehem as the place of Jesus' birth (Matt 2:1; Luke 2:4), but it stands in direct contradiction to the dominant Nazareth tradition of all of the gospels (Mark 1:9; 6:1–6; John 1:45–46; Acts 10:38; also Mark 1:24; 10:47; Luke 18:37; John 18:5, etc.). The virgin birth (Matt 1:18–25; Luke 1:26–38) also appears only in the infancy narratives and is in tension with the statements elsewhere that imply a normal birth (Gal 4:4; John 6:42; indirectly also Mark 6:1–6).

The statements in the infancy narratives that appear to justify an absolute chronology likewise have no historical value. The census (Luke 2:1–3) is based on a Lukan error,[2] and there is no way to define the star of Matt 2:1–12 astronomically,[3] since there is no such thing as a star that rises in the east, then moves at a human pace from the north in a southerly direction (i.e., from Jerusalem to Bethlehem) in order then to remain stationary over a house.

In their totality, therefore, the infancy narratives do not offer us access to the earliest childhood of Jesus. What we can know about Jesus historically remains limited to the time of his public activity, beginning with his baptism at the hands of John the Baptist and ending with his crucifixion at the hands of Pilate. This information consists, furthermore, of incidental items about his background and his family. As we have seen, all four evangelists agree that Jesus comes from Nazareth, information confirmed by Acts 2:22; 3:6, etc. In Mark 6:1 the evangelist clearly is thinking about Nazareth, since he has already named Nazareth as the place from which Jesus came (1:9, 24). The Synoptics and John agree (Mark 6:1–6; John 1:45; 6:42) that Nazareth was the home of his parents, Joseph and Mary (or, in the Semitic form of her name, Miriam). It is possible that Joseph had died before Jesus appeared publicly, since, outside the infancy narratives, Joseph is mentioned less frequently than Mary, and then only in references to his family background (where, again, the Synoptics and John agree: Luke 4:22; John 1:45; 6:42). The parents of Jesus had four other sons and at least two daughters (Mark 6:3; 1 Cor 9:5; John 2:12; 7:1–9).[4] Jesus' father was a woodworker, an occupation that Jesus also learned (Mark 6:3).[5]

Jesus' name goes back to Joshua, the successor of Moses. It was a popular name in those days as, indeed, all biblical names were. The brothers of Jesus, e.g., bear names of the patriarch Jacob and his sons. That Joseph's family was able to claim Davidic descent is perhaps historical (cf. Rom 1:3; Matt 1:1–17 par.; Eusebius, *Hist. eccl.* 3.20.1–6).[6] In the time of Early Judaism most people wanted to have a family tree, even if it was a recent creation. Davidic descent did not mean, however, that one belonged to a leading family, and it certainly did not automatically mean that one was a messianic pretender.

Jesus probably left his family home in Nazareth in order to go to John the Baptist. Josephus similarly withdrew to the desert to live for three years with the hermit Bannus (*Life* 7–12). Had people been required in those days to carry an identification card, in the case of Jesus one would have read *single, with no permanent address,* although the latter would have been true only after he left home.

When did Jesus appear publicly, and how old was he at the time?[7] Luke 1:5; 3:1–2, 23, and John 2:20 combined with 8:57 give possible answers. According to Luke, Jesus was about thirty years old when, in about 28 CE, John the Baptist and, then soon thereafter, Jesus appeared. John suggests the same date, but here Jesus is already fifty years old. To be sure, his age is approximate in both cases, and we cannot be completely certain of the dates we derive from the texts. Furthermore, Luke is not always trustworthy when he synchronizes his narrative with world history. To be more precise: He often was wrong.[8] With both Luke and John we simply have no way of knowing what the source of their information was. There is a general tendency to regard the date as approximately correct and to prefer Luke's statement about the age of Jesus to that of John.[9] Given the nature of our sources, any attempt to be more precise involves so many hypothetical constructs that in the final analysis its allegedly unambiguous result is too uncertain to be of any use.[10]

Most people place the death of Jesus in the year 30 CE, and this date fits well with the chronology of Primitive Christianity, especially that of Paul.[11] All of the gospels state that Jesus was executed during a Passover festival, and all of them agree that he died on a Friday, i.e., the day before a Sabbath. Beyond that, however, there are problems surrounding the date. The synoptic gospels (to be more precise: Mark's passion narrative, which the others follow) identify the Friday in question as the fifteenth of Nisan (Mark 14:12–16), while for John it is the fourteenth of Nisan (John 13:1, 29; 18:28; 19:14, 31). There is no way to harmonize this discrepancy.

Both versions make theological statements. In Mark, Jesus is able to celebrate his last meal with the disciples on the previous evening as a Passover meal. According to John, Jesus is the true Passover lamb, since he dies on the cross at the very moment when the Passover lambs are slaughtered in the temple (John 19:31). Thus his farewell dinner with the disciples cannot be a Passover meal (John 13:1ff.). Since Mark's claim that the last supper was a Passover meal is part of his redactional framework, it is likely that we should not follow him here. The heart of the Markan Lord's-Supper tradition (Mark 14:22–25), as well as all other Lord's-Supper traditions (1 Cor 11:23–26; John 6:51c–58; *Did.* 9–10), does not presuppose the setting of a Passover meal. If John is correct here it would explain the early belief that Christ is the Passover lamb of Christianity— that is to say, that his death, occurring as it did at the same time as the slaughter of the Passover lambs, took the place of that slaughter (1 Cor 5:7). This early tradition, independent of the Johannine circle, strengthens the vote for the Johannine version in John 18–19.

An additional argument in support of the Johannine dating of the event is that it is more likely that Jesus would have been executed on the day before the Passover rather than on a high holiday, when the Romans out of consideration for the Jews would have avoided executions if at all possible. It is likely that as a rule the Romans respected local holidays in the provinces and, e.g., did not hold court sessions on such occasions. In about 14 CE M. Agrippa released Jews from any obligation to participate in legal proceedings on Sabbath days (Josephus, *Ant.* 16.168). The release of Barabbas would be appropriate just before the festival (although it probably had nothing to do with a Passover amnesty), since he could then take part in the Passover celebration (cf. §6.3). Of course, while all of these possibilities are plausible, they cannot offer any certain proof. Since John's dating of the event also carries a theological accent, there is at least the suspicion that it too is a theological creation. Then we must be satisfied with the conclusion that Jesus was crucified during his visit to Jerusalem on the occasion of a Passover celebration, probably in the year 30 CE.[12]

With these two fixed dates we can calculate then how long Jesus was publicly active. Depending on how we count the beginning and ending year, we end up with a period of two to three years. John's probable view that Jesus went to Jerusalem on three occasions to celebrate the Passover (John 2:13; 11:55; 12:1) would confirm a figure of three years.[13] Mark, on the other hand, is aware of only one journey to Jerusalem (following a long period of activity in Galilee) for the Passover at which Jesus died. Thus Mark's account would suggest that Jesus was active as an ambassador of the Kingdom of God for about one year. Of course, our beginning and ending dates, i.e., the years 28 and 30 CE, are only approximate, and the information about the travels of Jesus in the Fourth Gospel could well be a literary device that the evangelist uses to organize his material.

Could then Mark be right that Jesus was active for only one year? It is possible, but by no means certain, for in Mark too the sequence Galilee-Jerusalem serves as the framework for the gospel and is theologically important. Of course, the way Mark uses the Galilee-Jerusalem motif does not exclude the possibility that the chronology is historical; there are other considerations as well. What we know about Jesus fits well within the time span of about a year. In terms of their narrative perspective and local coloring the overwhelming majority of the individual units of tradition best fit in Galilee. The fact that very little material—mainly the passion narrative—clearly belongs in Jerusalem strengthens the suspicion that Jesus was in Judea/Jerusalem only once. We need to remember also that literary connections are visible behind the present text of the Fourth Gospel, which some explain by postulating a semeia-source, others by assuming an earlier original gospel.[14] In any case, here also the material was arranged around a time frame of one year, much as is the case with the Synoptics. In any case, the probabilities speak for Mark rather than for John, a conclusion that is strengthened when we consider the rejection and hostility that Jesus encountered and that ended in his crucifixion (cf. §3.2.4). That kind of opposition as a rule moves quickly to a resolution.

The lament over Jerusalem in Matt 23:37 par. and Luke 13:34, on the other hand, could speak against Mark. If we take it literally and historically, this indictment of the city presupposes that Jesus had been in the city several times. Yet, the temporal statement *how often* is probably topical, and the unit as a whole is likely a later creation of the church (cf. §3.2.4). Furthermore, we need to remind ourselves that all of the recognizable traditions behind the literary surface of the gospels were formed independently of each other and therefore do not justify any unambiguous conclusions about the length of the activity of Jesus. An episodic reification of Jesus in an individual event is not an example of an existing curriculum vitae; it presents rather a complete Jesus.

That fact makes it possible for us to obtain somewhat more reliable information about several of the places where Jesus was active. Since an episodic narrative style uses the elements of time, place, and an inventory of characters to build a narrative framework, it offers, among other things, geographical points of reference. They are certainly not to be used uncritically, but in many cases they are historically valuable. In this context Nazareth naturally first comes to mind. That Jesus was rejected in his hometown in Galilee (Mark 6:1–6 parr.) is supported by the tension between him and his family, for which there is evidence elsewhere (cf. Mark 3:31–35 parr.; John 7:1–9). It can hardly be a later fiction since, once some members of the family had become part of the Christian community after Easter (Acts 1:14; 1 Cor 9:5; 15:7), it is unlikely that the church would have repeated such an unfavorable account of the family's earlier attitude had it not had some basis in reality. Furthermore, the rejection of Jesus by the people of Nazareth would best explain why Jesus centered his activity not in his hometown but along the northwest coast of the Sea of Galilee (thus Matt 4:18; 15:29; Mark 1:16; 7:31; John 6:1), the Lake of Gennesaret (Luke 5:1, or, according to John 21:1, also called the Sea of Tiberias). The three sites Capernaum, Chorazin, and Bethsaida are located here. Capernaum especially plays a positive role in the activity of Jesus (Matt 8:5–13 par. and John 4:46–54; Mark 1:21–31 parr.; 2:1–12 parr.; John 2:12), although all three villages are known as objects of Jesus' condemnation (Matt 11:20–24 par.; cf. §3.2.4). It is not clear why Capernaum received special attention. It may be that John 2:12 is an indication that Mary's family lived in Capernaum, but there is no way to confirm this special tradition.

The other place names in the gospels all pose problems for the historian.[15] Taken as a whole, however, they support the conclusion that the upper region of the Lake of Gennesaret is the primary location of Jesus' activity. That he was active in *all of Galilee* (e.g., Mark 1:28, 39) is Mark's own creation.[16] Jesus probably did not spend any time in the Hellenistic cities in Galilee, Sepphoris, and Tiberias (also Magdala), as indeed he generally avoided non-Jewish territory.[17] He worked primarily in the area ruled by Herod Antipas (Luke 13:31–32) and in the border regions of the neighboring lands of Herod Philip, to which Bethsaida probably belonged. Between these two areas there were the customary tax offices of which, e.g., Mark 2:14 parr. speaks. Also the frequent references to *the lake* in all gospels (cf. by way of example Mark 2:13; 3:7; 4:1; 5:21; 6:32, 45–51) point to the general area indicated by the place names.

Where the disciples came from is also relevant to this discussion. As far as we know only one of them came from Judea—Judas Iscariot, *the man of Kerioth*, in southern Judea. Peter was married in Capernaum (Mark 1:30), but he came from Bethsaida, as did Andrew and Philip (John 1:44; 12:21). Capernaum probably was also the home of James and John (thus Matt 4:12–13, 18–22, although admittedly Mark 1:16–20 has no place name). It would be safe to speculate that other disciples came from that same area. We should also mention here Mary Magdalene (Mark 15:40, 47; 16:1; John 20:1, 18). Thus the followers of Jesus who were closest to him, and whom he probably had known earlier, came from the northern area of the Sea of Galilee. What we know about the disciples of Jesus corroborates our conclusion, therefore, that Jesus limited his activity to a small area.

Along with the geographical references from the life of Jesus, relatively frequently we come across statements about specific persons. The inner circle of disciples, which we have just mentioned, plays, of course, a special role. According to the model stories in Mark 1:16–20 parr., Jesus calls young men directly from their everyday life into a life of discipleship. John 1:35–51 offers a different account. Here disciples of John the Baptist—i.e., people who, temporarily at least, had already given up their domestic existence—find their own way to Jesus and even recruit other followers. Both things may have happened in individual cases to which we no longer have access. It is safe to say, however, that people who wanted to take the initiative in following Jesus were turned away (Matt 8:18–22 par.) or that the demands of discipleship were too much for some people (Mark 10:17–22 parr.). In any case, according to the gospels the inner circle of disciples had to leave everything (cf. Mark 10:28) and live with Jesus outside settled society with neither a fixed place of residence, nor a means of livelihood, nor family ties (cf. in addition §5.2).[18] To be sure, it is questionable how much the disciples actually fulfilled this requirement. The mission instructions in Mark 6:7–13 parr. and Luke 10:1–16 par., in any case, reflect primarily the situation of the mission to Israel after Easter. They offer formal regulations for matters with which Jesus probably dealt pragmatically.

Certainly Jesus was homeless, but since he was active in and around the hometowns of some of the disciples, he and they probably often spent the night with relatives of one of the disciples (thus Mark 1:19–30 parr.). It is likely that they at least saw family members frequently on such visits. In view of the geographically limited area in which Jesus moved, they must have met friends and relatives frequently. They sat together at meals that Jesus staged (cf. §4.3.2), or they got together whenever the news of a miracle was making the rounds (cf. §4.3.3). Also it is nowhere written that Jesus and his circle slept only under the stars, which, incidentally, would not have been a problem with the mild climate at the lake. Of course, Jesus and an unknown number of the disciples were not married (or should we say, not yet married?), but that is not true of Peter and probably others as well (Mark 1:29–30). On the whole, statements such as Mark 3:35 parr.; Matt 8:22 par.; Luke 14:16 par. reveal an antifamily bias, but Peter is not required to dissolve his marriage (1 Cor 9:5). Finally, Jesus had no possessions, but there is no report that any one of the disciples, like the young man in Mark 10:17–22, was required to sell everything. Yet it is noteworthy that after Easter some of the disciples continued the life-style of the Lord (1 Cor 9:5, 14; *Did.* 11–12), even though the call to discipleship initially involved only a connection to Jesus for the limited time during which he proclaimed and practiced the inbreaking of the Kingdom of God.

Although our sources do not permit complete clarity on the issue, it is probable that Jesus gathered an inner circle of twelve disciples around himself and that other disciples spontaneously joined the group for brief periods of time. 1 Cor 15:5 certainly does not justify the hypothesis that the twelve were first formed as a group at Easter. According to this early confession, it appears that the Easter witnesses named in 1 Cor 15:5–7 all had known the pre-Easter Jesus of Nazareth.[19] If that is the case, inclusion of the twelve in the list implies that they were an identifiable group before Easter. By contrast, the number eleven in the Easter narratives (e.g., Matt 28:16; Luke 24:9, 33) is an editorial inference from the number twelve minus the traitor, Judas. After Easter the twelve played almost no role at all as a group (Acts 1:21–26; 6:2. Cf. Gal 2:6–9). If *the twelve* was a fixed pre-Easter designation, a usage that Mark 3:14; 14:10, and John 6:70–71 support, then it was not necessary for Judas to be omitted from 1 Cor 15:5. The group was a nascent institution and not simply a later invention based on the number twelve.

A compelling argument for the pre-Easter existence of the twelve as a group is the open admission that Judas, the traitor, was a member of the group (Mark 14:10, 43 parr.; John 6:71, etc.).[20] Peter, who denied his lord (Mark 14:66–72 parr.; John 18:17, 25–27), is the leading figure of the group and appears first in any list of the twelve names (see below).[21] When Jesus is arrested, the entire group flees (Mark 14:50 parr.; but note how John changes the story in 18:8–11). Of course, the number twelve is not mentioned in this context, but all of the evangelists leave no doubt in their editorial work that they are thinking of the twelve. Is it conceivable that one could make up such a scandalous account after the event?

Against this view one could argue that Jesus in the gospels often appears alone or that the disciples are only props on the stage, but these elements are stylized, literary features designed to emphasize Jesus and his activity rather than the historical recollection that Jesus acted alone. Furthermore, the disciples assume a special importance both in the narrative and on the historical level when, e.g., they are sent on a mission (Mark 6:7–13) or when they are present at the last supper (Mark 14:17–15 parr.) and at the arrest (Mark 14:43–50 parr.). Finally, the twelve are mentioned as a pre-Easter group in a number of varying and independent contexts: in the Markan passion narrative (Mark 14:43), which at one time existed independently; in the pre-Markan list of disciples in Mark 3:16–19 parr.; indirectly in the Johannine signs source (John 6:13; cf. also Mark 6:43); and by the Fourth Evangelist himself (John 6:67, 70–71; 20:24). This wealth of witnesses supports the conclusion that the twelve as a group were part of Jesus' activity in Galilee (and Judea).

To be sure, the lists of the names and surnames of the twelve, which always begin with Peter and end with Judas, pose some problems. The Synoptics and Acts differ in the order, the additions to the names, and, less often, in the names themselves (Mark 3:16–19 parr.; Acts 1:13). John offers still other differences (1:19–51; 6:66–71; 12:21–22). This variety probably originated in the post-Easter churches, where the better-known disciples were given greater prominence. Another feature that can be attributed to the later church is the designation of the disciples as apostles. Since the term appears infrequently in Mark, Matthew, and John (Mark 3:14; 6:30; Matt 10:2)[22] and is widely used only in Luke (6:13; 9:10; 17:5; 22:14), it is reasonable to conclude that the expression was first used to describe the Easter witnesses (1 Cor 9:1; 15:7).

Once we have concluded that it was Jesus who called the twelve into existence, we must ask how he understood the group. Clearly the answer has something to do with the number twelve, suggesting as it does an Israel that is made up of twelve tribes. The concept was still a living, if fictitious, idea in Jesus' time.[23] To be sure, each of the three synoptic statements about the function and meaning of the twelve (Mark 3:14–15; Matt 19:28 par., and Matt 10:5–6) is so problematic that we should not try to derive information from them about the historical Jesus.[24] We must be content with the general consideration that, just as for Jesus all of Israel is lost (cf. §3.2.2), so he chooses the twelve as an affirmation that his message of salvation is for all Israel. One can go further and suggest that Jesus chooses the twelve in order to make a statement about salvation history only by ignoring the fact that elsewhere Jesus frustrates the salvation history expectations of his listeners (cf. §§3.2.2; 3.2.7; 4.2; 4.3).

Finally, there has been a great deal of discussion recently about the role that women played in the group that Jesus gathered around himself.[25] It is clear that women do not appear in any of the lists of the disciples. Of course, immediately after mentioning the twelve, Luke refers to women who were among those who followed Jesus, without explicitly calling them disciples (Luke 8:1–3). Indeed, the term disciple is used of a woman only in Acts 9:36. This largely redactional material is unique to Luke, but it receives some support from Mark 15:40–41 parr., where the women at the foot of the cross are introduced as persons who "when he was in Galilee followed him and served him." Thus the names of several women are early on connected with events surrounding the passion. It is not the disciples, but women such as Mary Magdalene, Mary, the mother of James, and the Mary of Joses, along with Salome (Mark 15:40–41; cf. §6.3), who alone are mute but attentive witnesses of the death of Jesus. Obviously they had come with Jesus and the disciples from Galilee to Jerusalem for the Passover. This journey seems to have been for the singular purpose of participating in the Passover, since elsewhere women's names and female characters consistently appear only in connection with miracles tied to specific sites[26] and with other events of a similar nature.[27] This general description speaks for the view that, although Jesus healed women at certain locations (§4.3.3), recognized them as adherents, was received in their homes, and made use of their service at meals (cf. Mark 1:31), he did not include them with the disciples in his travels. He also probably celebrated his table-fellowship (cf. §4.3.2) for the most part only with men, a conclusion that is supported by the typical table-fellowship scenes from Luke 14:16–24 par. and Mark 2:15–17 parr. along with the farewell supper in Mark 14:12–25 parr. and John 13 and the masculine invective *tax collectors and sinners* (Matt 11:19 par.).

On the other hand, the old Jesus material frequently preserves parallel examples in which Jesus cites men and women with equal emphasis (Luke 4:25–27, cf. §3.2.4; 11:31–32 par., cf. §3.2.4; 12:22–31 par., cf. §4.2.3; 15:1–10 par., cf. §4.2.4; 17:34–35 par., cf. §3.2.2). This material appears to be a clear indication that, although Jesus challenged social custom only to a limited degree, inwardly he had a new attitude toward women. Nowhere does he say anything negative about women, and it was in that culture already offensive enough that he permitted himself to be seen associating freely with women in the villages (cf., e.g., Sir 25:13–26; 26; 42:9–14; *T. Reuben* 4–5; *'Abot* 1:4–5; 2:7; *Adam and Eve*; *b. Qidd.* 70a).[28] The approaching Kingdom of God placed in a new light all of the social distinctions that were taken for granted in an Early Judaism that was conditioned by Torah piety and culture.

There is little dispute about the public activity of Jesus in the synagogues as it is described in the gospels. In his trial before the high priest, the Johannine Christ summarizes his activity with the words, "I taught always in the synagogue and in the temple" (John 18:20). Mark gives the impression that Jesus continually sought out the local synagogue—indeed, that next to his open-air teaching activity he chose the synagogues as the primary setting for his public speaking (e.g., Mark 1:21, 29, 39, etc.). In Luke 4:16–30 Luke expands Mark's Nazareth pericope (Mark 6:1–6) programmatically as a synagogue scene so that it becomes for him one of the significant pericopes for his own picture of Jesus.

Yet, on closer examination there are reasons to doubt this description of Jesus' teaching activity. Most of the statements that put Jesus in a synagogue are redactional transitions and summary statements of the evangelists (Mark 1:21, 29, 39; 3:1a; Matt 4:23; 9:35; 13:54; Luke 4:15; 13:10; John 6:59; 18:20). Since the synagogue references in Mark 1:23 and 6:2 also probably come from the evangelist, there is no certain evidence in the oldest material in the gospels that Jesus taught in the synagogues. That being the case, it is doubtful that Luke's portrayal of the synagogue scene in 4:16–30 can be used even as evidence for

Jesus' general activity. We will, therefore, not go wrong if we envisage the preaching of Jesus as taking place for the most part in the open and in private homes.

In addition, in Galilee, in contrast to the Diaspora, there are few archaeological remains of synagogues prior to the first Jewish revolt against the Romans. By no means can we assume that every place that Jesus visited had a synagogue.[29] Indeed, the opposite is probably the case. This conclusion, independent as it is of our analysis of the gospels, offers strong support for the supposition that Jesus' custom of visiting the synagogues was part of the later fleshing-out of the life of Jesus as the gospels imagined it.

NOTES

1. On the infancy narratives cf. U. Luz, *Matthew*, 101–51 and F. Bovon, *Lukas, ad loc.*
2. Cf. E. Schürer, *History*, 1.399–427; G. Lüdemann, *Paul*, 9.
3. U. Luz, *Matthew*, 127–41.
4. Only Mark mentions the daughters. For sociohistorical reasons he does not name them, and other writers completely ignore them.
5. Occupational designations were usually quite general in Antiquity, and they do not necessarily conform to modern occupations. According to the *Protevangelium of James* (9:3), Joseph built houses. While the word carpenter does not appear there, we should note that, according to Josephus (*Ant.* 15.390) and 2 Kgdms 5:11, a carpenter is a craftsman in the building trade who works with wood and stone. According to *Jub.* 11:23–24, a carpenter is someone who makes wooden tools for farming. Homer (*Iliad* 5.60–61) describes a carpenter as an artisan.
6. This view may well also lie hidden behind John 1:45–46.
7. On the following, cf. the detailed discussions in J. Blinzler, *Trial*; H. W. Hoehner, *Aspects*; J. Finegan, *Handbook*; and G. Ogg, *Chronology*.
8. Cf. G. Lüdemann, *Paul*, 8–19. Lüdemann, however, is frequently hypercritical.
9. Of course, if it could be demonstrated that 2 Sam 5:4 (where David is thirty years old when he becomes king) played a role in Luke's calculation, then his figure would be a messianic statement. In any case, the calendar of Dionysius Exiguus, which he created in 525 CE at the instigation of Pope John I, with its designation *anno domini*, is based on a harmonization of dates that modern biblical criticism has shown to be wrong.
10. This criticism especially applies to A. Strobel's arguments.
11. Cf. J. Becker, *Paul*, 17–32.
12. In the debate over the Markan or Johannine dating people have expended a great deal of energy in astronomical calculations, but the mathematically precise dates at which they have arrived by this method fit, at best, only approximately into the calendar that was actually used in those days. The actual beginning of the month was determined through empirical observation of the first light after the new moon, and we can only guess how they determined the intercalation of this time. Even if we concede that we cannot deter-

mine the exact day, astronomical calculations will not help us in deciding between Mark and John.

13. Cf. J. Becker, *Johannes*, on these texts and on John 6:4.

14. Cf. J. Becker, *Evangelium*, 1.36–38; 134ff.

15. The villages of Caesarea Philippi appear only in the redactional beginning of Mark 8:27–30 parr. Nain is mentioned only in Luke 7:11. Cana is part of John's special material (John 2:1, 11; 4:46; 21:2). The region of the coastal cities of Tyre and Sidon (Mark 7:24, 31; Luke 6:17) in those days extended eastward into the interior. It is not said that Jesus was active in the cities themselves. The same is true for the loose alliance of the *Ten Cities*. According to Mark 5:20 and 7:31 Jesus visited only the area around the Decapolis.

16. The popularity of Jesus as it is given in summary form, e.g., in Mark 3:7–8 and 6:55 is also geography in the service of Mark's theology.

17. Cf. A. Alt, *Stätten*.

18. Cf. G. Theissen, *Social Reality*, 33–59; 60–93; T. Schmeller, *Brechungen*; J. Sauer, *Rückkehr*, 44–49, 211–19.

19. In the narrative world of the Easter legends of the four gospels the witnesses also are all people who had known the pre-Easter Jesus.

20. Cf. the works by W. Vogler, H.-J. Klauck, and G. Schwarz.

21. The literature on Peter is extensive. Cf. the articles by E. Dinkler and R. Pesch.

22. In the Fourth Gospel the term appears only in 13:16, where it describes a general function rather than an office.

23. Postexilic examples of the Twelve Tribes as a religious concept come from Deutero-Isaiah (Isa 49:6), the Chronicler (1 Chr 2:1–2; 12:24–37), and Sirach (Sir 36:10). In the post-Maccabean period there appear such texts as *Ep. Arist.* 32:39, 46–50; *Ps. Sol.* 17:26–29; 42–45; *T. 12 Patr.*; Josephus, *Ant.* 11.107; 11Q xix 57.2–13.

24. On the discussion of this issue cf. the surveys offered by W. Trilling, "Entstehung," 213–22, and M. Trautmann, *Handlungen*, 167–233.

25. Cf. the surveys in B. Witherington, *Women*, and J. Blank, "Frauen."

26. Cf. from the synoptic gospels Mark 1:29–31 parr.; 5:21–43 parr.; 7:24–30 par.; Luke 7:11–17; 13:10–17.

27. Cf. Mark 14:3–9 parr.; Luke 10:38–42.

28. Along with Luke it is clear that the Fourth Evangelist is especially concerned to include women in his scenes, but the traditions lying behind the text prevent any certain conclusions about Jesus' behavior. Cf. J. Becker, *Evangelium*, Exkurs 14.

29. Cf. H. C. Kee, "Transformation," 4–9. On Jerusalem cf. Acts 6:9 and K. Galling, *Textbuch*, Nr. 56. Blinzler, J. *Trial*, 101–8.

3

Israel under Judgment

3.1 JOHN THE BAPTIST AND THE COMING
WRATH OF GOD

Barnet, P. W. "The Jewish Sign Prophets—A.D. 40–70," *NTS* 27 (1981) 679–97.

Becker, J. *Auferstehung im Urchristentum.*

———. "Buße IV," *TRE* 7 (1981) 446–51.

———. *Täufer.*

Behm, J. "Metanoia," *DTh* 7 (1940) 75–86.

Böcher, O. "Johannes der Täufer," *TRE* 17 (1988) 172–81.

Brandenburger, E. "Gerichtskonzeptionen im Urchristentum und ihre Voraussetzungen," *SUNT* 16 (1991) 5–54.

———. *Studien zur Geschichte und Theologie des Urchristentums.* SBAB 15. Stuttgart: KBW, 1993. 289–338.

Dibelius, M. *Die urchristliche Überlieferung von Johannes dem Täufer.* FRLANT 15. Göttingen: Vandenhoeck & Ruprecht, 1911.

Dobbeler, S. von. *Das Gericht und das Erbarmen Gottes.* BBB 70. Frankfurt: Athenäum, 1988. For a review by J. Becker, see *ThLZ* 114 (1989) 737–38.

Ernst, J. *Johannes der Täufer: Interpretation—Geschichte—Wirkungsgeschichte.* BZNW 53. Berlin/New York: de Gruyter, 1989.

Gnilka, J. "Die essenischen Tauchbäder und die Johannestaufe," *RdQ* 3 (1961/62) 185–207.

Jeremias, J. "Elijah in Later Judaism," *TDNT* 2 (1964) 928–34.

Kazmierski, C. R. "The Stones of Abraham," *BiBl* 68 (1987) 22–40.

Kraeling, C. H. *John the Baptist.* New York: Scribners, 1951.

Lang, F. "Erwägungen zur eschatologischen Verkündigung Johannes des Täufers," in: *Jesus Christus in Historie und Theologie.* Festschrift H. Conzelmann. G. Strecker, ed. Tübingen: J.C.B. Mohr (Paul Siebeck), 1975, 459–73.

Lichtenberger, H. "Täufergemeinden und frühchristliche Täuferpolemik im letzten Drittel des 1. Jahrhunderts," *ZThK* 84 (1987) 36–57.

Lindeskog, G. "Johannes der Täufer," *ASTI* 12 (1983) 55–83.

Lührmann, D. *Die Redaktion der Logienquelle.* WMANT 33. Neukirchen-Vluyn: Neukirchener Verlag, 1969.

Lupieri, E. F. "John the Baptist in New Testament Traditions and History," *ANRW.* W. Haase and H. Temporini, eds. Berlin/New York: de Gruyter, 1992, II 26.1, 430–61.

Manson, T. W. "John the Baptist," *BJRL* 36 (1953/54) 395–412.

Merklein, H. "Die Umkehrpredigt bei Johannes dem Täufer und Jesus von Nazareth," in: idem, *Studien zu Jesus und Paulus.* WUNT 43. Tübingen: J.C.B. Mohr (Paul Siebeck), 1987, 109–26.

Michel, O. "Die Umkehr nach der Verkündigung Jesu," *EvTh* 5 (1938) 403–13.

Müller, Kh. "Gott als Richter," in: *Weltgericht und Weltvollendung.* H. J. Klauch, ed. QD 150. Freiburg/Basel/Vienna: Herder, 1994, 23–53.

Murphy-O'Conner, J. "John the Baptist and Jesus: History and Hypotheses," *NTS* 36 (1990) 359–74.

Reiser, M. *Gerichtspredigt.*

Rudolf, K. *Antike Baptisten.* SSAW 121/4. Berlin: Akademie, 1981.

Schlatter, A. *Johannes der Täufer.* W. Michaelis, ed. Basel: Reinhardt, 1956.

Schubert, K. "Die Entwicklung der eschatologischen Naherwartung im Frühjudentum," in: *Vom Messias zum Christus.* K. Schubert, ed. Freiburg: Herder, 1964, 1–54.

Schütz, R. *Johannes der Täufer.* AThANT 50. Zurich: Zwingli, 1967.

Scobie, Ch. H. H. *John the Baptist.* London: SCM, 1964.

Tilly, M. *Johannes der Täufer und die Biographie der Propheten.* BWANT 137. Stuttgart: Kohlhammer, 1994.

Vielhauer, P. "Johannes der Täufer," in: *Religion in Geschichte und Gegenwart* Vol. 3. 3rd ed. Tübingen: J.C.B. Mohr (Paul Siebeck), 1959, 804–8.

Webb, R. L. *John the Baptizer and Prophet: A Socio-Historical Study.* JSNT.S 62. Sheffield: JSOT, 1991. Cf. the review by J. Becker in *ThLZ* 118 (1993) 31–33.

Welten, P. "Buße II," *TRE* 7 (1981) 433–39.

Wink, W. *John the Baptist in the Gospel Tradition.* MSSNTS 7. Cambridge: Cambridge University Press, 1968.

Wolff, H. W. "Das Thema 'Umkehr' in der alttestamentlichen Prophetie," in: idem, *Gesammelte Studien zum Alten Testament.* TB 22. 2d ed. Munich: Kaiser, 1973, 130–50.

3.1.1 A Survey of the Sources

No one engaged the attention of Jesus as thoroughly as did John the Baptist—no one from Israel's past (e.g., Abraham, Moses, David, or one of the prophets), no one from among the contemporaries of Jesus. Matthew 11 par., which is from the sayings source, offers most of the relevant material here. The baptism of Jesus (Mark 1:9 parr.), clearly a historical event, also establishes the close relationship between Jesus and this prophet. Furthermore, the contemporaries of the Baptist and Jesus openly compared the two men (Matt 11:18–19 par.; cf. also Mark 2:18 parr.; 6:14–16 parr.). Such a comparison was made inevitable by the fact that for a time the two of them worked together—an activity confirmed by a special tradition in John 1:35–51 according to which disciples of the Baptist became disciples of Jesus. In a special way Luke also offers in Luke 1 a late testimony to the relationship between Jesus and John. It is clear that, because of this relationship between the two men, after Easter there was competition between Jewish Christian groups and Baptist groups. Without such competition we would be hard put to explain such traditions as Mark 2:18–22 parr.; Luke 1; Acts 19:1–7, and John 1; 3:22–30.

Thus all gospels justifiably assign to the Baptist an important place in their works. Mark, the first evangelist, follows the ancient view that the essence of a person's life is shown by that person's public activity. For this reason, among others, the Baptist appears at the beginning of this gospel and again at the end of the passion narrative (with the Easter testimony). In their gospels Mark's core-porters, Matthew and Luke, added infancy narratives to the beginning of Mark, but Luke still makes clear that he knows precisely where Jesus' public beginning lies (Acts 1:1, 5, 22; 10:37; 11:16; 13:24–25). Even though the Fourth Evangelist prefaces his narrative about the Baptist with a hymn, he includes in this prologue a commentary on the hymn in which he mentions the Baptist (John 1:6–8, 15). He also includes a later comparison between Jesus and the Baptist (John 10:40–42). A final consideration is that the sayings source begins with the Baptist's message of judgment and ends with Jesus' message of judgment (Luke 17:23–37 par.). Beginning and ending the collection of the sayings of Jesus with the same motif was doubtless intentional. Given this evidence of a connection between Jesus and the Baptist, we must deal with the relationship, if we are not simply to spiritualize Jesus as "without father, without mother" (Heb 7:3).

It is true, of course, that the Jewish author Josephus, while he describes the Baptist as a Hellenistic teacher of virtues, is completely silent about a relationship between him and Jesus (*Ant.* 18.117–19). Of course, since Josephus suppressed the Baptist's message of judgment (as, incidentally, Mark and the Fourth Evangelist also did), we must critically weigh his historical reliability. Yet he is probably right when he suggests that Early Judaism regarded the Baptist as a prophet in his own right, independent of Jesus. Clearly John regarded himself as an independent agent. He did not understand himself as a beginning of or presupposition for Jesus; it was Jesus who took the initiative in the relationship. For the Baptist, Jesus was but one of many converts who accepted him and whom he had baptized. It was only after Jesus had begun to act on his own that tension emerged between the two—a tension that included agreement as well as differences and that, according to Matt 11:18–19, influenced popular opinion about the two men.

The relationship that Jesus established with the Baptist was based on the content that John's message of judgment and Jesus' proclamation had in common. It was, therefore, not of a personal-christological nature. It was not until after Easter that the relationship was described in personal-christological terms by describing the Baptist, e.g., as the forerunner who prepared the way for Jesus (cf. Mark 1:2–3 parr.). In addition, in the synoptic tradition it is only by means of a later Christian interpretation of the *stronger one* who will come after John (Mark 1:7–8 parr.) that a positive word about Jesus is attributed to the Baptist, and the open question from Matt 11:2–3 par., "Are you the coming one, or should we look for another?" does not fit well with this statement. The Fourth Evangelist substantially expanded this kind of christological testimony of the Baptist by completely denying him any independence at all and by making of him only a witness to Jesus as God's Son (John 1:23, 27–34, 36; 3:27–30). Of

course, the Christians after Easter had a reason for subordinating the Baptist to
Jesus christologically as they did, since, as we have said, Jesus himself took the
initiative in joining the Baptist (Matt 11:2–19 par.), in being baptized by him
(Mark 1:9 parr.), and, above all, in appropriating the Baptist's message of judgment. Thus after Easter the Baptist became a forerunner for Jesus, a description
to which he certainly would have objected had he still been able to speak.

3.1.2   The Coming Wrath and Judgment by Fire

The sayings source begins with two separate, carefully formed traditions from
the preaching of John the Baptist: a word of censure and judgment in Matt 3:7–
10 par. and a word of judgment in Matt 3:11–12 par. Each has its own vocabulary
and perspective, yet they share a number of characteristics: the same structural
sequence of present and future, the identification of the *fruit worthy of repentance*
with baptism, and a final emphasis in each case on different images of judgment
by fire. This material enables us to describe the essence of John's message of
judgment relatively well, since both units, even though they were preserved in
Christian tradition, do not contain Jesus or Christian components (with the exception of the Christianizing addition in Matt 3:11 par. about which we will
speak in §3.1.4).

In its earliest form Matt 3:7–10 reads:

1a   Brood of snakes,
 b   who told you to flee the coming wrath?
2a   Bring conversion-appropriate fruit!
 b   And do not presume to say among yourselves,
 c   "For a father we have Abraham!"

3a   Because I say to you:
 b   God can from these stones raise up children to Abraham!
4a   Already the ax is laid at the root of the trees.
 b   Every tree that does not bring good fruit
 c   Will be cut down and thrown into the fire.

The text is preserved almost identically in Matthew and Luke. We can ignore their
differing introductions, since they are redaction. The few variant readings probably are
Luke's changes, and only one of them is of any consequence: Luke makes of the fruit of
conversion a plural expression (*fruits corresponding to conversion*), probably because of
the examples that follow in Luke 3:10–14.[1]

The words of censure (1ab; 2abc) and words of judgment (3ab; 4abc) are similarly
structured. The censure begins with a customary address, which qualifies the hearers (a
formal analogy is Isa 1:10; 30:1), along with an accusing question, which contains the
central catchword *wrath*. Then follows the prophet's opposing position, formed first positively (2a) and then negatively (2bc). (The catchwords are *fruit* and *Abraham*.) The
judgment word then takes up again the sequence wrath-fruit-Abraham in reverse order

from Abraham-fruit-fire. It focuses on two points. First, the idea that one can no longer appeal to Abraham is heightened by a reference to a divine miracle. Then the threatening imminence of judgment is intensified with the temporal emphasis first in prominent position and with a visual image. Together they make clear the hopeless situation of the hearers.

The second judgment word, Matt 3:11–12 par., is translated in §3.1.4.

John lives in the certainty that the *coming wrath* (Matt 3:7b par.) immediately threatens, without exception, the entire people of Israel of his day.[2] The term clearly is for him the key word around which everything else is oriented. That is to say, the Baptist is convinced that his primary task is to develop this central idea. In this regard he stands in a prophetic tradition, since Israel's prophets not infrequently structured their proclamation around a central concept.[3]

Nowhere does the Baptist explain why God is angry. He is compelled to declare to his hearers that they cannot escape the wrath of God (Matt 3:7–9 par.), and he explains the relationship between judgment and his call to baptism (Matt 3:11 par.). He discusses in connection with the coming judgment, therefore, other themes that require explanation, but he does not explain what Israel has done that would make God so angry. He offers no reason for the coming judgment. He confronts Israel as apodictically and with the same kind of aggressive self-confidence as Jeshua ben Ananias showed with his message of judgment when, in the years after 64 CE, he announced the fall of Israel (Josephus *J.W.* 6.300–1):

1a *Woe from the rising,*
 b *Woe from the setting,*
 c *Woe from the four winds!*
2a *Woe to Jerusalem and the temple,*
 b *Woe to all who are bridegrooms and brides,*
 c *Woe to the whole people.*

Josephus reports that this prophet of judgment simply repeated these words and refused to talk about anything else or to have any other human contact. Examples of similar prophetic judgments were not foreign to Israel, especially in preexilic times. One can draw a line, e.g., from Amos (5:18–20; 7:8; 8:2) and Hosea (1:6, 9) through Isaiah (6:11; 22:14) and Jeremiah (1:14), although postexilic prophecy tended primarily to be prophecy of salvation rather than of judgment.

What all of these prophets have in common is that they threaten all Israel with destruction. Characteristic of this prophecy is the fundamental certainty that judgment is coming and that it will come over all Israel. When the setting in Matt 3:7, contrary to Luke 3:7, limits the pronouncement of judgment to "many of the Pharisees and Sadducees," it contradicts the actual content of the Baptist's message, which is a general word to the children of Abraham (Matt 3:9). Thus one of the difficult aspects of John's pronouncement of judgment is that without exception all Israel is threatened by the divine wrath. John neither mentions an individual sin, nor is he thinking only of part of the nation. Rather, the people of God, as they now live, stand fundamentally and totally exposed before the coming wrath. When Paul, as a former Israelite, in full agreement with his Jewish contemporaries (*m. Sanh.* 10:1), states that God cannot renounce the promises and the call that he had given the patriarchs for Israel (Rom 11:29), he illustrates how intolerable the Baptist's words must have been for his hearers.

Thus John chooses neither the threat of judgment preceded by a statement of guilt, such as is in Mark 12:1–8 + 9 and 1 Thess 2:15–16b + 16c, nor the conditional parenetic warning of judgment that one finds, e.g., in *Sib. Or.* 4.161–69: "O ill-starred mortals, let not these things be, and drive not the great God to divers deeds of wrath . . . , God will grant repentance and will not slay: He will stay his wrath once more if with one accord ye practice precious godliness in your hearts."[4] Nor does John limit his condemnation to a lost portion of Israel by describing two different judgments, one for sinners and one for righteous, as do, e.g., *1 Enoch* 1–5 and the Essenes (1QS iii 13–iv 26). Nothing even approaching a promise of salvation crosses his lips, such as "Blessed are you righteous, for your salvation draws near!" (cf. Matt 5:3–12) or the announcement that the righteous will rejoice over the downfall of the sinners (as, e.g., *1 Enoch* 27:3; 62:12). Instead, for him all Israel in its present condition stands without exception under God's wrath. Were we to soften the absolute nature of this judgment, we would miss how intolerable the message must have been for John's contemporaries.

The Baptist portrays the coming wrath with two images. The ax is already chopping at the roots of the trees (cf. Jer 46:22). Trees that do not bear fruit will be cut down and thrown into the fire (Matt 3:10 par.). The winnowing fan is already in the hand of the one who harvests the grain. The chaff that is thus separated from the grain will be burned (Matt 3:12 par.). The two common farming procedures are typical images of judgment from Israel's prophetic tradition (cf. on the one hand Isa 5:24; Nah 1:10; Mal 3:19; and, on the other, Isa 10:18–19; Jer 21:14; Dan 2:35; Ezek 21:2–3; Zeph 2:2; Zech 11:1–2), but the Baptist put his own stamp on them just as he did with the image of the baptism of fire (Matt 3:11 par.). That the fire motif appears three times with different connotations in such a brief space is convincing evidence that it was characteristic of the Baptist, even though it appears only in Q and is missing in Josephus, Mark, and the Fourth Gospel. It will also have been typical of John that he does not use the third fire image common to prophecy, viz., the process of smelting metal (cf., e.g., Isa 1:25; Mal 3:2–3). Clearly it was too closely related to the aspect of refining or purifying. John wants to make sure that there is no possibility of misunderstanding: The coming judgment will be destruction.[5]

Moreover, the Baptist does not speak of a world conflagration (as do, e.g., 1QH iii 19ff.; *Sib. Or.* 4:172–78; 2 Pet 3:7). Indeed, in no way does he regard the judgment as a cosmic catastrophe. He assumes (along with Isa 66:15–16; *T. Zeb.*

10:3) the continuing existence of creation. (The same is true, incidentally, of Jesus' proclamation of the Kingdom of God. Cf. Matt 8:11–12 and §3.2.4 below.) Those who are baptized naturally will continue to live on the earth, since the judgment by fire applies only to the trees that do not bear fruit and to the chaff.

Nor is John vague about the time of this catastrophic judgment that is coming to contemporary Israel.[6] It is imminent. The fruit has already been harvested. The trees are already marked that have borne no fruit. Their roots are laid bare; indeed, the ax that is about to fall is already imbedded in one of the trees. The person who is going to do the chopping must simply begin work, and that will happen any moment. Who is going to leave an ax hanging on a tree for any length of time! "Already the ax is laid at the root of the trees" (Matt 3:10 par.). The *already* at the beginning of the sentence shows how urgent is the expectation. The other image communicates the same urgency. The stalks of grain have already been brought from the field to the threshing-floor. The threshing has even begun already. Indeed, the winnowing fan is in the hand of the worker. Any minute he will begin to separate the wheat from the chaff by winnowing, and then he will burn the chaff (Matt 3:12 par.). The images make it unmistakably clear: Israel's history is finished. Israel stands before the final judgment. In the next split second the catastrophe will begin.

With his threat of judgment the Baptist has changed the prophetic tradition of the Day of Yahweh. For Amos it was a "day of darkness and gloom" (Amos 5:20; cf. Joel 2:2; Zeph 1:15). Frequently it is a day of wrath and of the fire of anger (Isa 13:3, 9, 13; Ezek 7:3, 8, 19; Hab 3:12; Zeph 1:15, 18, etc.). It is a day on which Yahweh comes as judge (Mal 3:2), and frequently it is described as being *near* (Isa 13:6; Ezek 7:7; 30:3; Joel 2:1; Nah 1:6, etc.). It can strike the nations (cf., e.g., Isa 13; Ezek 30; Zech 12–14), but in Amos 5:18–20, Isa 2:12–17, Zeph 1:2–2:3, and elsewhere it comes over Israel itself.

Since Amos's preexilic pronouncement of judgment (Amos 8:2) and Deutero-Isaiah's exilic pronouncement of salvation (Isa 40:1–5; 43:16–21), Israel's prophecy is familiar with the phenomenon of imminent expectation. It is especially widespread in the Seleucid (198–63 BCE) and Roman (63 BCE–135 CE) periods. The hope for an imminent end is primarily documented in these years in apocalyptic, Essene, and Zealot groups as well as among Early Jewish exodus-prophets. In apocalypticism, Daniel sets the tone for many who came later (Dan 10:14; 11:40; 12:1–13). Near the end of the period 4 Ezra is a forceful example of the apocalyptic view that world history is coming to an end (4 Ezra 4:26; 5:55; 14:16; 2 Apoc. Bar. 23:7; 82:2; 85:10). The Qumran community has similar views (1QpHab vii 1–2, 7–14; CD 1:11–12; cf. 1QM i 11–12). The Zealots fight against Rome to establish an eschatological theocracy (cf. especially Josephus, *J.W.* 5.458–59). Several prophets want to use the interim to activate the beginning of the new era by repeating miracles of the Exodus (cf., e.g., Josephus, *Ant.* 20.97–98, 188; *J.W.* 2.261ff.; 7.437ff.). Of course, not all Jewish groups in this

time held such views. We have no evidence that the Sadducees thought eschatologically, and in their case it would be highly improbable that they did. Still, we
can be confident that many people were open to a portrayal of the present as the
time just before the end.

Nevertheless, it should be clear that a general eschatological mood is not the
same thing as a heightened imminent expectation such as that of John the Baptist.
In apocalypticism people believe that they are part of the last or the penultimate
generation (as, e.g., Dan 10–12). One waits and prepares for the end, but the
events that are going to usher in the end have not yet happened. The present is
even extended a bit so that one can describe it as a period of time. Even Qumran
expects similar events before the end (1QpH vii 7). With the Baptist it is different. For the Baptist the future is so near that there is nothing between it and his
proclamation. He sees the storm brewing. The sky is so threatening that the first
flash of lightening is going to strike at any moment.

3.1.3   Israel's Wasted Salvation History

In the view of the Baptist, therefore, God's condemnation leaves Israel no
hope for a future. Is there a chance that it can save itself in spite of its sentence of
judgment? In Matt 3:7–9 par., the Baptist assumes that his hearers would admit
that they stand under judgment, but that they are depending on Abraham to shield
them from the judgment's fiery arrows.

As a matter of fact, there is in Early Judaism a broad consensus that, in
contrast to the attitude of the Pharisee in the parable of the Pharisee and the tax
collector (Luke 18:11–12), does not quickly jump from divine election to human
merit, but recognizes Israel's continuous failure to keep the covenant and is able
to criticize its own disobedience toward the covenant God. This ability of Israel
and of the individual Israelite to engage in self-criticism is due to the influence
that the Deuteronomic view of history in its varying forms still exerted on Israel's
self-understanding.[7]

A good example of this attitude is the penitential prayer in Nehemiah 9, where
Israel confesses its sins and the offenses of its ancestors. In spite of God's
patience, their complete stubbornness led to the major catastrophes over the
various generations of Israel. Neh 9:33 expresses the core of the matter: "You are
just in all that has come upon us, for you have acted faithfully; but we have been
godless." The same idea is expressed in Tobit's hymn of praise: "Blessed be God
who lives forever, and his kingdom! For he punishes and shows mercy. . . .
There is no one who can escape his hand. . . . He will punish us for our iniquity
and will again show mercy and gather us from all the nations" (Tob 13:1–5). *Ps.
Sol.* 17:5, to cite a third example, describes the capture of Jerusalem by the
Romans in 63 BCE as the result of Israel's sins and as God's just judgment. These
examples show how the people with every new judgment that they experienced
were able to attribute it to their own failure and then to use it as a new oppor-

tunity for repentance. In this way the Deuteronomic view of history kept the possibility of repentance permanently open.

Within the context provided by that kind of confession of guilt, Early Judaism frequently appealed (again under the influence of the Deuteronomic view of history) to the patriarchs or to the other election traditions—the Exodus and the David-Zion traditions for whose sake God continually had mercy on the people.[8] Again we cite a few examples. Neh 9:7–8 reads: "You, Lord, are God, who chose Abraham . . . and gave him the name Abraham . . . , and you . . . made with him a covenant." Then the very next paragraph appeals to the Exodus tradition (Neh 9:9–15; cf. Dan 9:15). Tobit 13 is based on the David-Zion tradition (cf. also Dan 9:16, 19). The first of the Eighteen Benedictions blesses the God of the patriarchs, while Benediction 6 offers a confession of guilt with a petition for forgiveness. *Bib. Ant.* 9:4 expressly formulates: "God will not remain in his anger and will not forget his people forever . . . and he has not for nothing ended the covenant with our fathers." Similarly *T. Levi* 15:4 says: "And if it were not for the sake of Abraham, Isaac and Jacob, our fathers, not one of my seed would remain on the earth." Finally, *'Abot* 2:2 says: "The merit of the fathers . . . helps them, and their righteousness endures forever" (cf. also *Ps. Sol.* 9:9–11). Referring to the traditions of election, therefore, is in Israel and Early Judaism a common way of reassuring one's self of divine grace following a moral lapse.

That reality makes the Baptist's intention clear. He could reckon with the probability that many of his hearers would accept the heightened sense of sin that was part of the Deuteronomic view of history and that most of them would be familiar with the accompanying prophetic threat of judgment with its variations on the Day of Yahweh.[9] He also could reckon, and justifiably so, with resistance when he denied his audience their accustomed way of claiming salvation because of Israel's election traditions: "Do not presume to be able to say, 'We have Abraham as our father'" (Matt 3:9 par.). Repeated repentance, which until now has been an open possibility, is no longer an option. God will no longer gather together Israel's broken pieces for the sake of Zion's election (Mic 4:6–7); now God thinks the unthinkable: Salvation will pass Israel by. The constant accumulation of guilt has used up Israel's store of salvation. Israel stands helpless before the divine judgment, because the God of the covenant now will no longer forgive for the sake of the patriarchs. This reality explains why the Baptist calls his contemporaries a brood of snakes (Matt 3:7 par.). The metaphor calls attention to Israel's calamity in marquee lights. Israel is thoroughly and fundamentally lost. Of course, God will remain true to his promises to Abraham, because God can, with an extravagant miracle, raise up children to Abraham from stones, the deadest material of the wilderness (Matt 3:9b par.).[10] Thus on God's side the covenant is never annulled, but God can fulfill the covenant's promises without involving contemporary Judaism. God can remain true to himself without taking into consideration Abraham's current descendants.

Nor can we temper the sharpness of this view by referring to such texts as 4

Ezra 7:102–15 and *2 Apoc. Bar.* 85:12. As such texts demonstrate, it is occasionally claimed in Judaism that the individual Israelite will no longer be able to repent at the final judgment. God's mercy, poured out for so long for the sake of the ancestors, will come to an end, because on that day individuals will be rewarded only for their own deeds. The Baptist's judgment, however, is much more fundamental: God can take away wholesale from all Israel the promise made to the fathers and can, without Israel, fulfill that promise with a miracle. The authors of 4 Ezra and *2 Apoc. Bar.* would vehemently reject such an idea.

What, then, in view of the coming judgment and the impossibility of an appeal to Abraham is the meaning of the Baptist's call to repentance? The answer lies in bringing together the *fruit of repentance* that John demands and baptism as a baptism of repentance (Matt 3:11 par.; Mark 1:4 parr.). Repentance takes place as baptism. Baptism is the appropriate act of repentance. We can also best understand this statement in terms of the Deuteronomic view of history.[11]

The Baptist's hearers were familiar with the call to repentance as the Deuteronomic view of history understood it. In this view repentance was possible because there were covenants with God to which sinful Israel could flee. Thus the same Israel that had failed God and violated the covenant could take refuge in God's faithfulness. For the sake of the covenant God will punish but not completely reject Israel, because God cannot be unfaithful to himself. In this context repentance means to acknowledge God's judgments as just without reservation (Neh 9:33; *Ps. Sol.* 2:15–18; 3:3; 8:7–8; Dan 9:7, 14, etc.). At the same time one acknowledges that one's present misery is the just consequence of one's own failure (Neh 9:2, 16; Dan 9:7–8, 11; 1QS i 22–25). One then submits one's own sinful status to the mercy of the God of the covenant (Neh 9:19; *Ps. Sol.* 2:15–16; 7:7–10; Dan 9:7–9; Benediction 6 of the Eighteen Benedictions, etc.). Naturally, one then immediately had to turn to the fear of God, which could only mean that one would keep the covenant and the law (Neh 9:26; Tob 13:6; 1QS i 7–9, 16; Josephus, *Ant.* 9.13.2, etc.). A consequence of this Deuteronomic theology was that the Old Testament prophets also became preachers of repentance whose call to return to the Law was rejected repeatedly (Neh 9:26; Josephus, *Ant.* 9.13.2).

Of course, the Baptist's hearers, who as a rule came to him with this understanding, will have been offended by his message. A typical Deuteronomic preacher of repentance would not have used the future to criticize Israel, but would have interpreted its present suffering as the result of previous judgments on Israel and thus would have understood its present guilt as but one more example in a long line of continuing obstinacy. Still, they might have had some tolerance for a prophet who announced the end of Israel's history in light of the future.[12] What they could not tolerate was that John prevented all recourse to Abraham and to God's promises associated with Abraham. That kind of message made him an enemy and troubler of Israel (cf. 1 Kgs 18:17; 21:20). The Deuteronomic view of history was aware at crucial points of the deep tension in Israel's salvation history between the people's failure and unwillingness to repent on the one hand and, on the other, the mercy that God continually granted because of Israel's divine election. The basis of the salvation history itself, however, was never questioned.

Since in this salvation history the Law was an essential content of the covenant, we must ask what John's attitude toward the Law was. Was it not a betrayal of the God of the covenant, when John connected repentance not with the Torah, but with the new act of baptism? As a matter of fact, repentance and baptism did take on new meaning for John. His call to repentance was no longer one of a historical series of repentance movements that might yet be followed by others. It was, rather, a single, end-time act that, instead of being part of the flow of salvation history, offered a new eschatological possibility of salvation in light of the impending judgment, thereby terminating the value of the Deuteronomic view of history. Likewise, John's baptism differed from all other ritual washings in Israel (including the Essene washings with which it is often connected), because it was a process in which John immersed the penitent rather than an act of self-baptism (Mark 1:4–5 parr.). Like repentance, but unlike all ritual baths, baptism was a single, unrepeatable act.[13] Without describing its positive consequences in any greater detail, John simply presented baptism as an act that would protect an individual from the imminent eschatological judgment that was coming over all Israel. The coming judgment so dominated John's preaching that he refers only obliquely to salvation for those who are baptized. The image of a grove of fruit trees naturally allows for the possibility that some of the trees actually do bear fruit (they are doubtless those who are baptized), but the focus of the clause is the destruction of the trees that do not bear fruit (Matt 3:10 par.). Of course, winnowing makes sense only if grain and chaff are separated, and the wheat that is gathered into the barn also is an implied reference to those who have been baptized. Still, the prophet directs the attention of his hearers to the chaff that is burning (Matt 3:12 par.). John's repentance and baptism are neither anchored in salvation history nor are they the basis for a positive promise of salvation to follow. As a new reality, baptism takes the place of the old promise, but its content is limited to the double confession that God's judgment is just and that the one who is baptized stands before God as a sinner. Since Israel is at the zero hour, this baptism appears as the only possibility of escaping judgment, but that is not the same as a statement of salvation that would offset the dominating theme of judgment. Such a statement probably is missing, because John is concerned to emphasize that empirical Israel has used up its salvation history and thus the traditional hopes for a final salvation that were part of that salvation history are no longer available.

Such an understanding of John's baptism implies that it is at least indirectly an attack on the temple cult. The legitimacy of the cult rested on the repeated petition for divine blessing and mercy that was grounded in salvation history. It is precisely this theological perspective that John disputes when he offers his eschatological baptism as a new gift that takes the place of the salvation history that

Israel has squandered. Israel claimed that only God can forgive, and that he does it at the temple, the place of his choosing. The Baptist counters that, since it is zero hour in Israel, God offers through John baptism as the place that God has created as the last possibility of forgiveness.

According to John 1:28, John baptized "in Bethany beyond the Jordan," and John 3:23 adds that it was "in Aenon near Salim." Unfortunately, these statements are deficient on two counts: They appear only in the Fourth Gospel, and we cannot identify them archaeologically. What we can perhaps conclude from them is that the Baptist was active at the edge of the wilderness (Mark 1:4 parr.), which in his day belonged to Peraea and which was the region in which, according to Israelite tradition, the wilderness generation died out—i.e., did not get to enter the promised land (Num 27:12–23; Deut 32:48–52). If that is the case, it would add to our knowledge of John in two ways. John was imprisoned by Herod Antipas, and Peraea was part of his territory. The wilderness to the east of the Jordan River could demonstrate symbolically how Israel stands under judgment and no longer can lay claim to the promises. Still, as we have said, there is no firm evidence for these considerations.

We are in a better situation with regard to what the Baptist ate and wore (Mark 1:6 parr.). His diet and clothing are crude, signs of an uncultured existence outside the land that Israel occupied. The coat of camel's hair and rawhide girdle are often associated with Elijah (2 Kgs 1:8), but it is more likely the general costume of a prophet (*Mart. Isa.* 2:10–11). In Sir 40:4 a coat of skins is the opposite of a turban and golden diadem (cf. Matt 11:8). Locusts and wild honey are desert rations, which even John's contemporaries understood as an expression of an ascetic life-style (Matt 11:18 par.; cf. Mark 2:18). There is no reason to doubt that they correctly understood the Baptist in this regard. With his whole way of living the Baptist reveals how serious is the situation of judgment in which his contemporaries live. Even his life-style is an expression of repentance (cf. 1 Kgs 21:27–29; 2 Chr 7:13–14; Joel 2:12–14; *T. Jud.* 15:4; *Ps. Sol.* 3:8).

3.1.4   The Announcement of the Stronger One
Who Is to Come

Thus far the Baptist's message of judgment has contained no issues that raise serious problems with regard to the interpretation of the text. The question posed in Mark 1:7–8 and Matt 3:11–12 par. of the stronger one who is to come, on the other hand, is a knotty problem. The announcement of this stronger one appears in two traditions, Mark and Q. Of even greater import is the fact that it clearly shows the marks of Christian interpretation, although the reconstruction of the original form of the Baptist's words remains a matter of controversy. As a rule, the tendency is to regard Matthew as the one who best preserves Q and to attribute Luke's variations to his dependence on Mark. When we compare the texts of Matthew and Mark, it seems that Mark offers a syntactically simpler text than Matthew's more complicated structure and at the same time shows more Christian influence. The approximate Q version, which can serve as the beginning point for further analysis, is as follows:

1a *I* baptize *you* with water,
  b *but the one coming after me is stronger than I,*
  c *for him I am not worthy to untie his sandals.*

2a He *will* baptize *you with [Holy Spirit and]* fire;
  b *His winnowing fan is (already) in his hand.*

3a *And he will cleanse his threshing floor.*
  b *And he will gather his wheat into the granary,*
  c *but the chaff he will burn in an unquenchable* fire.

There is broad agreement that, as a minimum, the three words in brackets are a Christian addition to the Baptist's message. The opposition between water-baptism and spirit-baptism, which is used elsewhere to distinguish between John's baptism and Christian baptism (cf. John 1:33; Acts 19:1–7), confirms this conclusion as does the fact that the statement about the spirit[14] appears in the context as a foreign intrusion.[15] Furthermore, the rest of that line matches with syntactic precision the first line and stands in opposition to it. The opposition is sharp: Only water-baptism can save people from fire-baptism; without John's baptism one will be lost in the baptism by fire. That is why, the text argues, the baptism of repentance with water is so necessary. In the same way that water controls fire, baptism quenches the wrath of judgment.

Also at issue is whether the motif of loosing the sandal is intended to sharpen the distance between Jesus and the Baptist, i.e., whether, similar to the Christian addition in John 3:29–30, the words were put in the Baptist's mouth. Indeed, we need to ask whether comparing John with another, stronger figure makes sense only if the other figure is Jesus. Clearly the Christian community had a compelling interest in their relationship. Yet, even when we concede that the reference to a stronger figure made good sense from a Christian perspective, we must explain why the comparison both in image and word is not specifically Christian. Must we not make a distinction here between the later Christian understanding of the text and its original meaning? In the Christian elements of the synoptic material about the Baptist, where is there an allusion to this comparison between John and Jesus? Nowhere in the process of Christianizing the material do we see language that could explain this double motif of the stronger one and the menial act of removing the sandals. Although the double comparison makes sense from a Christian perspective, it is without analogy, and a Christian origin for it can in no way be proven. We need to keep the possibility open, therefore, that the unusual character of the statement could come from the Baptist.

In that case, the one who is to come is the one who will appear in connection with the judgment, i.e., the one who will administer the baptism with fire. Nothing more is going to happen between the present water-baptism of John and this figure's future fire-baptism. Indeed, the winnowing fan is already in his hand.

Who, then, is this person who is going to carry out the destruction? It could, of course, be God. That would correspond to the prophetic tradition and to the concept of the day of judgment that is precisely *the Day of Yahweh* and *the day of his coming* in judgment (Mal 3:2).[16] In addition, Early Judaism is aware of figures who perform God's functions in his stead, although in the case of judgment it is always clear that it is God's judgment. There is good reason to take a look at these figures, since anthropomorphic language about God's sandals and about his hand carrying out the harvest, e.g., winnowing, would be unusual, as least for Early Judaism. One tended to avoid references to God in such human terms. Nor does Ps 108:10 offer any help,[17] since the psalm is not contemporary with the Baptist and there is not the slightest indication that John was thinking of this text. Nor does the psalm mention God's harvesting activity, which John described in such human terms. Furthermore, we must ask why the Baptist felt such pressure to distance himself as intensively and as boldly as he does twice in Matt 3:11 par., when it was in Early Judaism already self-evident that God without question and without exception so greatly surpassed everybody. If the Baptist were using such comparisons to express his inferiority to God, he would be belaboring the obvious. It is much more likely that he is thinking of some other figure who is going to execute judgment in place of God and in God's name. Indeed, his language implies as much. In Matt 3:9 par. he is able to refer directly to God. Why does he not speak in Matt 3:11 in the same way?

Figures that on the basis of proven Early Jewish traditions might come into question are the Son of Man (Dan 7:13–14 and the further development of the figure in *1 Enoch* 37–71; Mark 13; cf. §4.4.2),[18] the Davidic Messiah (e.g., *Ps. Sol* 17; Benediction 14 of the Eighteen Benedictions; cf. §4.4.1), Michael (Dan 12:1; 1QM xvii 6–7; *T. Dan* 6; *As. Mos.* 10:2), Melchisedek (11Q xiii), and Elijah (Mal 2:17–3:15).[19] Now the Baptist certainly will not be thinking about a figure identified with national-political expectations as, e.g., the Davidic Messiah. He would not at all fit in with the Baptist's overall conception. The figure whom, next to God himself, the Baptist's statements would best describe is the Son of Man. He *comes* with the clouds of heaven (Dan 7:13; Mark 13:26–27; *Did.* 16:8; cf. *1 Enoch* 69:29 and similar texts). According to the images of *1 Enoch*, the Son of Man is purely and simply the judge, a powerful and majestic figure (*1 Enoch* 46:6; 49:2–3; 52; 61:8–13; 69:29, etc.). His judgment is formed on the basis of the Day-of-Yahweh tradition (cf. by way of example 50:2; 51:2–5; 54:7–10) and is described as, among other things, a judgment of fire (48:9 and elsewhere). The connection between repentance and judgment also appears (50:4–5). He is obviously so closely identified with God that his judgment is God's judgment; indeed, he is chosen by God (45:3–4; 46:3–4), and he sits on God's judgment seat (51:3; 61:8, and elsewhere). His judgment takes place on earth and restructures the relationships on earth (51:1–5; 69:28). The expectation is that when this Son of Man comes others will wash his feet as a sign of honor for him and as an act of their own humiliation (e.g., *Jos. As.* 7:1; 20:1–5; Herodotus 6:19, etc.). To do that they must untie his shoes and take them off. Not infrequently untying the shoes and washing the feet are mentioned together in this sense (*Mek. Exod.* 21:2 [82a]; *b. B. Bat.* 53b; *b. Ketub.* 96a; Plutarch, *Pompeius* 73E). According to the Baptist's own self-evaluation, he is not worthy even to humble himself in this service of honoring the one who is coming. In view of John's declaration that Israel's salvation history is bankrupt, the Son of Man figure here also has the advantage that his coming is described nowhere in Jewish literature as the fulfillment of an election tradition in Israel's salvation history. Finally, it makes better sense if the Baptist contrasted himself with the Son of Man than with God, since they had in common humanlike qualities (Dan 7:13; *1 Enoch* 46:1); between John and God there was only an obvious distance and difference.

Accordingly, the similarity between the Baptist's statements and the Son of Man tradition is so impressive that we must give serious consideration to understanding the figure of the judge in John's message as the Son of Man. Another thing that speaks for this interpretation is the way Jesus also used the Son of Man tradition in his proclamation of judgment (cf. §4.4.2). It is likely that he was the Baptist's heir in this regard. If that is the case, it would explain the relationship between the preaching of the Kingdom of God and the Son of Man sayings of judgment in the Jesus material.

3.1.5 The Baptist as a Prophet of Judgment

When we set out to understand John in the context of Early Judaism, it makes sense historically to ask how he measured up against the three major intellectual-spiritual powers of his day: the Deuteronomic view of history, wisdom's way of understanding the world, and the apocalyptic explanation of reality. In view of what we have said in §3.1.3, it is unlikely that John was a Deuteronomic preacher of repentance. Neither he nor his hearers understood him that way. Nor did the wisdom tradition have any noticeable influence on him.

Are we able to say the same thing about apocalypticism? Clearly the judgment theme, especially with the figure of the Son of Man, plays a central role in apocalypticism, so that we can see connections here. Even if the Baptist borrowed well-known apocalyptic motifs, however, that does not yet prove that he was an apocalyptist. We must distinguish between being influenced by an intellectual tradition and belonging to a group, as, indeed, we distinguish between borrowing a motif and one's own self-understanding. Given that distinction, the Baptist was certainly no apocalyptist. The intensity of his judgment against Israel departs significantly from apocalypticism, which in a time of crisis affirms new hope for Israel. John also does not describe judgment as the final break in a history that consists of successive periods; he merely eliminates the difference between future and present. He does not ask in apocalyptic fashion when the end is coming in order then to give the answer himself: It is coming soon, after the following things happen . . . (Dan 8:13–14; 12:6–7). He simply knows that the judgment is so near that it is beyond discussion and that there is no room for an intervening period of time. The apocalyptist looks from his situation of crisis toward an end that will bring salvation; the Baptist looks from the near-at-hand end to the present. And where in apocalyptic literature is there such a claim to authority as the Baptist makes? An apocalyptic author writes from within a situation of crisis whose crisis quality consists, among other things, in the fact that there is no longer any authority capable of bringing a revelation. For that reason the apocalyptist must make use of and hide behind an ancient authority figure. By using the I-form of address (Matt 3:9 par.) John claims authority for himself. From this point of view there are for John no doubts about revelation or authority. In the apocalyptic view of the world the present is empty of salvation and thus in need of comfort. In the Baptist's view, from the perspective of the coming judgment his baptism is the new, unrepeatable, and final chance for salvation in a degenerate present that stands under judgment.

To distinguish John from his apocalyptic contemporaries in this way is to understand him as standing in the prophetic tradition of Israel and Early Judaism. To be sure, this phenomenon is still too multilayered for us to describe John in general simply as a prophet (cf. Mark 11:32 parr.; Matt 11:9 par.; also John 1:6).[20] The fundamental conviction that stamps the message of the Baptist makes him a prophet of judgment who stands in a history of prophetic judgment in Israel and Early Judaism. As a prophet of judgment he is at the same time a baptizer (about which Josephus agrees) who extends to all who are threatened by the impending judgment one final possibility of salvation (cf. Amos 5:4; Isa 7:9). John's life away from culture and society (Mark 1:6 parr.; Matt 11:18 par.) is in keeping with this prophetic stance. With his own life he acts out in advance the situation Israel will be in when its zero hour arrives.[21] By avoiding all culture and by living in the wilderness he publicizes Israel's situation. Since John expects that all Israel will be lost in the coming judgment, we need not try to identify him with one of Early Judaism's movements and groups. For him they are as obsolete as is Israel's salvation history itself.

We might modify that opinion slightly if the Baptist understood himself in terms of Mal 3:1, 23–24, as the Elijah who is to come again and/or if he understood himself to be the fulfillment of the voice crying in the wilderness of Isa 40:3. It is true that, according to 1QS viii 12–16, the Essenes described their own existence in terms of Isa 40:3, and it could well be that John used the text in a similar way. The use of Isa 40:3 in Mark 1:3, however, comes from a source common to Mark and John in which the Baptist has already been given a Christian interpretation (Mark 1:3, 7–11, with the same sequence in John 1:23, 26–27, 29, 32–34). There are signs of a similar process in the Benedictus of Luke 1:68–

79, where a Jewish-Christian addition (vv. 76–79) is attached to a general Early Jewish hymn in vv. 68–75. The Christian addition refers to the Baptist and to Christ and uses Isa 40:3 (=Luke 1:76b) to identify the Baptist as the forerunner of Jesus, much as the tradition does that lies behind Mark and the Fourth Gospel. An analysis of the use of Mal 3 leads to a similar conclusion. In Mark 1:2 and the Q material in Matt 11:3, 10, 14 par., the Malachi text serves to underscore the Christian appropriation of the figure of the Baptist. Thus there is no compelling reason to identify John and Mal 3 historically, and we must conclude that both prophetic texts reflect a Christian interpretation of the Baptist; they provide no evidence for John's own self-understanding.

3.2   THE ANNOUNCEMENT OF JUDGMENT IN THE PROCLAMATION OF JESUS

Becker, J. *Täufer.*

Blinzler, J. "Die Niedermetzelung von Galiläern durch Pilatus," *NT* 2 (1958) 24–49.

Brandenburger, E. "Gericht Gottes III," *TRE* 12 (1984) 469–70.

Broer, I. "Die Parabel vom Verzicht auf das Prinzip von Leistung und Gegenleistung (Mt 18, 23–25)," in: *A cause de l'Evangile.* Festschrift J. Dupont. Paris: Publications de Saint-André Cerf, 1985, 145–64.

Burckhardt, J. *Griechische Kulturgeschichte* I. 2d ed. Deutscher Taschenbuchverlag 6075, 1982.

Dalman, G. "Viererlei Acker," *PJ* 22 (1926) 120–32.

Derrett, J. D. "Law in the New Testament: The Parable of the Unmerciful Servant," *RIDA* 10 (1963) 3–19.

Härle, W. "Die Rede von der Liebe und vom Zorn Gottes," in: *Die Heilsbedeutung des Kreuzes für Glaube und Hoffnung der Christen.* ZThK.B 8. Tübingen: J.C.B. Mohr (Paul Siebeck), 1990, 50–69.

Jeremias, J. "Elijah in Later Judaism," *TDNT* 2 (1964) 928–34.

Lohfink, G. "Das Gleichnis vom Sämann (Mk 4,3–9)," in: idem, *Studien zum Neuen Testament.* SBAB 5, Stuttgart: KBW, 1989, 91–130.

Luz, U. "Jesus und die Pharisäer," *Jud* 38 (1982) 229–46.

Meyer, R. and H. Fr. Weiss. "Pharisaios," *TDNT* 9 (1974) 11–48.

Reiser, M. *Gerichtspredigt.*

Weiser, A. *Die Knechtsgleichnisse der synoptischen Evangelien.* StANT 29. Munich: Kösel, 1971, 75–122.

Zeller, D. "Das Logien Mt 8,11f/Lk 13,28f und das Motiv der 'Völkerwallfahrt,'" *BZ* NF 15 (1971) 222–37; 16 (1972) 84–93.

3.2.1   *The Baptist's Heritage*

Our understanding of the message of Jesus depends, in part, on how we evaluate the influence of John the Baptist on Jesus. The general trend today is to

tone down or even eliminate Jesus' message of judgment. Current literature on
Jesus often deals with Jesus' words of judgment only in passing or not at all. It is
claimed that the important thing is to emphasize Jesus' message of salvation, or,
based on the writer's own theological position, it is argued that pronouncements
of judgment simply do not fit in with the kind of unconditional acceptance of
people that Jesus practiced. Especially those persons who want a Jesus who is
relevant in humanistic, political, liberation, or psychological terms ignore Jesus'
statements about judgment. As was often the case with the Enlightenment of the
eighteenth and nineteenth centuries, speaking about the wrath of God is no longer
acceptable. It is at best part of the historical side of Jesus that tacitly can be
ignored. In vogue are only love and unconditioned acceptance, and one has no
use for negative judgments about people.

There are a number of reasons for not following such a trend. In the Synoptics
the message of judgment is quantitatively and qualitatively part of the fabric of
Jesus' proclamation. While critical analysis from a tradition-historical point of
view reduces the amount of material somewhat, a remnant remains for the
proclamation of Jesus that simply cannot be argued away. For historical reasons
alone we cannot ignore the theme of judgment in Jesus. What kind of historical
view of Primitive Christianity would we be left with if we juxtapose a message of
Jesus that was purified of all traces of judgment and a dark and brooding Primitive Christianity that so easily and in so many ways speaks of God's judgment?

We also must ask why speaking about God's love is less anthropomorphic
than is speaking about God's wrath. Is not love reduced to a laissez-faire attitude
without commitment when it makes no demands? Love strives for what is good
and healing; it is the enemy of what is evil and destructive. Its reverse side must
of necessity be wrath. Even keeping in mind the limitations of all human language, a Christian view of God must speak of wrath as well as of love.[22] God is
not mocked (Gal 6:7) is an idea that the classical language about God's holiness
retains (Matt 6:9 par.). Furthermore, the post-Easter church continued this theme
without missing a beat. 1 Thess 1:10 offers the earliest (pre-Pauline) evidence,
then with Rom 1:18–3:20 Paul contributed the text that has had the greatest
lasting influence.

Persons who find that they cannot simply ignore Jesus' message of judgment
still frequently try to reduce it substantially by claiming that Jesus pronounces
judgment only on those who reject him. It is undeniable that there is early
material on this theme (see §3.2.4), but what justifies limiting the theme of
judgment in Jesus to this issue? An examination of the relevant texts will show
that Jesus' message of judgment is more comprehensive (§3.2.2).

Finally, Jesus' message of judgment is blunted by those who describe him
only as the physician who is there for the sick, but whom those who are well do
not need, or as the one who calls sinners but not righteous people (Mark 2:17
parr.; cf. §4.3.2). Limiting the meaning of those statements in that way sets one
on a collision course with the earliest Jesus material, which pronounces judgment

on all Israel (§3.2.2), and it requires a major break between the Baptist and Jesus. It also ends up with a Jesus whose statements on the theme were limited to what was conventional in his day. It was for Jesus' contemporaries a truism that there were always sinners in Israel who needed to repent and who were in need of God's grace.

The best place to begin an examination of Jesus' message of judgment is his close relationship to the Baptist. Jesus was baptized by John. When Mark interpreted that event christologically as a secret epiphany (Mark 1:10–11 parr.), he suppressed the primary and historical meaning of Jesus' baptism, viz., that with his baptism Jesus affirmed the Baptist's pronouncement of judgment not only in a general sense, but also for himself. Yet, the gospel tradition preserves only an indirect allusion to this original sense, because Matthew is forced to deal directly with the objection that christologically, from the early church's point of view, Jesus should have baptized John (Matt 3:14–15). Matthew is aware that it was an offense to the early church that Jesus of all people should be baptized by the Baptist as a penitent—that he himself repented in view of the judgment that threatened everybody. Jesus' baptism was such a problem for the author of the Fourth Gospel that he avoids any direct reference to it (John 1:29–34).

Thus to begin with, accepting baptism is an expression of agreement with the Baptist's message. That conclusion, however, based on the fact of the baptism itself, is only a beginning point for our discussion, for there is ample evidence that Jesus took over the Baptist's message of judgment, reworked it, and made it part of his own proclamation.

We can anticipate the discussion by summarizing the agreement between the Baptist and Jesus as follows: Jesus agrees with John that all Israel is facing judgment. The trauma of this hopeless situation lies especially in the fact that one can no longer appeal to Israel's historical election. Only a new beginning by God can bring relief, a beginning in which God graciously makes a new commitment to those who are lost. Judgment is threatening and imminent. Jesus may not sharpen the sense of immediate judgment as much as does John (Luke 3:9, 17 par.), but both his pronouncement of judgment and his view of the Kingdom of God that precedes it have a sense of immediacy. Finally, in his message of judgment, as indeed in his entire ministry, Jesus, like John, appears as a prophet. In terms of his own self-understanding he is not an apocalyptist (cf. §4.2.2).

For all practical purposes Mark limits Jesus' relationship with the Baptist to the baptism itself (Mark 1:1–15). For the earliest evangelist, Jesus decides on his own initiative to be baptized, spends, as it were, a few minutes with John, and then after his baptism immediately goes on his way. Similarly Mark makes a clean break between the work of the Baptist and Jesus' activity. It is on his own authority that Jesus begins to work publicly with a message that is independent of John, and he does so only after the Baptist is imprisoned (Mark 1:14–15). There is no connection between Jesus' message of judgment and the Baptist—indeed, the Baptist's message of judgment is missing; it is at most implied (Mark 1:5).

Then the Baptist is executed, independently of Jesus, while the latter is active in
Galilee (Mark 6:14–16). The Fourth Evangelist offers a noticeably different
version. For one thing, Jesus and John have only brief contact when the Baptist
identifies Jesus on the occasion of his baptism, which is never explicitly mentioned in the narrative (John 1:29–34). For another, John and Jesus are immediately active at the same time. Indeed, Jesus baptizes as does John (John 3:22–
30; 4:1–3). Disciples of John come to Jesus (John 1:35–42), and, because of the
competitive nature of their baptizing activity, there are tensions between the
followers of Jesus and John (3:22–30). The Gospel of John says nothing about
the Baptist's death, and, since it completely ignores the Baptist's proclamation of
judgment, it has nothing to say about how Jesus' message of judgment might
have been related to John's.

It appears that Mark energetically Christianized the material he had received
(Mark 1:3, 7–11 = John 1:23, 26–27, 29, 32–34; cf. §3.1.5) in order to create the
impression that Jesus was independent of John. We should not follow Mark here,
because the statement that Jesus baptized was hardly a Christian invention (John
4:1), especially since it is quickly, but belatedly corrected in John 4:2. Therefore,
we must reckon with the probability that Jesus spent a longer length of time with
the Baptist and that the two of them baptized simultaneously at the beginning of
Jesus' activity. Mark's picture is so powerful that even today it still has great
influence, but it is a literary creation. The historical reality was somewhat
different.

That being the case, we should consider the possibility that Jesus was a
disciple of the Baptist for a period of time.[23] Baptizing in the same way John
does implies a great deal of agreement with his message, especially when, as we
have shown, John's baptism had no analogy in Early Judaism. Where else would
Jesus have come across it? How else are we to explain the agreement in their
message of judgment? The caution of many interpreters of Jesus on this point
probably is the result of the influence of Mark's account, which clearly is a
christological creation. Yet, whatever one's decision about this particular case,
the consensus remains that we can best understand Jesus in the context of Early
Judaism along the lines of the Baptist's model. Like the Baptist he is independent
of the regular groups in Israel and is part of Israel's prophetic tradition. Within
this tradition he is able to act authoritatively on his own.

The best way to understand Jesus' message of judgment is to begin with the
recognition that Jesus shares the Baptist's view that all Israel is lost (§3.2.2). In
doing so we will see, however, that this basic conviction plays a different role for
Jesus. That insight leads then to a section (§3.2.3) that deals with those sayings in
which Jesus, unlike the Baptist, speaks of two possible outcomes of judgment. The
new element is the offer of the Kingdom of God as the final and eschatological
chance of salvation. Those who reject this Kingdom of God will, according to other
words of Jesus, not escape judgment (§3.2.4). In addition, Jesus, like the Baptist,
demands repentance, i.e., he calls the people of Israel to orient their lives in a new
direction in view of the seriousness of the hour. Jesus forms this call differently,

however, than does John (§3.2.5). All of these individual aspects of Jesus' pronouncement of judgment imply a different reason why the people of Israel are deserving of judgment, i.e., a different understanding of Israel's sin (§3.2.6). A final section then summarizes our most important conclusions (§3.2.7).

3.2.2 All Israel under Judgment

For Jesus, the Israel to which he brings his message of salvation is not an Israel whose relationship with God and covenant faithfulness are in relatively good condition. His personal and new announcement that God's salvation for Israel is at hand begins, rather—in full agreement with the Baptist—with the declaration that contemporary Israel has thoroughly squandered its covenant promises. That for the chosen people election has turned into the threat of judgment is clear from the double saying about the Galileans whom Pilate slaughtered and the people of Jerusalem who were killed (Luke 13:1–5). In the best tradition of Old Testament prophecy, Jesus transfers their fate, totally and without exception, to all Israel:

1a   Those Galileans, *whose blood Pilate mixed with their sacrifices,*
 b   do you think that they were greater sinners than all Galileans?[24]
2a   No, I say to you: If you do not *repent,*
 b   you all *will die in the same way!*
3a   Or those eighteen, on whom the tower in Siloam fell and killed them,
 b   do you think that they were greater sinners than all the inhabitants of Jerusalem?
4a   No, I say to you: If you do not *repent,*
 b   you all *will die in the same way!*

The prophetic attack with its twofold example formally parallels the word of the Baptist, both in style and content. "Do you think, . . . no, I say to you . . . ," is stylistically like Matt 3:9. The call to repent in order to keep from being lost stands in continuity with the Baptist. The two headline events probably were common knowledge in Jesus' day.[25] The first case was doubly incendiary: Pilate interferes in Israel's sacred, cultic activity, then the *arrogant kingdom* (Twelfth Benediction of the Eighteen Benedictions) captures what were probably anti-Roman revolutionaries. The second example has obvious significance because of Siloam's historical importance. If this case is to be connected with Josephus's comment (*Ant.* 18.60; *J. W.* 2.175) that the Roman Prefect, Pilate, commissioned work on the aqueduct, then he also would have been indirectly involved in the second example. The first case contains volatile material. That it is given first may reveal a Galilean perspective. The authenticity of this tradition is seldom questioned, since, with the exception of the apophthegmatic introduction, the unit contains no signs of Christian influence, and the examples can scarcely be dismissed as fabrications.[26]

Thus all Israel is caught in a negative relationship with its God from which there is no escape. Jesus is concerned only with this relationship to God, for he takes no stand on the thorny issue of Roman rule (for which *Pilate* is a code word), or on risk management at construction sites. He presupposes, rather, the widespread popular opinion that anything that limits life, including premature death, is the consequence of human behavior—that, in other words, human reality is to be understood in cause-and-effect terms. The question that the disciples pose in John 9:2, whether the man was blind because of his own sin or that of his parents, reveals the same attitude that lies behind Luke 13:2, 4. Thus popular opinion understands the two catastrophes neither in the context of the political tension between Rome and Israel, nor as an issue of responsible behavior at a construction site. Instead, it places the events in a theological world, which is concerned about the connection between human sin and divine judgment.

Jesus' answer employs a twofold stratagem. First, he takes a question that was limited to the persons involved in two individual events and expands it to include all Israel. All Israelites now living will die just as suddenly and unexpectedly (cf. Luke 17:26–29 par.). Then, in the second place, Jesus takes a question about the effect of the previous behavior of those who died prematurely, orients it toward the future, and applies it to Israel's fate in general. Thus in a roundabout way Jesus uses the cause-and-effect connection to reject the popular understanding. Once the individual case becomes an example of all cases, then calculation on the basis of cause-and-effect relationships becomes invalid. The point of the saying repeats the Baptist's basic message, but with a clear difference. Of less importance is that Jesus does not use John's powerful image of fire—an image that, by the way, he avoids elsewhere as well. What is theologically important, however, is that Jesus talks about the future in conditional terms: "If you do not . . . , then . . . "[27] The Baptist proceeds from the certainty that "judgment is unavoidable, therefore . . . " Jesus' new fundamental conviction is that the offer of the Kingdom of God brings with it the possibility of salvation. That salvation presupposes, of course, that repentance involves accepting his message. Repentance is turning to him. Between the judgment and the present will occur the establishment of the Kingdom of God (cf. §4.2.2). Thus Jesus' expectation of an imminent judgment, while it threatens the present generation, is not as intense as that of the Baptist had been.

A sudden and unexpected loss of life is also an element in the parable of the rich farmer (Luke 12:16–20):

1   *The land of a certain* rich man *bore well.*
    And he reasoned in himself, "What shall I do, since I have no place where I can gather the fruits?"
    And he said, "This is what I will do: I will tear down my barns and build larger ones, and I will gather there all my grain and my (other harvest) goods.
    Then I will say to my soul, 'Soul, you have many goods laid up for many years. Take your rest, eat, drink, be glad!'"

2   *But* God *said to him, "You fool, this night they will demand your life from you! The things which you have prepared, to whom will they belong?"*

The rich man at the beginning stands in opposition to God, who has the last word. The structure of the unit is simple. The situation is stated in a simple sentence, which is then followed by three statements from the wealthy landowner: a request for a solution to a problem, a decision about how to overcome the problem, and a statement about the anticipated consequence of the solution. The solution that he chooses appears to be the right one, but it contains a hidden problem, which becomes evident in the unexpected ending of the story, when the man's threefold soliloquy is followed by the terse "but God said to him." The problem is that the rich farmer speaks only to himself, without even considering a relation to God, while God in the closing word demands precisely this relationship and then pronounces judgment on the man. Forgetting God, therefore, is the primal sin that causes the man to lose his life. The farmer actually deals with his bountiful harvest as one would expect a farmer to act (Prov 10:5; 24:3–4; 28:19); his behavior is perfectly normal, similar to Luke 17:27–28. Furthermore, the rich landowner is challenged about his relationship to God just as he is about to put his decision into practice. Thus he has not yet had a chance to enjoy the rest about which he spoke to his soul.

As in the case of Luke 13:1–5, there are no indications that the material has been reworked from a Christian perspective, although the way the parable ends might lead one to think of the Son of Man who judges the world. The harsh message of judgment extends the Baptist's pronouncement of judgment and, with its hopeless finality and terrible immediacy, is unique in Early Judaism.

Avoiding the first person pronoun in God's speech corresponds to the usual way of speaking about God in Early Judaism. Naturally what is meant is that God himself will demand the man's life.

Instead of the kind of hair-raising examples from Israel's present that Luke 13:1–5 offers, what we have here is a story based on a traditional wisdom idea. A fool is someone who lacks divine wisdom, i.e., who is godless (cf. Ps 14:1). This farmer is godless, because he foolishly thinks that he can make his life secure by earthly means. He forgets the creator as the one who gives life and who holds people accountable for their life. However, Jesus is not simply a wisdom teacher who warns people not to forget God in their work and in their success. The harsh suddenness of the divine protest in the midst of great fortune parallels Luke 13:1–5 and several texts that we will discuss below (cf. especially Luke 17:26–29). As in Luke 13:1–5, an individual case is expanded to apply to Israel in general, and an instance of a sudden death, such as happens occasionally in history, is interpreted in terms of the final judgment that, unexpected and imminent (*tonight*), threatens all Israel.[28] Thus with this parable Jesus criticizes not the ethic of a particular profession, but an attitude that is typical of every human being.

The parable in Luke 16:1–8 takes us into the world of the large estates that were common in Galilee:

*1   There was a certain rich man who had a manager. And this one was
     accused of wasting his possessions.
     And calling him, he said to him, "What is this I hear about you?
     Render the account of your management, for you can no longer be
     manager."*

*2   Then the manager said to himself, "What shall I do, since my master
     is taking the management away from me? I cannot dig, and I am
     ashamed to beg.
     I know what I will do, so that after I am no longer manager, they will
     take me into their houses."*

*3   And he summoned each of his master's debtors and said to the first,
     "How much do you owe my master?" He said, "A hundred baths of
     oil." But he said, "Take your bill and sit down and quickly write
     fifty."
     Then he said to another, "You, and how much do you owe?" And he
     said, "A hundred cors of wheat." He tells him, "Take your bill and
     write eighty."*

The parable begins with short sentences but becomes more expansive in the final
dialogues. It falls into three parts—(1) the manager is accused and removed, (2) the
manager makes a decisive plan, (3) the manager carries out his plan—each of which is
further divided into two aspects. The narrator wants the hearer to be clear about the
manager's fate and about his energetic efforts to save himself. In his life-threatening, zero
hour situation, this manager does everything to make a future possible for himself.

It is clear that Luke 16:8b–13 consists of the church's commentary with which it tries
to extract parenetic lessons for itself from a situation that is unusual—indeed, offensive,
but what about 16:8a? Is the master's praise part of the narrative world of the parable, or
does the narrator become the interpreter? In the first case the master who praises would be
the landowner (cf. 16:3, 5); in the second case he would be the Lukan Jesus. Can the one
who has just dismissed his manager for irregularities that have come to his attention praise
him when immediately thereafter he acts so deceitfully? Furthermore, we are not told
(contrary to v. 1) how the landowner learns what happens in vv. 5–7. Thus v. 8a is the first
commentary in the process of appropriating this difficult material. It agrees that the
manager is indeed dishonest, but one can still learn something of value from his clever,
intelligent behavior when he finds himself suddenly standing at the edge of the abyss.

The management of an estate with an absentee landlord was largely a matter of trust.
There were no books subject to audit. As a rule there was no way the owner could oversee
his manager's behavior, nor was there a way the manager could give account of himself. If
the manager believes the charges, the manager is dismissed immediately,[29] in which case
he must give an account of the present economic condition of the property. That is the
situation presupposed by vv. 3–7. First the manager uses a motif from ancient comedy to
describe what it is that he does not want to happen.[30] Then he decides that he will gain
revenge for being thrown out that way by having the debtors change their bills of debt,
which they had written in their own handwriting and which he, as the one who granted
them credit, had certified. Thus he permits the debtors to reduce the amount of debt, again
in their own handwriting.[31] In both cases, incidentally, the value of the reduced amount is
about the same, about five hundred dinars.[32] With his generosity the manager assures the

gratitude of his business partners and thus hopes that his present disaster will have a positive outcome.

The church's struggles in vv. 8–13 reveal that the parable was difficult for Christians to digest. If the church had created the parable, the corrective explanations of vv. 8–13 would not have been necessary, and had the parable originated in Early Judaism, the church would have ignored it. These verses reveal, therefore, that the church accepted the parable, almost against its will, because it had the authority of authentic Jesus material. Once again, the pronouncement of judgment at the beginning of the parable parallels the Baptist's point of view, and to that degree it is unique in Early Judaism.

In this case as well, from one minute to the next the manager loses the ground of his existence. It simply disappears. Unlike the rich farmer, however, who faces only judgment, the manager can do something about his situation. He acts with the same decisiveness that Jesus demands of all his hearers in Mark 9:42–48. Jesus offers no moral judgment about the manager's machinations (cf., however, v. 8: "the unjust steward"); it was unlikely that any of his hearers would have ever been in the situation of repeating the manager's behavior, and, naturally, all agreed that what was done was forgery. The case of shady dealings with its shocking aftereffects is simply designed to demonstrate that everyone stands in a similar zero hour situation and that one can escape only by taking the decisive action that the message of Jesus requires.

Jesus also presents this idea of judgment with biblical examples that were used frequently in Early Judaism with pronouncements of judgment.[33] One thinks, e.g., of the traditional threat of judgment in Luke 17:26–29 par. (cf. §4.4.2), which calls attention to the way Noah's generation and Lot's contemporaries in Sodom suddenly were threatened with divine judgment. As in Luke 13:1–5, that judgment is coming to all without exception is emphasized twice at the end of the two examples. The inexorable nature of this judgment is underscored by the omission of any reference to Noah's and Lot's salvation. Their departure is mentioned simply to identify the time of judgment so that all others can recognize the unexpected suddenness as their own situation. As a rule Early Judaism portrays the generation of the flood and the inhabitants of Sodom and Gomorrah as unusually wicked (cf. *Jub.* 20:5; *T. Naph.* 3:4–5; *m. Sanh.* 10:3). Jesus portrays the normalcy of their lives without any moral judgment, however, by listing ordinary human events (cf. Jer 29:5–6). This description corresponds to the tendency we have observed in the previous judgment texts. For Jesus, being lost is thus different from simply failing to measure up to a standard of moral values (cf. §3.2.6). In addition, for Israel the flood generation and the Sodomites are Gentiles. When the text puts Israel on a par with them it ignores Israel's unique status among the nations. Thus Israel's election through the patriarchs (cf. Mark 3:9b par.) is no longer a theme that could be of any help for Israel.

In summary, with a broad repertory[34] from different areas Jesus presses the issue that, unless it responds to the Kingdom of God, which is at hand, Israel as a whole is lost. With eloquent silence he excludes any recourse to the fathers and thereby to Israel's election and covenant promise, and he puts contemporary Israel on a par with the nations (Luke 17:26–29). The Baptist had explicitly forbidden any appeal to Abraham. In the texts we have looked at, Jesus did not directly forbid such an appeal, but in other places he implies as much. In Luke 18:9–14a, e.g., the Pharisee begins his prayer expressly with thanks for his election, but the tax collector can name no reason why God should be gracious to him. It is he, however, rather than the Pharisee, who is heard. The younger son in Luke 15:11–32 also knows that he has squandered any right to be a son (15:19a). Such a right must be granted him anew by the father (15:22).

3.2.3 Judgment's Dual Outcome

The substance of the previous section is that all Israel stands under judgment. Luke 13:1–5 implied, however, that judgment is conditional—that Israel might not yet be at the point where its judgment is final and where there absolutely can be no exceptions. Are there other statements that support this tendency even more?

The question leads naturally to Luke 17:34–35. Luke offers the material at the end of a judgment discourse that begins with 17:20, the essential elements of which he derives from the sayings source. Contained in the discourse is a Jesus tradition that refers to the generation of the flood and to the Sodomites and that explicitly states that in those days everyone perished (§3.2.2). Then the discourse concludes with the following early, independent material:

1a *In that night there will be* two *(men) in one bed,*
 b *the one will be taken,*
 c *the other will be left.*
2a Two *(women) will be grinding in the same house,*
 b *the one will be taken,*
 c *the other will be left.*

That the two examples sound alike both in their language and in their structure should be clear to everyone. The unit provides tension and variety by juxtaposing men and women, bedroom and work room, and (indirectly) night and day. There are other good examples in which men and women are paired as opposites (§3.2.4: Luke 4:25–27; 11:31–32 par.; §4.2.3: Matt 6:25–34 par.).

The traditional unit reveals no evidence that it has been reworked by the post-Easter church. Especially noteworthy is that the passive reference to God in both cases is not interpreted christologically. The text is much closer to Early Judaism than to the church. We attribute it to Jesus because of its coherence with the other judgment material that we have claimed for Jesus.

While the conditional statement of judgment in Luke 13:1–5 deals with two extraordinary events, Luke 17:34–35 par. reflects life's normalcy. In that regard the text agrees with Luke 17:26–29 par. (§3.2.2). For the first time, however, we are dealing with the possibility of two different results of judgment formulated symmetrically. That possibility does not mean, of course, that one-half of the people will be saved and one-half lost. The purpose of the saying is to focus attention on the suddenness of judgment and on the fact that its outcome cannot be predicted rather than to make a statement about the relative percentages of the saved and the lost in the final judgment. In addition, the tradition, like that of Luke 13:1–5, says nothing about why such a statement is even possible, given the lost condition of all Israel. Thus at first there appears to be no reason for the softening of the position of the Baptist and of Jesus as presented in §3.2.2.

Things are different when we look at Mark 9:43–48:

1a And if your hand *offends you,*
b   cut if off!
c   It is good for you to enter life maimed,
d   than to go away into Gehenna with two hands [v. 43e].
2a And if your foot *offends you,*
b   cut it off!
c   It is good for you to enter life lame,
d   than to be thrown into Gehenna with two feet.
3a And if your eye offends you,
b   tear it out!
c   It is good for you to enter into the Kingdom of God with one eye,
d   than to be thrown into Gehenna with two eyes [v. 48].

The sentence structure and choice of words need no special description, since they contain little variety. Matt 18:8–9 obviously combines the first two examples from Mark 9. In so doing, not only does Matthew forget to make the object of *tearing out* in 18:8 plural, he ends up with a sentence that is clumsy and too long. Mark 9:48 is an addition based on Isa 66:24, and it is missing in Matt 18:9 and 5:29. The last line of Mark 9:43 probably is also part of this addition.

Matthew offers the examples of eye and hand again in 5:29–30, where in keeping with the context the eye appears first. (The saying is probably from Q rather than from Matthew's special material.) Compared with Mark, Matt 5:29–30 shows signs of having been edited (cf., e.g., *right* eye). In view of Matt 5:29–30 we can no more exclude the possibility that all versions are based on two variants (hand-foot, hand-eye) than we can exclude the possibility that Mark's group of three is the original from which all variants are derived. Fortunately, it is the basic structure, rather than the number of examples, that is decisive for determining the statement's intent.

The text shows no specifically Christian influence. With the exception of Philo (*Det.* 175), there are only limited parallels in Jewish and Hellenistic material. The crudely hyperbolic statement, which does not even begin to consider the reasonableness of the demand, is not for everybody, even though the text could be understood as a Jewish statement.[35]

The hyperbole of the statement is especially provocative. Taken literally, it demands that Jesus' hearers mutilate themselves. Since the goal of the Kingdom of God is healing (Luke 11:20), the crude demand is designed to attract attention.

Israel must take seriously the last chance that is being offered to choose life (i.e., the Kingdom of God) before it is too late. This material is, in other words, another tradition that describes symmetrically the either-or between heaven and hell and that demands from the hearers a total and consistent decision so that they do not waste their last chance—the chance that Jesus offers them with the Kingdom of God. Thus the assertion that all Israel will be destroyed is made relative as soon as Jesus mentions the Kingdom of God.

This conclusion is confirmed by the tradition in Luke 12:8–9 par. in which confessing and denying Jesus in the present serves as the criterion by which one is judged by the Son of Man in the final judgment. Thus the saying describes the future consequences of a person's present attitude about a particular issue. We will reserve a detailed discussion of this text for our later discussion of the Son of Man (§4.4.2); of interest here is that the saying pictures a forensic judgment with a double result. Which outcome people can expect depends on their present attitude toward Jesus. Once again, therefore, Jesus' new offer of salvation opens the possibility of modifying the judgment that is coming on all Israel.[36]

By way of summary we can say that, given Israel's lost condition, Jesus' message offers the only possibility of bringing light into a world of darkness. But wherever this light does not result in a new orientation of life, the darkness is final. We now turn to the texts which speak of this finality.

3.2.4   The Consequences of Rejecting Jesus

Contrary to Mark's euphoric description of the popular reaction to the Baptist's appearance in Mark 1:5 parr., many people doubtless took offense at his proclamation of judgment and reacted to it with anger. Josephus reports that many inhabitants of Jerusalem reacted violently to the solitary prophet of judgment, Jeshua, who was active during the first Jewish uprising against Rome (cf. §3.1.2). We should not be surprised, therefore, if Jesus' severe pronouncements of judgment had evoked similar reactions. Yet, the gospels report nothing of the kind. They are unanimous in describing the hostility toward Jesus as a reaction against his acceptance of those who were lost and his understanding of the Law, both of which were related to his preaching of the Kingdom of God. This absence of tension over the issue of judgment is doubtless due in part to the fact that the preaching of the imminent Kingdom of God lay at the heart of his activity. Another factor, however, is probably the fact that the way Jesus lived in light of the coming Kingdom of God attracted more attention than did his pronouncement of judgment (cf. §§4.3.2 and 4.3.3).

Still, Jesus experienced reserve, resistance, and rejection that were neither accidental nor incidental to his preaching of judgment. We need to remember that the description of Jesus' popularity (e.g., Mark 1:32–38 parr.; 1:45 parr.; 2:2 parr.; 3:7–8 parr.; 3:10 parr.) reflects the interest of narrators who were part of the later Christian community and who had a reason for claiming that Jesus was popular with the people. It is noteworthy that, in spite of this concern, the church remembered the reserve and hostility that Jesus evoked (much as it remembered the failure of the disciples in his passion), and it is likely that this description of the reaction to Jesus is historically reliable.

The substance of Mark's claim that Jesus was rejected in his hometown of Nazareth at the beginning of his Galilean activity is trustworthy (Mark 6:1–6 parr.; cf. §4.3.3). Given the outline of his narrative, however, it appears too late, for it does not explain why Jesus began his work in Capernaum (Mark 1:21–34). A likely explanation is that Jesus was active in places like Capernaum, Chorazin, and Bethsaida because he had been rejected in Nazareth. That he was rejected by his own family can be verified historically, since both his mother (Acts 1:14) and his brother James (1 Cor 15:7; Gal 1:19; 2:9) became part of the Christian community after his death (cf. §2). Other members of the family do not appear at all in the church after the death of Jesus, at least as Luke describes the church in the early chapters of Acts.

The people of Galilee also had their reservations about Jesus. It was they whom Jesus quotes as having described him, with justification, as a *glutton and drunkard* and a *friend of tax collectors and sinners* (Matt 11:19 par.). Such language hardly reflects warm-hearted agreement. Nor is the accusation of demon possession (Mark 3:20–22; Luke 11:14–16 par.; cf. John 7:20; 8:48, 52; 10:20; cf. §4.3.3) neutral; it describes the one so designated as a false prophet. The accusation is stereotypical in Early Judaism,[37] and it may well have been directed against Jesus. When Matthew says that the later missionaries to Israel suffer the same fate as Jesus, he agrees with John 15:20 (Matt 10:23–24: "When they persecute you in the [one] city, flee to another. . . . The disciple is not above the teacher"). Even though both evangelists reflect post-Easter conditions, they likely preserve an aspect of Jesus' own experience. Finally, the report preserved in Luke 13:31 that Herod Antipas was planning to kill Jesus can hardly have been spun out of thin air. Herod had, after all, in the case of John the Baptist already demonstrated his ability to liquidate people who made him uncomfortable (Mark 1:14; 6:14–29; Josephus, *Ant.* 18.116–119).

To be sure, there are reasons to doubt that the Pharisees were as continuously hostile toward Jesus as the gospels, beginning with Mark, repeatedly emphasize. For one thing, it was after 70 CE that the Pharisees became the official, standard-setting representatives of Judaism. Anyone writing during this period, as the evangelists did, would naturally think of the Pharisees as the personification of the hostility toward Jesus. Furthermore, in Jesus' day there was probably much more variety among them than one would assume from the typical formulations of the gospels, which refer to "the Pharisees," as a single entity. It is probable that prior to 70 CE they did not play the dominant role in Early Judaism that the evangelists give them. Thus we must judge the historical validity of the gospel references to Pharisees on a case-by-case basis, remembering that frequently it is easy to demonstrate both from a literary point of view as well as in terms of the history of the tradition that the Pharisees who appear in the gospels are both anachronisms and stereotypes. Mark gives a graphic example in 2:1–3:6 (cf. 2:6, 16, 18, 24; 3:2, 6).

On the other hand, the parable of the Pharisee and the tax collector in Luke 18:9–14 does not exactly picture the Pharisee in a positive light. The same thing is true of the older son in Luke 15:11–32, whose portrayal is, at the very least, similar to that of the Pharisee (cf. Luke 15:29, 18:11–12; §4.2.4), and who also complains in no uncertain terms when the younger son is graciously received. Such texts, and others like them, indicate that the Pharisees for their part distanced themselves from Jesus. It is only in Luke's redactional material that Jesus is entertained by Pharisees in their houses (Luke 7:36; 11:37; 14:1) in keeping with Luke's suggestion elsewhere of cooperation between the Pharisees and Jesus (e.g., Luke 13:31). That no other gospel suggests this kind of relationship justifies the conclusion that Luke's portrayal is not historical. In addition, we should remember that the Lukan Paul in Acts is more Jewish-Pharisaic than was the historical Paul. There are, furthermore, indications outside the gospels that there was much more tension between Jesus and the Pharisees than Luke portrays. Two or three years after the death of Jesus, Paul persecutes the Christian community as a Jew who was trained in the Pharisaic tradition (Phil 3:5–6), and it was former Pharisees who, according to Acts 15:1, 5, criticized the Gentile Christian life of Antioch as contrary to the Law. Are we to believe that just a few years earlier the Pharisees found nothing wrong with Jesus? In any case, we should discard along with other modern legends the idea that Jesus himself was a Pharisee.

The clear impression of the gospels is that Jesus was a man who experienced resistance and hostility. Thus it is not surprising that he himself had something to say about the phenomenon. He does so indirectly with the figure of the angry older son in Luke 15:25–32, but also with the grumbling of the workers in Matt 20:10–15 or with the motif of the rejected invitation in Luke 14:16–24 to which the master of the house reacts with anger. He speaks more directly to the issue in Luke's special material in Luke 4:25–27 in which Jesus temporarily refuses to perform miracles in Israel in especially sharp language:

1a Many widows *lived in the days of* Elijah in Israel,
b   *when the heaven was shut up three years and six months,*
c   *(and) when a great famine came over the entire land.*
d   *But to none of them was Elijah sent,*
e   *except to* Sarepta in Sidon *to* a widow.

2a *And there were* many lepers[38] in Israel *under* Elisha, *the prophet.*
b   *But none of them was cleansed, except* Naaman, the Syrian.

This double word with which Jesus temporarily refuses to perform miracles in Israel has in common with the judgment sayings that we will be discussing next not only the pairing of examples but also the counterpoint between Israel and the Gentiles. Here the pairing is between a longer and a shorter example (5 + 2 = 7 lines). Juxtaposed in the two examples are widows and male lepers (cf. Luke 11:31–32 par.; 17:34–35 par.) as well as Elijah and his pupil, Elisha. The former goes into a foreign country; the latter heals the Syrian in Israel.

Of these Old Testament examples (1 Kgs 17; 2 Kgs 5) only Elijah's miracle is cited elsewhere in Primitive Christianity (Jas 5:17–18; cf. Rev 11:6). The exhortation to pray in James, however, is so different from the theme of Luke 4:25–27 that we cannot assume that the texts reflect the same tradition. It is equally clear that the use in Early Judaism of the Elijah-Elisha stories and especially of the figure of Elijah in the formulation of Israel's hope[39] nowhere demonstrates this kind of polarity between Israel and individual Gentiles. The synoptic tradition also uses the Elijah theme elsewhere only in a christological context that does not appear in Luke 4:25–27. Nor are we to understand the pairing of these examples as an expression of the tension between Jewish and Gentile Christians. The issue in Luke 4:25–27 has nothing to do with a missionary preaching that turns from the Jews to the nations. The purpose is, rather, to explain why in the present moment (cf. the statement of the time in 4:25) miracles are being withheld from Israel. Since both miracles are exceptions, the focus remains on Israel. In addition, Primitive Christianity attributes the healing of leprosy only to Jesus (an exception is Matt 10:8, which is influenced by Matt 11:5), so that the example of Naaman most likely comes from the activity of Jesus (Mark 1:40–45 parr.; Matt 11:5 par.; Luke 17:12–19). Finally, both the form and the content of these paired examples are similar to the judgment sayings that we will discuss next. Thus we cannot deny this material to Jesus, especially since (to emphasize it once again) it does not make use of the usual synoptic interpretation of Elijah in christological terms.

Luke 4:25–27 is not a judgment saying in the narrow sense of the word, but the refusal to perform miracles is an aspect of present judgment. Could the material be a reaction to Jewish complaints in which Jesus provides miracles for non-Jews rather than for Jews? The miracle story of the healing of the centurion's servant in Capernaum (Luke 7:1–10 par.) speaks of the surprising faith of the Gentile centurion—a faith that, according to Luke 7:9, was not to be found *in Israel.*

We begin a discussion of the phenomenon with two traditions that are judgment sayings in the narrower sense of the word: the woes pronounced on the Galilean cities in Luke 10:13–14 par., which stand in the tradition of the Old Testament prophecies of judgment, and the word against *this generation,* whose fate in the judgment will be worse than that of the Queen of Sheba and the Ninevites (Luke 11:31–32 par.). In the first case the issue is that the miracles of Jesus were not appropriately respected. In the second case, it is the proclamation of Jesus that did not get the attention it deserved. Together they are reminiscent of the substance of Luke 10:23–24 par. (cf. §4.2.2):

1a   Blessed the eyes, which see *what* you see,
  b   and the ears, which hear *what* you hear!
2a   Amen, I say to you:
  b   Many prophets and kings wanted to see what you see,
  c   but did not see it,

3a   and to hear what you hear,
b   but did not hear it.

The text understands Jesus' healings and proclamation of salvation as the eschatological fulfillment of the hope of the Old Testament prophets and kings (cf. §4.2.2). Thus it pronounces blessed the eyes and ears that witness this final, definitive offer of salvation. The reverse side of that blessing is the woe on those who reject this salvation. Their judgment is not that something new is imposed on them but, rather, that they are condemned to remain in the lost condition in which, without the message of the Kingdom of God, they have been living for such a long time (cf. §3.2.2). They wasted their chance to escape their disastrous future.

It is likely that the woe over the Galilean cities (Luke 10:13–14 par.) in its earliest form was as follows:

1a   Woe to you, Chorazin, *woe to you,* Bethsaida!
*b   Because if the mighty deeds had been done in Tyre and Sidon that
      have happened among you,*
c   they would have repented in sackcloth and ashes.
*d   Nevertheless it will be endurable for Tyre and Sidon in the judgment,
      but not for you.*

2a   And you, Capernaum,
b   do you really expect to be exalted to heaven?
c   You will be cast down to Hades!

If we imagine the double saying back into a Semitic original, we come up with a form of 4 + 3 = 7 lines in which in the four-line unit the first and fourth lines serve as parentheses. It is possible, then, to understand the comparative in the fourth line as a Semitism[40] with the sense that the woe does not describe degrees of lostness; rather, it excludes from salvation altogether. The closing three-line unit is difficult to translate.[41] Our reconstruction is based on the assumption that Luke comes closer to preserving the original form.[42]

The authenticity of the saying is a matter of controversy.[43] It is difficult to think of an analogy from the post-Easter church, however, for associating two small cities of Galilee, whose occupants belong to chosen Israel, with the heathen cities of Tyre and Sidon, whose inhabitants serve as the prime example of God's judgment on shameless impiety, because they had inflicted so much damage on God's people (Isa 23; Ezek 26–28; Joel 3:1–8; Zech 9:2–4, etc.). There is also in the history of Primitive Christianity after Easter not the slightest reference to Chorazin and Bethsaida. The biting hyperbole is also suggestive of Jesus, since other sayings of his are equally pointed (e.g., Mark 9:43–48 parrs.; 10:25 par.). Again, there are no parallels from the post-Easter mission to Israel. Finally, the connection with Luke 10:23–24 par. is important. Corresponding to the view that it is Jesus who ushers in the time of salvation is the harsh judgment that those who reject his activity will be finally lost. It is easier to assume that, since Jesus had condemned these places so harshly, there was no post-Easter mission at all in them than to argue the opposite position, viz., that the saying was attributed to Jesus, because Christian missionaries had no success in the villages.[44]

The text is in quiet agreement with the Baptist, i.e., it is formulated with no regard for Israel's election in its salvation history, but it is in agreement with Amos's pronouncement of judgment (Amos 9:7–8). Since the text presupposes that Jesus' announcement of the Kingdom of God is the only thing that can save Israel, the consequences of rejecting this last chance are unavoidable. Of course, the statement is formulated first of all with reference to the two Galilean villages.[45] Its purpose is to make them aware of the disaster that awaits them, not to assure Tyre and Sidon that their fate will be better. The statement about Capernaum is reminiscent of Isaiah's taunt of the king of Babylon: "You said in your heart, 'I will ascend to heaven . . . I will sit on the mount of God. . . . ' But you will be brought down to Sheol" (Isa 14:13–15). The text is similar to Jesus' statement, and it expands Israel's comparison with the nations in the first woe by describing Capernaum's future fate with the same colors that Isaiah used to describe the Gentile king. Thus it is likely that Jesus consciously used the language of Isaiah 14 and that he expected his hearers to recognize it. The point of the statement, at least by implication, is that initially Capernaum wanted to be *exalted* by receiving Jesus, but it then rejected Jesus' message and earned his condemnation. Thus the parallel pronouncements of judgment are directed to places in and around which Jesus' activity had been especially intensive. They presuppose that Jesus had worked there. The judgment sayings provide a kind of closure on Jesus' activity[46] in towns in which he obviously had not been successful.[47]

The same thing is probably true of the more general threat of judgment in Luke 11:31–32 par.:

1a *The* queen of the South *will be raised*
 b *at the judgment with this generation*
 c *and will condemn it.*
2a *Because she came from the ends of the earth*
 b *to hear the* wisdom of Solomon.
 c *And behold, more than Solomon is here!*

3a *The* men of Ninevah *will rise up*
 b *at the judgment with this generation*
 c *and will condemn it.*
4a *Because they repented at* Jonah's preaching.
 b *And behold, more than Jonah is here!*[48]

The two sayings are so nearly identical that they must have had a common origin. The dynamic of the sayings is that they focus attention first on a female, then on males— indeed, first on a queen, then on citizens. She comes as a Gentile to Israel to seek out the great king Solomon who possesses divine wisdom. The Ninevite Gentiles, on the other hand, are visited by an Israelite prophet who speaks to them about God. The queen comes to hear; the Ninevites actually repent.

That the theme of Israel and the nations is used so harshly against Israel speaks once again for the probability that the material comes from Jesus. It also presupposes the same understanding of history and of the end-time as do Luke 10:13–14, 23–24. Nowhere else does Primitive Christianity show an interest in the Queen of Sheba. Even the Ninevites are not mentioned again until *1 Clem.* 7:7. We may assume a Semitic original.[49] The way the text confronts Israel with the exemplary behavior of non-Jews has an eloquent parallel in Luke 10:30–35. Important representatives of Israel, viz., a priest and a Levite, fail, while a Samaritan knows what to do. Thus he shames Jesus' Israelite hearers.

Jesus suggests a final judgment in terms of a courtroom scene that clearly is familiar to his hearers. In this scenario, the Queen of Sheba (cf. 1 Kgs 10:1–13) and the Ninevites (cf. Jonah) will rise up, i.e., they will stand, as is customary, before the judge in the final judgment. Against the contemporaries of Jesus, who will also be standing there, these Gentiles will bring charges that will lead to their conviction. A similar judgment scene appears in *T. Benj.* 10:6–10, where God judges first Israel, then the nations. In this final judgment God uses the elect from among the nations to convict Israel in the same way that he had used the Midianites to convict Esau. While the texts are similar, there is an obvious difference. In the *Testament of Benjamin* it is not an entire generation of Israel that is condemned. With the term *this generation*, however, Jesus continues a tradition that speaks wholesale of an entire generation.[50] (The immediate context always reveals that the term is used in a pejorative sense.) Once again we need to emphasize that the judgment saying is focused on Israel; it has no interest in the fate of the queen or the Ninevites. We should not overlook the fact that the words reveal a deep pessimism over the results of Jesus' activity.

It is occasionally alleged that the final lines of the two sayings contain a direct christological statement and that, therefore, the text could not come from Jesus. The "more than Solomon . . . more than Jonah" should be understood, however, as neuter formulations. The issue with Solomon is his wisdom, and the issue with Jonah is his preaching. Thus the two final lines are to be understood as saying that with the appearance of Jesus more is at stake than was the case with Solomon's wisdom and Jonah's preaching. Now what is at stake is the salvation that is being ushered in with the Kingdom of God. Thus the statement reflects the same understanding of judgment that we saw at the beginning of this section in the beatitude of Luke 10:23–24 (in addition, cf. §4.2.2). Accordingly, the two final lines reveal that the woe over the Galilean cities presupposes that they have lost their best, last chance to be saved.

Both the woe over the Galilean cities and the threat of judgment over *this generation* compared Gentiles favorably with contemporary Israel. It was the comparison that made the statement especially harsh. A similar comparison appears in Matt 8:11–12 par. about the participation in the eschatological banquet in the Kingdom of God.

1a   Many *will come from east and west*
 b   *and will recline at the table with Abraham, Isaac, and Jacob in the Kingdom of God;*

2a but you *will be thrown out,*
 b *there will be weeping and gnashing of teeth.*

Matthew preserves a series of opposites (nations-Israel, come–be thrown out, take part in the meal–be in misery) that Luke breaks up for contextual reasons. Luke 13:29 is left hanging in an impossible position. Since Luke demonstrably eliminated the catchword *(the) many* in 13:30 (cf. Mark 10:31; Matt 19:30), it is likely that he did the same thing in v. 29. In addition, Luke added the prophets to the meal and included all four directions of the compass (on the east-west motif cf. Isa 43:5–6; Bar 4:37, etc.). On the other hand, such expressions as *sons of the kingdom* (Matt 8:12; cf. 13:38) and *outer darkness* (cf. Matt 22:13; 25:30) are in Matthew's handwriting.

The first unit of two lines directs the hearer's attention to the expectation of an eschatological feast of salvation filled with the abundance of paradise. The hearer who was familiar with the Bible would be reminded of Isa 25:6: "On this mountain [Zion] the Lord of hosts will prepare for all nations a feast of rich foods, a feast of aged wines, of rich, marrowy foods, of aged, purified wines." The concept is too widespread, however, for us to assume that the text is a direct reference to Isaiah. Indeed, it is a standard religious theme in Early Judaism (cf. *1 Enoch* 62:13–16; 4 Ezra 9:19; *'Abot* 3:16; 4:16; Rev 19:6–9; also *T. Lev.* 18:11; *1 Enoch* 25–27; *Sib. Or. Pro.* 84–86). Nor would Jesus' contemporaries be surprised by a list of illustrious guests, with the patriarchs (mentioned because they are the traditional bearers of the promise) as the most honored guests. The patriarchs' prominent role in Israel's story secured for them in Early Judaism a special place near God (*1 Enoch* 70:4; different in *T. Benj.* 10:6–7). The idea was common in Jewish eschatology that sinners and the godless would not be admitted to the feast. Such unworthy persons would be thrown into the place of damnation (such as, e.g., the Valley of Hinnom; cf. Isa 66:23–24; *1 Enoch* 26–27), where they will suffer unending torment.

Still, the threat sounds notes that would have been as unbearable for Early Jewish ears as they were inescapable. The standard melody was that Israel and the patriarchs would feast together, with the nations, or parts of them, joining the celebration in honor of God and of his chosen people. This saying, however, reverses the order, with the nations mentioned first, then Israel's exclusion second. Equally significant is the observation that the saying does not address the nations themselves; instead, it speaks to Israel, describing the nations who are streaming to the banquet. Thus present Israel is being addressed directly, but only in order to threaten it with exclusion from the feast. These observations are consistent with the way the above-mentioned texts contradicted Israel's usual understanding of its privileged position by reversing the theme of Israel and the nations.

A further important feature of the threat is that it mentions the patriarchs, but relates them positively to the nations instead of to Israel. The patriarchs cannot keep Israel from being excluded; neither can Israel cite the patriarchs in its defense. One thinks of the position of the Baptist, who denied his contemporaries

any appeal to Abraham as their covenant father (cf. §3.1.3). For the Baptist, God
was able to raise up children for Abraham from the stones of the desert. Jesus
refers to the nations in support of the same basic idea. It is equally noteworthy
that, while the saying seems to presuppose the Zion tradition, it says nothing
directly about Zion and about the Valley of Hinnom as the place of condemnation. Thus the Kingdom of God is interpreted without direct reference to Zion's
role in Israel's salvation history. It is an offensive, albeit hidden, potential of the
text that it implies that one experiences the Kingdom of God in a final sense not
by making a pilgrimage to Zion but, rather, by entering the Kingdom of God (cf.
§4.2.3).

A final consideration in our understanding of the text is that it addresses Israel.
That is to say, it is a threat against the Israel of Jesus' day rather than a promise to
the nations. The nations are simply props on the stage, analogous to the Baptist's
stones, designed to underscore God's unlimited possibility in the hope that Israel
might still wake up and respond to Jesus' message of the Kingdom of God before
it is too late. Of course, it is not by accident that Jesus mentions the nations here,
since, as we will show (§§4.2.3, 5.4), his proclamation of the Kingdom of God is
to be understood within the framework of all creation.

This understanding of the threat coheres so well with Jesus' proclamation that,
for that reason alone, we can accept it as an authentic word of Jesus. In addition,
we can offer the following control test: Since the idea that in the last days the
nations would flow to Zion for their salvation had no relevance for Gentile
Christianity once it accepted 1 Thess 4:13–18, our text could have originated
only in Jewish Christianity. Yet, it is impossible to imagine that Jewish Christians, who still understood themselves as belonging to Israel, would have created
a saying that implicitly excluded them from the final salvation. The tension in our
text between Israel and the nations is simply not conceivable in the history of the
post-Easter church.

The sayings of Luke 10:13–14 par. and 11:31–32 par., which are so similar to
the judgment-prophecy of the Old Testament, underscore the inexorable finality
of judgment. Although Matt 8:11–12 par. contains a threat against Israel, it does
not exclude the possibility that Israel can still take the threat seriously. Thus the
exclusion from the eschatological feast is not necessarily final. The parable of the
unmerciful servant in Matt 18:23–34 offers a similar point of view. While the
narrator does not sweep the severity of judgment under the rug, he hopes that
none of his hearers will be lost:

*1a   A man wanted to settle accounts with his servants. When he began the
      reckoning, one was brought who was a* debtor *of ten thousand talents.
      When he had nothing with which to pay his debt, the master
      commanded that he be sold, along with his wife and children and
      whatever he had, so that the debt could be paid.*
  *b   The servant fell to the ground as a supplicant and said, "Be patient
      with me, and I will repay everything!"*

c   But the master had mercy *on that servant, released him, and canceled his debt.*

2a *But when that servant went out, he found* one of his fellow-slaves, *who owed him one hundred denarii. He seized him, choked him and said, "Pay what you owe me!"*

b   *Then his fellow-servant fell to the ground and pleaded with him, "Be patient with me, and I will repay you!"*

c   *But he would not agree. Instead, he went and* threw him into prison, *until he should repay the debt.*

3a *Now when his fellow-servants saw what had happened, they were greatly upset, and they reported to their master everything that had happened.*

b   *Then his master summoned him and said to him, "You wicked servant!* I canceled your entire debt, *when you asked me (to do so). Wouldn't it have been right for you to have* mercy on your fellow-servant, *just as I had mercy on you?"*

c   *And his master was* angry *and turned him over to the torturers until he should repay everything owed to him.*

Setting the limits of the parable is relatively easy. Verse 35 is Matthew's interpretation, which, along with vv. 21–22, provides the framework for the parable. Verse 35 and the reference to the king in Matt 22:2, which is missing in the parallel in Luke 14:16, justify the conclusion that 18:23a also comes from Matthew's hand.[51] Luke 14:16–24 demonstrates that the general expression *a man* can introduce a parable about a master and his servant. Since, of course, the parable presupposes the milieu of a great king, it is conceivable that Matthew's source began with the words *a royal man.* Such a possibility is worth considering, but it is by no means compelling.

Matthew's language appears again in the transitional v. 31a.[52] The verse is not really needed, except for the fact that without it we would not know how the master learned of the servant's behavior (cf., e.g., Luke 15:25–27). Under no circumstance should we conclude from this observation, however, that the entire conclusion of the parable is Matthew's addition; given the tension between vv. 23–27 and 28–30, the authority figure must appear again, since the two sections create a problem that demands a solution.

The place of v. 34 is a matter of controversy. It is true that the statement brings closure to the narrative tension of the story, when the evil servant after his good fortune becomes a tragic figure. Also appropriate to the style, however, would be an open-ended conclusion at v. 33 (cf. Matt 20:13–15; Luke 15:31–32). The question is whether that kind of open ending is intended. In its present form all three stages of the narrative contain the judgment motif, but without v. 34 it would be missing from the third part. Noteworthy is the way the judgment motif is played out among the changing personal relations. In the first scene the great king pardons the satrap and releases him from his debt. In the second scene the satrap is unforgiving with a petty debtor. The third scene parallels the first two perfectly, when the great king sentences the satrap.[53] It is also possible that the polarity between mercy and anger is intended (18:27, 34). It is true that with v. 35 Matthew moves in the direction of v. 34, but vv. 34 and 35 talk about completely different things. To be sure, the torturers are a new element in the story, but they appear as a natural element within the narrative's milieu (see below). What great king of Antiquity did not have torturers! In v. 35 Matthew nowhere indicates that he understands the story as an allegory, so that consideration is not a factor in separating v. 35 from v. 34.

Appropriately, in v. 34 the great king changes his earlier decision. This element of the narrative world probably reflected the real-life experience of the world of the ancient hearers. When the facts of a situation change, a great king can change his decision; indeed, one would expect that of him. In addition, v. 33 would be an unsatisfactory ending. Either the fate of the fellow servant in v. 30 must be reversed or the behavior of the evil servant sanctioned. It is not enough that the unjust servant is exhorted to think about his behavior. If the story ended with v. 33 without changing the fate of the fellow servant, the king's sovereign act in the first scene would, by the end of the second scene, appear to be arbitrary. Finally, if we were to remove v. 34 from the parable, we would have to attribute all of the texts that we are dealing with in this section (§3.2.3) to the church. In that case we would have to justify historically and theologically why we attribute such pronouncements of judgment to the church but not to Jesus. In any case, we should reject as worthless the desire to distinguish between a cheerful Jesus and a gloomy church.

The structure of the parable is easily recognizable. There are three scenes: (1) master-servant, vv. 23–27; (2) servant-fellow servant, vv. 28–30; (3) master-servant, vv. 31–34. Each scene has three parts. The first two scenes are parallel in structure and opposite in content. Then the third scene repeats the beginning (vv. 23–25) against the background of the second scene. Naturally, this composition is intentional as is the fact that the servant, who in vv. 26 and 30 is a speaking and acting agent, then becomes a mute and passive object. There is no second chance. He cannot make good his failure in the crucial situation (v. 30). The servant confronts the hearer in each scene. His behavior and his fate are what ties the three scenes together. While in the second scene he throws away his future, in the first and third scenes it is the master who makes sovereign decisions about the servant. Thus while he is the one who acts with sovereign authority, it is the servant on whom the hearers have their attention fixed—to the bitter end.

The material presupposes conditions that are obviously Oriental but hardly Jewish. One thinks, for example, of the ten thousand talents (i.e., sixty million denarii, whereby a denarius is the normal wage of a day-laborer [Matt 20:2]!) and the posture of submissiveness in v. 26 (falling on the ground),[54] and of the punishments (sale of family and possessions). According to Lev 25:39–40 and Deut 15:12, such punishments are not typical for Israel, in spite of the apparent temporary practice recognized in Neh 5:1–7 (cf. also Isa 50:1; Ps 109:7–13). They certainly are not as normal as the narrator in Matt 18:23b, 34 presupposes. Thus the parable's authority figure is a sovereign to whom satraps are subordinate and who (yearly?) demands his share of the produce. The contrast between the astronomically high debt and the paltry sum of one hundred denarii provides dramatic effect. The difference is comparable to that between the investment portfolio of an exorbitantly wealthy person and pocket change. Equally stark is the contrast between the satrap's humble attitude and pleading in v. 26 and his threatening behavior and harsh punishment in vv. 28, 30. Clearly the man did not understand that in v. 27, in an unexpected and unrepeatable situation, he was granted new life purely as an act of mercy and that he therefore could not continue to live as he had previously lived. His gigantic debt was forgiven, even though he had only asked for permission to defer payment, and, given the amount of the debt, even that request was perhaps unrealistic. Yet, he could not even grant the petty official's request for a delay in the repayment of a small amount

(vv. 26b = 29b), when he should have expressed the new life mercifully granted him by showing mercy to others (v. 33). Thus in the course of the narrative the issue of debt/guilt [German: *Schuld*, transl.] shifts from material debts to the guilt the servant bears in his misunderstanding of life. He is wicked because he failed to give the slightest thought to what the forgiveness of v. 27 implied for his own life and for human life in general. He refused to lead the new life that was granted him in v. 27.

Nothing more can be done to help those who have gambled away the offer of acceptance that the Kingdom of God extends to those who are lost. Thus the consequences of such behavior are in the third scene unambiguous and unavoidable. The parable is one of the few pieces of parabolic material that ends so negatively, with no ifs, ands, or buts. The finality of the judgment is sealed. Only the servant is punished (in contrast to v. 25 his family is spared), and, given the size of his debt, he will never again taste freedom. At least that is the understanding of the narrator, who intentionally ignores the possibility that the imprisoned and tortured satrap could lay his hands on hidden treasures or might have sympathetic relatives and friends. Only on the surface is the issue money. That the debt will never be repaid while the servant is in prison shows that now, under the executioner's shadow, he must drink the final dregs of his wasted life, because he did not learn from his master's earlier gift of grace how to live graciously. The Kingdom of God gave him only one chance, and it will not come again. Thus Matt 18:23–34 is a parable that in its substance belongs to the words of judgment that Jesus directs at those who have not accepted his message. It does not pronounce judgment on a particular individual or group, but it thoroughly and energetically warns people that the same thing will happen to them if they lose the new understanding of life that comes with the Kingdom of God. It impresses on the hearer that there is a necessary correlation between the gift of life and the way life is lived. Thus receiving forgiveness has a twin sister, viz., the obligation to extend that same forgiveness to others (cf. §5.2.3).

Finally, in spite of the ambivalence toward Jesus and the rejection of his message, he remained convinced that what he had begun would lead in the end to a positive result. This confidence is clear in the parable of sowing and harvesting in Mark 4:3–8:

1a *Behold, the sower went out to sow.*
 b *And the sowing happened in the following way:*
2a *Some fell* on the way,
 b *and the birds came*
 c *and devoured it.*
3a *And other fell* on rocky ground *[v. 5b, c],*
 b *and when the sun rose*
 c *it was scorched [v. 6c].*

4a   And other fell among the thorn (seeds),
 b   and the thorns came up
 c   and choked it,
 d   and it gave no fruit.
5a   And other (seed) fell onto good ground,
 b   and it gave fruit, coming up and growing,
 c   and bore thirty, sixty, and one hundred fold.

It has long since been adequately demonstrated that the parable's allegorical interpretation in Mark 4:13–20 comes from the early church;[55] and that the call to hear in vv. 3a and 9 is part of the framework rather than of the parable also should need no justification. The single relative clause in v. 5b and the typical Markan link *(and) immediately* in v. 5c disturb the unit's structural parataxis. The repetition of the style of v. 5c in v. 6b shows that the latter also is an editorial explanation. When these redundant additions are removed, a natural outline remains.[56] The fate of the seed is traced four times. Each time it is described in retrospect, i.e., a familiar process that is repeated every year is described in the past tense. On three occasions (viz., with the pathway through the field, with the rocky ground, and with the ground overrun with weeds) the sowing ends in failure; on one occasion (with the good ground) it is successful. Paralleling the three kinds of failure are the three levels of success, each of which is increased by thirty, except in the third case, when the thirty is rounded off by an additional ten. One hundred represents in round numbers the highest possible amount. The harvest the narrator projects is within the realm of the average, when one considers that when a kernel of grain germinates it can produce several side-shoots from the main sprout. If an ear contains about thirty kernels, then we would need a stalk with three shoots.[57] There is even a pattern to the fate of the different seeds. The first does not even germinate, the next one grows only a little, the third reaches about one-half its expected height, while the fourth seed reaches full growth. We note in addition that each of the negative cases is structured according to its beginning situation (line a), a description of the danger (line b), and its end (line c). In the case of the third seed a fourth line is added ("and it gave no fruit"), which both in form and substance underscores its difference from the seed on the good ground. The difference is one of quality rather than quantity. It is not that only one-fourth of the seed bore fruit. What is imagined, rather, is quite normal. Since in Palestine one sowed before one plowed,[58] the path is a short-cut through the field that has been trampled down over the winter months, the stones lie hidden in the ground, and one cannot even see the seeds of the weeds. Of course, the majority of the field is good ground.

The narrator is interested neither in the sower nor the land, only in the beginning and ending of the process—what is sown and what the yield of the harvest is. Year in and year out seed always faces an uncertain fate, but normally there is a good harvest. (The possibility of a total failure due to drought or a locust plague is intentionally ignored in the narrative.) This reality explains both the diffuse situation with which the story begins and also the confidence that there will be a successful harvest. Jesus' activity was subjected to the same kind of initial ambivalence in which only a fine line separated faith and indignation (Matt 11:6 par.), acceptance and rejection of his words and deeds, but this ambivalence did not diminish his confidence that, as the parable makes clear, what he had begun would reach its goal. An advantage of the parable is that instead of looking ahead to the arrival of the Kingdom of God, it looks back on a farming procedure as a normal experience. Thus the parable grounds hope and confidence on something that is verifiable by experience. By telling it Jesus claims the same hope for the Kingdom of God. As certainly as sowing leads to harvest, God will complete in the Kingdom of God what Jesus has begun.

3.2.5 The Meaning of Israel under Judgment

Jesus shares with John the Baptist a fundamental attitude about the contemporary generation of Israel. It is such a complete failure before God that it no longer has any claim on God's covenant promises. In the case of the Baptist this conviction derived from his basic certainty that impending judgment threatened all Israel. Unlike the Old Testament prophets (e.g., Isa 1:10–17, 21–23; Amos 1:6–2:16), in the extant tradition he does not indicate that he is thinking of individual sins. Jesus accepts this condemnation of all Israel. When he confronts Israel with the reality of an imminent and inescapable divine judgment, he makes the same general pronouncement that the Baptist makes (§3.2.2).

Yet, Jesus goes beyond the Baptist. Israel's disqualification cannot be reduced simply to a moral evaluation of Israel's daily life. Of course, Jesus does not commend the dishonesty of the steward in Luke 16:1–8; instead, he emphasizes his determination. Of course, Jesus does not approve of the younger son's life in the Diaspora as it is described in Luke 15:11–19; from an ethical point of view, the elder son does not need to repent. However Jesus may interpret individually the Torah's standards (cf. §5.3), a life apart from its ethic would be for him an absurdity. Still, it is noteworthy that he does not follow the Early Jewish line of describing the flood generation and the Sodomites as unusually wicked. He simply states that sudden judgment came over their daily life without evaluating it morally (Luke 17:26–29 par.; cf. §3.2.2). Nor is the younger son in Luke 15:11–32 disqualified on moral grounds, in spite of what for Jewish standards was extremely negative behavior. It is the older son who later condemns the younger son (15:30a). And it is not said of the rich landowner in Luke 12:16–20 (cf. §3.2.2) that he is hard-hearted and greedy. His plans for the future are ethically neutral, yet God's judgment strikes precisely in this situation. The commonsense wisdom of this parable underscores how the large landowner is foolish, or godless: He makes his plans as if he were the lord of his life, without considering that it is God the creator who is responsible for giving and sustaining life (cf. Matt 5:45 par.; Luke 12:22–31 par.), even ending life (e.g., Luke 13:1–5). Because the farmer does not see himself as a creature before God, his attitude toward life is fundamentally false. His life consists of nothing more that collecting treasures without thinking of God (cf. Matt 6:24 par.). Thus Israel's problem is not that it violates individual commandments of the Torah; it lies much deeper. Israel's relationship to God, its understanding of life before God, is so broken that it has used up its election. As a result, it must now listen while it is compared with the godless Gentile world, as intolerable as that comparison may be.

Yet, Jesus goes even further. He calls attention to Israel's failed relationship with God by indicating what criteria he uses when he judges Israel so severely. His coordinates are not the norms of the typical daily life with its necessary compromises. He is not interested in rigorously sweeping out the dark corners of daily life. In this sense he is not a social reformer; his contribution lay, rather, in helping people in the course of their daily lives come to terms with hostility and their own weaknesses (cf. §5.1–5.3). His standard against which every relationship to God is measured, however, is the perfection and holiness of God itself (cf. Matt 6:9 par.; §5.2.4). Thus it is not human individuals who determine how their relationship to God might be shaped; God's sovereignty alone determines what in this case is appropriate (cf. §5.3.3).

Jesus underscored in particular three points of view on this theme. The first begins with the creator's perfection. God's concern for the welfare of creation is focused on granting life rather than on the plans that humans have for their lives (Matt 5:45 par.; Luke 12:22–31 par.). The second point of view focuses attention on the God who out of his own graciousness grants lost persons a new life that overcomes their lost condition (Luke 15:11–32; 18:9–14). The third point of view focuses on the way human beings maneuver between their life as creatures and their final destination. Just as God is there for humans as creator and gracious redeemer, so must they live completely for God (e.g., Mark 9:43–48 par.; Matt 6:24 par.; Luke 12:22–31 par.), grant to others the same goodness they have experienced (e.g., Matt 5:43–48 par.; 18:23–34), and not repay God's goodness with anger and complaining (Luke 15:25–32; Matt 20:1–16). Thus human sin is actually a matter of not letting God be God as he chooses to be.

What was offensive about Jesus was his proclamation of the imminent Kingdom of God as graciousness that precludes judgment. In varying ways three parables deal with what was likely the common reaction of his contemporaries: Matt 20:1–16; Luke 15:11–32; and Luke 18:10–14. What they have in common is that all of them are aware of a negative reaction to Jesus that understands God in covenant-legalistic terms. Since, according to this view, it is what people do and what happens to them that determines their fate, God's task is simply to confirm in his judgment what has already been determined. Jesus has a different view of God. In the final judgment God does not merely ratify what humans have planned for their lives. Instead, with Jesus he creates new relationships by means of his present graciousness. In his election of the lost he refuses to abandon people to their own failed history. God is God not because he sees a cause-and-effect relationship between the way people act and what happens to them, but because he himself has a gracious word to say about the situation. The person who takes offense at this God is truly lost (Matt 11:6).

In the parable of the workers in the vineyard (Matt 20:1–16; cf. §5.2.2) this tension is described as follows: It is explicitly stated at the beginning (v. 2) that there was full agreement about the work to be done (i.e., the behavior expected) and the pay to be received (i.e., what will happen as a result). Verses 3–7 imply that the workers engaged later in the day were treated the same way. Yet, what happens in vv. 8–15 runs counter to what the outline of the story has led the hearer to expect. While paying the same wages to all the workers does not violate the agreement with those who worked all day, it does violate the principle of fairness in dealing with the other workers (v. 12!). That there is such disparity in the amount of work done for the same pay is scandalous. Furthermore, it would ruin any labor market. Should the same thing happen the next day, all of the workers will wait until the eleventh hour to show up for work. The costs would be extremely high, and the output for the day would be ruinously low. The cunning with which Jesus shapes the narrative world in order to confront the hearer with the offense of God's sovereign graciousness is as admirable as it is clear that, where this graciousness of God is present, defining one's relationship to God in terms of what one does and the rewards one receives belongs to the old world that existed before the Kingdom of God drew near.

In the parable of the father and his two sons (Luke 15:11–32; cf. §4.3.1) the younger son by his own admission is a total failure. In his misery he knows that he has lost the legal standing that was his by virtue of his birth. He repents in order to obtain a new legal standing with his father, one that he has not yet ruined. He wants to assume the position of a servant simply in order to live. He knows that he has forfeited his position as a son, but he hopes that his willingness to be a laborer will gain him acceptance. Thus he sees his relationship to his father only in terms of his behavior and its consequences. The father, on the other hand, as an act of pure mercy reestablishes his fatherhood toward the returning prodigal, so that the latter once again is a son. Then the son confesses his failure and realizes that his offer to become a servant is no longer relevant. He has learned that his relationship to his father is based on the father's will rather than on what he himself does or expects.

In evaluating himself and his brother, the older son also appeals to the principle that people reap what they sow (Gal 6:7). Of course, he is by far in the better position, for his evaluation of himself in terms of what he has done and what he deserves is the opposite of that of his shiftless brother (v. 29b). From his point of view he is also justifiably angered over the fact that his father gives a feast for the good-for-nothing brother, although he has never given one for him. For him the natural order of things has turned insane, and he complains to his father about this theater of the absurd. The father's answer is twofold. First, he denies the older son also the right to define his relationship to his father in terms of his own behavior. He says: You are always with me, i.e., our relationship is based on my presence as your father. To be a father is qualitatively different from distributing possessions and paying wages. Nor is a goat something that the older son has to negotiate angrily by calling attention to how much he has worked (v. 29). The father's possessions already belong to him. Secondly, the father repeats v. 24, i.e., he summons the older son to share his joy. Whether the latter learned his lesson is left open.

The parable of the Pharisee and tax collector in Luke 18:10–14a is the third of our parables:

1   *Two men went up into the temple to pray; one (was) a Pharisee, the other (was) a tax collector.*

2   *The* Pharisee *stood by himself and prayed, "God, I thank you that I am not like other people, rapacious, unjust, adulterers, or even like this tax collector. I fast twice each week, I tithe everything I have."*

3   *The* tax collector *stood far off and would not even raise his eyes to heaven. Instead, he beat his breast and said, "God, have mercy on me, the sinner."*

4   *I tell you, this one went down (from the temple mount)* justified *to his house,* not that one.

In view of the impending judgment (Luke 17:20–37) Luke uses two parables to warn his readers about two typical dangers (18:1, 9). Luke 18:9 is Luke's introduction to the parable of the Pharisee and the tax collector in which he underscores the danger of thinking of oneself as righteous and its companion attitude, condescension. Such an attitude would be disastrous for the church, because when it comes to judgment the principle is: Those who exalt themselves will be humbled; those who humble themselves will be exalted (18:14b). Within this Lukan framework the Pharisee in the parable represents arrogance and the tax collector humility. This understanding of the parable, however, which seems so compelling in Luke's framework, is secondary. Arrogance and humility are not the key to the parable. We must especially reject the frequent generalization that *the* Pharisees are described here as arrogant men who look down on other people. Reading into the parable a wholesale condemnation of Pharisees reduces the Pharisee in the parable to an unhistorical caricature. The parable itself no more classifies the character of Pharisees and tax collectors than does Luke 10:29–37 describe all Samaritans as especially helpful and all members of the temple staff (priests and Levites) as uncharitable (cf. §5.3.2). While it is not completely a historical accident that the narrator chose a Pharisee and a tax collector as opposites (see below), other figures could have been chosen to achieve the same purpose. The point is that, even though all Israel stands under judgment (§3.2.2), in the midst of a hopeless situation God is free to create the possibility of grace.

The parable has four parts: two prayers that are framed by an introduction and a conclusion. The first part introduces two men praying, i.e., they are engaged in the formally religious practice of their relationship to God. The final part is a commentary that evaluates the relationships to God described in the two middle parts in such a way that the hearer learns what kind of conversation with God is successful and what kind is unsuccessful.

Since the verb tenses in the narrator's commentary in Luke 18:14a differ from Luke's future orientation in v. 14b toward the final judgment, v. 14a must be pre-Lukan. The verbal formulation of *to justify* is documented in Early Judaism (4 Ezra 12:7; *Bib. Ant.* 3:10). There is no reason to assume Pauline influence on the sentence; indeed, its Semitic style indicates otherwise.[59] Furthermore, the flow of the parable leads naturally to the conclusion expressed in Luke 18:14a. The contrast between the two men is intentional, and it is natural that the second one who prays is regarded favorably. Linguistically the parable's framework is also balanced (*go up to the temple–go down*). Thus the author of the commentary in v. 14a is the Jesus who tells the parable. That the parable itself fits with Jesus' proclamation is clear not least of all from its similarity in content with the parables in Matt 20:1–16 and Luke 15:11–32).

Most contemporaries of Jesus would have agreed that Pharisees were quick to criticize tax collectors and to distance themselves from them (Luke 18:11c). Without discussing its legitimacy, Jesus uses this widespread attitude as the background for his scene, much as the hostility between Jews and Samaritans lies in the background of Luke 10:29–37 without actually being mentioned. Another creative force lying behind the parable is Jesus' own experience with the Pharisees, who, since they don't particularly like the tax collectors, take offense at Jesus for being, as they rightly judge, the *friend of the tax collectors and sinners* (Matt 11:19; cf. §4.3.2). Of course, the parable is not designed to be an apology for Jesus' behavior in this situation; it has, rather, its own concern, which could be expressed as well with another pair of contrasting characters such as, e.g., a Jewish Sadducee and a sick Galilean.

The Pharisee's relationship to God, as it is expressed in his prayer, reflects a point of view that within Early Judaism was both possible and appropriate (cf. *b. Ber.* 28b). Clearly he represents a common attitude among the hearers. According to this attitude, his prayer (morning or afternoon) in the temple as the place where God is near is exemplary, with thanks for God's election coming first. God and the Pharisee combined their efforts to make it possible for the Pharisee to express his identity by distancing himself from all sinners and tax collectors (v. 11; cf. 1QH vii 34; *'Abot* 1:7). Along with his obedience to the Torah through internalizing the will of God, he cites his additional achievements as expressions of a life lived successfully according to God's will (v. 12). Thus the Pharisee is at peace with God and with himself. There is no essential difference between him and the older son in Luke 15:25–32, for the latter also defines his sonship in terms of untiring diligence (cf. Luke 15:29 with 18:11–12). This similarity, along with the way the prayers of the two men in the temple are juxtaposed, is a clear indication that the Pharisee's prayer is not a caricature.

The tax collector's prayer (18:13) also lies in the realm of what was possible in those days. We should not suppose that Jesus regards the second man as an especially conspicuous sinner among his contemporaries; texts such as Luke 13:2–4 speak against such an assumption (cf. §3.2.2). Nor should we wonder whether the depth of his feeling of sin might not have been exceptional in his day; such texts as 1QS xi 9–xii 15 and 1QH i 24ff. show that that is not the case. Nor should we assume that such an act of repentance was completely unattainable (cf. §3.1.3 and examples from §§4.1.4 and 4.1.8). Thus the tax collector also formulates a prayer that is not all that unusual. We might describe it as a shorter version of the return of the younger son in Luke 15:11–24. Of course, the tax collector, unlike the younger son, does not presume to fantasize how he might create for himself a new beginning (with a life as a servant). He merely lives with the thought that the God whom he addresses in prayer could be gracious to him, simply because he is God. This God's grace is his only possibility of salvation.

Decisive is that these two prayers express two relationships to God that are mutuality exclusive. It is not the case that they represent different possibilities in the course of a checkered life; in the view of the narrator, only the second prayer represents the position of all people before God. The purpose of the parable is to underscore that idea. Thus the contrast between the two praying men is to be resolved in favor of the tax collector. The Pharisee (and that means every hearer of Jesus) must learn to do the same thing that was demanded of the older son in Luke 15:31–32. Unless he undergoes that kind of change of attitude, he and his prayer are lost. Thus the relationship that the Pharisee claims to have with God is worthless. It is the opposite of the way Jesus sees every person's true situation before God. Since the tax collector's penitential prayer reflects this situation (Luke 13:1–5; cf. §3.2.2), his prayer is the attitude toward God that is appropriate for everyone. He does the only thing possible when, unconditionally and exclusively, he turns to the God who simply wants to be the God who saves those who are lost.

Jesus' announcement of the Kingdom of God initiates the beginning of salvation—the transition to something that is qualitatively new (§4.2.2). What has previously existed is now obsolete, including the covenant legalism with its principle of conduct and reward. Since all are lost, salvation is possible only by God's mercy. Conduct and reward will no longer play a role in the age of salvation, because its character will be determined solely by God's gracious gift. According to Jesus, those persons who continue to think in covenant-legalistic terms face the Baptist's threat of judgment, i.e., the wrath of God (cf. also Luke 13:1–5 in §3.2.2). They can escape judgment only by letting God be what God wants to be, viz., a gracious God who receives that which is lost.

3.2.6   The Difference between Jesus and the Baptist

The freedom and independence that Jesus exhibited vis-à-vis the things that existed before he introduced the new age of salvation appear also in his relationship with John the Baptist, the area in which he demonstrably was most closely related to the old order. The continuity between Jesus and the Baptist is clear (cf. §3.2.1), but Jesus builds his own structure on John's foundation. This new interpretation of the Baptist's message is based on the following accents.

For Jesus, the Baptist stands on the threshold of the new age of salvation, but he still belongs to the old order (cf. Matthew 11: 11, 19 and 4.2.2). Jesus is fundamentally convinced that it is the Kingdom of God that will usher in this new age of salvation. The Baptist's basic conviction about Israel becomes in the mind of Jesus the description of what Israel's situation will be after the Kingdom of God. Yet, the God of Jesus is a God who wants to nullify this lost condition even before the judgment arrives. John bore witness to a God whose wrath encompassed all Israel. Jesus represents a God whose work and essence are essentially gracious. Without minimizing God's wrath over Israel's failure, Jesus identifies this graciousness as the reason for and the content of the coming salvation. Jesus does not challenge the Baptist's authority, but neither does he accept the judgment that John announced as God's last word to his people. Instead, Jesus is convinced that, since Israel as a whole is condemned, his task is to proclaim God as the final savior of those who were lost. For the God of Jesus, Israel's failure is nothing short of a challenge to show that he is a God who gives life and salvation. Human beings can in no way keep God from exercising his freedom to side with the Good, for God's creative graciousness far surpasses human misery.

Thus Jesus is also able to speak of judgment in conditional terms. Indeed, for him judgment can have parallel results. God will turn graciously toward lost Israel one last time, but nothing more can be done to help those who reject this final gracious act.

Jesus' new fundamental conviction brings with it a changed way of understanding the present. It is no longer the final moment of the old age before an imminent judgment; it is the beginning of the new age of salvation. Judgment is still temporally near, but the threatening imminence is weakened. Jesus no longer emphasizes that it will come suddenly in the midst of normal daily activity.

He also reformulates the Baptist's call to repentance. The announcement of impending judgment on all Israel still leads to a call to repentance (albeit without the demand for baptism), but Jesus uses different language to call for a decision on behalf of the Kingdom of God.

The Baptist spoke of *the wrath that is to come*, and of destruction by fire. We have no evidence that he actually used the word *judgment*. Jesus, on the other hand, appears not to have talked about coming wrath and destruction by fire, although after Easter the church would speak once more of God's wrath (cf. 1 Thess 1:10; Rom 2:5, 8; 5:9; John 3:36, etc.). Jesus himself talks about the (final) *judgment*, about *perishing*, about *being denied* in a forensic act of judgment, or about *being left behind*. He also has clearly different metaphors from the Baptist's fire, which consumes chaff and unfruitful trees. Another new element in Jesus is that, when Israel rejects its last chance for salvation, he compares it unfavorably with the nations.

Why does the Baptist belong to the old order? It is because he still measures human life in terms of behavior and its consequences, and thus because of the coming judgment he can offer Israel no hope for the future. Jesus, on the other hand, measures human reality in terms of the Kingdom of God—a kingdom characterized by the gracious nearness with which God wants to abolish the human misery caused, in part, by the system of works and rewards. In the light of this kingdom the entire system of works and rewards is declared to be obsolete and inappropriate.

In short, Jesus restructures and reevaluates John's message of judgment in light of his understanding of the impending Kingdom of God.

NOTES

1. For detailed evidence in support of these conclusions cf. S. von Dobbeler, *Gericht*, 45, 51, 71–72.

2. Thus John thinks in a synchronic framework. He has no concept of a resurrection of all Israelites to judgment; the judgment of which he speaks does not extend diachronically back into the history of Israel.

3. Zephaniah's central concept of the Day of Yahweh (Zeph 1:14), and Amos's catchword *justice and righteousness* (Amos 5:7, 23–27; 6:12–14) are both similar to the Baptist's message.

4. Cf. similar formulations in Zeph 2:3; Mal 3:7b; Tob 13:6, etc. [English translation of the Sibylline text is from R. H. Charles, *The Apocrypha and Pseudepigrapha of the Old Testament*, Vol. 2 (Oxford: Clarendon, 1913) 396.]

5. Thus John does not use the concept of a forensic judicial process as do, e.g., Joel 4:2, 14; Dan 7; *1 Enoch* 62:3; 90:20.

6. John shows no interest at all in the Gentiles. He thus is not thinking of a general judgment of the nations such as one finds in Matt 25:31–46.

7. On the Deuteronomic view of history cf. O. H. Steck, *Israel*, and S. von Dobbeler, *Gericht*, 83ff.

8. Another typical tradition that Israel used in appealing for divine mercy was the motif of God as the creator and ruler of the world who directs everything for good (cf. §§4.1.8; 4.2.3). We do not discuss it here, because the Baptist does not make use of it.

9. The heightened sense of sin in 1QH, which is cast in the framework of human impotence and which is sharply dualistic (cf. H. Lichtenberger, *Menschenbild*), obviously is not a factor in the Baptist's message.

10. For other examples of that kind of divine miracle, see *1 Enoch* 98:4; Ovid, *Met.* 1.395–415.

11. One gets the impression that the call to repentance in Early Judaism appears largely in connection with the Deuteronomic view of history and that, therefore, it stands in continuity with the Old Testament (cf. P. Welten, "Buße II"). *Sib. Or.* 4.158–169 is a text outside this tradition, which is often cited in connection with the Baptist, but it should not be connected with the Baptist's movement as closely as H. Lichtenberger does in "Täufergemeinden."

12. On this difference cf. E. Brandenburger, "Gerichtskonzeptionen," 51–52.

13. There is no evidence for proselyte baptism before 70 CE.

14. Naturally, there is evidence in Early Judaism for the Holy Spirit as an agent of eschatological cleansing (1QS iv 20–21). In the present context, however, that kind of Jewish, and especially Baptist, expression would be abrupt and isolated. It makes immediate sense only as a Christian expression.

15. There is little to commend the suggestion that we regard only the adjective *holy*

as a Christian addition and then translate the Greek (or Aramaic) word for *spirit* as *wind*, (most recently O. Böcher, "Johannes," 175). It is true that wind can be an agent of judgment (Isa 4:4; Ezek 13:11–13; *1 Enoch* 100:13; Sir 39:28, etc.), but that motif does not fit well in this context, since one would have to read into the text the idea that winnowing requires wind. Thus the suggestion is problematic for three reasons: First, it must dissolve the fixed Christian association of *holy* and *spirit*. Then it must give the word for spirit a meaning that is foreign to the context. Finally, it must assume a highly indirect allusion to the motif it alleges to find in the text.

16. Cf. in addition the evidence cited by R. L. Webb, *John*, 222ff.

17. M. Reiser, *Gerichtspredigt*, 172.

18. Mark 13 clearly is compatible with Jewish views, but the suggestion that it is based on a Jewish original (13:7–8, 14–20, 24–27) is too conjectural.

19. On the most recent discussion, cf. R. L. Webb, *John*, 228–260.

20. On prophecy in Early Judaism, cf. J. Becker, *Täufer*, 41ff.; P. W. Barnet, "Sign Prophets"; R. L. Webb, *John*, 307ff. On Jesus' form of prophecy cf. §4.4.3.

21. Another example of a prophet of judgment is Jeshua ben Ananias (Josephus, *J. W.* 6.300ff.), who in different form, but just as graphically, lived out his unique existence outside normal society. One thinks also of Bannus (Josephus, *Life*, 7–12), although he clearly was not a prophet.

22. Cf. W. Härle, "Rede."

23. A similar situation is that of Josephus, who spent three years as the pupil of the hermit, Bannus (*Life*, 10–11).

24. On the reconstruction of the unit's beginning, cf. M. Reiser, *Gerichtspredigt*, 233–234.

25. J. Blinzler, "Niedermetzelung," 24ff. However, his attempt to date the events is too hypothetical.

26. For more on the question of authenticity, cf. J. Becker, *Täufer*, 87–88; M. Reiser, *Gerichtspredigt*, 232–233.

27. H. Merklein (*Botschaft*, 36) has correctly emphasized this conditional element in Jesus' language about the future.

28. Cf. J. Jeremias, *Parables*, 165.

29. Thus the *quaestio facti* is not even posed in Luke 16:1–2.

30. Cf. J. Burckhardt, *Kulturgeschichte* I, 228.

31. Contra J. D. M. Derrett, who sees in the text the enforcement of the prohibition against usury. Cf. M. Reiser, *Gerichtspredigt*, 285ff.

32. J. Jeremias, *Parables*, 181.

33. Cf. D. Lührmann, *Redaktion*, 75–83.

34. Cf. also the exorbitant debt in Matt 18:24–25. The allegory of the evil workers in the vineyard in Mark 12:1–12 parr. and especially the Matthean (allegorized) version of the parable of the great feast in Matthew 22:1–10 pronounce judgment on Israel. (Luke 14:16–24 contains a corresponding word of judgment only in v. 24, which is secondary.) But it is impossible to attribute the two texts to Jesus. When they transfer salvation history from Israel to the church and thereby look back on the work of Jesus as a thing of the past, they clearly reveal a post-Easter perspective. On the parable of the tenants in the vineyard, cf. U. Mell, *Winzer*, 74ff.

35. On the question of authenticity, cf. most recently J. Sauer, *Rückkehr*, 271–276.

Sauer attributes the text to the Palestinian church, however, since he regards such pronouncements of judgment as incompatible with Jesus' sovereign interest in those who are lost
(p. 274). For him *offending* in all of the synoptic texts is the church's technical language
for causing someone to defect from the Christian message. On his first argument, cf.
above, §3.2.1. With regard to the second argument, we can note that the verb is used also
in Luke 7:22–23 par. in what in other regards is authentic Jesus material. Only by first
reading it into the text can we find in Mark 9:43–48 parr. and Luke 7:22–23 parr. the idea
that believing members of the church must be warned against apostasy.

36.   Naturally, there are other synoptic texts that describe the result of judgment in
symmetric or parallel terms, but texts such as Matt 13:24–30, 36–43, 47–50; 25:1–13,
31–46 (all special M material) and the Q traditions Luke 12:42–46 par. and 19:12–27 par.
are hardly authentic Jesus material. Their post-Easter orientation is too pronounced, be it
in the form of Matthew's understanding of the church, or the problem of the delayed
parousia, or both together. Furthermore, it is probably the case that the idea of a general
judgment based on human deeds such as we find in these texts became the dominant view
in the later years of Primitive Christianity. Jesus expresses it differently. For him all
judgment based on human deeds leads to the judgment that the Baptist proclaims. Salvation comes, however, from confessing him in the present (Luke 12:8–9 par.). Thus it is the
acceptance of the Kingdom of God, rather than the weighing of people's deeds, that opens
up the possibility of salvation.

37.   Cf. *Sib. Or.* 3.815; Josephus, *J. W.* 2.259; 6.303, 305; Matt 11:18.

38.   On leprosy as a general term for skin diseases, cf. J. Gnilka, *Jesus*, 123–124.

39.   On the material and the literature, cf. J. Jeremias, "Elijah"; P. Billerbeck, *Kommentar* IV, 764ff.

40.   On this possibility, cf. J. Jeremias, *Parables*, 142.

41.   Our translation follows M. Reiser, *Gerichtspredigt*, 209–210.

42.   Cf. the discussion in M. Reiser, *Gerichtspredigt*, 207–208.

43.   For the issues, cf. J. Becker, *Täufer*, 98ff.; M. Reiser, *Gerichtspredigt*, 210ff.

44.   On the Galilean churches after Easter, cf. the differing descriptions from L.
Schenke, *Urgemeinde*, 198 and J. Becker, *Urchristentum*, 28–29.

45.   Pronouncements of woes on cities or areas appear already in the Old Testament
(M. Reiser, *Gerichtspredigt*, 210). For concrete examples in which the city is addressed in
the second person singular see *Sib. Or.* 3.303, 319, 323; 4.99, 105.

46.   Since R. Bultmann's *Tradition*, it is customary to attribute to the church all of
Jesus' sayings that speak of his work as a whole or that look back on his activity. Of
course, it can hardly be denied that the church was active in this way. Since, however,
every person is capable of making summary statements and of referring to the past, it is an
open question whether Jesus or the church formulated the synoptic material. We have, in
any case, no real parallel for Jewish or Gentile Christian missionaries cursing entire cities
when their message was rejected. Clearly that does not happen in Mark 6:11 par., and Luke
13:34–35 par. is a special case. The saying belongs to the special words of judgment over
Jerusalem and is a reaction to the death of Jesus rather than the rejection of missionary
activity. Cf. in addition the next note.

47.   We can hardly attribute to Jesus the lament over Jerusalem in Luke 13:34–35 (cf.
O. H. Steck, *Israel*, 53–56 and E. Rau, *Jesus*, 26ff.). It would be exceptional in the earliest
Jesus material if the preexistent wisdom were to speak through the mouth of Jesus. Nor are

the saying's view of history and implicit christology (Jesus as the final messenger of wisdom) compatible with the proclamation of Jesus (cf. §§4.2.2 and 4.4.1). The Lukan woes in Luke 6:24–26 are also conscious additions that do not go back to Jesus, even if they may well be pre-Lukan (F. W. Horn, *Glaube*, 122–130).

48. Our reconstruction of the text follows M. Reiser, *Gerichtspredigt*, 192–193.

49. M. Reiser, *Gerichtspredigt*, 194.

50. See, e.g., on the flood generation, Gen 7:1; the wilderness generation, Deut 1:35; 32:5; Ps 95:10; and the generation of the last days in *Jub.* 23:14–16. The frequent references to *this generation* in Q do not justify denying all corresponding texts to Jesus, especially since Mark 8:12 is independent of Q (cf. also Acts 2:40; Phil 2:15).

51. Cf. A. Weiser, *Knechtsgleichnisse*, 75–76.

52. A. Weiser, *Knechtsgleichnisse*, 83–84.

53. Cf. H. Merkel, "Gottesherrschaft," 152–153.

54. Thus we cannot attribute these two features to Matthew as Gnilka suggests (*Jesus*, 100).

55. Cf. J. Jeremias, *Parables*, 77–79.

56. Cf. G. Lohfink, "Gleichnis," 92–98.

57. Cf. Dalman and G. Lohfink, "Gleichnis," 111–116.

58. Cf. J. Jeremias, *Parables*, 11–12.

59. Cf. J. Jeremias, *Parables*, 141–142.

4

The Approaching Kingdom of God as the Present Beginning of Salvation for Lost Israel

4.1 THE CONCEPT OF GOD'S RULE AS KING IN ISRAEL AND IN EARLY JUDAISM

Becker, J. *Das Heil Gottes*. StUNT 3. Göttingen: Vandenhoeck & Ruprecht, 1964, 190–217.

Bejick, U. *Basileia: Vorstellungen vom Königtum Gottes im Umfeld des Neuen Testaments von der Makkabäerzeit bis zur frühen Kirche*. TANZ 13. Tübingen: Franke, 1994.

Bousset, W. and H. Gressmann. *Religion des Judentums*, 213–42.

Camponovo, O. *Königtum, Königsherrschaft und Reich Gottes in den frühjüdischen Schriften*. OBO 58. Freiburg: Universitätsverlag; Göttingen: Vandenhoeck & Ruprecht, 1984.

Carmignac, J. "Roi, Royauté et Royaume dans la Liturgie Angqlique," *RdQ* 46 (1986) 178–86.

Coppens, J. *La Royauté, le Règne et le Royaume de Dieu*. BETL. Leuven: University Press, 1979.

Dalman, G. *Die Worte Jesu*. 2d ed. Leipzig: J. C. Hinrichs, 1930. Reprinted Darmstadt: Wissenschaftliche Buchgesellschaft, 1965, 75–119.

Füglister, N. "Die Verwendung und das Verständnis der Psalmen und des Psalters um die Zeitwende," in: *Beiträge zur Psalmenforschung*. J. Schreiner, ed. FzB 60. Stuttgart: KBW, 1988, 319–84.

Janowski, B. "Königtum Gottes in den Psalmen," *ZThK* 86 (1989) 389–454.

Jeremias, J. *Das Königtum Gottes in den Psalmen*. FRLANT 141. Göttingen: Vandenhoeck & Ruprecht, 1987.

Koch, K. "Offenbaren wird sich das Reich Gottes," *NTS* 25 (1978–1979) 158–65.

―――. "Gottes Herrschaft über das Reich des Menschen," in: *The Book of Daniel*. A. S. van der Woude, ed. BETL 106. Leuven: University Press, 1993, 77–119.

Ladd, G. E. "The Kingdom of God in the Jewish Apocryphal Literature," *BS* 109 (1952) 55–62, 164–74, 318–31; 110 (1953) 32–49.

Lattke, M. "Zur jüdischen Vorgeschichte des synoptischen Begriffs der 'Königsherrschaft Gottes,'" in: *Gegenwart und kommendes Reich*. Festschrift A. Vögtle. P. Fiedler and D. Zeller, eds. SBS 6. Stuttgart: KBW, 1975, 9–25.

Lindenmann, A. "Herrschaft Gottes/Reich Gottes IV," *TRE* 15 (1986) 196–218.

Michel, D. "Deuterojesaja," *TRE* 8 (1981) 510–30.

Plöger, O. *Theocracy and Eschatology*. Richmond: John Knox, 1968.

Schmidt, W. H. *Alttestamentlicher Glaube in seiner Geschichte*. NStB 6. 7th ed. Neukirchen-Vluyn: Neukirchener Verlag, 1990.

Schnackenburg, R. *Rule*, 1–75.

Schüpphaus, J. *Die Psalmen Salomons*. LGHJ 7. Leiden: Brill, 1977.

Schwemer, M. "Gott als König und seine Königsherrschaft in den Sabbatliedern aus Qumran," in: *Königsherrschaft Gottes und himmlischer Kult im Judentum, im Urchristentum und in der hellenistischen Welt*. M. Hengel and A. M. Schwemer, eds. WUNT 55. Tübingen: J.C.B. Mohr (Paul Siebeck), 1991, 45–118.

Steck, O. H. *Friedensvorstellungen im alten Jerusalem*. ThSt 111. Zürich: Theologischer Verlag, 1972.

Theisohn, J. *Der auserwählte Richter*. StUNT 12. Göttingen: Vandenhoeck & Ruprecht, 1975.

Umemoto, V. "Die Königsherrschaft Gottes bei Philon," in: *Königsherrschaft Gottes und himmlischer Kult im Judentum, im Urchristentum und in der hellenistischen Welt*. M. Hengel and A. M. Schwemer, eds. WUNT 55. Tübingen: J.C.B. Mohr (Paul Siebeck) 1991, 207–56.

Willis, W. (ed.) *The Kingdom of God in 20th-Century Interpretation*. Peabody, MA: Hendrickson, 1987.

Zenger, E. "Herrschaft Gottes/Reich Gottes II," *TRE* 15 (1986) 176–89.

4.1.1 Jesus and Early Judaism

The central concept of Jesus' preaching is found in his unique way of speaking about God's kingship.[1] In our earlier discussion of the Baptist's message (§3.1.2) we noted that the selection of a leading motif is not at all unusual in the prophetic tradition. When Jesus chose his signature word he did not have to introduce it to his hearers as a new concept. Indeed, all of the prophets were similar in this regard. None of them created a new vocabulary. They structured their message in a situation of dialogue. That is to say, the prophets and their hearers were always part of a cultural-religious community in which such catchwords already had a traditional meaning on which they both drew. The prophets chose words that everyone was familiar with precisely so they could use this common understanding to say things that were unique, irritating, or unexpected. By reinterpreting the traditional material, by creating shifts in emphasis, by using the language in unexpected ways, the prophets were able to express their own uniqueness. In the same way, Jesus presupposed a general understanding of the Kingdom of God in order to put his own stamp on the concept.

Few people have seriously argued that the proclamation of Jesus was not grounded in Early Judaism. Frequently, however, two additional observations are made. First, it is claimed that prior to Jesus no one structured an entire message around the Kingdom of God. It is also argued that the expression appears only seldom in the Old Testament and in Early Judaism, and then not as a technical term. These observations are then used to justify ignoring the prehistory of Jesus' central concept, and an understanding of what Jesus wanted to say is derived for the most part only from his proclamation itself.

Now no one denies that examining the message of Jesus itself is of the highest importance, but looking at the message in isolation has serious dangers. How are we to know why Jesus' hearers were so amazed at his message? How can we determine what he agreed with and what he changed? Does not such a process pull Jesus by the roots from his historical context and thereby, without any controls, run the risk of modernizing him? Instead of recognizing that Jesus spoke in a give-and-take situation that had diachronic depth, we look only at his words, which, unencumbered by the weight of a historical situation, we now interpret in terms of their present relevance.

With regard to the second observation, we will concede only that our evidence for the abstract noun *Kingdom of God*, like that for other abstract nouns in Hebrew, is relatively late. Obad 21 provides what is probably our earliest documentation, but the term appears frequently.[2] The Sabbath-hymns from Qumran, which first became known only a few years ago, use the word frequently and offer impressive and final proof against the claim that the abstract noun was used infrequently prior to Jesus.[3]

Yet, there is an even more substantive criticism to be made of this second assumption. It is important to recognize that Hebrew thinking is not organized around concepts and that the understanding of God's rule as king existed long before the emergence of the abstract noun. There was an entire way of speaking that included such practices as referring to God as king or as royal lord and using verbal formulations for ruling. Also relevant are words associated with kingship (e.g., God as lord and judge), royal attributes and insignias (e.g., palace, throne, royal court, glory), royal metaphors (e.g., the king as shepherd), and typically royal functions (granting peace and judging enemies).[4] It is clear that Israel and Early Judaism talk extensively about God's rule as king to describe his relationship with heaven and earth as well as to portray his special relationship to Israel.

Against this background, however, a special feature of Jesus' way of speaking is immediately obvious. He only uses the abstraction *Kingdom of God*. He never refers to God as king, and he never uses verbal forms to describe God's rule. One also never hears the adjective *royal*.[5] Jesus concentrates the entire conceptual field of God's kingship into one single technical term.

The first observation—that God's kingship had never been a central concept prior to Jesus—makes sense only if one keeps in mind the corrections that we have just offered to the second observation. It is true, of course, that no prophet uses the expression *Kingdom of God* as a key term. In the case of Deutero-Isaiah, however, there are good exegetical reasons to speak of a theology of the coming kingdom of God[6] (which we will do later in §4.1.3). We also need to remember the apocalyptist Daniel for whom the dominant motifs were God's powerful rule of history and final saving reign (cf. §4.1.5). Daniel's concept is reinterpreted and developed with the same fundamental emphasis on God's rule in the images of *1 Enoch* and in the targums on the prophets (cf. §4.1.5).

We should not overlook the fact that the theology of Zion was widely known in Jesus' day (cf. §4.1.2). Its center is clearly the concept of God as king, the earliest literary expression of which is found in Isa 6. It would be difficult to exaggerate the importance of this concept for the history of the theology of Zion after Isaiah. It became the symbol around which the theology expressed its unfulfilled hope (cf. §§4.1.3 and 4.1.4), and along the lines of which apocalypticism interpreted and transformed the theology (cf. §§4.1.5–4.1.7).

It was not only the scribe studying sacred texts who was familiar with the theology of Zion. From the Sabbath hymns of Qumran it is probably safe to conclude that it also influenced the worship in the temple cult in Jerusalem. The temple was the natural place for this theology, and the Zion psalms (Pss 46; 48; 84; 87) and royal Yahweh Psalms (Pss 47; 93; 96–99) have their probable setting in the temple cult. Of course, it is likely that in the time of Early Judaism the Old Testament Psalter was not simply the hymn book for the temple and synagogue worship.[7] With the exception of a few psalms that clearly were intended for cultic use (e.g., Pss 29; 30; 120–34), there is no clear proof that the entire Psalter was used in public worship. It is possible that the Psalter in this period served more as a book of devotional reading and of instruction in the school and in the family (cf. Ps 1 as an introduction; Wis 18:8–9; 4 Macc 18:10–19). Yet, precisely because of this popular usage their contents, including the concept of God as king, would have been familiar to the people. Another phenomenon that we need to consider here is that in the time of Late Judaism there were many prayers, most of them probably literary constructions, in which the theme of the Kingdom of God was used with a relatively fixed inventory of motifs (cf. by way of example Tob 13; Sir 51:12; *Ps. Sol.* 17; 2 Macc 1:24–29; *As. Mos.* 4:1; Benediction Eleven of the Eighteen Benedictions).[8] Even if these prayers to a great degree were literary products, they came easily to mind for authors who were familiar with Early Judaism's prayer life. Of course, the Eighteen Benedictions are themselves a direct and trustworthy witness for that prayer life.

Given this evidence, it is reasonable to conclude that Jesus' hearers were familiar with the concept of God's kingdom in some form of the theology of Zion and that they were exposed to this theology not simply from reading literature. With its various expressions, at the center of which stood the theological affirmation of God's reign as king, the theology of Zion was part of the religious air that people breathed. Moreover, although there was no single, far-reaching way of talking about God's rule as king, the theology of Zion gave them concrete images with which to express it. Even with the changes that history brought, certain things among those images remained constant. We may conclude, therefore, that Jesus' central concept of the Kingdom of God evoked widespread associations that were already well-formed. We turn now to a brief survey of these images.[9]

4.1.2 *Yahweh, the King, and Zion*

We begin a discussion of the texts at the place where the idea of God as king originated in Israel. The concept of a royal God is most certainly of Canaanite and Ugaritic origin, and it was transferred to the God of Israel at a time when Israel lived a settled life as a nation and had to come to terms with the religions of the land. Relatively clear remnants of this process of assimilation are preserved in Pss 29; 48; 69; 96; 98; 145; 146. When the Solomonic temple was constructed in the former Jebusite city of Jerusalem, the official temple theology began to use its inherited Canaanite traditions to transform Yahweh into the one divine king. Evidence for this use is the cherubim-throne as God's royal throne in the temple (cf. Pss 47:9; 99:1 and, of course, Isa 6 as the earliest example).

What were the central points of this earliest theology of Zion? If in the surrounding world El was the king of the gods because he ruled over all gods (an idea preserved in Ps 95:3), Israel's God now becomes the only god and king, although he is surrounded by a large court (Isa 6; Ps 103:19–22). Here then are the roots of the later idea of angel hierarchies as we know them in Daniel, *1 Enoch* 37ff., 1QM, and the Sabbath hymns from Qumran (cf. also Luke 12:8–9 and §4.4.2). Here also is the beginning of the view that the earthly and heavenly cult are celebrated together (e.g., 1QH xi 13–14; 4QFl i 4) and that this endless cultic unity between heaven and earth is the goal of all of history (Chronicles; *Jubilees*).

Since as the king of all heavenly beings God ruled the gods of the nations, it followed that the nations themselves were subordinate to Yahweh as king (Ps 2). This new way of understanding Yahweh's kingship suggested, then, another theme, which became a leading motif in the development of Yahweh's kingship, viz., the polarity between Israel and the nations, especially the kings of the nations. As we can see in the prophets after Isaiah, in Daniel, in *1 Enoch*, and in 1QM, Yahweh became the one who governed the affairs of nations and rulers.

Now the king of the gods, Baal, ruled the world from the mountain of the gods in the north (cf. Ps 48:3). He had established his power by military might, and spatially and temporally had become a kind of universal ruler. This mythological motif became a third way of determining Yahweh's kingship: He is the king of the earth (Ps 47:8), and he has this power forever (Ps 29:10). From these expansions of the theology of Zion it was but a short step to the idea that Yahweh was the lord of all creation (Pss 29; 104). Thus a theology of creation became an expression of Yahweh's rule as king. Unlike Baal, of course, Yahweh did not achieve his supremacy by being victorious in war. Instead, Israel used its early election traditions, along with creation ideas, to justify elevating Yahweh to this position of universal supremacy.

A final important development was that the Jerusalem temple now became the earthly seat of God's kingship over the entire world and especially over Israel (Pss 24; 47). The temple and the city of Zion became, at least in terms of their theological claims, the center of the world. It was here that the God of the entire world was enthroned—the God who in a special way had chosen Israel. There were, of course, different ways of highlighting this election. Within Israel the priesthood was singled out for special honor and put in charge of the temple. People also began to emphasize 2 Sam 7 and to regard David and his dynasty as the political representatives of Yahweh as king. Of course, the prophetic movement was able to criticize both of these institutions. Isa 6 is, if nothing else, a criticism of the monarchy![10]

These four basic expressions of the preexilic theology of Yahweh as king determined the further development of the theology of Zion down to the time of Jesus and beyond. It would be interesting to examine the variety among these motifs, the way they influenced each other, and their actual development in the political history of Israel as they influenced evolving views of kingship and led to various theological positions. We must be satisfied, however, with this outline of the more important expressions of Yahweh's kingship.

4.1.3 God's Kingship as an Object of Hope

Prior to the Exile the theology of Zion was focused exclusively on historical events, and it served to legitimize the status quo. Such use of the imagery no longer made sense, of course, after the fall of the Davidic monarchy and Israel's loss of independence. Prophecy after Isaiah directed its attention to this negative turn of events and developed a hope according to which God's actual and decisive demonstration of power had not yet happened. This transformation has come to be known as the eschatologizing of the Zion tradition. Once this decisive step was taken (decisive also for the preaching of Jesus), we begin to come across not only eschatological statements that refer to God as king; we also frequently find in the sources a tension between God's present and future reigns. Sometimes the emphasis is on the present (cf. once again the Sabbath hymns of Qumran); at other times the future is dominant (e.g., *T. Dan.* 5:13; *As. Mos.* 10). As a rule, however, the view is that God rules already as king, but not until the near future will he do so in any complete sense (e.g., Daniel).

The earliest and decisive figure in this transformation of the theology of Zion is Deutero-Isaiah (Isa 40–55). His message is a proclamation of good news for the Zion whose inhabitants still live in exile (Isa 40:1, 9–10; 41:27). The king of Israel (which is now the way it is put) will care for his people in a new way (41:21; 43:15; 44:6). Deutero-Isaiah emphasizes Yahweh's kingship in a way that makes clear why one can expect that care from him. He is the holy ruler and king (43:15; 44:6) of the classical theology of Zion (Isa 6:3, 5). He rules over the nations and directs the kings (41:2–3; 43:14–15; 45:1). Indeed, he is in control of history and creation (40:3–4; 41:4; 43:3, etc.). Before him the gods are nonentities (Isa 41:21–29; 44:6). The theology of Zion is also familiar with these statements (Pss 2; 104).

According to Deutero-Isaiah, God soon will demonstrate his power as king for the benefit of Israel (52:7). God is not only king over the gods as nonentities, he not only rules over history and creation in a general sense; he also shows himself to be king by creating something new for Israel—something so new that one will forget the old (43:18–19). By leading Israel out of exile God reveals himself in a new, previously unknown way as king. As Israel's king, God is Israel's savior (49:14; 44:6). This work as savior is a continuation of God's work as creator, so that the new reality that he creates is not something that can be understood in terms of the previous salvation history; it is to be described, rather, only in terms of creation (40:3–4, 28; 43:14–21).[11]

This concept not only provides the important channel through which the theology of Zion became the bearer of a new hope for the future; at the same time it creates two additional provisions that will play an important role in the preaching of Jesus. One condition is that the demonstration of God's kingship for which people were waiting is to be understood in terms of God's work as creator and his related activity as the lord of history. The other is that this activity as ruler is focused on his function as Israel's saving king.

Deutero-Isaiah's basic conviction remains dominant in the subsequent history of prophecy; there is agreement that God's final, unique act of kingship is still in the future. Compared with Deutero-Isaiah, however, there is less emphasis on creation. A form of nationalism that is concentrated on Zion-Jerusalem and that portrays the polarity between Israel and the nations in especially ostentatious terms rules the day. Representatives of this development are Isa 24–27, 33; Obadiah; Mic 2:12–13; 4:6–8; 7:14–17; Zeph 3; and Zech 12–14.

More richly developed as a motif is one particular tone that Deutero-Isaiah had sounded, viz., that as king God is Israel's savior and grantor of mercy (cf. Isa 25:9; 33; 12:23–24; Zeph 3:12, 15, 19; Mic 4:6–8; 7:18–20). The nations, on the other hand, will be lost (Isa 24:21–22; 25:10; 26:21; 33:3–4, 12–13, 19; Obad 8–21; Zeph 3:6–8:15; Mic 7:16–17; Zech 12–14). According to Isa 25:6–7, however, after the judgment they will participate in the salvation-banquet. Yahweh is especially gracious to forgive Israel's guilt (Isa 27:9), so that the chosen people will be free of all burdens when they participate in the final salvation, which is portrayed as a banquet (Isa 25:6–7) or, more generally, as a time of the abundance of paradise (Isa 33:20–24). This salvation will be a time without war, sickness, hunger, and it will be free of all creature needs (Isa 25:8; 26:19; 27:2–5).

4.1.4 Zion's Restoration in Early Judaism

It is beyond dispute that, from the Exile to the first uprising against Rome (or even to the second uprising), a representative mainstream of Early Jewish statements about God's kingship follows the lines that were laid down in the prophetic movement after Isaiah. There is a relatively fixed cluster of motifs with the following basic affirmations (which, to be sure, do not always appear together). In the present the nation lives in misery, oppressed and scattered. This suffering is God's punishment on sinful Israel. However, the God who already rules creation and history will restore Israel. That is to say, he will build a glorious Jerusalem and temple and will return the scattered Jews to their homeland. The nations stand under judgment, but some of them will make a pilgrimage to Zion to serve Israel's king and his people. This sequence of statements appears in Tob 13 in a prayer that makes frequent reference to God as king.[12] Variations of this concept appear in *1 Enoch* 93:3–10; 91:11–17. Cf. also 2 Macc 1:24–29; *1 Enoch* 25:3–5; *Jub.* 1:27–28 (see on this text also 16:17–18), and *Sib. Or.* 3.767–80 (cf. 3.46–60 with its judgment of the nations). We can also include *As. Mos.* 10 if we read this small apocalypse as ignoring the usual distinction between the heavenly throne of the king of the world and the Zion-temple as the location of the presence of Israel's king among his people.[13] Then Israel is elevated to the heavenly dwelling of God as the place from which he reigns as king (*As. Mos.* 10:8–9). Thus the place where sinners are punished is not only the Hinnom Valley (Isa 66:23–24; *1 Enoch* 26–27); it is the entire world (*As. Mos.* 10:10). Instead of looking horizontally from Jerusalem out to the Hinnom Valley, Israel looks vertically from heaven down on the earth.

Now, of course, if we were so inclined we could supplement this hope that we find so well represented in Tob 13 with other Early Jewish eschatological elements. One thinks of a personified hope for an end-time ruler of which, in the context of the nationalistic texts just cited, the anticipation of an eschatological Davidic ruler is an especially good example (cf. §4.4.1). *Ps. Sol.* 17 is the first to refer to such a figure as *Messiah*, and also is the first to cite 2 Sam 7, Nathan's promise to David, as the decisive reference for the hope for an eschatological ruler. Beginning with Solomon, the palace and temple were part of the city of David to whom Nathan had declared in the name of Yahweh that his descendants would rule forever. For the enemies of the Hasmoneans, part of Israel's misery was that this Davidic throne had been deserted since the Exile, while its hope was that this misery would end with a final, royal appearance of God on behalf of Zion. Compatible with this hope was the figure of a Messiah ben David based on 2 Sam 7.

The framework of *Ps. Sol.* 17:1, 3, 46 asserts that God is Israel's king forever, but in a special sense the coming Messiah will be the representative of this kingship (17:32, 34).[14] As Israel's merciful savior, who as king is judge of the nations (17:3), God will raise up the Messiah to be the ruler of Israel (17:21). He will expel the nations from Jerusalem and from the land of Israel (17:22, 28, 30), gather the holy nation (17:26), and make them sons of God in the true sense (17:26–27). The Gentiles will come to Israel to pledge fealty and to pay tribute (17:30–31).[15]

In its essential points Sir 51:12a–o and the Eighteen Benedictions share this same view (cf. also *Sib. Or.* 3.652ff.). In its own way the *Targum of Jonathon* on the prophets is also centered on Zion and is messianically focused.[16] This work is especially consistent both in the process of eschatologizing God's rule as king begun by Deutero-Isaiah and in looking forward to a Davidic ruler in the end-time. Although God is already king, the catchword *kingdom* or *reign* is not used to refer to his present rule; it is obviously being saved for the eschatological

Kingdom of God, which has not yet appeared. This kingdom will bring the divine power and glory to their final realization (*Tg. Isa* 40:10; 52:7–8). Together they will effect everlasting blessing, but they will also bring about judgment on the idolaters (*Tg. Isa* 24:23). This revelation of the Kingdom of God (God himself and his appearing recede into the background) will take place in Zion-Jerusalem (*Tg. Mic* 4:7–8) and will have universal dimensions; it will be a genuinely worldwide kingdom (*Tg. Isa* 2:2). Zion also will be the residence of the eschatological Messiah, whose rule will replace the present kingdoms (*Tg. Mic* 4:7–8; *Tg. Zech* 4:7).

Of course, those persons who looked for a priestly eschatological figure from the tribe of Levi and a royal eschatological ruler from the tribe of Judah (cf. §4.4.1) could use the material as it is preserved in Tob 13 in the service of their concept of two messiahs. *T. Dan.* 5:4–13 (cf. *T. Benj.* 9:1–2; 10:6–10) is an especially good example. The blessings in 1QSb also illustrate this phenomenon, although (probably because of the special genre) they offer the various motifs in a more limited form (cf. in their contexts especially 1QSb iii 5; iv 25–26; v 21).

4.1.5 Kingdom of God and Son of Man

In Daniel's apocalyptic interpretation of world events, language about the Kingdom of God from the perspective of universal history serves to explain the history of the world in terms of the God of Israel. With an eye on the kingdoms of this world, which fall like a row of dominoes, the apocalyptic hope looks toward the final Kingdom of God. This kingdom is personified in the Son of Man; it is established by God's activity; and it prepares the saints of the Most High (i.e., Israel) for perfection (Dan 7).

Of primary importance for Daniel is the view that God participates in the existing world through his eternal dominion as king from which he entrusts to the kings (and nations) power, strength, honor, and a share in creation (Dan 2:37–38). God's kingdom is eternal and continues from generation to generation (cf. §4.1.2), and he demonstrates his rule by permitting kingdoms to rise and fall (Dan 3:31–33; 2:37–45). A constant emphasis is that with unlimited sovereignty God gives power to whom he will (4:14, 21–24, 29; 5:21). By contrast, all gods are worthless nonentities that can accomplish nothing (Dan 2–3; cf. §4.1.2). When a king to whom God has granted power worships foreign gods and does not give the honor to the God who holds the life and destiny of all human beings in his hands (5:23), God will take his power away (Dan 5:18–30). Whoever serves God faithfully will be as wise as Daniel (Dan 2), and God will save him from all dangers (6:1–29), so that before the God of Daniel all people must tremble (6:27).

Thus the essence of this God's governance is the recognition that Darius writes to all peoples in his register: The God of Daniel "is the living God, and he endures forever; his kingdom cannot be destroyed, and his dominion has no end.

He saves and he sets free; he performs signs and wonders in heaven and on earth" (6:27–28). This perspective is not that of an Israelite who views Israel and its saving history from Jerusalem and the temple and then looks outward to the surrounding nations. Here Israel's God from the very beginning is understood programmatically as king of the world. The author of Daniel understands himself to be an Israelite world-citizen in a heathen kingdom, and from this perspective he regards all reality as an aspect of his God's royal governance of the world.

Of course, this eternal world-rule does not extend the ebb and flow of history into eternity. Instead, God sets an end to history with the same sovereign power with which he ruled within history. God's judgment over the world is already determined, and the last mighty act of God's rule of the world will be his transfer of a final and ultimate kingdom to the one who is like a son of man (Dan 7:13–14; cf. §4.4.2). In contrast to the previous kingdoms, which were symbolized by animals, it will be a genuinely humane kingdom. It cannot be destroyed, and it will be the kingdom for the saints of the Most High. All other powers must serve him and be subordinate to him (Dan 7:27)—an idea that is suggestive of a theme from the Zion tradition (cf. §4.1.4).

In Daniel this concept of God's rule of the world as king pushes into the background the elements of the theology of Zion that were focused on Israel's own salvation history. Of course, Israel's uniqueness is not completely missing; it is simply part of the setting (cf., e.g., Dan 1). It appears that the basic themes that Israel appropriated from Canaan in its early days in order to create the theology of Zion receive a new and unexpected importance. Daniel's thought-world evolves within the horizons of the Persian idea of a universal kingdom, which is grounded theologically in Ahura Mazda's work as creator and king.[17] In that way the focus on God's rule in terms of creation becomes dominant, and Israel's election traditions recede into the background. Of course, Daniel does live after Deutero-Isaiah, and the hope for a final demonstration of God's power as king, which is documented in Dan 7, is also Deutero-Isaiah's.

In the parabolic addresses of *1 Enoch* 37–71 we find another instance of Daniel's understanding of reality with the same emphasis on divine rule and a special reinterpretation of Dan 7. At first glance the addresses appear to have next to no interest in God's kingship.[18] Only *1 Enoch* 63:2–3 refers to God as king, and only *1 Enoch* 41:1 speaks of the kingdom that will be allotted at the end of time. As a result, in the discussion of the background of Jesus' message about God's rule (as king), the parabolic addresses of *1 Enoch* have been ignored and have been brought into the discussion only in connection with the sayings about the Son of Man (cf. §4.4.2). Such a procedure is unacceptable in view of the methodological rule that one must consider not only the lexical evidence, but also the text's outlook, its perspectives, and its background traditions. Applying this rule is especially important in the case of the two texts cited.

1 Enoch 63:2, 4 contains the doxological confession that the world's kings and potentates make at the final judgment. It is, in essence, what the history of the world has brought them to in the final judgment and thereby what the reader can anticipate. At the moment of their punishment the world rulers praise "the lord of spirits, the lord of kings, the lord of the mighty," and they confess that they "should have glorified and praised the lord of kings and him who is king over all kings." The theme comes, of course, from Daniel (Dan 2:44, 47; 4:34; 7:26–27), and it is hardly accidental that the entire prayer in some of its individual motifs is reminiscent of Dan 3:33; 4:31; 6:27.

1 Enoch 41:1 also points to Dan 7 to the degree that, as in Dan 7, the kingdoms will be redistributed at the final judgment. In addition, just as Dan 7:13–14 refers to the transfer of eschatological rule to one who looks like a son of man,[19] *1 Enoch* 62 depicts a transfer of power involving the same persons that parallels the judgment scene of *1 Enoch* 63. It is said of the Son of Man that he rules over all (62:6; cf. Dan 7:27). Thus, Daniel's theme of the Kingdom of God that is victorious in the end is developed programmatically in the parabolic addresses.

In the same context (62:2, 3, 5) it is emphasized that the Lord of Spirits sets his Elect One, the Son of Man, on *the throne of his glory*, so that he may execute the final judgment and be the eschatological king (62:6!). The throne motif takes up once again Dan 7:9–14,[20] and the history of its tradition as the throne on which God sits as king goes back to Isa 6 (cf. also 1 Kgs 22:19; Jer 14:21; 17:12; *1 Enoch* 14:18–20; *As. Mos.* 10:3).[21] It is also probably the case that the frequent references to the *throne of his glory* throughout the parabolic addresses have the purpose of describing the various scenes as the activity of a king. A comparison of *1 Enoch* 62–63 with Ps 110:1, 5–6 shows that the throne imagery makes use of this psalm to express the transfer of royal authority to the Son of Man.

Relevant here is another distinguishing feature of the worldview of the parabolic addresses that is compatible with Daniel. The world is divided into heavenly and earthly historical realms. Heaven is characterized by an immense number of heavenly beings, which are God's ministering spirits (*1 Enoch* 39:12–13; 40:1–10; 47:3; 60:1–2; 61:6; Dan 7:10) and which, as in Isa 6, surround the throne.[22] On earth attention is focused primarily on the kings. They receive their power from God, who is their lord and king and who holds them accountable in the final judgment (*1 Enoch* 46:4–5; 62; Dan 7:23–27).[23] In Daniel God's kingship encompasses both of these realms (Dan 7:9–10), while *1 Enoch* uses different language for God and the Son of Man. God is the *lord of spirits* (e.g., 37:2, etc.) and *lord of kings and lord of the mighty* (*1 Enoch* 63:2), who *is king of all kings* (63:4). Then God grants the Son of Man authority as king over the heavenly (*1 Enoch* 61) and the earthly relationships (*1 Enoch* 48; 62).

Doubtless we could with greater precision describe how the parabolic addresses make use of Daniel. We could also note that they make use of other Old Testament traditions in addition to Daniel. One can no longer claim, however, that the parabolic addresses are only marginally interested in the concept of God as king. On the contrary, it is clear that they are a continuation of the Kingdom of God theme as it appears as the central theme of Daniel. Given the cloudy tradition-historical relationships in the parabolic addresses, of course, it would be risky to try to formulate the perspective of the redactor. Still, it is tempting to regard Daniel's concept of the kingdom, with its variations, as the common thread running through the diversity in *1 Enoch*.

4.1.6 The Annihilation of Belial in the End-Time

One of the features of the future orientation of the Zion tradition after Isaiah is the anticipation that the nations will mount an assault against Jerusalem that will be defeated by Yahweh, the King of Zion (Ezek 38–39; Joel 3; Zech 14, etc.). The War Scroll (1QM and the fragments from 4Q), which is basically a pre-Essene document, takes over this concept with its tradition of the Day of Yahweh and a holy war in such a way that it also reinterprets statements from Dan 11–12.[24] In the process the mythical figure of Belial becomes God's (and Michael's) dualistic opponent, so that a final struggle takes place between two power blocks. This war, which will take place both on the earth and in the heavens, will be fought between God, Michael, all the angels, and Israel on the one side and, on the other side, Belial and his army, along with the nations.

Power is wielded on both sides, of course, but only God's exercise of power is described as that of a king (several times in 1QM xii; xix). Traditional references to the rulers of the nations as kings also appear (1QM i 4; xi 3, etc.), but the authority of Belial and of Michael is described only in general terms and not with the language of kingship. Linguistically, 1QM maintains the uniqueness of God's sovereignty.

That God will establish his eternal kingship at the end of time by defeating his dualistic opponent is new in 1QM,[25] but, as the three hymnic elements in 1QM xii; xiv 16–18; xix, illustrate, the work also preserves the essential motifs of the traditional Zion material. God dwells in his heavenly palace (xii 1–2), surrounded by his royal court (xii 1, 4–5, 8; xix 1). He is holy (xii 8; xix 1), eternal king (xii 3), king of glory (xii 8; xix 1), and god of the gods (xiv 16). Zion-Jerusalem is the earthly reflection of this divine reign (xii 13; xix 5). God's eschatological dominion is realized as Israel's dominion (xii 16; xix 6–7). God will judge the nations (xii 5, 9–12; xix 2–4), so that they will be able to serve Israel (xii 14; xix 6).

Parallel to the material from 1QM is a little apocalypse from *T. Dan.* 5:10–13 in which God wages the final war against Beliar, after which he establishes eternal peace, restores Jerusalem, returns the exiled Jews, and dwells in the midst of his people as Israel's Holy One and king.

By way of summary we can say that the War Scroll, which has pre-Essene roots, and the *T. 12 Patr.* demonstrate that the anticipation of an eschatological realization of God's rule as king could be expressed within the framework of a dualistic worldview both in Qumran and in Early Judaism at large.

4.1.7 Kingdom of God and Resurrection Hope

For most of its history the Zion tradition maintains the sense of Israel's historical continuity—i.e., it assumes that only that generation of Israel that is alive at the end will experience God's salvation and the kingdom of peace. Only at a late date do occasional descriptions of the establishment of the final kingdom appear that include in its participants not only the persons who will be living at the time (primarily Israel), but also the dead who will be raised to experience this salvation.

What is likely the earliest reference to this hope, Isa 26:19, appears in an apocalypse (24–27) that, although not a unity, contains elements of the Zion tradition. The apocalypse speaks not only of the resurrection of the dead, but of the destruction of death itself (25:8). If we are correct that the parabolic addresses of *1 Enoch* 37–71 anticipate the future reign of God as king (§4.1.3), we can see this resurrection hope there also in 51:1 (46:6; 48:9–10). An especially impressive text is *T. Benj.* 10:6–10. According to this text, the first persons to be raised from the dead will be three figures from primeval times: Enoch, Noah, and Shem; then the three patriarchs, mentioned by name; then the twelve sons of Yahweh, who will worship the King of Heaven. Finally, all persons will be raised, some to glory, others to shame.

All three resurrection texts belong to Early Jewish apocalypticism. Yet, even in those texts that move beyond apocalypticism and speak of a personal resurrection of individuals immediately after their death, God's kingship and the hope for eternal life can coexist (2 Macc 7:9; Wis 3:1–8; Philo, *Spec. Leg.* 1.207). Here God's kingship is regarded as everlasting.

4.1.8 God's Permanent Role as King in Creation and History

According to our presentation in §4.1.2, under the influence of Canaan's El and Baal religion Yahweh became king because he was the creator of the world and the lord of history. Yahweh's eternal kingship then became Israel's assurance that the world and history were not left to themselves or to other gods and that Israel served a God who ruled both the world and history. Deutero-Isaiah later issued a challenge to forget all that had been and that presently was, and he spoke of a demonstration of divine kingship that was yet to come. The new and special quality of this kingly rule would transcend all that had gone before and would therefore make a break with the past. Thus Deutero-Isaiah began a process of eschatologizing the divine kingship—a process that involved a new way of understanding the future in terms of Israel's king. Prophecy and apocalypticism cultivated this way of thinking further.

Was it a given that one had to follow Deutero-Isaiah's lead? There are texts that continue to affirm faith in terms of an ongoing and unlimited reign of God, which began at creation and continued as a reliable and unbroken reality into the future. Many of the songs and prayers of Israel and Early Judaism express this kind of piety as if the major shift in course after Isaiah had never happened for them. The texts involved are primarily individual or group prayers of thanksgiving and petition and doxologies from the community gathered for worship.

An impressive example of this kind of material is Enoch's supplication in *1 Enoch* 84:2–6. Its typical structure begins with an introduction that praises God (vv. 2–3). The content of the praise is at the same time the basis for the petition, which is expressed in the third part (vv. 5–6). The middle section portrays the situation of need that is to be overcome (v. 4). The praise of God contains typical motifs from the theology of Zion. In particular it takes up the concept of the transcendence of God's kingship from Isa 6 in a way that is hardly accidental:

1a   *Blessed are you, Lord (and) King,*
 b   *great and mighty in your greatness,*
2a   *Lord of the whole creation of the heaven,*
 b   *King of kings and God of the whole world.*
3a   *Your deity, kingship, and majesty abide for ever and ever,*
 b   *and your dominion throughout all generations.*
4a   *And all the heavens are your throne for ever*
 b   *and the entire earth your footstool for ever and for all time.*
5a   *For you have made (everything) and you rule everything,*
 b   *and absolutely nothing is too hard for you . . .*[26]

Then the petition repeats the king motif:

> *And now God and Lord, Great King, I implore and beseech you to fulfill my prayer . . .*

Convinced of the incontrovertible permanence and greatness of God's power as king, a power described primarily with creation terminology, the worshipper is able to pray: Such a king can and will fulfill my request![27]

Simon's supplication in 3 Macc 2:1–20 offers the same structure (praise of God, 2:1–12; present disaster, 2:13–15; appeal for deliverance, 2:16–20). Here, however, God's kingship (2:2, 13) is related only marginally to his work as creator and is based more on his historical deeds leading to the election of Jerusalem and his residence in the temple. Since God is a just king who punishes the transgressors and rescues the lowly and the oppressed, here too one can appeal to his mercy.[28]

With some urgency these motifs also appear in Judith's supplication (Jdt 9:12), admittedly with a different structure, since God's kingship dispenses with the final point. God is praised as the God of the lowly and helper of the oppressed, as comforter of the weak, as protector of the outcasts and savior of the despairing. Then the prayer ends: "You, Lord of heaven and earth, Creator of the waters and King of all your creation, hear my prayer!" We find the same theology in the prayers of Mordecai and Esther, which were added to Esth 4:17. Sometimes the Zion tradition shrinks to almost nothing as is the case in the individual prayer of Sir 51. These examples show how the concept of God's kingship provided the basis for appealing to God as the one who demonstrates that he is Israel's king in Zion and the king of the world by showing mercy, helping persons in distress, and judging the enemies of Israel.

That God is helper and deliverer is also a point of view that appeared as early as the Psalter of the Old Testament in places that speak of Yahweh as Zion's king, sometimes extensively, sometimes briefly: Pss 10:17–18; 22; 44:6–8, 27; 103:2–6; 145; 146.[29] As in 3 Macc 2, Yahweh, the king, creator, and lord of history, can also function as judge, primarily of Israel's enemies (Pss 5:9–11; 22; 68; 74; 95; 103; 145; 149; *Ps. Sol.* 2). God's activities as king and as creator also appear together in Pss 8 and 24.

The Sabbath hymns from Qumran assume a special role in this section. These hymns praise God as the eternal, heavenly king and emphasize that God's kingship is of unlimited duration. God's kingship in creation and history is so conspicuous by its absence, that we are able to catch an unexpected glimpse into a view of the cult that is merely suggested in other texts of Israel and Early Judaism. The earthly cult shares in the heavenly cult by praising it in a way that largely ignores creation and history. The image of God that emerges is removed from involvement with the world and history and takes on contours that underscore in bold relief God's unapproachable distance from the world, his heavenly brilliance, and his royal court. *Jubilees* probably would have enjoyed that kind of worship. Likewise, the prayer of thanksgiving in the LXX addition to Dan 3:23, numbered as Dan 3:52–56, fits well with this understanding.

4.1.9 A Brief Review

A survey of the Old Testament and Early Jewish texts that speak of the kingship of Israel's God leads to a clear result: All branches of this theme lead back to the beginnings of the theology of Zion in the Israel of David and Solomon. The cluster of motifs surrounding the concept of God's rule as king remains relatively constant over the centuries in spite of the many shifts in Israel's history. Although we can no longer observe all the historical changes, and while there were numerous variations on the theme, all of the formulations that we can trace down to and including the time of Jesus reveal their solidarity with the theology of Zion. This firm conclusion is important for understanding how Jesus spoke of the Kingdom of God and how his hearers received his message.

4.2 THE ESSENTIAL ELEMENTS OF JESUS' UNDERSTANDING OF THE KINGDOM OF GOD

4.2.1   The Kingdom of God as the Central Concept of the Preaching of Jesus

The synoptic gospels and the sayings source are in complete agreement that, when they and their churches speak about the Kingdom of God, they are using a term that goes back to Jesus—a word that, indeed, he has chosen for them.[30]

The sayings source underscores the importance of the term in a number of ways: It uses it in connection with Jesus' first public word, the first of the beatitudes ("Blessed are the poor, because theirs is the Kingdom of God," Luke 6:20 = Matt 5:3); it uses the term to separate Jesus from John the Baptist and the time prior to John (Matt 11:11 = Luke 7:28); it emphasizes the Kingdom of God as the major concern of the disciples (Luke 12:31 = Matt 6:33); and when the disciples are sent out to preach, it uses the same catchword to describe their message (Luke 10:9 = Matt 10:7–8).

The sayings source follows Mark, who says essentially the same thing in 1:14–15. It is as a preacher that Jesus appears, and the content of his preaching is the Kingdom of God. The first extended address of Jesus in the Gospel of Mark is the parable in Mark 4:1–8, which further develops the programmatic statement of Mark 1:14–15. It does so by calling attention to itself as a paradigm for the preaching of Jesus and by stating that the Kingdom of God is the general theme of that preaching (Mark 4:11, 26, 30).

Matthew tempers this emphasis somewhat by claiming that the preaching of the kingdom was part of the Baptist's message (Matt 3:2 = 4:17), yet in Matt 4:17 he follows Mark 1:14–15. He takes over Q and Markan material and multiplies the references to Jesus' central concept not least of all by turning some of the parables into parables of the kingdom. In Matthew's case, of course, they are parables of the Kingdom of Heaven (cf. Matt 13:24, 44, 45, 47, 52; 18:23; 20:1; 25:1).

The Third Evangelist changes Mark and Q very little; for him also the message of the Kingdom of God begins with Jesus. Far removed from the approach represented by Matt 3:2, Luke understands the message of the Kingdom of God as part of the post-Easter mission's inheritance from Jesus, and he uses the term to express the continuity between Jesus and the church's preaching (Luke 4:43; 8:1; Acts 8:12; 19:8; 20:25; 28:23, 31).

All of which is to say that the synoptic gospels serve as a billboard for the

Kingdom of God; refusing to acknowledge it as Jesus' central concept, or even denying it to him altogether, would involve going against the unanimous witness of the synoptic tradition. We would then have to explain how the wealth of evidence and the unanimity among the witnesses came into existence. Of course, the Fourth Evangelist goes his own way with a christology that understands the preaching of Jesus in terms of revelatory addresses, so that he preserves only fragmentary references to the Kingdom of God (John 3:3, 5; also 18:36). Yet, by looking at the Gentile-Christian tradition that evolved through Antioch (which also minimizes the importance of the Kingdom of God), we can see how such a development happened. The hope for the parousia of the risen Lord gradually replaced the expectation of the Kingdom of God (cf. on the one hand 1 Thess 2:12; 1 Cor 6:9–10; Gal 5:21, and on the other hand 1 Thess 2:19; 3:13; 4:15, etc.). Indirectly, Matthew also makes the same shift (Matt 24:3, 27, 37, 39). Indeed, all of the synoptic gospels reveal that the Kingdom of God sayings were interpreted in christological terms, although such christological interpretations did not become dominant in the synoptic material (cf., e.g., Matt 13:41; 16:18; Luke 22:29–30; 23:42).

The tradition represented by Antioch and Paul even suggests when the statements about the Kingdom of God began to recede into the background. Since it must be related to the development of a kind of missionary preaching that was directed specifically to Gentiles (1 Thess 1:9), the transition happened in Antioch during the years when people were beginning to think of Christianity in Gentile terms, i.e., sometime before the Jerusalem conference of 48 CE (Acts 15; Gal 2:1–10)—and when people were beginning to do missionary work in the area around Antioch as is described in Acts 13–14. Denying the preaching of the Kingdom of God to Jesus would require that we explain how it originated so soon after Easter and why none of the Easter traditions (both confessional and narrative) make use of it.

Now the more we can demonstrate that Jesus distanced himself from Early Judaism and at the same time was reinterpreted by the post-Easter churches, the more we will have to conclude that the catchword *Kingdom of God* was central and typical for Jesus. Before we turn our attention to that task in §§4.2.2–4.2.4, however, it is important to make another observation: Other than the Kingdom of God, there is simply no other central concept, no other overarching theme, that could define Jesus's message. Jesus' theme is, quite simply, God and his kingdom. Jesus was no new teacher of the Torah, who by means of the love command reduced the law to a single principle. Nor was he a sage, who understood Israel's wisdom in a new way or a charismatic, miracle-working rabbi like Honi the Circle-maker. He did not live a particular kind of humanity characterized by social concerns.

One could extend this list of interpretations of Jesus almost at will, but each of them must submit to being measured by what the sources actually say about Jesus. A description of the figure of Jesus that does not include as its central element an interpretation of the Kingdom of God simply misses him altogether. Thus the first essential element for understanding the Kingdom of God is that this central concept is the essence of the entire message of Jesus throughout his total activity.

4.2.2   The Coming Kingdom of God as Integral Part of the Present

Bammel, G. "Erwägungen zur Eschatologie Jesu," *StEv* 3 = *TU* 88 (1964) 10–13.

Berkey, R. F. "Engizein, Phtanein, and Realized Eschatology," *JBL* 82 (1963) 177–87.

Bultmann, R. *History and Eschatology*. Edinburgh: University Press; New York: Harper & Row, 1957.

Burrows, M. "The Kingdom Come," *JBL* 74 (1955) 1–8.

Catchpole, D. R. "The Law and the Prophets in Q," in: *Tradition and Interpretation in the New Testament*. Festschrift E. G. F. Hawthorne and O. Betz, eds. Ellis. Tübingen: J.C.B. Mohr (Paul Siebeck); Grand Rapids, MI: Eerdmans, 1987, 95–109.

Clark, K. W. "Realized Eschatology," *JBL* 59 (1940) 367–83.

Conzelmann, H. "Eschatologie IV," *RGG* 3d ed. 1958, 2. 665–72.

Craig, C. T. "Realized Eschatology," *JBL* 56 (1937) 17–26.

Cullmann, O. *Christ and Time*. Rev. ed. London: SCM, 1962.

Delling, G. *Zeit und Endzeit*. BSt 58. Neukirchen-Vluyn: Neukirchener Verlag, 1970.

Dodd, C. H. *The Parables of the Kingdom*. Rev. ed. London: Collins; New York: Scribners, 1961.

Grässer, E. *Naherwartung*.

———. *Parusieverzögerung*.

———. "Zum Verständnis der Gottesherrschaft," *ZNW* 65 (1974) 3–26.

Häfner, G. "Gewalt gegen die Basileia?" *ZNW* 83 (1992) 21–51.

Hahn, F. "Die Bildworte vom neuen Flicken und vom jungen Wein (Mk 2,21f. parr)," *EvTh* 31 (1971) 357–75.

Hoffmann, P. "Zukunftserwartung und Schöpfungsglaube in der Basileia-Verkündigung Jesu," *SHS* 31 (1988) 174.

Kuhn, H. W. *Enderwartung und gegenwärtiges Heil*. StUNT 4. Göttingen: Vandenhoeck & Ruprecht, 1966.

Kümmel, W. G. "'Das Gesetz und die Propheten gehen bis Johannes'—Lukas 16,16 im Zusammenhang der heilsgeschichtlichen Theologie der Lukasschriften," in: *Heilsgeschehen und Geschichte*, Vol. 2. E. Grässer and O Merk, eds. MThSt 16. Marburg: N. H. Elwert, 1978, 75–86.

———. "Die Naherwartung in der Verkündigung Jesu," in: idem, *Heilsgeschehen und Geschichte*. Mthst 3. Marburg: N. H. Elwert, 1965, 457–70.

———. *Promise and Fulfillment: The Eschatological Message of Jesus*. SBT 1/23. 3d ed. London: SCM, 1957.

Linnemann, E. "Zeitansage und Zeitvorstellung in der Verkündigung Jesu," in: *Jesus Christus in Historie und Theologie*. Festschrift H. Conzelmann. G. Strecker, ed. Tübingen: J.C.B. Mohr (Paul Siebeck), 1975, 237–63.

Lohfink, G. "Zur Möglichkeit christlicher Naherwartung," in: G. Greshake and G.

Lohfink, *Naherwartung—Auferstehung—Unsterblichkeit.* QD 71. 4th ed. Freiburg/Basel/Vienna: Herder, 1982, 50–81.

Lorenzmeier, Th. "Zum Logion Mt 12:28; Lk 11,20," in: *Neues Testament und christliche Existenz.* Festschrift H. Braun. H. D. Betz and L. Schottroff, eds. Tübingen: J.C.B. Mohr (Paul Siebeck), 1973, 289–304.

Mell, U. "'Neuer Wein (gehört) in neue Schläuche' (Mk 2,22c)," *ThZ* (1996) 1–31.

Müller, Kh. "Apokalyptik/Apokalypsen III," *TRE* 3 (1978) 202–51.

Müller, U. B. "Vision und Botschaft," *ZThK* 74 (1977) 416–48.

Pesch, R. "Über die Authorität Jesu," in: *Die Kirche des Anfangs.* Festschrift H. Schürmann. R. Schnackenburg et al., eds. Freiburg: Herder, 1978, 25–55.

Schenk, W. "Naherwartung und Parusieverzögerung," *ThV* 4 (1972) 47–69.

Schlosser, J. "Die Vollendung des Heils in der Sicht Jesu," in: *Weltgericht und Weltvollendung.* H. J. Klauck, ed. QD 150. Freiburg/Basel/Vienna: Herder, 1994, 54–84.

Schmidt, W. H. and J. Becker. *Zukunft und Hoffnung.* Kohlhammer TB 1014. Stuttgart: Kohlhammer, 1981.

Schulz, S. "'Die Gottesherrschaft ist nahe herbeigekommen' (Mt 10,7/Lk 10,9)," in: *Das Wort und die Wörter.* H. Balz and S. Schulz, eds. Festschrift G. Friedrich. Stuttgart: Kohlhammer, 1973, 57–67.

Smend, R. "Eschatologie II," *TRE* 10 (1982) 256–64.

Theissen, G. "Der Bauer und die von selbst Frucht bringende Erde," *ZNW* 85 (1994) 167–82.

Vogler, W. "Die 'Naherwartung' Jesu," *ThV* 16 (1986) 57–71.

Vollenweider, S. "'Ich sah den Satan wie einen Blitz vom Himmel fallen' (Lk 10,18)," *ZNW* 79 (1988) 187–203.

Vorgrimler, H. "Zur Eschatologie Jesu," in: idem, *Hoffnung und Vollendung.* QD 90. Freiburg/Basel/Vienna: Herder, 1980, 32–45.

Weder, H. *Gegenwart und Gottesherrschaft.* BThSt 20. Neukirchen-Vluyn: Neukirchener Verlag, 1993.

Weiss, J. *Jesus' Proclamation of the Kingdom of God.* Philadelphia: Fortress, 1971 (1892).

Israel and Early Judaism understood time and history in terms of the concrete events that took place within them. According to the Torah, Israel spent forty years in the wilderness. Decisive is not the length of time, but the fact that it was the time of the wilderness wandering or the time of Moses. In this context Jesus naturally understood the Kingdom of God as the event that qualitatively changed time and history. He judged the present as well as history from the point of view of the Kingdom of God. For him the Kingdom of God determined the content and dimensions of both of these realities. This new reality intruding into history was the event that would change everything and at the same time cause everything to be understood from a new perspective.

In describing how the Kingdom of God defined in detail Jesus' understanding of time and history, one ordinarily debates the relationship between present and future in his preaching. Approaching the question that way, however, is short-sighted. At the very least we should include the past in the discussion and then ask the question: Where does Jesus set the defining break? Does it take place for him between the past and his own present, which he then integrates into the future? Or does it happen between now and then, so that the present is simply a continuation of the past, while the future, even if imminent, still has not appeared? The sources require that we choose the first of these alternatives.

It is true that people often resist this option, because they prefer to understand the final realization of the Kingdom of God as separated qualitatively from Jesus' own present, and they reject the idea that his initial activity on behalf of the Kingdom was the beginning of a gradual development that would lead in the end to salvation. This is not the place, however, to discuss issues of dogma or our own worldview. The decisive question must be: What possibilities of understanding existed for Jesus in his day? Jesus proclaimed the Kingdom of God as a present event (Luke 11:20) and at the same time used the term to talk about the final salvation that God would bring. When Israel and Early Judaism spoke of the establishment of a final salvation and of God's coming, what might they have meant?

In answering that question we should not permit the obvious diversity in Early Judaism to obscure the reality that there were some fundamental elements that could be changed little, if at all. We might regard them as part of the grammar with which people talked about the future. One of these constants was the widespread conviction that the final kingdom of peace and happiness had to be understood in terms of the present creation, with Zion as the center of salvation. The anticipated *shalom* would be the final fulfillment of God's covenant promises to Israel (with the nations participating to a lesser degree or not at all). By their very nature these promises are set in space and time, and they are valid for the generation that is currently living. It is true, of course, that this hope was expanded by speaking of a resurrection that would enable the dead to participate (e.g., Dan 12:2; *Bib. Ant.* 3:10; *T. Benj.* 10:6–7), or by talking of a heavenly Jerusalem (with the temple) that would come to earth (e.g., *1 Enoch* 90:28–42; *4 Ezra* 7:26; Rev 21), or even on occasion of envisioning Israel as the chosen people being transported to the starry heaven, which, of course, was part of the presently existing cosmos (*As. Mos.* 10; cf. §4.1.4). Seldom does one find the suggestion, however, that the final salvation will take place apart from or beyond this historical reality. (Examples of such exceptions are 1QH iii 29ff., which speaks of a cosmic fire that will destroy all creation, and 4 Ezra 13:29ff., which states that before the final salvation the world will return to the condition described in Gen 1:1–2).[31] John the Baptist assumed that creation would continue to exist without interruption (cf. §3.1.2), and the same was true of Jesus (cf. Matt 8:11–12 par. and above, §3.2.4).

It is clear, therefore, that the change that they were expecting would be characterized not by a change in reality as a whole or by a transformation of human nature. Historical reality as we know it would remain, but it would receive a new quality through God's eternal and immediate presence and through his gifts. This distinction is important for describing how Jesus understood the continuity between the Kingdom of God that is presently active and its final, future realization. That "(human) flesh and blood cannot inherit the Kingdom of God" (1 Cor 15:50) is a Pauline statement. It is Rev 21:1–2 that first says that Christians await a new heaven and a new earth. John (12:31–32; cf. 16:28) is the first to describe human redemption as leaving the world at death and being drawn to the exalted Christ who dwells above in God's world of light. Such distinctions between present historical reality and a future perfection are foreign to the preaching of Jesus. For him there is a natural continuity between the present reality and the coming perfection, because there is a self-evident relation between God as creator and the world, which constantly depends on him. The point of Jesus' proclamation is that from now on God's kingdom will be a reality in this world. The occasional and limited references to life beyond death (Matt 8:11; Luke 10:12; 11:31–32; 17:28–29) are to be subordinated to this basic conviction rather than set over against it.[32]

Another, equally decisive element of this perspective was that the end would not simply arrive at one moment, eliminating the old, evil, sinful order in a split-second miracle beyond imagination. Here, too, it is clear that, e.g., the Day of the Lord (cf. §3.1.2) is not a day of twelve or twenty-four hours; it designates, rather, a time of limited duration within which God would act as judge. It is measured not by the chronometer, but by the events that fill it with meaning.[33] No Early Jewish reader would have felt compelled to understand the events of Joel 2–3, where the Day of the Lord is described in detail as occurring on one calendar day. The apocalypse of ten weeks (*1 Enoch* 93:1–10; 91:11–17) limits the final events to the last three weeks of world history—first in Israel, then in the rest of the world, finally in heaven—after which eternal salvation will reign. According to the War Scroll from Qumran (1QM) the final struggle between the sons of light and the sons of darkness will last forty years. In 11Q xiii the final day lasts seven years. 4 Ezra 13:10–11 speaks of seven days. Such direct references to time are infrequent; in Early Judaism it is not chronometric time that is important so much as time's content. Still, while one should not overlook the importance of their subject matter and their symbolism, these references do indicate clearly that people expected the final events to last over a period of time. The life experience of ancient people was itself enough to keep them from imagining that an event such as the cosmic fire of 1QH iii 29ff. would happen in a single day. Everything had its time (Eccl 3:1–8). Those persons who did not regard the historical dimension of reality as simply abolished at the eschaton, would have no reason to deny that the final consummation would take place over a period of time. On the contrary, thinking of time in linear terms was necessary and normal. In fact, this extended period of time could serve as a framework within which one could link several previously unrelated eschatological events. One would then have a sequence of events that would occur in stages without having to choose from among the variety of traditional materials (*Sib. Or.* 3.656–795).

It is clear that the events that would establish the final salvation—that, indeed, themselves were eschatological events—would extend over a period of time. The next question is, then: When do these end-time events begin? Here, too, Early

Judaism was in basic agreement. Given the tacit understanding that God's rule of the present course of world events was hidden and indirect, those persons who stood under the influence of Deutero-Isaiah and the later prophets (see §4.1.3) were looking for God to intervene in history in a way that would be final, immediate, public, and qualitatively new. However one imagined the end, and whatever one expected to happen in detail, it was clear that God himself would have to appear and bring about a fundamental change from evil to good. This direct intervention of God could be in the form of a theophany in which God himself would appear in glory to judge the world (e.g., *1 Enoch* 1:3–9; *Sib. Or.* 3.669, 705, 709). Or God could send a special eschatological figure who would shape the coming judgment and salvation (e.g., the Messiah of *Ps. Sol.* 17 or the Son of Man of *1 Enoch* 37–71). Since this salvation was to last forever (i.e., be a continuous extension of time), it was necessary that history's negative forces (such as sin, death, evil, the devil, demons) be eliminated at the same time that salvation was being established. The question about the beginning of the end-time is, then: Where in the texts are the signals for the transition from God's indirect rule of the world to his direct rule as king at which time evil of all kind will be decisively defeated? The answer to this question must make clear at what point history becomes part of the old order, which, to speak in Deutero-Isaiah's terms (cf. §4.1.3), must be put in the past and forgotten. When does the change take place that marks the beginning of the new order as the time of the end?[34]

The end-time that begins with this change does not simply appear all at once in its final state as a *deus ex machina*. What qualifies it as the end-time is that the final salvation is now unstoppable and irresistible; it will prevail until God "becomes all things in all" (1 Cor 15:28)—that is to say, until the one determining reality in creation and history is God's sovereign rule, which will no longer tolerate evil. In Early Judaism sometimes human beings participate in this process. One thinks, e.g., of the War Scroll (1QM) and of the Zealots, who claimed that they were fighting against Rome on behalf of God's sovereign rule. As a rule, however, it is God alone who establishes his kingdom and who appoints his people its citizens. God acts alone to redeem his promises. This compelling sequence of revelatory events from the turning-point to the final consummation has a dynamic that simply cannot be delayed. God is absolutely unstoppable in his activity on behalf of all. It is also clear that, since no one would want to resist God, from the turning-point on this sequence moves toward God's final victory with an unwavering chronological necessity. This focus on a temporal movement toward a goal is so much a part of all the texts that it simply cannot be debated away.

Of course, when we talk in this context about expecting an imminent salvation-event, we must distinguish between the attitude after the turning-point and the attitude of those persons who before the turning-point imagine it to be near. For John the Baptist, e.g., God's judgment—i.e., the turning-point of history—is still in the future, albeit alarmingly near at hand (§3.1.2). As we shall see, for Jesus the turning-point has already happened. His anticipation of an imminent consummation proceeds from a different presupposition, since he believes that the age of salvation has already begun.

In the following arguments we will attempt to demonstrate that for Jesus the dividing line is between the past and the present and that the present and future constitute a continuous unity, since the coming Kingdom of God has already caught up with Jesus' present. If we are right, then Jesus' interpretation of reality brings a new perspective into the history of the interpretation of the Zion tradition with its concept of God as king. Jesus does not believe in a Kingdom of God that is present and eternal and that guarantees that the world and history will continue to be stabile and reliable; this noneschatological understanding of a Kingdom of God is completely foreign to him. Nor does he speak of a perpetual rule of God as king, which, admittedly hidden at present, will be revealed in a special way with finality and without mediation at the end of time; such a view represented the typical way of thinking in Early Judaism as well as the early rabbinic thinking, which came later. Nor does he focus exclusively, or even primarily, on a demonstration of God's power as king, which in the past has been only hoped for but which now, because it is so near, is impinging on the present in certain anticipatory signs; the only place that kind of partial realization of the Kingdom of God has ever existed is in the recent discussion among the exegetes. It is, rather, the case that Jesus makes the eschatological Kingdom of God real in the present in such a way that the turning-point for the time of salvation takes place here and now. The present is already end-time. Instead of confirming the status quo, Jesus establishes a new beginning that makes a break with the past—a break that is so radical that the past is rendered old, and the status quo is forced into a crisis. Modulating the concept of God's kingship that way was a radical departure from earlier expressions of the theology of Zion. There were, of course, other things that struck his contemporaries as different, but this change was fundamental. Prior to Jesus, everyone understood the Kingdom of God as something for which one had to wait, but Jesus declared his time to be the beginning of salvation itself, because already, in the present, the Kingdom of God was beginning to prevail.[35]

When we turn to the Jesus material itself, our first task is to emphasize those texts that justify the conclusion that Jesus understood his own time as the beginning of salvation. In this context an important element is the traditional Jewish belief that all of the powers that resist God in the world, including, e.g., the supreme Antagonist himself, would be deposed and destroyed.[36] Luke 10:18 offers a clear example from the early Jesus material:

I saw Satan fall from heaven like lightning.

It is generally agreed that the present context for this special Lukan material is secondary and that the saying goes back to Jesus. It refers to Satan's overthrow as a thing of the past (*I saw* . . .), while in Early Judaism it is always an event that has not yet happened.

Primitive Christian tradition also speaks of it as a future event (Rom 16:20; Rev 12:7–17). In all Jewish sources as well as in these two Christian texts it is God who brings about Satan's overthrow. In the context of John's special christology, John 12:31–32 relates it to what happens to Jesus Christ. Primitive Christianity identifies the beginning of salvation not with the life of the earthly Jesus, but with the resurrection of Jesus (1 Cor 15:20–28; John 12:31–32) and with the gift of the Spirit (cf. Acts 2:16–17; 1 Thess 4:8–9, 5:1–11, etc.). Thus Satan's overthrow is either connected with a christological description of Jesus' fate or it is expressed as a hope for the future. Luke 10:18 is unique, therefore, both in Judaism and in Primitive Christianity. It is also not completely unimportant that Luke 10:18 is similar to Luke 10:13–14 (cf. §3.2.4); in both cases the fall is an act of judgment.

Satan's fall neither happens by his choice nor is it accidental; it is a final judgment that God executes, much as in John 12:31 the ruler of this world is cast out (passive), or in Rom 16:20 God crushes Satan under the feet of the church. The comparison with lightning is probably less a matter of its visibility (cf. Luke 17:24) than it is a description of Satan's rapid fall from above to below, which, of course, is irreversible, since lightning never returns to heaven. It is conceivable that one might think here of a falling star (cf. *1 Enoch* 43:1–2; 44; *T. Sol.* 20:16–17).[37]

Is the saying the verbal reflection of a vision[38] or a prophetic interpretation that reasons from the exorcisms back to what made them possible?[39] Except for the visionary style of the Christ legend in Mark 1:10–11 parr., it would be the only vision attributed to Jesus. Interpreting the text as a vision would make it unique among the sayings of Jesus, since one can hardly imagine that the church would have repressed a visionary Jesus; the church itself had experienced such phenomena beginning with Easter. To be sure, there are visionary and auditory experiences in classical prophecy (Jer 1:14; Amos 8:2) that could serve as analogies, but the prophets were used to speaking in visionary language even beyond those experiences. In the case of Jesus a vision would remain a singular experience. We also should note that understanding Luke 10:18 as a vision would mean that Jesus pictured the world in dualistic terms. His statements about a power hostile to God are limited, however, to the exorcisms (cf. §4.3.3). Elsewhere his worldview is monistic. The thesis that Luke 10:18 represents a vision should be rejected, therefore, in favor of the view that it represents for Jesus the logical consequence of his miracles. However one decides on that issue, the sense of the verse is beyond dispute. It says that God has already deposed Satan in an act of final judgment.

This execution of judgment on the devil is identical with the positive statement of Luke 11:20 par.:

> *If I cast out demons by the finger of God,*
> *then the Kingdom of God has come upon you.*

It is generally recognized that Luke's version of the saying is older. When Matt 12:28 speaks of the Spirit of God instead of the finger of God, it is an example of the way the post-Easter church reinterpreted the time of Jesus in terms of its own experience of the Spirit.[40] That the two-line saying is rounded and self-contained is also generally recognized, and it does not need to be supplemented by reconstructing a scene from Luke 11:14, 17a, 20 par. Since the Jesus material tends to create apophthegms, we should distance ourselves from the reconstruction of an apophthegm. §4.3.3 contains an analysis of the context of Luke 11:20.

There is also great unanimity that the prophetic interpretation of time given with the saying comes from Jesus. Using the I-form, he describes himself not in the language of current Jewish expectations about end-time figures, but in terms of the end-time Kingdom of God. Such a description lies beneath the surface of the church's post-Easter christology. There also is no evidence in Judaism and early Christianity for relating the Kingdom of God and exorcisms in this way (cf. §4.3.3). Of special interest linguistically is that the Kingdom of God is the subject of a verb of movement. It is probably no accident that there are no Jewish parallels for this usage (see below), and only to a limited degree did the church continue it after Easter.[41]

The prophetic I-saying announces that salvation takes place on earth and in the present. Satan's fall from heaven in Luke 10:18 was the point at which God assumed eschatological power; now God makes that power real in human lives in Jesus' exorcisms. The inauguration of God's power as eschatological king may take time, but it is unwavering, and it determines the present. The establishment of his kingship on earth logically and consistently follows the establishment of his kingship in heaven. The exorcisms are not isolated incidents; they are but one aspect of the total reality that is given with the theme of the Kingdom of God— that is to say, of the coming reign of God as king (cf. §4.3.3).

There is no suggestion in the saying that the miracles are simply signs of a kingdom that is to come rather than the kingdom itself. We also misunderstand the word if we understand it as saying that the Kingdom of God is present only proleptically. Since the statement says that the victory over the demons is itself the establishment of God's kingdom, questions about the signs of its coming are no longer relevant. Portents of the Kingdom of God are simply not possible any more, because the kingdom itself has already made its appearance. Thus the character of the present is determined by its future; it is the beginning of the time of salvation itself. Before Jesus appeared one could ask, "When will the Kingdom of God appear?" Now one can show where and how it is already present. The verb *come upon*[42] does not mean that the Lord stands before the door of the present; it explains his presence in the present. Even with the miracles of Jesus the present is not the time for establishing and shoring up hope; it is the time to experience that what one has hoped for is now here.

Of course, we need to keep in mind that the verb is a verb of movement. The Kingdom of God is in the process of expanding to encompass everything, admittedly over a period of time. Soon it will have prevailed everywhere in the same way that it has already prevailed over the demons in Jesus' exorcisms. The kingdom is, in other words, a dynamic reality. Since it is the final destination of all reality, today's present can no longer become the past; it must always be integrated into the future. The past would be a time in which God is not near. The present cannot become the past, because the Kingdom of God and the present are combined.

Luke 11:20 expresses this idea graphically by speaking about the finger of God. The term may be reminiscent of Exod 8:15 (cf. also Ps 8:4); in any case the saying connects Jesus' deeds with God's present. When Jesus acts it is God's kingdom itself that appears, not a preview of the kingdom. It may be that a more relevant reference here is the *Targum of Jonathan* on Isa 40:10 where, following the establishment of God's reign at the end of time (cf. *Tg. Isa* 31:4–5), it is said: "Behold, Yahweh (is) God. He reveals himself as almighty, and the arm of his strength (i.e., his mighty arm, cf. Deut 5:15) rules." This strength is then described as a primarily redeeming power (*Tg. Isa* 24:23). Given that kind of statement, would we be justified in saying that God's kingdom has already come into the present with his finger—i.e., in a limited, but nevertheless direct, way— and that soon he will rule with his entire arm, i.e., with his full power? The so-called parables of contrast, about which we will be speaking next, would be compatible with this interpretation. Understanding the saying in terms of *Tg. Isa* instead of Exod 8:15 also has the important advantage that in this case we are reading texts together that make eschatological pronouncements.

Luke 10:18 and 11:20 demonstrate, therefore, that Jesus understands his present as the time when salvation begins. If we are correct on this point, then the Jesus material must contain traces of a break between the present and the past. As a matter of fact, the earliest Jesus material does indeed speak about such a caesura between the inbreaking Kingdom of God and the past, which as the existing order still influences the present apart from the kingdom, and it does so from three perspectives: generally, with reference to Israel's history; individually, in light of the Baptist's activity; and existentially, as a requirement for Jesus' disciples.

The Q saying, Matt 13:16–17 = Luke 10:23–24, contains the first perspective:

1a Blessed the eyes which see what you see,
b and the ears which hear what you hear!
2a Amen, I say to you:
b Many prophets and kings wanted to see what you see,
c but did not see it
3a and to hear what you hear,
b but did not hear it.

Only in minor details is our reconstruction of the Q version hypothetical.[43] Both evangelists have preserved the basic sense, so that issues involved in reconstructing the original form of the saying do not affect its meaning. The contexts in Matthew and Luke explain the differences between the two versions and, at the same time, confirm the saying's original independence. Its simple structure and balanced theme contribute to its concise, self-contained character.

This pronouncement of blessing on the witnesses who see and hear Jesus has two special characteristics that can also confirm the material's authenticity. Jesus shares the general view in Early Judaism that those who participate in the time of salvation of course are blessed (e.g., *Ps. Sol.* 17:44; *1 Enoch* 58:2–6; *Sib. Or.* 3.371), but he does not say as did his predecessors, "Blessed is the one who . . . " Instead, he identifies his contemporaries with the blessing. In contrast to other

Early Jewish sources he sees no reason to distinguish between the situation of the present hearers and the coming eschaton. In Early Judaism one expected that the blessings of salvation and God himself would be revealed at the end of time. For that reason verbs of seeing are emphasized (*1 Enoch* 62:3; *2 Apoc. Bar.* 51:7–8; 1 Cor 13:12, etc.) to point out that what previously was invisible would become visible. Hearing was important, if at all, only as a way of perceiving some of the noises that might accompany the establishment of the final state of affairs (such as thunder) or of hearing commands from heaven (e.g., 1 Thess 4:16; Rev 21:3). In the word of Jesus, however, seeing and hearing are parallel and of equal importance. They are equal ways of experiencing Jesus' activity in word and deed.

From the reference to prophets and kings it is clear that current happenings are end-time events. The prophets and kings, it is said, longed to see and hear what people now can see and hear (cf. 1 Peter 1:10–12). It was granted the earlier figures only to stand in the waiting room and to hope for the time of salvation, while Jesus' contemporaries are able to experience it directly. It is clear, therefore, that the present as the time of salvation is separate from the past, which was only the time of anticipation. Thus the difference between the past and the present is the difference between hope and experience. It is also clear, to repeat what we have said previously, that Jesus' words and deeds do not stand in a subordinate relationship to the time of salvation as if they were previews of coming events; they themselves qualify the present as the end-time.

The words of Matt 11:5–6 = Luke 7:22–23 say much the same thing:

1a Blind see again,
* b and lame walk.*
2a Lepers are cleansed,
* b and deaf hear.*
3a Dead are raised,
* b and poor have good news preached to them.*
* 4 And blessed is whoever takes no offense at me.*

Behind Matt 11:2–19 = Luke 7:18–35 a Q text is visible that brings together several independent traditions about John the Baptist. (Matt 11:7–19 contains three such traditions.) The text falls naturally into two sections: (1) John asks and Jesus answers, Matt. 11:2–6 par.; (2) Jesus takes the initiative in speaking about the Baptist, Matt 11:7–19. Originally Matt 11:5–6 had nothing to do with the Baptist. Instead of answering the question of 11:3, Jesus refers in general to the way all of his contemporaries reacted to him. End-time events are happening (see below), yet these phenomena are so ambiguous that people are able to reject him. John did not receive an answer that would satisfy him; the blessing pronounced on all contemporaries is a challenge to overcome Jesus' ambiguity with faith. Thus, the text presupposes that same situation that lies behind Mark 4:3–8 parr. (cf. §3.2.4).

The unit of seven lines is self-contained. Unlike Matt 13:16–17, the pronouncement of blessing on the followers of Jesus appears at the end of the unit. There are five acts that one can see and one event that one can hear (seeing and hearing appear in Matt 13:16–17 in the same order.) The good news to the poor is in essence the same as the preaching of Jesus in Matt 5:3 = Luke 6:20 (cf. §4.3.2).

There are no indications in Early Judaism that eschatological figures were expected to be healers; it was God's end-time revelation itself that would eliminate sickness and death. That anticipation is clear even in 4Q521,[44] the Early Jewish text that most likely has the closest similarity to Matt 11:5–6. Three things are listed in the second fragment from 4Q521: the prisoners will be released, the blind will see, the oppressed will be lifted up (Ps 145:7–8; cf. Isa 42:7). Then a little later it is said that God will heal the wounded, raise the dead, and proclaim good news to the poor. This last group of three shows marked similarity to Matt 11:5–6. In Matthew the first element of the Qumran text is developed, and the closing line is added.

The list of mighty deeds reminds Jesus' contemporaries of texts such as Isa 26:19; 29:18–19; 35:5–6; 42:18; the good news to the afflicted reminds them of Isa 61:1 (cf. also 29:19). Healing lepers and raising the dead also may well have made them think of Elijah and Elisha (1 Kgs 17:17–24; 2 Kgs 4:18–37; 5:1–19; cf. Luke 4:25–27 and §3.2.4). That Jesus' hearers would have been able to make such connections is clear from 4Q 521. To make such a statement, however, is to imply that Jesus intentionally chose words that would make them think of the Old Testament promises. The text does not simply enumerate statistically what Jesus has done. He is not concerned to make the results of his works a matter of record. Instead, he identifies them collectively as history's turning-point by describing them with the language that Old Testament prophecy used when it expressed its hope for the end of time. That identification makes Jesus' working and preaching activity the beginning of the eschaton. Prophecy's traditional hope is now realized. Thus Matt 11:5–6 par. makes the same claim for Jesus' activity as does Matt 13:16–17. The time before Jesus was the time of anticipation. Now, with him, begins the time of salvation as hope's fulfillment.

Once we have understood the text this way it is no longer a problem that the list of mighty deeds does not include the exorcisms that were so characteristic of Jesus. The text is not a summary of what Jesus has done, but an announcement that what the prophets were looking for has now been realized. Furthermore, Matt 11:5–6 speaks of overcoming illnesses, but it does not evaluate them. A glance at Matt 9:32–34 and Mark 7:31–37 shows that each of those texts has its own understanding of (almost) the same phenomena that are cited in Matt 11:5–6. In one case healing is described as an exorcism, in another as therapy.

This understanding of the text helps us to understand it as part of Jesus's preaching of the Kingdom of God. Since it does not specifically mention this central catchword of Jesus' proclamation, doubts are sometimes expressed about its authenticity. On closer examination, however, it is clear that several of the prophetic texts cited above are part of the postexilic anticipation of a new demonstration of God's kingship, i.e., of the tradition that interpreted the theology of Zion in terms of the end-time (cf. §4.1.3). Especially relevant here is 4Q 521, the Early Jewish text that is strikingly similar to Matt 11:5–6, since in the immediate context it speaks of God's everlasting kingship. God himself is the one who saves. Similarly, in Luke 10:18 and 11:20 we have seen that Jesus understands God to be the one who acts. That God is the agent is clear also in Matt 11:5–6 when it cites the miracles as describing the time—more precisely as defining the end-time—in the sense that the Kingdom of God is beginning to prevail in the present. Jesus is not named as the one who does the deeds; he is mentioned only in the closing sentence about taking offense. It is only in light of this final sentence that one learns who the miracle worker actually is. That Jesus is involved in the victorious Kingdom of God is the essential difference between Matt 11:5–6 and 4Q 521.

A final observation on Matt 11:5–6 is that, in view of the saying's character, the last line is to be understood in the same sense as Matt 13:16–17 par., viz., as a word of praise for the contemporaries of Jesus. They belong to the end-time that is being established by Jesus' activity and, if they do not take offense at him, they can share in the blessings of the end-time.

We can see the same break between the present and the past in those texts in which Jesus compares himself to the Baptist. We turn first to Matt 11:11 = Luke 7:28:

> *Truly I say to you:*
> *There has not arisen among those born of women a greater than John,*
> *but the smallest in the Kingdom of God is greater than he.*

Matt 11:7 = Luke 7:24 is an editorial introduction in which Q brings together three self-contained traditions, each of which has a central saying. Matt 11:11 par. is a pointed antithesis,[45] full of tension. Luke smoothes the beginning; Matthew adds *the Baptist* and changes *Kingdom of God* to *Kingdom of Heaven*.

It should be beyond debate that the opening words, "Amen, I say to you . . . " are typical of Jesus.[46] It is difficult to be certain, however, whether in an individual case the words come from Jesus or were added in the process of tradition. As a rule of thumb we can say that the introductory words, "Amen, I say to you . . . " are from Jesus if the following criteria are met: There are other reasons for attributing the material to Jesus; there is uniformity in the synoptic use of the material; there is no reason to attribute the material to one of the evangelists. Good examples of texts that meet these criteria are Matt 11:11 par.; 13:17 par.; Mark 11:23.

The first of the two main lines is bold to the point of audacity when it states that in all of creation God has permitted no one to be born who was greater than John the Baptist. (*Arisen* is the passive way of avoiding a direct reference to God.) By implication Abraham, Moses, David, and the Old Testament prophets are less than John. Indeed, the saying focuses on creation rather than on salvation history. The high value placed on the Baptist includes, among other things, approval of his statement that Israel's salvation history has run its course. Yet, John is no sooner praised above all others than his status is immediately diminished. When one's standard of judgment is the Kingdom of God rather than human history, a different picture emerges: Every member of the Kingdom of God is greater than John. By placing the smallest in rhetorical opposition to the greatest in all creation, Jesus says that the smallest human creature, if it belongs to the Kingdom of God, is greater than John. The statement clearly excludes John from the Kingdom of God. There is a separation between John and Jesus with his proclamation of the Kingdom of God.

Of course, except for Jesus no one in Judaism could have talked that way. At most one of the Baptist's followers could have echoed the first sentence; the second would have left him speechless. The post-Easter church also would not have been able to make this kind of statement, since, while it subordinated the Baptist to Jesus in the history of salvation, it did not make a break between them. Unlike the first sentence of the antithesis, it also assigned to John a positive role in salvation history.

In a similar way the so-called violence-saying of Matt 11:12–13 = Luke 16:16 emphasizes the seam between the time before Jesus and the Kingdom of God that is making its appearance with him. Unfortunately, it is difficult to determine its original form and some of its individual aspects. It may well be that its original meaning is lost to us forever. The view of history that it presupposes, however, is clear. The saying reads:

> The Law and the Prophets—until John.
> Since then the Kingdom of God prevails violently,
> and violent persons seize it.

For our purposes we can ignore the third line of this unusual statement.[47] Even in the second line the translation of the verb is strongly hypothetical. There is a play on words in the verbs in lines two and three that we cannot recapture in German. [The English words *violently* and *violent* capture something of the play on words. Tr.] Either it originated in the Greek version, or it is an attempt to imitate an Aramaic play on words that is lost to us.[48] That we cannot be sure what the saying means supports the view that the material is very old. Other arguments for attributing the saying to Jesus parallel those for Matt 11:11 par.

The Law and the Prophets was in the time of Jesus an established way of referring to the canon as it was accepted in all groups of Early Judaism (4 Macc 18:10; Matt 5:17; John 1:45; Acts 13:15; Rom 3:21, etc.), although it was usually understood that the Torah had preeminence. That the sentence introduced with this phrase has no verb is probably a Semitism. Connected to the phrase is an indication of time (*until John*) that prepares for the expression *since then*. The two temporal designations determine that between the *terminus ad quem* and the *terminus a quo* a line of demarcation is set. John stands on one side of the line as the end of an era; on the other side the Kingdom of God sets the tone. The two periods are separated from one another, because their contents are different. On the one side are the Law and the Prophets; on the other side is the Kingdom of God.

Matt 11:12–13 par. and Luke 10:23–24 help clarify what this division means. The time of waiting and hoping, including predictions of the future, lasts until John; what happens when the Kingdom of God appears is fulfillment. Thus the time after John is qualitatively new. Along with the Law and the Prophets John is part of the future's vestibule. With the arrival of the Kingdom of God this waiting period, which was not characterized by the Kingdom of God, is closed, and it is separated from the new age. The Kingdom of God brings with it a transformation into an eschatological quality in which only the Kingdom of God fills the time.

Matt 8:21–22 = Luke 9:59–60 offers an impressive example of how breaking with the past and the existing order can define the way one lives in the present. In the apophthegm a potential disciple offers to follow Jesus if he can first go and bury his father. In that culture this custom was so important that there was no reason to expect that Jesus would not grant the request. The possibility that one would not honor one's parent in such a situation would not even have entered anyone's mind.[49] Jesus' answer must have shocked and offended his hearers, therefore, when he said,

Let the dead bury their dead!

It is conceivable that the heart of the scene and Jesus' answer originally belonged together, although the setting also could be deduced from the word of Jesus itself. It is safer, however, to explain the saying simply on its own terms. Similar to Matt 9:9, Matthew prefaced Jesus' word with a typical introductory command, "Follow me!" Because of the setting with which he frames the saying (Matt 8:18, 23), he is also able to omit Luke's second half of the command ("but you go and proclaim the Kingdom of God"). In the post-Easter tradition, however, and not least of all for Luke, there is a tendency to connect verbs of preaching with the Kingdom of God (cf., by way of example, Luke 8:1; 9:2, 11; Acts 1:3; 20:25; 28:23, 31). It is true that the verb for *proclaim* in 9:60 appears nowhere else in the Third Gospel and that, therefore, one might claim it as pre-Lukan, i.e., Q material, but to be safe, in reconstructing authentic Jesus material we should limit ourselves to the heart of the saying as we offer it above.[50]

Since the unexpected harshness of such an unreasonable demand lies in the refusal to grant permission to honor the dead (cf. Tob 1:17–19; 2:3–9; 12:12–13; the conclusions of the *T. 12 Patr.*), the interpretation of this saying usually focuses on this violation of both custom and the Torah. There is, however, a reason for the offense that is given in the saying itself in the play on words: Those who are dead metaphorically should bury those who are dead physically. The sense is that all are dead who do not enter the Kingdom of God that is offered by the preaching of Jesus. These people may engage in the customary business of burying the dead, while those who have found the way to Jesus have experienced the individual turning-point of salvation that defines all time. As persons who have chosen life they no longer need to concern themselves with the physical

dead. In the Kingdom of God death is simply not an issue any more (cf. Isa 25:8;
also 35:10; 65:19–20, along with Rev 20:4 and §§4.1.3, 4.1.7), because when the
end-time Kingdom of God begins, death loses its power to define the present. The
new age that begins with Jesus renders impotent the things, including death, that
are no longer relevant.

That the old and the new are incompatible is the theme of the wisdom saying
in Mark 2:21–22 parr.:

> *1a   No one sews a* patch *of unfulled cloth on an old garment.*
> *b   Otherwise the new piece tears away from the old [v. 21c],*
> *c   and the tear becomes worse.*
> *2a   And no one pours new* wine *into old wineskins.*
> *b   Otherwise the wine bursts the wineskins,*
> *c   and the wine is lost (as) also the wineskins [v. 22d].*

It is obvious that the double saying that concludes the pericope Mark 2:18–22 is
thematically and formally independent. Only two small additions intrude into the formal
structure, and they use the opposites old/new to confirm the general theme. The formal
parallelism between the two sayings and the choice of examples from the complementary
worlds of the artisan and the farmer found in rural Galilee support the conclusion that the
two examples originated together.

At first glance the saying sounds like general, commonsense wisdom—a
collection of rules for the tailor and the vintager. Giving that kind of simplistic
advice to people who are familiar with the professions, however, is superfluous
and is tantamount to carrying coals to Newcastle. Precisely because this commonsense wisdom is so noncontroversial and self-evident, it must serve the
purpose of making equally self-evident a reality that is not yet clear. What we
have before us, therefore, are not two sentences that preserve knowledge gained
through experience; they are parabolic sayings designed to use a noncontroversial insight to win agreement for a controversial statement. The new understanding of time and history that comes with the Kingdom of God provides an
especially good situation for Jesus to use the parables. Beginning with Deutero-
Isaiah, the final demonstration of God's power as king could be described by
contrasting the old and the new in such a way that the old is devalued (Isa 43:19;
also 42:9; 48:6; cf. §4.1.3). This terminology may well have influenced the
choice of images in the double saying. In any case, in the context of the preaching
of Jesus the saying makes the affirmation that his message is incompatible with
the old order (cf. Luke 9:62) and that, therefore, the old and the new must keep
their distance from one another. One may repair the torn garment in another way,
and one may for a while fill the old wineskin with a less dangerous liquid, but
both the garment and the wineskin have been so damaged by time that the
weakness of old age is obvious. The new is downright dangerous for the old.

Thus the first important result of our investigation is that Jesus separates the present, the time in which the Kingdom of God is dawning, from the past. In so doing he nowhere makes use of the views of history that were current in his day, whether from the Deuteronomic (e.g., Neh 9), or from the wisdom (e.g., Sir 44), or from the apocalyptic (e.g., *1 Enoch* 93:1–10; 91:11–17) points of view. He does not attempt to create a place for himself within an existing outline of history. That sort of thing does not occur to him, because it is not his intention to move the flow of history closer to its end. Instead, he sees the hoped-for salvation of the future Kingdom of God as a present turning-point in history that overcomes all opposition. The present with its new quality is integrated into God's future and is separated from the past and from the present, which is still conditioned by the past.

Thus far we have mentioned only in passing that for Jesus the Kingdom of God was by nature a future reality. Yet, for our claim that Jesus incorporated the present into the future to have any meaning at all, it must be a given that the kingdom is a future reality. When we look once again at the earliest Jesus material from this perspective, we make first of all the negative observation that in talking about God's preservation of creation and history, Jesus, contrary to the mainstream of Early Judaism, never speaks of a (hidden) rule of God as king. The closest source to Jesus in this regard has been the *Targum of Jonathon* (cf. §4.1.4). It may be that Jesus avoids this customary way of speaking (cf. §§4.1.3–4.1.8) in order to bring the difference between the old and the new more sharply into focus. In any case, when Early Judaism spoke of God's final rule, it said that the rule, which had been hidden throughout history, then would become visible, would appear, finally would be established, or would be revealed.[51] Jesus, on the other hand, does not talk this way. Instead, he uses a way of speaking that is up to that point not common in Judaism. He makes (and this is our positive observation) the Kingdom of God the subject of verbs of movement.[52] Examples of this usage are the statements that the Kingdom of God *has come* (Luke 11:20) or that it *has come near* (Mark 1:15b parr.; cf. Luke 10:9 par.).[53]

Israel and Early Judaism could speak of God's coming in a theophany at the end of time (*1 Enoch* 1:9; 25:3; *Sib. Or.* 3:49) or of the Day of the Lord, which will come or which has drawn near (Joel 2:1–2; Zech 14:1–21; *Sib. Or.* 3.55–56, 60, etc.),[54] but they could not speak of the coming of the Kingdom of God (which was not yet present).[55] They did not understand that, while the Kingdom of God had always existed, only at the end of history would it be established absolutely and for all to see. Jesus, on the other hand, speaks of the activity of the Kingdom of God with verbs of movement (*to come, to draw near*). He describes the Kingdom as a new and dynamic reality that, similar to the Day of the Lord or God's final theophany, is a temporal event in the strict sense of the word—an event that is beginning to prevail and that in the end will lead to the final condition of salvation (Matt 5:3–4 par.; 8:11–12 par.).

We have already discussed Luke 11:20, one of the above-mentioned cardinal texts that are important for this aspect of the preaching of Jesus. Mark 1:15–16 also deserves a few comments.

The text reads:

1a   *Fulfilled is the time,*
 b   *and drawn near is the Kingdom of God.*
2a   *Repent*
 b   *and believe in the gospel!*

With this text Mark summarizes at the beginning of his gospel the message of Jesus. Now it has long been observed that the missionary preaching of Mark's church and the preaching of Jesus about which Mark knew are mixed together here. Themes of early Christian preaching are the fulfilled time (cf. Gal 4:4), the call to repent in response to the offer of salvation (cf. Acts 2:38; Heb 6:1–2), the call to faith (e.g., Phil 1:27; Heb 6:2–3), and the catchword *gospel* (cf. 1 Thess 1:5; Rom 1:1).

The reference to time at the beginning of the text is not to be understood in the sense that the measure of time has been filled and that therefore the Kingdom of God now will come. The point is, rather, that the time is fulfilled, because the kingdom is coming (much as 2 Cor 6:2 is based on 5:18–21). In the same way, because the gospel is offered, the call to repent can be announced.

With the help of Q (Luke 10:9 = Matt 10:7) we can isolate the statement about the Kingdom of God from this text, but what is the meaning of *has come*? Is the Kingdom of God on the way, i.e., at the door? Or is it characterized by present activity, as in the case of Luke 11:20? The prior reference to time would indicate that Mark, at any rate, understands the verb in the latter sense. Luke 10:9 (unlike Matt 10:7) also emphasized the present reality of the kingdom through the direct address (*to you*, cf. Luke 11:20). It is possible that the same Aramaic temporal word stands behind the different Greek verbs of movement in Luke 11:20 and Mark 1:15, in which case we could assume that both Mark 1:15 and Luke 11:20 speak of the kingdom as a present reality. Yet, these three considerations do not offer convincing proof, because they are not explicit in the sentence itself.

If, therefore, we are not to understand Mark 1:15 in the sense of Luke 11:20, then we must ask whether, in view of the obvious understanding of the kingdom as present in Luke 11:20, a statement about an imminent but not yet present future can be attributed to Jesus at all. In this case would not Luke 11:20 and Mark 1:15 be mutually exclusive? The answer is *no*, if we keep in mind what we emphasized at the beginning of this section, viz., that Early Judaism expected the final state of things to be established over a period of time. According to 1QM, at the beginning of the end-time Israel and the heavenly forces will go to war against all the powers that are hostile to God. In the midst of this final war God is addressed *in the glory of his kingship*, and he is petitioned to let his rule as king finally be known with mighty deeds (1QM xii). There exists in 1QM, therefore, the same kind of tension that exists between Luke 11:20 and Luke 11:2 par.— i.e., between the Kingdom of God that has already arrived and the request that it come—and we need not assume that a statement of realized eschatology such as

Luke 11:20 and statements about a future eschatology are mutually exclusive. There is room for each in a dynamic understanding of the Kingdom of God, so that it is possible that Mark 1:15 speaks of an immediate future. However one decides that question, Mark 1:15 remains a statement that presupposes that the Kingdom of God will be completed at some future time and that this future is drawing near.

In a pregnant statement, Luke 17:20–21 also states that the present is absorbed into the future:

1a   The Kingdom of God comes not with calculation [v. 21a];
* b   the Kingdom of God is (rather) among you.*

The saying is found only in Luke, and it was probably Luke who created its present setting (v. 20a). Luke also added v. 21a under the influence of 17:23. The prophetic pronouncement is self-contained and is structured antithetically.

In the first sentence Jesus uses his own language ("the Kingdom of God comes . . . ") to distance himself from a common view ("not . . . "). The question about signs and the time of the end is typical of Early Jewish apocalypticism (Dan 12:5–13; 4 Ezra 6:7; cf. Mark 13:4). It expresses not curiosity, but the despair of a crisis situation in which it seems that only God's final intervention can bring order into a chaotic situation. The question is: When will a future of salvation and health replace this unbearable present? The intervention is already a part of God's historical plans, but he has revealed these plans only to a few persons. Their task is to help people persevere during God's absence by sharing their knowledge about God's plans for history. Those who, instructed by the bearers of apocalyptic revelation, can understand the signs of the times are able to see how God's salvation is approaching. For them the present phenomena are signs of what is to come.

Jesus rejects this attitude about the coming Kingdom of God, because it presupposes a false understanding of reality. The present is not a time of crisis, waiting for a Kingdom of God that is to come; God is already present in a final way as king. The present is wasted when people spend their time looking for signs of God's future appearance. It is used appropriately when it is understood as the place for experiencing God's nearness, since the Kingdom of God has already come.[56] This turning-point necessitates a new understanding of reality. No longer does the present come before the future; now the present through God's initiative has become the place where one meets the final future. In other words, the Kingdom of God does not announce itself with signs; it has already happened. When Jesus makes the special statement that "God's reign as king is among" his hearers, he obviously intends them to understand the statement in the context of the Early Jewish anticipation that at the end God will live among his people and will be with them (Zeph 3:14–16; Zech 2:14–15; *Jub.* 1:17, 28; *T. Dan.* 5:13; 1QM xii 7–8; *Sib. Or.* 3.785–95; Rev 21:3–4). This hope is now fulfilled in Jesus' activity. Since Jesus' appearance effects this nearness of God that is expected for the end-time, the present is end-time. Present and anticipated future occur simultaneously.

Mark 2:19a makes the same declaration, although this original word of Jesus is buried in Mark 2:18–22 parr. as the core of a pericope with several layers of tradition.[57] The saying is in the form of a rhetorical question:

Can the sons of the bridechamber . . . fast?

While the unit is in the form of an apophthegm, the answer does not respond directly to the question. The present answer in vv. 19–20 focuses on the difference between the post-Easter time of fasting and the time of Jesus when one did not fast, while v. 18 raises the issue that the disciples of Jesus, unlike other disciples, do not fast. At the same, time vv. 19–20 reveals a post-Easter christology in allegorical form: The bridegroom is Jesus. When we strip away the temporal and allegorical declarations that presuppose a post-Easter point of view, what is left is the rhetorical question as we have translated it above. It is the beginning of a possible answer to the question in v. 18. Even when we concede that there is more than one layer of material in v. 18, nothing in that verse can serve as a core text that is as general and fundamental as v. 19a. Verse 19a is not simply a prohibition of fasting; it is also a concrete example of the principle that one's behavior must always be appropriate to the situation. Thus it is likely that v. 19a was an isolated saying of Jesus for which at an early date v. 18 was created as a setting. Then later in the process the independent double saying in 2:21–22 was added as commentary: The penitential fasting of the Baptist's disciples in light of the coming judgment (cf. §3.1.3) and the joyful meal of the time of Jesus in light of the Kingdom of God are as irreconcilable as are old and new in the two examples. Then a final editor expanded v. 19a to the form that we now read in vv. 19–20.

The sons of the bridechamber are the friends of the bridegroom who make up the inner circle of the wedding guests and who have the task of verifying the marriage. While they participate in the wedding excitement they cannot fast, because part of the joy of a wedding celebration is a joyful and abundant feast (John 2:1–10).[58] The wedding celebration is at the same time a metaphor for the end-time joy (Isa 62:5; Matt 25:1–13; John 3:29–30; Rev 19:7–9, etc.). It is against this background that we are to understand the sense of the rhetorical question for which the answer is obvious: "Of course they cannot fast!" Fasting at a wedding would not be appropriate to the situation, and no one should behave inappropriately—not even Jesus. Since his activity initiates the time for end-time joy, his behavior and that of his circle of followers must be appropriate to the situation. The accusation that Jesus was *a glutton and a drunk* (Matt 11:19 par.) may have been malicious, but it was essentially accurate. Jesus' table-fellowship was an expression of the festive joy of the end-time (cf. §4.3.2).

A second important conclusion of our study is then that Jesus understands the present as the turning-point for a victorious Kingdom of God, which as the fulfillment of history at the end of time is already leaving its mark on the present. The present is the beginning of God's final rule as king, and as such it is bound up with the future. In the full sense of the word—i.e., not simply in symbolic anticipation—the future salvation has arrived in the present.

The remaining question is: How did Jesus imagine the activity of the dynamically unfolding Kingdom of God in the time between the present turning-point and the kingdom's final realization? Do we find information on that subject in such texts as Mark 9:1 parr.; 13:30 parr.; and Matt 10:23, which make statements about the time of the end? Clearly one cannot say that Jesus said nothing about the course of the dynamic process. That Early Judaism and Primitive Christianity made such statements does not justify the a priori conclusion that Jesus could not have done so. We must follow the same line of argument here that we use with the question about Jesus' use of allegory (cf. §4.3.1): In principle he could have spoken allegorically, but other elements in the allegorical texts suggest that he did not. In the same way we must deal with the statements about time not in terms of a general principle, but by analyzing each individual text.

The evidence does not speak for Matt 10:23 as an authentic word of Jesus. The statement that the disciples will not have completed their mission to the cities of Israel before the world-judging Son of Man comes is special Matthean material attached to a context that the evangelist borrowed from Mark (Mark 13:12–13). On two occasions, in Matt 10:23a and 10:23b, the text assumes that the mission will take place in a situation of persecution, similar to the language of Matt 10:16–22. Yet, we have no evidence for that kind of persecution of Jesus and his followers prior to Easter. The two test cases of conflict related to Nazareth (Mark 6:1–6 parr.) and Herod Antipas (Luke 13:31–33) suggest just the opposite. On the other hand, such texts as Matt 5:11–12; Mark 13:9; Acts 7:58; 8:1; Gal 1:13, 22–23; John 15:18–16:4 reveal that the early churches were persecuted by Judaism. That persecution is a fertile ground for statements about an imminent end is clear from such works as 1 Peter and Revelation.

Mark 13:30 parr., along with 13:28–32, is part of an apocalyptic discourse about the beginning of the end-time. The verse is not an isolated single saying, since it is understandable only in the context of 13:4, 24–25, 29. In contrast to the words of Jesus, all stages of the tradition lying behind Mark 13 proceed from the assumption that the beginning of salvation still lies in the future and that the present is a time of suffering before the end. That anticipation itself is enough to deny the statement to Jesus.

The situation is more complicated for Mark 9:1 parr., which says that "some of the ones who stand here will not taste death until they see the Kingdom of God coming in power." Both the vocabulary and the form of the saying permit the possibility that it came from Jesus, but we should overlook neither the connection to Mark 13:30 nor the initial reference to *some*, which implies that not all will be involved. Does this limitation not devalue the beatitudes of Matt 11:5 par. and 13:16–17 par.? Mark 9:1 would be an anomaly in the proclamation of Jesus, while it fits exceptionally well with the early church's experience of the delay of the parousia.[59]

Finally, the only miracle of judgment in the synoptic material (cf. §4.3.3), viz., the cursing of the fig tree (Mark 11:12–14, 20–25 parr.), can be traced back to a saying that describes the time before the end as limited and brief. This word about the appointed time admittedly must be deduced from vv. 13–14, but its original form may have been:

1a   *And when he saw from a distance a* fig tree *which had* leaves,
 b   *he went to see if he could find something on it.*
2a   *And when he came to it,*
 b   *he found only* leaves *[vv. 13–14].*
3a   *And he answered and said to it:*
 b   *"Never again shall anyone eat* fruit *from you." [v. 14c]*

The reference to the season at the end of v. 13 is the part of the text that most likely was added as commentary. Mark needed the disciples in v. 14c because of 11, 12, 19, 20, but in v. 14a they are not even addressed.

The apophthegm is self-contained and rounded. Each of the three sentences begins with a paratactic *and*, followed by a participle. The verbs in the first two sentences are linked. The sequence *leaves, leaves, fruit* is intentional.

According to the Markan framework, even from up close Jesus can find only leaves on the tree; the fruit is not yet ripe. In response to this situation (*answered*) Jesus speaks directly to a nonhuman creature—behavior that is unique in the synoptic material.[60] No one will ever again harvest fruit from the fig tree, because there will not be enough time for its fruit to ripen before the end comes. The saying assumes a time span of only a few months, but even this precise a dating of the end can hardly be attributed to Jesus. The subject is too broad (cf., e.g., Mark 13:28–29), and the saying offers nothing peculiar to Jesus. Is it really conceivable that someone who describes the final fulfillment in terms of eating and drinking in the abundance of paradise (Matt 8:11–12; cf. §§4.2.3 and 4.3.2) would speak in such a discordant way about eating?

If, then, we cannot attribute to Jesus the sayings that speak of the time of the end, we must ask whether he understood the relation between the present turning-point and the coming fulfillment in some other way. The answer is yes. There is a series of authentic Jesus words that differ in outlook from the texts that we have just discussed. We are thinking especially of the parables of the mustard seed and the leaven (Mark 4:30–32 parr.; Matt 13:33 par.), of the seed that grows of itself (Mark 4:26–29), and of the parable of sowing and harvest (Mark 4:3–8 parr.; cf. §3.2.4). The original forms of the first three parables would have been something like:

1a   *[Mark 4:30] As a* mustard seed, *when it is sown on the ground,*
 b   *is the* smallest *of all the seeds on earth.*
2a   *But when it [is sown (and)] comes up*
 b   *becomes* larger *than all shrubs.*

3a   And it sprouts large *branches,*
  b   so that the birds of heaven can nest in its shade.

Mark 4:30, although pre-Markan, is an editorial introduction; its connection to v. 31a is awkward. Verse 32a repeats the verb *sown* from v. 31 unnecessarily and disturbs the flow of the sentence. Without these additions the structure is smooth. Each two-line unit makes a statement that presupposes the previous statement. The beginning and the ending offer a contrast.

The reference is probably to the *sinapis niger* (black mustard), which has an especially tiny seed and which grows to a height of about three meters, producing unusually large branches. Although the plant is well known, we have no reference prior to Jesus to the difference between a small seed and its large shrub. The birds may well come from the motif of the earth as a tree (Ezek 31:6, 13; Dan 4:9, 18). It is possible that 3a, b constitute an allegorical interpretation that has been added; if the two lines were removed, a complete parable would remain that formally would parallel Matt 13:33. Since, however, there is no firm evidence for such a conjecture, it is probable that we should leave 3a, b as part of the early form of the parable.

The first verb refers to a past action. The second, in v. 32, is in the present tense. Thus the narrator looks back to the event of sowing and ahead to the full growth, emphasizing the beginning and the end. The growth in the middle part is only mentioned as a condition for the final situation.

> *With what can we compare the Kingdom of God?*
> *It is like* leaven *which a woman took*
> *and kneaded into three measures of flour*
> *until it was* all *leavened.*

Noteworthy is the narrative style that looks back at a repeatable experience. The focus is on the leavening process, which works by itself. The Kingdom of God has begun with Jesus, and one can depend on it to prevail.

Three measures of flour would comprise about forty liters, but we should regard the figure as a typical, round number. The point is that there was a great amount of flour. The expansion of the Kingdom of God will be total and comprehensive:

1a   [Mark 4:26a] As a man casts the seed *on the* ground
  b   and sleeps and rises (again) night and day.
2a   And the seed sprouts and grows,
  b   but he does not know how.
3a   Of itself the earth bears fruit,
  b   first a stalk, then an ear,
  c   then full grain in the ear.
4a   But when the fruit permits,
  b   he immediately sends the sickle,
  c   because the harvest *has come.*

A glance at Mark 4:30 shows that the introduction can be posed in various ways and that it does not belong to the parable itself.

The farmer is active at the sowing and at the harvest. Between those two events the emphasis is on the process of growth, which is independent of human action, resulting in the usual sequence of sowing, growth, and harvest. Approximately in the middle, the expression *of itself* appears asyndetically at the beginning of a sentence. The parable functions to reassure the hearer that once the sowing has taken place the harvest is assured at the end of the usual growing period.

The growth comes from God, but it is not presented as a miracle; it is a normal dimension of God's maintenance of creation (Lev 21:5, 11; 1 Cor 3:6). The focus is intentionally limited to the central idea; no reference is made to cultivating the crop (weeding, watering) or to negative natural events (drought, pests). According to Early Jewish eschatology, trouble-free growth without human effort will not take place until the age of salvation (*2 Apoc. Bar.* 74:1).

Contrary to widespread Jewish tradition the metaphor of fruit is not given an ethical meaning; instead, it is used in the service of Jesus' theme of the Kingdom of God.[61]

Common to all four parables, with individual variations, is that they describe the repetition of common experiences from the life of farmers. Everyone is familiar with the world that they describe. Each parable contains a natural unit of time that is confirmed by experience. Under normal conditions it always takes the same amount of time for a mustard seed to grow into a bush. On the farm every woman knows how long it will take dough to rise. People who sow in the spring will harvest in the fall. In all four parables the beginning and the end of each unit of time are accented. In the parable of the seed growing of itself, the inactivity of the farmer in the time between the sowing and harvesting is emphasized. In the parable of the leaven, the narrative skips from the kneading of the leaven into the dough to the dough that has risen. The parable of the mustard seed hurries over the long period of growth with just a few words. In Mark 4:3–9 the negative things happen immediately after the sowing; in the case of the seed that produces a harvest the harvest comes right after the sowing. All of which is to say that beginning and end are closely connected in the narratives, although a time factor is involved in each instance and a development or dynamic process takes place. Within a process that is not subject to human influence (cf. the *of itself* in Mark 4:28) there is a direct relationship between the initial situation and the final result.

We may apply this inner structure to Jesus' understanding of time and of the Kingdom of God. Jesus' activity and the fall of Satan (Luke 10:18; 11:20) mark the beginning of a process that cannot be stopped; the Kingdom of God is spreading. With absolute confidence Jesus expects an end that is imminent, but that cannot be stated with any objective measure of time. Since the fall of Satan and the activity of Jesus have made the present history's turning-point, it is irreversible, and one can now view the beginning and its completion together. Between the beginning and the end there is a short period of time, but Jesus is not interested in describing its length; instead, he emphasizes that his activity will lead inexorably and immediately to the final completion.

We can summarize this section by saying that the earliest Jesus material reveals that for him the present is the turning-point of history. In his deeds the Kingdom of God makes its appearance with inexorable finality, and it will lead directly and with certainty to the ultimate consummation. God's end-time rule that is now appearing is qualitatively different from everything that has gone before. It is no longer an object of hope and prophecy; it can now be experienced. No one in Israel and in Early Judaism had ever before made such claims about the Kingdom of God.

4.2.3   Creation as the Focus of the Kingdom of God

Becker, J. "Jesu Frohbotschaft und Freudenmahl für die Armen," *BiKi* 33 (1978) 43–47.

Grässer, E. "Jesus und das Heil Gottes," in: *Jesus Christus in Historie und Theologie.* Festschrift H. Conzelmann. G. Strecker, ed. Tübingen: J.C.B. Mohr (Paul Siebeck), 1975, 166–84.

Haufe, G. "Gott in der ältesten Jesustradition," *ZdZ* 24 (1970) 201–6.

Hoffmann, P. "'Er weiß, was ihr braucht . . .' (Mt 6,7). Jesu einfache und konkrete Rede von Gott," in: *"Ich will euer Gott werden."* N. Lohfink et al., eds. SBS 100. Stuttgart: KBW, 1981, 152–76.

Kümmel, W. G. "Die Gottesverkündigung Jesu und der Gottesgedanke des Spätjudentums," in: *Heilsgeschehen und Geschichte.* E. Grässer et al., eds. Mthst 3. Marburg: N. H. Elwert, 1965, 107–25.

Müller, U. B. "Vision und Botschaft," *Zthk* 74 (1977) 416–48.

Sauer, J. *Rückkehr*, 304–12; 521–31.

Schmidt, W. H. and J. Becker. *Zukunft und Hoffnung*, KTB 1014. Stuttgart: Kohlhammer, 1981, 103–7.

Stegemann, H. "Der lehrende Jesus," *NZSTh* 24 (1982) 3–20.

Wischmeyer, O. "Matthäus 6,25–34 par," *ZNW* 85 (1994) 1–22.

Zeller, D. *Mahnsprüche*, 11.

The mainstream theology of Early Judaism is essentially focused on salvation history with its emphasis on Israel's election from among the nations and the various covenants (cf. Rom 9:4), especially God's covenants with Abraham, with the people at Sinai, and with David. God's exclusive choice of Israel means that the people are obligated to serve this God alone and that God will be faithful to his promises to the people. The drive toward Hellenization under Antiochus IV led to a renewed emphasis on Israel's salvation history among the Hasideans and Maccabeans as well as among groups such as the Essenes and the Pharisees, which developed in the period of restoration (1 Macc 1; CD 6:2–20; 1QS i 1–3, 12; *Pss. Sol.*). After the death of Herod the Great, the Exodus prophets and the Zealots put this theology into action. Of course, included in this emphasis on salvation history was the theology of Zion, which gave the concept of God's kingship its primary shape (cf. §4.1).

There was undoubtedly a great deal of variety in this main trend of Early Jewish theology; indeed, the variety was probably greater than our extant sources reveal. One important area of difference was the attitude toward the nations. Of special interest was the issue concerning the varying degrees to which the nations someday would share in the promises to Israel. One can find examples of severe hostility toward the nations (1QM; *T. Sim.* 6:3–4; 4 Ezra 6:56–59) along with different levels of acceptance (Isa 66:20–21; Jon; Tob 14:6–7; *Ps. Sol.* 17:30–31; *T. Jud.* 25:5; *T. Naph.* 8; *1 Enoch* 48:4–5; 90:30, 38). In *Sib. Or.* 3.663–731 one finds the idea that the nations will be destroyed alongside the idea that they will share in the promises to Israel. This issue along with its various positions extends even into the New Testament. As a Pharisee it is likely that Paul was as severely confrontational as were his later Judaizing opponents in Galatians and Philippians (cf. Gal. 1:13; Phil 3:4–6). Luke, on the other hand (e.g., in Luke 1–2), speaks for a Judaism that includes the nations in the promises of salvation granted to Israel.

Alongside this dominant salvation history emphasis with its variety of expressions there were also theological schemes, which did not turn on the axis of the God of Israel and his people—which chose rather as their conceptual system of coordinates the creator of the world and the humanity that belongs to him. Of course, the two impulses were not mutually exclusive in Early Judaism. No one would deny that the God of Israel is also the creator of everything, and a theology that is fundamentally oriented toward creation naturally can include elements of a theology of salvation history. Still, there is a decided difference between understanding reality with the particularism of, say, *Jubilees* and speaking almost totally with the language of a theology of creation as does the Wisdom of Solomon. Whether one believes that the created order was made only for the sake of Israel (4 Ezra 6:55–59) or one sees Israel as part of a creation that has the totality of reality as its own preeminent meaning (*1 Enoch* 1–5) is no small difference.

When we set out to find the locus for the view of God as world creator and sustainer and for an understanding of the world in universal-human terms, we are led to two of Early Judaism's main traditions: wisdom and apocalypticism.

The earliest witnesses from the wisdom tradition appear in the Old Testament—specifically in Jonah and in Job. Jonah, a man who confesses God as the Lord of all creation (Jonah 1:9), is sent to proclaim God's judgment on Ninevah, but God accepts the city's repentance because as the creator he has mercy on his creatures (Jonah 3:10; 4:5–11). The book of Jonah proclaims the creator's grace toward the worst heathen city because its inhabitants repent. That the creator has pity on his creatures is also a basic motif in wisdom psalms (e.g., Ps 145; *Ps. Sol.* 5). We have already noted above (§4.1.8) that this view of God appears in a number of prayers that speak of God's continuous kingship in creation and history. The Wisdom of Solomon offers another example of a view of God that is focused on creation. While it makes reference to Solomon's rule over God's people and to the building of the temple (Wis 9:7–8), what most characterizes Solomon is that he possesses the divine wisdom who sits with God on his throne and who is the authoress of all things (7:12, 15; 9:1–4). As a kindly spirit she fills the world (1:6–7), and she leads all who love her to true humanity (6:12–25).

Thus Solomon, who finds wisdom (7:1–21), becomes the genuine human being and king that God wants him to be, and he is able to teach all people to follow his example (1:1–5; 6:1–11; 9:1–18).

Apocalypticism also made a contribution to a theology based on creation. The apocalypse in *1 Enoch* 1–5 that originally existed independently is so focused on creation that the judgment that it proclaims is a judgment from the *God of the world* (1:4), i.e., the God who created everything and who lives forever (5:1)—a judgment that is coming over all humanity (1:7, 9). It makes no allusions to typical salvation history motifs. The final salvation contains only blessings of salvation oriented on the creatureliness of the blessed (*1 Enoch* 1:8; 5:7–9):

> *With the righteous he will make peace,*
> *And he will protect the elect,*
> *And mercy shall be upon them.*
> *And they shall all belong to God,*
> *And they shall prosper,*
> *And they shall be blessed,*
> *And God's light shall appear unto them.*

> *And for the elect there shall be light and joy and peace, and they shall inherit the earth. And then there shall be bestowed upon the elect wisdom, and they shall all live and never again sin, either through ungodliness or through pride. But they who are wise shall be humble. And they shall not again transgress, and they shall not be judged all the days of their life, and they shall not die of torment and wrath, but they shall complete the number of the days of their life. And their lives shall be increased in peace, and the years of their joy will be many in eternal joy and peace all the days of their life.*

The parabolic addresses of *1 Enoch* (cf. §4.1.5) fit this pattern. They address those who live on the mainland (*1 Enoch* 37:2). As the Lord of the world (58:4) God has given over the judgment of the world to the Son of Man, who will summon the kings of the world and the mighty of the earth to give account of themselves (62–63). The theme of Israel's special position is nowhere expressly mentioned. The final salvation, once again focused only on creation, is described as follows (*1 Enoch* 62:13–15; cf. also 58:2–6):

> *And the righteous . . . shall be saved on that day. And they shall never again see the face of the sinners. . . . And the Lord of spirits will abide over them. And with that Son of Man they shall eat and lie down and rise up for ever and ever. And the righteous . . . shall have ceased to be of downcast countenance, and they shall have been clothed with garments of glory.*

The description of the final salvation in *T. Lev.* 18:10–14, which at one time existed independently, is also appropriate here:

1a   And [the Lord, cf. v. 13] shall open the gates of paradise
b   and shall remove the threatening sword against Adam.
2a   He shall give to the saints to eat from the tree of life,
b   and the spirit of holiness shall be on them.
3a   And Beliar shall be bound by him,
b   and he shall give power to his children to tread on the evil spirits.
4a   And the Lord shall rejoice in his children
b   and be well pleased in his beloved ones for ever.
5a   Then shall Abraham and Isaac and Jacob exult . . . ,
b   and all the saints shall clothe themselves with exultation.

When we ask where Jesus fits in this panorama, we must begin with John the Baptist (cf. §3.1). Jesus inherits from the Baptist the unheard-of conviction that Israel has used up its salvation history (§3.2.2). In the face of this hopeless condition Jesus then brings the saving nearness of the Kingdom of God into the situation. For that to happen he must of necessity suppress the salvation history traditions of his people and describe the Kingdom of God in terms of all creation. Thus while Jesus belongs to that theological stance that is focused on creation, what he inherits from the Baptist gives him a unique position in that tradition.

A number of observations confirm and elaborate this thesis. It is clear from the entire synoptic tradition that Jesus did not formulate an outline of Israel's salvation history. While he is aware of Israel's history, he does not refer to God as the *God of the fathers*; Mark 11:10 parr. and 12:26 parr. do not reflect Jesus' opinion. Nor does he claim for the people of Israel a special role as the chosen people. *People* and *people of God* as terms of salvation history are not found in the oldest Jesus material. Furthermore, the way he uses *Israel* to refer to the people of God supplements these observations. We can say with some certainty that the term appears in the early Jesus material only in statements that are critical of Israel (Luke 4:25, 27; cf. also Luke 7:9 par.). Even those who would cite Matt 19:28 par. in this context will have to agree that this one saying is rather meager evidence, especially in view of the fact that the language of election appears nowhere else.[62] The same is true of the catchword *covenant*, since the only text that is even remotely debatable—the tradition of the last supper in Mark 14:22–25 parr. and 1 Cor 11:23–26 (cf. §6.2)—is a liturgical text and not a historical report. Since especially the covenant idea, which in Mark is related to Exod 24:8 and in Paul to Jer 31:31, most likely is characteristic of the post-Easter church (e.g., Rom 3:25; 2 Cor 3:7–11; Gal 4:21–31) but is not at home elsewhere in the preaching of Jesus, we cannot avoid the conclusion that the covenant motif in the supper tradition does not come from Jesus. Why should Jesus at the last supper have proclaimed a covenant theology when the clear evidence is that he had not done so previously—indeed, because of the influence of John the Baptist could not have done so?

The names of individual figures from Israel's history are also infrequent in the early Jesus material. Contemporary with or prior to the patriarchs, only Noah and Lot are mentioned (Luke 17:26–29 par.). The patriarchs themselves appear only in Matt 8:11 par.[63] References to Moses are also scarce, if not nonexistent. At most one might bring Mark 10:3–6 into the discussion, but the text has no interest at all in Moses as a person—only in the regulations that carry his authority (cf. in addition §5.3.3). Of the kings of Israel Solomon is mentioned (Matt 6:29 par.; 12:42 par.)—of the prophets Elijah, Elisha (Luke 4:25–27), and Jonah (Matt 12:41 par.). With the exception of Mark 10:3–6, all of these texts are pronouncements of judgment or, at the least, critical of Israel. Almost always, when Israel is compared with the nations it is to Israel's disadvantage (cf. §3.2.4). Nowhere is Israel granted a special position based on its salvation history.

When we examine Jesus' statements about the future in light of the promises made to Israel, it is immediately clear that Jesus did not use the themes of the promise of land, dwelling in the land free of foreign domination, and the return of the exiles. Nor does he speak of a special role for Jerusalem and the temple. Matt 8:11–12 par. (cf. §3.2.4) shows how he reformulates the Zion tradition for which traditionally those institutions were of central importance. Nathan's promise to the house of David (2 Sam 7) is also missing, as is the promise that whoever obeys the law will live. Jesus takes the place of the Torah as the standard of judgment (Luke 12:8–9 par.; cf. §4.4.2). The double effect of judgment that Jesus describes (cf. §3.2.3) is based not on covenant/legalistic criteria, but on one's acceptance or rejection of his message. In the minds of Jesus' contemporaries his omission of these themes doubtless justified their suspicion of him, for all of these key terms were in his day of acute topical interest.

Jesus does, of course, think of all Israel when he calls twelve disciples, but he is also convinced that without repentance this Israel is lost (cf. §3.2.2). He can, of course, divide Israel's history in a salvation history–like outline in which the time before him is the time of waiting and the time of his appearing is the time of fulfillment (Matt 13:16–17 par.; cf. §4.2.2), but he can also with Matt 11:7 (cf. §4.2.2) replace the perspective of salvation history with a focus on all humanity. No one can doubt that Jesus' hearers would hear such statements as Matt 5:3–5 par. and 11:2–6 par. (cf. §4.2.2) in terms of the blessings of salvation associated with the book of Isaiah, but he selects the material in such a way that the blessings consist in the removal of the general obstacles to life that face all people rather than in the fulfillment of specifically Israelite hopes identified with Zion or the Messiah. It is true that Jesus conducts no mission to non-Jews. He does not even feel the need to justify why he directs his message to Israel; it is for him simply self-evident. He also wants his contemporaries to understand that his message of the Kingdom of God is a continuation of the new direction set by

Deutero-Isaiah (cf. §4.1), but he dissolves the symbiotic relationship between the Kingdom of God and the Zion tradition. The latter lies fallow, while the former is interpreted in terms of creation. No longer is God's mercy toward Israel based on the traditions of election. Since Israel can no longer depend on God's demonstrations of grace toward the ancestors, its salvation history has come to an end. In the midst of this disaster and in the face of the final judgment that is threatening Israel, God is nevertheless present on Israel's behalf in the activity of Jesus, because as the creator he has mercy on his creatures (cf. §4.2.4).

That the Kingdom of God is to be understood in terms of creation is clear precisely in the areas in which Jesus presents the kingdom to his hearers (cf. §§4.3.1–4.3.3). None of the material in the parables that goes back to the preaching of Jesus addresses the issue of salvation history. There are only two parables that would even come into question here, viz., the Good Samaritan (Luke 10:25– 37; §5.2.3) and the Pharisee and the tax collector at prayer in the temple (Luke 18:9–14; §3.2.5), and both of them speak another language.[64] In the former case the most hated stepchild in Israel's history conducts himself in an exemplary way, while two special representatives of Israel's salvation history, a priest and a Levite, fail to meet the challenge. In the latter case the Pharisee, who stands in the continuity of salvation history, appears in a negative light, unlike the tax collector. In all other cases Jesus draws the material for his parables from the natural experiences of life in rural Galilee[65] and from the sociohistorical sphere.[66] Of course, this modern distinction is foreign to the ancient world. For Israel and Early Judaism both areas belong to God's creation. It is clear, therefore, that for Jesus there is a world of experience that is more fundamental and comprehensive than is the world of Israel's salvation history, viz., the world of one's own creatureliness. In view of Israel's lost condition, intensified by its squandered salvation history, it is this world in which the Kingdom of God is to be seen. It is the world of everyday creatureliness and not salvation history that serves as the context in which the Kingdom of God proclaimed by Jesus has drawn near and is to be experienced.

The same is to be said of the other two areas in which Jesus makes it possible for people to experience the nearness of the Kingdom of God—the table-fellowship in the villages of Galilee (cf. §4.3.2) and healing the sick (cf. §4.3.3). Sickness and hunger represent basic needs common to all creatures.

Such considerations make it possible to understand why for Jesus the Kingdom of God is not bound to the holy city and the temple, i.e., to the site that for Early Judaism represented the embodiment of Israel's unique position in God's salvation. Not long before Jesus appeared, Herod the Great invested a great deal of labor, time, and material in remodeling the temple, doubtless to a great degree from political motives. Jesus' attitude to the temple was reserved, if not actually critical (cf. §5.3.4). Jesus similarly grounded the command to love one's enemies in God's activity as creator (cf. §5.2.3). Comparing the Lord's Prayer (cf. §5.2.4) with the prayers of Judaism, from Tob 13 to the Eighteen Benedictions, reveals by contrast just how free the Lord's Prayer is of all salvation history motifs. The same is true of the first three beatitudes (Matt 5:3–5 = Luke 6:20–21). The Kingdom of God is there for the poor, and it will supply all their creature-needs (cf. §4.3.2).[67]

Finally, the exhortation of Matt 6:25–34 = Luke 12:22–31, a text that deserves an extensive treatment, expresses in an especially compelling way that the Kingdom of God means that it is precisely as creator that God draws near. Fortunately, the changes that were made in the text in the history of its reception by the church were by and large for the purpose of illustrating and elaborating, so that with only moderate reconstruction we can arrive at what was likely to have been the earliest text:

> 1a *[Matt 6:25a]* Do not be anxious *about your life, what you eat,*
> b *nor about your body, what you put on!*
> c *For life is more than food,*
> d *and the body (more) than clothing.*
> 2a Look at the crows*!*
> b *They neither sow, nor do they reap, nor do they have barns.*
> c *But God feeds them.*
> d *You are of more value than the birds! [vv. 27. 28a]*
> 3a Learn from the anemones,
> b *how they neither spin nor weave!*
> c *[v. 29a] Even Solomon in all his glory*
> d *was not clothed as one of these. [v. 30]*
> 4a Therefore, do not be anxious*:*
> b *What shall we eat, what shall we drink, what shall we put on?*
> c *The nations pursue all these things.*
> d *Your father knows that you need them.*
> 5a Seek *only* his Kingdom,
> b *and all these things shall be added to you! [v. 34]*

Each of the five sections begins with its own imperative. Since the entire unit has only these five imperatives, they serve to divide the sections formally. They also constitute a well-thought-out sequence. The rationale for the first prohibition (*Do not be anxious*) is given by the two commands that follow (*Look! Learn!*). That human anxiety about life and limb is unnecessary is illustrated by two phenomena from the rest of creation—the birds of the heaven and the plants of the earth, specifically by such ordinary birds and plants as crows and anemones. (It is not clear what kind of flower is meant; one usually thinks of some sort of lily.) The activities that, in contrast to human beings, they do not do are divided into the work of men (cf. Mark 4:3–9; Luke 12:16–21) and women. (For similar paired examples, see Luke 4:25–27; 11:31–32; 17:34–35.) In the fourth section the first imperative is repeated. Finally, the fifth imperative (*Seek!*) makes of the repeated prohibition a new and positive challenge in which the catchword *Kingdom of God* receives special emphasis.

Our reconstruction begins with the assumption that both evangelists found at the beginning of the unit a Q-transition that at one time provided its context within the sayings source. Matt 6:27, 28a, 30, 34 par. are parenetic expansions. With each new idea they reinforce the trend of the text, first by emphasizing that anxiety is useless, then by adding an argument from the lesser to the greater, and finally by recommending an economic solution to anxiety—a clear afterthought that is found only in Matthew. Since these additions contain a number of parenetic-rhetorical questions, it is possible that the corresponding questions in Matt 6:25–26 also are editorial reformulations. It is probable that, in order to heighten the parenetic urgency, the exhortations were prefaced with *I say to you* . . . (in Q?) and that the expression also was added in v. 29a par. It does not emphasize prophetic authority, and syntactically (as, e.g., in Matt 3:9 par.) it is not needed. It may well be that, as in Matt 8:11; 19:9, 23, where they are omitted in Luke's parallels, the words were added to strengthen the statement.

Concerning the question of authenticity, even though the language of the formulations is unique, it is clear that the wisdom tradition of Early Judaism provides the background for the material. Still, it is not unusual for Jesus to make use of wisdom material (cf. by way of example Luke 12:16–20 and §3.2.2). What is unexpected for wisdom thought, however, is the claim that the Kingdom of God renders all worry unnecessary (see below). The challenge to seek the Kingdom of God (rather than wisdom or the Torah as interpreted by wisdom) is unique (for Jesus cf. Matt 7:7–8) and in the context unexpected.

The text reflects a rural milieu and would fit well in a setting in Galilee. In any case, a comparison with 1 Thess 4:1–12 and 2 Thess 3:10–12 can show that it does not come from an urban setting. Such an observation does not mean, however, that the material originated in the radical, itinerant mission to Israel. The commissioning speeches of Mark 6:7–11 parr. and Matt 9:35–10:14 par. are characterized by precise instructions of which there is no hint in Matt 6:25–34 par. Nor does the latter text suggest leaving one's family for the sake of a calling or reducing one's precautions for life to a bare minimum. Itinerant radicalism minimizes the normal concern for one's life for the sake of the mission. Matt 6:25–34, on the other hand, for the sake of the Kingdom of God rejects all anxiety about one's own existence, and it does so in terms of life's ordinary activities (cf. the masculine and feminine activities in vv. 26, 28). In addition, Matt 6:25–34 is compatible with such texts as Luke 6:20–21 par.; 11:2–4 par., 9–13 par. We can proceed, therefore, on the assumption that this text is authentic Jesus-material.

Initially the address is a wisdom exhortation that warns against letting life be consumed by an anxiety born of poverty and want. How can life itself unfold if it is a slave of anxiety (cf. Ps 90:10, 15; Sir 40)? One cure for such anxiety is suggested by the reference to the father, i.e., to God as the creator of the world and thus as the father of the hearers. Since the Gentiles do not know him (1 Thess 4:5), they are of necessity responsible for everything. Those who know him, however, may depend on his paternal care (Pss 104; 145; §4.1.8). Thus the God who oversees human life reduces the need for worry to a minimum; indeed, he may even make it superfluous.

This theological statement from the text itself explains what is meant at the beginning by the assertion that life is more than food and clothing. Far from being an inner-worldly, anthropocentric statement, it is carried by the theological certainty that life is solely a gift of God and that in the final analysis he alone sustains or takes life (Gen 1–2; Ps 90). It is true, of course, that human beings must earn their own food and clothing by their own struggle and toil (Gen 3:17–

19; Ps 90:10; Eccl 1:3–4; 2:11; Sir 40:1–5), even when here also God is always graciously present (see above). Life is *more*, in the sense that it is totally and immediately dependent on God. This interpretation cannot be accused of prematurely inserting in the text what is said later, because what is later unfolded had long been generally recognized. Matt 6:32 says nothing that was new for the hearer in that day; instead, it simply affirms what everyone (including the redactor in v. 27!) with a worldview in the wisdom tradition already thinks.

This beginning position of v. 25 is then altered by the reference to the birds and the flowers[68] in such a way that it explains how God provides everything for them and how humans need not worry. Since in the hierarchy of creation humans are more than animals (thus, the first affirmation), God will care even more for humans. One must simply rely on this care. Indeed, when humans assume responsibility for their own care (thus, the second affirmation), they do not achieve the same quality of care that God shows the flowers. Where God is at work the result is better than is the work of humans. Thus it is clear that, first of all, in view of God's activity as creator the birds show that human care is unnecessary; in the second place, the flowers show that the quality of human care is inferior to that of God.

In wisdom terms the text could end here. Of course, a comparison with the texts of the wisdom tradition shows that this line of argument, even though it has the character of wisdom material, too abruptly forbids care. The wisdom texts simply do not say it that smoothly. They understand that human beings by nature are anxious about life; human concern can at best be tempered. The tenor of the wisdom approach to life is that human concern can be limited, but not eliminated. Indeed, those who are not anxious about life—who are not concerned about food, clothing, and shelter—are foolish (Prov 24:30–34; 28:19). The point in the word of Jesus must have something to do with the conclusion in Matt 6:33 = Luke 12:31, i.e., with the turning-point of history that is given with the approaching Kingdom of God (cf. §4.2.2). The best way to approach this closing statement is by remembering that the wisdom exhortation could end with Matt 6:32, but does not necessarily have to do so. It could end with an exhortation to seek wisdom or the Torah (Prov 2:4; Eccl 7:25; esp. Sir 1; 6:18–37; 24; Wis 9). It is precisely at this point in Matt 6 that the Kingdom of God appears.

Thereby a decisively new element enters the picture. One can seek wisdom and Torah any time. Now, however, this general exhortation to seek wisdom rather than worrying about food and clothing has become an immediate, eschatological call that demands unconditional obedience (cf. Matt 13:44, 45–46). The impending Kingdom of God, which already initiates the turning-point of salvation (cf. §4.2.2), claims absolute allegiance. Thus Matt 6:33 presupposes that Jesus' hearers know what he means by Kingdom of God. This final sentence once again gives them the basis for abandoning their anxiety about their means of livelihood. With this Kingdom of God the creator begins to rule—the creator who in the table-fellowship of Jesus (cf. §4.2.2) and in the eschatological banquet (Matt 8:11–12 par.) assumes responsibility for the care of his creatures. Where the coming Kingdom of God is already in the process of being realized, human anxiety is ended eschatologically, i.e., for all time (Isa 25:6 and §4.1.3). Wisdom knows that, because of godlessness, plague and blood, sickness and drought, natural pollution and social collapse, hunger and death are part of life in this world (Sir 40:9–10). Jesus claims, on the other hand, that whoever seeks the Kingdom of God is free of anxiety about life, since God without reservation provides for life's needs.

When we take into consideration what Jesus has to say about the creation theme it is clear that his statements about the Kingdom of God almost totally ignore motifs from Israel's salvation history—Jerusalem, the temple, the promise of the land, the return of scattered Israel, etc. His central catchword is characterized not by these standard themes, but by statements about creation. The terized not by these standard themes, but by statements about creation. The evidence for these statements is so clear and overwhelming that we may regard as valid the thesis that Jesus' message of the Kingdom of God is defined not by Israel's salvation history, but by the reality of creation. The chosen people Israel stands so severely under judgment that it is no longer possible for it to be saved as the chosen people; it can only be saved because the creator acts with sovereign grace on behalf of his creatures.

The consequences of this conclusion for various aspects of the preaching of Jesus are not insignificant. For one thing it confirms what we said earlier in connection with Matt 8:11–12 (in §4.2.2)—viz., that Jesus understands the final consummation as standing in continuity with the present empirical reality. We can further expect that the focus of the Kingdom of God on all creation will influence Jesus' attitude toward the non-Jewish world, a subject that we will discuss in §5.5. We already have enough evidence, however, to make the following observation: With all of Jesus' concern for contemporary Israel, we will find in him neither a priestly cultic attitude, as with the Sadducees and Essenes, nor a political-theocratic position, such as one finds in the Zealots. We should expect, rather, a tendency to minimize those features that would lead to a relationship of confrontation. When the exclusivity of salvation history gives way to the openness of creation, there is no longer any reason for confrontation.

We conclude this section with one final observation. Given the emphasis on creation in Jesus' message of the Kingdom of God, one might conclude that Jesus regarded the final consummation as a (modified) restoration of the condition of creation in its primal state (cf. *Barn.* 6:13).[69] The thesis would be as follows: Jesus goes back behind the story of Israel's election—indeed, even before Adam's sin—to the original creation as it is described in Gen 1–2, so that his understanding of the Kingdom of God consciously is based on the image of the original state of creation and humanity as it is presented in the early part of the Torah. We will also be discussing this problem frequently in later pages (cf. esp.

§5.3.1), but in view of what we have already observed we can say that all of the texts we have discussed have in common that they deal with creation as a present, empirical reality. The creation that serves as the setting for the Kingdom of God is discussed not as a lost paradise but as something that one experiences in the present. Jesus does not claim that the Kingdom of God will lead the present creation back to its original state. It is more likely that the kingdom's potential for change is to be understood in terms of the prophetic promises about creation (cf. Matt 11:3–5 par.). Of course, statements about the final perfection (as, e.g., freedom from hunger and sickness) can demonstrate a close similarity to the original paradise, since in individual details descriptions of creation's beginning and ending always have much in common. In view of our survey of the texts thus far, however, we have no evidence that Jesus had developed an idea of the restoration of creation.

4.2.4 The Kingdom of God as Salvation for the Lost

Fiedler, P. *Jesus*, 97–215.
Gnilka, J. *Jesus*, 98–117.
Hoffmann, P. " 'Er weiß, was ihr braucht . . . ' (Mt 6,7). Jesu einfache und konkrete Rede von Gott," in: *"Ich will euer Gott werden."* N. Lohfink et al., eds. SBS 100. Stuttgart: KBW, 1981, 153–76.
Pedersen, S. "Die Gotteserfahrung bei Jesus," *StTh* 41 (1987) 127–56.
Weder, H. *Gleichnisse*, 168–77; 249–52.

Thanks to the Third Evangelist, the biblically literate reader is familiar with Jesus' programmatic self-description at the end of the Zachaeus story: "The Son of Man came to seek and to save the lost" (Luke 19:10).[70] Receiving and saving the lost is also named in Luke 15:4, 6, 8–9, 24, 32 as the *leitmotif* around which Luke structures the three parables. Indeed, it is probably true in substance, if not in the form of a statement from Jesus about his own activity, that Jesus preached that the Israel that does not respond to his message stands under judgment and is therefore *lost* (Luke 13:3, 5; 17:27, 29). The Kingdom of God comes not to a relatively good world, which is capable of improvement; it comes rather (in a continuation of the message of John the Baptist) to recipients who will meet God only in judgment (cf. §§3.1; 3.2). Thus the impending Kingdom of God is always fundamentally directed toward the salvation of Israel.

In fact, Jesus probably used *Kingdom of God* only as a term of salvation, with the emphasis on deliverance and acceptance. At least the oldest layer of synoptic material uses the term only this way. Statements about judgment have a different vocabulary. In this regard Jesus moves in the direction of simplicity. While the tradition of Israel and Early Judaism does emphasize God's positive and redemptive reign as king, it also describes God's reign in terms of judgment (cf. §4.1). As opposed to its traditional meaning, therefore, Jesus limits the term *Kingdom of*

God. It has become for him a dynamic concept oriented toward the future
(§4.2.2); it is focused only on creation and no longer on a salvation history that is
oriented toward Zion (§4.2.3); and now the element of judgment that was part of
its traditional semantic background is no longer actualized.

That as king and creator God is also a rescuer of the oppressed and a helper of
the lowly—indeed, that he is gracious and long-suffering—is one of Israel's
fundamental faith convictions (cf. esp. §4.1.8). According to *Ps. Sol.* 2:30, 36, the
king in heaven is gracious to those who constantly call on him; he deals with his
own according to his mercy. In the same vein, Tob 13:10 calls on all to praise the
eternal king that he might show love for the afflicted from generation to generation. Likewise, according to *Ps. Sol.* 5:18, God's graciousness is upon Israel in
his kingdom. Thus God is "a gracious and merciful God, slow to anger and
abounding in steadfast love" (Jonah 4:2, 10–11); he is a God who forgives (Neh
9:17).

When compared with the preaching of Jesus, however, this series of statements about God as savior and helper is rather vague. Deutero-Isaiah and his
successors offer clearer parallels. The newly expected demonstration of God's
activity as king that begins with Deutero-Isaiah involves a change in the people's
fortunes. The Exile—a situation of judgment for the people—e.g., will end. The
message is that God will turn this disaster around so that it will work to Israel's
benefit (cf. §4.1.3). We have already noted (§4.1.3) that in the prophecy that
followed Deutero-Isaiah, God the king is described as one who saves and who
shows mercy, precisely in connection with the coming day of salvation. Noteworthy here is the forgiveness of Israel's guilt. Since what is envisioned is God's
extraordinary intervention on behalf of Israel, the similarity to the preaching of
Jesus is remarkable.

It is true, of course, that, backed by the Baptist's message, Jesus could no
longer pray the words of *Ps. Sol.* 9:8–11: "You are God, and we are the people
whom you have loved . . . show compassion . . . for we are yours, and do not
remove your mercy from us. . . . For you have chosen Abraham's seed before all
the nations. . . . You made a covenant with our fathers for our sake." In the eyes
of the Baptist and of Jesus, such divine mercy was no longer possible, since Israel
had wasted its salvation history. The Kingdom of God, proclaimed by Jesus as a
power that will prevent the disaster that Israel faces, is solely God's eschatological, creative self-expression. It is neither expected nor can it be explained by
anything in Israel's prior history; it creates a future precisely where the chosen
people had squandered their future. At the same time Jesus declares lost Israel to
be the stones from which, in the Baptist's words, God can raise up children to
Abraham (Matt 3:9 par.; §3.1.3).

This unique feature of the message of Jesus leads to a second observation.
Deutero-Isaiah comforts his people by proclaiming that God is creating a new
reality. Part of his message is the statement that Israel's bondage in the Exile has
ended, because Israel has experienced a double measure of God's wrath (Isa
40:2; 42:18–25). In a similar manner *Ps. Sol.* 17 prays for the establishment of

the messianic age. Because of Israel's sins it has been delivered into the hands of the Romans (17:5), but in their arrogance (17:13) the Romans went too far and persecuted Israel over the whole earth (17:18). As a result, God will transfer his punishment from Israel to the Romans and will let the age of salvation begin for Israel. With Jesus one looks in vain for statements to the effect that God's wrath toward Israel has run its course. Just as Jesus does not base God's mercy on the covenant, neither does he base it on the idea that God has punished Israel enough. Measuring Israel's sufferings vis-à-vis its sins is absolutely foreign to the message of Jesus. For him Israel has so destroyed its relationship to God that the quality of that relationship can no longer be quantified. The divine mercy can derive its motivation exclusively from God himself. As Israel's savior God's only obligation is to himself. For Jesus only God can be so gracious that, instead of saving by means of judgment, on his own initiative he saves from the (final) judgment.

In determining what it means to be lost and saved, where does Jesus place the accents? We have provided a partial answer (cf. §3.2, esp. §3.2.6) in the sense that the basic theme is the restoration of Israel's broken relationship with God. The Kingdom of God makes it possible for God once again to be God as he is and as he wants to be, viz., as the sole guarantor of life and as the sovereign dispenser of mercy (cf. Luke 11:2 par.). Jesus eliminates the understanding of God's holiness as condemnation of Israel every bit as radically as he emphasizes God's mercy solely and without reservation. The tax collector's prayer in Luke 18:13 ("God, be merciful to me, the sinner") is typical of Jesus' attitude both to the human sinner and to God as the one who wishes to be gracious. The dialogue and the action between the younger son and his father in Luke 15:20–21 reflect the same view; here the father's mercy appears even before the son confesses his sin. Finally, the unconditional and complete forgiveness of the debt in Matt 18:24–27 is an example of merciful compassion.

Two problem areas define this theocentric focus with greater precision. The first problem deals with the relation between Jesus' activity and God's forgiveness. Jesus publicly respects God's sovereign right to be the only one who forgives sins, since he himself nowhere forgives sins. This much discussed and controversial assertion turns on our interpretation of Mark 2:1–12. With the exception of Luke 7:48 and John 7:53–8:11, we can find no other picture of Jesus forgiving sins, and those two texts hardly represent authentic Jesus material. Among other things, the break between the summarizing statement in Luke 7:47 and the performative language of 7:48 indicates that 7:48–50 comes from a different hand (probably that of Luke himself) than does the pericope. This conclusion is almost as widely accepted as is the view that the non-Johannine material in John 7:53–8:11, because of its complicated history and novelistic character, could not come from the life of Jesus.

We are left, therefore, with Mark 2:1–12. Now without the verses 5b–10, the story of the healing of the paralytic is a typical and self-contained miracle story that achieves its goal in the praise of God with which it concludes. It is the polemic in vv. 5b–10 that (with syntactic awkwardness: v. 10!) makes of the miracle a demonstration of Jesus' authority to forgive sins. Thus the dialogue that is woven into the story is later than is the miracle story, and it is out of the question that it should contain authentic words of Jesus. When Jesus accepts sinners into his fellowship (§4.3.2), but reserves the privilege to forgive sins to the God who reveals himself in the coming Kingdom, he is consistent in his position that sin happens *before God* and that God alone can restore the broken relationship. In this regard he is in agreement with Israel's basic belief (Exod 34:7; Isa 43:25; 44:22; cf. also the Jewish objection in Mark 2:6–7; Luke 7:49).

The other problem deals with the fact that Jesus did not publicly speak of an end-time theophany as the form in which God approaches people. God's eschatological nearness consists for Jesus in the kingdom that is coming on behalf of men and women rather than in the vision of God's immediate presence. Such a vision is missing in such texts as Matt 8:11–12 par.; Matt 5:3–6 par.; Luke 6:20–21; Matt 6:9–13 par. (Matt 5:8 does not come from Jesus). One can compare *1 Enoch* 62:14: "And the Lord of Spirits will abide over them, and with that Son of Man they shall eat and lie down and rise up for ever and ever." Here the distinction between God's realm above and the human realm below is maintained even in the final consummation. The eschatological theophany that one finds, e.g., in *1 Enoch* 1:3–9 or Rev 21 was not universally expected in Judaism.

When we return to the main question of how Jesus understands what it means to be lost and saved, the first thing to recognize is that his hearers stand as total persons, with their full creatureliness, before God as creator and redeemer. The Kingdom of God is concerned with the whole person: with health, with the fundamental needs of life, with interpersonal relationships, with a heart that is undivided before God. The final realization of the Kingdom of God also does not look toward a new reality beyond the present created order. It intends, rather, a transformation of the existing reality and the conditions of life that are associated with it (cf. §§4.2.2; 4.2.3), which is why Satan's fall from power (Luke 10:18) and expelling the demons (Luke 11:20) must be part of the final establishment of God's rule. The goal of the kingdom, therefore, is the wholeness and integrity of creatures (§4.3.3). In addition, all the normal situations of need will come to an end. The Kingdom of God will do away with poverty, hunger, and all of life's experiences that cause human suffering (Luke 6:20–21). Human beings will be able to depend on God to care for them and to provide for their needs (cf. Matt 8:11–12 par.; Luke 12:22–31 par.). Finally, society will be changed, although references in the preaching of Jesus to the social order are sporadic and isolated. Naturally, the banquet of salvation will occur in joy and harmony (Matt 8:11–12 par.; Mark 2:19a). We probably will not go wrong if we assume that human temptation and greed also will no longer be present (cf. Luke 11:4 par.; Matt 5:27–28). Both in their details and in their general tone these statements fit well with our earlier examples of a salvation hope based on creation (§4.2.3).

All in all we must say, however, that the preaching of Jesus effectively concentrates on the present hearers and invites them to experience the present beginning of salvation without pressuring them to worry about how its final state should be described. The final salvation is normally described in detail when the present is regarded as hopeless, or at least when there are few signs of hope. In such times of hardship the portrayal of the anticipated age of perfection serves to nourish hope and to give people a reason to persevere. When, on the other hand, what is hoped for is capable of being realized as a present experience, it is the experience itself that takes center stage, while interest in what the end will look like recedes to the background.

Nowhere in the Jesus material is the present into which the Kingdom of God is coming as a saving power more impressively presented as the time in which God himself seeks lost Israel than in Luke 15. What especially carries the first two parables of that chapter, the parables of the lost sheep and of the lost drachma, are that in each case the lost possession appears only as an object that is sought and that the joy is experienced by the persons who found what they had lost. The first parable (Luke 15:4–5 = Matt 18:12–13) reads:

> *What man of you, who has a hundred sheep and who loses one of*
> *them, will not leave the ninety-nine in the desert and go after the one*
> *that is lost until he finds it?*
> *And when he has found it, he lays it on his shoulders and rejoices.*

Analyzing the layers of tradition in Luke 15:1–10 is more difficult than one might wish. We begin with the generally recognized assumption that the core of Matt 18:12–13 = Luke 15:4–5 comes from the sayings source. Beyond that, it is possible that Luke also found 15:8–10 in Q and that Matthew omitted it, because it was not compatible with his so-called church order in Matt 18; his interest in persons clashed with the subject of money. Without fear of contradiction, of course, we can attribute Luke 15:11–32 to Luke's special material.

If we are correct that the parables of the lost sheep and the lost drachma, with their parallel structures, come from the same source, it is likely that 15:2, 7, 10 offer clues about the original setting in Q and their meaning in Q. In any case vv. 7 and 10 come from the same hand. It is also clear that vv. 7 and 10 could not have been the original interpretation of the parables, even though they do not show Lukan syntax and thus are older than Luke. Sheep and coins are lost and they are found; they do not repent. Nor does the apophthegmatic introduction in 15:1–3 (or, perhaps, for Q in v. 2) belong to the parables. The approach of the tax collectors and sinners (15:1) and their acceptance at the table-fellowship (15:2) do not reflect the situations in the parables, where the focus is on seeking and finding lost objects. In the parables one does not eat with the objects that are found; the finders rejoice, and they express their joy by inviting others to join them.

Of course, it is likely that this last motif is secondary in the parable of the lost sheep. While it makes sense in the parable of the lost drachma (15:9), it is more than a little strange in 15:6. The previous scene takes place in the wilderness, not in a village (cf. Luke 2:8), and the reaction in 15:6 is exaggerated. It is appropriate in 15:9 if we can assume that the woman lost one of her coins reserved for an emergency (see below). If v. 6 was created under the influence of v. 9, then we must also ask whether at one time v. 5 was a syntactic parallel to v. 9a. A comparison with Matt 18:13 shows that Matthew's version is different at this point, although his changes are conditioned by the context, and his *Amen, I say to you . . .* frequently is a Matthean formulation. On the other hand, because of the comparison he drew, he could not make use of the detail about the sheep being carried on the shoulders, which appears only in Luke 15:6.7.[71] A reconstruction of the original parable, therefore, would involve a mixture of Matt 18:13 and Luke 15:6.[72]

The narrator focuses the hearer's attention exclusively on the activity of the shepherd, who has a flock of sheep of moderate size. The round number of one hundred is, of course, a standard number. One of his sheep, i.e., one percent of his flock, wanders off. It is not exactly a great loss, yet no shepherd who is not totally irresponsible would simply give up a lost sheep. Such behavior would violate practicality and the ethic of shepherding. He leaves the flock (naturally, under someone else's care) and begins his search. The reason and the initiative are his alone. It is not that the sheep has a special value that necessitates the search; it belongs to the shepherd's flock and it is lost—that is reason enough. The joy comes from the successful search; it is natural that success makes one happy. Thus the parable portrays a normal event with which everyone can identify. When they affirm what Jesus says, however, they have already made contact with the Kingdom of God that Jesus represents, for they understand that God has been searching for them, that he has found them, and that he rejoices over the successful search. Thus they are part of the present beginning of salvation with which God has taken the initiative in looking for the lost and now rejoices over his success. Within the hearers' understanding is the special recognition that it is Jesus who makes the Kingdom of God happen. They are not simply reminded in general about what God does; Jesus' activity is revealed to them as the turning-point in which God offers them salvation. They are invited to identify what Jesus does with God's activity. What is formulated in Luke 11:20 par. (cf. §4.2.2) as a prophetic announcement of the time ("If I cast out demons by the finger of God, the Kingdom of God has come to you") is expressed in Luke 15:4–5 in the form of a parable.

The parable of the lost drachma (Luke 15:8–9) reads as follows:

> *If a woman who has ten drachmas loses one of them, does she not*
> *(then) light a lamp and sweep the house and search diligently until*
> *she finds (the drachma)?*
> *And when she has found it, she calls together her (female) friends and*
> *neighbors*
> *and says, "Rejoice with me, for I have found (my) drachma which was*
> *lost!"*

As is the case with Luke 15:4–5, the parable, which describes a normal event and understandable behavior, begins with a rhetorical question about the spontaneous search for a lost object and then in the second sentence describes the natural joy when it is found. The structural similarity between the two parables along with the polarity of man and woman (cf. §3.2.3) and of open wilderness and house, could support the conclusion that Jesus formed the two stories as matching parables. The thesis must remain open, however, since its assumption—that the two parables were already together in Q—is only a hypothesis, albeit an attractive one.

The woman lives in poverty. There is no mention of a husband or of children, and it may well be that she lives alone. The emergency coin is her only reserve against disability and sickness. The drachma is a Greek silver coin that was the approximate equivalent of the Roman dinar, a silver coin that was one day's wage for a day laborer (Matt 20:2). The woman's reserve, therefore, was quite small. Since she lives in a small room whose only source of light is probably the door, she lights an oil lamp to aid in her search. She sweeps with a broom of palm branches in hopes that the coin will make a noise on the hard floor made of stone or rammed earth.

Again, the narrator focuses only on the woman's activity. She seeks and she rejoices; the drachma in v. 8 and the women in v. 9 are simply props on the stage. The story begins with the woman acutely disturbed over her loss so that she immediately begins an intensive search. Anyone would have done the same in her place. Then finding the coin makes her so happy that she lets all of the women in her immediate neighborhood know of her good fortune, and she calls them to celebrate with her. That is the way it is in a small village. Jesus' hearers know that in that situation they would have acted the same way. Spontaneously they identify with the only person who plays an active, seeking role in the parable.

In identifying with the woman they affirm Jesus' advocacy of the Kingdom of God that is coming with finality. In this kingdom God is looking for the lost, and in this kingdom God rejoices when he finds what is lost. When the narrative world of the parable parallels the seeking and the rejoicing that are happening in Jesus' activity, the hearers identify with and agree with that activity.

Thus the God of the kingdom that Jesus proclaims is a God who rejoices when he finds people who have been lost. In this sense Jesus brings God near for his contemporaries. How the nearness of this Kingdom of God is mediated will be our subject in §§4.3.1–4.3.3.

4.3 THE KINGDOM OF GOD BROUGHT NEAR

4.3.1 The Kingdom Brought Near in the Parables of Jesus

Becker, J. "Zum Verständnis der Gleichnisreden Jesu," *Kiele Entwürfe für Schule und Unterricht* 11 (1990) 9–20.

Berger, K. "Materialien zu Form und Überlieferungsgeschichte neutestamentlicher Gleichnisse," *NT* 15 (1973) 1–37.

Biser, E. *Die Gleichnisse Jesu*. Munich: Kösel, 1965.

Crossan, J. D. *In Parables: The Challenge of the Historical Jesus*. New York: Harper & Row, 1973.

———. "Parable and Example in the Teaching of Jesus," *Semeia* 1 (1974) 63–104.

Dodd, C. H. *The Parables of the Kingdom*. Rev. ed. New York: Scribners, 1961.

Eichholz, G. *Gleichnisse der Evangelien.* 4th ed. Neukirchen-Vluyn: Neukirchener Verlag, 1984.

Fiebig, P. *Altjüdische Gleichnisse und die Gleichnisse Jesu.* Tübingen: J.C.B. Mohr (Paul Siebeck), 1904.

_____. *Die Gleichnisreden Jesu im Lichte der rabbinischen Gleichnisse des neutestamentlichen Zeitalters.* Tübingen: J.C.B. Mohr (Paul Siebeck), 1929.

Flusser, D. *Die rabbinischen Gleichnisse und der Gleichniserzähler Jesus,* vol. 1. JudChr 4. Bern/Las Vegas: Peter Lang, 1981.

Harnisch, W. *Gleichniserzählungen.*

_____. (ed.) *Gleichnisse Jesu.* WdF 366. Darmstadt: Wissenschaftliche Buchgesellschaft, 1982.

_____. (ed.) *Die neutestamentliche Gleichnisforschung im Horizont von Hermeneutik und Literaturwissenschaft.* WdF 575. Darmstadt: Wissenschaftliche Buchgesellschaft, 1982.

Jeremias, J. *Parables.*

Jülicher, A. *Gleichnisreden.*

Jüngel, E. *Paulus und Jesus.*

Klauck, H.-J. *Allegorie und Allegorese in synoptischen Gleichnistexten.* NTA 13. Münster: Aschendorf, 1978.

Kurz, G. *Metapher, Allegorie, Symbol.* KVR 1486. Göttingen: Vandenhoeck & Ruprecht, 1988.

Linnemann, E. *Parables of Jesus: Introduction and Exposition.* New York: Harper & Row; London: SPCK, 1966.

Nethöfel, W. *Theologische Hermeneutik.* NBST 9. Neukirchen-Vluyn: Neukirchener Verlag, 1992, 92–126.

Pöhlmann, W. "Die Abschichtung des Verlorenen Sohnes (Lk 15:12f) und die erzählte Welt der Parabel," *ZNW* 70 (1979) 194–213.

_____. *Der Verlorene Sohn und das Haus.* WUNT 68. Tübingen: J.C.B. Mohr (Paul Siebeck), 1993.

Rau, E. *Reden in Vollmacht.* FRLANT 149. Göttingen: Vandenhoeck & Ruprecht, 1990.

Ricoeur, P. "On Biblical Hermeneutics," *Semeia* 4 (1975) 29–148.

_____. "Stellung und Funktion der Metapher in der biblischen Sprache," in: idem and E. Jüngel, *Metapher.* EvTh.S. Munich: Kaiser, 1974, 45–70.

Schulnigg, P. *Rabbinische Gleichnisse und das Neue Testament.* Bern: Lang, 1988.

Sellin, G. "Allegorie und 'Gleichnis'," *ZThK* 75 (1978) 281–335.

_____. "Gleichnisstrukturen," *LingBibl* 31 (1974) 89–115.

Via, D. O. *The Parables.* Philadelphia: Fortress, 1967.

Weder, H. *Gleichnisse.*

Early in his gospel (Mark 1:14–15) Mark defines the essence of the message of Jesus as the preaching of the Kingdom of God. Soon thereafter he concludes his first main section with the first major address of Jesus in which he presents the message of the Kingdom of God as speaking in parables (Mark 4:2, 33–34). For Mark, Jesus' message of the coming kingdom is closely related to the practice of speaking in parables. The same is true of Matthew, who consistently identifies parables as parables of the kingdom, even in those cases when demonstrably they were not previously identified as such (e.g., Matt 22:2). Luke's special material preserves almost half of the parables attributed to Jesus. The sayings source and the *Gospel of Thomas* also are aware that Jesus spoke in parables. Given this evidence, and especially based on the three important and independent sources of Q, Mark, and Luke's special material, we can conclude that Jesus' message was expressed in a special way in his parables. It is also worth noting that in the gospels only Jesus speaks in parables.

Comparative studies help us evaluate this evidence. It goes without saying that the culture of Antiquity and, in a special way, Judaism and Hellenism have a fondness for parables in the general sense of the word and, thus, for the teller of parables. The popularity of this form of address in Jesus' immediate environment—i.e., in Early Judaism, especially in wisdom and apocalypticism, along with the early rabbinic discussions about the law—is beyond dispute. It is also true that Jesus frequently retold and shaped anew traditional parabolic material. In this sense he was part of an existing culture of story telling.[73] It should be noted, however, that Jesus stood out among his contemporaries for the frequency of his use of parables.

Yet, it is not the quantity of the material that is decisive for Jesus. In a way that distinguishes him from the storytelling culture of his day he was able to master in a specific way the inner formation of the parable so that it focused the attention of every hearer on the message that was contained within the narrative world. (One can especially observe this quality when he makes use of earlier material.) In so doing he avoided the usual illustrative, didactic, or hortatory use of storytelling. Whether it was material that he had simply remolded, or whether it was an original parable, he invested it with such a power that it was able to stand on its own. In his activity as a miracle worker he did more than simply offer people occasional assistance; he incorporated his miracles into the comprehensive scope of the Kingdom of God (Luke 10:18; cf. §4.3.3). In the same way, he usually wove the narrative web of his parables in such a way that they made it possible to experience the nearness of the coming Kingdom of God. With his parables he established the reality of the Kingdom of God in the reality of the world of human experience in the narrative. Thus parabolic speech became a formative way of speaking that, along with the table-fellowship and the miracles, made the Kingdom of God happen as a saving experience. Sometimes his words disclosed the meaning of his actions; sometimes they themselves functioned as actions. In the course of the following discussion we will document this claim.

Of course, we cannot attribute the synoptic material to Jesus in its entirety. In each instance one must test whether and in what form we can trace material from its literary stage back to Jesus. In this regard parables are the same as other kinds of material (cf. §1). Over the past century or so, however, a widespread consensus has emerged that a large portion of the synoptic parables in their core material comes from Jesus. Recent attempts to break out of this consensus have not been successful.[74]

Thus Jesus' parables and Jesus' message of the Kingdom of God belong together. The kingdom comes to Jesus' hearers as parable. We should not understand this relationship in an exclusive sense, however, as if the parable were the only appropriate medium for proclaiming the Kingdom of God. For one thing, the nearness of God that is both promised and realized in the Kingdom of God can be produced in other forms of speech (e.g., prophetic words) and in Jesus' actions. For another, it would be a misunderstanding if all of Jesus' parables were understood exclusively in the narrow sense as parables of the kingdom. If nothing else, the existence of parables of judgment (cf. §3.2) shows that that understanding simply is not true. Just as the proclamation of the Kingdom of God defines Jesus' preaching and behavior, so do his parables derive their special character from the kingdom, and without a doubt many of them make the nearness of the Kingdom of God come to life in an especially appealing way.

With such a statement we have already suggested that the parables of Jesus do not disclose general truths or elucidate general anthropological or sociological phenomena. Nor are they autosemantic works of art whose meaning is disclosed in the subjective process of receiving and experiencing them. The parables of Jesus offer, instead, a distinct narrative style that comes from an author who uses them in a unique way in the service of his specific message of the Kingdom of God, and he does so in order to effect identifiable changes in the behavior of his hearers. They are, therefore, an integral part of a particular message and of a special event in a particular historical setting. That is not to say, of course, that we can identify a parable's historical setting by reconstructing individual scenes and situations in the life of Jesus. The settings provided in the synoptic gospels are the editorial creations of their authors, even if occasionally at some level they may preserve an aspect of historical truth. We must also take into consideration that Jesus probably told his parables more than once, so that we should not imagine that there was such a thing as an original production. It remains true, however, that the parables must be included in a comprehensive understanding of the preaching of Jesus and that they help to define that preaching. Indeed, to a large degree the parables constitute this comprehensive understanding.

That the parables are historically rooted does not keep the evangelists from reshaping them and adapting them to the post-Easter concerns of the gospels. In the process the parables often received a new meaning that did not necessarily conform to their original meaning, in the same way that other narrative materials in the culture and, indeed, other synoptic forms were changed in the process of transmission. The evangelists are not conscious of a tension between a parable's original meaning and its later interpretation. For them Jesus' historically conditioned message and the new understanding of the gospel in the time after Jesus are united in the parables.

The evangelists normally present the parables in their works as instruments that disclose the message of Jesus to the disciples as well as to all of his hearers. The purpose of the parables is to create understanding. They invite the hearers to reorient their lives; indeed, they make the hearer a part of the story, as one can see from a random reading of scenes from, say, Luke 14 or 15. Mark's so-called secrecy theory offers a different understanding (Mark 4:10–12). Here the distinction is made between an outer and an inner understanding. Outsiders do not understand the parables. Insiders receive additional instruction without which the parables remain inaccessible. The power of a narrative to stand alone, indeed to create insight spontaneously, and a parable's dependence and partial helplessness in the secrecy theory are mutually exclusive. The latter is a Markan creation while the former is characteristic of the preaching of Jesus. Jesus speaks in parables in order to engage all hearers without distinction, to open them to the reality of the Kingdom of God, and to effect change in their lives. The parable, by itself, can do these things.

Related to Mark's understanding of the parable is his interpretation in Mark 4:13–20 of the parable of sowing and harvesting. What is especially noteworthy in the unit is a vocabulary that differs from that of the parable; it is the language of the early Christian mission.[75] The interpretation follows Mark 4:3–8 line for line in an allegorical style of interpretation, even when the fit is awkward. The many birds, e.g., become one Satan, and the thistles are reinterpreted as three different vices. It has long been recognized that the three parables in Mark 4:3–8, 26–29, 30–32 thematically and substantively constitute a single group. No interpretation is added to the two latter parables; they are permitted to speak for themselves. The same could be said of Mark 4:3–8, for what is right for the others should also be right for Mark 4:3–8. The allegorical interpretation of the parable of the sower, therefore, is secondary both in terms of its content and in terms of the history of its transmission. In spite of this fact, Mark 4 dominated the history of parable interpretation so radically that until the end of the last century the allegorical method set the standard for understanding the parables of Jesus.

If, then, Mark 4:13–20 is a later interpretation of Mark 4:3–8, we must ask whether they are two different forms of address. As we shall see, this question is of fundamental importance, because it is crucial to understanding how Jesus made the Kingdom of God available to his hearers. Primitive Christianity, as a child of its culture, did not have the vocabulary for distinguishing among various forms of parabolic speech: similes, parables, comparisons, allegories, or riddles. There were only one or two general words for all the forms. Nor did an Early Christianity that had no interest in the discussion of rhetorical matters make use of what an Aristotle or a Quintilian had to say on the subject. In trying to describe the synoptic phenomena, therefore, we must enlist the help of the current scholarly discussion, and in the following comments we must be more precise in defining what we mean by parabolic material and parabolic speech.

We begin with allegory. Allegory is not a form or a genre; it is a way of speaking that is formally analogous to a metaphor. For a time it was largely forgotten in parable research that the allegory is in principle a rhetorically neutral kind of speech; like others it can be bad or good.

The assumption that Jesus created no allegories (which, as we will later see, is valid) does not justify the conclusion that allegories are inferior to other ways of speaking. Within the rhetorical culture of Early Judaism, Jesus could well have made use of allegorical speech. The question is why, surprisingly, he did not do so.

Our observations on Mark 4 have led to the conclusion that the allegorical interpretation of Mark 4:3–8 is a later addition. For our discussion, then, we must distinguish between primary and secondary allegories—between allegories in the strict sense (e.g., Mark 12:1–9) and allegorizing (e.g., Mark 4:13–20). The ancient world is also well acquainted with such subsequent allegorical interpretations, e.g., as a hermeneutic technique in the interpretation of dreams. The superficial meaning of the dream hides a deeper sense, which can be discovered only through allegorical intervention. Woven into a first understanding of a dream that has no generally understandable message is a second understanding that can be laid bare only by interpretation or revelation (Dan 2, 7). From the initial level of the dream, the interpretation derives clues that point to a deeper level, which is both visible and hidden. At this deeper level then, the abstruse references, the loose ends, and the irrational descriptions in the initial text come together to form a cogent statement.

Canonical texts also were interpreted in this way in Antiquity when their surface meaning caused problems. Homer's view of the gods was too archaic, and thus offensive, for an enlightened Hellenism. By interpreting the anthropomorphic statements about the gods allegorically, one was able to recognize a hidden meaning behind them, which reduced the offending language about the gods to temporary statements that were not intended to be understood in the first place. Hellenistic Judaism, e.g., wanted to preserve the Torah's ritual laws, but at the same time it felt obligated to justify them to contemporaries who regarded them as strange. Thus people like Philo and Aristobulus allegorized the laws in terms of Hellenistic virtues. When Christianity also interprets its normative texts allegorically (as in Mark 4:13–20 or Gal 4:21–31), it is using the methods of interpretation of its day. More precisely, it is conforming to the popular use of texts; the allegorical interpretation of Primitive Christianity had not yet reached the sophistication of the philosophical hermeneutic of a Philo or an Origen.

Unfortunately, the example of Mark 4, where the allegorizing interpretation is separate from and follows the original text, is the exception in the synoptic material. As a rule the texts themselves have been changed and retold in such a way that they appear to be allegories, even though in reality they are allegorized mutations of nonallegorical texts. A good example is the parable of the great banquet (Matt 22:1–14; Luke 14:16–24; cf. §4.3.2). Since Matthew and Luke offer differing allegorical interpretations of the parable, it is relatively easy to reconstruct the nonallegorical original text by comparing their texts. The original is a parable that can speak for itself.

What is the nature of allegorical speech? As we have already suggested, it begins with an initial narrative world from which then it moves to a world of declarative statements. Thus the initial narrative level serves a subordinate function; it is the underlying world that is important. The hearer is able to reach this underlying world by means of a network of metaphors that the narrator inserts into the first level of the text. The king, the wedding feast, and the son in Matt 22:1, e.g., appear at the beginning of the narrative as metaphors for God, for the banquet of salvation, and for Christ. Allegorical speech presupposes a culture in which such metaphors are common. Only in such a culture can a conversation take place between the narrator and the hearer. Usually, however, hearers do not think of reading a text allegorically unless they are provided with additional aids, since metaphors also appear in other kinds of texts. In Gal 4:24, e.g., Paul can state explicitly that he is now going to allegorize. Comparing one statement with another is also a typical method (Gal 4:24; Mark 4:13–20). Frequently the narrative jumps directly to the second level (Matt 22:6–7). It is also the case that sometimes the first level contains illogical elements. (In Matt 21:34, 36, 37, e.g., it is not necessary that two servants and then the son are sent.) An allegory needs, therefore, various kinds of clues that lead from the initial world to the underlying world. Finding this underlying world as a unified whole is the decisive step in the process of interpretation.

Did Jesus create allegories or allegorize other texts? The answer is no, because wherever we find allegorical speech in the gospels, without exception (and this is the only valid criterion) the content always reveals the concerns of the post-Easter church. Given this reality, we can then ask ourselves why Jesus did not make use of allegory. It is clear that Jesus does not want to use the world of Galilee as a point of departure from which he then would alienate it and use it in the service of another world. Instead, he wants to short-circuit the world of his contemporaries with the Kingdom of God (cf. Luke 11:20). Instead of using one of them as an entry into the hidden meaning of the other, he wants to bring the two together in the closest possible relationship. He does not urge his hearers to find a launching pad from which they can take off into God's world and leave their own world. Instead, he wants to open them to the possibility that salvation will begin right now and exactly in this world.

This observation supports our conclusion that Jesus did not make use of allegory. In addition, we should note that allegory presupposes the existence of authoritative texts that one cannot ignore, but that one wants to understand differently. Clearly Jesus uses a different method for dealing with the tension between an authoritative tradition and a new way of experiencing reality. A good example is the way Jesus deals with the Torah (cf. §5.3), where, unlike Philo, he makes no use of allegory. Jesus does not need to speak allegorically, since he believes himself to be authorized to describe God's will on his own authority. Furthermore, he does not regard parabolic material as canonical, since he claims for himself the right to create parables using no other criterion than the Kingdom of God. It is the post-Easter church that begins to regard the Jesus material as authoritative texts that must be preserved and reinterpreted. It is the post-Easter situation in which the conditions for allegorizing first exist.

Once we have eliminated allegories and allegorizing as forms of speaking that Jesus used, our next task is to explain how we are to understand similitudes and parables, since, as is generally recognized, it is above all in these forms that we are dealing with Jesus' own language. They are not typical ways of speaking; they are independent forms with a particular narrative structure, which the concepts of comparison[76] or metaphor[77] are not adequate to explain.

Those who understand similitudes and parables in terms of comparison see them as plastic speech, which makes a statement by means of a single point of comparison. What connects the image and the point that it makes is the bridge of similarity and abstraction. The hearer is expected to be able to extract from the image the point that is intended. The validity of this understanding is that it recognizes that the narrative structure of similitudes and parables has a goal. It cannot be made to say whatever one wishes; it points, rather, toward a single, coherent meaning. The purpose of synoptic similitudes and parables, however, is not to create an image from which one then derives a point by means of abstraction. The point of the similitude or parable is in the story itself. It draws the hearers with their worlds into the narrated world so that without warning they discover that they are part of the story and they come to a new understanding of themselves and their time. The experience of hearing reveals to the hearers the truth of their own lives and of the historical moment. In this way the Kingdom of God comes to people through the narrated world, since in the story there are aspects of the Kingdom of God that draw the hearer into their own reality. Parables make the Kingdom of God real for the hearer.

The value of understanding parables in terms of metaphor is that it does justice precisely to this dimension of the parable. In a metaphor the image and its meaning are closely interwoven. The metaphor makes it possible to grasp a new insight immediately. Instead of depending on the intellectual work of abstraction and looking for a point, it looks for immediate agreement or rejection. One cannot predict what result it will have, because it allows room for emotions and fantasy. Metaphors are shared cultural agreements whose meaning cannot be defined. They have fluid boundaries with a relatively stabile core; their structure, therefore, is the opposite of that of the earth with its fluid core and its hard surface.

Now this quality of the metaphor is, in fact, very similar to the similitude and to the parable. We must question, however, the tendency to identify the form of the parable so exclusively with metaphorical speech in general, which appears in many forms, including, e.g., allegory. It is preferable to distinguish between forms (such as parables, fables, poems) on the one hand and ways of speaking (allegories, metaphors) on the other. The essential structure of a form is internal to itself; it is independent of the communicative situation. Metaphor, on the other hand, flows from the process of communication. It is not a self-contained declarative statement. Above all, a metaphor exists for the moment; it is never a sequence of events structured in a narrative that is directed toward a point.

This characteristic, on the other hand, is decisive for similitudes and parables. They are not simply expanded metaphors; they must be described in terms of their own internal relationships, i.e., in terms of their own narrative structure. Since in this regard they are analogous to fables,[78] it makes sense to compare these two forms from this perspective. Of course, the difference between the two is obvious. The fable humanizes the world of animals in order to mirror human behavior in an alien form, while similitude and parable consciously limit themselves to the world of human beings. Nothing happens in them that is not part of the world as the hearers understand and experience it. There are no animals that talk and act like humans. One encounters the Kingdom of God in this world just as it is.

Within this commonality, then, we can differentiate between similitude and parable. Similitudes tell about typical events, normal experiences, everyday scenes. They capture the normal world, its regularity and order, which everyone can experience at any time and on which one can depend. Jesus uses this reality as an expression of what is normative and dependable so that his hearers will be open to the reality of the Kingdom of God with the same level of trust. Such typical scenes make available the nearness of the Kingdom of God, which, according to Jesus, deserves the same trust, because, e.g., the creator whose order is described in the so-called parables of contrast (Mark 4:3–8, 26–29, 30–32) is the God who is bringing his kingdom.

Parables, on the other hand, are interested in a particular case. They focus not on what is typical, but on what is unusual in the world of experience. A frequent term used to illustrate the point is that something extravagant surprises the normal order and shatters it so radically that one's previous understanding of the world is shaken and one must look for a new orientation. Of course, the parable does not flee into the world of fable, or myth, or fairy-tale; from the possibilities of normal experience it simply chooses the unusual rather than the typical. When in the course of everyday life the nonrecurring and the abnormal stand out, when the unexpected runs counter to the typical and creates the possibility of new experiences, one has the beginning of a connection to the preaching of Jesus, since he is concerned to make real precisely the unexpected nearness of the Kingdom of God in the everyday world of those who are lost. Parables are well-suited, therefore, to express in narrative form what was so important for Jesus. When they bring near what is unusual in the message of Jesus, they also bring near the unexpected Kingdom of God in the midst of the everyday world.

Both similitudes and parables are linear. That is to say, their sequence of events is chronological and irreversible. With a few strokes the narrator says only what is absolutely necessary. This economy of words helps the hearers concentrate so that they can move straight to the point of the narrative without distraction and focus on what is essential. The sequence of events increases the concentration, and the hearers experience the chronological progression as a logical necessity that makes clear the inner point. They recognize the point by trusting the goal-directed flow of the narrative. When they follow the story's development, suddenly and on their own they see Jesus' message about the Kingdom of God, and they are brought near to it.

Without diminishing the recognition that similitudes and parables are among the most valuable jewels of the Jesus material, we need to caution against exaggerating their importance. Jesus is not primarily a teacher who only incidentally worked miracles and initiated table-fellowship. The turning-point of salvation is not a mind game that ignores the three-dimensional world, the body, and social realities. It wants to redefine and to change the entire world of human experience—both the historical and the social. This grounding of the kingdom in all of human life has been part of the tradition without exception from Deutero-Isaiah's proclamation of God's new intervention as king on behalf of Israel down to Jesus himself.

It is also noteworthy that similitudes and parables make possible new actions in the world of concrete experience. They are not ideas about truths; their actions are truth as the course of an event. Thus they reproduce actions that as a paradigm of life offer a new understanding of life. Proclamation and life-formation are one.

Nor are the plots of the parables chosen at random. It is certainly no accident that the frequent appearance of banquets in the parables, with the emphasis on inviting and accepting (e.g., Luke 14:16–24 par.; 15:11–32), parallels Jesus' own table-fellowship. Indeed, it is likely that those who heard Jesus' parables could not fail to think of his table-fellowship in the villages. Jesus' affirming actions and his forgiving speech come together; God's nearness is both promised and practiced. Table-fellowship is putting into practice the openness of which the parables speak; it is the openness of the Kingdom of God that is becoming real in the turning-point of history.

A consequence of this insight is that the parenetic overlay that covers much of the parabolic material, like its allegorical interpretation, comes from the early church. The parable of the unjust steward in Luke 16:1–7 (cf. §3.2.2) did not originally serve as the basis for a parenetic exhortation about wealth; it challenged the hearers to examine their standing before God and to consider what they should do about it.

Finally, we must ask whether, given this understanding of parables, it makes sense to group the four Lukan texts in Luke 10:30–37; 12:16–21; 16:19–31; 18:10–14 together as *exemplary stories*. In support of this designation it has been argued that these four texts differ from parables, since in each case the narrated world offers an exemplary figure with whom the hearer can identify. Such an argument has merit only if one understands the parable as a comparison whose point is given by drawing a parallel. A different understanding of what a parable is relieves us of the need to regard these four texts as a special group.

Given the understanding of the parables of Jesus that we have outlined here (if we can ignore for a moment the parables of judgment), their purpose was to make real the saving nearness of the Kingdom of God so that those who were lost could be saved. No text better expresses this purpose than does the parable of the father who had two sons (Luke 15:11–32; cf. our earlier comments in §3.2.5). The special Lukan material reads:

1   A man *had* two sons. *And the younger of them said to his father,* *"Father, give me the share of the property that is coming to me." He divided his possessions.*

2a   *And not many days later* the younger son *gathered everything and departed to a far country. And there he squandered his property in loose living.*
     When he had spent everything, a severe famine came over the land, and he began to be in want.
     And he went and hired himself out to a citizen of that country, who sent him into the fields to take care of the pigs. And he longed to ease his hunger with the husks that the pigs ate, but no one gave him (anything).

2b   *Then he came to himself and said, "How many of my father's hired servants have more than enough bread, while I am starving. I will rise up and go to my father and say to him, 'Father I have sinned against heaven and before you. I no longer deserve to be called your son. Take me on as one of your hired servants.'"*

2c   *And he arose and came* to his father. *But while he was still far away, his father saw him and had compassion. And he ran and fell on his neck and kissed him.*
     But the son said to him: "Father, I have sinned against heaven and before you. I no longer deserve to be called your son."
     But the father said to his slaves: "Hurry! Bring the best robe and put it on him, and put a ring on his hand and sandals on his feet. And bring a[79] *fatted calf, slaughter (it),* and let us eat and be merry. For this my son was dead and is alive . . . "
     And they began to celebrate.

3a   *But* his older son *was in the field. And as he was coming to the house, he heard music and dances. And he called one of the (house) servants to ask what was going on. He said to him: "Your brother has come, and your father has killed a fatted calf because he has received him back in health." Then he was angry and did not want to go in.*

3b   *But* his father *went out and spoke with him.*
     But he answered his father: "Look! I have served you so many years. And never have I disobeyed you. But you never gave me (even) a goat that I might celebrate with my friends. But when this your son came

*who squandered your possessions with harlots, you (even) slaughtered
for him a fatted calf."
But he said to him: "(My) child, you are always with me. And
everything that I have is yours. We must celebrate . . . ,* because this
your brother was dead and now he is alive . . . "

Luke 15 is structured in such a way that one after another two similitudes and a parable
emphasize the joy (15:5–7, 9–10, 23–24, 29, 32) at finding (15:4–6, 8–9, 24, 32) what
was lost (15:4, 6, 8–9, 24, 32). This arrangement is doubtless editorial, and at the end of
§4.2.4 we have commented on the details and on the strata. What is clear in Luke 15:11–
32 is that no one goes out looking for the younger son; he returns on his own initiative. It is
likely, therefore, that the combination of the motifs *lost-found* in 15:24, 32 is due to Luke's
redaction. More complex is the motif of joy, since the vocabulary is varied. One verb
appears only in the material in 15:11–32 (15:23–24, 29, 32). The other term appears in the
preceding text (15:5–7, 9–10) and in v. 32. We probably will not go wrong if we regard v.
32 as an editorial addition. While the text has a number of Lukanisms, they appear to be
stylistic rather than substantive changes.

Attempts to separate Luke 15:25–32 on literary-critical grounds ignore the narrative
structure and the background of the material.[80] Efforts to deny that the parable came from
Jesus also have not been successful.[81] Indeed, the narrative is a classic presentation of
Jesus' core affirmation, and the elements of his message that were offensive to Early
Judaism are woven into the parable.

It is a matter of common knowledge that a father can claim as his own two
sons who go in opposite directions, so that one of them chooses the best, the other
the worst of life; one of them represent the ideal of a normal life, the other is a
miserable failure. This common wisdom is passed on by the sages to train the
young and to maintain the existing order. The order in this case is the life of the
farmers who live on the land that God once gave Israel. The situation is different,
therefore, from that of the owner of the large estate in Luke 16:1–8 (cf. §3.2.2),
who lives in the city and turns his land over to a manager. There one owns the
land simply as a business investment. In Luke 15, on the other hand, we are
dealing with a farm that has been in the family for generations—with the life of a
free landholder with an extended family that includes servants and slaves (cf. *T.
Iss.*; Sir 7:15).

Of course, the legal possibility of divestiture[82]—in this case the early distribu-
tion of an inheritance[83] so that a son could begin a new life elsewhere—itself
demonstrates the difficulty of earning a livelihood on a farm. That the Jewish
Diaspora (about four million in the Roman empire) was so much larger than the
Jewish population in Israel (about five hundred thousand) testifies to the harsh
life in Israel. Those who emigrated for economic reasons knew that the official
explanation for Israel's dispersion among the nations was that it was a sign of
God's judgment that would not be lifted until the end of time (cf. §4.1.4). Still,
many people left the land in order to improve their fortunes, and they often lived
better than did the ones who stayed at home (Sir 29:22 and *T. Iss.* 6:2 offer a
polemic against the practice). Thus Jesus' hearers are familiar with those who
cling tenaciously to the ideal of farming on Israel's native soil, with those who

simply regard the land as a business investment, with the entrepreneurial émigrés, and with the theological judgment about the Diaspora. It is into this complex jumble that Jesus tells his parable.

Where does Jesus stand in this situation? We should expect him to avoid taking sides among these competing values. A parable only talks in any detail about what it thinks important. Jesus avoids any discussion of legal questions in order to focus on the relationships among the father and the two sons. He also ignores questions about the Diaspora or farm work. The younger son is a failure simply because he led an unusually dissolute life (15:13; cf. Prov 28:7), consorting with prostitutes (15:30; cf. Prov 29:3; Sir 9:6) and thus squandering his inheritance instead of establishing a life in the Diaspora that would enable him to be self-sufficient. It is this behavior alone that is his sin before God and his father (15:18). He is censured, because in his wild excess he wasted the inheritance that other members of the family had earned by the sweat of their brow (Gen 3:17–19). As we shall see, that he is censured does not mean that the hard-working older son is praised.

That kind of excess leads to poverty and loss of one's independence (cf. Prov 10:4; 12:24; 13:18). For one thing, the younger son cannot avoid life's natural injustice. It may well be that he left home to avoid the famines that frequently came over Israel, yet he gets caught in a famine. For another, the once-free son has to become a hired hand (cf. *T. Iss.* 6:1-3), engaged in work that for a Jew is appallingly unclean (Lev 11:7–8). Herding pigs is also hardly a rewarding occupation. He lives in filth and is hungry. Still, no one takes note of his misery even though his hunger drives him to eat pig swill.

His life thus reaches its lowest point. If he is not to die a miserable death in a foreign land in cultic impurity, he must act soon to change his situation. The fallen son evaluates his situation, comparing it not with his earlier life in his father's house and not with the present life of his father and brother, but with the hired servants on his father's farm. He hopes to achieve a position as a hired servant by confessing his guilt to his father. He knows that he can expect no more. Indeed, whether he receives even that much depends solely on the anger or the grace of his father. With this uncertainty he sets out on his journey.

The returning son does not even need to knock at the door of the house that, through his own fault, is no longer his. He does not need to wait to see whether he may enter. His father comes to him, running across the distance between them, and, free of anger and accusations, he compassionately puts his arms around his ragamuffin son, who then makes his confession of guilt and acknowledges that he no longer deserves to be a son. There is no longer any talk of being a hired servant for, without responding to his son, as soon as the father hears the word *son*, he begins giving orders that make things happen. The festive robe restores the son to his position as son; the signet-ring is a sign of authority; the shoes mark him as a free man, since slaves do not wear shoes (cf., e.g., Gen 41:42). In addition, he gives a party. Fatted calf, music, and a dance for men are expressions of his joy at having his dead son alive again. The father's behavior must have caused a lot of head-shaking. Is he not upsetting the ordered life of the entire family? Can he justify this kind of extravagance to the other son?

The older son, after he has finished working in the field (a sign that it is evening; cf. Matt 20:2a), also starts walking home. The formal parallel between Luke 15:20 and 15:25 is intentional. When he hears the celebration in the distance, one of the house servants tells him what is going on. He reacts with anger and with strong disapproval.

The father goes to meet him also (cf. 15:20, 28), but the son, as his father's hard-working, number-one servant, sees that the very foundation of the household's life is falling apart—viz., the duty of the entire family to work day-in and day-out in order to make the future secure—the duty not to spend anything unnecessarily, not even a goat, and certainly not to waste a fatted calf giving a party for a gambler. If the practice of gratuitously overlooking selfishness and wastefulness becomes widespread, the stability of family life on the farm will come unraveled. His anger is justified because it comes from his responsibility for the extended family—a responsibility that obviously only he fulfills. The prodigal, therefore, is no longer his brother, even if the patriarchal decision of the father to restore him as son is irreversible.

The father makes no effort to enforce a standard of fairness. He does not decide, e.g., that the younger son should work for three years, learning his lesson about the corporate responsibility of farm life while his older brother takes an all-expense-paid trip around the world. While no attempt is made to justify an act of grace that is at odds with the ethic of farm life, and while no attempt is made to contradict the older brother's arguments, neither does the narrator confirm the older brother's ethic. Instead, a view of life characterized by obedience and work is corrected by a new life-stance, which the father makes the basis for his relationship with his younger son. That the father-child relationship is not a matter of keeping score on work and extravagance is something that is true even for the older son, and in the case of the younger son, there is a new *world order* (cf. the *must* of v. 32), which the father establishes by his own sovereign authority: When people return from the dead, it is time to celebrate.

Since, according to Jesus, everyone is dead who lives apart from the Kingdom of God that is already defining reality (Luke 9:60 = Matt 8:22; cf. §4.2.2), what he formulates in Luke 15:24, 32 is nothing less than God's eschatological order, which characterizes this salvation. It is a salvation that is attainable only when God takes the initiative and accepts the one who is lost (cf. §§3.2; 4.2.4). The narrator intends for the younger son to be a role model, not in his dissolute life but as one who is granted new life. Everyone is invited to the banquet even as are the younger son and, later, his brother (cf. §4.2.3). The older son's protest creates a dilemma for the hearers, however, when it suddenly confronts them with an issue that forces them to take sides and to declare where they stand. Does this new understanding of God and of what it means to be human not call into question everything that they previously had stood for? If the world is to be ruled along the lines laid down by the new relationship between the father and his returning son, then no one will follow the diligent older son's example. One thinks of the way the objection of the complainers in Matt 20:11 is countered by the landowner's determination to be gracious, or of the Pharisee in Luke 18:11–12 for whom the tax collector parallels the younger son. Everywhere the hearers turn they are confronted with the choice between unlearning what they have believed to be true or turning away in disgust (Matt 11:6).

How does the older son react to the father's invitation? One looks in vain for an answer. The story is open-ended, and one cannot help but think of the Pharisee praying in the temple; Luke 15:29 clearly parallels Luke 18:11–12. Still, the presence of the complainers in Matt 20:11–12 cautions against concluding that Luke 15:11–32 is directed only against Pharisees. The invitation is for anyone who thinks like a Pharisee. The absence of a description of the older son's reaction does not mean that only the members of a specific group are challenged to choose between the new world of the Kingdom of God and the old world. A Pharisaic hearer will get the point, but the parable requires all hearers to understand themselves anew in light of the father's gracious acceptance. Like a wrestler trying to pin the opponent to the floor, the parable tries to force the hearer to enter the Kingdom of God, which is made near in the parable itself.

4.3.2 Jesus' Table-Fellowship as Admission to the Kingdom of God

Becker, J. "Jesu Frohbotschaft und Freudenmahl für die Armen," *BiKi* 33 (1978) 43–47.

Bösen, W. *Jesusmahl—Eucharistisches Mahl—Endzeitmahl.* SBS 97. Stuttgart: KBW, 1980.

Dunn, J. D. G. "Jesus, Table-Fellowship, and Qumran," in: *Jesus and the Dead Sea Scrolls.* J. H. Charlesworth, ed., 254–72.

Fiedler, P. *Jesus,* 119–53.

Herrenbrück, F. *Zöllner,* 228–81.

Hofius, O. *Jesu Tischgemeinschaft mit den Sündern.* CwH 86. Stuttgart: Calwer Verlag, 1967.

Jeremias, J. "Zöllner und Sünder," *ZNW* 30 (1931) 293–300.

Kiilunen, J. *Die Vollmacht im Widerstreit: Untersuchungen zum Werdegang von Mk 2,1–3,6.* AASF.DHL 40. Helsinki: Suomalainen Tiedeakatemia, 1985, 127–82.

Klinzing, G. *Die Umdeutung des Kultus in der Qumrangemeinde und im Neuen Testament.* StUNT 7. Göttingen: Vandenhoeck & Ruprecht, 1971.

Koch, D.-A. "Jesu Tischgemeinschaft mit Zöllnern und Sündern," in: *Jesu Rede von Gott und ihre Nachgeschichte im frühen Christentum.* Festschrift W. Marxsen. D.-A. Koch et al., eds. Gütersloh: Mohn, 1989, 57–74.

Kratz, R. G. "Die Gnade des täglichen Brotes," *ZThK* 89 (1992) 1–40.

Merklein, H. *Botschaft,* 45–51.

Priest, J. "A Note on the Messianic Banquet," in: *Messiah.* J. H. Charlesworth, ed., 222–38

Sanders, E. P. "Jesus and the Sinners," in: idem, *Jesus and Judaism.* Philadelphia: Fortress, 1985, 174–211.

Schottroff, L. and W. Stegemann. *Jesus,* 6–17.

Smend, R. "Essen und Trinken—ein Stück Weltlichkeit des Alten Testaments," in: *Be-*

iträge zur Alttestamentlichen Theologie. Festschrift W. Zimmerli. H. Donner, R.
Hanhart, R. Smend, eds. Göttingen: Vandenhoeck & Ruprecht, 1977, 446–59.
Trautmann, M. *Handlungen*, 132–66.
Völkel, M. "'Freund der Zöllner und Sünder'," *ZNW* 69 (1978) 1–10.
Youtie, H. C. "Publicans and Sinners," in: idem, *Scriptiunculae I.* Amsterdam: A. M.
Hakkert, 1973, 284–317.

From the post-Isaiah apocalypse in Isa 25:6 to Rabbi Akiba's statement in *'Abot*
3:16 we can trace the belief that God's eschatological activity as king means that
at the end of time the righteous will enjoy a banquet of salvation of inestimable
abundance. Indeed, the end-time as a whole will be characterized by an excess of
food and drink, especially of fat foods and old wines (cf. §4.1.2; Isa 25:6), which
the people will consume with great joy (*T. Lev.* 18:14) in a setting of peace and
harmony for humans and animals (Isa 62:8–9; 65:17–25; *1 Enoch* 10:18–22).
Since the earth will produce food continuously (*Bib. Ant.* 3:10), there will be no
interruption in the abundant flow (*1 Enoch* 62:14). One will be able to enjoy once
again the fruit of the tree of paradise, which without pause will bear life-giving
fruit (*T. Lev.* 18:11; *1 Enoch* 25–26), or one will receive manna from heaven
(*Sib. Or. Pro.* 84–86). Even the primal animals Leviathan and Behemoth will
serve as food (*1 Enoch* 60:6–10, 24; 4 Ezra 6:49–52), demonstrating that they
are no longer a threat. *Sib. Or.* 3.744–61; 785–94 is able to bring together a
number of these motifs in almost baroque detail. Peace among and with the
animals is described in a further development of Isa 11:6–9. There will be an
abundance of food—much grain, wine, and oil. Manna will fall from heaven.
The trees will bear fruit, the animals will provide meat in abundance. Drought
and hunger will be no more. Great joy will cover the entire earth. It is expressly
said that all of these things are the work of the creator who rules the world as king
(*Sib. Or.* 3.704, 717–18, 767, 783, 785).

Along with this apocalyptic picture of the end-time emerges a broader wisdom
tradition in Israel and Early Judaism according to which God is the one who in
history blesses all persons with food and especially provides the poor and the
hungry with bread (Ps 132:15; 146:7). Here it is not a matter of God's intervention at the end of time to alleviate human need; it is rather the continuous
providential care of the creator that enables his creatures to live. It is God's
gracious and merciful work as creator with which he provides food (Ps 145:8–9,
15–16). God is praised as the one who satisfies human need by producing
sustenance from the earth and wine that makes glad the human heart (Ps 104:14–
15). The worshipper of Ps 136 recites the blessings of creation and salvation
climaxing in the praise of God as the one who provides food for all flesh. God's
providential care is especially identified with his kingship (Pss 146; 147). *Ps. Sol.*
5:8–18 bears eloquent witness:

> *For if I hunger, I will cry unto you, O God;*
> *and you will give to me.*

> *You nourish birds and fish . . .*
> *Kings and rulers and peoples do you nourish, O God.*
> *And who is the help of the poor and the needy, if not you, Lord?*
> *. . . . But your gift is great in goodness and wealth . . .*
> *Upon the whole earth is your mercy, O Lord, in goodness . . .*
> *Blessed is the glory of the Lord, for he is our king.*

Looking back over his life, Joseph remembers God's care in *T. Jos.* 1:5:

> *I was beset with hunger,*
> *but the Lord himself nourished me.*

Because Jesus' message was fundamentally oriented toward the coming Kingdom of God (§4.2.2), he thinks primarily in terms of the apocalyptic motifs, but he also integrates wisdom material into his message (Matt 6:25–34; cf. §4.2.3). As one can see in Matt 8:11–12 par. (§3.2.4), the multifaceted apocalyptic material left its imprint on Jesus's concept of the end only in a simple form, similar to *'Abot* 3:16. We should not allow the warning tone of the text to obscure the significance of its positive dimension for our understanding of the preaching of Jesus. It is of more than marginal importance, given the way Jesus emphasizes at the last supper the festive drinking of wine in the end-time (Mark 14:25; cf. §6:3) and given the way the earliest form of the beatitudes in Matt 5:3–5 = Luke 6:20–21 alludes to a banquet of salvation. This earliest form reads:

1a *Blessed (are) the poor,*
  b *for the Kingdom of God (will be) yours.*
2a *Blessed (are) the hungry,*
  b *for you will be filled.*
3a *Blessed (are) the ones who cry,*
  b *for you will laugh.*

There is general agreement that the first four beatitudes belong to Q, but since the fourth differs linguistically from the other three and reflects the situation of persecution that the early church faced, we are able to claim only the first three beatitudes for the earliest Jesus material. Luke's change from the third to the second person offers an unusual mixed form. Since it is the more difficult reading, we should regard it as the earliest stage of the tradition. Makarisms seldom appear in the second person; usually they are in the third person (also with Jesus; cf. Matt 11:5–6 par.; 13:16–17 par.; cf. 4.2.2). The Lukan *now* that appears in the protasis of the second and third beatitudes is missing in the first, and it may well be occasioned by Luke's tendency to balance the here and the beyond, the present and the future (cf. Luke 16:1–31). It is likely that no verb appeared in Aramaic in the apodosis of the first makarism and that we should understand it in a future sense, parallel to the second and third beatitudes. The two versions of the third beatitude (Luke: cry-laugh; Matt: mourn–be comforted) are not substantially different (cf. Rev 18:11, 15, 19), and Luke may well have mixed the two variants in Luke 6:24b, 25b. Luke's concrete formulation fits better with the second beatitude—an argument that carries even more weight if one regards the second and third beatitudes as explicit examples of the more general first beatitude.

That the Kingdom of God will result in a final banquet of salvation that fills the hungry and brings joy is a statement that parallels exactly Matt 8:11–12 par. The focus is exclusively on creation rather than on Zion (cf. §4.2.3). There are no signs of the church's self-understanding or its christology. The text speaks universally, and with its passive voice it implies that God is the agent. It differs also from Judaism, which reserves its blessing for the chosen righteous who are faithful to the Torah (*1 Enoch* 82:4; *Ps. Sol.* 4:23; 4 Ezra 7:45) or in general for the Israel that will take part in the final salvation (*Ps. Sol.* 17:44). The Jesus material begins with human want, which God's gracious act in the form of the Kingdom of God transforms at the end of time into its opposite. There is no valid reason for doubting the authenticity of this material, especially since the poor appear again in Matt 11:5–6 (cf. §4.2.2) and the miracles of the age of salvation described there also highlight human creatureliness.

The beatitudes do not describe how the hearers' election and corresponding righteousness are going to be of benefit in the end-time; they simply comfort the poor, i.e., the hungry and those who weep, in the here-and-now with the assurance that the Kingdom of God (i.e., God himself) is going to change their condition of deprivation into its opposite. It is an unexpected promise of salvation, with no justification in the human condition, whose basis and initiative lie solely in the Kingdom of God. The makarisms do not presuppose a reversal of conditions in the end-time so that those who now are prosperous will be miserable and those who suffer now will know the joy of salvation (*1 Enoch* 92–107; Luke 16:19–31). That kind of thinking comes from outside the text. The word of comfort contains no hint of a balancing of accounts; it speaks rather with the awareness that it is solely because of God's initiative that one will experience an unexpected change of fortunes. Creatures overwhelmed by troubles receive a word of good news for which there is no basis in their previous experience. They will share in gifts that result from God's activity, but it will not be granted to them to see God's all-equalizing world rule. Since they are pronounced blessed in the present, it is likely that Jesus bases the word on the approaching Kingdom of God, which has already begun as salvation's turning-point. Otherwise, the suffering hearers could well feel patronized, or even ridiculed, by the word, since no other reason is given (e.g., election, being righteous) why they should experience such a change in fortunes. There is, therefore, an inner connection between the expected final state and the present pronouncement of blessing on the poor. It is exactly the same connection that exists between the anticipated banquet of salvation and Jesus' Galilean table-fellowship.

Although it is somewhat less obvious, one runs into the same relationship in the Lord's Prayer (Luke 11:2–4; Matt 6:9–13; cf. §5.2.4). It begins with the double request for the final realization of the Kingdom of God, and then in the second section it speaks about the human condition: the need for sustenance, the entanglement in guilt, and the exposure to temptation. The first of these needs has an obvious affinity to the beatitudes, with which the prayer also shares an emphasis on the Kingdom of God. Praying the Lord's Prayer is a personal response to the proclamation of the Kingdom of God. Since it is a community prayer rather than an individual prayer, it may well have been a table prayer of Jesus' adherents. Is not their table-fellowship an anticipation of the final realization of the Kingdom of God? As persons invited by God to eat together do they not celebrate a meal that within the present turning-point of salvation reflects the brilliance of the final banquet of salvation? What else in the activity of Jesus could serve as a both repeatable and distinct setting for the Lord's Prayer?

Finally, the issue of anxiety about food, which is no longer necessary when one seeks the Kingdom of God, appears also in Matt 6:25–34 par. (cf. §4.2.3). Since the Kingdom of God also means that the creator provides for his creatures, it sheds a different light on the concern for food and clothing. The rule that those who do not work should not eat (2 Thess 3:10, 12) is thus rendered inoperative. Everyone is invited to the meal and may eat whatever is there as a gift from God. Such a statement, of course, is not a general social rule that in antithesis to a wisdom-based work ethic is intended to establish a code of conduct for the whole world. It describes, rather, a personal way of acting that is temporarily appropriate, because the end-time salvation has begun as the Kingdom of God, which alone and everywhere is in effect and in which God feeds his creatures.

We have intentionally begun our discussion of Jesus' table-fellowship with a discussion of creature-needs; it is a feature that is consistently overlooked. There is a common understanding of this table-fellowship that immediately focuses on the new community that it represents and that as a result defines its character in terms of the acceptance of the marginal and the outcast. The problem with such an interpretation is that it describes the essence of the table-fellowship from the point of view of hostile outsiders. That Jesus was *a friend of tax collectors and sinners* (Matt 11:19 par.) is a charge that his opponents hurl at Jesus. Such a pejorative description of the table-fellowship of Jesus emphasizes what was visible and offensive from the outside while ignoring the way the participants experienced the event.

The inclusive dimension of the meal was, of course, important for Jesus, but it should not dominate our understanding of the table-fellowship. It is helpful here if we remind ourselves of the Early Jewish tradition (cf. §4.1.8) in which God is regarded as the one who provides creature-gifts and at the same time is the one who is unceasingly gracious toward the sinner. The combination corresponds to the second section of the Lord's Prayer. The thanksgiving hymns of Qumran offer a special example of this theological connection. Statements about the utter dependency of all human creatures that emphasize the distance between God and humans appear alongside descriptions of the sinfulness and the need for redemption on the part of human beings whom God helps with his righteousness (cf., e.g., 1QH i 21–ii 1; xi 2ff.; xii 24ff.). While Jesus does not speak of the worthlessness of human beings as does Qumran, neither Jesus nor Qumran shares the basic belief of Early Judaism that God's care of his creatures and his redemptive work are two separate acts of the one creator.

With this insight we are in a position to define with greater precision what it means for Jesus to include the marginalized into his fellowship. He receives them into the Kingdom of God, which is already at work, which addresses people in terms of their total needs as creatures, and which is inclusive of all Israel. While he has a special concern for the poor and the outcast, we should not understand those persons simply in terms of social categories, nor should we conclude that Jesus favored them or even directed his message exclusively to them. They serve, rather, as special examples of how the Kingdom of God is directed to all Israel, much as Jesus uses the extreme example of love of one's enemy to demonstrate what love should be (cf. §5.2.3). When the poor are cited along with tax collectors and sinners (see below), the focus is on something other than social deprivation. Since one stands before God as a whole person, poverty and being a sinner represent two quite compatible human needs. It should also be clear that when Jesus accepts the message of John the Baptist, he affirms that one's position as a sinner before God takes precedence over all other possible needs.

Almost without exception the usual social interpretations of Jesus' table-fellowship regard it as a symbolic event that anticipates the Kingdom of God that will soon arrive. It represents the kingdom in both a literal and figurative sense and anticipates what has not yet happened. We could not disagree more with this understanding of the table-fellowship. Not only does it bring to the texts ways of speaking that are foreign to them; it contradicts Jesus' understanding of time. If the turning-point of salvation has already begun (§4.2.2) so that with Jesus God's final rule is already being realized, then there is no real choice between literal and figurative. The Kingdom of God happens in the table-fellowship.[84] In the same way that the parables and the miracles of Jesus bring the Kingdom of God near so that people experience the claims of the Kingdom in them, the table-fellowship is nothing less than the event in which God the creator himself assumes responsibility for the eschatological care of his creatures and is merciful toward sinners. Now that the turning-point of salvation has taken place, God's end-time nearness is present, and from it the final banquet of salvation that will last forever will soon develop.

The synoptic gospels bear frequent witness to Jesus' table-fellowship, which, incidentally, plays only a marginal role in the Gospel of John (John 12:2). There are references to it in the sayings source (Matt 11:18–19 = Luke 7:33–34; Luke 10:7 = Matt 10:11; Luke 14:15–24 = Matt 22:1–10) and in the gospels of Mark (Mark 1:31; 2:15–17; 2:18–22; 3:20; 7:1–8; 14:3–9), Matthew (in its use of Q and Mark), and Luke (Luke 8:1–3; 10:8, 38–42; 13:26; 14:1–24; 15:1–2). Even when we allow for the historical uncertainty of some of this evidence, its range across all four sources justifies the conclusion that conducting common meals and attributing specific meaning to them was especially characteristic of Jesus. There are no convincing analogies to this table-fellowship in Early Judaism.

There is, of course, the general rule that one should share one's food with the poor (Tob 2:1–2; 4:16; *T. Iss.* 3:8; 5:2; 7:5 etc.), and it is equally clear that in Antiquity eating together is regarded as a special expression of harmony (cf. 2 Kgs 25:27–30),[85] but Jesus' table-fellowship was unique in three ways: Its eschatological setting as the realization of the coming Kingdom of God and its inclusion of persons designated as sinners have no parallels in his world. There is also no analogy to the regular repetition of such meals in the villages of Galilee. These features are especially true when one compares the table-fellowship of Jesus with the community meals of the Essenes, which occur as cultic meals under the oversight of a priest and according to the strictest purity regulations.[86] In the Judaism of that day one can hardly imagine a more obvious contrast to the table-fellowship of Jesus.

We can quickly summarize the rest of what can be known about these common meals. Obviously they did not take place out in the open, as the stories of the miraculous feedings might have us believe (Mark 6:35 parr.; 8:3–4 par.; John 6:1–3), but in a house (Mark 1:31 parr.; 2:15 parr.; 14:3 parr.; Luke 10:38; 14:1; 19:5; cf. also Luke 14:16–24; John 12:2–3). Nowhere is Jesus himself the host; he and his disciples are guests. It is tempting to surmise that as the distinguished guest Jesus would have broken the first bread and would have said the prayer. That would explain most naturally why in the narrative world of the Easter legend in Luke 24:30 Jesus was recognized in the breaking of the bread. It may well be that the fellowship meals of the primitive church, which were not without some connection to the table-fellowship of Jesus, reveal the same influence when, without any cultural basis, they are described as *the breaking of the bread* (Acts 2:42, 46). That Jesus broke the bread is also recalled in the feeding miracles (Mark 6:41 parr.). The prayer may well have been a popular blessing of the day, but, as we have already noted, Jesus' table-fellowship would have been a good setting for the Lord's Prayer. In that case the Kingdom of God would have been named, which had the power to make all things holy (cf. the double petition at the beginning of the prayer)—to make holy gifts of God out of food that may well have been unclean (the petition for bread) and to render holy the tax collectors and sinners (the petition for forgiveness of sins and deliverance from temptation). Whether the Lord's Prayer was offered in this setting or not, however, it should be beyond dispute that the food that the residents of the village brought together was received as gifts from God so that God was the implicit host of the fellowship meals.

All residents of the house and village were possible participants in the meals, since Jesus was sent to all Israel. Of course, it was unlikely that women ate at the table with the men. More typical scenes would be the service of Peter's mother-in-law (Mark 1:31) and the women of Mark 14:3 and Luke 7:37 who came to the table to perform special acts of love. That Mary was one of the listeners and did not serve the guest in Luke 10:38–42 is cited as an exception. The houses in which the meals took place must have been large enough and prosperous enough to accommodate a large group; at least Mark 2:15 parr. and Luke 14:1 presuppose such a setting. If we can assume that in addition to the members of the family Jesus and his disciples were present along with others who joined the group, such fellowship meals were by no means small events, especially in view of Jesus' insistence (preserved in his parable Matt 22:9 = Luke 14:21) that outsiders should be permitted to participate (Mark 2:15 parr.; Matt 11:19 par.; Luke 15:2; cf. also Luke 14:1–24).

The guests certainly included the poor (Matt 5:3 par.; 11:5 par.) and the sick (Luke 14:21 par.) and, of course, those persons who caused Jesus to have a reputation as a friend of tax collectors and sinners (Matt 11:19 par.). It is probably no accident that this inclusiveness is reminiscent of Isa 25:6, where the boundaries of the chosen people are opened to the nations so that they also can participate in the final banquet of salvation. In Matt 8:11–12 par. (cf. §3.2.4) Jesus offers a polemical reinterpretation of that hope. Still, Jesus' inclusiveness, which ignored social distinctions, must have been highly offensive. For one thing, how can he include everyone and still claim that his table-fellowship represents God's eschatological kingship? For another, in spite of Isa 25:6, does not the establishment of God's final rule require the separation of righteous and sinners and of clean and unclean (*1 Enoch* 38:2–3; 45:5; 62:12–13; *Ps. Sol.* 17:27, 32, 44–45; *T. Lev.* 18; *T. Jud.* 24, etc.)? How could Jesus simply ignore this ironclad eschatological rule?

The emphasis on typical negative groups points in several directions. Poor is not a religious badge of honor as is often the case in Early Judaism, beginning with the prophecy that stood in Isaiah's tradition (Isa 61:1–2; cf. also *Ps. Sol.* 10:6; 1QM xi 9–10; 1QH v 22; 4QpH xii 3–10; 4QpPs 372:10). The concept of spiritual poverty is excluded by Matt 5:3–6 par., where the poor suffer material deprivation so that they hunger and weep. They also appear in Matt 11:5 par. and Luke 14:21 in connection with specific sicknesses. When Matthew expands the first beatitude by adding *in spirit* to the poor, he obviously knows that without that addition an understanding of economic poverty is unavoidable. Indeed, when all three Synoptics speak of the poor, the context consistently indicates material poverty. There is also no evidence in the early Jesus material for claiming that material poverty was a religious sign of special humility before God. Nor can we use Isa 61:1–2 to read such a meaning into Matt 5:3 and 11:5. Isa 61:1–2 does not reveal to us what Jesus thought; the Jesus texts reveal, rather, how Jesus understood Isa 61:1–2. To be poor means specifically that one cannot even find work as a day laborer—that one must live by begging, because one is too sick to work (Acts 3:2 offers an example).

The combination of tax collectors and sinners appears nowhere outside the Synoptics, not even in Early Judaism. It combines the designation of a profession and a wholesale generalization. It probably means tax collectors and all other suspicious people. They are suspicious, because they belong to the people who do not observe the Law (cf. John 7:49). That kind of accusation naturally comes from those who are faithful to the Law—from Pharisees, for example (cf. Mark

2:16; Luke 15:1–2; John 7:45–52; 9:13, 34). Thus in Luke 18:10–14 (cf. §3.2.5) the righteous Pharisee is juxtaposed to the sinful tax collector. The tax collectors who here receive wholesale condemnation are by no means an impoverished lot. Since their profession is of no interest to the post-Easter church—indeed, is not even a problem—we can safely conclude that Jesus consorted with tax collectors and that his relationship with them was conspicuous. The persons involved were private Jewish tenants, along the Hellenistic model, who in Galilee leased from Herod Antipas the right to collect various kinds of taxes and fees. They paid for their lease a year in advance with the expectation that at the end of the lease they would have collected enough taxes to have earned a profit. The various taxes in Palestine certainly were an oppressive burden, and the tax collectors were always suspected of maximizing their income at the expense of the people. All tax collectors, not simply the individual tax collector of the parable, had the reputation of being thieves, of being greedy and hard-hearted, and of not taking seriously their own civil and religious taxes. Surrounded as they were by the aura of wholesale suspicion, it was naturally assumed that they were in religious violation of the Torah. Possession obtained through unlawful means, tax fraud, and failure to pay the temple tithe all rendered their income unclean. They very soon were in serious conflict with the Law. Nowhere in the Synoptics is the Zealot accusation explicit that the tax collectors served a heathen occupying power. At the most such a claim would apply to Judea, where Pilate ruled and collected taxes for Rome. Thus the tension between Israel and Rome is not a factor in evaluating the participation of the tax collectors in the table-fellowship of Jesus. Tax collectors and Gentiles appear together only for Matthew's church (Matt 5:44–45; 18:17). Likewise, tax collectors and prostitutes appear together only in Matthew (Matt 21:31–32). Matthew is also the first to include a tax collector among the disciples of Jesus (Matt 10:3). Since all other lists of disciples are silent on the subject, this statement from Matthew is also of no historical value.

Thus Jesus emphatically and intentionally included those persons in his table-fellowship whom the official Judaism of his day would have preferred to exclude. One can see in the parable of the supper (Luke 14:16–24 = Matt 22:2–10) just how natural this opening was for him, just how unexpected it was for this target group, and just how offensive it was for others :

1 *A man prepared a meal. And at the hour of the meal he sent a servant to say to those who had been invited, "Come, because everything is already prepared."*

2 *But all of them together began to make excuses. The first one said to him, "I bought a field, and I just have to go out to see it. Please excuse me!" Another said, "I have bought five yoke of oxen, and I am on my way to check them out. Please excuse me!" Another said, "I have married a wife, and therefore I cannot come." And the servant returned and reported these things to his master.*

3 Then the master of the house became angry and said to his servant: "Go quickly out into the streets, and bring back here whomever you find.!" And the servant went out and did as he was commanded, so that the house was full.

The material from the sayings source, for which there is a version in *Gos. Thom.* 64, is offered by Matthew and Luke in widely different versions. In Luke 14:16–21a Luke preserves what is essentially old material, and in Matt 22:8–10 Matthew stays closer to the source. Matthew is responsible for the metaphors *king, wedding, son,* which define the content of the Kingdom of Heaven (22:2a). The double plurality of servants is another metaphorical salvation history motif. Because it divides history into periods, it shortens Luke's illustrative three excuses (Luke 14:18–20). They did not lend themselves to being allegorized. Matt 22:7 alludes to the destruction of Jerusalem in 70/71 CE. This statement, which temporarily leaves the narrative world, is anticipated by the unusual treatment of the messengers in 22:6 and then receives its divine judgment in 22:8. In 14:16–21a, therefore, Luke does a better job of preserving the structure and diction of the parable (with the possible exception of an expanded v. 16), especially since in several cases Matthew clearly presupposes the Lukan text.

For his part, in 14:21b–23 Luke has created two stages of salvation history that do not appear in Matthew and the *Gospel of Thomas.* First, people of the city are invited (Jewish-Christian mission). For reasons we are not told, this first invitation does not fill the room, but it serves to prepare the way for a second invitation outside the city (Gentile-Christian mission). Luke makes this change by creating two invitations out of a source that originally was similar to Matt 22:9–10. We can come close to this source by calculating how the changes in Matt 22:2–8 affected the formation of 22:9–10 and then assuming several additional variations.

Matt 22:11–14 is a secondary expansion, and Luke 14:24 is influenced by the setting in 14:1, 3, 5, 7, 12, 15, 16a. In general we can say that the totally different contexts of the parable make it clear that both frameworks are secondary. On the other hand, the sense of the parable fits well with the situation posed by the preaching of Jesus.

The parable recites how the unexpected but complete rejection of an invitation leads understandably to anger, which, in turn, leads to the equally unexpected, sovereign decision that the festivities will still take place. The determination to celebrate overcomes all obstacles, because at issue is God's Lordship, which will not be denied. Those who reject the invitation and refuse to join the celebration place themselves beyond the pale. The parable begins by portraying a typical situation. The simple and uncomplicated opening scene for a banquet suddenly become a hopeless situation, because without exception all of the persons without whom the banquet cannot take place refuse to come. Three excuses are given. In and of themselves they are joyful and good activities, and they increase in quality—first, farmland; then, five yoke of oxen, i.e., animals; finally, a wife. Still, they are questionable excuses, because, as Luke 14:17 suggests, the invited guests had ample advance knowledge of the date. If one is not planning to keep the engagement, should one not let the host know ahead of time? Why have they all without exception planned something else? The celebration is in danger of being a total failure. The head of the house overcomes the crisis with an imaginative second invitation to a wide circle of people who originally had not been considered. Yet, what is astonishing is that they are not regarded as substitutes, recruited in an emergency; they are treated as full guests who fill the house so that an authentic rather than a substitute celebration can take place.

The narrator hopes that the parable will lead to a quiet debate within the hearers. They are familiar with Jesus' table-fellowship. They know that he thinks that people should celebrate the turning-point of salvation and that the Kingdom of God is so powerful that it is going to achieve its goal. They also know the ridicule and invective that have been directed at Jesus' table-fellowship because of his friendship with the tax collectors and the sinners. They realize that they are the unexpected guests and that this reproach is also directed at them. They are not to blame for their participation in the table-fellowship, because it is what God wants. Those who have excluded themselves from the fellowship have made the worse choice. When they pursue the normal activities of the world (cf. Luke 17:26–27), they reveal priorities that ignore the importance of a present that the table-fellowship characterizes, and they fail to recognize that the Kingdom of God is in their midst (Luke 17:20–21) and demands of them a radically new orientation of their lives.

The themes of acceptance and offense appear also in the typical meal narrative of Mark 2:15–17 parr., which, in spite of its topical nature, preserves some authentic elements of Jesus' table-fellowship:

1a   And it happened that he was reclining at the table in "a" house,
b   and many tax collectors and sinners reclined with Jesus and his
*   disciples [v. 15c].*
2a   And the scribes of the Pharisees [v. 16b] said to his disciples:
b   "Is he eating with tax collectors and sinners?"
3a   And Jesus heard (it) and said to them: [v. 17b]
b   "I came not to call righteous, but sinners."

In Mark's gospel the call of Levi (Mark 2:13–14 parr.) is already connected with eating with tax collectors, but the other calls to discipleship (Mark 1:16–20 parr.) do not result in a meal. The connection is awkward in Mark 2:15; *his house* should refer to Levi, but in its present form it refers to Jesus. Thus 2:15–17 was originally an independent unit.[87] In 2:15c and 16b the pericope has received two editorial expansions, probably from Mark. As is often the case, Jesus' answer is a collection of different kinds of sayings.

The first answer in 2:17b is unexpected in the context. It is a previously individual saying—more precisely, a proverbial wisdom saying—which is related to the context only through the use of the plural (tax collectors and sinners/sick). Based on the context, this maxim is often interpreted metaphorically, but that way of using a metaphor is foreign to the Synoptics. It is more likely that the reference to the sick is an analogy used to justify Jesus' concern for the tax collectors and sinners: One should not be surprised that the tax collectors and sinners are Jesus' target group, since comparable things take place in other areas of life. Of course, we should note that v. 17b focuses on the sick, while in v. 16 it is Jesus who is the point of controversy, not the tax collectors and sinners. It is Jesus who must justify his behavior as, indeed, he does in the following answer.

The second answer has a christological orientation, and it responds to the double term *tax collectors and sinners* in vv. 15–16 with the shorter *sinners*. It also implies that the

Pharisees are among the righteous, so that the connection *Pharisees-righteous* (Matt 23:28; Luke 18:9–14, etc.) builds a second bridge to the context. The sense of the saying is then: Are you offended that Jesus removes the separation between the righteous and sinners (Ps 1)? This offense is precisely the reason he was sent. Of course, v. 17c is by itself an easily understandable summary of Jesus' activity, especially since the contrast between righteous and sinners is typical of both Early Judaism and Primitive Christianity (cf. by way of example Luke 15:7). Since it was generally known in the church that Jesus ate with tax collectors and sinners (Matt 11:19 par.; Luke 15:2), the scene may have been added later to the saying when there was a general tendency to make apophthegms from the words of Jesus. In any case, the scene is not simply a creation based on v. 17c. Instead, what was commonly known about his typical behavior is justified with the addition of an independent christological statement. Whoever prefaced this confrontational answer with v. 17b weakened the response by suggesting that Jesus' concern for the tax collectors and sinners was no more unusual than was the activity of a physician. The sharp statement remains, but it now describes a behavior that others can also do.

The three-part outline (introductory scene, crisis, authoritative solution) is easily recognized. The paratactic connections are missing only where direct address is used in the reproach and its refutation.

Jesus represents the violation of the Law, the Pharisaic scribes represent the Law and the righteousness that the Law requires. A righteous person does not sit in the circle of those who scoff at the Law and despise it (Ps 1:1). A sinner, on the other hand, has no business in the fellowship of the righteous (Ps 1:5). Excluding the godless persons (Ps 1:6) serves, therefore, to establish and preserve the identity of the fellowship of the righteous. Jesus reverses this principle. He creates a community whose identity depends on integration. Its basic principle is the inclusion of the lost (Luke 18:10–14). This narrative, which was expanded by the church, preserves the recollection that Jesus practiced God's mercy in a way that ignored boundaries and that came into conflict with the representatives of the Law.

The church also knew that Jesus' table-fellowship distinguished him from John the Baptist, as Matt 11:16–19 = Luke 7:31–35 demonstrates:

1a   *"You are" like children sitting in the market place*
 b   *who call to each other and say:*
2a   *"We piped for you, but you did not dance."*
 b   *"We wailed for you, but you did not mourn."*
3a   *For John came neither eating nor drinking, but you say, "He has a demon."*
4a   *The Son of Man came eating and drinking,*
 b   *but you say, "Behold, a man who is a glutton and a drunk,*
 c   *a friend of tax collectors and sinners."*

Interpreters have long struggled to explain the relationship between the introduction with the term *this generation* (Matt 11:16a = Luke 7:31) and the parable of Matt 11:16b par. We can avoid this problem only by assuming that this typical beginning (Luke 13:18, 20; Mark 4:30) was added in the sayings source. When we further consider that in 11:18,

19, under the influence of 11:17, Matthew changed the direct address of the verb (thus Luke), we must assume that the unit began with the direct address. The present Q introduction serves to signal that Matt 11:17 par. is to be read as an allegory and that 11:18–19 par. gives the interpretation of the allegory (formally, Matt 4:1–23 parr. has the same sequence). The Q ending in Matt 11:19e = Luke 7:35 also belongs to this stage of the tradition.

Frequently the attempt is made to separate Matt 11:16–17 par. from Matt 11:18–19 par., but since vv. 16–17 offer at the most a rather trite put-down of Jesus' contemporaries, they hardly would have been passed on by themselves. When we recognize that the Q introduction is secondary, we do not need to understand vv. 16–17 as a parable, and the problems of interpretation that lead to decomposition disappear.

Special problems are posed by the reference to the Son of Man, who is identified with the Jesus who is active on earth (Matt 11:19 par.). *The Son of Man came . . .* is reminiscent of texts such as Mark 10:45 = Matt 20:28 and Luke 19:10, which are christological statements projected back onto the Jesus of the past. In Matt 11:15–19, however, nothing suggests a christological distinction between the Baptist and Jesus. What is essential to the text is their different behavior, and that would be clearer if there were no title of honor. Should we as an exception read *Son of Man*, therefore, with the meaning *I* or *a person such as I* rather than as a title? Certainly that is not the way the church understood it. The church understood *Son of Man* consistently as a title of honor. The close proximity between *Son of Man* and *man* in the text is another irritation (Mark 2:27–28 offers an analogy). Finally, we should call attention again to the similarity with such texts as Mark 10:45 (see above). While there is no proof, we can at least surmise that the text originally read "I have come . . . " and that an allegorizing church substituted a statement of honor. Further support for this conjecture is the observation that the synoptic Jesus nowhere else uses the title Son of Man to distinguish himself from the Baptist. Supported by this hypothesis, we can attribute this material to Jesus. It hardly came from Jesus, however, in its present form (cf. §4.4.2).

Children are sitting in the marketplace, but, since they cannot agree on what they want to do, they are not playing. Some of them begin to play a flute, but no one dances. Others try the opposite tack, suggesting that they play at funeral instead of a wedding dance. They begin the mournful cry for the dead, but the rest of the group will not beat their breasts in sorrow. Since they cannot agree on any of the suggestions, nothing happens. That makes no one happy, since normally children want to play.

The scene reflects the situation in which Jesus' contemporaries find themselves. The Baptist called them to fast as an act of penance in light of the coming judgment, but they rejected him with an invective that denied to him any religious legitimacy. Then Jesus offered them a joyful meal (the sequence is chiasmic, reversing the order of the children's play), but they ridiculed him. Because they cannot make up their minds, they get nothing.

This prophetic invective makes use of two criticisms of Jesus made by outsiders. (In Luke 13:1–5 Jesus cites another popular opinion in order to correct it. Cf. §3.2.2.) The two expressions relate to the table-fellowship and interpret each other. Of course, the description of Jesus as a pleasure-seeking glutton is an intentional exaggeration. It is more likely that the meals consisted of simple peasant food. They were, however, joyful occasions. As early as Deuteronomy, eating in God's presence is equated with being joyful before God (Deut 12:7, 12, 18; 15:20; 16:11, 14). Eating and being filled are divine gifts related to dwelling in the land of Israel (Deut 6:11; 8:10, 12). Joel promises that in the future Israel will once again eat and be filled as a sign that God is in Israel's midst and that he alone is God (Joel 2:26–27). There is no way an Israelite can imagine the eschatological banquet other than as a joyful meal (Isa 24:23; 25:6–8; T. Lev. 18:11, 14, etc.). In view of the belief that the turning-point of salvation has happened, this excitement is a natural part of the table-fellowship of Jesus (cf. Luke 15:23, 25).

Jesus' opponents were not the first to find fault with the joyful mood at mealtime. The pleasure-seeking glutton, the carouser, the drunkard had always been negative figures (Deut 21:20; Prov 23:20–21; As. Mos. 7; T. Jud. 14, 16; Luke 15:13, 30; 16:19; cf. also Rom 13:13, etc.). Practically all of the texts warn that that kind of wild living leads to lawlessness and to impurity and reveal that the epithets in Matt 11:19 par. are simply two sides of the same accusation.

It is noteworthy that, according to Acts and the letters of Paul, the post-Easter church nowhere had to defend itself against similar criticism, yet in their retrospective descriptions of the time of Jesus the Synoptics continually claim that his table-fellowship was controversial (e.g., Mark 2:15–17 parr.; 2:18–22 parr.; Mark 7:1–23 parr.; Luke 15:1–2). Our historical analysis shows that Jesus himself also dealt with such criticisms (e.g., Luke 14:16–24 par.; 15:11–32; probably also Matt 11:19 par.). The range of evidence that we have looked at reveals the following issues related to the Law: disregard for the distinction between the righteous (persons faithful to the Law) and sinners (persons who despised the Law) in accepting the lost (e.g., Matt 11:19 par.; Luke 15:11–32) and carelessness in questions of ritual purity when dealing with persons (Matt 11:19 par.; cf. Matt 22:9–10 par.) and things (Mark 7:15 parr.; cf. Luke 10:7–9; cf. §5.3.4).

Our discussion of the table-fellowship in this section began with Jesus' own understanding, then looked at the concrete features of the table-fellowship, and finally dealt with the rejection and criticism from the opponents. We should not leave the subject without saying something about the participants and the role they played in the table-fellowship. Why did they agree to participate in meals in which everyone ate together, and why did they feed Jesus and his disciples? It is not enough to point out that the solidarity that serves as a kind of insurance against bad harvests and sickness is greater among the poor than it is among those who have resources that protect them against such risks. We must remember that Jesus expected to be fed along with his entire entourage of disciples and that, given the limited geographical scope of his activity, it is likely that he appeared frequently in the same village (cf. §2). Why did they not regard him as a lazy parasite? Another way of asking the question is: What was it that Jesus had to offer them? Certainly the miracles were a factor (§4.3.3).[88] In a world of sickness with no medical care they would be especially important, and in every village there would be people who wanted to be healed. There would always be an occasion, therefore, to exchange healing for food. Yet, Jesus doubtless offered them more than healing. He made their concerns God's concerns. He subjected their drab lives to the excitement of the coming Kingdom of God. Contrary to all expectation, it was they rather than the mighty who were the recipients of this message, and in Jesus they were able to experience in their daily lives the kind of noble figure ordinarily denied them.

4.3.3 The Miracles of Jesus as the Establishment of the Kingdom of God

Annen, F. *Die Dämonenaustreibungen Jesu in den synoptischen Evangelien.* ThBer 5. Zürich: Zwingli, 1976, 107–46.

Betz, O. and W. Grimm. *Wesen und Wirklichkeit der Wunder Jesu.* ANTJ 2. Frankfurt: Peter Lang, 1977.

Böcher, O. *Christus Exorcista.* BWANT 96. Stuttgart: Kohlhammer, 1972.

Busse, U. *Die Wunder des Propheten Jesus: Die Rezeption, Komposition und Interpretation der Wundertradition im Evangelium des Lukas.* FzB 24. 2d ed. Stuttgart: KBW, 1979.

Delling, G. "Das Verständnis des Wunders im Neuen Testament," in: *Wunderbegriff.* A. Suhl, ed. Darmstadt: Wissenschaftliche Buchgesellschaft, 1980, 300–17.

———. *Antike Wundertexte.* KIT 79. 2d ed. Berlin: de Gruyter, 1960.

Fiebig, P. *Antike Wundergeschichten zum Studium der Wunder im Neuen Testament.* Berlin: de Gruyter, 1911.

———. *Jüdische Wundergeschichten des neutestamentlichen Zeitalters.* Berlin: de Gruyter, 1911.

Fuller, R. H. *Interpreting the Miracles.* London: SCM, 1963.

Gallagher, E. V. *Divine Man or Magician: Celsus and Origen on Jesus.* SBLDS 64. Chico, CA: Scholars Press, 1982.

Gutbrod, K. *Die Wundergeschichten des Neuen Testaments.* 3d ed. Stuttgart: Calwer Verlag, 1972.

Hahn, F. "Jesu Wort vom bergeversetzenden Glauben," *ZNW* 76 (1985) 149–69.

Haufe, G. "Hellenistische Volksfrömmigkeit," in: *Umwelt des Neuen Testaments I.* J. Leipoldt, W. Grundmann, eds. 7th ed. Berlin: Evangelische Verlagsanstalt, 1985, 68–100.

Heitmüller, W. *"Im Namen Jesu."* FRLANT I 2. Göttingen: Vandenhoeck & Ruprecht, 1903, 132–85.

Hull, J. *Hellenistic Magic and the Synoptic Tradition.* SBT 2/28. Naperville, IL: Allenson, 1974.

Kahl, W. *New Testament Miracle Stories in their Religious-historical Setting.* FRLANT 163. Göttingen: Vandenhoeck & Ruprecht, 1994.

Kampling, R. "Jesus von Nazareth—Lehrer oder Exorcist," *BZ* 30 (1986) 237–48.

Kee, H. C. *Miracle in the Earl Christian World: A Study in Sociohistorical Method.* New Haven, CT: Yale University Press, 1983.

Kertelge, K. *Die Wunder Jesu in der neueren Exegese.* ThB 5. Munich: Kösel, 1976, 71–105.

———. *Die Wunder Jesu im Markusevangelium.* StANT 23. Munich: Kösel, 1970.

Kirschschläger, W. "Exorzismus in Qumran?" *Kairos* 18 (1976) 135–53.

Koch, D.-A. *Die Bedeutung der Wundererzählungen für die Christologie des Markusevangeliums*. BZNW 42. Berlin/New York: de Gruyter, 1975.

Latourelle, R. *The Miracles of Jesus and the Theology of Miracles*. New York/Mahwah, NJ: Paulist, 1988.

Léon Dufour, X. (ed.) *Les miracles de Jésus selon le Nouveau Testament*. Paris: Editions du Seuil, 1977.

Mills, M. *Human Agents of Cosmic Power in Hellenistic Judaism and in Synoptic Tradition*. Sheffield: JSOT, 1990.

Müller, U. B. "Vision und Botschaft," *ZThK* 74 (1977) 416–48.

Nielsen, H. K. *Heilung und Verkündigung*. AThD 22. Leiden: Brill, 1987.

Pesch, R. *Jesu ureigene Taten? Ein Beitrag zur Wunderfrage*. QD 52. Freiburg/Basel/Vienna: Herder, 1970.

Petzke, G. "Die historische Frage nach den Wundertaten Jesu," *NTS* 22 (1976) 180–204.

———. *Die Traditionen über Apollonius von Tyana und das Neue Testament*. SCHNT 1. Leiden: Brill, 1970.

Reitzenstein, R. *Hellenistische Wundererzählungen*. Berlin: de Gruyter, 1906. Repr. 1963.

Schenke, L. *Die Wundererzählungen des Markusevangeliums*. Stuttgart: KBW, 1974.

Schürer, E. *History*, III 342–79.

Schürmann, H. "Die Symbolhandlungen Jesu als eschatologische Erfüllungszeichen," *BiLe* 11 (1970) 29–41.

Seybold, K. E. and U. B. Müller. *Sickness and Healing*. Nashville: Abingdon, 1981.

Smith, J. Z. "Towards Interpreting Demonic Powers in Hellenistic and Roman Antiquity," *ANRW*. Berlin/New York: de Gruyter, 1978, II 16.1, 425–39.

Smith, M. *Jesus the Magician*. San Francisco: Harper & Row, 1978.

Suhl, A. (ed.) *Der Wunderbegriff im Neuen Testament*. WdF 295. Darmstadt: Wissenschaftliche Buchgesellschaft, 1980.

Theissen, G. *The Miracle Stories of the Early Christian Tradition*. Philadelphia: Fortress, 1983.

Thiede, D. L. *The Charismatic Figure as Miracle Worker*. 2d. ed. Missoula, MN: SBL Seminar on the Gospels, 1973.

Trunk, D. *Der messianische Heiler*. HBS 3. Freiburg: Herder, 1994.

Twelftree, G. H. *Jesus the Exorcist*. WUNT II/54. Tübingen: J.C.B. Mohr (Paul Siebeck), 1993.

Weder, H. "Wunder Jesu und Wundergeschichten," in: idem, *Einblicke ins Evangelium*. Göttingen: Vandenhoeck & Ruprecht, 1992, 61–93.

Wegner, U. *Der Hauptmann von Kapernaum*. WUNT II/14. Tübingen: J.C.B. Mohr (Paul Siebeck), 1985.

Weinrich, O. *Antike Heilungswunder*. RVV 8, 1. Berlin: de Gruyter, 1909. Repr. 1969.

To no miracle worker in all of Antiquity were as many miracles attributed as there were to Jesus. All four gospels, including their sources (the synoptic sayings source and the Johannine signs source), without exception bear witness to Jesus as a powerful miracle worker (Mark 1:32–34, 39; 2:12; 3:7–12; 4:41; 6:53–56; Matt 8:16–17; 9:35–38; 14:34–36; 15:28–31; Luke 4:40–41, 44;

6:17–19; John 10:41–42; 20:30–31, etc.) who cannot escape the crowds, who enlists the help of his disciples in driving out demons (Mark 3:13–15 parr.; Luke 10:17–20), and who knows that there are others who do similar deeds (Mark 9:38–41 par.). At the same time he resists the demand for miracles (Matt 12:38–42 par.; Mark 8:11–13 parr.). He also must deal with the charge that he is in league with the devil (Mark 3:23–30 parr.; Matt 9:32–34). Where he is not accepted, he cannot heal (Mark 6:5–6 parr.). He also believes that a successful exorcism can be undone if the demons return (Matt 12:43–45 par.). Nowhere is it said, however, that Jesus' power was not sufficient to perform a miracle (as, e.g., in Mark 9:18b, 28–29). There are no reports of failures that could be attributed to Jesus. On the contrary, it was said of him: "He has done everything well" (Mark 7:37; cf. John 9:32–33, etc.). He is known everywhere as a worker of miracles (Mark 6:2; Luke 4:23).

This widespread view, of course, is not identical with the historical reality of Jesus, but there is no reason to ignore this dimension of his activity or to assign to it a marginal role. If eating and drinking (Matt 8:11–12 par. and §4.3.2) reveal the corporeality of the Kingdom of God, then the other side of that corporeality—the issue of health—should not be ignored. As early as Ps 146:5–10, providing food and healing appear together as activities of the creator. In order to develop some critical criteria in this area—i.e., in order to clarify the extent of Jesus' miracle-working and how he himself regarded it—we will do well to divide the material into three strands: the summary reports of the evangelists, the miracle stories themselves, and the sayings about Jesus' miracle-working activity.

The use of summary reports is not yet a feature of the sayings source; Mark is clearly the first to use this literary technique (Mark 1:32–34 parr.; 3:7–12 parr.; 6:53–56 parr.), and Matthew and Luke take it over from him. Taken by themselves these summary statements are not based on early material. They convey that picture of Jesus that was created by the evangelists and that they wanted to disseminate. On the literary level, next to the summary reports it is the relationship between the miracle stories and other kinds of material that best reveals how the evangelists regarded Jesus as a miracle worker. Mark places the greatest emphasis on Jesus' miracles. He offers a compelling image of Jesus' miracle-working activity by describing the Son of God as the one who restores the peace of paradise (Mark 1:9–13) and as the strong one who in a final struggle defeats the demons who are ruled by Satan (Mark 3:20–27). His coreporters do not necessarily follow him in this regard. With them the emphasis is more on Jesus as prophet and teacher. They accomplish this shift not by reducing Mark's miracle material, but primarily by increasing substantially the nonmiraculous material in their gospels.

With but a few exceptions (e.g., Luke 14:1–6, or perhaps Matt 12:22–23 = Luke 11:14), the miracle legends probably have their roots in the oral tradition that preceded the evangelists and the sayings source. Here they would have served the purpose of missionary propaganda (e.g., Mark 1:28, 45; 5:19–20) or perhaps of christological reassurance (e.g., John 2:10; 20:30–31). They establish Jesus' authority as a teacher (Mark 1:21–27; 4:33–41) and justify the church's practices (Mark 2:1–12 parr.; 3:1–6 parr.). They are even used in the service of the church's parenesis (Mark 8:22–26). Of course, the uses that the church makes of the miracles influences the way the stories are formed. Those who are interested in recruiting adherents will emphasize the greatness and the number of the miracles, as will those who are competing with similar claims (Acts 8; 13–14). John illustrates how highlighting the miraculous can serve christology. The five versions of the feeding miracle (Mark 6:30–44 parr.; 8:1–10 par.; John 6:1–15) serve as an example of the way a miracle could expand. Even in the case of the different stories of blind healings we must reckon with the probability of variations of the same story (cf. Matt 9:27–31; Mark 10:46–52 par.).

We must further observe that none of the miracle legends is cast in the form of a personal report from Jesus or presents itself as the account of eyewitnesses. Not only is the entire miracle tradition formed in a detached, third-person style; it is composed of many different structural types, even if we should not rush to standardize the units.[89] If it is true anywhere, then it is certainly true here that the narrated world and the historical world are not identical.

It is especially conspicuous that Jesus' central concept of the Kingdom of God appears in none of the miracle stories. Indeed, the whole area of eschatological hope seems to be totally missing. (Only Luke 11:20 par. is an exception.) One gets the impression that, as is the case with other ancient miracles, these miracles can happen spontaneously anywhere in history. Nowhere are they related to the eschatological Kingdom of God that is being realized. This omission is especially noteworthy, since the missionary preaching of the early church was familiar with the idea that the end was near. It is not surprising, of course, that there is no connection between the Kingdom of God and the miracle stories in the Gospel of John, because the catchword *Kingdom of God* plays only a marginal role here (the exception is John 3:3, 5.), but one cannot say the same of the Synoptics. Nor can the claim that christology suppressed eschatology, true as it is, explain the entire phenomenon, since there are numerous miracle stories in which both the theme of the Kingdom of God and an explicit christology are missing (e.g., Mark 1:29–31 par.; 1:40–45 parr.; 2:1–5a, 11–12 parr.; 3:1–5; 7:24–30 parr.; 8:22–26 parr.). There are, therefore, multiple factors at work here. We cannot even exclude the possibility that on occasion a non-Christian legend about an itinerant miracle worker was retold from a Christian point of view and for that reason contains nothing about the message of Jesus.

When we look at the kinds of miracles involved, our first and most obvious result is a negative observation: In the early material Jesus performs no miracles to save himself (cf. Matt 4:5–7 par.; Mark 15:31–32 parr.) or to punish others (cf. Luke 9:52–55; Acts 5:1–11).[90] He rejects the demand that he legitimate himself with a miracle (Luke 11:29–32). Christological epiphanies (e.g., Mark 1:9–13 parr.; 6:45–52 parr.; 9:2–10 parr.), because of their thoroughgoing christological character, also will not have been part of the earliest synoptic material. As is also the case with the relatively few miracles dealing with nature (e.g., Mark 6:32–44 parr.; 8:1–10 par.; John 2:1–10; there are no animal miracles at all), the epiphanies appear nowhere in the rather extensive and oldest layer of the sayings material, about which we will soon have more to say. Their absence from the early traditions is not accidental, since epiphanies, nature miracles, and especially raising the dead (Mark 5:21–43 parr.; Luke 7:11–17; John 11:1–44) are all dimensions of the picture of Jesus that reveal the church's own Easter experience.

Finally, the connection between the miracle stories and the church's need to justify its own practices is hardly part of the early material. The texts involved are Mark 2:1–12; 3:1–6; Luke 13:10–17. In the case of Mark 2:1–12, the healing of the lame man, vv. 5b–10 are a later insertion into the story (cf. §4.2.4). Mark 3:1–6, the healing of the man with a withered hand, follows Mark 2:23–28 as the second violation of the Sabbath—one that takes place intentionally and provocatively *with stretched-out hand.* His enemies were already lying in wait for Jesus. Furthermore, the Sabbath pronouncement in 3:4 is a separate saying; without it Mark 3:1b, 5c, d offer a self-contained miracle story. The same is true of the story in Luke 13:10–17 of the healing of the bent-over woman. One can easily separate the miracle story (13:11–13) from the conflict over the Sabbath (13:14–17).

It is, therefore, the healings (examples are Mark 1:29–31 parr.; 1:40–45 parr.), which, incidentally, are the most numerous miracle stories, and the exorcisms (examples are Mark 1:21–28 parr.; 7:24–30 par.) in which, in spite of all of their variety, we will find aspects of the historical reality of Jesus. The two ways of shaping a miracle story are not necessarily to be seen as alternatives, even if there are no exorcisms in the Old Testament and in the Gospel of John.[91] Where they are missing, as a rule it is safe to conclude that belief in demons was not in vogue or that for some reason it was suppressed.[92] Yet, even when people believed in demons they did not necessarily regard all sickness as the result of demon possession. There could be many reasons for sicknesses (cf. Matt 9:32–33 and Mark 7:32–35). It was also often the case that the typical methods of an exorcist could appear in a healing story (e.g., Matt 8:9 par.; Luke 4:39, contrary to Mark 1:31), or that, as we see in Matthew, exorcisms could be changed into healings.

Our decision about the degree to which Jesus was a worker of miracles will ultimately depend on our analysis of the sayings, since it is here that we have the best evidence for authentic Jesus material. The material involved is from the sayings source (Luke 7:22–23 par. [§4.2.2]; 10:13–15 par. [§3.2.4]; 10:23–24 par. [§4.2.2]; 11:20 par. [§4.2.2]; 11:24–26 parr.; 11:29–32 parr.; 14:5 par.; 17:6 par.), from Mark (Mark 3:4 parr.; 3:21–22 parr. [cf. Matt 9:34]; 3:23–27 parr.; 6:1–6 parr.; 11:22–23 par.), and from Luke's special material (Luke 4:25–27 [§3.2.4]; 10:18 [§4.2.2]; 13:32). Most of these texts deal with Jesus' miracles as healings or exorcisms in which sick people recover unexpectedly. Even those texts that do not explicitly speak of healings imply them (e.g., Luke 10:13–15 par.). The sayings thus confirm what we observed in the miracle legends, viz., that Jesus appeared as a therapist or physician (in the ancient understanding of the words) and as an exorcist. This activity was as much a part of his public life as were the parables and the table-fellowship.

Now this miracle activity of Jesus, unquestionable as it is, must be understood in the context of the ancient world in which all sorts of unusual phenomena are explained in terms of a world and a history permeated by the numinous. One explains events not in terms of a network of cause-and-effect relationships from which natural laws are abstracted, but in terms of divine powers that make life possible and of demonic forces that destroy and limit life. In Judaism, e.g., the stars of heaven, the seasons, and the plants are divine works, which serve the creator as persons, so that everything happens as God has commanded (*1 Enoch* 2:1–5:3; cf. Job 38; Pss 107, 135, 145, 148, etc.). Or the demons are spirits that torment people with sickness (*Jub.* 10:1–14; 2Q 26; 4Q 203). Where numinous powers hold sway, momentary suspensions of the ordinary by the unusual, while not everyday events, are always possible and thus can be used to explain human experience. Job affirms before God nothing more than what every Israelite thought, when he confesses: "I know that you can do all things; nothing can be denied you which you desire" (Job 42:2; cf. Gen 18:14). Of course, God can also make use of a Moses to perform miracles (Exod 7ff.). It is furthermore possible for human beings to influence the numinous that is active in all things: Unclean spirits must submit to the one who is holy (Mark 1:23–28). God's angels know how to heal people of demonic damage (Tob 6, 8, 10). Joshua can make the sun stand still (Josh 10:12–13). Water can be changed to wine (John 2:1–10). When the numinous fills everything and holds everything together, it does not in principle matter when and where the miraculous happens—whether it is to an individual human, in history, in nature, or in heaven. Some miracles, of course, are more difficult than others. Raising someone from the dead (as in John 11) is especially difficult, while subduing a fever (as in Mark 1:19–31) is not so amazing. It is likely that making the sun stand still would belong to the super-heavyweight division.

Naturally, such astonishing events are going to remain fixed in a group's collective memory. One passes them on in the form of oral tradition; one also writes them down. On the one hand, the group collects stories about the deeds of persons gifted with divine qualities (Exod 7–12; 2 Kgs 4:18–5:27; Apollonius of Tyana). On the other, it is interested in which exorcistic techniques, which prayers, which formulas work when dealing with numinous powers. Here also there is a rich oral tradition and an entire literary form (*Jub.* 10:12–14; Josephus *Ant.* 8.2.5; 4Q 510, 511, etc.).

With a great deal of variety, most of which came from different understandings of the gods, this numinous way of understanding the world was true for all of Antiquity. While the belief in the old classical gods faded somewhat in the

Hellenistic age, while the early empirical medicine among the Greeks began to develop its own ways of understanding the phenomena of sickness, and while educated Stoics could integrate the standard understanding of the numinous into their worldview only with some difficulty, there was not (yet) a new and competing model for understanding the world. Instead of rejecting the prevailing understanding, people made compromises. If for a time attendance at the temples of the Capitolium was low (cf., e.g., Pliny, *Ep.* 10.96), mystery religions, divination, and magic blossomed all the more. The work of a physician and that of a miracle worker were not opposites; their activities overlapped. Even an educated writer such as Pliny the Elder includes reports about the miraculous (*Nat. Hist.* 7.13–14, 27ff., 64–65, 179). We should further note that the enlightened tendencies in Hellenistic-Roman culture had little impact on Early Judaism. If Israel's attitude toward the medical profession[93] is any indication, Hellenistic culture was more likely to be rejected than appropriated.

There were, of course, in late Antiquity expressions of skepticism such as Marcus Aurelius' "incredulity about the talk of miracle workers and magicians concerning conjuring, exorcisms, and such things" (*Med.* 1.1.6). Josephus, on the other hand, claims to have seen a Jewish exorcist successfully demonstrate his art to one of Marcus Aurelius' predecessors, Vespasian (*Ant.* 8.2.5). According to Tacitus (*Hist.* 4.81) Vespasian himself performed two miracles. In Antiquity one was always trying, often without success, to distinguish between fraud and the miraculous and between what was reported and what really happened.

Yet, precisely in the face of this ambivalence it is clear that not only Jesus and the primitive church (cf., e.g., Rom 15:18–19; 1 Cor 12:10), but also Early Judaism[94] and Hellenism as a whole[95] knew from their own experience the phenomenon of marvelous and spontaneous events. There were famous miracle workers before, contemporary with, and after Jesus—such people as Pythagoras, Menecrates, Apollonius of Tyana, the Samaritan Simon Magus, Honi the Circle-maker, or Hanina ben Dosa. Even those persons who no longer share Antiquity's numinous view of reality and who deny to it any truth at all must accept this historical judgment, regardless of how they might explain the phenomena.[96]

When we look at the activity of Jesus within this ancient understanding of the world and in light of the evidence for spontaneous and astonishing phenomena, the first thing to notice is that Jesus was the only one who placed the episodic and chance experience of miracles into a single, comprehensive context, viz., the Kingdom of God. His miracles themselves become experiences of the rule of the God, who is presently at work establishing his kingdom. One can see this understanding in such texts as Luke 10:18; 11:20; Matt 11:5–6; 13:16–17 (already discussed in §4.2.2). Alongside the parables and Jesus' table-fellowship, his miraculous deeds constitute a third area in which one can experience the Kingdom of God that is being realized.

Early Judaism also expected that God's final reign would be characterized by miracles that would enable people to participate in the eschatological community as whole persons (e.g., Isa 35:5–6; *Jub.* 23:26–30; *1 Enoch* 5:8–9; 4 Ezra 8:52–54; cf. §§4.1.3; 4.2.2),[97] since obviously there can be no life-inhibiting realities in the age of perfection (cf. Isa 33:24; Mic 4:7–8). The trials of the present age—a short life span, suffering and hardship, sickness and injustice—will be absent in the age to come, because Satan will be defeated and God's blessing and salvation will be immediately present (*Jub.* 23:11–31). In the days of Jesus the Essenes excluded all sorts of unclean and sick persons from their gathering, because they regarded such persons as smitten by God and because they believed that the angels of holiness were present in the gathering.

Jesus' understanding of miracles, according to which they are expressions of the Kingdom of God, is also missing in the post-Easter churches. Although miracles still happen (cf. Acts 5:12–16), they are expressions of the Spirit (Rom 15:19; 2 Cor 12:12; cf. Acts 13:9), and they take place *in the name of Jesus* (Acts 3:6) or as the result of prayer (Jas 5:14); they are no longer understood as acts of the eschatological Kingdom of God.

It is this understanding of the miracles as expressions of the immediacy of God's eschatological kingdom that explains why as a rule Jesus neither drives out spirits by means of rituals, formula and prayers, or magical names nor uses (secret) healing techniques and miracle-producing instruments. Since Jesus knows such phenomena all too well, it is surprising that they appear only marginally in the Jesus material (e.g., Mark 5:6–13; 7:33–34; 8:23–25). Jesus does not go around with a bag containing the literature and the paraphernalia needed to work miracles. Such things are ordinarily typical of miracle stories, and their absence undoubtedly reflects the activity of Jesus himself according to which he performs miracles *with the finger of God* (Luke 11:20; cf. §4.2.2) and thus understands his deeds as expressions of God's nearness and kingdom. For him an authoritative word was enough (Mark 1:25–26, 41–42; 7:29; 9:25–26; 10:52, etc.). Ordinarily in the world of Jesus a simple word was not enough.

It is equally clear that, since Jesus heals people in their corporeality as creatures, his healing activity presupposes a holistic view of human beings. God's eschatological kingship comes to expression not only verbally in the form of proclamation; it is a three-dimensional, concrete event. As there was a direct relation between Jesus' table-fellowship and the final banquet of salvation, so there must be a relationship between overcoming bodily imperfections in the present and the anticipated perfection of the final age. The Kingdom of God that is being realized in the activity of Jesus makes persons whole as a promise of the final perfection of the kingdom. This relationship between Now and Then is so dominant for Jesus that he does not speak of a general resurrection of the dead or of a general transformation of the living that will initiate the final perfection (Mark 12:18–27 parr. and Luke 14:14 are late texts). While it is true that such texts as Matt 8:11 par., 12:41 parr., and Mark 14:25 parr. show that Jesus could ignore the limitation of death in individual cases, we have no evidence in the earliest Jesus material of a general resurrection of the dead to judgment or to eternal life related to a new, resurrected body. One is well advised to regard all such statements in the gospels as the result of the experience of Easter (cf. 1 Thess 4:13–18; 1 Cor 15, etc.). For Jesus the Kingdom of God that is now being experienced and its final fulfillment are so closely related that the healing of the sick is an aspect of this kingdom that does not need to be supplemented by another act, such as a resurrection or a transformation.

We need to correct, therefore, the recent tendency to understand Jesus' miracle-working activity in an instrumental sense, viz., as a temporary means of declaring solidarity with and inclusiveness toward society's outcasts. According to this understanding, integration and solidarity serve as the bridges over which Jesus becomes relevant for today, but the ancient instrument for achieving integration and solidarity has been replaced by modern means. Against such a view we must insist that for Jesus sickness, suffering, and death (cf. Isa 35:10; 65; 19:23; Rev 20:14; 21:4, etc.) will no more be part of the Kingdom of God than will hunger and poverty (cf. §4.3.2). Because the goal of the kingdom is to restore human perfection, overcoming sickness and death is Jesus' primary concern as a miracle worker. This concern is so central in the sayings that we cited above, that surprisingly the themes of integration and solidarity nowhere appear.

We should not conclude, however, that the miracles of Jesus did not perform an inclusive function or that they were not intended to restore people to community. When traditionally various sicknesses were regarded as God's curse (Deut 28:59–61; Isa 1:5), persons so stricken automatically were excluded from the community. In the case of various diseases of the skin, the Law even required segregation (Lev 13:45–46). The Temple Scroll from Qumran describes the way this rule was likely enforced in Early Judaism (11Q xix 45.12–13; 48.14–15). The same was true of the blind (Deut 28:28–29; 1QSa ii 5–7). When Jesus affirmed the sick and freed them from their defect, this must have been understood as establishing community. We should understand Jesus' miracles, therefore, much as we understood his table-fellowship—as the eschatological restoration of life and as inclusion in the end-time community.

For understanding Jesus' worldview it is furthermore important to note that dualistic statements appear only in connection with the exorcisms. Frequently such dualistic texts as Luke 10:18 and 11:20 (cf. §4.2.2) have been used to justify the conclusion that Jesus worked from a totally dualistic worldview and that he understood his activity as a struggle against Satan for the purpose of establishing a monistic final state, or even of restoring the perfection of paradise (cf. *Barn.* 6:13), but the dualistic attitude is not found in the miracle tradition as a whole, since the material about Jesus' healing activity knows nothing about it (cf., e.g., Luke 7:22–23 parr.).

To get a clear overview of the situation we can begin with the three areas in Early Judaism that contain clearly dualistic ideas and that at the same time are represented by significant texts. They are *Jubilees*, 1QS iii 13–iv 26, and the *Testaments of the Twelve Patriarchs. Jubilees* represents a partial dualism, since only a limited number of evil spirits are permitted to tempt people temporarily (*Jub.* 10:5–11). These evil spirits are the dualistic opposites of the good angels. Both angelic armies directly or indirectly serve the divine administration of the world (*Jub.* 2:2; 7:27; 10:1–11; 15:30–32; 48:9, 12, etc.). The host of evil angels will be judged at the end of time, but until then they tempt human beings to sin (*Jub.* 1:20–21; 7:27; 12:20). They cause sickness, while the good angels provide instruments of healing (*Jub.* 10:11–12). 1QS 3–4 explains reality in terms of a predestined dualism. Before the creation of the world God created two opposing armies of angels, which carry out what has been predetermined for the human race. The issues about which they struggle are sin vs. good deeds, impurity vs. purity. There is no direct reference to sickness and health. The final destruction of the evil army is predestined. In the *Testaments of the Twelve Patriarchs* dualism appears in the service of parenesis. It sharpens the issue of life under the Law, and it warns against sin. Michael and his spirits and Beliar and his followers stand opposed to each other (*T. Lev.* 19:1; *T. Jud.* 20:1–5; *T. Dan* 6:1–5; *T. Ben.* 6:1–2). Beliar's army tempts people to do evil (*T. Dan* 6:1–2; *T. Benj.* 6:1–2), but does not cause sicknesses. The evil spirits are destined for final destruction (*T. Dan* 5:10–11).

A comparison of these ideas with the Jesus material quickly reveals agreement only in the destruction of the evil spirits at the final judgment. There is no reference in the early Jesus material to an army of good angels.[98] Most significant is that the demons do not tempt people. There is no discussion of good and evil deeds in terms of demonology. The human heart is tested, but not to determine whether it has been influenced by evil spirits. Nor is there any speculation about the origin of evil spirits—either in the context of the interpretation of Gen 6 or as preexistent beings. They simply appear as agents that are destructive of human health. The damage they do is eliminated by the Kingdom of God in the end-time, which is just beginning. We must conclude, therefore, that Jesus is not to be understood in the setting of Early Jewish dualistic thought. His view of reality, like that in Israel and in Early Judaism at large, is nondualistic; it is a monistic understanding of creation. Jesus shares with the people in general the belief in demons that cause sickness. They are a limited but disruptive threat to the goodness of creation—a threat that the eschatological Kingdom of God is beginning to eliminate.

Three synoptic texts might appear to contradict this description of Jesus: Matt 6:13b, Mark 8:33 parr., and Luke 10:18. In the first text, the long version of the third we-petition in the Lord's Prayer (Matt 6:13b: "but deliver us from the Evil One") certainly does not belong to the earliest form of the prayer. Although Matthew may have understood the expanded petition as a reference to the devil (cf. Matt 13:19, 38–39) rather than with a neuter meaning ("but deliver us from the condition of evil"), the core of the petition that Matthew and Luke have in common understands temptation as coming from God ("and lead us not into temptation") rather than from a satanic power. The rejection of Peter as Satan

(Mark 8:33 parr.) is stereotypical language for disqualifying false teachers (cf. Acts 13:10; 2 Cor 11:13–15) and, whether the statement is authentic or not, cannot be used to claim for Jesus a dualistic worldview. Finally, although the word about Satan's fall (Luke 10:18) makes no direct reference to demon-caused sicknesses, the context (Luke 10:17, 19) reveals that Luke understood it in those terms, and there is no reason to question Luke's understanding.

The references to the sicknesses are unfortunately superficial and imprecise, and are limited to popular descriptions. They have next to no clinical value, because they simply allude briefly to that part of the sickness that is visible and external, they never distinguish between symptoms and causes in the modern sense, and they never offer an even approximately adequate case history. Nor do we have anything like an overview of the general health of the population so that we might determine which diseases were typical then or which diseases do not appear in the synoptic healing stories. As a rule the synoptic references to sickness are general, summary statements from which one may not demand too much. We should be cautious, therefore, in trying to imagine how the spontaneous healings happened and which results might be explained, e.g., as due to the power of suggestion.

With a greater degree of certainty we can describe how Jesus viewed the relation between sickness and human failure—an issue that was always current in Antiquity. Sickness could be no exception in a world in which one's behavior and one's fate were so connected that people assumed that what happened was in part the result of one's own behavior. In John 9:2 the disciples ask Jesus, "Rabbi, who sinned, this man or his parents, that he was born blind?" The question reveals an attitude that was widespread in Early Judaism. In the *Testaments of the Twelve Patriarchs*, e.g., almost all of Jacob's sons find that their misdeeds lead to sickness (*T. Rub.* 1:6–8; *T. Sim.* 2:6–4:6; *T. Lev.* 6:7; *T. Jud.* 16:3; *T. Iss.* 2:1–2; *T. Zeb.* 5:1–5; *T. Dan* 5:7–8; *T. Gad* 5:9–11). *T. Gad* 5:9–11 even goes so far as to say that Gad's liver disease was caused by his mistreatment of Joseph with the explanation that "by what things a man transgresses, by the same also he is punished." While it may be that not all of Jesus' contemporaries would have accepted this specific cause-and-effect explanation of sickness, there can be no doubt that the more general form of describing sickness as the consequence of the sick person's behavior was customary. 4QOrNab 1:1ff. offers a typical and expressive example of the general attitude. According to this text, the king of Babylon, Nabonidus, suffered with a severe illness for seven years. After he prayed to the Most High and received forgiveness for his sins, he recovered "as a matter of course."

Did Jesus take a position on this understanding of sickness? Within the sayings that refer to miracles and within the miracle stories the evidence is overwhelmingly negative. To be sure, in the prophetic debate of Luke 13:1–5 (§3.2.2) he touches on the issue of explaining people's death by their previous behavior when he uses those who had died as the basis of a warning for the future. Jesus

announces a way of escaping the fate that threatens everyone. The escape lies in
the nature of the God who does not equate human behavior with a person's fate.
On the basis of his active graciousness God establishes his eschatological salvation in such a way that it alone determines human fate (cf. §3.2.6). Since God's
eschatological nearness is unlimited and eternal, the issue of behavior and its
consequences is superfluous and is no longer appropriate. For this reason Jesus
does not understand his miracles within the context of a system of behavior and
consequences; they are for him solely expressions of the Kingdom of God that is
there for human beings (Luke 12:8). It is no accident, therefore, that his orientation toward life is based not on human deeds and their results, but on the
Kingdom of God, which is moving in a new direction. Reality is to be explained
not in terms of what has caused the present world, but in terms of the future that
God is in the process of creating.

A few of the miracle stories (Matt 8:5–13 par.; Mark 7:24–30 parr.; Luke
17:11–19) as well as some of the sayings material on miracles (Luke 4:25–27;
10:13–14) deal with the same theme that we observed earlier (§3.2.4) in connection with the statements of judgment—Israel's relationship to the nations. The
miracles that Jesus performs on Gentiles are exceptions, but they present people
who, contrary to expectations, can serve as models for Israel.

This material is part of a larger theme that seems to characterize the miracles
of Jesus—the relationship between faith and unbelief. It is an issue that appears
differently in Early Christianity than it does in the surrounding world.[99] The
rejection of Jesus in his hometown of Nazareth (Mark 6:1–6a parr.) may well
have a historical basis. The claim is made that, because of the offense taken in
Jesus and because of the people's lack of faith, Jesus was unable to heal anyone.
The pre-Markan tradition may have looked something like the following:

1a *[6:1a] And he comes to his home town [6:1c, 2a].*
 b *And the many who heard him [6:2c] said,*
2a *"Whence has this one these things?*
 b *And what the wisdom that is given to him? [6:2–3]*
3a *Is not this one the carpenter,*
 b *the son of Mary?*
4a *And the brother of James, Judas, Joses, and Simon?*
 b *And are not his sisters here with us?"*
5a *And they took offense at him [6:4].*
 b *And he could not do any miracles there [6:5b], because of their*
    unbelief.

Our analysis of Mark 6:1–6a[100] begins with the recognition that the maximlike statement in 6:4 that a prophet has no honor in his own country, like Mark 2:17b (§4.3.2), is a
late addition to the text. It is the only statement of Jesus in the pericope, and its appeal to
general experience serves to soften the harsh reality of Jesus' rejection in Nazareth. Mark
6:5b also tempers the harshness by conceding that Jesus was indeed able to heal a few.

Mark introduces the pericope by connecting it to the previous unit and by including the disciples (cf. 3:13–19; 6:7–13), who play no further role in the narrative. He reworks the scene in v. 2 along the lines of 1:21–22. Mentioning the miracles reminds the readers of the miracles in Mark 1–5. The reference prepares the reader for v. 5a and reinforces the miracle theme that is so important for Mark. Mark probably also had a hand in the formation of v. 6a (cf. Mark 5:10). On the other hand, such terms as *hometown, the many* (elsewhere only in 9:26), *wisdom, carpenter* (i.e., an artisan in the building trade), and *unbelief* (elsewhere only in 9:24 as pre-Markan tradition) are non-Markan, although they are essential to the text. The names of Jesus' relatives are also definitely pre-Markan.

That Jesus is not the central figure makes the pericope unusual in Mark. The people of Nazareth dominate the scene, and Jesus is the subject of the action only in the two sentences that frame the unit. It is probably assumed that people knew where Jesus lived, so that Nazareth does not need to be mentioned by name. The crowd speaks as one person—a feature characteristic of popular stories and found often in the parables. Thus Mark 6:1–6a is one of the few synoptic units (for others cf. primarily the material about John the Baptist) in which Jesus is not the dominant actor.

The double sentence with which the pericope concludes summarizes why the tradition was formed and passed on. Taking offense at Jesus is an expression of the unbelief of the people of Nazareth who reject the message with which Jesus comes to them (cf. the double sentence at the beginning). By rejecting his message they reject him. Their attitude of unbelief keeps him from being able to heal the sick in that place. Rejecting Jesus and his message of the Kingdom of God makes it impossible, therefore, for him to act to bring healing to people (cf. Luke 4:25–27). Before Jesus can appear as an exorcist and worker of miracles, people must accept his proclamation and execution of the Kingdom of God that is at hand.

The miracles of the gospels offer numerous variations on this theme of belief as a precondition for the miracles of Jesus. The Fourth Gospel presents faith (with a christological cast) as the result of the miraculous deed (cf. John 2:11; 6:14; 20:30–31) and thus is similar to such Hellenistic authors as Plutarch and Strabo. The Synoptics, on the other hand, offer a sequence that is not typical in the ancient world. Before Jesus acts, he asks the two blind men in Matt 9:27–31: "Do you believe that I can do this?" (Cf. Acts 14:9.) Jesus helps the paralytic in Mark 2:1–5a, 11–12 parr., because he sees the faith of the people. After a moving conversation with the Gentile centurion, Jesus states that he has not found such faith in Israel and then proceeds to heal in such a way that the centurion receives what he had believed would happen (Matt 8:5–13 par.). The father of the epileptic son says to Jesus: "If you can do anything, have compassion on us and help us!" When Jesus answers that anything is possible to the one who believes, the father reacts: "I believe; help my unbelief!" (Mark 9:14–29 parr.). Miracle stories frequently conclude with the observation that faith was a factor in the miracle (Mark 5:34 parr.; 10:52 parr.; also Matt 15:28; Luke 17:19). According to these examples, therefore, unless there is a relationship of trust the possibility of a miracle does not even exist.

That this view approximates Jesus' own attitude is shown by the saying about the power of faith that has been preserved in two versions (Mark 11:23 = Matt 21:21; Luke 17:6 = Matt 17:20). Assuming that Matthew harmonized the two variants, we can focus on Mark 11:23 and Luke 17:6. In one case of hyperbole it is a mountain that is transported; in the other it is a mulberry tree. The motif of moving a mountain in the sense of doing the impossible is common (cf. 1 Cor 13:2; *b. Sanh.* 24a), while the motif of the tree is unusual. We should attribute the former, therefore, to the church and the latter to the earliest Jesus material. It reads:

> 1a *If you had faith as a mustard seed,*
> b   *you would say to this mulberry tree:*
> 2a *"Uproot yourself and (trans)plant yourself in the sea!"*
> b   *And it would obey you.*

Each of the evangelists has altered the form of the sayings source so much that a reconstruction is difficult, but the meaning is easily recognizable. The power of faith, comparable to the power of an especially small mustard seed, should be enough to transplant a tree with a large expanse of roots from the land to the sea.

In the same way that unbelief keeps the Kingdom of God (Luke 11:20) from bringing health to the sick in Nazareth (Mark 6:1–6 parr.), faith makes possible unimaginable changes, much as in the miracle stories trust in Jesus makes it possible to experience his miracles. Faith is the existential place that the Kingdom of God chooses as the basis for its work. Since it gives God room to work, it possesses unlimited and unexpected possibilities. Faith becomes the possibility of the God for whom everything is possible. For that reason "everything is possible to the one who believes" (Mark 9:23 parr.). Faith changes the world, because it counts on God's kingdom, which is changing the world.

It is thus clear why Jesus had to reject the demand for a clear sign before one would believe him. The tradition is preserved in both the sayings source (Matt 12:38–42 = Luke 11:29–32) and in Mark (Mark 8:11–13 parr.). Even the Fourth Gospel retains traces of the demand (John 2:18; 6:30–31) as well as of Jesus' special way of refusing the demand (2:19–25; 6:32–34). (Cf. also 1 Cor 1:22.) John 6:30–34 makes clear what lay behind the demand for a sign. It was the desire for an unmistakable, miraculous divine event that would give a positive answer to the legitimacy question before the speakers themselves acknowledge the other's claim to special divine authority. In this sense many contemporaries of Jesus looked for a repetition of the miracles of the Exodus (John 6:31; Josephus, *Ant.* 20.97–98, 188; *J.W.* 2.291ff.; 7.438ff.). Given the frequency with which the tradition appears in the gospels, it is highly probable that Jesus was confronted with that kind of demand for a sign, perhaps more than once. Inquiries and proofs of that nature were not unusual for prophetic claims (cf. 1 Sam 10:1–16; 2 Kgs 19:29–31).

It is difficult to reconstruct in any detail how Jesus answered the demand. It is probable, however, that the formal refusal of Mark 8:12 was less likely to be passed on than was the more content-rich answer of the sayings source with its reference to Jonah (Luke 11:29 par.). The Markan answer, therefore, will be a trimmed-down version. Matthew interprets the reference to Jonah in terms of Jesus' death and resurrection (Matt 12:40), the sayings source in terms of the imminent judgment of Jesus as the Son of Man (Luke 11:30b–32). Since both interpretations show the clear signs of editorial activity and breathe a post-Easter spirit, we can claim for Jesus only the core of Matt 12:39 = Luke 11:29 (to which Matt 16:4 is assimilated). According to this statement Jesus refuses to give to those contemporaries who reject him any legitimizing sign except the *sign of Jonah*. What does Jonah do? God sent him to Nineveh to preach repentance. The sign that Jesus offers his contemporaries, therefore, is his call to repentance (cf. §3.2). Instead of insisting on their demand for a sign, they should recognize their own lost condition. They can demand a sign and thus block their salvation, or they can accept Jesus' description of their condition and thus open themselves to the salvation that the Kingdom of God brings.

The accusation that Jesus performed exorcisms in secret league with the satanic power is an expression of unbelief—indeed, of hostility. While questioning his legitimacy may formally leave open the possibility of affirming him or rejecting him, this accusation is an open attempt to discredit him. The charge is often leveled against prophetic claims (Matt 11:18 par.; Josephus, *J.W.* 2.259; 6.303, 305; *Sib. Or.* 3.815, etc.). It also is used in the Gospel of John against Jesus (John 7:20; 8:48, 52; 10:20), and a form of it appears in the early Christian polemic against opponents and heretics (John 8:44; Acts 5:3; 13:10; 1 John 3:8; Rev 2:9, 13; 20:2, 10). Other miracle workers such as Apollonius of Tyana or Pythagoras also attracted the accusation in the form leveled against exorcists. Justin (*Dial.* 69:7) also reports that Jews rejected Jesus, because they suspected him of witchcraft. Given the evidence, it is historically plausible that Jesus' activity subjected him to similar charges.

Materials in the form of a defense against such charges—i.e., a direct counterpolemic—are included in Mark 3:20–35 and Matt 12:22–37. Among them are two traditions that probably are quite old: Matt 12:24, 25a, 27 = Luke 11:15, 17, 19 and Mark 3:24–26 parr. The first apophthegm reads:

1a   *And some (?) said:*
  b   *"By Beelzebul, the ruler of the demons, he expels the demons."*
2a   *And he . . . said to them: [Matt 12:25b, c = Luke 11:17–18]*
  b   *"If I expel demons by Beelzebul,*
  c   *by whom do your sons expel them?"*

The second saying has the following form:

1a Every kingdom that is divided against itself will become desolate.
* b And every house that is divided against itself cannot survive.*
2a If therefore Satan is divided against himself,
* b How can his kingdom survive?*

In 3:20–35 Mark structures a large scene that is framed by Jesus' rejection by his relatives (3:20–21) and by his statement about his new relatives (3:31–35). Mark connects the relatives' charge that Jesus is beside himself with the accusation of the scribes that he is possessed by Beelzebul and drives out demons with the prince of demons (Mark 3:22). The two charges receive a threefold answer in Mark 3:23–26, 27, 28–29.

Matthew and Luke have so much in common with each other and are so different from Mark that it is likely that they are dependent on the sayings source. An exorcism (Matt 12:22–23 = Luke 11:14) provides the setting for the charge that Jesus is in league with the devil (Matt 12:24 = Luke 11:15). As early as Q, Jesus' answer was composed from different materials. The first two parts respond directly to the accusation (Matt 12:25–26 = Luke 11:17–18; Matt 12:27 = Luke 11:19), while the two following units deal with the same theme but are no longer polemical (Matt 12:28 = Luke 11:20; Matt 12:29 = Luke 11:21–22). With Matt 12:30 = Luke 11:23 the composition of the sayings source concludes the section.

The sayings source begins with an early apophthegm, which has as its core the accusation (from whom?) that Jesus drives out demons by Beelzebul (Matt 12:24 par.) and Jesus' response (cf. formally Mark 3:4 parr.), which takes up the catchword *Beelzebul* (Matt 12:27 par.). Inserted between the charge and the response is the saying about Satan's kingdom (Matt 12:25b–26 par.), which puts the devil in a different light and which robs the response in Matt 12:27 of its effectiveness. In Mark's tradition there is no saying that corresponds to Matt 12:27, even though the different names for the devil are preserved in Mark 3:22 and 3:23–26. Mark also created the scene in 3:20–21 himself, based on 3:31 and 6:31, and he harmonized the accusations of Mark 3:21b and 22a. It was probably Q who first used the nonspecific miracle story of Matt 12:22–23 par. to provide the setting for the sayings. Matt 9:34 is derived from the accusation of Matt 12:24.

Mark 3:23–26 and Matt 12:25–26 par. are witnesses of the same tradition. Mark was more aggressive in making additions at the beginning and at the end. Luke likely omitted material in the middle, while Matthew expanded the reference to the household to include the sequence kingdom, city, house = family.

Matt 12:28 = Luke 11:20 is an independent saying that we have already discussed in §4.2.2. In Q, Matt 12:29 par. serves as a commentary on 12:28, while in Mark 3:27 it is an independent tradition. This parabolic word about breaking into the house of a man who knows how to protect himself is a general illustration, but in the present form it is understood allegorically and christologically. Jesus has already bound Satan, and he now plunders the people who belong to Satan. Since the saying stands in tension with Luke 10:18 (§4.2.2), according to which it is God who deposes Satan, we should attribute it to the church rather than to Jesus.

Both traditional units presuppose that Jesus and his opponents were in agreement that they both could perform exorcisms. Mark 9:38–41 also implies that Jesus conceded as much for others. When differing camps engage in the same activity, they are going to compete (cf. Acts 8:4–13). One way of dealing with the competition is to deny that the opponent is on the good side—in short, to say that he is a seducer, a magician, that he has made a pact with the devil, etc. The result is the typical situation captured by Matt 12:24, 25, 27 par. There is no evidence for the name Beelzebul elsewhere in Early Judaism, and it was probably a popular expression in the area of Galilee in which Jesus performed his exorcisms.[101] Since it appears only one other place in Matthew's special material (Matt 10:25), it is probable that the accusation of Matt 12:24 par. in fact was made of Jesus (similar to Matt 11:19 par.). Jesus deflects the charge with a question that makes use of the opponents' language. Since the opponents do not accuse themselves of having made a pact with the devil, but claim that they derive the power to cast out demons from God, like it or not they must concede the same for Jesus.

The saying about the kingdom of Satan clearly presupposes an attack from Jesus' opponents, especially since it ends with a question that is a countercharge. With the saying, Jesus establishes both in vocabulary and in substance the connection between Satan and the demons that is suggested in Luke 10:18 and 11:20 (§4.2.2). Since he formulates the saying with his own words, it is difficult to recognize how (in contrast to Matt 12:27) the opponents formulated their criticism. Their attack is simply implied, and we must read between the lines to discover its substance. A good beginning point in the search is the word that the sayings source includes in the same context, viz., Luke 11:20 par.: "If it is by the finger of God that I cast out demons, then the Kingdom of God has come to you" (§4.2.2). When Jesus identified his activity as an exorcist with the Kingdom of God, the opponents appear to have affirmed the opposite: It was the kingdom of Satan. One could then use this associative distortion against Jesus. If Jesus claims to establish the eschatological Kingdom of God, instead of performing only a few miracles, must he not cure all sickness, since God's kingdom means total perfection? Does not Jesus himself reveal that he is only too aware of the problem posed by his small and diffuse beginning (cf. Mark 4:2–8, 26–29, 30–32 in §4.2.2)? Could he really be surprised when his opponents said to him that they were not convinced that his miracles were the beginning of God's final victory— when, indeed, they claimed that those miracles were a devil's trick (cf. the offense motif in Matt 11:6 par.)? If this is the case, then the charge against Jesus was that he was the devil's impostor (cf. 2 Cor 11:13–15)—that his exorcisms were a satanic deception in which the devil permitted Jesus to appear to defeat him in a few select instances. Once convinced, the people then would be easier targets for Satan, and Jesus would secure not Satan's defeat, but his mastery.

If we can assume that such a charge has been made against Jesus, his answer becomes more understandable. His polemical response begins with what in those days was generally understood: Harmony is the best guarantee for the continued existence and the prosperity of any community. Discord, on the other hand, is toxic for every social structure and leads eventually to its death. Jesus builds his argument on this generally accepted insight. He reasons that even if his opponents were right, that would mean that Satan's kingdom was at an end, since a divided kingdom is for all practical purposes already a destroyed kingdom. The opponents' attack fails, therefore, because of its own inner weakness. They are unable to discredit Jesus by appealing to the offense of his claim to represent the Kingdom of God. Their charge against him simply cannot invalidate his own explanation of his exorcisms.

The New Testament miracle tradition consistently presents Jesus as a miracle worker, while for the most part the disciples either appear as statistics or are missing altogether. Still, Mark 9:14–29 parr. demonstrates that later Christian storytellers had no problem assuming that people expected the disciples to be able to work miracles. Mark 3:15; 6:7 parr. and Matt 10:8 par. similarly report that Jesus himself authorized the disciples to teach and to heal. Could the portrayal of Jesus as almost the sole worker of miracles not reflect more a christological bias than a historical reality? If Jesus affirms the activity of an outside exorcist, would he not also encourage the same kind of activity among the disciples (Mark 9:38–39 = Luke 9:49–50)? Our evidence does not permit a certain conclusion one way or the other, but it is at least reasonable to leave open the question whether the disciples might also have worked miracles.

4.4 JESUS AS MEDIATOR OF SALVATION AND ESCHATOLOGICAL PROPHET OF THE KINGDOM OF GOD

4.4.1 Jesus and the Expected Messiah ben David

Becker, Joach. *Messianic Expectation in the Old Testament*. Philadelphia: Fortress, 1980.

Berger, K. "Zum Problem der Messianität Jesu," *ZThK* 71 (1974) 1–30.

———. "Die königlichen Messiastraditionen des Neuen Testaments," *NTS* 20 (1973/74) 1–44.

———. "Zum traditionsgeschichtlichen Hintergrund christologischer Hoheitstitel," *NTS* 17 (1970/71) 391–425.

Charlesworth, J. H. "The Concept of the Messiah in the Pseudepigrapha," *ANRW*. Berlin/New York: de Gruyter, 1982, II 19.1, 188–218.

Collins, J. J. *The Scepter and the Star: The Messiahs of the Dead Sea Scrolls and Other Ancient Literature*. New York: Doubleday, 1995.

Dahl, N. A. "Messianic Ideas and the Crucifixion of Jesus," in: *Messiah*. J. H. Charlesworth, ed., 365–81.

Greschat, H.-J., et al. *Jesus—Messias? Heilserwartungen bei Juden und Christen*. Regensburg: Pustet, 1982.

Grundmann, W., F. Hesse, A. S. van der Woude, and M. de Jonge. "chrio, etc." *TDNT* 9 (1974) 493–580.

Horsley, R. A. "'Messianic' Figures and Movements in First-Century Palestine," in: *Messiah*. J. H. Charlesworth, ed., 276–95.

Horsley, R. A., and J. S. Hanson. *Bandits, Prophets, and Messiahs: Popular Movements at the Time of Jesus*. Minneapolis: Winston, 1985.

Jonge, M. de. *Jewish Eschatology, Early Christian Christology and the Testaments of the Twelve Patriarchs*. New York: Brill, 1991.

Karrer, M. *Der Gesalbte*. FRLANT 151. Göttingen: Vandenhoeck & Ruprecht, 1991.

Kellermann, U. "Die politische Messiashoffnung zwischen den Testamenten," *PTh* 56 (1967) 362–77, 426–48.

Klausner, J. *The Messianic Idea in Israel from Its Beginning to the Completion of the Mishnah*. New York: Macmillan, 1955.

Koch, K. "Messias und Menschensohn," *JBTh* 8 (1993) 73–102.

Landmann, L. (ed.) *Messianism in the Talmudic Era*. New York: Ktav, 1979.

Levey, S. H. *The Messiah: An Aramaic Interpretation*. Cincinnati: Hebrew Union College Jewish Institute of Religion, 1974.

Lichtenberger, H. "Messianische Erwartungen und messianische Gestalten in der Zeit des Zweiten Temples," in: *Messias-Vorstellungen bei Juden und Christen*. E. Stegemann, ed. Stuttgart: Kohlhammer, 1993, 9–20.

Mendels, M. "Pseudo-Philo's Biblical Antiquities," in: *Messiah*. J. H. Charlesworth, ed., 261–75.

Müller, U. B. *Messias und Menschensohn in jüdischen Apokalypsen und in der Offenbarung des Johannes*. StNT 6. Gütersloh: Mohn, 1972.

Oegema, G. S. *Der Gesalbte und sein Volk*. SIDL 2. Göttingen: Vandenhoeck & Ruprecht, 1994.

Schäfer, P. *Der Bar Kokhba-Aufstand*. TSAJ 1. Tübingen: J.C.B. Mohr (Paul Siebeck), 1981, 51–77.

Schunk, K.-D. "Die Attribute des eschatologischen Messias," *ThLZ* 111 (1986) 641–52.

Schürer, E. *History*, II 488–554.

Seebass, H. *Herrscherverheißungen im Alten Testament*. Bthst 19. Neukirchen-Vluyn: Neukirchener Verlag, 1992.

Starcky, J. "Les quatre étapes du messianisme a Qumran," *RB* 70 (1963) 481–505.

Stuhlmacher, P. "Der messianische Gottesknecht," *JBTh* 8 (1993) 131–54.

Waschke, E.-J. "Die Frage nach dem Messias im Alten Testament," *ThLZ* 113 (1988) 321–32.

Woude, A. S. van der. *Die messianischen Vorstellungen der Gemeinde von Qumran*. SSN 3. Assen: Van Gorcum, 1957.

Zeller, D. "Zur Transformation des Christos bei Paulus," *JBTh* 8 (1993) 155–67.

Zobel, M. *Gottes Gesalbter: Der Messias und die messianische Zeit in Talmud und Midrasch*. Berlin: Schock. Jüdischer Buchverlag, 1938.

All of the gospels, but especially Matthew, claimed that as David's descendant Jesus was the promised Messiah (for which *Christos* is the Greek form; the term means *the Anointed One*). This understanding regards the Old Testament as a book of christological promises from prophets, all of whom, from David's contemporary Nathan to the late, postexilic prophets, predict the coming Messiah. A study of the postcanonical Jewish and rabbinic literature during the nineteenth and twentieth centuries has expanded this position until it was assumed that a broad stream of Israelite-Jewish hope had at one time been focused on the Davidic Messiah. The expectation that an anointed one from the line of David would come at the end of time was not only regarded as the personified center of Jewish hope; it also was understood to be part of Jesus' self-understanding and the post-Easter christological efforts. It followed then almost by necessity that at the very least Jesus' contemporaries expected him to be the promised Messiah ben David. Indeed, for many people it was this popular expectation that caused, perhaps even forced, Jesus to regard himself as the Messiah. At the very least people claimed that the Jewish-Christian church was justified in using this conceptual world of the Davidic messiahship to formulate their confession of Jesus as the Messiah who had come. The modern Jewish-Christian conversation has also in part accepted as its central issue the alternative between the Christian confession of the Messiah who has already come or the Jewish hope for a Messiah who is yet to come.

Yet, this concept, which is so unified and because of its simplicity so manageable, is in need of serious correction. Indeed, its very foundations are flawed. For this reason we must survey anew the entire terrain for a discussion of Early Jewish messianic expectation. Even the Old Testament promises of a ruler are a complex set of sayings.[102] In no way do they constitute a continuous sequence of promises pointing toward a new Davidic ruler in a quasi-eschatological time, and they certainly were not all understood that way at all times in Early and Rabbinic Judaism. Furthermore, these texts do not present either the only or even the decisive center of postexilic expectation. Indeed, the dominant expressions of hope are those which do not even use messianic figures to make concrete their expectations for the future. Long before the time of Early Judaism the view was widespread in postexilic Judaism that God himself would accept his chosen people without a mediating figure.

In the same way, a highly complex picture emerges in Early Judaism. With the Maccabean Revolt a new phase of eschatological hope began in many circles (e.g., Daniel and 1QM; 1 Macc offers a different view). Soon after the Maccabean victory new groups emerged in Early Judaism, but these groups did not necessarily supplant the circles that had held the older views. This new diversity almost of necessity led to different formulations of eschatological hope. Many of these new witnesses of Early Jewish hope continued to get along without a personal eschatological mediator of salvation and to let God alone be responsible for saving his people (cf., e.g., 1QM; *Jub.*; 1 Macc; 2 Macc; *1. Enoch* 1–5; 93:3–10 + 91:12–17; 92–104; 1QH iii 19ff.; *As. Mos.*; *Sib. Or.* 4.161–90; Wis). It is not at all surprising that among them were those projections of the future that spoke of God's eschatological kingdom (cf. §4.1), since the originator of the hope for a final demonstration of God's power as king, Deutero-Isaiah (§4.1.3), nowhere speaks of a special mediator of salvation alongside God. His decision in this regard had long-term effects. One was much more likely to come across descriptions of the content of salvation (e.g., restoration of God's people or an end-time characterized by the abundance of paradise) than end-time figures with whom the coming salvation was identified. It was not the case, therefore, that Jesus and his Galilean followers were under some sort of historical compulsion to think of his activity in messianic terms. That historical pressure is a construct that the first Christian generations played a major role in creating. Their interpretation of the person of Jesus in terms of a personalized christology led them to read the hope of the Old Testament and of Early Judaism in personal, individualized terms. The desire to identify God's activity with the fate of Jesus—a desire born of the Easter experience—oversimplified, therefore, a complex historical process.

Yet, our problem is posed not simply by the diversity in Early Jewish eschatology, which in contrast to Christianity did not necessarily look for a particular end-time person. We must recognize the diversity and independence even of those statements in which the hope of Early Judaism was personalized and not jump to premature, oversimplified conclusions. There simply was no such thing as *the* Early Jewish messianic hope, which may have been expressed here or there in different ways. There were competing expectations, each of which was conceptually independent. There probably were also circles in which the different concepts were preserved and which promoted their preferred options without necessarily making exclusive claims. Within this situation the groups sometimes influenced each other; sometimes they rejected one another's views. We must furthermore recognize that during the entire time span that we identify with Early Judaism not all of the possibilities were at the same time and always present. All indications speak for this kind of complexity, even though we can no longer trace the history in any detail. The texts of Qumran especially illustrate this process. As witnesses of one particular group, they present their own unique individualized hope as opposed to other Early Jewish groups. At the same time they reveal that within the approximately two-hundred-and-twenty-year history of this group new eschatological images could develop while others were suppressed.[103]

Now in discussing the many ways Early Judaism could make concrete its hope, it is important to remember the role and the importance of Israel's scriptures in this period—in this case especially of the Torah, the Prophets, and the Psalter. It was the fundamental conviction of Early Judaism that God's will was fixed in these scriptures. It is often forgotten that this will did not only deal with what human beings were required to do; there was widespread agreement that God's will was not limited to ethics. It encompassed the entire world and its history. It also included God's goal of salvation for Israel and the human race. It only made sense, therefore, to inquire of the holy scriptures what they had to say about the future and not simply to determine how one should observe God's commandments in the conduct of one's life. Thus the hermeneutic principle developed that what the prophets had to say referred not to their own time, but to the end-time of the future. Those persons who believed that they were living in or near this end-time were able to find that the events of their own time were not only predicted; what is even more important is that they were interpreted (an example is 1QpHab).

Against this background the diversity of hopes for the future achieved not only an abundance of possibilities; it also was concentrated in a specific direction. People could not simply assert what the future would be like; they had to take into consideration the prophetic dimension of the scriptures and to prove that their statements were scriptural. Statements about the future were thus based on the scripture, and the scripture becomes the prophetic voice that through exegesis opens the future.

As a matter of course, the statements about the future that were focused on a person were part of the Early Jewish consensus. Of the numerous persons who were expected to play a role in the events at the end of time none was a new creation. All of them came out of an exegesis of the scriptures. For all of them, therefore, one can cite the core text(s) and further scriptural proof texts that legitimized their claims. *Ps. Sol.* 17, e.g., bases its description of the king from the line of David on the word of Nathan in 2 Sam 7 (cf. also 4QFlor). Nor can there be any doubt that the figure of the Son of Man in *1 Enoch* 37–71 is a direct interpretation of Dan 7:9–10, 13–14 (cf. esp. *1 Enoch* 46:1–2; 47:7; 69:27). Qumran's expectation of two messiahs claimed Zech 4:14 for its authority. CD 7:18–19 refers to the One Who Searches the Law as the *Star out of Jacob* of Num 24:17. The concept of an eschatological Melchizedek in 11Q 13 includes Gen 14 in the future hope. Since one needed more than one witness to establish the truth, it was important to be able to cite other texts. Of course, the more certain and clear the witnesses, the better was their position among the competing views of the future. The circles responsible for the description of the royal figure in *Ps. Sol.* 17 also used at the very least Ps 2 (cf. *Ps. Sol.* 17:22–24), Isa 11:2–5 (cf. *Ps. Sol.* 17:29, 32–37), Isa 42:4 (cf. *Ps. Sol.* 17:37), and, of course, several of the main texts from the Zion tradition. The parabolic discourses of *1 Enoch* made use of Isa 11:2–9 (cf. *1 Enoch* 49:3–4; 62) and Isa 42:6; 49:6 (*1 Enoch* 48:4). Nor should we forget Ps 110:1, 5–6 (*1 Enoch* 61:8; 62:2). In both cases we can see that several of these proof texts were claimed for different concepts. Isa 11 was claimed for the Davidic Messiah (cf., e.g., *Ps. Sol.* 17:29ff.; 1QSb ii 22ff.; *T. Jud.* 24:5–6; 4QpIsa 11ff.; *Sib. Or.* 3.767ff.) and for the Son of Man (cf. *1 Enoch* 49:1ff.). Num 24:17 was claimed for the royal Messiah (cf., e.g., 1QSb ii 22ff.; *T. Jud.* 24:5–6; *Sib. Or.* 3.49) and the One Who Searches the Law (cf. 4Q 174). Isa 42:6; 49:6 was claimed for the Davidic Messiah (cf. *T. Jud.* 24:6), the eschatological high priest (*T. Lev.* 18:9), and the Son of Man (*1 Enoch* 48:4). All of these saving figures were to help realize Israel's *shalom*. Since the Torah, e.g., would still be valid in the final salvation, *Ps. Sol.* 17 gave the decisive responsibility for the Torah to the Messiah (17:26–29, 37–40, 43). In 4Q 174 it is the One Who Searches the Law who has this responsibility. Since there were limits to the way these concepts could be varied, along with the multiple use of scriptural texts it was always possible that the eschatological figures might assume one another's functions or that the functions of one person might be distributed to several of them.

The phenomenon that most notably set Early Judaism apart from Primitive Christianity may well have been the fact that in Judaism one could not only describe a single figure of salvation at the end of time—perhaps the eschatological king of *Ps. Sol.* 17 or the Son of Man–Judge of the World of *1 Enoch* 37–71; one also had room for several end-time persons in the same concept of the future. The Qumran texts speak of two eschatological anointed figures—one a high priest, the other a king (e.g., 1QS ix 10–11; CD 20:1)—and along with them (indeed, in 1QS ix 10 intentionally given the prominent position) an eschatological prophet who is described in terms of Deut 18:15 (cf. 4Q 175), i.e., as a prophet like Moses. It was Primitive Christianity's exclusive concentration on Christ that first reduced this tradition to a single person, although admittedly John the Baptist (§3.1.4) and Jesus (§4.4.2) in their inner-Jewish orientation (along with others in Early Judaism) had spoken of only of one figure.

Given what we have seen in this brief outline, we should not only make an occasional comparison with Primitive Christianity; we must also take another look at the way the Old Testament prophets expressed their hopes for God's future rule. Such a comparison makes it clear that during the Hasmonean period the cards for such end-time figures of salvation were reshuffled. One indication of such a change is the increase in the number of potential figures that could be used to describe the future. New central concepts appear (such as *Messiah*), about which we will speak below. Another important indication is that, while the prophetic promises of God's rule are limited to individual traditions, now all of the scriptures are used to describe the coming figures who will fulfill Israel's hopes. The pool of potential texts, in other words, has changed. 2 Sam 7, e.g., plays for all practical purposes no role in the four major traditions about a coming ruler: Isa 9; 11; Mic 5; Zech 9:9–10. Now, however, it becomes the central text for *Ps. Sol.* 17. Num 24:17—to offer a second example—also is given its (diverse) messianic dignity. We could multiply such examples, but perhaps these observations will suffice to demonstrate that the previous eschatological bearers of salvation underwent a transformation in the Hasmonean period. It appears then that after the first revolt against Rome there was a period of harmonization in which this diversity was restrained. In any case, the period from the Hasmoneans to the first revolt is characterized by a great deal of variety, and it was under these conditions that Jesus appeared and the early church formed its first christological concepts.

It would be helpful if we could attribute each of these Early Jewish views to a definite group of that period. As we have already indicated, however, such an effort creates problems. The joint appearance of a priestly and a royal Messiah is, of course, clearly Essene, and it fits well with the priestly orientation of the Qumran community. Where, however, do *T. Lev.* 18 and *T. Jud.* 24 belong? *Ps. Sol.* 17 may well represent Pharisaic views. Are we then justified in saying that the messianic hope of the Pharisees was tied to the figure of a Davidic Messiah? A text such as *Sib. Or.* 3.49, 652ff. should caution us against limiting the view to the Pharisees. It may well be that the Son of Man of the parabolic discourses of *1 Enoch* belonged to an apocalyptic circle gathered around the (fictional) teacher

Enoch. Where then did John the Baptist get this hope (§3.1.4)? Particular eschatological views may have been typical for a group in the sense that most of its
members held them and that for a time at least they represented the group's
views, but it is unlikely that any group ever had exclusive claims to them. The
sacred scriptures to which all end-time figures had to appeal belonged, indeed, to
everyone. As a matter of principle it was impossible, therefore, for the members
of any given group to claim exclusive ownership of their future hopes.

This sketch of the Early Jewish views from the perspective of their relationship to the scriptures can now serve as the basis for describing the differences
among the various eschatological figures. Within this context we can then examine the special question about which of these figures are to be regarded as
messianic, i.e., as *anointed*, and what such a designation even means. While
anointing is one good way of emphasizing the importance of an eschatological
figure, the designation is not determinative, because the authority of the various
figures depends primarily on their grounding in the scriptures.

The catchword *Messiah* first appears as a substantive to designate an eschatological figure in *Ps. Sol.* 17:32; 18:1, 5, 7. It appears nowhere, therefore, in
the Old Testament. The eschatological figures of Early Judaism that might (occasionally, but not necessarily always) be designated in some form as anointed[104]
were the royal ruler, the Son of Man, the eschatological high priest, and a
prophetic figure. The anointing attributed to these figures emphasized that they
were commissioned and empowered by God himself. Nowhere is there a narrative description of an act of anointing.[105] The figures are not anointed with oil in
a sacred act; they appear as persons who have always been anointed. The concept, thus robbed of its concrete setting, functions more to underscore that one
has been authorized and equipped by God and that one is, therefore, set apart
from other humans. Since the term is used somewhat as an abstraction and can
appear in statements about kingship, the priesthood, prophecy, and the figure of
the Son of Man, we should give primary importance to the other characteristics
of these figures. There is no such thing as *the Anointed One*. There are different
eschatological expectations focused on a king, a high priest, etc., who sometimes,
but not necessarily always and everywhere, can be designated as anointed ones. It
is this understanding alone that takes into account the well-known quality of
Israelite-Jewish thought, viz., that one comprehended the world not with abstract
ideas, but with concrete and visible images (§4.1.1). It also explains why the
authors of Early Judaism in describing these figures consistently made use of Old
Testament texts that did not speak directly of a Messiah.

When we examine the contents of the individual eschatologies, the image of a
royal figure (along with the Son of Man) becomes especially important for the
Jesus material. Its oldest and most extensive treatment is given in *Ps. Sol.* 17 (and
18). The psalm (which certainly is not a unity) presupposes that God is the
supreme king (*Ps. Sol.* 17:1–3, 34, 45–46), but within that context it unfolds the
promise of an anointed (17:32) king (17:21, 32, 42) chosen by God (17:42),

based on Nathan's promise to David (17:4–5; 2 Sam 7). Nathan's promise appears in a prominent position early in the psalm in order to expose and criticize the Hasmonean dynasty (*Ps. Sol.* 17:6, 20).[106] Other texts cited in support of this eschatological David are Ps 2 (*Ps. Sol.* 17:22–24, 30) and Isa 11 (*Ps. Sol.* 17:37). Here and in all other texts he is always a human being with a human genealogy (cf. Justin, *Dial.* 67:2), and he is here equipped with a special blessing of the Lord, viz., with God's holy spirit, with understanding, with strength, and with righteousness (17:37–38). He is thus able to defeat Israel's foreign rulers simply with the *word of his mouth* and to purify Jerusalem from all inner uncleanness (17:22–25, 35). His rule will enable the twelve tribes to live in Israel once again in obedience to the Law and in righteousness (17:26–28, 32–33), so that Israel will be made whole again. The nations will become Israel's vassals and will deliver tribute to Jerusalem (17:30–31). Thus Israel's present servitude to a foreign power will be reversed and will become mastery over the nations. These ideas are all variations from the repertoire of motifs offered by the hope for salvation within history as it was represented by the Zion tradition (§4.1.4). This same king, who is always characterized as a strong figure (never weak, and certainly not a suffering figure), also appears in 1QSa ii 11–12; 1QSb v 20ff., and other Essene texts. It is noteworthy that the Essenes reworked the War Scroll to include an eschatological figure (4Q 285 6:1–10; 7:1–5).[107] Other texts that speak of this Davidic king are Sir 51:12a–o; *Sib. Or.* 3.49,[108] 652–62; Philo, *Praem.* 95; and Benediction Fourteen of the Eighteen Benedictions.[109]

To the degree that this prayer was intended to forge a consensus between the two rebellions against Rome, the petition reveals that people regarded the appearance of a Messiah ben David as something that was distinctly possible. During this period, therefore, such a hope probably characterized a cross section of the population. If the *Targum of Jonathan* on the Prophets dates from the first century, we can include it among the witnesses for the Davidic Messiah, which were important around the time of Jesus (§4.1.4). Paul, the former Pharisee, also reveals indirectly that he is familiar with this hope, since he applies it to Jesus Christ.[110] In fact, it is part of the Son-of-God formula that he takes over in Rom 1:3b–4. Regardless of how we might reconstruct the formula, it is so filled with the motifs that one finds in Pss 2; 110; Isa 11:2; *Ps. Sol.* 17:37 that Paul is clearly the recipient of a Christianized form of the Early Jewish hope for an eschatological Davidic ruler. That Paul himself also can evoke such connotations is clear from Rom 15:7–12, where he interprets the Christ title with, among other things, Isa 11:10, and from Rom 9:5, 33; 11:26, where he makes use of the Zion tradition to outline the figure of Christ.

In this context we must also mention Bar Cochba, whom Rabbi Akiba in the second revolt against Rome declared to be the royal Messiah.[111] Since, however, he was not descended from David, his messiahship was supported not with the promise to David in 2 Sam 7, but with Num 24:17, a text that already had a long history as a messianic text ("A star shall come out of Jacob, and a scepter shall rise out of Israel").[112] It appears that Bar Cochba is the exception rather than the rule. Prior to the second revolt there were no other references to a non-Davidic, anointed ruler.[113] Indeed, in the entire period between the Maccabees and Bar Cochba messianic claims were made for no living person. The messianic hope is focused on the future.

That Bar Cochba was unique is clear, especially when we recognize that the various leaders of revolutionary groups prior to 70 CE were not messianic pretenders, as is sometimes claimed,[114] even though they claimed royal status. It is one thing to want to be a king, quite another to claim to be the eschatological Anointed One. Josephus, who is the only source for the appearance of these revolutionaries between the death of Herod and the first open revolt against Rome, speaks exclusively of royal claims that were raised in opposition to the Roman occupation (*J.W.* 2.56–58; 4.510, 573ff. and the parallel texts in *Ant.*). That Josephus intentionally repressed the messianic ambitions of the revolutionaries is an argument, but not evidence. Josephus says in *Ant.* 17.10.8 that "Judea was a robbers' hideout. And wherever a group of insurgents gathered, they immediately chose a king." In this case at least he was not thinking in messianic terms, since one does not elect a Messiah. The Messiah is sent by God or at the very least summoned forth by a prophet or by someone knowledgeable in the scriptures. At the most one might perhaps attribute a messianic context to Menahem, since he entered Jerusalem *like a king* (*J.W.* 2.434, 442), but what else would one expect from someone who lays claim to royal honors when he appears in the city that is the traditional seat of the king? If he does not enter as a king, no one is going to take his claims seriously. It makes more sense to understand these *kings* in Maccabean-Hasmonean rather than in messianic terms. Philo also designates those persons kings who usurp power by force of arms (*Virt.* 218; *Praem.* 53). The attempt to understand these persons as messianic figures must offer some unmistakable clues from the texts to support the claim, and that evidence simply does not exist.

The Son-of-David issue leads to another kind of problem, since David's son Solomon was the center of reflection on how to achieve a successful life. Early Judaism regarded Solomon as especially gifted with wisdom (e.g., Wis 7–8), which included, among other things, the ability to use healing plants and to drive out demons (Wis 7:10–11, 20; 11Q xi 1; *Bib. Ant.* 60:3; Josephus *Ant.* 8.45ff.). Thus in Wis 6:1, 4, 9 Solomon calls on the other kings, who themselves serve God's kingdom, to seek this wisdom as he has done, so that they might rule justly. Indeed, in Wis 7:27 Solomon looks beyond his own life when he asserts that in every generation wisdom seeks friends of God and prophets in order to dwell in them and to effect in them the gifts of wisdom. It is in this sense—and not in messianic terms—that Jesus is referred to as David's son in the miracle stories (cf. §4.3.3). He is praised, in other words, as the descendant of the wise Solomon (Mark 10:47–48 parr.; Matt 9:27; 15:22). The royal ruler of *Ps. Sol.* 17 never performs miracles in Early Judaism.

When we turn our attention from the issue of the expected anointed king to the other anointed figures, of greatest importance is the hope for a Son of Man. We will devote a separate section to the Son of Man in §4.4.2; here we are interested only in the two sources that refer to him as anointed—*1 Enoch* 48:10 and 52:4. Neither of them is without problems: 52:4 interrupts the context, while the reference to the Anointed One in 48:10 appears suddenly; indeed, in terms of its meaning it is superfluous. There is no reason to assume that they are Christian interpolations. The clear individual sense of 52:4 should be a reason not to understand the similar text of 48:10 collectively[115]—i.e., as a collective reference to righteous persons, who elsewhere in *1 Enoch* 47–48 are always described with a plural formulation. Since in other instances the parabolic addresses also are not from one hand, we should probably understand 48:10 and 52:4 as Jewish additions to the text, which have the same meaning. In that case the Son of Man would not have been understood in the original parabolic discourses as an anointed figure, just as we find no reference to anointing in Dan 7, the literary model for the parabolic addresses. As the work passed through Jewish hands, however, this oversight was corrected, since people were of the fundamental conviction that eschatological figures of high position must be especially equipped by God. This conviction alone justifies the editorial addition, since there is nothing in the text that would indicate that it was contaminated with ideas about the royal figure of *Ps. Sol.* 17.

The primary witness for the anointing of high priests is the Priestly document of the Pentateuch (Lev 4:3, 5, 16; 6:15, etc.). It appears to have been practiced into the Seleucid period,[116] unlike the anointing of kings, which had been abandoned much earlier. In any case, the Hasmoneans anointed neither the king nor the high priest. It is probable, however, that the Hasmonean, Hyrcanus I (135–104 BCE), laid claim to the offices of king, high priest, and prophet.[117] By contrast, the Essenes, whose beliefs about the future were formed in this period, intentionally separated the three offices, and they secured the authority of the eschatological figures with anointing (1QS ix 10–11; CD 20:1). They claimed that their beliefs were faithful to the Bible and at the same time critical of the present age. They had no influence on the synoptic tradition.

The function of a prophet was occasionally, if not often, defined by anointing (1 Kgs 19:16; Isa 61:1–2). On only one occasion in Early Judaism, however, were eschatological prophets identified as anointed—viz., in the Melchizedek tradition in 11Q xiii, which makes use of Isa 61:1–2. There is no reference to an anointed prophet in the synoptic material.

Given this survey of Early Jewish views, we are ready to ask whether Jesus understood himself (or whether others understood him) as an eschatological messianic figure, and, if so, what connotations the term had. The discussion centers on three Markan pericopes—Peter's confession (Mark 8:27–33 parr.), the controversy about the Son of David (Mark 12:35–37 parr.), and Jesus's confession before the Sanhedrin (Mark 14:60–64 parr.).

Peter's confession is a three-part unit (8:27–28, 29–30, 31–33) of atypical form with which Mark begins the second part of the Galilean ministry of Jesus. It was also Mark who with artistic creativity composed the unit from different kinds of material. The answer of the disciples in v. 28 had appeared earlier in 6:14–15. The command to silence is typical of Mark (1:34; 3:11–12, etc.), and the prediction of the passion in v. 31 appears with little variation in Mark 9:31; 10:32–34. That the titles *Christ* and *Son of Man* appear together (8:29, 31) is likewise a characteristic of Markan theology (Mark 14:61–62). It is also noteworthy that Son-of-Man and passion sayings do not appear in pre-Markan material. The question is, then, whether Mark made use of individual traditions in his composition. Such a possibility is conceivable for Mark 8:27, 29, since John 6:66–71 offers an independent parallel. Instead of the title *Christ*, however, John contains a version of Peter's answer that is unusual for Johannine christology: "You are the Holy One of God." Of course, there is in Mark also no prior preparation for the use of the Christ-title. (It appears previously only in 1:1.) It is probable, therefore, that we have two independent versions of a preliterary tradition.

That probability is reinforced by the fact that the style of a titulary confession also appears elsewhere in primitive Christian tradition (cf. Mark 3:11; John 1:49; 4:19). It appears again in John 11:27 with the Christ-title. The frequency with which such titles appear suggests that they were part of Primitive Christianity's confession. Only within such a context does it make sense to refer to Jesus in such an absolute way as the Christ without any further explanation. In Early Judaism one had to ask which of the eschatological figures is the Anointed One. In Christian circles it was clear that only Jesus should receive this designation, since every Christian had long since become used to hearing the title *Christ* used in connection with what were for Jesus the defining experiences of death and resurrection in the sense of the early confession of 1 Cor 15:3b–4. Finally, we should note that Mark 8:29 is the only synoptic text in which the pre-Easter disciples make a confession of faith in Jesus.

The question about the Son of David in Mark 12:35–37 parr. appears in a setting that the evangelist himself created (12:35a, 37b). What remains is a haggadic question that formally poses a previously unsolved problem. Outsiders (the scribes) believe in a Davidic Messiah. Their views contradict, however, what David himself, assumed to be the author of Ps 110:1, says when he refers to the Christ not in the subordinate position of *son*, but in the superior position of *Lord*. The text is quoted according to the Septuagint, and the Lord is thus understood in Christian terms as the exalted Lord of the church. Only from this perspective does the problem even exist that the pericope intends to solve. Since the exalted Lord, Jesus Christ, is superior to David, his later subordination to the primal ancestor, David, is obsolete. The Christian Christ, therefore, is Christ and Lord of all in a much more comprehensive way than the scribes, in the sense of *Ps. Sol.* 17, expected the Messiah to be.

Jesus' confession before the Sanhedrin in Mark 14:60–64 parr. is part of the passion narrative. A diachronic analysis of the text that takes into consideration

Mark's contribution to the narrative reveals that Jesus' confession belongs to the latest, i.e., the Markan level (§6.3). There are, in addition, other reasons for not making use of this open claim of messiahship on the part of Jesus, which appears only here in Mark, in understanding Jesus' own historical self-understanding. Within the high priest's household there were no later Christian witnesses. Followers of Jesus at most could have deduced what had happened from the public accusation made the next morning in the trial before Pilate. Furthermore, as we have just noted, Mark was the first to combine Messiah and Son-of-Man statements. Finally, Jesus' implicit identification with the coming Son of Man in the second part of his confession is unhistorical (§4.4.2). It presupposes that even before his death Jesus expected to be exalted, when the most that can be documented is that he might have had a premonition of his death (§6.2). The disciples experienced Easter as something radically new—not as the fulfillment of what Jesus had predicted. If for that reason we can eliminate from consideration the reference to the Son of Man in Mark 14:62b, the only thing that remains is Jesus' agreement that he is the Anointed One (14:61–62a). Such a claim hardly ranks as blasphemy punishable by death. Only the claim of a human being that he soon will be equal with God (14:62b!) would be deserving of such a punishment. Furthermore, the claim that Jesus is the Anointed One is a precise answer to a general, inner-Jewish question, since the narrative does not indicate which eschatological anointed figure the questioner means. The high priest asks a question, therefore, which later Christians are going to ask, and the answer that he receives from Jesus is the confession of the later Christians, simply reworded as an I-statement. Jesus' affirmation, in other words, is the later church's confession, put into his mouth in order to explain his fate and his future.

Such a negative judgment about the messianic claim of Jesus[118] (however one might understand the content of that claim) fits well with the earliest impulses to create christological confessions after Easter.[119] We can best explain the diversity of christological concepts that were attached to Jesus after Easter by concluding that Jesus himself had made no unequivocal christological statements that could serve as the basis for the church's reflection. The earliest evidence for this reflection furthermore shows with reference to the earliest Easter confession (Rom 10:9; 1 Thess 1:10, etc.) and similar traditions such as Rom 1:3b–4; Phil 2:6–11; 1 Tim 3:16 that Jesus' christological exaltation began with Easter. His previous life, now regarded as his earthly life, is understood as the precondition for his exaltation, but no special quality is attributed to it apart from the special circumstances of his death.

4.4.2 Jesus and the Eschatological Son of Man

Aufrecht, W. E. "The Son of Man Problem as an Illustration of the techne of New Testament Studies," in: *Origins and Method*. Festschrift J. C. Hurd. B. H. McLean, ed. Sheffield: JSOT, 1993, 282–94.

Black, M. "The Messianism of the Parables of Enoch," in: *Messiah*. J. H. Charlesworth, ed., 145–68.

Borsch, F. H. "Further Reflections on 'the Son of Man'," in: *Messiah*. J. H. Charlesworth, ed., 130–44.

———. *The Son of Man in Myth and History*. Philadelphia: Westminster, 1967.

Casey, M. "'The Jackals and the Son of Man (Mt 8,20 par Lk 9,58)," *JSNT* 23 (1985) 3–22.

———. "The Son of Man Problem," *ZNW* 67 (1976) 147–54.

Collins, J. J. *The Apocalyptic Imagination: An Introduction to the Jewish Matrix of Christianity*. New York: Crossroad, 1984.

Colpe, C. "Ho Huios tou Anthropou," *TDNT* 8 (1972) 400–77.

———. "Der Begriff 'Menschensohn' und die Methode der Erforschung messianischer Prototypen," *Kairos* 11 (1969) 241–63; 12 (1970) 1–16; 13 (1971) 1–17; 14 (1972) 241–57.

Coppens, J. *Le Fils de l'homme néotestamentaire*. BETL 55. Leuven: University Press, 1981.

Fitzmyer, J. A. "The New Testament Title 'Son of Man' Philologically Considered," in: idem, *The Wandering Aramean*. SBLMS 25. Missoula, MT: Scholars Press, 1979, 143–60.

Fuller, R. H. *The Foundations of New Testament Christology*. Glasgow: Collins, 1978 (1965).

Hahn, F. *The Titles of Jesus in Christology: Their History in Early Christianity*. New York/Cleveland: World, 1969, 15–53.

Haufe, G. "Das Menschensohnproblem in der gegenwärtigen wissenschaftlichen Diskussion," *EvTh* 26 (1966) 130–41.

Higgins, A. J. B. *The Son of Man in the Teaching of Jesus*. SNTS MS 39. New York: Cambridge University Press, 1980.

———. "Is the Son of Man Problem Insoluble?" in: *Neotestamentica et Semitica*. Festschrift M. Black. E. E. Ellis and M. Wilcox, eds. Edinburgh: T & T Clark, 1969, 70–87.

———. *Jesus and the Son of Man*. London: Lutterworth; Philadelphia: Fortress, 1965.

Hoffmann, P. "Jesus versus Menschensohn," in: *Salz der Erde—Licht der Welt*. Festschrift A. Vögtle. L. Oberlinner and P. Fiedler, eds. Stuttgart: KBW, 1991, 165–202.

———. *Studien zur Theologie der Logienquelle*. NTA NF 8. 3rd ed. Münster: Aschendorf, 1982, 82–102; 142–58.

Kim, S. *"The Son of Man" as the Son of God*. Tübingen: J.C.B. Mohr (Paul Siebeck), 1983.

Koch, K. "Messias und Menschensohn," *JBTh* 8 (1993) 73–102.

———. *Das Buch Daniel*. EdF 144. Darmstadt: Wissenschaftliche Buchgesellschaft, 1980.

Kümmel, W. G. "Das Verhalten Jesu gegenüber und das Verhalten des Menschensohns," in: idem, *Heilsgeschehen und Geschichte*, vol. 2. MThSt 2. Marburg: N. H. Elwert, 1978, 201–14.

Lindars, B. *Jesus Son of Man*. London: SPCK, 1983.

Maddox, R. "Methodenfragen in der Menschensohnforschung," *EvTh* 32 (1972) 143–60.

Müller, K. "Menschensohn und Messias," *BZ* 16 (1972) 161–87; 17 (1973) 52–66.

Müller, M. *Der Ausdruck "Menschensohn" in den Evangelien.* Leiden: Brill, 1984.
———. "The Expression 'the Son of Man' as Used by Jesus," *StTh* 38 (1984) 47–64.
Müller, U. B. *Messias und Menschensohn in jüdischen Apokalypsen und in der Offenbarung Johannes.* StNT 6. Gütersloh: Mohn, 1972.
Neugebauer, F. *Jesus der Menschensohn.* Stuttgart: Calwer Verlag, 1972.
Nickelsburg, G. W. E. "Son of Man," in: *Anchor Bible Dictionary.* Vol. 6, 137–50. New York: Doubleday, 1992.
Pesch, R. "Über die Autorität Jesu," in: *Die Kirche des Anfangs.* Festschrift H. Schürmann. R. Schnackenburg et al., eds. Freiburg: Herder, 1977, 25–55.
Polag, A. *Die Christologie der Logienquelle.* WMANT 45. Neukirchen-Vluyn: Neukirchener Verlag, 1977, 102–17.
Sjöberg, E. *Der Menschensohn im äthiopischen Henochbuch.* Lund: Gleerup, 1946.
Theisohn, J. *Der auserwählte Richter.* SUNT 12. Göttingen: Vandenhoeck & Ruprecht, 1975.
Tödt, H. E. *The Son of Man in the Synoptic Tradition.* Philadelphia: Westminster, 1965.
Vanderkam, J. C. "Righteous One, Messiah, Chosen One and Son of Man in 1 Enoch 37–71," in: *Messiah.* J. H. Charlesworth, ed., 169–91.
Vermès, G. "The Present State of the 'Son of Man' Debate," *JJS* 29 (1978) 123–34.
Vielhauer, P. *Aufsätze zum Neuen Testament.* ThB 31. Munich: Chr. Kaiser, 1965, 55–91, 92–140.
Vögtle, A. "Bezeugt die Logienquelle die authentische Redeweise Jesu vom 'Menschensohn'?" in: idem, *Offenbarungsgeschehen und Wirkungsgeschichte.* Freiburg: Herder, 1985, 50–69.
———. *Die "Gretchenfrage" des Menschensohnproblems.* QD 152. Freiburg/Basel/Vienna: Herder, 1994.

Even a cursory reading of the synoptic gospels reveals that the term Son of Man is the most frequently used christological title applied to Jesus. A more careful reading reveals that the texts in which this title appears constitute, from the perspective of the evangelists, a clearly recognizable semantic field. Jesus is active on earth as the Son of Man (Mark 2:10); as the Son of Man he faces his death and resurrection (Mark 8:31); and he will return as the Son of Man to judge the world (Mark 14:62). Mark first created this complex in literary form, and in this regard Matthew and Luke followed him.

In this form, of course, the complex of Son of Man statements reveals its post-Easter origin. The stereotypical yet detailed statements of Mark 8:31 parr. (and 9:31 parr.; 10:32–34 parr.) make sense only as a retrospective attempt to come to terms with events that have already happened. Even if we must acknowledge that in principle anyone in Early Judaism might have hoped for life after death, an announcement such as that of Mark 14:62 that one will come soon to save and to judge the world is clearly the post-Easter hope for the parousia of the one who at Easter was exalted to the position of the Son of Man. Anyone who would attribute to Jesus both a detailed knowledge of his impending death and such an unusual view of his task after his death must be able to justify that claim in light of the finite conditions to which every human life is subject. The synoptic Son of

Man statements cannot be cited uncritically to demonstrate whether or how Jesus used the term.

To pursue that question we must begin once again with the gospels at the literary level. The Son of Man sayings in the synoptic material without exception demonstrate two consistent facts that are of supreme importance for our further analysis.[120] One is that the term Son of Man appears exclusively in the mouth of Jesus. Apart from him, no one in the Synoptics refers to the Son of Man. The second is that, according to the Synoptics, Jesus himself uses no other term for a traditional eschatological figure. It is other persons who speak of such figures. No attempt to forge a consensus on what for many is the insoluble Son of Man problem should proceed without a satisfactory explanation of these two related facts.

Two additional phenomena provide a basis for understanding this double observation. For one thing, it is likely that the earliest post-Easter christological understanding of Jesus described him in terms of the functions of the Son of Man,[121] who at Easter was exalted, who will soon come to save his church, and who at the same time will be equipped with divine authority as judge. While the work of the Son of Man is attributed to the exalted Jesus, the title Son of Man does not appear directly. Outside the Synoptics it plays a role only in the revelatory sayings of Jesus in the Fourth Gospel, in Stephen's vision in Acts 7:56, and in Rev 1:12–16 and 14:14. This first Son of Man christology clearly can be documented for the early Jewish and Aramaic-speaking church (1 Cor 16:22). It also was part of the earliest missionary preaching to non-Jews (1 Thess 1:9–10) and was used by Paul in his missionary activity (1 Thess 1:9–10; 4:13–18). It was, therefore, hardly a marginal phenomenon; it was widespread in the earliest post-Easter christological development. The second observation is that, while there are direct christological statements in these post-Easter witnesses for the Son of Man christology, the identification of Jesus as the Son of Man is not at all clear in the synoptic material. It is implied, but never explicitly stated. For this reason many of the scholars who believe that Jesus referred to himself as the Son of Man assume that he used the term as an intentionally veiled reference.

Unless we can come up with clear evidence to the contrary, these four observations must set the direction for our analysis of the individual Son of Man sayings. Given the first two observations, along with the emergence of the earliest post-Easter christology as a Son of Man christology, we begin with the recognition that some of the Son of Man sayings go back to Jesus himself. The post-Easter use of the Son of Man title, therefore, was an act of continuity with Jesus. It is, furthermore, likely that Jesus used the term to refer to someone other than himself. Such a conclusion relieves us of the necessity of attributing to the texts a secrecy strategy that they themselves do not claim. It also has the advantage of interpreting the Son of Man statements analogous to the Messiah statements (and all other direct christological statements), which recognize Easter as the origin of direct christological pronouncements (§4.4.1).

We gain considerable support for this interpretation if we can assume that the Stronger One announced by John the Baptist was the Son of Man (§3.1.4). In that case, there was then a consistent line of development from John through Jesus to the early church in understanding history in terms of the figure of the Son of Man. John proclaimed the imminence of the judgment that the Stronger One would carry out in God's name. Jesus shared this view of the coming judgment, but he proclaimed that prior to the judgment the Kingdom of God would effect the salvation of the lost (§3.2). The early church also expected this final judgment. For it, however, the Son of Man and World Judge was Jesus the Savior, who had been inaugurated into this role at Easter. There is, therefore, a continuum in the expectation of a judgment initiated by the Son of Man with three unique variations represented by the Baptist, by Jesus, and by the early church. Supporting this interpretation is the not insignificant observation that the title *Son of Man* designates an eschatological figure that had already been formed in Early Judaism without the connotations of Israel's classical salvation history. This factor was especially important for the Baptist and for Jesus, since they began with the conviction that Israel had squandered its salvation history (§§3.1.3; 4.2.3).

This basic approach to the interpretation of the synoptic Son of Man statements has the advantage of being the least complicated of the suggested interpretations. Those who would claim that Jesus made no Son of Man statements[122] must explain why immediately after Easter it was the Son of Man tradition that was used to create the first christological concept and why at the same time in the synoptic material Son of Man statements—with some frequency, and not simply as a marginal term—come only from the mouth of Jesus. Those who would further claim that Jesus referred to himself indirectly as Son of Man must explain why he elsewhere spoke openly about his activity and the coming Kingdom of God (§§4.2; 4.3; 4.4.3), but avoided a direct reference to himself as Son of Man.

A separate question arises when we look for the Early Jewish background against which Jesus and early Christianity formulated Son of Man statements. Do Dan 7 and the Early Jewish texts that develop its themes provide the semantic framework for understanding the synoptic Son of Man sayings? Or should we—especially with regard to the statements about the present activity of the Son of Man—begin with an exclusively idiomatic usage according to which *Son of Man* was a figure of speech that was already used in Early Judaism in place of the first person singular? This latter possibility can be modified in different ways.[123] While this claim was initiated by the insights of various Aramaic specialists[124] and is popular among New Testament scholars, it cannot be maintained on philological grounds, since no one has yet documented that such a linguistic possibility existed in Aramaic at the time of Jesus.[125] Furthermore, what we might gain from such a view for understanding the synoptic material has highly negative consequences. If we argue that the synoptic Son of Man tradition began with an idiomatic usage, we must accept in exchange so many new and insoluble problems and must assume such a complicated history for the synoptic Son of Man tradition that one hypothesis would lead to another until they were completely out of control.

We must continue to look for the background for the synoptic Son of Man sayings in the tradition initiated by Dan 7, therefore, even though this way also has numerous problems of interpretation. It is at the very least clear that the Son of Man is to be understood in terms of Dan 7:13, where, after God's judgment comes over the world empires, and in contrast to the animallike figures that represent them, a figure appears that looks *like a son of man* (i.e., like a human being) to whom the eschatological authority is given. This description corresponds to the normal language of visions. In the later interpretation of the vision the figure is understood collectively as the eschatological people of God (Dan 7:22, 27), but after Daniel this collective understanding never reappears; Dan 7:13 is consistently understood in an individual sense. For this reason, among others, it is occasionally suggested that there was behind Dan 7:13 an earlier, noncollective concept describing in visionary language the figure of an angel without a title.[126] Independently of each other the Septuagint and *Tg. Dan* 7:13–14 probably also understood the figure individually.[127]

There is no ambiguity in the way this understanding is developed in the parabolic addresses of *1 Enoch* 37–71 (cf. §4.1.5). Here there is a clear distinction between the Son of Man and the eschatological community of salvation (*1 Enoch* 38:1–3; 45:1–4, etc.). The Son of Man is also introduced with the visionary language of Dan 7:13 and is compared with an angelic being (46:1), so that beginning with the paraphrase of Dan 7:13 in *1 Enoch* 46:1 the figure is referred to as *that Son of Man* or *the Son of Man* (46:2–3, etc.). Thus in the absence of the particle of comparison what originally was a visionary comparison used to describe a figure came to be the designation of an individual. The process is formally similar to the manner in which the description of God as one who had *a head of days* (i.e., an aged head; cf. Dan 7:9, 13) later became a personal designation of God as the Head of Days (46:1; 47:3, etc.). One can see a similar comparison between the way God is consistently called the *Lord of Spirits* (37:2 and more than one hundred other instances; cf. Dan 7:10) and the way the Son of Man is designated as *the Elect* (39:6, etc.) or *my Elect* (45:3–4). There is no doubt that in the present text both designations refer to the same person.[128] It is questionable, therefore, whether a separate tradition lies behind each term, but we can leave that question open here.

Who is the Son of Man of the parabolic discourses? He is clearly a heavenly figure, like an angel, and not a human figure.[129] He is chosen to represent God in the final judgment. His judgment is universal. It has negative consequences for all sinners (45:3–6; 46:4b; 50:2; 69:27–29), but especially for the kings of the world empires (46:4–8; 62–63). He gathers the righteous, on the other hand, into his eschatological community and will be their ruler and the guarantor of their salvation (45:3–4; 47:4; 48:1–7; 51; 58; 61; 69:26–29). Just as he is chosen, so the righteous are the Elect (38:2; 61:4 and 45:3, etc.). He is "the staff on which they stay themselves and not fall" (48:4). Until the final judgment, however, he is hidden and is revealed only to "the holy and the righteous" (48:6–7; 62:7). They know that when he appears on the throne of his glory (69:29) he will bring about their salvation (50:1; 62:8, 13–16) and that after the judgment he will celebrate with them the banquet of salvation (62:14). While the Son of Man, like other eschatological agents of salvation (and, above all, like the Davidic Messiah), can be anointed (cf. §4.4.1), he is not simply another version of the Messiah; he is an independent conception of an eschatological agent of salvation. The decisive difference is that the Messiah is descended from David and part of the theology of Zion. The Son of Man, on the other hand, is a preexistent, supernatural figure given the task of judging the entire world at the end of history (cf. §3.1.4), who is to be understood in terms of the tradition of God's world-rule that goes back to Daniel (§4.1.5).

Evidence of the Daniel Son of Man tradition appears also in other Early Jewish apocalyptic works. 4 Ezra and *2 Apoc. Bar.* are clear witnesses of the tradition. Neither work can be used in the interpretation of the earliest synoptic Son of Man statements, since they both date from the time between the two Jewish revolts against Rome. We have a somewhat different situation with the so-called little synoptic apocalypse in Mark 13.[130] There is a depth to this Jewish Christian text that justifies at least the suggestion that it is based on a Jewish source (Mark 13:7–8, 14–20, 24–27).[131] Yet, even those who are not prepared to find such a source must concede that this text stratum shows an independence vis-à-vis other synoptic Son of Man statements and at the very least is a Jewish Christian witness for the Early Jewish Son of Man tradition. The Son of Man christology of the Jewish Christian primitive church after Easter (e.g., 1 Cor. 16:22; 1 Thess 1:10; cf. also Acts 7:56) also reflects the background of the Early Jewish Son of Man tradition.[132] From the Jewish Christian beginnings of the Johannine church we also have traditions that have been influenced by a Son of Man christology (John 3:35–36; 14:2–3). Next to Mark 13 and the texts cited with 1 Cor 16:22, they reveal the existence of a third independent Jewish Christian tradition that offers its own reworking of a Jewish Son of Man christology.[133] Finally, we need to remember that the Stronger One predicted by the Jewish prophet, John the Baptist, is probably to be interpreted as a Son of Man tradition (§3.1.4).

We may conclude, therefore, that the Book of Daniel, which as a whole was influential in Early Judaism and Christianity to a degree that can hardly be exaggerated, in Dan 7 reveals a hope that gave rise to its own special tradition. Sometimes the evidence for this tradition is direct, sometimes indirect. The earliest stage of Jesus' Son of Man sayings, preserved in the sayings source, breathes the spirit of this Early Jewish Son of Man tradition. The sayings at this stage quote directly neither from Dan 7 nor from the parabolic discourses of *1 Enoch*, but they make use of what probably in that day were widespread and basic views about the Son of Man. They presuppose that the hearers do not need to be informed what connotations were implied by the catchword *Son of Man*. The speaker expects, rather, that the hearers from within a semantic field familiar to them will be able to recognize what is unique about the sayings.

When we look at the synoptic material that represents a Son of Man tradition, common to all the texts is that *Son of Man* is a title of exaltation for Jesus.[134] The observation is still valid, furthermore, that the sayings fall naturally into three groups: statements about the coming Son of Man, statements about the presently active Son of Man, and statements about the Son of Man who must suffer and who will be raised.[135] This last group of sayings especially bears the imprint of Jesus' own fate (cf. Mark 8:31 parr.; 9:31 parr.; 10:33–34 parr.; Mark 9:9 = Matt 17:9; Mark 10:45 = Matt 20:28; Mark 14:21 parr.; Mark 14:41 = Matt 26:45). In Mark these sayings are for the most part the result of Mark's editorial work, and they have no parallels in the sayings source. The statements about the presently active Son of Man share with this group the fact that for all practical purposes they show no influence of the apocalyptic Son of Man tradition. They are interested, e.g., in Jesus' authority as the Son of Man (e.g., Mark 2:10 parr.; 2:28 parr.) in situations in which the larger context simply implies that it is, of course, Jesus who is the Son of Man. This group of sayings does appear also in the sayings source (Matt 8:20 = Luke 9:58; Matt 11:19 = Luke 7:34). Here it is also assumed that the term *Son of Man* is a designation of Jesus. The two groups probably originated when the post-Easter belief that Jesus had been raised from the dead, which led the church to identify Jesus with the coming Son of Man, stimulated the church to apply the same designation to the Jesus who had been active on earth and who had suffered.

With its various motifs the group of statements about the coming Son of Man shows the greatest similarity with the Early Jewish Son of Man tradition. It furthermore shares with the Early Jewish material the future-oriented character of the language about the Son of Man who has not yet appeared. Of course, hardly anyone will claim that all of the sayings of this group came from Jesus. Yet, several of the texts can probably stand the test of critical analysis sufficiently so that there is no reason to deny Jesus' authorship. One such text is Luke 17:26–30 = Matt 24:37–41. The earliest form of this threat of judgment may have read:

1a *And as it was in the days of* Noah,
  b *so it will be in the "day" of the Son of Man:*
2a *They ate, they drank,*
  b *they married, they were given in marriage,*
3a *until the day when Noah entered the ark.*
  b *Then the flood came,*
  c *and all were destroyed.*

4a   *Likewise as it was in the days of Lot,*

  b   *"so it will be in the day of the Son of Man":*

5a   *They ate, they drank,*

  b   *they bought, they sold,*

  c   *they planted and built.*

6a   *But on the day that Lot went out of Sodom,*

  b   *it rained fire and brimstone from heaven,*

  c   *and all were destroyed.*

In Luke 17:20–18:8, the Third Evangelist composed an address about the final judgment, in which the catchword *Son of Man* dominates (17:22, 24, 26, 30; 18:8). This Son of Man is the one who will bring about the salvation of the elect (17:31–35; 18:7–8) and will abandon the others over to corruption. The Son of Man will come suddenly and in ways that one cannot understand (Luke 17:23–24) in order to establish God's kingdom (17:20–21). A comparison with Matt 24:26–28, 37–41 reveals that the core of this address comes from the sayings source. In only one instance does the order of the sentences differ (Luke 17:37c = Matt 24:28). The Son of Man statements in Luke 17:24, 26–27 are part of this core material.

The example of the flood in Luke 17:26–27 = Matt 24:38–39 shows that Matthew put his own imprint on the text and that he combined and heavily edited the apocalypse from Mark 13 and the material about the final judgment from Q. It is likely, therefore, that Luke's second example of judgment—about the destruction of Sodom (Luke 17:28–30)—was originally in Q, but was omitted by Matthew. That Matthew tightened the material is confirmed by the way he preserves the reference to the Son of Man in the Noah example (Matt 24:37) and at the same time reworks the Son of Man statement from Luke 17:30, which there rounds out the Lot example, to conclude the Noah example. Since the Noah example made the same point as the Sodom example, it was easy for Matthew to shorten the material. The flood-generation and the Sodomites are, by the way, the traditional examples for the divine judgment.[136]

If we assume that the order in the sayings source was Luke 17:24, 37c,[137] 26–27, 28–30 as the core of the judgment address (followed by Luke 17:31–35 par.), we can subject this Son of Man tradition to further analysis. In its present form the text has in Luke 17:24, 30 a framework that is intentional in which the *revealing* of the Son of Man in 17:30 takes up the not-to-be-grasped appearance from 17:24. No one can miss his coming; everyone will see it. Something different is suggested by 17:26–27, where the focus is only on the day[138] of the Son of Man as the time of judgment, since on this day all will be destroyed. The text speaks of the Son of Man, in other words, in two different ways. If we then attribute the framework to the sayings source, since the two examples of judgment make good sense by themselves, it only remains to ask whether the second example in Luke 17:28 at one time had a Son of Man sentence corresponding to 17:26b. It could very well have been used in the formation of 17:30. The parallel formation of the two examples speaks for such a view.

Can we attribute both examples to Jesus?[139] The basic statement agrees perfectly with Luke 13:1–5 and related texts (§3.2.2). Only those who deny all Son of Man sayings to Jesus can claim that these sayings were created in the Jewish Christian community, and their sole reason is the appearance of the catchword *Son of Man*. Such reasoning, however, would be a case of *petitio principii*. Another reason for attributing the sayings to Jesus is that they offer not the slightest suggestion that Jesus understands himself as the Son of Man. On the contrary, Jesus speaks of the unexpected day of judgment as the day of the Son of Man (cf. *1 Enoch* 46:3–4; 62:2–3) without showing any further interest in the Son

of Man. According to the text, Jesus predicts the coming judgment structurally parallel to
the Baptist's proclamation of judgment in Matt 3:7–10 par. Neither of them (i.e., neither
Jesus nor John) has anything to do with the execution of the judgment.

The text portrays the flood generation and the inhabitants of Sodom in an
unusual way—not as especially egregious sinners, as the Old Testament text does
(Gen 6–7; 18–19), but in terms of the simple normality of their lives, much as
Jeremiah writes in his letter to the exiles (Jer 29:5–6). Suddenly and unexpectedly there comes into this normal situation a judgment that leads to destruction—a
judgment from which no one can escape. What is described parallels the parables
of the rich farmer (Luke 12:16–20) and of the unjust steward (Luke 16:1–8) as
well as the examples in Luke 13:1–5 (cf. §3.2.2). With the flood generation and
the Sodomites it is a case of judgment on persons who are not Israelites. That
their judgment is an example of Israel's lost condition is also typical of Jesus'
way of speaking to his contemporaries (examples in §2.3.4). Since he does not
describe how the judgment will take place, the figure of the Son of Man is a
personified sign of the judgment, but beyond that is not an object of description.
Of concern is not how the judgment will be accomplished, but that the present is
immediately threatened. For this reason Jesus can make the same statement
without referring to the Son of Man (§3.2.2). We might surmise that this double
saying is directed at a particular attitude among Jesus' hearers. They could easily
be thinking that, in spite of the preaching of judgment from the Baptist and from
Jesus, things have not changed—life is still normal. Why then should they pay
attention to what John and Jesus had said? Jesus responds: You are making the
same mistake that the people made in the days of Noah and Lot; judgment by
water and by fire came on those people in the midst of their normal lives.

The reference to the Son of Man in this double saying presupposes that the
hearers were familiar with it, at least in general terms. The term is not introduced
as a new concept; it is briefly stated without explanation. The saying does not
refer to the statement of comparison in Dan 7:13 (*like a Son of Man*), but simply
assumes that *Son of Man* will be understood as a well-known term for the
eschatological agent of judgment. It presupposes, therefore, a stage of the tradition even beyond the parabolic discourses of *1 Enoch*, where in reference to Dan
7:13 *that Son of Man* is spoken of (see above). The personal designation *Son of
Man* in the Jesus material assumes that everyone will know that this Son of Man
and the final judgment belong together. In this regard there is substantive agreement with the parabolic discourses. There is also agreement with the Son of Man
saying that more than any other has dominated the scholarly debate, viz., the
saying in Luke 12:8–9 (Matt 10:32–33; Mark 8:38) about confessing and
denying:

1a   Amen, I say to you:
b   Everyone who confesses *me before people,*
c   that one also the Son of Man will confess before the angels of God.

2a But whoever denies *me before people,*
b that one also the Son of Man will deny before the angels of God.

There is widespread acceptance of this suggested earliest form of the saying along with the assumption of its independence from its context.[140] It may be that the final line from Luke 12:9b ("that one will be denied before the angels of God"), which with the help of Mark 8:38 we have reconstructed against Luke, should read as Luke has it. That reading would not change the meaning, however, since the passive style of the language of an Oriental court should be understood to parallel Luke 12:8b. That kind of rapid transition between active and passive formulations is also characteristic of the parabolic discourses of *1 Enoch* (cf., by way of example, 50:2–5; 51:2; 61:8; 62:2–3, 10; 69:27) precisely when describing the activity of the Son of Man.

This prophetic statement about the future fits in well with the sayings of Jesus that speak of judgment that has double consequences (§3.2.3). A difference, however, is that the saying from Luke 12:8–9 focuses on the criterion on which the judgment will be based, while the other statements describe the unexpected appearance of judgment, which will either include people in or exclude them from salvation and then call on the people to do everything possible to share in the coming salvation.

If we set aside for a moment Jesus' reference to himself, the statement in Luke 12:8–9 is in its form a typical apocalyptic-wisdom teaching in which a person's positive or negative behavior is rewarded (or threatened) with a corresponding consequence. What in the wisdom tradition is a typical, this-worldly relation between a deed and its consequence (Prov 22:8: "Whoever sows evil will reap calamity") becomes in apocalypticism, which because of its own experience can no longer believe in this-worldly justice, the hope for a balancing of the scales in God's final judgment: "Do righteousness on earth, that you may find it (righteousness) in heaven" (*T. Lev.* 13:5). New Testament statements in the tradition of apocalypticism also make use of this view of a final, divine judgment that will balance the scales. One thinks, e.g., of Jas 2:13: "Judgment is unmerciful to the one who shows no mercy." Matt 7:2 says similarly: "Judge not, in order that you not be judged." Of course, the balancing can also occur antithetically in the case of kinds of attitudes, i.e., simply by reversing the position: "Humble yourselves before the Lord, and he will exalt you" (Jas 4:10). Formulated as a double-sentence it comes out: "Whoever exalts himself will be humbled; whoever humbles himself will be exalted" (Luke 14:11 = 18:14).

Whether the correspondence between behavior and consequence is analogous or antithetical, the statement always assumes that the human being's relationship to God's judgment is asymmetrical. God determines the terms of judgment, in other words, in absolute sovereignty. Apocalypticism sees itself as commissioned to teach the divine fundamental rule that it has received by revelation. Human beings may not choose between this and another order of things. They are able to make choices only within this order of things as long as God's patience permits.

For this reason, when describing the relationship between this present life and the coming judgment, apocalypticism always speaks of a person's grounding in either good or evil. One is either righteous or a sinner. Exalting one's self or humbling one's self (cf. above, Luke 14:11), e.g., is not an individual act, but a fundamental attitude before God throughout one's entire life. Kings are deposed and destroyed by the Son of Man "because they neither extol nor praise him, nor humbly acknowledge whence they received the kingdom" (*1 Enoch* 46:4–5). Their permanent self-assurance, in other words, is their downfall.

That each person's life has a fundamental orientation toward either good or evil provides, then, the context for understanding the antithetical *confessing* and *denying* in Luke 12:8–9 (cf. John 1:20). Since nothing in the text suggests a situation of persecution, there is no reason to understand the words in terms of the special situation of Christians before pagan judges. Both words suggest a much broader meaning. Indeed, their use in the parabolic discourses of *1 Enoch* supports the view that they describe one's basic attitude. According to *1 Enoch* 45:2 people are sinners "who have denied the name of the Lord" (cf. 46:7). No one will be able to help such people on the judgment day, because "they have denied the Lord of Spirits (and his Anointed)" (48:10). In 67:8, 10 such denial is the equivalent of godlessness. In the judgment doxology of *1 Enoch* 63:4–7 the condemned kings *confess* that they previously *have neither confessed nor glorified* the Lord of Spirits as their Lord. The parabolic discourses use the terms *confess* and *deny*, therefore, to describe fundamental orientations of life (cf. also Heb 11:13). This usage provides an excellent background for understanding Luke 12:8–9, especially since this synoptic text, like the parabolic discourses, speaks of the Son of Man.

In understanding Luke 12:8–9 we further need to determine what role the Son of Man plays in this statement. Is he himself the judge, or is he a witness in the divine court? At first reading one might draw the latter conclusion, reasoning that the Son of Man testifies by confessing and denying before God what he knows about the human beings. Apart from the terms *deny* and *confess*, however, there is no basis in the text for this understanding, given the lack of information about the Son of Man. The two verbs, which initially describe basic, human, life orientations, are chosen here to underscore the correspondence between a person's confession or denial and that of the Son of Man. In the Son of Man clauses they are subordinate and dependent on the earlier clauses. They were not chosen, therefore, to describe with precision the legal function of the Son of Man in a trial. When Jesus *confesses* in Matt 7:23 that he never knew the false prophets, he does so as a judge; the statement is a verdict, not simply the testimony of a witness. We must understand the confessing and denying of Luke 12:8–9, therefore, as a performative verdict that creates what in Luke 17:34–35 is described as *being taken* and *being left*, or what is meant in Mark 9:43–48 par. by *entering life* or *going into Gehenna* (cf. §3.2.3). In the great judgment scene of Matt 25:31–46, with a simple command the Son of Man assigns the righteous and the sinners to the eschatological Kingdom of God or to final destruction (25:34, 41). These words pronounce the same final verdict that is meant in Luke 12:8–9. The Son of Man in Luke 12:8–9 functions, therefore, as a judge. A major advantage of this interpretation is that it agrees with the view of the Son of Man held by John the Baptist and the early primitive church and, according to Luke 17:24, 26–27, formulated by Jesus.

The view of the heavenly royal court in Luke 12:8–9, like the alternatives posed by the double saying, also belongs to the Son of Man tradition of Early Judaism. As early as Zech 14:5 God is described as coming as judge "with all heavenly beings." Dan 7:10 also pictures the ruler of the world surrounded by an incalculable number of angels in a scene in which the Son of Man appears (7:13–14). The parabolic addresses then speak of the heavenly court (*1 Enoch* 4:1; 47:3; 60:2) in which the angels actively participate in carrying out judgment (53:1–54:6; 56) and praise God while the Son of Man is engaged in the act of judgment (61:1–13).[141] It is not surprising, therefore, that the angels are mentioned in Luke 12:8–9, even though they appear nowhere else in the extant early Jesus material.

Since in all of the texts just cited the heavenly court is a sign of royal majesty and power, the figure of the Son of Man is related to God's kingship in both Daniel and in *1 Enoch* (§4.1.5). From this standpoint, therefore, there is no reason to see a tension, as is frequently done, between the synoptic Son of Man tradition and the statements about God's kingship. While Jesus' early Son of Man sayings may not directly mention the Kingdom of God, there is no doubt that such a connection exists in Early Judaism. We may assume, therefore, the same connection for Jesus and his hearers.

Recognizing these ties between Luke 12:8–9 and the traditions of Early Judaism makes it possible for us to see what is unique in Jesus' statement. Jesus does not simply repeat the prevailing view; he supplements what is commonly known with a new criterion by which people are to be judged, viz., their positive or negative relationship to him. Wisdom and apocalypticism teach in a formal way their criteria for the judgment that will take place (either in this world or at the end of history). A sage or an apocalyptist is interchangeable with any other member of his group, since he himself is not the subject of his teaching. His criterion is, e.g., whether one has honored or dishonored the creator (*1 Enoch* 46:5; 63:7) or in general whether one fears God (*'Abot* 1:3), has committed specific evil deeds (*1 Enoch* 53:2; 62:11–12; 99:11–15) or human works in general (*1 Enoch* 61:8; *Bib. Ant.* 3:10). Of course, in many cases the Torah is the criterion (*'Abot* 2:1, 7, 8, 16; *T. Ash.* 6; *1 Enoch* 5:1–4). In the Deuteronomic view of history the prophets can be added to the Law as the standard of judgment, when their summons to obey the Law is not heard (Neh 9:26). This last case in which a personalized standard is offered that is dependent on the actual standard of the Law comes the closest to Luke 12:8–9. Here the teaching takes on a prophetic tone when the speaker ties the fate of the present hearers to his own person. What does the Teacher of Righteousness say, who claims special revelation for himself (1QH ii 13; iv 26–27; vii 7, 10)? "You will declare all of my enemies guilty, separating through me the just and the guilty" (1QH vii 11b). Or: "I have been a snare for the godless, but healing for all who are converted from sin" (1QH ii 8). These statements of the Teacher of Righteousness with their prophetic-sounding claims have the greatest similarity with the I-statement of Luke 12:8–9. Just as he weaves a prophetic consciousness into the psalms that he composes, so Jesus expresses his prophetic authority within typical wisdom-apocalyptic teaching.

Does Luke 12:8–9 then invite the reader to identify Jesus as the Son of Man? While it is true that those who are convinced that the two are identical can read the statement that way if they wish, the text itself does not make that claim. The flow of the statement suggests that it is not Jesus who identifies himself with the Son of Man, but the Son of Man who identifies himself with Jesus, but this interpretation also would be premature. The general trend of such instruction is in the direction of establishing a criterion for judgment, so that the people who receive the teaching will know what is at stake and how they should live their lives. The point lies specifically, therefore, in the correspondence between the present human deed and its later consequence. The identity of the standard is to be understood on this level. Jesus is described *only* as an object of human relationship, and the corresponding judgment that the Son of Man executes is directed to the persons who have this relationship to Jesus. The Son of Man himself has no direct personal relationship to Jesus. In that case, however, Jesus and the Son of Man are two different persons; one of them appears now, the other later. In the present Jesus makes it possible for people to determine their relationship to good and evil. In the approaching judgment the Son of Man will ratify this commitment that people have made. If Jesus and the Son of Man are different in Luke 12:8–9, we will include the text in the preaching of Jesus, because immediately after Easter the two have not yet been identified (1 Cor 16:22).

Thus Luke 12:8–9 makes good sense within the proclamation of Jesus. Jesus understands himself in a special sense as the prophet of the end-time who is able to make the Kingdom of God real in the lives of people (Luke 10:18; cf. §4.2.2). This Kingdom of God that is beginning to be realized offers them the only possibility of escaping the coming judgment (§3.2.2). They can, however, still take offense at Jesus and his message (Matt 11:6; cf. §4.2.2). Such *denying* means that they will not escape the judgment, since the judgment of the Son of Man will be based on this rejection. On the other hand, those who find their way to Jesus—i.e., who *confess* him—escape the sin/judgment trap in which they were previously caught (§4.2.4). They become part of the salvation offered by the Kingdom of God, and the Son of Man will not change their status.

It is likely that we have discussed the core of the Son of Man sayings that can be attributed to the proclamation of Jesus. Claiming as authentic Jesus material other words from the group of sayings dealing with the coming Son of Man would be too hypothetical, if not downright problematic. Even if we were to do so, we would not gain any new information, so that limiting our discussion to Luke 12:8–9 and 17:26–30 is no real loss. We have learned that Jesus can formulate statements about judgment with and without referring to the Son of Man. He has no interest in describing either the judgment process or the person of the Son of Man. Thus he does not always and everywhere personalize the judgment. The significance of the judgment is more important for his hearers than are descriptions of scenes from the judgment. When the Son of Man appears, he is a personal embodiment of judgment. For Jesus this traditional understanding of the Son of Man says enough about him. It enables him to underscore the unexpected dimension of judgment and to work out the eschatological situation of decision in which Jesus' contemporaries stand. We should note in conclusion that those who claim that Jesus made no Son of Man statements create for themselves major problems in other places, but they do not substantially change the preaching of Jesus, since the essence of Luke 12:8–9 and 17:26–30 also appears in other early Jesus material.

4.4.3 Jesus' Relationship to the Kingdom of God

Aune, D. E. *Prophecy in Early Christianity and the Ancient Mediterranean World.* Grand Rapids, MI: Eerdmans, 1983.

Böcher, O. "Propheten, Prophetie 3. Neues Testament," *EKL* 3 (1992) 1345–49.

Bowman, J. "Prophets and Prophecy in Talmud and Midrasch," *EvQ* 22 (1950) 107–14; 205–20; 255–75.

Brox, N. "Das messianische Selbstverständnis des historischen Jesus," in: *Vom Messias zum Christus.* K. Schubert, ed. Freiburg: Herder, 1964, 165–201.

Cadbury, H. J. "Jesus and the Prophets," *JR* 5 (1925) 609–22.

Davies, P. E. "Jesus and the Role of Prophet," *JBL* 64 (1945) 241–54.

Dunn, J. D. G. *Jesus and the Spirit.* 2d ed. London: SCM, 1978.

Fascher, E. *Prophetes.* Gießen: Töpelmann, 1927.

Fenneberg, W. "Die Frage nach Bewußtsein und Entwicklung des historischen Jesus," *ZThK* 97 (1975) 104–16.

Frankemölle, H. "Jesus als deuterojesajanischer Freudenbote?" in: *Vom Urchristentum zu Jesus.* Festschrift J. Gnilka. H. Frankemölle and K. Kertelge, eds. Freiburg/Basel/Vienna: Herder, 1989, 34–67.

Friedrich, G. "Prophets and Prophecies in the New Testament," *TDNT* 6 (1968) 828–61.

Greif, J. C. G. "Abba and Amen: Their Relevance to Christology," *StEv* 5 = *TU* 103 (1968) 3–13.

Hahn, F. *The Titles of Jesus in Christology: Their History in Early Christianity.* New York/Cleveland: World, 1969.

Hengel, Martin, *Nachfolge und Charisma.*

Hoffmann, P. "'Er weiß, was ihr braucht . . .' (Mt 6,7). Jesu einfache und konkrete Rede von Gott," in: *"Ich will euer Gott werden."* N. Lohfink et al., eds. SBS 100. Stuttgart: KBW, 1981, 151–76.

Jeremias, G. *Der Lehrer der Gerechtigkeit.* StUNT 2. Göttingen: Vandenhoeck & Ruprecht, 1963.

Leivestad, R. "Das Dogma von der prophetenlosen Zeit," *NTS* 19 (1973) 288–99.

Limbeck, M. "Jesus als Prophet," *BiKi* 31 (1976) 9–12.

Meyer, R. *Der Prophet aus Galiläa.* 2d ed. Darmstadt: Wissenschaftliche Buchgesellschaft, 1970.

——. "Prophecy and Prophets in the Judaism of the Hellenistic-Roman Period," *TDNT* 6 (1968) 812–28.

Nebe, G. *Prophetische Züge im Bilde Jesu bei Lukas.* BWANT 7. Stuttgart: Kohlhammer, 1989.

Nützel, J. M. "Zum Schicksal der eschatologischen Propheten," *BZNF* 20 (1976) 59–94.

Schlosser, J. *Le Dieu de Jesus.* LeDiv 129. Paris: Cerf, 1987.

Schnackenburg, R. "Die Erwartung des 'Propheten' nach dem Neuen Testament und den Qumran-Texten," *StEv* = *TU* 73 (1959) 622–39.

Schnider, F. *Jesus der Prophet.* OBO 2. Freiburg: Universitätsverlag; Göttingen: Vandenhoeck & Ruprecht, 1973.

Steck, O. H. *Israel und das gewaltsame Geschick der Propheten.* WMANT 23. Neukirchen-Vluyn: Neukirchener Verlag, 1967.

Webb, R. L. *John the Baptizer and Prophet: A Socio-Historical Study.* JSNT.S 62. Sheffield: JSOT, 1991.

If Jesus understood himself neither as the Messiah ben David (§4.4.1) nor as the Son of Man (§4.4.2), then we must try to describe his activity in terms of the rich legacy of prophecy in Israel and in Early Judaism.[142] In so doing we must acknowledge up front that there is no clear evidence that Jesus referred to himself as a prophet. The same can be said of others, however, who clearly functioned as prophets. Prophets do not typically say, "I am a prophet." Instead, they speak and act as prophets, i.e., as persons who have experienced God and whose authority comes directly from God. It is usually others who speak of them as prophets and who in so doing recognize their mission. Those persons who do not acknowledge them designate them either as false prophets or not as prophets at all. John the Baptist, e.g., perhaps did not refer to himself as a prophet, but he spoke in prophetic style (§3.1.2). The people regarded him as a prophet (Matt 11:32 parr.), but Josephus did not (*Ant.* 18.117–19). Some people regarded Jesus also as a prophet (Mark 6:15 parr.; 8:28 parr.; Luke 24:19; Acts 3:22–23), but the statements attributed to the Pharisees in Luke 7:39 and John 7:52 reveal that this opinion was not universally held.

For Early Judaism and its understanding of the prophets it was of special importance that the classical period of Israel's prophecy ended with the canonization of the writing prophets (Sir 45–49; Sir Prologue 1–14; 4 Ezra 14:44–45). In the Hebrew Bible the tendency also existed to describe as prophets great figures from Israel's history who were close to God—persons such as Abraham (Gen 20:7) or Aaron (Exod 7:1), and, of course, Moses (Num 12:6–8; Deut 34:10). Thus anyone who scanned *the Law and the Prophets* (Matt 5:17; 11:13; Luke 24:27, 44) would have the immediate impression that Israel's canonica-classical period was a time when God led Israel continuously through prophets.

Early Judaism regarded itself as subordinate and inferior to this classical period. It lived from the memory of this important time, and it had no intention of rivaling it in any way. It was claimed, among other things, that there were no longer any prophets among the people (Ps 74:9; Dan 3:38 [LXX]; 1 Macc 9:27) or that the prophets had fallen asleep (*2 Apoc. Bar.* 85:3). Later *Sotah* 13:2 says: "When Haggai, Zechariah, and Malachi, the last prophets, had died, the Holy Spirit disappeared from Israel; nevertheless the Bath Qol (i.e., God's indirect voice) was heard." Such statements do not mean, of course, that there were no longer any prophetic claims in Early Judaism. History is always much more complex than generalizations would suggest. Such statements about prophecy always have a secondary purpose of claiming for one's self a different kind of divine authority such as, e.g., the Law. *2 Apoc. Bar.* 85:3 continues, e.g.: "We have nothing now save the Mighty One and his Law." Josephus and the New Testament give ample evidence that prophecy had not simply disappeared in Early Judaism (cf. §3.1.5).

A natural corollary of the view that, compared with the classical period of prophecy, the present was (relatively) free of prophecy was the belief that prophecy would flourish once again in the end-time. "The prophets of the Mighty God" will themselves be judges and kings in the final Kingdom of God (*Sib. Or.* 3.780–82). People were also of the conviction that the purpose of the Old Testament prophets was not so much to proclaim God's judgment and salvation to their own time as it was to predict what would happen to Israel and the world at the end of time (1QpHab vii 1ff.; similarly Luke 4:17–21; Acts 2:14–21; 2 Cor 6:2; 1 Pet 1:10–12, etc.). Since Moses and David were also understood as prophets, one could examine the entire canon for descriptions of the end, including descriptions of the prophetic figures that would appear in the end-time. Some, e.g., appealing to Deut 18:15–22, looked for a prophet like Moses (1QS ix 9–11; 4QTest 1–8), while others set their hopes on a returning Elijah (2 Kgs 2:1–12; Mal 3:1; 3:13–14; Sir 48:10).

In the circles that believed that the end was imminent, the hope for the return of prophecy could actually lead people to take action in the present. The Exodus prophets, e.g., tried to stage a reenactment of the miracles from the time of Moses and Joshua in order to usher in the age of salvation and to legitimize their own mission. Theudas collected a group of followers at the Jordan River in order to repeat for them the Jordan miracle (Josephus, *Ant.* 20.97–98). Another prophet, whom Josephus does not name, led his followers into the wilderness promising them miracles and freedom from all suffering (Josephus, *Ant.* 20.118). One could easily multiply such examples.

Such present prophecy, of course, did not have to identify itself with a figure from the canonical text. It could simply announce certain events (Josephus, *Ant.* 13.311ff.; 15.373ff.; 17.345ff.; Acts 11:27–30), or it could proclaim disaster and judgment, as in the case of John the Baptist and Jeshua ben Ananias (cf. §3.1), or salvation, as in the case of the Teacher of Righteousness (1QH ii 8, 13, 17–18; iv 5–6, 10; v 9–11; vii 7, and 1QpHab ii 1ff.; vii 1ff.).[143]

This last figure, the Teacher of Righteousness, reveals a quality that had appeared as early as the late phases of Old Testament prophecy, viz., the charismatic's appeal to sacred texts (cf. Isa 34:16).[144] The revelation that he claims to have received without mediation is the true interpretation of the Torah. Rabbi Akiba also speaks with prophetic authority when he interprets the Torah, specifically Num 24:27, in terms of Bar Cochba and declares him to be the eschatological Messiah.[145] Josephus states in general of the Essenes that they received their prophetic understanding through their interpretation of the scriptures (J.W. 2.159).

Where does Jesus fit in these various prophetic claims? An appropriate answer must begin with three fixed realities. One is that Jesus did not simply make an occasional prophetic observation; his entire activity in Galilee and Jerusalem was an expression of his special authority and mission. As was the case with John the Baptist, he did not have a full-time profession alongside which he functioned part-time as a prophet. Another given is that John provided the impulse for Jesus' own appearance as a prophet; Jesus is the product of a prophecy that existed before him. Equally clear is that Jesus intensified the Baptist's anticipation of an imminent end so much that he integrated the present into the beginning end-time events. He does not stand, therefore, within an ongoing history, making comments about the course of that history. Instead, he announces the beginning of God's kingdom in the present. When this kingdom has completely arrived, history will end.

Given these realities, it makes sense to ask whether Jesus regarded himself as one of the eschatological prophetic figures such as a returning Elijah or a prophet like Moses. The answer in both cases is a firm no. Not only is there not the slightest evidence that he did so; neither figure has anything in common with Jesus's activity. Given that activity, it would make more sense to relate Jesus to the bearer of good news in Isa 52:7 and 61:1. Indeed, the overtones of Old Testament texts in Matt 5:3–5 par. and 11:5–6 par. (cf. §§4.3.2; 4.2.2) suggest that Jesus described the beginning age of salvation with motifs from Deutero- and Trito-Isaiah, i.e., with what he regarded as the prophecy of Isaiah. It is one thing, however, to describe the present as the realization of prophecy about the end-time; it is quite another to claim that the speaker is one of the earlier prophets. The texts give no indication at all of this second understanding.[146] That Jesus intended the former is plausible, since Early Judaism elsewhere also uses such motifs to uncover the fulfillment of end-time prophecies. To claim the latter, however, would require that we be methodologically consistent and interpret Luke 11:20, which is usually assumed to be the *finger of God* of Exod 8:19, with a sense that no one gives it, viz., that Jesus is the reappearing Moses.[147] It is appropriate here to remind ourselves that Jesus did not understand himself to be the suffering servant of Isa 53, since the two texts, Mark 10:45 and 14:24 (cf.

§6.2), hardly qualify as authentic Jesus material. It is clear, therefore, that Jesus did not understand himself in terms of a personalized prophetic description of the end-time. The only thing that he had in common with that kind of personalized prophetic expectation is that he also understood himself as one commissioned to usher in the final age. In that regard he is an eschatological prophet.

What we have already said about Jesus and the Kingdom of God makes it possible for us to sharpen this description. Jesus is the end-time prophet of God's rule over Israel and over all creatures—a rule whose beginning coincides with Jesus' appearance. Since this Kingdom of God is the eschatological nearness of the benevolent creator who is concerned to save those who are lost, we can go a step further and say that Jesus is an eschatological prophet of salvation. This explanation has the unquestioned advantage of capturing Jesus' uniqueness within the history (and especially the prophecy) of Early Judaism. Another not insignificant advantage is that it does not have to resort to such expressions as *christology in execution* or *indirect christology* in order to describe Jesus' self-understanding. The problem with such terms is that they are post-Easter christologies in disguise.[148] It is precisely because of this point that our description has a twofold advantage. It understands Jesus within the context of Early Jewish prophetic phenomena, but it also provides a basis from which the post-christological reflection could begin to understand Jesus anew with eyes sharpened by the experience of Easter.

It is not enough, therefore, to call Jesus an exorcist and healer or, more generally, a charismatic or a teacher and rabbi. His miracles are only one aspect of his activity, and the term *charismatic* is much too vague and general to describe Jesus with precision. Jesus taught, of course, and it is quite possible that others addressed him with a title of respect such as *rabbi*. From his understanding of the Law, however, it is clear that Jesus was no rabbi in the Early Jewish sense of the term. His understanding of reality was based not on a study of the Torah (cf. §5.3) but on his fundamental certainty about the Kingdom of God, which was about to be realized. This quality clearly distinguishes Jesus from the Teacher of Righteousness, whose revelation consisted of uncovering the true meaning of the Torah from a study of the Scripture. Nowhere in Jesus did this kind of connection exist. Nor has anyone ever been able to demonstrate a relationship between Jesus and Israel's priesthood. If anything is incontrovertible from the Jesus material, it is that there is not the slightest connection between Jesus and the theological self-understanding of the Jerusalem priesthood. No Jew who had a close relationship to the priesthood or more generally to the temple could treat the purity laws as Jesus so obviously did (§5.3.4). There is, therefore, no basis for the occasional suggestion that Jesus had a close relationship with a community like that of the Essenes who were oriented toward the priesthood.

Given the distinctions we have drawn in §3.1.5 between John the Baptist and Early Jewish apocalypticism, no one should be surprised when we make the same claims for Jesus. We need not repeat here what we said there. Scarcely anyone in

Jesus' day had not been influenced by the apocalyptic book of Daniel, which was accepted into the prophetic canon and which provided an important impulse for the acceptance of apocalypticism in Early Judaism. Its basic attitude became just as canonical as was that of the other two major intellectual movements of the time—the Deuteronomic view of history and wisdom's understanding of the world. Moreover, the three understandings of reality frequently drew on one another. Jesus was influenced, of course, by these movements. His expectation of the Son of Man came from apocalypticism (§4.4.2). The banquet of salvation as a concrete expression of the final perfection of the Kingdom of God goes back to the apocalyptic text of Isa 25:6. Admittedly, the apocalyptic elements, which are not limited to these two motifs, cannot obscure the reality that Jesus' fundamental certainty about the present appearance of the eschatological Kingdom of God and his own sense of authority separate him by light years from the typical apocalyptic attitude. The apocalyptist creates a fiction to promote his own views behind the authority of earlier men of God. Jesus is authorized to say *I*. The revelation of apocalypticism is a scribal work that appears in literary form (4 Ezra 14:37–48). Jesus proclaims an oral message.[149] He is, in other words, a prophet rather than an apocalyptist.

Having clarified what Jesus was not, we need to focus once more on him as a prophet. Can we describe his prophetic self-understanding in more detail? First of all we need to remind ourselves that Jesus shared the view about a classical time of prophecy in the past. Israel's canonical prophets are for him proclaimers of the end-time in a time of waiting and hoping for the end (Matt 13:16–17; cf. §4.2.2). He also is able to speak of the canon as *the Law and the Prophets* (Matt 11:12–13; cf. §4.2.2). Of course, his relation to the period of classical prophecy and to the canon was not that he merely continued what had been and that his norms were simply what he had received from the canon. His prophetic consciousness leads him to understand his activity in terms of something qualitatively new. For him the earlier prophets had talked about what was to come, and they had taught the people to hope. He actualizes this coming reality and sets into motion the fulfillment of the hope. For him the canon was the unquestioned authority for the past, but now the focus is on the Kingdom of God, which sets new standards and new goals. From this focus he derives the freedom to act independently. Because of this inner authority he refuses to join any of the groups within Early Judaism, and he is able to address all Israel. His view is that all persons must orient themselves toward the Kingdom of God and live totally from that kingdom, even as he does. Whoever does not say yes to it without reservation has lost everything. He sees no other possibility.

With three observations we can summarize the way the person and activity of Jesus are tied up with the Kingdom of God. First of all, out of his conviction that through him the Kingdom of God is irreversibly and finally present he makes possible for his hearers an experience of God by making God's eschatological nearness a present reality for them in word and deed. Since all are lost, he submits everything to the power of the final Kingdom of God that can restore everything. In this way he accomplishes, according to his understanding, the turning-point of salvation in which all things—the present, the objective world, each concrete person, and society—are subjected directly to the coming Kingdom of God. This direct link is not a secondary experience based on earlier ecstatic experiences, visions, or dreams; Jesus' concern to create a healing connection between lost people and God is so grounded in the world of everyday experience that it has no place for such experiences.

A second observation deals with the relationship between Jesus' basic attitude and his own fate. Jesus knows that his death will not keep the Kingdom of God from being realized and that he will be able to share in it in spite of his death (Mark 14:25; cf. §6.2). Jesus did not preach himself; he proclaimed the Kingdom of God, and he promoted it with his own actions. He is so identified with the kingdom that he is convinced that he can no longer lose the salvation that it offers.

Finally, his activity is relevant not only for the present, historically conditioned situation; it has consequences for a person's salvation beyond the final judgment. According to him, in other words, the standard by which a person will be judged in the final judgment will be that person's relationship to the person of Jesus (Luke 12:8–9; cf. §4.4.2). Those who respond positively to Jesus and to his message of the Kingdom of God not only experience God's graciousness in the present; they also, like Jesus himself, will be secure in it forever.

NOTES

1. The sayings source Q, Mark, and Luke all agree in this regard. Only Matthew as a rule avoids this formulation (exceptions are Matt 12:28; 19:24; 21:31, 43) and replaces it with Kingdom of Heaven in order to speak as indirectly as possible of God, as was done increasingly in Judaism after 70 CE. Among the relatively early parallel examples of Matthew's usage are *3 Apoc. Bar.* 11:2 and *y. Qidd.* 59d. Cf. also *'Abot* 1:3, where the fear of God is referred to as "the fear of Heaven." On this entire problem see G. Dalman, *Worte*, 75ff.

2. Cf. W. Bousset and M. Gressmann, *Religion*, 214; O. Camponovo, *Königsherrschaft*, 450ff.; A. M. Schwemer, "Gott," 45–46, 62–63, 70; K. Koch, "Offenbaren," 158ff.

3. Cf. A. M. Schwemer, "Gott," 45ff.

4. Lattke makes a start in this direction ("Vorgeschichte," 9–10).

5. Only Matt 5:35 (cf. Ps 47:3) speaks of the city of the great king, and Matt 18:23 and 22:2–14 allegorize the king as a metaphor for God. By comparing the first text with James 5:12 and the third text with Luke 14:16–24 one can see that the First Evangelist himself is responsible for this usage. In 18:23 Matthew probably changed his source much

as he did in 22:2 (cf. §3.2.4). Those who argue differently must explain why it is only Matthew who (three times!) uses this formula.

6.   Even if this formulation too easily reminds us of Jesus, the general impression that Zenger thereby expresses is doubtless correct ("Herrschaft Gottes," 182).

7.   Cf. in more detail Füglister, "Verwendung."

8.   Since many prayers describe or refer to God as king, even if only in passing, I have chosen for illustrative purposes here only a selection in which the theology of Zion plays a role. Other examples will appear in the following discussion.

9.   In the following pages we will discuss only those texts that were contemporary with or earlier than Jesus and for which we can make the case that they were part of the world of Jesus and his hearers. We will omit, e.g., such writings as the works of Philo (cf. most recently V. Umemoto, "Königsherrschaft").

10.   E. Zenger, "Herrschaft Gottes," 180–81.

11.   On the discussion about Deutero-Isaiah, cf. D. Michel, "Deuterojesaja," and E. Zenger, "Herrschaft Gottes," 182–83.

12.   The abstract noun *Kingdom of God* also appears in Tob 13:2. Tob 13 is a text with a complex background. On the current discussion cf. A. Strotmann, *Vater*, 28–30. Tob 13:1b–6a, which is probably the earliest core of the text, already begins and ends with language about the divine kingship.

13.   Probably the text should not be understood in dualistic terms, since there is no struggle between opposites. Attention is focused, rather, on God's solitary work to which he also appoints Michael (*As. Mos.* 10:2). The devil, who is mentioned only in the introduction (vv. 1–2), was obviously Israel's oppressor in the period of Israel's history that is now drawing to a close. (*Tristitia* in 10:1 is to be understood as a reference not to Israel's mood but to the devil's activity, i.e., with the sense of *oppression.* Cf., e.g., 1QS iii 14, 21–22.) Unlike 1QM, the devil here is not the commander of the hostile force in the final struggle; indeed, there is no final struggle. Nor does he have a special relationship to the nations. Cf., in contrast to 1QM, vv. 2, 7, 10.

14.   The attempt to describe the framework as a late editorial criticism of the psalm's messianic expectation is not convincing (*contra* J. Schüpphaus, *Psalmen,* 64–65). The point of the framework is that the earthly king acts as the extended arm of the heavenly king (cf. Benediction 15 of the Eighteen Benedictions).

15.   In his enthusiasm to describe the Messiah and his work, the poet forgets to tell of the restoration of the temple. In the context of the Zion tradition such an oversight is unforgivable. Can one actually conceive of the hallowing of the nation and the city (*Ps. Sol.* 17:26, 30, 32, 43) without a temple? The king judges the chosen people, but he does not make them holy. Thus as an act of hostility toward the Sadducees the temple theme is banished to the background.

16.   K. Koch has called attention to the importance of this work for comparison with the preaching of Jesus ("Offenbaren"). We are justified in citing this targum here, because the beginning of the history of its translation dates from before 70 CE.

17.   On this subject cf. K. Koch, "Gottes Herrschaft."

18.   After a long period of controversy, a broad consensus appears to have emerged concerning the approximate date of *1 Enoch* and the question whether it is of Jewish or Christian origin. The parabolic addresses are Jewish. Whether there is Christian influence

cannot be verified, but the material's relationship to Old Testament texts, especially Daniel, is fundamental (cf. also Ps 110; Isa 49). Also clearly describable are references to *Jubilees, 2 Apocalypse of Baruch*, and the Sabbath hymns of Qumran. Incorporating these texts and traditions is a purely Jewish process. The parabolic addresses developed in stages in the two centuries that marked the transition to the Common Era, certainly before 70 CE. On this consensus cf. above all the discussions by F. H. Borsch, M. Black, and J. C. Vanderkam in: Charlesworth, *Messiah*. Cf. in addition S. Uhlig, *Henochbuch*, 574; W. G. Kümmel, *Jahre*, 353–60). The following comments take into consideration the literary layers to the degree that the Noachian sections (*1 Enoch* 39:1–2a; 54:7–55:2; 60; 65:1–69:25), the Wisdom insertion (*1 Enoch* 42), and the present conclusion (*1 Enoch* 70–71) are used only when they document something that is also found elsewhere. For the rest of the material it is a defensible thesis that the material is a conceptual unity in which disparate elements that have different histories came together.

19.   This formulation is taken over in *1 Enoch* 46:1, but elsewhere in the parabolic addresses the simile becomes the personal designation *the Son of Man* (cf. §4.4.2).

20.   Cf. especially *1 Enoch* 47:3 and 60:2 with Dan 7:9–10.

21.   *1 Enoch* 46:4–5 speaks analogously of the thrones of the human kings.

22.   The Sabbath psalms from Qumran provide impressive parallels to this heavenly kingdom.

23.   Daniel and the parabolic addresses accuse the kings of the same sins: misusing power, worshipping foreign gods, and persecuting the true worshipers of God (*1 Enoch* 46:7–8). Underlying this accusation is the same basic structure that one finds in Daniel, in which the earthly realities are seen as a world of tense relations between heathen, sacrilegious kings and the pious worshipers of God who live under their rule.

24.   That statements from Daniel appear frequently after *1 Enoch* 37–71 is hardly accidental. It would be difficult to exaggerate Daniel's influence on Early Jewish apocalypticism and on Primitive Christianity.

25.   1QM is not a unity. The following discussion interprets the text in its present, final form.

26.   The titles of God that follow come from the wisdom tradition. The structure is similar to Abraham's prayer in *Jub.* 12:19–20: (1) invocation of God as creator (v. 19a, b); (2) description of the human situation (v. 19c); (3) petition (v. 20). To be sure, there is no direct reference to God's kingship in the first section, but part two contains the words, "I have chosen you and your kingdom."

27.   Cf. in addition Ps 29, where in vv. 1–10 Yahweh is praised as king of creation, and then v. 11 concludes, "The Lord give strength to his people! The Lord bless his people with salvation!" Relevant here is also *1 Enoch* 9:4–11 in which first God's kingship in creation is celebrated (vv. 4–5), then a situation of misery is described (vv. 6–9), and, finally, instead of formulating a petition it is asked why God permits such things to happen (vv. 10–11).

28.   Cf. also *As. Mos.* 4:2–4 with the same themes and structure: Praise of God as king of the world and especially as king of Israel's history as the chosen people (4:2); description of the crisis (4:3); brief petition (v. 4: "Regard [the problem] and have compassion on them, O God of heaven").

29.   Of course, this special understanding of divine kingship in terms of God's

saving activity and compassion was part of God's kingship as early as Deutero-Isaiah (cf. §4.1.3). Cf. in addition Tob 13:2, 6–7, 10; 2 Macc 1:24; 3 Macc 6:4; Sir 51:1–12. An impressive monument to this theme is the song of praise that appears in the Cairo manuscript B as an addition of Sir 52:12.

30.   H. Merklein gives a well-structured survey of the evidence (*Handlungsprinzip*, 21–30).

31.   For more on the subject cf. U. B. Mell, *Schöpfung*, 119ff.

32.   Contrary to these texts, it is unlikely that Jesus is responsible for such sayings as the word of comfort in Mark 13:31 (cf. Matt 5:18) or the saying of Mark 12:25 on which the Jewish-Christian discussion in Mark 12:18–27 is based. (On this problem cf. 1 Cor 15:35–57.) Mark 12:25 is in conflict with Matt 8:11–12, and Mark 13:31 appeals to the continuing words of Jesus as a source of comfort in light of the delayed parousia.

33.   Cf. esp. H. Stegemann, *Essener*, 288–89.

34.   For an example of this expression cf. *1 Enoch* 50:1: "In those days a change will occur for the holy and elect."

35.   Cf. D. Flusser, *Jesus*, 87.

36.   Cf. among others 1QM xv 12–xvi 1; *Jub.* 23:29; *As. Mos.* 10:1–2; *Sib. Or.* 3.796–807; *T. Lev.* 18:12; *T. Jud.* 25:3; *T. Dan* 5:10–11.

37.   Thus S. Vollenweider, "Satan."

38.   Thus U. B. Müller, "Vision."

39.   Thus, e.g., P. Stuhlmacher, *Theologie*, 82.

40.   J. Becker, *Epoche*, 29–30.

41.   Cf. H. Merklein, *Botschaft*, 18–19.

42.   Cf. most recently H. Merkel, "Gottesherrschaft," 143–44; H. Weder, *Gegenwart*, 26ff.

43.   Cf., e.g., H.-W. Kuhn, *Enderwartung*, 193–94.

44.   Cf. H. Stegemann, *Essener*, 50–51.

45.   On the saying's cohesion, cf. U. B. Müller, "Vision," 432–33.

46.   Cf. the overview in R. Pesch, "Autorität," 30–33.

47.   On the reconstruction of the Q version, cf. H. Merklein, *Handlungsprinzip*, 80ff.; J. Gnilka, *Jesus*, 150–51.

48.   D. R. Catchpole's attempt ("Law") to create a single new line from a combination of lines two and three ("since then the Kingdom of God is proclaimed") results in a sentence with a good meaning, but it does so by eliminating the text's difficulties. Such an approach creates methodological problems.

49.   For comparative material and a discussion of the question of authenticity see M. Hengel, *Nachfolge*, 9–17; J. Sauer, *Rückkehr*, 196ff.

50.   Since Matt 11:5–6 par. lists the proclamation of the good news among the mighty deeds that accompany the Kingdom of God, one cannot make too much of the claim that Jesus never used verbs of proclamation in connection with the catchword *Kingdom of God*.

51.   Cf., e.g., Dan 2:44; *As. Mos.* 10:1; *Sib. Or.* 3.46–48; *Tg. Isa* 24:23; *Tg. Mic* 4:7; *Tg. Zech* 14:9.

52.   See H. Merklein, *Botschaft*, 18–19; 23.

53.   Cf. in addition Luke 11:2 = Matt 6:10; Luke 16:16 = Matt 11:12–13; Luke 17:20–21.

54.   Thus the world-judging Son of Man *comes* at the end of this age (Dan 7:13; cf. *1 Enoch* 69:29; Mark 13:26 parr.; Rev 1:7; 22:7, 12, 20), or the wrath (of judgment) of the end-time is *coming* (Matt 3:7 par.; 1 Thess 1:10).

55.   The exception, Mic 4:8, makes clear both in the Masoretic and in the Greek texts that it is not that a new reign of God is coming, but that the old reign is coming again.

56.   Cf. M. Weder, *Gegenwart*, 39–40.

57.   Cf. U. Mell, "Wein."

58.   1 Macc 1:25–28 and the pronouncement of judgment of a Jeshua ben Ananias (cf. §3.1.2) reveal that it was only in exceptional cases that a wedding was not a joyful occasion.

59.   Cf. J. Becker, *Epoche*, 96ff. 4 Ezra 4:26 offers an analogy from an apocalyptic tradition: "if you live long you will marvel, because the aeon is hurrying swiftly to its end."

60.   Mark 11:23; Luke 17:6 are hyperboles. Cf. §4.3.3.

61.   Cf. P. von Gemünden, *Vegetationsmetaphorik*, 192.

62.   The reference to the *chosen* in Matt 22:14; Mark 13:20, 22, 27; Luke 18:7 is an example of the language of the later church.

63.   Mark 12:26 parr. and Luke 16:19–31 hardly constitute authentic Jesus material.

64.   This statement assumes that Mark 12:1–11 parr. is not from Jesus. Cf. U. Mell, *Winzer*, 474ff. Luke 16:19–31 is also not a parable of Jesus. The traditional Jewish material is unusual for Jesus. Luke takes over a Jewish Christian tradition that has wisdom and Ebionite characteristics. On the discussion of this parable see F. W. Horn, *Glaube*, 81–88; 144–54.

65.   Cf. the following six items: Mark 4:3–8 parr.; 4:26–29; 4:30–32 parr.; Matt 13:33 par.; Luke 12:16–21; 15:4–7 par.

66.   See the following ten units: Matt 13:44; 13:45–46; 18:23–35; 20:1–16; Luke 11:5–8; 14:16–24 par. (in its original form); 15:8–10; 15:11–32; 16:1–8; 18:1–8.

67.   These examples demonstrate that Jesus limits his use of the creation theme to human beings. He views the nonhuman parts of creation only from an anthropocentric perspective.

68.   Structurally such comparisons are common in the wisdom material. Cf., e.g., *Ps. Sol.* 5:5–12 and in addition D. Zeller, *Mahnsprüche*, 89–90.

69.   Cf. the discussions by U. B. Müller, "Vision"; H. Stegemann, "Jesus"; J. Sauer, *Rückkehr*.

70.   Cf. the limited but similar sayings in Matt 1:21; 10:6; 15:24.

71.   The action is quite normal. Cf. J. Jeremias, *Parables*, 134.

72.   Compared with Luke, Matt 18:12 is secondary. Cf. H. Weder, *Gleichnisse*, 170–71.

73.   Comparative materials from the narrative culture are available in the works by K. Berger, P. Fiebig, D. Flusser, J. Jeremias, W. Pöhlmann, E. Rau, and P. Schulnigg.

74.   See, as an example, the recent discussion on Luke 15:11–32. Cf. W. Pöhlmann, *Sohn*, 153–83.

75.   Documented by J. Jeremias, *Parables*, 77–79.

76.   Thus A. Jülicher in his epoch-making work, *Gleichnisreden*, which dominated parable research for a generation.

77.   Thus E. Jüngel, H. Weder, et al.

78. Compared, appropriately, by W. Harnisch, *Gleichniserzählungen*, 16ff.

79. The definite article is used in a general sense (also in 15:27, 30).

80. Cf. the most recent major works on the text by E. Rau, *Reden*, and W. Pöhlmann, *Sohn*.

81. Cf. W. Pöhlmann, *Sohn*, 153–83.

82. Cf. W. Pöhlmann, "Abschichtung."

83. As a rule the older son received two-thirds of the inheritance, the younger son one-third.

84. Cf. P. Pokorný, *Entstehung*, 29; W. Nethöfel, *Hermeneutik*, 104–9.

85. Cf. P. Billerbeck, *Kommentar*, IV 2, 611ff.

86. Cf. G. Klinzing, *Umdeutung*, 106–43; H. Stegemann, *Essener*, 264–67.

87. For a discussion in more detail, see D.-A. Koch, "Tischgemeinschaft," 59–63.

88. By contrast, John the Baptist performed no miracles (John 10:41) and provided for himself (Mark 1:6).

89. See the foundational work by G. Theissen, *Miracle Stories*, who, however, sometimes succumbs to the danger of standardizing the material.

90. The apparent exception in Mark 11:12–14, 20–21 parr., is not originally a miracle of punishment. Here an apophthegm without a miracle (11:13–14) was later recast as a miracle (11:20–21).

91. On the evidence from Antiquity for demon possession and exorcisms see D. Trunk, *Heiler*, 243ff.

92. Because of his polemic against itinerant prophets, Matthew avoids Mark's emphasis on exorcisms by omitting some of them and by changing others to healings. Cf. D. Trunk, *Heiler*, 236–39.

93. Cf. K. E. Seybold and U. B. Müller.

94. Cf. G. Delling, P. Fiebig, M. Mills, and D. Trunk.

95. Cf. G. Haufe, R. Reitzenstein, G. Petzke, J. Z. Smith, D. L. Tiede, O. Weinrich.

96. Of course, explaining away the miraculous with rationalistic interpretations is the least acceptable option.

97. We have no evidence, however, that the Messiah or Son of Man was expected to perform miracles.

98. Angels appear only in a marginal role in the judgment in Luke 12:8–9 parr. (cf. §4.4.2).

99. Cf. the discussion in Theissen, *Miracle Stories*, 129–40.

100. Cf. the survey of current research that J. Sauer offers along with his own arguments (*Rückkehr*, 157–63).

101. Beelzebul is the name of an old Ugaritic deity, which means Sublime or Grand Lord. Early Judaism reduced such foreign deities to demons (cf. 1 Cor 8:4–5; 10:20). In addition, the names of the gods were sometimes changed to put them in a bad light (cf. Dan 12:11; Mark 13:14). Beelzebul, e.g., was changed to Beelzebub or Baalzebub, which means Lord of the Flies (cf. 2 Kgs 1:2–16 and the variant reading of Mark 3:22).

102. Cf., e.g., H. Seebass, *Herrscherverheißungen*.

103. Cf. the helpful discussions of the developmental history offered by J. Starcky, "étapes," and H Stegemann, *Essener*, 284ff.

104. Outstanding men of God from the past were also designated as *anointed* (1QM

xi 7–8; CD 2:12; 6:1). The chosen people themselves can be described the same way (*Sib. Or.* 5.68). For other evidence, however, (excluding the Septuagint) the situation is complex (cf. M. Karrer, *Gesalbte*, 228ff.).

105.   One did not even begin to speak of anointed eschatological figures in Early Judaism until long after actual acts of anointing in the installation of someone like a king or a high priest were no longer performed (M. Karrer, *Gesalbte*, 95ff.). Enoch's anointing in *2 Enoch* 22 enables him to enter the seventh and highest heaven (22:4, 6–7). Even the books that he is to write after the experience have a new source of revelation; they are dictated by the archangel (22:11–12).

106.   The stance of *Ps. Sol.* 17 is thus the opposite of the friendly attitude toward the Hasmoneans exhibited by 1 Macc.

107.   Cf. H. Stegemann, *Essener*, 287–88.

108.   Cf. Schürer, *History*, 2.504–5.

109.   It may be that the hope for a messianic ruler lies behind Josephus, *Ant.* 17.43ff. (Schürer, *History*, II 505), but the text is difficult. It is probably safe to say, however, that the Septuagint interprets Gen 49:10 and Num 24:7, 17 as messianic texts.

110.   Cf. J. Becker, *Auferstehung*, 18ff.; D. Zeller, "Transformation," 159ff.

111.   Cf. P. Schäfer, *History*, 148–51.

112.   Cf. 1QSa ii 18ff.; CD 7:18f.; 4QFlor.

113.   A possible later reference is *Sota* 9:9–15.

114.   The claims of M. Hengel have been influential in this regard (*The Zealots: Investigations into the Jewish Freedom Movement in the Period from Herod I until 70 A.D.* Edinburgh: T. & T. Clark, 1989). Recently J. D. Crossan has discussed the texts as messianic texts (*Jesus*, 270–84).

115.   Thus the recent suggestion from M. Karrer, *Gesalbte*, 240–41, who also gives a brief survey of current research.

116.   Cf. M. Karrer, *Gesalbte*, 147ff.

117.   Discussed in greater detail by P. Schäfer, *History*, 67–69.

118.   We will contend in §6.3 that the inscription on the cross is not relevant for the question of the messiahship of Jesus.

119.   Cf. J. Becker, *Epoche*, 25–26, 38ff.

120.   Cf. A. J. B. Higgins, "Problem," 84; also A. Vögtle, *Gretchenfrage*, 168ff.

121.   Cf. J. Becker, *Epoche*, 50ff.

122.   This view is impressively defended by P. Hoffmann ("Jesus") and A. Vögtle (*Gretchenfrage*).

123.   Those who see various layers of tradition in the synoptic Son of Man sayings, e.g., are able to argue that the process began with the idiomatic usage, while the understanding represented by Dan 7 influenced the tradition at a later stage.

124.   The recent discussion was initiated by G. Vermés in 1973 with the publication of his English edition of *Jesus the Jew*.

125.   Cf. J. A. Fitzmyer, "Title"; W. G. Kümmel, *Jahre*, 348–51; 520–25; A. Vögtle, *Gretchenfrage*, 31–64.

126.   This appealing thesis is defended, e.g., by J. J. Collins, *Imagination*, 81–85, and K. Koch, *Daniel*, 220–21.

127.   On this subject see K. Koch, "Messias," 82–83.

128. Cf. J. J. Collins, *Imagination*, 148–49.

129. When Enoch is installed as the Son of Man in *1 Enoch* 70–71, a later view is added to the text that was not in the original parabolic discourses.

130. For an analysis cf. E. Brandenburger, *Markus 13*.

131. The text does not identify Jesus as Son of Man, and it portrays what one would expect in a typical Jewish apocalyptic description of the future.

132. Cf. J. Becker, *Epoche*, 50ff.

133. When we look at somewhat later Jewish-Christian texts, we find in Rev 1:13–18 a later witness for a completely independent Son of Man christology.

134. The term *Son of Man* first appears as a description of Jesus' humanity in Ign. *Eph.* 20:2 and *Barn.* 12:10.

135. This division goes back to R. Bultmann, *Theology*, 30, and is widely accepted. G. Haufe ("Menschensohnproblem") gives an informative survey of the current discussion of the three groups.

136. Cf. D. Lührmann, *Redaktion*, 75–83.

137. Our analysis assumes that Luke is responsible for Luke 17:25. With reference to Luke 17:37c, Matthew's order is original.

138. Luke changes the form to the plural (cf. the Lukan verse 17:22) to make it agree with 17:26a (it is singular in 17:29, 31). Matthew introduces the early Christian concept of the parousia (24:37, 39).

139. For a discussion of the question cf. J. Becker, *Täufer*, 90–95.

140. Cf. R. Pesch, "Autorität," 26–39; A. Vögtle, *Gretchenfrage*, 14–21.

141. Cf. also the Son of Man tradition in Mark 13:26–27; Matt 13:41; 16:27; 1 Thess 3:13; 2 Thess 1:7, where the same motif appears.

142. Some object that the view that Jesus stood in the line of the prophets has long since been disproven. Their claim is right to a degree, but it misses the point. The issue is not that Jesus stood in direct continuity with classical prophecy; it is that he was part of the prophecy of his own day, which had its own relationship to Old Testament prophecy.

143. R. Meyer ("Prophecy and Prophets in the Judaism of the Hellenistic-Roman Period," *TDNT* 6 [1968] 823–26) offers further examples.

144. Dan 9 serves as an impressive example.

145. P. Schäfer, *History*, 148–51.

146. It is questionable whether there was in Late Judaism an identifiable tradition looking for a bearer of good news according to Isa 61:1–2 (J. Becker, *Täufer*, 53–54). On understanding Jesus as the bearer of good news cf. also H. Frankemölle, "Jesus," and J. Becker, *Epoche*, 25–26.

147. This usual assumption is discussed in §4.2.2.

148. In §4.4.1 we have already criticized the general category of *messianic*.

149. Cf. J. Becker, *Täufer*, 41–43.

5

The Understanding and Formation of Life in Light of the Kingdom of God

Bald, H. "Eschatologische oder theozentrische Ethik?" *VF* 24 (1979) 35–52.

Becker, J. "Das Ethos Jesu und die Geltung des Gesetzes," in: *Neues Testament und Ethik.* Festschrift R. Schnackenburg. H. Merklein, ed. Freiburg/Basel/Vienna: Herder, 1989, 31–52.

Betz, H. D. *Essays on the Sermon on the Mount.* Philadelphia: Fortress, 1985.spret

Dautzenberg, G. "Über die Eigenart des Konfliktes, der von jüdischer Seite im Prozeß Jesu ausgetragen wurde," in: *Jesus und das jüdische Gesetz.* I. Broer, ed. Stuttgart: Kohlhammer, 1992, 147–72.

Dillmann, R. *Das Eigentliche der Ethik Jesu.* TTS 23. Mainz: Matthias Grunewald, 1984.

Eichholz, G. *Auslegung der Bergpredigt.* BSt 46. 5th ed. Neukirchen-Vluyn: Neukirchener Verlag, 1982.

Guelich, R. A. *The Sermon on the Mount.* Waco, TX: Word, 1982.

Hiers, R. H. *Jesus and Ethics: Four Interpretations.* Philadelphia: Westminster, 1968.

Hoffmann, P. and V. Eid. *Jesus von Nazareth und eine christliche Moral.* QD 66. Freiburg/Basel/Vienna: Herder 1975.

Lohfink, G. *Jesus and Community: The Social Dimensions of Christian Faith.* Philadelphia: Fortress; New York: Paulist, 1984.

Manson, T. W. *Ethics and the Gospel.* London: SCM; New York: Scribners, 1960.

Neuhäusler, E. *Anspruch und Antwort Gottes.* Düsseldorf: Patmos, 1962.

Pokorný, P. *Der Kern der Bergpredigt.* Hamburg: Evangelischer Verlag, 1969.

Sanders, J. T. *Ethics in the New Testament.* Philadelphia: Fortress, 1975.

Schmeller, Th. *Brechungen,* 66–70.

Schnackenburg, R. *The Moral Teaching of the New Testament.* New York: Herder & Herder, 1965.

Schrage, W. *The Ethics of the New Testament.* Philadelphia: Fortress, 1987.

Schulz, S. *Neutestamentliche Ethik.* ZGB. Zürich: Theologischer Verlag, 1987.

Strecker, G. *The Sermon on the Mount.* Nashville: Abingdon, 1985.

———. *Handlungsorientierter Glaube.* Stuttgart: Kreuz, 1972.

Weder, H. *Die "Rede der Reden".* Zürich: Theologischer Verlag, 1985.

Wendland, H.-D. *Ethik des Neuen Testaments.* GNT 4. Göttingen: Vandenhoeck & Ruprecht, 1970.

White, R. E. O. *Biblical Ethics.* Atlanta: John Knox, 1979.

Wilder, A. N. *Eschatology and Ethics in the Teaching of Jesus.* Rev. ed. Westport, CT: Greenwood, 1950.

Windisch, H. *Der Sinn der Bergpredigt.* UNT 16. 2d ed. Leipzig: Hinrich, 1937.

Wrege, H. T. *Die Überlieferungsgeschichte der Bergpredigt.* WUNT 9. Tübingen: J.C.B. Mohr (Paul Siebeck), 1968.

5.1 BASIC QUESTIONS ABOUT THE ETHIC OF JESUS

No element of early Christian tradition has had a greater influence on subsequent history than Jesus' call to a new understanding of life and his instructions on how to live out that understanding. This influence is due not least of all to Matthew and his Sermon on the Mount, whose provocative sentences (such as the call to love one's enemy) have not only dominated the discussion of ethics within the Christian community; they have also influenced the wider cultural dialogue about the ethical life. Yet, it has been the widespread popularity of precisely this part of the preaching of Jesus that has led other worldviews and understandings of human life to appropriate the Jesus materials for their own purposes. As a result, these materials have been subjected to a thoroughgoing reinterpretation. Modern interpreters of Jesus cannot avoid this history since, indeed, they are part of it.

In order to come to an understanding of this dimension of the preaching of Jesus in a way that is as controlled and methodologically sound as possible, we must keep two things in mind in addition to the methodological considerations that we enumerated in Chapter 1. For one thing, we may not separate Jesus' statements about his ethic from his preaching of the Kingdom of God. Isolating one set of statements from another has been done all too often in a way that has resulted in a distortion of the material. We will have occasion to make frequent reference to this concern in the following sections. In the second place, we must subject the language and the paradigms that we use to describe the Jesus material to strenuous criticism in order to keep from subjecting Jesus' statements prematurely to a conceptual world that is foreign to them.

Part of this latter problem is the question of whether Jesus even intended to teach ethics. At the very least we must say that Jesus' message does not contain an ethical system; nowhere does he pose theoretical considerations about which of life's possibilities are to be affirmed, how and under what conditions they are to be justified, or how these options measure up against one another. He offers no theoretical discourse about norms, reasons, or situations, and he does not even hint of an interest in how ethical judgments are formed. He is not concerned about defining all possible areas of human activity in terms of their ethical claims. He does not ask about the best way to construct an ethical system and how one should proceed in an ethical presentation. We look in vain in Jesus for these and other requirements that one would bring to a modern ethical system. He took nothing from Aristotle, the founder of systematic ethics. Jesus is neither a philosopher nor a systematic theologian.

Morality is also a concept that we probably should avoid in our description of Jesus, since this word refers more to traditional norms that lie behind jurisprudence—norms that form community, give it cohesion, and belong to its general culture. One could describe ancient teachers of wisdom (such as those who produced Sirach, *Ep. Arist.*, *T. 12*), e.g., as representatives of morality. Their purpose is to preserve the norms, customs, and rules of behavior that have stood the test of time—perhaps even to make them relevant for the continuing life of the community. The proclamation of the Kingdom of God, on the other hand, throws the world in its present form into crisis. Something new is clamoring for attention. With Jesus, therefore, there is a tension between Early Judaism's way of life as he knew it and normative claims laid on people. Because of this tension his ethic is characterized by responsible, discomforting, and, to the outsider, unusual decisions that he requires of those who would accept his message. Morality lives primarily by means of synchronic and diachronic incorporation into the norms of a group, not by individual reflection and personal evaluation of the norms. This tension between Jesus' preaching and practice of the Kingdom of God on the one hand and the existing order on the other is for him so fundamental and preeminent that referring to the undeniable existence of wisdom traditions in the oldest Jesus material carries little weight against it. It is the pioneering, eschatological Kingdom of God that determines the meaning and function of the wisdom material, not the other way around. Jesus is not primarily a sage in the wisdom tradition; he is a prophet of the beginning end-time who sets into motion the final divine drama.

Nor should we characterize the life-shaping dimension of the proclamation of Jesus in terms of Jewish Halacha. In the time of Jesus, Halacha is associated with the continuous reflection on the Torah (Ps 1; cf. Rom 2:17–18) and the effort to actualize the Torah in daily life. This reflection is a fundamental orientation of one's life, without interruption and without exception, to the Sinai Torah. Here the basic principle was "Fulfill the Law, and you will live" (cf. Deut 9:4; 30:15–16). At Sinai Israel received the Torah as the proclamation of God's will, and from that point on it is the authority that sets the standards for all human conduct. Thus Halacha and Torah-obedience are intimately related. Yet, with the exception of the material unique to Matthew (Matt 5:17–19; 7:12c; 19:17b; 23:2–3), only in Mark 12:28–34 parr. does the Torah appear as a normative program designed to govern all of life, and even this tradition of the dual commandment of love probably does not go back to Jesus (cf. §5.2.3). A Jesus tradition that in its core is authentic says rather that the Law and the Prophets lasted until John and that they belong to the time that, now that the Kingdom of God has appeared as the end-time, lies in the past (Luke 16:16 par.; cf. §4.2.2). However Jesus may have determined his relation to the Jewish Law in individual cases (§5.3), one thing is clear: He is no scribe (rabbi, sage), who could summarize his entire message to his contemporaries by saying: "Observe . . . the commandment of the Lord, and keep his Law!" (*T. Dan* 5:1; cf. *T. Iss.* 5:1; *T. Naph.* 8:10, etc.). His proclamation of the Kingdom of God that is drawing near unquestionably has a different intention. His purpose is not to transmit previous understandings of the Law and its interpretation in detail, but rather to measure all reality, including the way people shape their lives, by the Kingdom of God itself. For the sake of historical clarity, therefore, we should not speak of a Halacha of Jesus.

It is, furthermore, not appropriate to describe the ethical preaching of Jesus as parenesis. The parenesis known both to Antiquity and to Christianity is a loosely structured but by no means unsystematic collection of individual exhortations that reflect an existing social structure. The exhortations themselves appear in abbreviated form and are more likely simply to be asserted than explicitly justified (e.g., Rom 12–13; James; *Didache*, etc.). Since parenesis functions to preserve as comprehensively as possible for a given community its existing rules of behavior, it is not obligated to justify its exhortations; it can simply describe what has been valid and what should continue to be valid. Parenesis makes explicit the conventional norms that are practiced in a community's daily life in order to internalize them and to ensure their continued existence. The Sermon on the Mount is a classic example of how Jesus material can become parenesis, but Matthew and his church are responsible for this parenetic form of the material. The Jesus material that is preserved in the Sermon on the Mount and elsewhere is not originally parenesis. Thus our objections to using the terms *morality* and *Halacha* are equally relevant for parenesis.

Describing Jesus' ethic as an eschatological divine law avoids all the problems associated with the catchwords *morality*, *Halacha*, and *parenesis*. Jesus' norms, in other words, are the Magna Carta of God's final judgment. They serve neither to provide principles of behavior nor to refine human understanding of the Torah; instead, they authoritatively reveal the radical nature of God's end-time forum of judgment. Jesus does not evaluate the human condition of lostness in terms of violations of the Torah; he measures people instead against God's perfection and holiness (§3.2.6). We are to understand Jesus' norms in terms of the end-time Kingdom of God that is in the process of being realized. They are articulated, therefore, within an eschatological context. It is true that we cannot easily use the forensic concept of justice to describe Jesus (Matt 5:21–22 provides too limited a basis). It is also true that according to his message it is precisely the experience of the saving power of the creator who is in the process of establishing his final rule that makes it possible for people to behave in a way that is appropriate to that kingdom (cf. e.g., Matt 5:44–45 par.; 6:25–34 par.; 18:23–35). When he was asked to define his eschatological standard of judgment, Jesus did not recite a catalog of norms; he called people to follow him as the one who in the present is establishing the final Kingdom of God (Luke 12:8–9 par.; §4.4.2).

In our search for a concept that can best capture that dimension of the preaching of Jesus that lays a claim on human life, we can still do no better than the concept of ethic. As a rule, one's ethic is determined by a personal conviction, from which are derived the power and the direction for life. The term does not carry the theoretical connotations associated with the term *ethics*. It is open enough that it is not as focused on traditional norms as is the catchword *morality*; it avoids the attachment to the Torah that is characteristic of *Halacha*; and when compared with *parenesis* it has the advantage of being able to incorporate the prophetic and eschatological dimension of the preaching of Jesus. Jesus' ethic is prophetic in the sense that it is spoken by a prophet; it is eschatological in the sense that its initial impulse comes from the Kingdom of God, which is asserting itself in the end-time. It is, in short, the structuring of life in view of history's turning-point, which has already occurred and the realization of salvation, which is imminent.

There is, to be sure, a special quality to Jesus' prophetic and eschatological ethic. Although Jesus speaks to his contemporary Israelites in their actions as moral agents, as a rule he does not try to define their behavior in concrete, individual situations. (Luke 12:13–14 is typical for him.) He does not engage in casuistry; he does not analyze situations; he negotiates no compromises; he does not weigh values against one another; he offers no catalog of norms or behaviors; he does not debate a norm's value for a community. He makes no use of "if . . . , then . . . " sentences. The only situation he recognizes is the situation that is created by the approaching Kingdom of God and that is totally dominated by his presence. Nowhere does he identify, as Paul does in 1 Cor 6:1–11, what is the best (but also the most difficult) option, what must be avoided, and where one might find a middle way as a compromise. He does not consider situations in which one must choose between competing, mutually exclusive values (cf. Phil 1:21–26). He speaks consistently in aphorisms and has no interest in collections of rules for the total life of a community such as one finds in Matt 5–7 or Rom 12–13.

Given these limitations, what positive statement can we make about Jesus' intention? The demands of Jesus directed to people who are struggling to live well—sometimes successfully, sometimes unsuccessfully—come to them in the form of general rules such as the love of one's enemy (Matt 5:44–45 par.), the prohibition of judging (Matt 7:1 par.), or the fundamental choice between serving God or mammon (Matt 6:24 par.). People hear of observable behavior in specific situations (Luke 6:29), or of one's obligations as a vassal (Matt 5:41 par.), or they experience Jesus as an interpreter of the Law (e.g., Mark 10:11–12 parr.). Yet, a person's relationship that is addressed (whether personal, as in the case of the enemy, or impersonal, as in the case of one's possessions), or a specific area of behavior (controversy, indebtedness), or the special case of a legal regulation (marriage and its dissolution) is always treated in a way that transcends the individual case and focuses attention on a fundamental principle. Among the many examples of the love commandment (family, friendship, nation, stranger, enemy), e.g., Jesus does not discuss how one should act in even the most equivocal case. Instead, he makes this most uncomfortable test-case the basis for describing a fundamental attitude for self-understanding in every situation. The statement about a peasant's obligation in a vassal relationship in Matt 5:41 par. is not designed to foster submissive obedience by supporting the position of a landowner, or a ruler, or the commander of an invading army. Instead, this concrete example from a limited area of behavior becomes a question to the individual about the understanding of life out of which one lives. We could illustrate this point with many other examples.

When Jesus addresses persons as moral agents, therefore, his words would be misunderstood if they were used directly, either then or now, to describe his requirements for every possible area of activity. With such statements he is not defining in detail his followers' political, national, social, or economic obligations. Indeed, his statements are intentionally designed to keep people from using them that way by forcing the hearers to move beyond the question, What shall I do? to the question, Who am I? or, even better, Who am I in light of the impending Kingdom of God? so that they can commit themselves in new and better ways to the formation of a successful life. Jesus does not create a list of rules for his followers, which they then automatically and uncompromisingly must obey in every situation. Instead, he forces them to ask, Of whose spirit am I a child? and then, within the limits of their answer, he gives them the freedom to shape their own lives.

Dealing with ethic at this deeper level relieves Jesus of the pressure of commenting on every ethically relevant case. Instead of offering a list of all possible situations, he paradigmatically offers examples of the all-encompassing reality that underlies the individual cases. While his choices are hardly selected at random, we should not expect him to offer a systematic presentation. What we will more likely find is a sense of direction for the formation of one's life. This would mean, by the way, that he also is not interested in the issue of sanctions in human society. He is concerned only with the total scope of divine judgment and mercy. From this perspective the focus is on the decisive question: Who am I before God and my neighbor?

To be sure, the relationship between the Kingdom of God and human behavior that we have suggested poses several problems that need to be addressed. The primary problem is the question of whether the nature of the traditions even permits such a clear-cut option. From a history-of-traditions point of view, are not the prophetic proclamation of the Kingdom of God and wisdom sayings completely independent of one another? Are not, to put it in systematic terms, eschatology and ethics in Jesus relatively unrelated? Does not Jesus perform the parallel functions of prophet and sage (rabbi) at the same time? The answer to this question is: Neither can we permit the two strands of tradition to run parallel to one another nor can we play one off against the other. Nor can we seek a third way (emphasizing, e.g., Jesus' concept of God,[1] the human situation of decision,[2] or Jesus' self-understanding[3]) as a way of harmonizing the two traditions. The most consistently valid approach in reconstructing the preaching of Jesus is to recognize that his understanding of the Kingdom of God is the central element from which his entire proclamation becomes transparent.[4] Not all parables, e.g., contain the term *Kingdom of God*, yet the inner evidence for their themes and their intention demonstrates such a closeness to the Kingdom of God that we are justified in saying that parabolic speech in a special way reveals the Kingdom of God (cf. §4.3.1). Since, furthermore, it is characteristic of Jesus that the concept of God as creator and the Kingdom of God are related in a special way (§4.2.3), it should not surprise us that wisdom creation-traditions are used to describe God's will. In addition, when claims are made of people concerning the shaping of their lives, what is important is whether and to what degree their norms correspond to the Kingdom of God. If we can demonstrate this statement, then our claim that Jesus' approach to ethic is determined by the Kingdom of God is confirmed not only by fundamental reflection and by argument from analogy, but also by an examination of the content of the ethic in each individual case.[5]

Yet, to understand the ethic of Jesus in terms of the Kingdom of God—i.e., from the perspective of Jesus' eschatology—and thus to subordinate especially the wisdom material to this concern is to be confronted with a new problem: What does such an eschatological ethic have to do with normal life? Is it perhaps limited to that segment of time between Jesus' proclamation and the complete realization of the Kingdom of God? Is Jesus' ethic an interim ethic[6] in the sense that it is valid only for the time between Jesus' appearance and the end? In dealing with this question we need to remember that Jesus separates the present from the past, but understands the final consummation of history in continuity with the Kingdom of God that is presently asserting itself (§4.2.2). From this perspective the term *interim* is misleading, indeed, inappropriate, since it regards the time from the proclamation of the Kingdom of God to its coming as a separate period of time and creates a break between the present and the future. *Interim* suggests a time of waiting for a future that is imminent, but that is yet to appear. Jesus understands his present, however, as the beginning of the future, which will continue until the final banquet of salvation. His ethic, therefore, is an end-time ethic at least in the sense that, effective immediately, he intends it to be permanent. He certainly does not believe that at the final banquet God will propagate a new way of social living that is different from that of the present in which he is beginning to realize his saving rule. Furthermore, Jesus' ethic is determined not by the shortness of the time until the end, as the interim terminology suggests, but by the content of the Kingdom of God itself.[7] The forgiveness of the debts in Matt 18:23–35 (cf. 3.2.4) is designed to bring the forgiven servant to the inner conviction that he should share his forgiveness. It is not the case that a heightened expectation of the end eliminates such worldly concerns as debts.

While Jesus' ethic cannot be limited to an interim period, there remains the possibility of limiting it to a special group—perhaps to the followers of Jesus or even to Israel. Here also we need to examine the evidence carefully. There is no doubt that Jesus addresses contemporary Judaism and, as a rule, gives special attention to those who followed him. Yet, as clear as it is that he makes no missionary journey outside Israel to a place like Syria, it is equally clear that he develops an ethic that encompasses all of humanity. The love of one's enemy (Matt 5:44–45 par.), e.g., is grounded in creation, and it is a Samaritan, not an Israelite, who demonstrates exemplary love. The ethical themes with which Jesus deals consistently are general, human concerns. Indeed, this emphasis was anticipated by the Early Jewish wisdom tradition, which plays such a major role in the understanding of the will of God in the preaching of Jesus. This evidence corresponds precisely to the theological focus on creation in the Kingdom of God whose final banquet of salvation will also include the nations (Matt 8:11 par.). Corresponding to the universal dimension of the Kingdom of God is a will of God that is concerned with all humanity. For obvious reasons, after the death of Jesus Primitive Christianity developed an ethic that was concerned with the Christian community and that treated the rest of humanity only marginally. Yet, we would be swimming against the current of the preaching of Jesus (not to mention the Primitive Christianity that followed him) were we to attribute to it an ethic of exclusivity that is limited to a small group. Jesus does not create a special group in Israel; he addresses all Israel, yet he does it in such a way that he proclaims God's will for his creation.

Is perhaps God's will different in the present than it was prior to the appearance of Jesus? Or is it the case that God's will has been the same since the beginning of creation, only that Jesus is now drawing special attention to it? The clear break between present and past (§4.2.2) cautions against assuming that Jesus regards the will of God as always the same. Nor is Jesus' attitude toward the Torah, as controversial as this subject presently is, such that, to put it carefully, he simply expands it and interprets it as a Law that is always valid for creation and humanity as well as for Israel (cf. §5.3). It is noteworthy that he himself does not raise the issue of continuity with the Torah, but that he evaluates everything in terms of the essence of his message of the Kingdom of God, viz., God's gracious nearness to the lost,[8] and that he thereby consciously accepts a tension with the Torah in, e.g., questions of ritual purity (§5.3.4). On the other hand, Jesus naturally is not concerned consistently and exclusively to emphasize what is new in his ethic. *New at any price* is not his slogan. Continuity with what is old does not bother him, as many of his ethical statements can demonstrate (§5.3). Still, such continuity is not a programmatic goal; instead, when it appears it is the result of Jesus' commitment to the Kingdom of God, which from now on determines everything.

To say that Jesus' ethic is an attitude formed in light of the impending Kingdom of God is not to say that it in any way causes the kingdom. The ethic does not consist in human efforts to make God's rule happen. It is the Kingdom of God itself that brings near his rule (§4.2); God and God alone makes it happen. All are lost, and no one can escape the judgment. Only the Lord of judgment can decide on behalf of lost persons whether and how he will grant them salvation. In spite of all its diffuse beginnings (Mark 4:1–8) God's rule appears irresistibly *of itself* (Mark 4:28). The power with which Jesus drives out demons *by the finger of God* (Luke 11:20) also derives solely from God's nearness. The food of Jesus' table-fellowship comes from God for those persons who strive for the Kingdom of God (Matt 6:25–34; cf. §4.2.3).

The human role, on the other hand, does not consist simply in waiting patiently for the harvest (Mark 4:27). Asking for the coming of the Kingdom (Matt 6:10 par.) is an active process; even persevering to the end and praying are, by themselves, not enough. Discipleship involves a special way of living. Those whose debts have been forgiven are to forgive the debts that their neighbors owe them (Matt 18:23–35). Whoever has experienced God's love and sees it reflected in God's activity as creator should act that love out in the area of human relationships (Matt 5:44–45 par.). These examples do not change the reality that God alone can graciously heal his relationship to human beings and that no human agent can reinforce or supplement God's sovereignty. They do make clear, however, that those persons who have experienced God's nearness can and should create new relationships among themselves and that Jesus expects this kind of human involvement in the Kingdom of God. Indeed, he requires even more of the twelve by authorizing them to drive out demons even as he does (Mark 3:14–15; Luke 9:1–2; 11:20).

That is not to say, however, that Jesus demands so much more from the disciples that we should speak of a two-tiered ethic, viz., a radical ethic for those who are disciples in the narrow sense and a less demanding ethic for his sympathizers in the villages of Galilee.[9] We can reckon with that kind of double standard only by assuming that the post-Easter mission to Israel presupposed by the instructions of Mark 6:7–13 par. and Luke 10:1–16 par. and that the three cardinal demands of giving up home, profession, and family were for all practical purposes institutionalized for the circle of the twelve. Given the nature of the sources and the earliest material that they contain, we can hardly make such an assumption (cf. above, §2). Life in the circle of the twelve was probably more loose and unregulated; the later, post-Easter special regulations are for them not yet a regular practice. If we posit the possibility of a group of persons between the inner circle and the followers who lived in the villages—a group that occasionally traveled with Jesus—the possibility of a two-tiered ethic becomes even more confusing. It is important to keep in mind that the twelve are a visible symbol that the proclamation of the Kingdom of God is directed to all Israel. They are not a select group chosen from Israel; they represent all Israel, and it is in the service of that ministry that they are called temporarily to be disciples.

Since the Kingdom of God is for all Israel, the behavior that is appropriate to that kingdom is required of all Israel. The more severe requirements for the inner circle of disciples that we find in the earliest material have one simple explanation. Just as Jesus himself risked his family relations for the sake of the Kingdom of God (Mark 6:1–6 par.), disciples must also give up all family obligations for the duration of their discipleship. Peter is not to care for his wife, and the potential disciple in Luke 9:60 is not to be concerned about his dead father (cf. Luke 14:26). Just as Jesus trusts himself to God's care and in principle demands of all his followers the same carefree attitude in view of the impending Kingdom of God (Matt 6:25–34), disciples who proclaim the kingdom (Matt 10:7–8=Luke 10:9) also must live conspicuously and concretely without a purse[10] and without luggage (Luke 10:4). They are not ascetics in the style of John the Baptist (Mark 1:6 parr.); they may count on and accept hospitality in a village. Indeed, that is the way God's care becomes real for them (cf. §4.3.2).

Our discussion of the question of a two-tiered ethic for Jesus should not focus exclusively on the disciples; it should also consider those persons commonly known as sympathizers. To call them sympathizers is not to suggest that they are only marginally related to the message of the Kingdom of God. On the contrary, they are totally involved in the initial establishment of God's rule. Jesus is convinced that God will establish his eschatological rule in all Israel. Those persons who participate in Jesus' table-fellowship are not in a no-man's land between discipleship and rejecting his claims; in their experience of the Kingdom of God they are subjected to all of the claims that that kingdom brings to life.

By way of summary, the most that we can say is that Jesus may in a very limited sense imply what we might call a special ethic for his closest disciples. In view of the nature of our sources it makes more sense, however, to speak of a single ethic of Jesus and then to assume for the members of the inner circle that they begin to demonstrate already the kind of life that will be appropriate to the Kingdom of God when it comes in its fullness, viz., a life that is totally oriented toward the Kingdom of God and that trusts totally in God's care.

Finally, we should say a word about the Jesus who brings to people the demands of this ethic. He is related to it in two ways. He is a person whose own life is determined by the Kingdom of God and who himself lives for the kingdom. He is also the prophetic authority who formulates the ethic and who presses its claims. Naturally the two functions belong together for Jesus. Since his authority is the Kingdom of God for which and in which he lives, he himself becomes the living authority of the ethic of this kingdom. He thus claims the same authority in proclaiming God's will that he claims, e.g., in the healings with which he establishes the kingdom (Luke 11:20). This observation makes it possible to recognize that Jesus and his ethic appear in the culture of Early Judaism alongside the ethical stance represented by the line of thinking *covenant Law–keeping the Law–receiving life*. There is, therefore, an inner-Jewish tension that can by harmonized only by ignoring the sense of the texts of the earliest Jesus material.

5.2 UNCOMPROMISING DISCIPLESHIP AS AN EXPRESSION OF GRATITUDE

5.2.1 Joyful Discovery and Uncompromising Decision

Becker, J. "Buße IV," *TRE* 7 (1981) 446–51.

Behm, J. "Metanoia," *DTh* 7 (1940) 75–86.

Berger, K. "Materialien zur Form und Überlieferungsgeschichte neutestamentlicher Gleichnisse," *NT* 15 (1973) 1–37.

Braun, H. "'Umkehr' in spätjüdisch-häretischer und in frühchristlicher Sicht," in: idem, *Gesammelte Studien zum Neuen Testament und seiner Umwelt.* 3d ed. Tübingen: J.C.B. Mohr (Paul Siebeck), 1971, 70–85.

Derrett, J. D. M. "Law in the New Testament: The Treasure in the Field (Mt 13,44)," *ZNW* 54 (1963) 31–42.

Eichholz, G. *Gleichnisse der Evangelien.* 3d ed. Neukirchen-Vluyn: Neukirchener Verlag, 1979, 192–99.

Hengel, M. *Nachfolge.*

Jülicher, A. *Gleichnisreden.* II 202–14, 581–85.

Knütel, R. "'Der Schatz im Acker' und 'die bösen Weingärtner'," *Juristische Schulung* 26 (1986) 950–57.

Kuhn, H. W. "Nachfolge nach Ostern," in: *Kirche.* Festschrift G. Bornkamm. D. Lührmann and G. Strecker, eds. Tübingen: J.C.B. Mohr (Paul Siebeck), 1980, 105–32.

Limbeck, M. "Jesu Verkündigung und der Ruf zur Umkehr," in: *Das Evangelium auf dem Weg zum Menschen.* Festschrift H. Kahlefeld. Frankfurt: Knecht, 1973, 35–42.

Löning, K. "Die Füchse, die Vögel und der Menschensohn (Mt 8,19f par.; Lk 9,57f)," in: *Vom Urchristentum zu Jesus.* Festschrift J. Gnilka. H. Frankemölle and K. Kertelge, eds. Freiburg/Basel/Vienna: Herder, 1989, 82–102.

Merklein, H. "Metanoia," *EWNT.* 2d ed. (1992) 1022–31.

———. "Die Umkehrpredigt bei Johannes dem Täufer und Jesus von Nazareth," in: idem, *Studien zu Jesus und Paulus.* WUNT 43. Tübingen: J.C.B. Mohr (Paul Siebeck), 1987, 109–26.

———. "Der Jüngerkreis Jesu," in: *Die Aktion Jesu und die Re-Aktion der Kirche.* Kh. Müller, ed. Würzburg: Echter Verlag, 1972, 65–100.

Michel, O. "Die Umkehr nach der Verkündigung Jesu," *EvTh* 5 (1938) 403–13.

Schnackenburg, R. *Moral Teaching,* 25–53, 73–81.

Schniewind, J. *Die Freude der Buße.* KVR 32. 2d ed. Göttingen: Vandenhoeck & Ruprecht, 1960.

Schulz, A. *Nachfolgen und Nachahmen.* StANT 6. Munich: Kösel, 1962.

Suss, T. "Nachfolge Jesu," *ThLZ* 78 (1953) 129–40.

Weder, H. *Gleichnisse,* 138–42.

Jesus responded to the Baptist's call to a final and comprehensive repentance as a total reorientation of one's life in light of the coming wrath (cf. §3.1.3); indeed, he himself submitted to baptism as an act of repentance. In the context of his own preaching of judgment, the call to repentance appears then as a summons to all Israel (cf. §3.2.2). Of course, when Mark connects Jesus' preaching of the Kingdom of God with the call to repentance in 1:15 by saying, "The time is fulfilled and the Kingdom of God has drawn near; repent and believe in the gospel," he is summarizing the early Christian missionary preaching (cf. §4.2.2). We nowhere find the message of the imminent Kingdom of God connected with the call to repentance in light of that kingdom in an authentic saying of Jesus. The popular claim in books about Jesus to the effect that he transformed the Baptist's call to repentance so that the earlier repentance in light of the impending judgment becomes in the mouth of Jesus a repentance as a consequence of the offer of salvation simply is not supported in this form by the texts.

What is true in this claim is that Jesus in fact did expect from his hearers an uncompromising and total reorientation of life in view of his offer of salvation. While he expresses this expectation in various ways, he nowhere does so with the word *repentance*. We find him using this word only in the context of judgment. For Jesus we must distinguish, therefore, between the call to repentance and the call to decision. The decision for the Kingdom of God that he demands comes from an experience of salvation that the kingdom offers. It is a grateful response, which knows that it is called to a new life—a shaping of life based on joy and freedom from judgment. Repentance, on the other hand, is an expression of life lived under the threat of judgment; it is remorse based on guilt and anxiety. Neither case is satisfied with a partial change. Both desire an unrepeatable and thoroughgoing reorientation of life. Yet, each has its own conceptual world and its own vocabulary.

The call to decision in view of the Kingdom of God that has already drawn near is developed from three points of view. Sometimes Jesus speaks of the decision's severity—its uncompromising nature. On other occasions he focuses on the need to calculate the cost of discipleship;[11] in view of the severity of the demand, one must stop to consider whether one is being swept along by temporary enthusiasm. Still other times Jesus emphasizes that being overtaken by the Kingdom of God is such a happy experience that the decision itself is overwhelming joy with life-transforming consequences.

The severity of the call to decision appears in hyperbolic exaggeration in Mark 9:43–48 parr. (cf. §3.2.3): One must sacrifice anything that keeps one from entering the Kingdom of God—whether it is a hand, a foot, or an eye—for nothing short of total commitment can hope to be successful. Since what is at issue is a person's total well-being, there are no other values that should stand in the way. One must be prepared to sacrifice all. It is not simply a matter of being prepared to give up one's favorite things; since all too often it is one's own self that stands in the way, severity may be required against one's self. The point of the hyperbole is that the actual decision takes place with regard to the self.

Next to this demand comes the requirement that one free one's self from all care about financial security and the quality of life for the sake of the greater goal of seeking the Kingdom of God (Matt 6:25–34 par.; cf. §4.2.3). Indeed, if one is to be committed at all, both intensively and exclusively, to the Kingdom of God that is being realized, this goal must be all-consuming. A partial commitment will simply result in the kingdom being lost. Only by seeking the Kingdom of God with total trust and with undivided energy can one lay claim to the promise that as creator God will care for all one's needs by establishing his final rule. Anything less than total commitment would reveal a doubting of God's ability to keep his promise. One would deny God as the creator and would exclude oneself from the approaching Kingdom of God.

Other harsh requirements appear in the synoptic descriptions of the call to discipleship. There are frequent references to the potential disruption of family ties or even to renouncing marriage (Mark 10:29–30; Luke 14:26; Luke 9:61–62; Matt 19:12). Since ancient people understood themselves primarily in terms of the family, such demands struck them as harsh, requiring as they did that they become homeless persons (Matt 8:20 par.).[12] In view of what is certainly the authentic tradition in Matt 8:22 = Luke 9:60 (cf. §4.2.2), doubtless we have here a feature of Jesus' inner circle. To be sure, each of the texts cited has problems that keep us from attributing it to Jesus with any degree of confidence. In any case, our earlier observations about the disciples (§2) and about the table-fellowship (§4.3.2) make it clear that with such sayings Jesus was not describing discipleship as a way of life that was hostile to the family.

Also controversial is the harsh saying about discipleship as the bearing of one's cross (Luke 14:27 par.; Mark 8:34 parr.). In light of the crucifixion of Jesus a metaphorical understanding of bearing one's cross is likely, yet any pre-Easter meaning of the saying is purely hypothetical.[13] Nor can we attribute to Jesus the other words about discipleship that involve the sacrifice of one's life (Mark 8:35–36 parr.; 10:38–39 par.), since they presuppose a life-threatening situation, which, according to our sources, did not exist for the disciples in Galilee prior to Easter. It is true that according to Luke 13:31 Herod Antipas wanted to seize Jesus, but his plan was never realized, and in any case it did not involve the disciples of Jesus. After Easter the situation changed, and there is ample evidence for persecutions of Jesus' followers in this period (Acts 7:54–60; Gal 1:13–14, 23–24; Josephus, *Ant.* 20.200; Mark 10:35–45 par.; Matt 5:11–12 par.; Mark 13:9–13, 19–20 parr.; John 15:18–16:15, etc.). It is probable, therefore, that these discipleship sayings, even in their core, originated in the history of the early church and do not go back to the time of Jesus.

The situation is different, however, with the warning against entering the life of discipleship without first evaluating one's ability to persevere in the undertaking. The abrupt termination of discipleship has severe consequences, as Luke 14:28–32 makes clear:

1a   Who of you, wishing to build a tower, *does not first sit down to count the cost, whether he has enough for completion?*

   b   *So that when he has laid the foundation he is not able to finish (the*
         project), and all the observers begin to mock him [v. 30].
   2a *Or what king, going* to attack *another king* in war, *does not first sit*
         down to consider whether he is strong (enough) with ten thousand
         (men) to confront the one who with twenty thousand is coming against
         him.
   b   *And if he is not, while the other is still a long distance away, sends a*
         delegation to ask for peace.

The similar syntactic structure of the two examples suggests that they originally belonged together (cf. the examples in §§3.2.2–3.2.4). Within this formal arrangement there
are some intentional differences. On the one hand is a farmer who plans to build a tower on
his field (cf. Mark 12:1) that he obviously intends to use in his business. On the other is a
king who is confronting the threat of war. One makes his plans free of external pressure;
the other faces a hostile army. The petty farmer may become an object of ridicule in the
village; the great king may lose his lands and his throne. In different ways the two figures
face stand before an either-or.
   The images are typical for that day (Epictetus, *Diss.* 3.15.10–12), which, of course,
does not mean that Jesus could not have used them (cf. §4.3.1). The material in any case is
older than is the Gospel of Luke, since both the narrow application in Luke 14:33, (34),
and the broader interpretation of Luke 14:30 speak for the appropriation of traditional
material. Since the two examples are focused less on winning disciples than on advising
others to think seriously about what they are about to do—since they call for sober
calculation instead of enthusiasm—the probability is that they are closer to Jesus than to
the early Christian mission.

   The text effectively shows by contrast how the early church formed the
account of the call of the disciples in Mark 1:16–20 parr. There the church is
concerned to emphasize the authoritative and irresistible demand of its master.
Luke 14:28–32, on the other hand, serves as a counterpoint. It also deals with the
issue of discipleship, but it permits only a discipleship that excludes the possibility of a premature yes. Only those persons should become disciples who have
thoroughly considered whether they are capable of fulfilling the demands of
discipleship. The theme of the double parable in Matt 13:44–46 (cf. *Gos. Thom.*
76; 109), on the other hand, is that for the sake of such a supreme goal one should
risk everything on one throw of the dice with unquestioning joy and inner
conviction:

   1a *The Kingdom of God is like a* treasure *hidden in a field,*
   b   *which* a man *found and hid (again).*
   2a *And in his joy he goes*
   b   *and* sells everything *he has*
   c   *and* buys that field.

   3a *Again, the Kingdom of God is like a* merchant,
   b   *seeking beautiful* pearls.

4a   When he found an (especially) valuable pearl,
 b   *he* sold everything *that he had*
 c   *and* bought it.

Again, the two parables reveal a structure that formally is almost identical. Yet, the different ways they begin (" . . . treasure . . . , which a man found . . . " and " . . . merchant, who . . . when he found a . . . pearl") along with their separate traditions in the *Gospel of Thomas* have frequently led to the conclusion that they once circulated independently. Yet, the secondary character of both parables in the *Gospel of Thomas* could just as well indicate that they were separated here or at some point on the way to the *Gospel of Thomas*. The variations in the way the parables begin in Matthew may also have been intentional. Since it is not a field and a merchant, but two total processes that are compared with the Kingdom of God, the variety in their beginnings may be regarded as a narrative device designed to create tension. When we remember that the early Jesus material often contains doublets (cf. §§3.2.2–3.2.4), the scale tilts toward an original doublet also in this case. Otherwise we would have to explain the identical structure of the two texts with the unnecessarily complicated assumption that one of them was later changed to parallel the other.

The formally parallel narratives intentionally contain additional tensions. A worker in a field (probably a day laborer) and a (rich) pearl merchant are juxtaposed. One of them in the course of his normal work in the field discovers something for which he is not looking. The other intentionally seeks something, and his persistence is rewarded with success. The accidental discovery leads to serendipitous joy. The reward for persistence reveals a cool and calculating decision.

Just as the merchant prepared and carried out the purchase with what was likely an Oriental poker face according to customary business practice, according to current law and custom the day laborer also does nothing wrong.[14] As the recent discovery of the copper scroll from Qumran (3Q 15) demonstrates, a treasure in a field is by no means unusual in Early Judaism. Burying valuables was a relatively secure way of protecting them from robbery and confiscation (Philo, *Virt.* 85). What the business man does is also normal in that culture. Good pearls were quite valuable and were often worth a fortune. We can probably assume, therefore, a graduation from the first to the second parable; in the case of the pearl merchant there is a higher level of intensity.

In order to make a point, it is said of both figures that they sold *everything*. Just as the traveling merchant normally would sell all of the valuables that he had with him, the day laborer will change into cash everything that he can possible do without. Both must proceed unobtrusively and slowly so that the market will not recognize that the value of the fields is depressed. Neither of them plans to keep the treasure and the pearl; they will sell them for the greatest possible profit. This reality is intentionally glossed over, however. What is emphasized is the sacrifice to reach the goal. That the process is described only to the point at which the purchase is made intentionally directs attention to the point of the parables.

Both parables contain frequently used motifs.[15] It would be premature, however, to suggest that they do not come from Jesus, since we often find the reformulation of traditional materials in the parables of Jesus (cf. §4.3.1). Indeed, several things speak for attributing the parables to Jesus. The Kingdom of God is presented as a presently obtainable reality. The treasure and the pearl are not things yet to be discovered; it is their prior discovery that is the occasion for further activity. This process corresponds with Jesus' view of the Kingdom of God (cf. §4.2.2). The usual world of experience and the narrative world are not identical, as we have just demonstrated in relation to the ending. This conscious tension is necessary in order to include in the narrative flow of the parables

Jesus' motif, also found elsewhere, that one must accept the Kingdom of God without reservation. In the parables themselves the characters do not sell the treasure and the pearl after they have obtained them, since the Kingdom of God is the ultimate goal for which one makes the decision. We may conclude, therefore, that both traditional motifs are used in the service of Jesus' own view of the Kingdom of God and that he is their author.

The behavior of the two protagonists in the parables is determined by their surprising discovery—a discovery of such immediate intensity that they spontaneously realize they are faced with a decision that will determine their entire future. It is as if they had an inner compulsion to win the game. Their discovery and the chance to change their lives are so enticing that they are prodded to give their all. They grasp their once-in-a-lifetime chance, and they win! Every hearer thinks: I would like to have a chance like that. If I did, I would risk everything and would think only about winning.[16] Then once the hearers have been drawn into the events of the parable and have spontaneously identified with the protagonists, they remember the way the parable began: "The Kingdom of God is like. . . . " This kingdom so convinces the hearers of its inner quality that they immediately recognize that they have only to make the right decision to realize their life's fulfillment. This conviction will lead them to risk everything and to decide to enter the Kingdom of God without reservation and with all their energy, since only with that kind of total involvement can they be certain of success. In this way the double parable develops the power to convince that is implicit in the behavior that is described—a power derived from the desire of every hearer to experience the same kind of discovery.

The willingness to act, which in the framework of the two parables follows from one's attitude toward what is discovered and its special quality, calls attention once again to the harsh dimension of the message of Jesus, which appears in such sayings as Luke 9:57–62 par. or Mark 9:43–48 par. Matt 13:44–46 offers a complementary point of view—what we might call the inner side of the outer demands. We should not simply dwell, therefore, with one group of texts and emphasize only the side of the prophetic demand and the radical obedience that it calls forth. We must recognize that this external perspective is carried by an inner conviction that lives because the reality of the Kingdom of God itself works in people to bring willingness, joy, and self-evident recognition to fruit in discipleship. To *enter* the Kingdom of God (Mark 9:47; 10:15, 25)[17] demands much of people, but the Kingdom of God itself provides the power for the decision, because it offers something of great value—indeed, of supreme value—viz., a person's ultimate redemption.

From this perspective we can understand that the decision and its consequences are to be described as an expression of gratitude. Such a statement presupposes a twofold recognition. For one thing, Jesus does not summon people to decision in order to make it possible for the Kingdom of God to come. His call is not similar to the claim of Rabbi Simeon ben Yohai (ca. 150 CE) that redemption would come if Israel were to keep the Sabbath perfectly two times (*b. Sabb.*

118b *Bar.*). The only precondition for the coming of the Kingdom of God is God's decision. The human decision is a reaction after the event. It is an entering into a Kingdom of God that is already near, not a preparation for its coming. To experience its contingent nearness (Luke 11:20; cf. §4.2.2) is to be called to orient one's life toward this situation that God has newly created. For another thing, this experience of the nearness of God's rule is characterized by the salvation of the lost; it is, in other words, an offer of salvation (§4.2.4). One's *natural* reaction to this salvation can only be gratitude and joy in the sense that both of them become creative forces in the life of the one who is saved from judgment.

5.2.2 Gratitude and the Concept of Reward

Bornkamm, G. "Der Lohngedanke im Neuen Testament," in: idem, *Studien zu Antike und Urchristentum II*. BhEvTh 28. Munich: Kaiser, 1959, 69–92.

Dietzfelbinger, Chr. "Das Gleichnis von den Arbeitern im Weinberg als Jesuswort," *EvTh* 43 (1983) 126–37.

Hezser, C. *Lohnmetaphorik und Arbeitswelt in Mt 20, 1–16*. NTOA 15. Göttingen: Vandenhoeck & Ruprecht, 1990.

Schottroff, L. "Human Solidarity and the Goodness of God: The Parable of the Workers in the Vineyard," in: *God of the Lowly: Socio-Historical Interpretations of the Bible*. W. Schottroff and W. Stegemann, eds. Maryknoll, NY: Orbis, 1984, 129–47.

Schnur, H. C. *Fabeln der Antike*. 2d ed. Darmstadt: Wissenschaftliche Buchgesellschaft, 1985.

Weder, H. *Gleichnisse*, 218–30.

This kind of decision for the kingdom, which leads to a fundamental, life-determining attitude of thanks, leaves no room for the idea that at the end of the day God grants an appropriate reward for each good deed. Indeed, given Jesus' opinion about Israel, what could it offer that would be deserving of a reward (cf. §3.2)? Furthermore, where in Jesus' view of the eschaton is there room for the idea that the present world is the vestibule from which one then later enters the dining room (*'Abot* 4:16)? Since, for Jesus, the eschaton is already beginning in the present (cf. §4.2.2), anything that later could be given as a reward is already present as a gift.

Still, there is enough confusion in the debate about the issue of rewards for one's performance that it deserves our attention. While the relationship between human deeds and divine reward is known in the Old Testament and Early Judaism prior to 70 CE, it is only infrequently documented (cf., e.g., Ezek 29:19–20; Prov 11:3, 16–17; 26:27; Sir 2:8–9; 51:30; *1 Enoch* 103:3; 108:10). It appears not much more often metaphorically as *to reckon something* (Gen 15:6; *Jub.* 14:6), *to grant the inheritance* (*Ps. Sol.* 15:10), *sowing-reaping* (*T. Lev.* 13:6; Gal 6:7–8), receiving the *crown of victory* after the *contest* (Wis 5:15–16; 4 Macc 17:11–16; 1 Cor 9:24–27), or repayment for something one has done (1 Sam

24:20).[18] It assumes a dominant role only in the early texts of the Mishna (e.g., *'Abot*), where the imagery is based on a typical work relationship (*'Abot* 2:15–16; 4:10). One's entire life is regarded as an employer-employee relationship in which God will pay for work that has been done. While the evidence for the existence of this metaphor in Judaism in the time of Jesus is weak, the former Pharisee Paul (Rom 4:4; 1 Cor 3:8, 14), the Jewish-Christian sayings source (Matt 5:11 = Luke 6:22–23), and Matthew's Jewish-Christian church (Matt 5:12, 46; 6:1–2, 5, 16; 10:41–42) demonstrate that Christianity knew this imagery as part of its Jewish heritage.

To be sure, this interpretation of human life in terms of the metaphor of a reward for one's accomplishments is usually moderated in special ways. One is aware, e.g., that human beings cannot really sign a labor contract with God, since God is their Lord and creator, while they are creatures and servants. There is a warning, therefore, against doing God's will simply to receive a reward (*'Abot* 1:3; 2:8), for from God's point of view he is not obligated to pay a reward. Thus one should obey the Torah simply for God's sake (*'Abot* 2:12). Nor is the reward really understood as repayment that can be calculated for the number and quality of one's good deeds. (Cf., however, statements such as *'Abot* 2:1, 15–16). As a rule the eschatological reward, on the one hand, has nothing to do with a tangible reality; it is more a matter of life itself and its quality. The righteous person receives not a quantifiable thing, but a perfected life. On the other hand, it is frequently emphasized that God's reward far surpasses one's own human accomplishment. It is less a repayment in the strict sense of the word than it is an expression of God's mercy (4 Ezra 8:31–36, 48–92; *'Abot* 3:15). Of course, God's mercy comes more to those who can be rewarded, while eternal condemnation comes to those sinners who have earned no reward; for them there is no mercy (4 Ezra 7:31–35; 8:55–62; 9:10–13; *'Abot* 2:15; 3:11, 15). Thus the normal, human labor relationship is modified at critical points when it is applied to God's relationship with human beings. Within this modified usage the concept of reward emphasizes how important human activity is—and not only in the study of the Torah or in the way one speaks (*'Abot* 1:17).

When we put the preaching of Jesus in this Early Jewish context, the reward motif with its related themes appears seldom. Luke 17:7–10 clearly illustrates the first of the above modifications of the work-reward metaphor in Early Judaism when it emphasizes that a master can expect his servant to do what the master says without being thanked for it. It is this reality that serves as a model for the human relationship to God. Luke 17:7–9 reads:

1   *Who of you, having a servant for plowing or shepherding, will say to him when he comes from the field (into the house), "Come quickly and recline at the table"?*

2   *Will he not say to him, "I want something to eat; prepare it! Put on*

> *an apron and serve me until I have eaten and drunk. Then you can*
> *eat and drink"?*
>
> 3 *Does he thank the servant for doing what he was told to do?*

The three rhetorical questions that call for the answers *no one, of course*, and *of course not* do not need the parenetic application of Luke 17:10, and they certainly do not need the negative judgment of the servants as *unworthy*. The questions themselves make clear that all servants—even the best—work without thanks simply because they are servants. The argument makes sense in terms of the social relationships of the day—relationships that are neither approved nor disapproved. The relationships are simply used to shed light on the relationship between God and human beings.

We cannot with certainty guarantee a critical minimum here that goes back to Jesus, since Jesus, Early Judaism, and the church were all able to make this statement. This consensus, however, should not keep us from claiming the text for Jesus. The opening words *who of you . . .* is not atypical of him (Luke 11:5, 11; 14:28; 15:4). The same is true for the three-point outline, which he uses elsewhere in parabolic materials (e.g., Luke 10:25–28; 14:16–24; 16:1–9). The careful formulation of the material is reminiscent of his skill as a teller of parables (cf. §4.3.1). As far as the content is concerned, there is no reason to attribute to Jesus a view of the relationship between God and humans different from the one that appears in Luke 17:7–9.

While Luke 17:7–9 remains within the Early Jewish consensus, the situation with the parable of the workers in the vineyard (Matt 20:1–15) is more complex. On the one hand, the parable can be understood as a variation of the view that rewards are an expression of God's mercy. On the other hand, the text takes the discussion in a new direction. The text reads:

> *1a* *A house master went out early in the morning to hire workers (day laborers) for his vineyard. After agreeing with the workers for a denarius for the day, he sent them into his vineyard.*
>
>   *b* *He also went out about the third hour and saw others standing around in the marketplace, and he said to them: "You go into the vineyard too, and I will pay you whatever is right." And they went.*
>
>   *c* *He did the same thing again about the sixth and the ninth hour. And about the eleventh hour he went out (again) and found others standing, and he says to them: "Why are you standing idly here the whole day?" They answer: "Because no one hired us." (So) he says to them: "You go into the vineyard too."*
>
> *2a* *At evening the master of the vineyard says then to his steward: "Call the workers and pay their wages, starting with the last ones up to the first ones."*
>
>   *b* *Then the ones (hired) at the eleventh hour came and each received a denarius. And when the first ones came, they thought they would receive more, but each of them also received a denarius.*

3a *After they had received their wages, they complained against the
    house master and said: "These last ones worked only one hour, but
    you treated them the same way you treated those of us who bore the
    burden and the heat of the day."*

b   *But he responded to one of them and said: "Friend, I am not treating
    you unfairly. Did you not agree with me to work for a denarius? Take
    what is yours, and go. I want to give these last ones the same thing I
    gave you. Do I not have the right to do what I want with my own
    things? Or is your eye evil, because I am gracious?"*

The introduction in Matt 20:1a is part of Matthew's special material (cf. Matt 13:31,
33, 44–45, etc.), and the gnomic final verse could stand alone (cf. Matt 19:30; Luke
13:30). The rest of the material, however, offers no reason for decomposition. Even the
threefold division of the parable (hiring the workers at different times, payment of the
wages, the controversy over the payment) follows naturally from the flow of the narrative.

As is often the case, the material of the parable is traditional; indeed, it was used often
in rabbinic circles.[19] It is obvious from a comparison of the materials that the images[20] are
traditional and that the threefold structure appears frequently. Of course, what is unique in
Matt 20:1–15 is equally clear. For one thing, none of the Jewish parallels deals with a
conflict between reward and kindness in the way that Matt 20:1–15 does. None of them
offers, therefore, a parallel to the twofold question of 20:15. For another thing, all rabbinic
texts are formed in terms of regular, repeatable standards. The situations portrayed, therefore, are possible cases that might happen over and over. That is not the case with Matt 20.
The event is not repeatable, because once the word gets out that he has paid hourly
workers and day laborers the same thing, the next day he will get only hourly workers. The
task will not be finished, and what is done will be too expensive. Repeating the experience
would lead to bankruptcy. Determinative for Matt 20:1–15, therefore, is the singularity of
the situation along with the fact that the graciousness can happen only once. In the third
place, all rabbinic parables follow one of two basic questions: When is payment relatively
just? Under what conditions is the employer obligated to pay a reward? When, in other
words, is one obligated to thank him? Matt 20 poses a different question: Can one protest
against graciousness freely given, or does such graciousness not require a new understanding of life?[21]

These three essential differences between Matt 20:1–15 and the rabbinic materials
justify attributing the parable to Jesus. The significance of the differences is not that the
parable calls one to view the world through the eyes of love.[22] It is that the essence of the
approaching Kingdom of God is graciousness and that the purpose of this graciousness is
once and for all to create new relationships between God and Israel (cf. 4.2.2; 4.2.4). This
situation, which Jesus' hearers know, determines what he wants to say to them with the
parable. He creates the narrative flow of the parable, therefore, in order to reveal this
present unique situation under a particular aspect from the inside out.

Jesus appears to enjoy the familiar scene with which he begins the parable;[23]
he describes in painful detail the typical arrangements made for typical wages.
Everyone can and should be familiar with such a scene. Everything in the parable
must begin normally. (A denarius is barely enough to feed a normal family for
one day.) The further hirings at the third, sixth, ninth, even at the eleventh hour,
appear more artificial, but the story is supposed to be unusual.[24] The motif of fair

wages that is woven into the parable (v. 4) and the scolding of the workers hired last (v. 6) serve as clues to the hearers, who receive no clearer information, that a just accounting is a tricky thing. At the same time they are confirmed in their assumption that people who work different lengths of time will be paid differently. Why else would the different times be in the story? Yet, there is also the nonsense associated with the one hour's work. Even a drachma (one denarius = four drachmas) is, when compared with the agreement of Matt 20:2, much too much. How is the employer going to deal with the situation? Will he not take into consideration the quality of the work as well as the time involved?[25] That is to say, will he not mix quantitative and qualitative criteria? The hearers are anxious to find out how the Gordian knot with which the first part of the parable closes will be solved. Yet, they are convinced that no matter how it is done, it will involve a fair settlement, since a promise is a promise (v. 4!).

After the long first section, the second is more dramatic and compact. The scene is structured artistically so that when the evening comes the last workers are the first to receive their wages. Those who worked one hour receive a denarius. Was that not precisely what had been promised those who worked all day? Of course, a hearer might think that therefore the wage for each worker will be one denarius per hour, but would such generosity not be too strange and thus more than one could expect? Even at the rate of one drachma per hour the payment would have been overly generous. Yet, whatever the narrator may have hoped the hearers would expect, he sets them up for a surprise. With a single stroke he negates all of their expectations. The offense is sudden and complete. Everybody receives the same wages. The fox led the hounds on a wild goose chase and then suddenly doubled back on his tracks.

Yet, the narrator does not leave the scene. He knows how strong is the sense of fair play in his hearers when it comes to payment for work done. He knows that they are quite willing to make room for graciousness as long as it is just.[26] The third and shortest part of the parable deals with this issue in the form of a dramatic dialogue with an open question. It begins with a protest from those who have the greatest reason to complain about their absurd treatment. For two reasons they understandably are upset with their pay. They work twelve times as long for the same amount of money, and they work during the heat of the day. If the employer is to be just at all, the length of time and the difficulty caused by the heat must be taken into consideration. The narrator lets the workers raise the issue, because he knows that many of the hearers are thinking the same thing. At the same time he has uncovered the problem created by the unequal wages. Everything depends on how the owner responds.

He begins by reminding the complainers of his agreement mentioned at the beginning of the parable (20:2) and which he has kept to the letter, but since the protesters (and all of Jesus' hearers) have never questioned that fact, this explanation is superfluous and has nothing to do with the issue that has violated their sense of justice. When one considers the fact that the same pay was given for different amounts of work, it is precisely the correct adherence to the agreement that is the source of such a great injustice. This aspect of the problem is glossed over with eloquent silence. The same thing happens a second time, when the landowner, who has just clarified his relationship to the day laborers, now describes his relationship to the hourly workers and asserts his right to do as he pleases with what he owns. Of course he can do what he wants with his possessions; no one has questioned that. From this perspective there is no difference between his relationship to the complainers and his relationship to those who received the most. Therein lies the dilemma. No one intends to criticize the answer of the employer in that regard, and yet the problem has not been solved, because those who worked the longest have not yet received an answer to their protest. They would be satisfied, if the employer were able to explain his graciousness in the context of what is fair and right. He refuses to do that, however, because he understands his graciousness only in terms of his own sovereign will. When the landowner insists on the absolute freedom to be gracious, the only possible solution to the dilemma lies in the words to the protesters: "Or is your eye evil, because I am gracious?" Those who rebel against the graciousness will have reasons to do so—reasons raised by this question that focuses on the self-understanding of the complainers.

The question is also directed immediately to Jesus' hearers. Once it has arrived at this point, the narrative can speak with power only if it is understood in the context of the Kingdom of God. The above-mentioned three unique features of the parable derive from this setting. The final question, of course, does not ask in a moralizing way whether the complainers are just a little bit jealous. Such a banality would rob the parable of the force of its inner logic. Nor should we read into the ending a call to mutual solidarity.[27] The day laborers do not want to take anything from the hourly workers. Based on their sense of what is fair and right, they want more for themselves. Their anger is not directed against those who were paid too much; it is against him who does not treat them so that justice and graciousness are compatible.

They must work out, therefore, a new relationship to the employer who acts solely on his own graciousness. Since he refuses to abandon this sovereign graciousness, they must either move from this offense to a new understanding of themselves and the world or they must continue to live with their dilemma. In terms of Jesus' specific understanding of the Kingdom of God, that means that they have only one last chance for salvation, viz., to turn to this sovereign, gracious God. Were they to do so, they would recognize that their demand for justice is based on an obsolete principle. Indeed, the real reason why Jesus is not concerned with fairness and why he has the employer say nothing about that issue is his conviction that all Israel is lost (cf. §3.2). This lost condition can be changed only by the Kingdom of God, which graciously draws near to those who are lost (§§4.2; 4.3). For those who stand outside this reality this graciousness will not make sense, and it will be subjected to charges of unfairness. The final question confronts Jesus' hearers, therefore, with the choice between opening themselves to the Kingdom of God or siding with the complainers. The parable clearly poses the choice. The graciousness of the Kingdom of God is not based on the general understanding of justice; instead, whatever this graciousness creates is just.

By way of summary, we can place our exegesis of Matt 20:1–15 alongside Luke 15:11–32 and Luke 18:9–14 (cf. §3.2.5). In all three cases the same approximate theme appears. By juxtaposing greater and lesser degrees of achievement in its beginning scene, Matt 20 deals with the issue of the sovereign graciousness according to which everything else is to be measured. Luke 15 juxtaposes a failed life and a life that on the basis of the current ethic must be judged as successful. When the lost son is accepted even before he makes his speech, both sons are challenged to come to terms with a new world order based solely on an understanding of reality structured on the father's mercy (cf. §4.3.1). Finally, in Luke 18:9–14 the polarity is formed by the Pharisee who is faithful to the covenant and the Law and the repentant tax collector, and it is the tax collector who is justified (cf. §4.2.4). Common to all three variations is, among other things, that from an initial polarity a crisis is created by a new way of shaping human life. Out of the crisis emerges a new understanding of reality based on the Kingdom of God—an understanding focused solely on God's graciousness.

What we can say in retrospect on the issue of rewards in the preaching of Jesus is that, because of his all-encompassing attitude toward God's graciousness in the approaching Kingdom of God, the ethical life can only be understood as the necessary response to this divine initiative. The human concern that God's mercy should correspond with human behavior is no longer relevant, since those who have escaped the final judgment and have entered the Kingdom of God that is being realized are able to be happy beyond belief. What could they still need? They no longer have to structure their lives around goals, since they already have *everything* (Matt 13:44–46).

5.2.3 The Grateful Sharing of Forgiveness

Becker, J. "Feindesliebe—Nächstenliebe—Bruderliebe," in: idem, *Annäherungen*, 382–94.

————. *Untersuchungen zur Entstehungsgeschichte der Testamente der zwölf Patriarchen.* AGAJV 8. Leiden: Brill, 1970.

Berger, K. *Gesetzesauslegung.*

Bornkamm, G. "Das Doppelgebot der Liebe," in: idem, *Geschichte und Glaube I.* BeTh 48. Munich: Kaiser, 1968, 37–45.

Brandenburger, E. *Das Recht des Weltenrichters.* SBS 99. Stuttgart: KBW, 1980.

Broer, I. "Das Ius Talionis im Neuen Testament," *NTS* 40 (1994) 1–21.

Burchard, Chr. "Das doppelte Liebesgebot in der frühen christlichen Überlieferung," in:

Der Ruf Jesu und die Antwort der Gemeinde. Festschrift J. Jeremias. E. Lohse, ed. Göttingen: Vandenhoeck & Ruprecht, 1970, 39–62.

Dietzfelbinger, Chr. *Die Antithesen der Bergpredigt.* TEH 186. Munich: Kaiser, 1975.

Dihle, A. *Die goldene Regel.* SAW 7. Göttingen: Vandenhoeck & Ruprecht, 1962.

Ebersohn, M. *Das Nächstenliebegebot in der synoptischen Tradition.* MThSt 37. Marburg: Gewert, 1993.

Fuller, R. H. "Das Doppelgebot der Liebe," in: *Jesus Christus in Historie und Theologie.* Festschrift H. Conzelmann. G. Strecker, ed. Tübingen: J.C.B. Mohr (Paul Siebeck), 1975, 317–29.

Harnack, A. von. *The Mission and Expansion of Christianity in the First Three Centuries.* London: Williams & Norgate, 1908.

Hoffmann, P. *Frühgeschichte,* 73–94.

———. "Tradition und Situation," in: *Ethik im Neuen Testament.* QD 102. K. Kertelge, ed. Freiburg/Basel/Vienna: Herder, 1984, 50–118.

Küchler, M. *Frühjüdische Weisheitstraditionen.* OBO 26. Göttingen: Vandenhoeck & Ruprecht, 1979.

Kuhn, H.-W. "Das Liebesgebot Jesu als Tora und als Evangelium," in: *Vom Urchristentum zu Jesus.* Festschrift J. Gnilka. H. Frankemölle and K. Kertelge, eds. Freiburg/Basel/Vienna: Herder, 1989, 194–230.

Légasse, S. *"Et qui est mon prochain?"* Le Div 136. Paris: Cerf, 1989.

Lührmann, D. "Liebet Eure Feinde (Lk 6, 27–36/Mt 5, 39–48)," *ZThK* 69 (1972) 412–38.

Mell, U. *Die "anderen" Winzer.* WUNT 77. Tübingen: J.C.B. Mohr (Paul Siebeck), 1994.

Moffatt, J. *Love in the New Testament.* New York: R. R. Smith, 1930.

Nissen, A. *Gott und der Nächste im antiken Judentum.* WUNT 15. Tübingen: J.C.B. Mohr (Paul Siebeck), 1974.

Piper, J. *"Love Your Enemies".* MSSNTS 38. Cambridge: Cambridge University Press, 1979.

Pohlenz, M. *Die Stoa.* 2d ed. Göttingen: Vandenhoeck & Ruprecht, 1959.

Sauer, J. "Traditionsgeschichtliche Erwägungen zu den synoptischen und paulinischen Aussagen über Feindesliebe und Wiedervergeltungsverzicht," *ZNW* 76 (1985) 1–27.

Schmal, G. "Die Antithesen der Bergpredigt," *TThZ* 83 (1974) 284–97.

Schneider, G. "Die Neuheit der christlichen Nächstenliebe," *Tthz* 82 (1993) 257–75.

Schottroff, L. "Gewaltverzicht und Feindesliebe in der urchristlichen Jesustradition (Mt 5,38–48; Lk 6,27–36)," in: *Jesus Christus in Historie und Theologie.* Festschrift H. Conzelmann. G. Strecker, ed. Tübingen: J.C.B. Mohr (Paul Siebeck), 1975, 197–221.

Sellin, G. "Lukas als Gleichniserzähler," *ZNW* 65 (1974) 166–89; 66 (1975) 19–60.

Strecker, G. "Compliance—Love of One's Enemy—The Golden Rule," *ABR* 29 (1981) 38–46.

Theissen, G. *Social Reality,* 60–93.

Wouters, A. *" . . . wer den Willen meines Vaters tut."* BU 23. Regensburg: Pustet, 1992.

We need to remind ourselves of two characteristics of Jesus' ethic that we have already noted. Jesus deals with ethical themes in a casual, almost accidental way (§5.1), and the behaviors that he requires are to be understood as a grateful response to God's eschatological initiative (§5.2.2). This latter principle appears nowhere so forcefully as in those statements of Jesus that call his disciples to share the grace and freedom that they have received in the form of love, reconciliation, and forgiveness. Indeed, the statements dealing with these themes form a kind of *cantus firmus* within the traditional material and thus are an exception to what we said earlier about the casual, accidental nature of the material. This exception should not be surprising. If the essence of the Kingdom of God is God's gracious and liberating gift, which calls forth a human response, it follows that love will be the fundamental attitude of life—an attitude with self-evident consequences.

To be sure, when we subject to historical analysis the synoptic material that is available for a closer examination of this theme, we find that it is burdened with two problems. The early Christian churches, which justifiably saw themselves as entrusted with the task of transmitting the material and obeying its ethic, expended a great deal of energy in applying the statements to themselves and thus reformulating the material (down to and including 1 Cor 13). In the effort to ensure continuity, they failed to distinguish clearly between the material from Jesus and their own reformulation of that material. There are also significant ties between Jesus and his Early Jewish context. While Jesus may have been unique in the way he consistently based his ethic on God's transforming graciousness, which is available in the Kingdom of God, there can be no doubt that Judaism contributed significantly to his understanding of the love command, to his demand for mercy, and to his call to forgiveness as well as to his prohibition of anger and revenge. Of course, neither Jesus nor Christianity claimed that the love command and related exhortations were originally Christian. Still, many non-Christians observed as outsiders how serious the Christians were about the love command.[28] No one will seriously question that this theme was part of Jesus' message; indeed, it was an especially appropriate way of describing the human response to God's gracious rule in the end-time.

The parable of the so-called unmerciful servant (Matt 18:23–34; cf. §3.2.4) offers an impressive portrayal of this response. One expects that the satrap, after his large debt has been forgiven as an act of pure mercy, will grant mercy to those who are under him. The expression of mercy should lead to a basic orientation of life in which mercy plays a dominant role. The Lukan church's pericope of Jesus' meeting in the house of Simon the Pharisee with the woman who was a well-known sinner (Luke 7:36–48) captures this same attitude of Jesus.[29] Visible acts of love here reveal that one has received from God a love that is dependable and that empowers—indeed, compels—one to perform acts of love. We must further recognize that anyone who, like Jesus, saw God's wrath and judgment coming over all Israel (§3.2) and who offered in their stead a God who was drawing near with end-time salvation, would not regard as appropriate human responses such behavior as judging and anger, since they belonged to the old world that was passing away. Such activities simply had no place in the Kingdom of God. It is no accident, therefore, that, according to Matt 7:1 par. and 5:21–22, Jesus rejected judgmental or angry speaking and acting.

In its earliest form Matt 7:1 reads:

Do not judge,
and you will not be judged.

The unit Matt 7:1–5 par.; Luke 6:37–42, is divided into two parts by the plural (Matt 7:1–2 par.) and singular (Matt 7:3–5 par.) forms of address. The second part not only loses the focus on the divine judgment; it also changes the absolute prohibition of judging into a pragmatic warning against judging too hastily. With its threefold reference to *your brother*, it offers rules for living in the Christian brotherhood. Matt 7:3–5 is, therefore, a separate church tradition. The material in Luke 6:37–38 that goes beyond Matt 7:1–2 may well also be a separate unit. In the same context Matthew created 7:2a under the influence of 7:1, which means that Matt 7:1, 2b par. existed as a prior unit. Even this connection was not original, however, since Matt 7:1 deals with judging in and of itself, while Matt 7:2b introduces a quantifiable measurement. Furthermore, Matt 7:2b exists elsewhere as a separate tradition (cf. Mark 4:24; *Sota* 1:7; *Gen. Rab.* 9 [7b]; *Tg. Yer. II* Gen 38:26, etc.). We can conclude, therefore, that the general statement of Matt 7:1 = Luke 6:37a was the beginning point of the tradition. All subsequent additions serve to temper its radical nature.

It was Matthew who for parenetic reasons first made of the second line a final clause with the sense: Each of you should yourself refrain from judging, since each of you should fear judgment. If, as we may assume, the passive form of the verb alludes to God's sovereignty as judge, the statement says that God will appear as judge without fail whenever people judge—not merely when they judge prematurely or in a partisan manner or, e.g., when they serve as their own judge. The statement is reminiscent of the parable of the unmerciful servant in Matt 18:23–34 in the sense that after he had been granted new life solely because of his master's mercy, the servant fell back into his old life and thereby risked once again his own destruction. Thus Matt 7:1 says that there is no reason whatsoever for someone who has escaped from judgment to engage in any kind of judging. Those who do are still living in the old age, which stands under God's judgment. Those, on the other hand, who live in the age of the emerging King-dom of God live exclusively from a God who has mercifully suspended the judgment that by rights they should have received. Why should they do some-thing that God has long since stopped doing to them? Must they not reflect this divine turning-point in their own behavior? Matt 7:1 does not have as its goal a restructuring of the state's legal system. The verse begins, rather, with a personal, pragmatic concern in order to cause the hearer to think seriously about the reason for the new life in the Kingdom of God. It demands of the followers of Jesus that they live as persons who, sustained by unexpected mercy instead of harsh judg-ment, reflect on how they themselves are to live with their neighbors.

With this statement about judging, Jesus includes in his message of the King-dom of God a variation of a traditional theme of Early Jewish exhortation where there is general agreement that an injured party is justified in expecting the condemnation of the sinner (*T. Gad* 4:3). The demand for punishment is part of an understanding of justice based on the need to have a balance between behavior and its consequences (*T. Gad* 5:10–11; *T. Zeb.* 5:3); every wrong deed must have negative consequences. The question, of course, is: Where does retaliation end? The best course of action is to leave judgment in God's hands (*T. Gad* 6:3; Sir 10:6b; *2 Enoch* 50:3–4) and to eliminate hate from one's own heart (*T. Gad* 6:1). In any case, one should not take revenge against one's own brothers (Lev 19:18; Prov 20:22; 24:29). Those who judge must know that the Lord will deal with them even as they deal with their neighbor (*T. Zeb.* 5:3). For this reason they should judge the neighbor as good (*'Abot* 1:6b) and put themselves in their neighbor's shoes (*'Abot* 2:4b). God will remember the sins of those who take vengeance on another, but God will forgive those who forgive (Sir 28:1–2).

It is clear that this Early Jewish admonition presupposes that any wrong doing must lead to sanctions and that the question then is: What best ensures a community's healthy survival, in view of the ambivalence of all human existence, when should this judging be left up to God and, on the human side, forgiveness and forbearance be allowed to rule? While the word of Jesus is similar to this view in many of its motifs, it has a new context, viz., an understanding of God's rule of the world according to which God's mercy precludes the need for a judgment in which there is a balance between deeds and their consequences. Within this context the prohibition of judging receives then its new sharpness.

We find a similar idea of Jesus associated with the catchword *anger* cited in the first of the antitheses (Matt 5:21–22; cf. §5.3), where even the smallest expressions of anger stand under divine judgment. The focus is not on the issue of justified or unjustified anger, but on anger itself as a possibility for human existence. Nor does the text speak of degrees of sanctions; instead, judgment is applied in its totality to the one who is angry. Every angry person stands completely under God's wrath. This statement, which has the same sense as Matt 7:1 par., also is to be understood in the context of Jesus' message. An angry God and a human life that is governed by wrath are signs of the age prior to John the Baptist; since John the graciousness of the Kingdom of God precludes wrath. Should, therefore, the person who has been seized by the Kingdom of God not act out of graciousness rather than out of anger?

This awareness of a new eschatological saving order is also preserved in the church's tradition of unlimited forgiveness as it appears in Matt 18:21–22 = Luke 17:3–4. There are considerable differences between the texts, but the two versions agree that members of the church must be willing to forgive each other without reservations. Matthew's version exhibits a conspicuous hyperbole. When Matthew reworks the material in the form of an apophthegm, he has Peter ask whether forgiveness, which is in principle boundless, should not be limited for the sake of church discipline. The answer that Matthew places in Jesus' mouth goes back to Gen 4:23–24. In his song of vengeance Lamech demands for himself a seventy-seven-fold vengeance after Cain has received only a sevenfold vengeance. In contrast to this unlimited revenge, Peter, who thinks that sevenfold forgiveness should be sufficient, is given the obligation of unbounded forgiveness. In the church order the world of unlimited revenge is thus replaced by its opposite: unlimited forgiveness. Luke's version, which probably better corresponds to the sayings source, obligates the hearer to respond to a sevenfold offense in one day with sevenfold forgiveness. Here also seven has the sense of always. The requirement is, of course, impractical—cf., e.g., the immediately preceding instructions in Matt 18:15–18—but one can hear in it an echo of the message of Jesus. Where God's graciousness is boundless, the measure of the human response also can only be unlimited.

In close proximity to the prohibition of judging or anger is Matt 5:39b–42 = Luke 6:29–30, an exhortation in the style of a wisdom saying:

1a   To the one who strikes you on the cheek
  b   turn also the other!
2a   And from the one who takes your cloak
  b   do not refuse your undergarment!
3a   And whoever tries to force you to accompany him *one mile,*
3b   go with him two!

From Luke it is clear that Matthew's antitheses are not original. The style is similar in all three parts. We can assume that Matt 5:41 was in the sayings source, since the sequence physical blow, theft of essential clothing, and forced labor makes sense. This understanding presupposes that Matthew's version of the middle example, which speaks of legal seizure rather than of theft, is secondary. His wording is complicated; Luke's version, on the other hand, fits well syntactically with the other cases. It is also clear that Matt 5:42 ("Give to him who begs from you, and do not turn away from him who would borrow from you") is a parenetic addition, since it deals with a general willingness to give and to lend, unlike the other three cases, which in a pointed way require that one surrender twice the original damage. It is a universal wisdom exhortation (Sir 4:3–4; Tob 4:7, etc.) to engage in personal charity.

Were the three examples brought together at a secondary stage of the tradition? Against this frequently made assumption are the identical syntax, the arrangement in a group of three, the logical sequence of the themes, and the identical way of responding. Since the three examples and the responses to them are without serious parallels in Judaism and Christianity, there is no reason not to attribute them to Jesus.

The content of the sayings transcends the wisdom style in which they appear. What they offer is not rules for everyday living, but unrepeatable examples of a behavior that is absolutely foreign to common sense, which are not even willing to acknowledge that they are playing into the hands of evil. At the same time they are examples of experiences that people could well have in the villages of Galilee and against which they would have no effective defense. In the responses to such unexpected demands from the powerful, the issue is not simply nonviolence, as Matthew suggests in 5:39a. More is demanded than simply accepting the abuse. The clue to what this *more* is comes from recognizing that we do not have casuistic *if, then* sentences that describe regular behavior. We have instead unexpected impositions designed to surprise and shock the hearers themselves. The statements are in a sense parabolic cases (cf. §4.3.1), which reveal the situation of the hearers in a new dimension. They are to imagine how they themselves would be changed if they were to act this way.[30] At most they might be expected to accept the aggression and to turn over to God the issue of revenge (*2 Enoch* 50:3–4; Rom 12:19–20). If, however, the God of Jesus is no longer interested in revenge—if he is interested in establishing his rule with graciousness instead of restoring the balance of justice—then the Kingdom of God requires of its people that they give up even their most hidden hopes for a righting of the wrongs they have suffered (e.g., in the form of a restoration of their fortunes at the end of time). They should see themselves as people who completely eliminate from their lives the righting of wrongs. Indeed, they themselves are able to live solely from an understanding of life based on the forgiveness of the sinner (§§3.2; 4.2.4) and not on a careful balance between deeds and consequences.

An especially forceful expression of the human response to God's initiative is the command to love one's enemy as it is transmitted in Matt 5:44–45 par.:

1a   Love your enemies,
b   and you will be sons of your father.
2a   For he makes his sun rise on the evil and the good,
b   and he makes it rain on the just and the unjust.

There is a general consensus that Luke 6:27–36 should determine the analysis of the text.[31] Matthew divided the material that he found in the sayings source into two antitheses, which he himself created. He then arranged it at the end of his series of antitheses as the climax to the unit on the interpretation of the Law that began with Matt 5:17–20. Luke creates of the material a church parenesis in support of his effort to establish in the church a spirit of unselfish giving that is different from the common Hellenistic custom. In the sayings source the first material after the unit on the Baptist is a cycle that begins with the beatitudes, moves to the themes of the love of the enemy and the prohibition of judging, and ends with typical concluding exhortations (Luke 6:12–49 par.). The theme of the love of the enemy in particular is understood in terms of the external persecution that is threatening the mission to Israel.

The text of the sayings source is composed of various materials, as one can see, e.g., from the change from singular to plural in Luke 6:30–31. The parallels to individual sentences from the early Christian parenetic material also show that we are dealing with a process of some length. Especially the imperatives in Matt 5:44 = Luke 6:27–28, which in their present context support the command to love one's enemy, are later interpretations in the style of individual parenetic exhortation. The command concerning the persecutors and enemies not only goes back to the last beatitude (Matt 5:11 = Luke 6:22, thus Q); it is a typical early Christian way of applying the general command concerning the love of one's enemy to specific aspects and thus making it usable (cf. *Did.* 2:7; Ign. *Sm.* 4:1; Polyc. 12:3; cf. even *T. Benj.* 3:6). A comparison of Luke 6:28a with texts such as Rom 12:14 shows how typical and general it is. Luke 6:27c is widespread in Antiquity (cf., e.g., the image of Joseph in *T. Jos.*; Seneca, *De Otio* 1.4). After Luke repeats the commandment to love one's enemies in 6:35a, he adds a typical Lukan explanation that repeats 6:33–34 in a new form. All of these considerations support the conclusion that the simple command to love one's enemy in Matt 5:44 par. and its motivation in Matt 5:45 par. at one time constituted a separate unit.

The inner conciseness of this unit rests on the fact that the command, which brings together the verb *love* with the object *enemy* in a way heretofore unknown in the Old Testament and Judaism, was so unusual that from the very beginning it needed to be justified. While the rationale given in Matt 5:45 par. has an approximate Stoic parallel (Seneca, *De Benef.* 4.26.1, quoted below), for reasons of both language and content it cannot have served as a model for Matt 5:45 par. The catchwords *love* and *enemy* do not appear, and the deity is able to treat all people equally only because the benefits earned by thankful people of necessity must be shared with the others (*De Benef.* 4.28.1ff.). Equal treatment occurs, therefore, not as an expression of graciousness toward all, but because the relationships require it, when good people are to receive benefits from the gods. Since the creation motif is important for the preaching of Jesus, especially in the form of the providential care that we find in Matt 5:45 par. (§4.2.3), it is easy to understand Matt 5:45 par. as an example of this theme. For the most part, therefore, attributing Matt 5:44–45 par. to the preaching of Jesus is not disputed.[32]

This conclusion is further supported by the observation that the motivations given for the command are used nowhere else in early Christianity. Even the *love* of one's *enemies* appears infrequently and only in connection with Matt 5:44–45 par (the addition to *Did.* 1:2; *2 Clem* 13:4; *Ep. Apost.* 18).[33] Tertullian's later claim (*Ad Scap.* 1) that only Christians loved their enemies while all others loved their friends (cf. also *Ep. Diogn.* 6:6; Justin, *Apol.* 1.15.9–10) is not all that clear in early Christianity. People clearly knew that the command was hard, and they divided it into segments in order to tone down its harshness by, e.g., forbidding vengeance, while expecting God to execute vengeance (Rom 12:20–21), or by limiting love to the requirement to pray for one's enemies (see above).

Finally, the use of the expression *sons of God* is unusual. According to Matt 5:45a par., one becomes a son of God by acting as God does in creation. The sonship is neither grounded in Israel's salvation history (Exod 4:22; Hos 3:1; 11:1; Deut 7:13; *Jub.* 2:20; *'Abot* 5:14; Rom 9:4) nor is it understood in terms of an Early Christian experience of the Spirit or a post-Easter christology (Rom 8:14–15, 23, 29; Gal 3:26; 4:6–7). It reflects instead a wisdom style (Sir 4:10–11; Wis 2:16–18). Whoever internalizes God's wisdom as creator is like God, i.e., his son. That Jesus avoids both a salvation history and a pneumatological understanding is, therefore, another special feature of the saying.

When Jesus said, "Love your enemies," it was immediately clear to him and to his contemporaries that this formulation was to be understood as a new interpretation of Lev 19:18: "You shall love your neighbor as yourself; I am the Lord." Jesus thus took his place (indirectly, to be sure) in a long-standing tradition in Israel that based the love command on the Torah.[34] The declaration of God's authority (*I am your God*) that appears frequently in Lev 19:9–37 at the end of imperatives may even have been what led Jesus to add a theophorus promise in support of his command to love one's enemies. Of course, Jesus does not directly quote the Torah. While the same can be said of much of the Early Jewish parenetic material on the love command,[35] it is significant that Jesus does not claim the authority of the Torah at all in support of his reformulation of the command. Indeed, he makes no use of the authority of the Torah when he speaks. He bases his command solely on God's constant action on behalf of human beings and distances himself from the appeal to the Torah in such Early Jewish texts as the *Testaments of the Twelve Patriarchs*, which described the love of God and of one's neighbor as a summary of the Torah (e.g., *T. Jos.* 10:5–6 and 17:1– 18:4; also *T. Dan* 5:1–3; *T. Benj.* 3:1–5; 10:3, etc.). Mark 12:28–34 parr., like the *Testaments*, offers the double command as a summary of the Torah. Here the use of the Torah to legitimate the command is undeniable—a use that clearly distinguishes the material from Matt 5:44–45 par. While the Torah hovers quietly in the background of Matt 5:44–45 par, it in no way serves as the saying's fundamental basis. Jesus functions not as a teacher of the Torah, but as an interpreter, in the wisdom tradition, of God's sustaining rule of creation—a rule that, according to him, everyone can recognize without the books of the Torah.

Nevertheless, Jesus' call to love one's enemy serves as a common denominator, since it serves as an appropriate and positive formulation of the tendency of the texts with which we are dealing in this section. Generally speaking, these texts serve as the only exception to the more casual way Jesus usually deals with ethical themes, since they are especially suitable for capturing the basic intention of his ethic, and among this series of texts no tradition is better able to bring all of them together than is the command to love one's enemy. That is not to say that the command summarizes the Torah; it rather marks the basic direction for the ethic of Jesus as it emerges from his own understanding of the Kingdom of God (see below).

The command to love one's enemy does not serve to expand the definition of the neighbor, so that it would include first one's fellow Israelite (which was the usual understanding of *neighbor* in the culture of Israel and Early Judaism; cf. even Lev 19:18),[36] then the sojourner and proselyte, and finally a third group. If that were the case, then the enemy would be the last member in a series of persons whom one should love. Such an expansion of the concept of *neighbor* would then for the first time connect the command to love with the person of the enemy.

While such a process would fit in well with Early Jewish thinking, it cannot have been determinative for Jesus. He brings together the terms *love* and *enemy* not to expand the circle of those whom one is to love, but to move away from that kind of thinking to a totally new orientation of love. Only the enemy is named. The enemy takes the place of the neighbor whom one would ordinarily expect to be the object of love. He is not the last item in a list that begins with the neighbor, but the sole focus of the statement. He who by choosing the verb *love* made people think of Lev 19:18 (*to love* is, by the way, not a common word in the oldest Jesus material), is bound to surprise his hearers when he continues as Jesus does. Since the noun *enemy* is an important word nowhere else in the early Jesus material, we must assume that Jesus consciously chooses it in contrast with the *neighbor* of Lev 19:18. Such a change needs, of course, to be justified, and Matt 5:45 par. serves that purpose. The function previously performed by the concept of the neighbor is now taken over solely, and without fanfare, by the enemy. The result is that neither is there a series of love objects, ranked by importance, nor is any object excluded from love. It is clear from the naming of the enemy that all persons, equally and without exception, are objects of love. Such an understanding is especially consistent with the tendency of the remaining texts of this section. While it does not formally contradict the Torah in Lev 19:18 (since the neighbor is still included in the love), it thoroughly avoids thinking of the objects of love in terms of their order of importance, as is the case even in Lev 19:9–37.

The concept of the neighbor has fixed connotations in the salvation history of Israel and Early Judaism; he is almost always a fellow member of the nation, i.e., a descendant of Abraham. The enemy of Matt 5:44 plays no corresponding role in Jewish thought. The term can represent any number of enmities: personal, professional, social, salvation-historical, or political. Love must, like God, be universal and under no circumstances permit exceptions. Just as God throughout all creation provides without exception the necessities of life for all people, the followers of Jesus, even though they are addressed as Israelites, must think and act in terms of all creation. The command to love one's enemy no longer thinks in terms of the history and the social identity of Israel; it focuses instead on a universal creation to which all of God's creatures belong. This focus on creation is in harmony with what we have seen in Jesus' understanding of the Kingdom of God (§4.2.3), and in the absence of salvation history terminology in his message (§§3.2.2; 4.2; 4.3).

Finally, we need to look at those from whom this brief imperative demands love. They are not instructed to love their enemies as the means to an end. One does not love the enemy, e.g., in order to get him to give up his enmity (such as one finds, e.g., in the so-called dehostilization of 'Abot R. Nat. 23:1). Nor is love presented as an especially effective way to overcome one's own egotism (the self-control of a text like T. Gad 6:1). Nor is one called to love all people because they all have the same dignity, as Stoicism claims[37] (Seneca, Epist. 95:33, 52–53; Epictetus, Diss. 1.3.2; 1.9.1–7; 2.22.3), or because one is no better than the enemy and is often complicit in the enmity (Sir 28:1–2). One can find these and similar considerations in the text only by putting them there. In contrast to such rationalizations, Jesus' command is simply presented as something that is self-evident. One is to live this way, because it is indisputable and convincing that this is the way God acts.

If the command were presented as a Law or a wisdom-exhortation with specific instructions on how to act, we would be faced with the same kinds of problems contained in the prohibitions against judging and anger. To make it practical, one must do as the Christian church did—one must discuss individual kinds of behavior and various levels of love (cf. Rom 12:14–21; Did. 2:2 [addition]; Matt 5:38–48 par.). In so doing, the churches were able to draw on the rich inheritance of Early Judaism to interpret the love command. The strength of this Early Jewish tradition lay in its ability to test practical, community- building solutions—i.e., to keep in mind the limits of what is possible for the individual and what is dangerous for the community and thus to avoid solutions that were too idealistic-utopian. This is the way a teacher of the Torah or a parenetic instructor always has to work.

Jesus is not concerned, however, with the social structure of a group and its relation to outsiders. He is not testing the power of love to create community for the people of God on its pilgrimage through the ages, as the *Testaments of the Twelve Patriarchs* had done for the Jewish people in the Diaspora. He is not Paul, who performed a similar service for his mission churches in Hellenistic cities (Rom 12–13; Gal 5:13–6:20). Jesus is concerned, rather, in light of the Kingdom of God that is already intruding into the present, to confront people who as social beings live in relation to God and the neighbor with the issue of the understanding of life on which their behavior is based. Is their understanding of reality appropriate to the inbreaking Kingdom of God?

When Jesus takes up the essence of the discussion about the love command in Early Judaism and in Antiquity in general, he creates for consideration an uncompromising and heretofore unheard-of demand.[38] The enemy replaces the neighbor as the fundamental orientation of one's behavior. The demand is designed to offend and thus to attract attention. Where in such a demand is there room for the traditional concern for reciprocity or the balance between accommodation and firmness? The new perspective requires that one be as sovereign as God is. He does not let human evil determine how he must react; he gives the things that are necessary for life independent of such considerations. Those persons who act as God does can no longer understand themselves as sender and echo in a relationship of giving and taking; they can no longer base their conduct on a careful calculation of acts and their consequences for themselves and for others. They must surrender all such considerations of fair play. They learn from experience that, like all creatures, they live from God's provisions, over which they have no control—gifts that the creator continuously provides, regardless of whether their lives are good or evil. God does not react to various human designs for living. He acts in total freedom to provide what is necessary for life, and one is called on to act the same way, always and everywhere. The imperative is thus an invitation into a sovereign freedom that commits itself to provide what is conducive to life in the same way that God does. That it is God's example that obligates people to act similarly keeps the invitation to freedom from becoming an expression of egotism. When God acts as creator, he is his own standard. By acting as God acts, creatures receive their standard from outside themselves.

To act as God does in his preservation of creation, in his patience and graciousness, his forgiving nature and benevolence, is an idea that is not at all uncommon in Early Judaism and in Antiquity. In *Ep. Arist.* 190, in language that is reminiscent of Ps 145:15, the king is encouraged to care for his people and in so doing to consider how "God bestows his benefits on the human race, providing for them health and food and all other things in due season" (cf. also *Ep. Arist.* 253–54). Philo summarizes the same argument (*De Virt.* 168): "Furthermore, he

(Moses) taught . . . that one should follow God's example as much as possible, without overlooking anything, in order to be as much like God as it is possible to be." The *Tg. Yer. I* on Lev 22:28 pronounces: "You must be holy, because I, your God, am holy." Rabbi Meir has God say to Moses (*Shemot Rabba* 2b on Exod 17:8): "Be like me: As I repay evil with good, so also you should repay evil with good." Finally, one thinks of Seneca (*De Benef.* 4.26.1) who says: "If you want to be like the gods, do good even to those who are ungrateful, for the sun rises even on the evil, and the seas are open even to pirates."

The line of argument is thus sufficiently widespread. What makes it unusual in Jesus' case is the special reference to the love of one's enemy, although the focus on creation always includes the possibility that one is thinking of human beings. Of course, the argument from creation, supported by God's activity, is not uncontested, since one can also appeal to creation as normative to support a different line of argument. Creation shows, e.g., that each creature loves its own kind (Sir 13:15–19). Or one can point out that people are not capable of the creator's graciousness (*Ps. Sol.* 5:8–15). Furthermore, does not the creator's equal treatment of his creatures at least make it possible to call into question his just rule of the world (Eccl 9:2–3)? Such examples demonstrate that people were able to experience the creator's governing of the world in different ways. When we ask, as we must, about the source of Jesus' certainty on this question, the probable answer is that he derived his unequivocal conviction from the gracious quality of the Kingdom of God that is drawing near. Jesus regards the creator's government of the world with a clear bias. He is not a teacher of a world order (cf. *1 Enoch* 1– 5; *T. Naph.* 2:8–3:5), but the prophet of the Kingdom of God. The appeal to creation is important for him, because it corresponds with his experience of a gracious God who is in the process of establishing his kingdom. It is the experience of salvation that enables one to see creation clearly.

The parable of the Good Samaritan (Luke 10:30–35) provides another, unusual treatment of the love command from the oldest Jesus material (admittedly, without explicitly mentioning love),[39] which reinforces the essential observations we have made on Matt 5:44–45 par.:[40]

1   *A man went down from Jerusalem to Jericho, and he fell among
    robbers who stripped him and beat him. Then they went away, leaving
    him half-dead.*
2   *By chance a priest came down that way, and when he saw him he
    passed by on the other side. In the same way a Levite also came to
    the place. He saw (the one who was half-dead) and passed by on the
    other side.*
3   *But a certain traveling Samaritan came upon him. When he saw him
    he had compassion. He went to him and bound up his wounds,
    pouring oil and wine (on them), put him on his own animal, brought
    him to an inn and cared for him. And on the next day, he took out two*

denarii, gave them to the innkeeper, and said, "Take care of him. And whatever you spend in addition, I will repay you when I return."

Everyone knows that the road from Jerusalem in the uplands down to Jericho in the Jordan Valley passes through a wilderness area that is infested with robbers.[41] Of course, that there are several robbers in this story while the others appear as individuals is part of the narrative structure. People do not travel alone in that kind of region. The first traveler is unnamed. Throughout the story he is simply the object of others' actions, either life-threatening or rescuing actions. Nor does he speak, even though he has reason both to curse and to give thanks. The storyteller thus has no interest in him beyond the fact that he is attacked and rescued. He is simply a person who needs compassion, who is identified neither as a Jew nor as anything else.

The situation is different with the other three persons. Two of them are important representatives of the temple and the Torah, who as such, as will soon be clear, represent the Jews as the chosen people. Ordinarily the hearer would expect the third person in the series to be a Jew—someone with whom the Galilean listener would identify, but the narrator refuses to provide such a simple solution. He leads the hearer to expect an anticlergy point and then surprisingly does not develop it. Instead, he introduces a member of the hated stepchild of Israel's saving history, a half-Gentile who lives between Galilee and Judea and whose very proximity is a provocation. It is true that in 128 BCE under John Hyrcanus the Jews had destroyed the competing temple on Mt. Gerizim, but the Samaritans still revered the mountain as the site of Isaac's sacrifice (Gen 22) and their holy mountain. The official version of Israel's history was that Jews and Samaritans had nothing to do with one another (John 4:9); more precisely: they were enemies (Sir 50:25–26; Josephus, *J.W.* 2.232–46). *Samaritan* became a religious term of contempt (John 8:48), and *Samaritans* and *Gentiles* could be dismissed with one breath (Matt 10:5).

It is a Samaritan then, and not a Jew, who does what is necessary—indeed more than is necessary, more than anyone could have been expected to do. He is the personification of concern and helpfulness, which is why the third part of the parable is the longest. One can just hear the story grating on the ears of the Galilean listeners. What is Jesus trying to say to them? Has he not already played off the nations against Israel (Luke 4:25–27; 11:31–32 par.; Matt 8:11–12 par.; cf. §3.2.4)? At any rate, there is no question in his mind that, since Israel has wasted its saving history (§3.2.2), God is able to use the nations to shame Israel (*T. Benj.* 10:10). Those who were expecting the sequence priest-Levite-Jew are in crisis because of the Samaritan's appearance. The enemy is the focus of one's orientation not merely as the object of love; this quasi-Gentile forces one to take the enemy seriously also as the subject of love. When one is called to act as God the creator does (Matt 5:45 par.), and when suffering persons are seen as creatures (Luke 10:30), then the creator's will for his creation is that both the subject and the object of love are to understand themselves as creatures. Thus everyone is potentially both the subject and the object of love, and love is always and everywhere, without reservation, the basis of human relations. It is this message that Jesus' listeners are to hear. They are to identify with the Samaritan, even if the very thought makes their hair stand on end.

5.2.4   Life as Trust in the Reliability of the Creator and Redeemer

Berger, K. "Vaterunser," in: *Sacramentum mundi*. Vol 4. Freiburg: Herder, 1969, 1147–52.

Brown, R. E. "The Pater Noster as an Eschatological Prayer," in: idem, *New Testament Essays*. Garden City, NY: Doubleday, 1968 (1965), 275–320.

Dalman, G. *Worte Jesu*, 283–365.

Deichgräber, R. *Gotteshymnus und Christushymnus in der frühen Christenheit*. StUNT 5. Göttingen: Vandenhoeck & Ruprecht, 1967.

Dorneich, M. (ed.) *Vater-unser Bibliographie*. Freiburg: Herder, 1982.

Elbogen, J. *Der jüdische Gottesdienst in seiner geschichtlichen Entwicklung*. 4th ed. Hildesheim: Georg Olms, 1962.

Fiebig, P. *Das Vaterunser*. BFChTh 3013. Gütersloh: Bertelsmann, 1927.

Greeven, H. *Gebet und Eschatologie im Neuen Testament*. NTF III 1. Gütersloh: Bertelsmann, 1931, 72–101.

Hengel, M. *Property and Riches in the Early Church: Aspects of a Social History of Early Christianity*. Philadelphia: Fortress, 1974.

Jeremias, J. "The Lord's Prayer in the Light of Recent Research," in: idem, *Prayers*, 82–107.

Kuhn, K. G. *Achtzehngebet und Vaterunser und der Reim*. WUNT 1. Tübingen: J.C.B. Mohr (Paul Siebeck), 1950.

Limbeck, M. *Von Jesus beten lernen*. Stuttgart: Religiöse Bildungsarbeit, 1980.

Lohmeyer, E. *The Lord's Prayer*. London: Collins, 1965.

Manson, T. W. "The Lord's Prayer," *BJRL* 38 (1955/56) 99–113, 436–48.

Marchel, W. *Abba, Père! La prière du Christ es des chrétiens*. AnBib 19. 2d ed. Rome: Biblical Institute, 1971.

Mell, U. "Gehört das Vater-Unser zur authentischen Jesus tradition? (Mt 6, 9–13; Lk 11, 2–4)," *BThZ* 11 (1994) 148–80.

Pool, David de Sola. *The Kaddish*. Leipzig: R. Haupt, 1909.

Schnackenburg, R. *All Things Are Possible to Believers: Reflections on the Lord's Prayer and the Sermon on the Mount*. Louisville: Westminster/John Knox, 1995.

Schürmann, H. *Das Gebet des Herrn als Schlüssel zum Verstehen Jesu*. 4th ed. Freiburg: Herder, 1981.

Strotmann, A. *"Mein Vater bist du (Sir 51,10)."* FTS 39. Frankfurt: Knecht, 1991.

Vögtle, A. "The Lord's Prayer: A Prayer for Jews and Christians?" in: *The Lord's Prayer and Jewish Liturgy*. J. Petuchowski and M. Brocke, eds. New York: Seabury, 1978, 93–117.

Why is Jesus able in such a carefree manner to demand of himself, his disciples, and his followers the kind of defenseless, highly vulnerable life that he portrays with the radical forgiveness of debts (cf. §5.2.3)? Why does he, instead of offering a work ethic for the farm family (cf. on Luke 15:11–32; §4.3.1) or for the day laborer (cf. Matt 20:1–15; §5.2.2), live in a separate group, eating and drinking in the villages without a care in the world for how he will keep body and soul together, support his family, or raise children? Why does he not outline a social order (the state, a legal system, social equality, etc.) beyond a reference to the banquet of salvation with the patriarchs (Matt 8:11–12 par.)?

The answer lies, as one would expect, in his understanding of the Kingdom of God. Life is being lived in conditions created by the Kingdom of God, which is in the process of being realized, but is not yet finally determinative for the creation and humanity, and this life is sustained by the trustworthiness of the one who is both creator and redeemer. His rule brings a reign of peace that has no room for enmity (§§4.1.3–4.1.6). His rule brings food and health for people (§4.3.2). His rule now takes the place of all other structures. All people should turn to this God, who is beginning to establish his rule, by placing their trust in his reliability. Jesus is trying to get people to structure their lives with this understanding of the world and of history and, thus, to practice this kind of trust. Looking forward to such a Kingdom of God (§4.1) is a deeply theocratic hope. By connecting his presence with the approaching Kingdom of God Jesus confronts people so strongly with his concept of a theocracy that their present life takes on theocratic characteristics. To trust God concretely over all things is the attitude that is in keeping with Jesus' understanding. According to him God has earned that kind of trust, since as creator he provides everything that is of importance for human fulfillment.

In the spirit of such trust Jesus pronounces the beatitudes on those who are poor and in need (Matt 5:3–6 par.; §4.3.2) and calls people to strive for the Kingdom of God, which renders all anxiety superfluous (Matt 6:25–34 par.; §4.2.3). Indeed, as Jesus so uncompromisingly formulates in Matt 6:24 = Luke 16:13, they are challenged to choose between their earthly possessions and God:

1   No one can serve two masters.
2a   For either he will hate the one and love the other,
b   or he will hold fast to one and despise the other.
3   You cannot serve God and Mammon!

It is generally agreed that the saying is independent and self-contained. The change from the descriptive presentation (1, 2ab) to the personal address (3) happens when a general, proverbial saying dealing with a specific case, viz., the alternatives between the masters, God and mammon, is applied to an actual group of hearers (*you*). Those who because of their own experience agree with 1, 2ab will find it reasonable to accept the special case (3) also. The sequence leading from 1 to 3 is also found elsewhere. Texts such as Eccl 1:8 and Sir 8:17 demonstrate that *can* and *cannot* do not necessarily presuppose Greek syntax, as is frequently claimed.

That the saying came from Jesus is supported by the observation that the choice between God and mammon is not tempered by reducing them to a *more* or *less*. Early

Judaism offers no parallel to this radical alternative.[42] The Torah protects private property (Exod 20:15, 17; Deut 5:19, 21). To be sure, beginning with the prophets (Amos 5:10–12; 8:4–8; Isa 5:8–10) there was criticism both of possessions unjustly acquired and of social oppression. In the wisdom tradition there was the warning that one cannot remain blameless in the quest for possessions (Sir 11:10; 31:5), and the apocalyptic tradition threatens rich sinners with final judgment (*1 Enoch* 34:6ff.), but nowhere is poverty praised or is the alternative posed between the God of Israel and human possessions. Even the Essenes were not materially poor; their community was wealthy, and they were interested in gaining wealth.[43] Early Christianity minimized the importance of possessions (as in 1 Cor 7:29–30; Phil 4:5–6), but nowhere did it require people to surrender them in order to become Christians.

We can attribute this word to Jesus also because it is consistent with the other materials in this section.

What begins with a gnomic wisdom saying unexpectedly ends with a demand for exclusivity in one's service to God—with what for Israel was the central theme of its existence.

It was understood in Early Judaism that, given Israel's history, one should *serve only God*. What that meant, however, was that one should not serve the other gods of the surrounding world (Exod 20:2–6; Deut 5:6–10; Isa 24; Judg 10:6–16, etc.). Judaism's interpretation of the figure of Abraham was an especially effective vehicle for presenting the claims of this exclusivity (*Jub.* 12; *Bib. Ant.* 6). Diaspora Judaism recruited proselytes who *served the only true God* and renounced all other gods. The figure of Aseneth in *Jos. As.* is a good example of such a proselyte.

This contrast between God and the gods, however, is not the concern of Matt 6:24. The worship of foreign gods is not an issue for the Galilean, Jesus, although it was not long before the Jewish revolutionary groups, including the Zealots, set about to drive all heathen influence out of Israel's land so that the God of Israel, his chosen people, and the land of Abraham's inheritance could come together in a rigorously theocratic realization of the first commandment (Josephus, *J.W.* 2.264–65, 408–10; *Ant.* 18.23). Jesus places the emphasis elsewhere, on an issue that is unusual for his hearers.

The accepted way of ensuring one's future security by accumulating possessions is for Jesus an expression of godlessness, because creation belongs to God, and he rules creation in order to provide for the needs of all creatures (§4.3.2). Since he cares for flowers and animals, provides food and clothing, and heals the sick, the service of mammon and the service of God are mutually exclusive. Those who seek the Kingdom of God, therefore, are to trust without reservation the promises of the God who will provide for all their needs.

The normal way of providing for one's future by accumulating family possessions appears also in Luke's special material (Luke 12:13–14):

> 1 *One of the members of the crowd said to him:*
> *"Master, tell my brother to divide the inheritance with me."*

2 *He responded:*
"Man, who appointed me to be your arbitrator or executor?"

The brief apophthegmatic dialogue is well rounded. It is clear that 12:15 is Luke's interpretation of what at one time was an independent unit and also provides a connecting link to the parable of the rich farmer (Luke 12:16–21). The unit 12:13–21 is thus Luke's composition.

Attributing the saying to Jesus is not without its difficulties. It is clear that Luke 12:13–14 was not universally applied in early Christian churches, since 1 Cor 6:4–5 shows at the very least that in individual cases one could appoint referees. Since, however, there is nothing unique to the preaching of Jesus in the material, we can attribute it to him only by comparing it with his attitude toward possessions.

We can surmise that the case posed to Jesus involved a situation in which, after the father's death, an older son has taken over the farm, one third of which was to belong to his younger brother (Deut 21:17). For some reason (probably because it would create financial difficulties for him) the older brother refuses to pay the younger brother for his share of the inheritance, so the younger one comes to Jesus and asks for help in getting what is due him. Jesus refuses to help him. His reason for refusing is in all probability not simply that every village has officials responsible for such things and that he is not competent to make such decisions. The problem is that the petitioner's attitude is anachronistic. Now that the Kingdom of God has begun to be realized, this kind of controversy is no longer appropriate. Striving for financial security belongs to the old world, and anxiety about one's life is now superfluous, because one can now depend on God's eschatological provision for one's needs (Matt 6:25–34 par.). Since this kind of trust is now the only appropriate attitude toward life, Jesus would betray his own mission if he were to become involved as an arbitrator in a dispute over an inheritance. It may be that Jesus drew on Exod 2:14 in formulating his answer.

Since those persons who seek to find security through accumulating possessions are incapable of trusting God to provide for life and the future, Jesus is able to formulate in Mark 10:25:

> *It is easier for a camel to go through the eye of a needle than*
> *for a rich person to enter the Kingdom of God.*

With a simple hyperbole Jesus asserts a religious impossibility by comparing it with an example from daily life.[44] The largest animal in Palestine is obviously too big for the smallest opening known in that culture. The difference in size is a graphic description of something that is impossible. It makes clear that a rich person simply cannot enter the Kingdom of God. The saying blissfully ignores the question of whether it does not place external limits on the Kingdom of God (cf. Matt 19:25–26), which by rights is irresistible (Luke 11:20; Matt 13:28). Of course nothing is impossible for God and his rule, but that is not an issue here. The speaker obviously did not intend simply to create a popular attack on the rich (cf. *1 Enoch* 94–96); he chose this comparison to make clear to everyone (!) that those who try to run their own lives and who do not trust the creator to care for them as he does for all creatures stand outside the effective influence of the Kingdom of God.

Corresponding to the trust in God who establishes his saving rule is the petitionary prayer that one offers in the confidence that one will be heard. Matt 7:7–10 par. encourages people to pray with the assurance that God will help. Two early units are buried in the text:

1a Ask, and it will be given you.
 b Seek, and you will find.
 c Knock, and it will be opened to you [v. 8]
2a What person among you,
 b whose son will ask for bread:
 c He certainly will not give him a stone?
3a Or he will ask for a fish:
 b He certainly will not give him a snake? [v. 11]

The two units are linked with the catchword *ask*, and each has its own commentary (Matt 7:8, 11). Their different styles and the ability of v. 7 and vv. 9–10 to stand alone suggest that originally each was independent. When reconstructing the text of the sayings source, the general tendency is to choose Matthew's reading over that of Luke.[45] The similarity to Jewish statements is obvious,[46] but it is equally clear that both traditions existed prior to the sayings source, since it is responsible for the commentaries of Matt 7:8, 11. Both sayings also are compatible with the other texts that we are discussing in this section. There is no reason, therefore, not to attribute them to Jesus.

The three invitations to turn (of course!) to God, reveal in the identically structured concluding clauses the certainty that God will not turn a deaf ear to such appeals (*Ps. Sol.* 5:8–15). How could he, according to Jesus, since with his kingdom he graciously made himself available to people! As early as Isa 65:24 the promise is made that God will answer even before the eschatological community calls. The two comparisons of Matt 7:9–10 strengthen the trusting attitude that asks in confidence. Is there really a father who would give his son not the usual staples of bread and fish (cf. John 6:9; 21:9–10, 13), but stones and snakes, which, while similar in appearance, are useless? Those who petition God may as a matter of course expect good things!

This confidence in God's response is also the subject of the parable of the friend who asks for bread in the middle of the night (Luke 11:5–7) and the parable of the self-centered judge who nevertheless vindicates the widow (Luke 18:2–5). However, in view of the complexity of the debate about the meaning and authenticity of the two units from Luke's special, material it is difficult to argue convincingly and unequivocally that the material comes from Jesus.[47] Given the early Christian view of prayer that we find in Matt 6:8; John 16:26–27; 1 Thess 5:17; Rom 12:12; Phil 4:6; Eph 6:18; 1 Pet 3:7; Jas 1:5, the basic idea of the two parables is hardly limited to Jesus. On the other hand, both parables are compatible with his view when one understands them in the context of God's concern for his creatures that is being realized in the approaching Kingdom of God. Then the attitude of the supplicants who are confident that God will grant their request is an expression of the appropriate human response to the kingdom.

Putting the two parables in this context means that they involve the hearer in reasoning from the lesser to the greater, a step that is so self-evident that one does not need the interpretations in Luke 11:9–13 and Luke 18:6–7, 8 to think of it. In the former case it is obvious that Luke used separate traditions as commentary. Yet, in the latter case as well, Luke 18:6–7, 8 offers two interpretations that were added by the later narrator (18:6a! Cf. 16:8). In their present form both of them reflect the early church's struggle with the delay of the parousia.[48] They help to make sense of the time of waiting, and in so doing they underscore the widow's persistence, which sharpens the focus on the confidence that one's petition will be granted. Thus both parables are to be understood solely on their own terms. The one says: If someone who is in an impossible situation because his friend asked for something that he urgently needed in spite of everything does not refuse the request, how much more will the God of the Kingdom of God not deny his creatures what they need for life. The other says: If even a self-centered judge, who really does not care what happens to the complaining widow, helps her just so he can get some peace and quiet, how much more will God, who is graciously disposed toward human beings, help those who need him. In both cases a needy person faces difficulties; in both cases the need is met because the petitioned, who are the only ones who can help the petitioners, do something that is out of character. In God's case, however, he does not have to overcome his nature in order to act graciously.

The sayings about one's attitude toward possessions and about trusting the God who gives everything are complementary clusters of sayings. They come together linguistically and existentially in the prayer of Jesus, which serves as an exercise in the practice of depending on God for all of life's necessities. According to Matt 6:9–13 = Luke 11:1–4 and *Did.* 8:2 Jesus created the prayer for his followers. Although it preserves in the form of a petitionary prayer the call of the early Jesus tradition to ask God in confidence for everything that is necessary for life, it is so short (in Aramaic it may have consisted of 15–17 words) that the concentration of petitions makes it difficult to demonstrate that it actually comes from Jesus. Along with the common view that Jesus created it, is has also been argued that it is a purely Jewish[49] or Jewish-Christian[50] prayer. We will consider these options in our interpretation of the earliest form of the prayer. It read:

1   Father,
2a   Your name be hallowed,
* b   your Kingdom come.*
3a   Give us today our bread for tomorrow,

b   *and forgive us our debts,*

c   *and do not lead us into temptation.*

This reconstruction of the text is based on the recognition that, in the address and the number of petitions, Matthew's longer text represents an expanded version. With the exception of the petitions for bread and forgiveness, where Matthew does a better job of preserving the originals, the individual petitions have a similar structure. Of course, no one knows exactly what the original petition for bread was, since the adjective (translated here as *for tomorrow*) poses philological problems, and we can only guess what its Aramaic equivalent might have been.

The unit has an orderly structure. Its inner unity is given by the simple address in each petition: twice *your* and three times in the imperatives of the we-petitions. The division into two you-petitions and three we-petitions is obvious. The two synonymous you-petitions are connected asyndetically; the three we-petitions, after beginning asyndetically, are linked with *and*. With the exception of the difficult petition for bread, the petitions in each group are similarly structured in Greek, and probably also in Aramaic. This precise structure justifies regarding the text as a unit and not breaking it down into smaller units.

The well-known doxology with which the prayer ends is most certainly a later liturgical addition that the Christian church borrowed from Jewish worship. Since the prayer of Jesus was a private, community prayer offered perhaps in connection with a meal (§4.3.2), there are two possibilities. If they recited the prayer together, it required no response. If Jesus prayed for the entire group, the community would have responded with a simple (or double?) *amen* (1 Chr 16:36; for the double *amen* see Neh 8:6; 1QS i 20; ii 10, 18; following a petition: Tob 8:8).

A survey of the prayer reveals that it contains no early Christian concerns. There is no christological reference (such as *Father of Jesus Christ* or *let the parousia of your son come*), nor are there references to the church and the Spirit. There is nothing here that is of special interest to the post-Easter church. The focus is on creation and its fulfillment and on the creature needs of the petitioners; the petition for food is even at the head of the list. It is clear, therefore, that the prayer is not an early Christian prayer. Of course, precisely for that reason a Jew could have prayed this way. He would have immediately noticed, however, that the prayer says nothing about his election and saving history (§§3.1.3; 3.2.2) and about Zion's restoration (§4.1.4).

Yet, is this not precisely what is unique about Jesus, that he calls into question Israel's claim to a Saving History (§3.2.2) and that he interprets the Kingdom of God in terms of creation (4.2.3)? Did not Jesus also use the Kingdom of God as the subject of verbs of movement—a practice for which we have no evidence in Early Judaism (§4.2.2)? And if anyone made the Kingdom of God the central concept of his preaching and measured all reality in terms of its impending fulfillment, it was he (§4.2.1). He proclaimed that this rule was already in the process of beginning (§4.2.2), but he also knew that this small, disputed beginning must lead to God's unconditional rule. Should he then with his followers not pray for this final coming?

One wonders why the request for bread stands prominently at the beginning of the we-petitions. It may be that Jesus' table-fellowship and its understanding had something to do with it (§4.3.2). Indeed, it may well be that all of the we-petitions were chosen and arranged as they were because they call attention to the areas of human need for which God must still provide between the dawning of the Kingdom of God and its final realization: hunger (§4.3.2), guilt (§3.2), and the temptation to which people are subjected when they cannot see the beginning of God's rule (Mark 4:2–8 parr., cf. §3.2.4); Matt 11:5–6 par., cf. §4.2.2). The prayer is thus a call to God for help offered by people who have tasted the Kingdom of God, which the all-sufficient God, as Jesus has described him, to give them everything that they ask for, viz., the quick realization of the kingdom's fulfillment.

Of all the possibilities, therefore, the major concerns of the prayer fit best in the context of the preaching of Jesus. There are absolutely no indications of a post-Easter context. Jews could pray this way, but the prayer made sense most naturally to them if they were followers of the Jew, Jesus. Our further interpretation of the prayer will confirm this thesis.

The position of the direct address, *Father*, dominates the entire prayer to such a degree that we must approach the prayer's contents by means of the Aramaic *abba*, which stands behind it (cf. cf. Rom 8:15; Gal 4:6). To understand it within the framework of Early Judaism,[51] we should consider a narrow focus, viz., whether and how God is addressed as father in Jewish prayers, as well as the broader question of how the concept of father was applied to God in general in Jesus' day.

The first exercise reveals that different ways of addressing God as father appear in Early Jewish prayers. In 3 Macc 6:3, 8, the title is inserted late or even at the end of the sentence. The sixth of the Eighteen Benedictions mentions *our Father* along with many forms of address in the other petitions. In Wis 14:3b one finds *you, Father* within a larger text. Sir 23:1, 4 begins a prayer with *Lord, Father, and Master* or *Lord, Father, and God of my life*. We have no examples from the fragments of prayers in Aramaic.[52] We may not conclude that Jesus was the only person to use *abba* in an Aramaic-language prayer. It is likely, however, that addressing God as father at the beginning of a prayer without further additions is unique among the extant sources.

The everyday reference to God as father on the part of his children also sheds light on these texts. The possibilities are *Lord* (*Jos. As.* 4:3, 6) or *my Lord and my Father* (*Jos. As.* 4:6, 12) or *Father* (*Jos. As.* 1:12; *Jub.* 12:1, 5; Luke 15:12, 21). It is immediately clear that the simple *Father* is the most intimate form of address. It was most likely the usual familiar form of address. We can conclude with regard to the prayers, therefore, that the simple address as *Father* implied nearness and intimacy. In general one can say that the more elaborate the form of address, the greater is the emphasis on the distance between God and human beings (e.g., *1 Enoch* 9:4–11; 84:2–6; 3 Macc 2:2–20; 6:2–15). It was this distance that Rabbi Simeon had in mind when he criticized Honi the Circle-maker for talking to God like a son to his father (*Taan.* III 8b). It does not show enough respect. Matthew reveals the same concern when he expands the simple address as father with the more respectful *our Father in heaven* (Matt 6:9). The Spirit-led cry of *abba* is for Paul, on the other hand, a sign of nearness and immediacy (Rom 8:15; Gal 4:6).

We will limit our examination of the wider use of *father* to refer to God to those observations that are important for understanding Jesus' prayer.[53] It is noteworthy that in Tob 13:2, 4 God's kingship appears in close proximity to the statement that *our Lord and our God* is at the same time *our Father* forever (cf. Ps 68:6, 25). *Our Father* has here a salvation history connotation as is often the case with God's fatherhood (e.g., *Jub.* 1:24–25; 19:29; 3 Macc 7:6; Sir 34:24). In other texts God is the father of creation (Wis 14:3; 1QH ix 35–36) with a special emphasis on his care of all creatures. Indeed, help and salvation play a major role in texts that refer to God as father, especially in prayers or situations of prayer (Sir 23:1–6; Wis 14:3; *Jos. As.* 11:13; 12:8, 13). The *targumim* also continue this emphasis (*Tg. Ps.-J. Exod* 1:19; *Tg. Gen.* 21:33; *Tg. Exod.* 17:11; *Tg. Num.* 21:9). In *Jos. As.* 12:12–15 and 1QH ix 32–36 being abandoned by one's earthly parents is contrasted with taking refuge in God's fatherly aid and its mercy.

Finally, we should not overlook the eschatological promise for history that we find in *Jub.* 1:23–25: God is going to be Israel's father, and the Israelites will be his children (cf. also *Ps. Sol.* 17:27).

With the exception of the salvation history components, all of these aspects point in the direction of Jesus' prayer. What is noteworthy is that the *abba* stands alone at the beginning of the prayer, with the references to God's rule and God's holiness coming later and subordinated to the *abba* through the use of *your*. The intimacy of the *abba*-address is not tempered by God's transcendence; instead, it makes God's glory part of the father's nearness. This relationship is the natural consequence of the turning-point, which, according to Jesus, one can already experience (§4.2.2) and which, according to *Jub.* 1:23–25, will bring a new relationship between God as father and his children. The dominating position of the prayer's address also influences the three we-petitions—the appeal to the father's care of his creatures, the appeal to his mercy, and the appeal to him as the place of refuge. All three are in keeping with the tone of the Early Jewish references to God as father. It may well be that there was a loosening of family ties among the followers of Jesus (§5.2.1). That God in such cases can become one's true father also continues an Early Jewish theme.

This interpretation is further confirmed when we examine the early Jesus material in which the activity of earthly fathers is compared with God's activity and in which God himself is presented in terms of a father. The latter is the case in Matt 6:25–32 par. (§4.2.3), where God cares as father for his creatures. Matt 5:44–45 par. (§5.2.3) offers a similar situation. Matt 7:9–10 also refers to the father who cares for his children. In the parable of the father and his two sons in Luke 15:11–31 (§4.3.1) the father's mercy is the key to the entire parable. These references all show that to refer to God as father is to see him as creator and as one who is merciful. Both images fit precisely with the prayer of Jesus.

It is clear, therefore, how Jesus understands the relationship to God of those who begin their prayer by addressing God as father. They experience the nearness of the dawning Kingdom of God in the trustworthiness with which God provides for their needs and shows mercy toward them. Calling God *father* captures the sense of this nearness. It identifies what one may and should expect from God.

The first two petitions following the address express a yearning that God's eschatological kingdom will finally be realized. Then follow three petitions that present to God the human need and weakness of the petitioners so that he will remove them. This sequence reflects the thrust of Jesus' message, where everything is seen in the light of the Kingdom of God that is being realized. The same thing is literally true for Jesus' prayer in the sense that it offers a comprehensive view of reality by naming before the God who is coming with his kingdom everything that should be brought before God. Everything that people may expect of the future is in the two you-petitions. Everything that still requires God's attention is in the three we-petitions. Together they say everything that needs to be said about the future and the present. The petitioners who come before God with this prayer use it to practice making transparent God and his future as well as themselves and their present. The premise for working this way on their understanding of reality is that nothing more is needed for salvation.

When we look for Early Jewish prayers or hymns with a similar claim to completeness,[54] what we find from Tob 13 to the Eighteen Benedictions is by no means insignificant (examples in §4.1.4). They have a common structure that is the opposite of the structure of Jesus' prayer. They begin by talking about the present with a salvation history perspective and then conclude with petitions for the future. No one knows for sure, but it may be that the Eighteen Benedictions achieved their formal structure after 70 CE.[55] In any case, they were organized around a conservative pattern in order to solidify a desired consensus. No one who is working toward a consensus is going to create an unusual structure. It makes sense, therefore, to compare the outline of the Eighteen Benedictions with Jesus' prayer.[56] When we do it is clear that Jesus reversed a traditional approach so that God's final demonstration of his rule as king came not at the end but at the beginning of the prayer and thus forced the present into a secondary position. Is that not the way anyone would think who understands the present as integrated into salvation's new beginning (§4.2.2)? This comparison also sheds light on another unusual feature of Jesus' prayer. A prayer that like Tob 13, or the Eighteen Benedictions, or the prayer of Jesus wants to be comprehensive is not going to omit anything it regards as essential. With the exception of Jesus' prayer all of these texts are focused on Israel's salvation history. That Jesus ignores it is hardly accidental; his silence on the subject is eloquent.

The Early Jewish Kaddish prayer provides a parallel to the double you-petition. In its earliest form it probably read:[57]

> His name be *glorified and* sanctified *in the world.*
> *May* his kingdom *be established soon.*

The similarity to the prayer of Jesus is striking. The sequence of the two petitions, the eschatological orientation, and the future hope focused on creation suggest that Jesus may have used this prayer as a model for his prayer. Of course, since Isa 6 (§§4.1.1; 4.1.2) it is not unusual for the language of God's reign as king to appear together with his holiness and his glory,[58] frequently even in prayers (3 Macc 2:2, 13; 1QM xii 7–10; *1 Enoch* 39:9–14, etc.). In *1 Enoch* 9:4–5, e.g., the holiness of the divine name and his kingly rule appear in the same order as in Jesus' prayer. It is clear in any case that Jesus drew on the language of prayer that was already in existence when he formulated his prayer. Creating prayers by using, among other things, traditional phrases was a custom in those days. That Jesus also made use of the practice would explain why language about the *Name of God* and its *hallowing* appears nowhere else in the early Jesus material. The language of preaching and the language of prayer are not always identical. Using this evidence as an argument against authenticity[59] is problematical, since we do not have enough early Jesus material to permit judgments based on statistics. Were we to apply this criterion consistently, we would filter out much of our critical minimum (cf. §1) and would deny to Jesus such material as the command to love one's enemies (§5.2.3).

What are the understandings of God, the world, and human beings that such a prayer presupposes? It trains the petitioners to think of a world that is not yet perfected in terms of the finality of God's rule initiated by Jesus so that they depend on God for everything. Neither petition leaves room for any kind of human activity, much as the seed in the parable in Mark 4:26–29 grows of itself without human involvement (§4.2.2). In the way it appeals to God as father the prayer requires the same thing that Jesus demanded in Matt 6:25–34 par.—that people give up their anxiety as creatures (§4.2.3).

As opposed to the nearness and intimacy suggested by the term *father*, the theme of God's holiness initially suggests distance. The numinous experience of God's perfection and transcendence in contrast to human impotence and impurity (Isa 6) leads to a description of God as the Holy One. But this distance can be overcome! Just as God's rule can be realized in the healing of sick people (Luke 11:20) so that they can become complete, so can the hallowing of God's name, which the father is to produce, make it possible that people become through this divine activity what they were intended to be before God. According to *1 Enoch* 1:3–4, 8, the demonstration of God's rule and holiness is that "with the righteous he will make peace, and will protect the elect, and mercy shall be upon them."[60] The two you-petitions in Jesus' prayer do not make explicit this connection with the God who will perfect everything for human beings, but the relation is there in the three we-petitions. Noteworthy is what the petitioner does not find in the you-petitions: the hallowing of God's name for the sake of his chosen people (e.g., Ezek 36:23–24; 2 Macc 1:24–29), a cultic understanding of holiness related to the Jerusalem temple, and a sanctification of human beings mediated by the Holy Spirit.

It is clear from the we-petitions that we are dealing with a noncultic, community prayer. The community has no visible shape, either in terms of a common salvation history or in terms of its present structure. This feature is consistent with the preaching of Jesus, which summoned all Israel independent of its salvation history and which did not intend to create a new group. What held the followers of Jesus together was the God who was opening himself to them and who soon would stage the eschatological banquet of salvation.

In a selection and sequence that we do not find elsewhere, the three we-petitions deal with human dependence on God for food, with release from the consequences of a failed life, and with support for the commitment to orient one's life toward the final realization of the Kingdom of God. The petitions mention everything that is important for people for whom the eschatological turning-point has happened. It is not yet given to Jesus' contemporaries to share in the abundance of the banquet of salvation, even though the God of Jesus has already invited them to it.[61] There is still enough ambiguity about God's dawning reign that its claims can be scandalous. The three we-petitions thus direct the petitioners to understand that they live between the beginning of God's rule and its final realization so that they will trust the father who cares for them.

5.3 THE TORAH AND JESUS' AUTHORITATIVE PROCLAMATION OF THE WILL OF GOD

Banks, R. *Jesus and the Law in the Synoptic Tradition.* MSSNTS 28. Cambridge: Cambridge University Press, 1975.

Becker, J. "Das Ethos Jesu und die Geltung des Gesetzes," in: idem, *Annäherungen*, 1–22.

Berger, K. *Gesetzesauslegung.*

Betz, H. D. *Essays on the Sermon on the Mount.* Philadelphia: Fortress, 1985.

Blank, J. "Lernprozesse im Jüngerkreis Jesu," *ThQ* 158 (1978) 163–77.

Booth, R. B. *Jesus and the Law of Purity.* JSNT.S 13. Sheffield: JSOT, 1986.

Braun, H. *Spätjüdisch häretischer und frühchristlicher Radikalismus.* 2 vols. BhTh 24. 2d ed. Tübingen: J.C.B. Mohr (Paul Siebeck), 1969.

Broer, I. "Jesus und das Gesetz," in: *Jesus und das jüdische Gesetz.* I. Broer, ed. Stuttgart: Kohlhammer, 1992, 61–104.

———. *Freiheit vom Gesetz und Radikalisierung des Gesetzes.* SBS 98. Stuttgart: KBW, 1980.

Catchpole, D. R. "The Synoptic Divorce Material as a Traditio-Historical Problem," *BJRL* 57 (1974/75) 92–127.

Dautzenberg, G. "Gesetzeskritik und Gesetzesgehorsam in der Jesustradition," in: *Das Gesetz im Neuen Testament.* QD 108. K. Kertelge, ed. Freiburg/Basel/Vienna: Herder, 1986. 46–70.

———. "Ist das Schwurverbot Mt 5,33–37; Jak 5,12 ein Beispiel für die Torakritik Jesu?" *BZ* NF 25 (1981) 47–66.

Dietzfelbinger, Chr. "Vom Sinn der Sabbatheilungen Jesu," *EvTh* 38 (1978) 281–98.

———. *Die Antithesen der Bergpredigt.* TEH 186. Munich: Kaiser, 1975.

Donner, H. "Jesaja 56,1–7," in: idem, *Aufsätze zum Alten Testament.* BZAW 224. Berlin/New York: de Gruyter, 1994, 165–79.

Eichholz, G. *Auslegung der Bergpredigt.* 3d ed. Neukirchen-Vluyn: Neukirchener Verlag, 1975.

Fiedler, P. "Die Tora bei Jesus und in der Jesusüberlieferung," in: *Das Gesetz im Neuen Testament*. QD 108. K. Kertelge, ed. Freiburg/Basel/Vienna: Herder, 1986, 71–87.

Flusser, D. "Jesus und die Synagoge," in: idem, *Bemerkungen eines Juden zur christlichen Theologie*. ACJD 16. Munich: Kaiser, 1984, 10–34.

Greeven, H. "Ehe nach dem Neuen Testament," *NTS* 15 (1968/69) 365–88.

Guelich, R. A. *The Sermon on the Mount*. Waco, TX: Word, 1982.

Hengel, M. "Jesus und die Tora," *ThBeitr* 9 (1978) 152–72.

Hinz, Chr. "Jesus und der Sabbat," *KuD* 19 (1973) 91–108.

Holtz, T. "Ich aber sage euch," in: *Jesus und das jüdische Gesetz*. I. Broer, ed. Stuttgart: Kohlhammer, 1992, 135–46.

Hübner, H. *Das Gesetz in der synoptischen Tradition*. 2d ed. Göttingen: Vandenhoeck & Ruprecht, 1986.

Karrer, M. *Der Gesalbte*. FRLANT 151. Göttingen: Vandenhoeck & Ruprecht, 1991.

Kister, M. "Plucking on the Sabbath and Christian-Jewish Polemic," in: *The New Testament and Christian-Jewish Dialog*. Festschrift D. Flusser. M. Lowe, ed. Jerusalem: Ecumenical Theological Research Fraternity, 1990, 35–51.

Klein, G. "Gesetz III," *TRE* 13 (1984) 58–61.

Kosch, D. *Die eschatologische Tora des Menschensohnes*. NTOA 12. Göttingen: Vandenhoeck & Ruprecht, 1989.

Kuhn, H.-W. "Das Liebesgebot Jesu als Tora und als Evangelium," in: *Vom Urchristentum zu Jesus*. Festschrift J. Gnilka. H. Frankemölle and K. Kertelge, eds. Freiburg/Basel/Vienna: Herder, 1989, 194–230.

Kümmel, W. G. "äußere und innere Reinheit des Menschen bei Jesus," in: idem, *Heilsgeschehen und Geschichte*. Vol. 2. Mthst 16. Marburg: N. H. Elwert, 1978, 117–29.

———. "Jesus und der jüdische Traditionsgedanke," in: idem, *Heilsgeschehen und Geschichte*. Mthst 3. Marburg: N. H. Elwert, 1965, 15–35.

Lambrecht, J. "Jesus and the Law," *EThL* 53 (1977) 24–82.

Limbeck, M. *Die Ordnung des Heils*. Düsseldorf: Patmos, 1971.

Lohse, E. "Ich aber sage euch," in: idem, *Die Einheit des Neuen Testaments*. Vol. 1. Göttingen: Vandenhoeck & Ruprecht, 1973, 73–87.

Lührmann, D. " . . . womit er alle Speisen für rein erklärte (Mk 7,19)," *WuD* 16 (1981) 71–92.

Luz, U. and R. Smend. "Jesus und die Pharisäer," *Jud* 38 (1982) 229–46.

———. *Gesetz*. KTB 1015. Stuttgart: Kohlhammer, 1981.

Merkel, H. "Markus 7,15—das Jesuswort über die innere Verunreinigung," *ZRG* 20 (1968) 340–63.

———. "The Opposition between Jesus and Judaism," in: *Jesus and the Politics of His Day*. E. Bammel and C. F. D. Moule, eds. Cambridge/New York: Cambridge University Press, 1984, 129–44.

Müller, Kh. "Beobachtungen zum Verhältnis von Tora und Halacha in frühjüdischen Quellen," in: *Jesus und das jüdische Gesetz*. I. Broer, ed. Stuttgart: Kohlhammer, 1992, 105–34.

———. "Gesetz und Gesetzeserfüllung im Frühjudentum," in: *Das Gesetz im Neuen Testament*. QD 108. K. Kertelge, ed. Freiburg/Basel/Vienna: Herder, 1986, 11–27.

Müller, U. B. "Zur Rezeption gesetzeskritischer Jesusüberlieferung im frühen Christentum," *NTS* 27 (1981) 158–85.

Mussner, F. "Das Toraleben im jüdischen Verständnis," in: *Das Gesetz im Neuen Testament.* QD 108. K. Kertelge, ed. Freiburg/Basel/Vienna: Herder, 1986, 28–47.

Neirynck, F. "Jesus and the Sabbath," in: *Jesus aux Origines de la Christologie.* J. Dupont, ed. 2d ed. BEThL 40. Leuven: Leuven University/Peters, 1989, 227–70.

Neusner, J. *Judentum.*

Noll, P. *Jesus und das Gesetz.* SGV 253. Tübingen: J.C.B. Mohr (Paul Siebeck), 1968.

Paschen, W. *Rein und unrein.* StANT 24. Munich: Kösel, 1970.

Räisänen, H. "Jesus and the Food Laws," in: idem, *The Torah and Christ.* SESJ 45. Helsinki: Finnish Exegetical Society, 1986, 219–41.

Robinson, G. *The Origin and Development of the Old Testament Sabbath.* BET 21. New York: Lang, 1988.

Schäfer, P. "Die Torah der messianischen Zeit," in: idem, *Studien zur Geschichte und Theologie des rabbinischen Judentums.* AGJU 15. Leiden: Brill, 1978, 198–213.

Schaller, B. "Die Sprüche über Ehescheidung und Wiederheirat in der synoptischen Überlieferung," in: *Der Ruf Jesu und die Antwort der Gemeinde.* Festschrift J. Jeremias. E. Lohse et al., eds. Göttingen: Vandenhoeck & Ruprecht, 1970, 226–46.

Schnackenburg, R. *Moral Teaching,* 56–65.

Schoeps, H. J. "Jesus und das jüdische Gesetz," in: idem, *Aus frühchristlicher Zeit.* Tübingen: J.C.B. Mohr (Paul Siebeck), 1950, 212–20.

Schrage, W. *The Ethics of the New Testament.* Philadelphia: Fortress, 1987, 40–68.

Stegemann, H. "Der lehrende Jesus," *NZSTh* 24 (1982) 3–20.

Strecker, G. *The Sermon on the Mount.* Nashville: Abingdon, 1985.

Stuhlmacher, P. "Jesu vollkommenes Gesetz der Freiheit," *Zthk* 79 (1982) 283–322.

Suggs, M. J. "The Antitheses as Redactional Products," in: *Jesus Christus in Historie und Theologie.* Festschrift H. Conzelmann. G. Strecker, ed. Tübingen: J.C.B. Mohr (Paul Siebeck), 1975, 433–44.

Taeger, J.-W. "Der grundsätzliche oder ungrundsätzliche Unterschied," in: *Jesus und das jüdische Gesetz.* I. Broer, ed. Stuttgart: Kohlhammer, 1992, 13–36.

Vouga, F. *Jésus et la loi selon la tradition synoptique.* Geneva: Gd. Labor et Fides, 1988.

Weder, H. *Die "Rede der Reden."* Zürich: Theologischer Verlag, 1985.

Westerholm, St. *Jesus and Scribal Authority.* CB.NT 10. Lund: Gleerup, 1978.

5.3.1 The Interpretation of the Torah and the Formation of Groups in Early Judaism

The issue of Jesus' attitude toward the Torah is an area of inquiry in current research about which there is an almost unimaginable diversity of perspectives and opinions. Such a complex issue always, but especially in the current situation, evokes a special sensitivity to personal prejudices and manipulations of the subject.[62] No one can seriously doubt that such biases are involved in the debate, but we should be suspicious when subjectivity is always attributed only to the other person. We are all partially blind to our own biases. At the same time, no one can interpret without preconceptions. While we must always and everywhere be aware of these phenomena, our primary task is to come to as accurate an understanding of historical reality as is possible by dealing directly with the texts and by weighing the arguments of other observers. Of course, the observation that others begin with preconceptions simply describes part of the process by which they arrive at their conclusions; it says nothing about whether those conclusions are historically true.

The wide-ranging disagreement over Jesus' view of the Law is also related to a number of difficult problems. One of them is the issue of the role of the Law in Early Judaism. More specifically: Where does Jesus' understanding of the Law belong in the range of options offered by the Judaism of which he was a part? A second issue is: Which synoptic material dealing with the Law is to be attributed to Jesus, and how is this theme related to the overall preaching of Jesus? We must further consider what Jesus' understanding of the Law might have to do with the way his life ended. Finally, we must ask how and whether Jesus' position and the history of post-Easter Christianity can be coordinated. Until we can offer comprehensive and consistent answers to this entire set of questions we cannot claim to have made a serious contribution to an understanding of historical truth.

In this section we will deal only with the first of these questions. We will try to portray, at least with broad strokes, the stage on which Jesus spoke and acted. In the following sections we will then consider the other questions.

From Nehemiah and Ezra to the first anti-Roman revolt, i.e., during the time of the Second Temple, we can divide Early Judaism into two major epochs. At the beginning of each period occurred a Torah-based restoration that determined its character. Representing the first renewal are the names of Nehemiah and Ezra under whom Jerusalem, with the Second Temple, which had been dedicated in 515 BCE, once again was confirmed as the only legitimate cultural center. Added to the new temple was the *Law of the God of Heaven*. It is probable that the term initially referred only to parts of our present Pentateuch, but the entire Pentateuch was soon canonized with the result that this first Early Jewish community was a temple- and Torah-based theocracy.

The Persian period gave way to the Hellenistic age. In 332 BCE Jerusalem surrendered to Alexander the Great without a struggle. During the second half of the third pre-Christian century, under the Tobiads, a period of Hellenization began, which was marked by a widespread relaxation of the Law.[63] When after the Battle of Panium (ca. 200 BCE) the Seleucid dynasty wrested control of Palestine from the Ptolemaic dynasty, the process of Hellenization became even more intense. The heavy-handed attempt to paganize the Jerusalem cult and the Jewish culture led to the Maccabean revolt (169–165 BCE), whose goal was the restoration of the cult in its ancient form as a program for propagating covenant and Law. The model for this movement was the zeal of Phinehas on behalf of the covenant and the Torah (Num 25, cf. 1 Macc 1–2; 2 Macc 5–6).

Because of their dynastic politics the Maccabees were unable to unite broad segments of Judaism under their leadership, and very quickly there arose a multiplicity of groups, among whom were the Sadducees, the Pharisees, and the Essenes. The result was that Judaism diversified as it never again did in all of Antiquity. The Maccabeans did, however, accomplish one thing: No Jew could ever again assert himself without demonstrating (and, if possible, convincingly proving) his faithfulness to the Torah and the cult. Among the groups there was, therefore, a common denominator that they might mutually deny to each other even while claiming it for themselves. Even Onias IV was forced to justify his establishment of a schismatic cult in the Egyptian city of Leontopolis by appealing to the holy scriptures (Josephus, *Ant.* 12.387–88; *J.W.* 7.420–43). And, of course, the Essenes also based on the scriptures what was in part a fundamental criticism of Judaism and especially of the cult. Even when claims to revelation were made that went beyond the scriptures, they respected the Torah. The revelation of a final apocalypse of ten weeks, e.g., does not challenge the validity of the Torah (*1 Enoch* 93:6, 10). The Teacher of Righteousness understands his special revelation as instruction in the Torah (1QH iv 10; v 11; vi 10; vii 6ff.). Anyone who rewrites Israel's salvation history claims to be defining and interpreting the Torah more precisely (*Jub.*; *As. Mos.*; *Bib. Ant.*, etc.).

This phase ended with the first revolt against Rome, which led to the destruction of the Second Temple and the city of Jerusalem at the hands of Titus. The Judaism that reconstituted itself under the leadership of the moderate wing of the Pharisees distanced itself from those groups that had been involved in the revolt and its catastrophic consequences. At the same time, again in the interest of restoring the old order, it formed an early rabbinic identity for which the normative Torah remained the basis even while it was being interpreted more strictly.[64] The temple and the temple cult no longer existed.

This brief outline provides a framework for understanding the nature of the diversity among the Early Jewish groups at the time of Jesus. It is a relationship characterized by rivalry and competition. Each group was totally committed to the Torah, at least according to its own understanding. Each group emphasized its own brand of Torah loyalty in opposition to the others. Each group energetically, even ostentatiously, promoted itself and sought to expand its influence among the people. It was, in short, a diversity that was characterized by intense competition rather than by multicultural tolerance and a liberal spirit.[65] While acknowledging the authority of both the Torah and the cult, a group could distance itself from other groups by, among other things, distinguishing between cultic laws and other laws. As a result there emerged a broad spectrum ranging from the Sadducees and Essenes to wisdom-oriented groups. The former emphasized purity laws, while the latter were more interested in the Torah's general ethic. What was especially incendiary was that with regard to individual laws the groups were able completely to reject one another's claim to Torah loyalty; indeed, they could question the legitimacy of the entire practical cult. The Essenes were not at all reluctant to refer to all other Jews as *sons of darkness*. At the same time the groups were able to arrive at some sort of accommodation so that they could preserve the nation's unity even though their rivalry sometimes stopped just short of violence, especially when someone questioned their faithfulness to the Torah.[66]

These frequently irreconcilable differences among Jewish groups between the Maccabean period and the revolts against Rome were so intense because Phinehas's zeal for the Torah, as it is described in Num 25, became the dominant model (1 Macc 1–2). Lawbreakers were to be controlled by all possible means, including the threat of and punishment by death. Thus the physical elimination of one's Jewish opponent occurred not only within the dynastic struggles of Herod's house, and not only during the political and military struggles of the revolt against Rome. The practice was also widespread of killing simply for the sake of the Torah (1 Macc 2:24; 3:5–6; 2 Macc 13:4–8; 3 Macc 1; 4 Macc 5–18; 1QpH 11–12; 4QpPr 37; Josephus, *J.W.* 1.13; 2.4–13; *Ant.* 13.340; 20.200, etc.).[67]

Virtually all of the groups were in agreement, however, when it came to defending Judaism as a national-religious force as opposed to non-Jews, especially as opposed to their occupation first by the Syrians and then by the Romans. The issue of their national identity as a chosen people took precedence over their internal quarrels. Nothing better documents this solidarity against the outside world than the fact that the large majority of Jews in that day were prepared to die for the Torah. The willingness of the Maccabeans to lay their lives on the line for the sake of the Torah had made such a lasting impression on subsequent generations (1 Macc 1–2; 2 Macc) that Josephus reports that the mark of a true Jew at that time was to die for the ancestral laws (*Ag. Ap.* 2.218). Precisely in this period a great many people sing the praises of the martyrs for the Law. See, e.g., Dan 3 (with the LXX additions); 6; 2; and 4 Macc; *Mart. Isa.* Josephus also furnishes numerous examples of the willingness of Jews to accept all kinds of suffering to keep the Law of Moses from being violated (e.g., *J.W.* 1.148–50; 2.152, 169–74, 192–98).

The diversification of the groups in this stage of Early Judaism was due in part to their historically conditioned decisions and their own resulting view of the history of Israel (for an example see CD 1–4). At the same time these differences grew out of different conceptions of the Torah and the will of God that it revealed. It is most likely this impulse that explains why all groups in Early Judaism possessed a Halacha that was based on a broad consensus while at the same time working out a Halacha unique to their own group. The question is: What is the relationship between Torah and Halacha?

Every group treasured the Halacha that they shared with others as well as their own Halacha so highly that they granted it the same divine authority as they granted the Torah itself. While they formally acknowledged that the Torah had final authority, they identified the Halachic tradition directly with the will of God. Halacha is interpreted Torah (e.g., CD 8:19). It is Torah faithfully reproduced and actualized (e.g., *Jub.* 2:17–33) and at the same time the *teaching of God's works*

(CD 2:14–16). It is God's unmediated word to Moses (*Jub.* 1:26–27; 2:1). It is a *return to the Torah of Moses* (CD 16:2), and, of course, it claims not to deviate in any way from Moses (Josephus, *Ant.* 4.197).[68] For this reason in their literary portrayals Torah and Halacha are not always carefully separated; indeed, in many areas they are indistinguishable (cf. *Jub.*; *T. 12 Patr.*; CD; 1QS v 1–ix 11, etc.), in the same way that Israel's salvation history time and again could be actualized and presented anew by means of partial quotations, analogous retelling of narratives, and new insights (e.g., *Lib. Ant.*; *Jub.*; *T. 12 Patr.*; *Jos. As*).

One frequently finds major blocks of material offering regulations about specific cases without any reference to scripture at all—indeed, without even the hint of such a reference, because the Old Testament does not deal with the case. There are, of course, other cases in which the reader expects that the regulation offered is supported by an appeal to the Torah (e.g., CD 4:21–5:3, 8–10; 9:2, 7; 10:16, etc.). In still many other cases the allusion to the Torah was so obvious for Early Jewish readers that it did not need to be stated explicitly. There is, therefore, adequate evidence to show that, with all the independent ways Halacha could occasionally go, substantively as well as formally it was related to the Torah. Halacha understands itself to be the interpretation of scripture, the legitimate development of the meaning of the Torah. The observation that Halacha does not always qualify as a direct deduction from a statement in the Torah and that it is not always explicitly exegesis does not justify the conclusion that Israel's Halachic teaching could stand alone on its own authority alongside the Torah.[69] Nor does it prevent us from referring to the Halacha as Torah interpretation in an untechnical and general sense, since it understands itself to be based on the Torah and claims that it unfolds the meaning of the Torah, casuistically expands it, and frequently openly appeals to the scripture for justification. This one-way movement from the Torah to the Halacha in no way keeps Torah and Halacha from outwardly claiming the same authority.

Thus the claim that the Halacha is *only* human opinion and not necessarily true to the Torah appears exclusively in polemical situations in which one group claims that another group does not correctly understand the Torah (*T. Asher* 7:5; *T. Levi* 14:4; *T. Iss.* 6:1–2; CD 3:4–9; Mark 7:8). It is not used to distinguish one's own Halacha from the Torah. The Halachic interpretations of others are paraded as contrary to the Law (*T. Levi* 10:2–3; 16:2; CD 5:21–6:1); people who hold such views are *stubborn* (CD 8:19; Mark 7:6–7). A group's own Halacha, however, is in keeping with its own understanding of the Torah, and it can claim for both the highest divine authority.

Altogether separate from this phenomenon is the question posed by outsiders concerning the degree to which the Torah interpretation of the day was faithful to its original meaning—how arbitrary it was in its dealing with the Law, indeed, whether in some cases it actually contradicted the Law.[70] We can say in general that during the period of the Second Temple there was more diversity in the Halacha than in the time after 70/71 CE and that the early rabbinic movement excluded Essene or Sadducean Halacha from before 70/71 that it believed to be contrary to the Torah. On the other hand, we must remember that only since the European Enlightenment has there been a historical awareness that not only can we read and receive historical texts; we must also learn to understand them objectively in their original setting. Where that distinction does not yet exist, it is the historian's task to begin by identifying as violations of the Law those interpretations that in the original polemical situation were regarded as such.[71] Whether those polemics were unnecessary is a separate question as, of course, is the question about who according to the Torah is actually right.

We must keep this brief outline in mind as a framework when we turn to the issue of Jesus' understanding of the Law. We begin by observing that no one in that day commissioned a scholarly opinion or charged a neutral commission with the task of examining whether his words and deeds fit within the variety of Early Jewish interpretations of the Law as an independent, historical development, or whether Jesus de facto put himself outside the pale of Judaism and thus was an apostate of sorts. That sort of question was not considered, since the issue was not historical impartiality. Jesus was simply one of the competing voices. Every group based its judgment about him on its own position, i.e., in partisan terms. The question was: Given our goals, do we want to coexist with him, or do we want to oppose him? Those who were not satisfied with the entire program were then quick to judge.[72] There is, therefore, no historical basis for the recent claim that, since Jesus' view of the Law fits within what we know of Early Judaism, the stories of conflict over the Law in all four gospels must have been later creations. The core of the conflict narratives may well reflect historical reality even in the extreme possibility that objectively seen (i.e., from the perspective of a neutral examination of the breadth of Early Jewish Torah interpretation) Jesus might be understood in these cases to be in conformity with the Torah. Given this theoretical possibility, we must keep three issues clearly separate: What did Jesus think about the Torah? What did his competitors think about him? How should the historian view the situation today in view of the range of possibilities in Early Judaism?

We must also keep in mind that judgments about Jesus were hardly based on thorough examinations of his total message or on extensive conversations with Jesus. It is more likely that people caught a glimpse of a healing on the Sabbath or of a banquet in a village or that they based their opinions on what others had to say about him. Further, it cannot be for us a historical issue, as the question is often debated, whether Jesus violated only the Halacha and not the Torah, or both Halacha and Torah, since for all Early Jewish groups Torah and Halacha are a unity with divine authority. Nor should we expect Jesus to offer a literal quotation from the Torah followed by a Halachic opinion. Instead, he makes single pronouncements that in their content are both Torah and Halacha that is in conformity with the Torah (cf. Matt 5:21, 27), in the same way that he in general never quotes the Old Testament literally, but offers an interpretive paraphrase with the claim that he correctly gives the sense of the scripture (cf. the implicit references in Matt 5:3–5 par.; 8:11–12 par.; 11:5–6 par., or in Matt 11:11:20–24 par.; Luke 4:25–27; 17:26–29 par.). We can also describe Jesus' polemical situation somewhat more precisely by observing that in Galilee he was dealing primarily with the Pharisees. In general, Josephus supports this conclusion (*Ant.* 18.15–17, 297–98) as indeed in essence the gospels also do (§3.2.4). Finally, we must consider the possibility that Jesus himself was not competing with the other groups in terms of their claims that their Halacha interpreted the Torah. It may be that instead of explicitly or implicitly appealing to the Torah in a way formally analogous to them he had a different way of describing the will of God, e.g., in terms of the Kingdom of God (§5.3.2). Yet, even if this was the case, the other positions would have been compelled to regard him as a competitor in the way he dealt with the Torah.

This is perhaps the best place to evaluate three totally different interpretations of Jesus' understanding of the Law, since they deal directly with the way we describe the Jewish understanding of the Law in that day. One view is that Jesus represented a *messianic* Torah that was the fulfillment of the Sinai Torah.[73] Matthew's understanding of the Sermon on the Mount may offer support for such a view (Matt 5:17–19). There is, however, no evidence in Early Judaism for the view that prior to and contemporary with Jesus one looked for a special Torah for the messianic age or that the Messiah would offer his own messianic interpretation of the Torah. What was expected was that the Messiah would apply the one Torah consistently (*Ps. Sol.* 17:22ff.; 1QSa ii 11–12) so that the messianic age would be characterized by a high degree of Torah obedience.[74] The few rabbinic texts that attribute to the Messiah a perfect understanding of the Sinai-Torah are late.[75] Jesus himself could not have held such a view of the Torah, since he did not regard himself as the Messiah (§4.4.3). To say in spite of these considerations that in a more open sense there was a messianic quality to Jesus' appearance and to his understanding of the Torah is to obscure the historical reality with a smoke screen. We can reject, therefore, such a label.

It is not only possible to try to understand the Torah of Sinai in terms of an eschatological Torah; one can also go from the Sinai-Torah back to a primal Torah of creation. According to this interpretation, within the Torah at large Jesus suspended (partially) the Sinai-Torah and proclaimed the Kingdom of God as the restoration of the primal age and its Torah.[76] He regarded the golden age of paradise as the purest expression of the divine will and thus took its norms as his point of departure. The salvation offered by the Kingdom of God would be a return to the primal age.

Yet, this paradigm also creates problems (cf. §4.2.3). It assumes an understanding of history for Jesus that posits a break between primal history and the time after the fall (in the sense of Gen 3 or 6). Yet, the break for Jesus occurs not between humanity's original condition and its fall, but between the present and the past (§4.2.2). Jesus cancels Israel's salvation history only in the sense that he denies his contemporaries the right to appeal to it (§3.2.2)—not, however, with regard to God's election of the patriarchs (Matt 8:11–12 par.) or the divine promises of the prophets (Matt 13:16–17 par.; Luke 7:22–23 par.; cf. §4.2.2). Jesus does not represent a view of history, therefore, that simply bypasses Israel's history and returns to the time of human origins. We should trust Jesus to be consistent enough that, had he done so, he would also have declared superfluous the circumcision that was part of the story of election (Gen 17). Would he then not also have had to be a vegetarian? Finally, we should note that *Jub.* 2:16–33 makes the claim (that certainly is not atypical for Early Judaism) that keeping the Sabbath is a commandment based on creation. When, however, for the sake of the Kingdom of God Jesus comes into conflict with the Sabbath-command (§5.3.4), how is his attitude compatible with his alleged move from the Torah of Sinai to the Torah of the primal age?

One could cite other concrete examples. When we return then to a consideration of the Early Jewish understanding of the Torah in general, it becomes clear that the widespread belief that the written Torah from Moses is identical with the natural laws of creation (i.e., with the orderliness of all things visible and invisible established by God at the beginning of the world) existed because people closely identified the Torah of creation and the Sinai-Torah.[77] Where then can the possibility exist that Jesus distinguished between a Torah of Sinai and a primal Torah?[78]

It is true, of course, to emphasize it once again, that a concept that portrays the final age with an absence of sin and sorrow can do so in part in terms of paradise. Jesus' eschatological banquet of salvation, e.g., has some features of the primal age, especially in its abundance of food. It is a separate question, however, whether Jesus intended to juxtapose the Sinai-Torah to a primal Torah. There is nothing in the early Jesus material that would indicate such a consistently critical distinction within the Torah.

Finally, there is at present a widespread tendency to describe Jesus' violation of the Torah as *unprincipled*.[79] As popular as this label is, it obscures the problem more than it helps. It is a term designed to refute the view that Jesus in principle abolished the Torah, but it does not clarify how Jesus dealt with the Torah. When it is used indirectly to avoid asking what the key is to understanding Jesus' attitude toward the Torah in general, we must protest against its use. When we recognize that the approaching Kingdom of God provides a conceptual world that also regulates Jesus' understanding of the Law (§5.3.2), we will not be able to regard his positive or critical attitude toward the Torah (or a mixture of the two) simply as accidental, pragmatic, or even careless. We will recognize instead that his central concern also influences his understanding of the Law. For the sake of historical clarity, therefore, we should totally avoid this term, especially since there is no corresponding expression in the debate about the Law in Early Judaism.

5.3.2   Kingdom of God and Torah

Our discussion of Jesus' understanding of the Kingdom of God (§4.2) led to the conclusion that it involved a new interpretation of reality for him. The Kingdom of God that is presently asserting itself is for Jesus a fundamental certainty that needs no justification and that is never presented as something that depends on other themes. Its authority is not derived; it asserts itself as its own self-authenticating authority. By so doing it claims to be the reality by which everything else is to be measured. In the presence of Jesus it becomes the measure of all things. It reveals who God wants to be for those who are lost. It determines which understanding of history and time is appropriate. It establishes what discipleship means and which basic human attitude is appropriate to the Kingdom of God. It makes sense, therefore, to describe Jesus as an eschatological prophet of the Kingdom of God (§4.4).

If that is an appropriate description, then it is clear that he was not a rabbi, scribe, or sage who understood everything in terms of Israel's covenant Torah and who challenged people to internalize the will of God that it revealed. He was not in that sense in direct competition with his contemporaries. When all groups in Early Judaism were forced by cultural-religious pressures to justify their existence by appealing to the Torah (§5.3.1), Jesus is notable for not doing what was expected. Nowhere does he defend his unique role as proclaimer of the Kingdom of God by offering it as his new understanding of the Torah. For him the Kingdom of God and its effects do not need to be legitimated by the Torah. The heart of Jesus' message does not consist of a demand to fulfill the Torah. To give a concrete example: Jesus does not say that one should keep the Law in one's heart and that one can best do that through the love of one's neighbor. Instead, he calls people to enter the Kingdom of God. It is within the Kingdom and its rules for living that people may understand themselves as lost persons who have been rescued and who are loved, and they are to share this understanding by the way they live their lives.

It is, therefore, the understanding of the world, of history, and of human beings that is given by the Kingdom of God that sets the direction for dealing with the Torah. Jesus neither ignored the Law, nor did he seize every opportunity to criticize it, nor did he fundamentally abrogate it. The Law is not his constant theme, driven perhaps by a love-hate relationship. Yet, neither is the opposite true. Given his view of the Law, Jesus does not fit easily in Early Judaism.

In the former case Jesus would, for all practical purposes, have excluded himself from Judaism. Since, however, his total message makes sense only within the context of Judaism, his understanding of the Law is also part of an inner-Jewish dialogue. It is, of course, a dialogue to which Jesus makes his own contribution and that makes his contemporaries uncomfortable, even angry. In post-Maccabean Judaism prior to Jesus one can think of no comparable example of such a critical attitude toward the Law. We can say, therefore, that Jesus adds a totally new dimension to the diversity within this Judaism—a dimension that expands the boundaries of what previously had been possible.

Those who argue the other case, claiming that Jesus lived in harmony with the Law, have more varieties and combinations of arguments available to them. The simplest option is to claim that Jesus was a Jew, therefore he must have been faithful to the Law. Unfortunately, this kind of historical conjecture occurs more frequently than one would like to suppose. Given history's contingency and variety, however, for methodological reasons we must ignore all such conjectures; they are convincing only when we assume that the particulars of historical processes must conform to what is customary. Or one can also negate the proclamation of the Kingdom of God that is making its presence known by robbing it of its central point. One can, e.g., ignore Jesus' unusual and offensive table-fellowship, which was in direct conflict with the Law. Or one can claim that Jesus' understanding of the Law had nothing to do with his message of the Kingdom of God and that we have to treat his interpretation of the Law as a separate issue. The problem with such an approach is that it gives up the possibility of any coherent portrayal of Jesus and understands him only in terms of his individual parts. Or one can reduce Jesus' criticism of the Law and collision with individual requirements to a single instance or to a very few cases and then declare that they are of negligible importance.[80] This approach is successful only when one claims that all of the situations of conflict over the Law in the gospels originated in the later churches and when one interprets Jesus' message of the Kingdom of God by means of the second approach mentioned above.

Finally, it is frequently the case that one knows that one can defend the thesis that Jesus was in harmony with the Law only in connection with a general skepticism about the possibility of saying anything more specific about Jesus. In that case, however, is it not better to avoid saying anything at all about Jesus' view of the Law? Why should we be concerned to emphasize that Jesus was completely faithful to the Law when we otherwise acknowledge such a small amount of authentic Jesus material? However one may combine these various arguments, one thing is clear: Those who do not want the Jewish Jesus who has an uncomfortable attitude toward the Torah of necessity end up with a Jewish Jesus who is so void of anything special that the history of Christianity that follows must be seen as a totally new phenomenon that has little or nothing to do with Jesus.

What comes then from the irreversible flow from the Kingdom of God to the Torah? With reference to the Law, where does the one-way street lead that begins with the Kingdom of God that sheds a new light on everything? We begin by reminding ourselves of Jesus' judgment that his contemporary Judaism had squandered Israel's salvation history (§§3.2.2; 4.2.3). Such a perspective distinguished Jesus from all other groups by preventing him from grounding his preaching in the covenant. The covenant and the Law, however, went hand in hand; indeed, the Law was the covenant's gift and obligation. The question is: What role does the Law play when it is separated from a covenant theology?

Before we answer that question, we must remind ourselves of another observation. The interpretation of the Law presupposes, among other things, a cause-and-effect relationship between one's behavior and its consequences. The one who keeps the Law receives the promise of life, while those who despise the Law receive judgment. Given Jesus' view that all were lost (§3), it follows that the Law's promise of the gift of life can never be fulfilled. Indeed, for Jesus the Law's promise must fail, since human existence allows no other possibility. In the parable of the Pharisee and the tax collector (Luke 18:10–14) Jesus denies to the law-abiding Pharisee the gift of life, which by rights he should have received (§3.2.4).

The acceptance of the lost, on the other hand, viz., those who are lost precisely because they have thus far failed to fulfill the will of God, is grounded solely in the Kingdom of God. The Kingdom of God thereby nullifies an explanation of reality based on rewards and punishments (§§3.2.2; 3.2.5). This explanation belongs to the old world, which is retreating before the advancing Kingdom of God. The Kingdom of God thus creates life unexpectedly where the course of one's life should have led directly to ruin. That means that the gift of life has been transferred from the Law of the covenant to the Kingdom of God precisely for the sake of the salvation of the lost. Those who divorce the statements about the Law from Jesus' proclamation of the Kingdom of God obscure this decisive core of the message of Jesus. Those who recognize this connection, on the other hand, will know that the Law is to be seen in a new light. Its theological grounding in the covenant is no longer valid. It cannot deliver on its promise of life. Salvation now comes from the God, who has drawn near in the Kingdom of God and who has eliminated the connection between behavior and its consequences. Salvation is the gift of life, unconditionally and finally, that is grounded in God alone.

If the Law's promise is not fulfilled, and if life is given apart from the Law, the question is whether for Jesus the Law is still the plain will of God concerning the norms by which people live. Now it is true that Jesus did not explicitly say that the Torah was not the will of God expressed in words. On the other hand, neither does he claim that one learns what the will of God is simply from the Law, for here also the Kingdom of God plays a dominant and energetic role. It is noteworthy that Jesus never measures human evil in terms of the Torah's prohibitions or commands. He does not use the Torah to show people how sinful they are; it is God's perfection against which they are seen to be lost (§3.2.5). The call to unconditional discipleship (§5.2.2), the grateful sharing of the forgiveness that one has received (§5.2.3), and life as trust in the dependability of the creator and redeemer (§5.2.4) are all aspects of an approach to life that in its deepest sense comes from the impending Kingdom of God and not from the Torah. The Kingdom of God, therefore, is not only the life-giving acceptance of the lost; it also itself contains norms for daily living. Furthermore, Jesus is able to establish these norms by virtue of his own authority.[81]

For Jesus, therefore, the will of God is an expression primarily of the Kingdom of God; it is neither given by the Torah nor subordinate to the Torah. For this reason Jesus does not require his disciples and hearers to study and obey the Law. They are to seek the Kingdom of God (Matt 6:33 par.; §4.2.3). Ordinarily one would expect a statement like Matt 6:25–34 to contain a call to seek wisdom (cf. Prov 2:4; 14:6; Sir 4:12–13; 6:27, etc.) with the implication that wisdom is to be identified with the Torah (Sir 24:1–2, 23). Instead, Jesus calls his hearers to strive for the supreme authority that conditions his understanding of all reality. To take the yoke of the Kingdom of God on one's self[82] is identical with life under the Torah for the early rabbis (*Exod. Rab.* 23 [84c]; *S. Lev.* 18:6 [337a]), but not for Jesus. His call to make a decision for the Kingdom of God and to risk everything for it is, therefore, an initiation into a life with a new set of obligations—a life that is independent of the Torah and whose authority comes from the Kingdom of God alone. While it is true that Jesus nowhere explicitly states that God's will and the Torah are two separate realities, it is equally clear that the Kingdom of God that is intruding into the present is on its own authority creating a new and original perspective for understanding God's will. Life in the Kingdom of God is defined not by seeking the Sinai-Torah that comes from Israel's past, but by the self-authenticating message of Jesus about the God who is near and who with finality saves that which is lost.

This message means that also from the perspective of the will of God the Law is to be seen in a new light. It is no longer the final court of appeal for the binding force of norms that correspond to the will of God. The Kingdom of God now takes precedence as its own independent source of norms. This observation underscores again the difference between Jesus and Qumran's Teacher of Righteousness. The Teacher also claimed to bring a special revelation, but for him the new revelation is an opening up of the presently dormant understanding of the Torah (1QH iv 10; v 11; vi 10; vii 6ff.). For Jesus what is at issue is precisely not a self-evident and new understanding of the Law of Sinai. He stands much closer to Trito-Isaiah when in Isa 56:1–7 the latter speaks to an end-time abrogation of the Torah in individual cases.[83]

Our discussion of the priority of the Kingdom of God over the Torah has led to two results. (1) For Israel to be saved from the impending judgment, the Torah had to relinquish its soteriological function to the Kingdom of God. (2) The Kingdom of God also brought into existence a new and independent source for the will of God. While these changes do not of necessity lead immediately to conflict over the Law, the new understanding certainly creates the conditions for conflict. It is not surprising, therefore, that the synoptic material describes conflicts over the Torah.

The first indication that these conflicts, assuming they happened, did not occur as random, isolated cases, but resulted from an intentional stance is the so-called violence saying of Matt 11:12–13 = Luke 16:16 (cf. §4.2.2). Here Jesus assigns *the Law and the Prophets*—i.e., the sacred scriptures of Early Judaism—to the time before salvation's turning-point, and he does so because of the new understanding of history that comes with the Kingdom of God. For this reason the saying is not simply a statement about the historical origins of the Law and the Prophets. In those days no Jew could have understood it that way, since the sacred scriptures were regarded not as a historical phenomenon, but as a reality that laid a claim on people in the present.[84] The issue, therefore, is the validity and meaning of the Torah during the time when the Kingdom of God is becoming a reality, and it is clear that the saying speaks not of continuity, but of a break between the past and the present.[85] It does not describe the nature of the break, but the parallel to the saying about the Baptist in Matt 11:11 par. (cf. §4.2.2) suggests that the Law's authority is not simply abrogated. Instead, the saying probably envisages a reduction of the Law in certain areas for the time that the Kingdom of God is in effect. Such a statement is already a marginal concept in Early Judaism.

The next question, of course, is: Is this reduction in the Law's scope limited to its work as a life-giving agent, or does it also include its norms for daily living? The answer can only come from an examination of what Jesus does and says. Matt 8:21–22 = Luke 9:59–60 (cf. §4.2.2) offers a call to discipleship that contains the same understanding of history that one finds in the so-called violence saying. Now that the time of the Kingdom of God is here one is to follow Jesus, even when it involves violating the command to honor one's parents, which in this case means that one does not bury the father who has just died. Such behavior must be seen as a blatant offense against Torah and Halacha. Matt 8:21–22 par. thus offers a concrete example of the so-called violence saying that makes it possible for us to evaluate what it means to violate the Law. If according to Jesus' view, which he does not justify by appealing to any other authority, it is important for the sake of the Kingdom of God to begin the life of discipleship immediately, then the higher demands of the Kingdom of God render the Torah invalid for this one case. Matt 8:21–22 par. does not say, therefore, that the decalogue with its command to honor one's parents has become generally meaningless.[86] Its view is more likely that there are circumstances in which the Kingdom of God and the Torah have competing claims. When that happens, the Kingdom of God takes precedence and denies the previously valid claims of the Law. In such a case, violating the Law fulfills the will of God instead of opposing it. In such examples the new element, which makes its own rules, is irreconcilable with the old order, even when it is the Torah that is involved (cf. Mark 2:21–22 parr.; §4.2.2).[87]

This rule applies not only to one's initial decision for the Kingdom of God; it also is in effect throughout the continuing process of making salvation real in people's lives. This dynamic is especially clear in Jesus' table-fellowship

(§4.3.2)—a provocative and permanent practice that we can hardly eliminate from his life. There are, furthermore, indications in the material that the salvation offered by the Kingdom of God time and again was realized in this table-fellowship. The tax collectors and sinners were included as a matter of course (Matt 11:19 par.). Accepting them this way of necessity clashed with the distinction between sinners and righteous, clean and unclean, that was based on the Law. It also meant that one was not always dealing with kosher things. Is it an accident that the grossly unclean younger son of Luke 15:11–32 is embraced by his father without any reservations and that not a single word is said about questions of purity? The illustrious society of Luke 14:21 (cf. §4.3.2) would not even pass a superficial test for purity, yet it is what the master of the house wanted. Early Jewish groups that based their identity on the Torah of necessity excluded people who were careless or scornful of the Law. The identity of the Jesus-people under the Kingdom of God as it appeared in the table-fellowship was exactly the opposite. It was based on unconditional acceptance; it integrated everyone into the group. Once it was accepted that all Israel was lost, one could no longer make distinctions within Israel that would exclude one subgroup as sinners in a special way. On the contrary, the very presence of those who were ordinarily excluded was a clear sign that the salvation of the lost was the chief attraction of the Kingdom of God and that, furthermore, the Kingdom of God would no longer permit the Law to lay down the conditions for salvation.[88]

A third example is a text that speaks about the final realization of the Kingdom of God, viz., Luke 12:8–9 (cf. §§3.2.3, 4.4.2). When in this tradition the standard of judgment is one's attitude toward Jesus rather than the will of God as revealed in the Law, the statement agrees with the two texts we have just cited: Jesus is the one who has brought the Kingdom of God to its present level of activity. Whoever identifies with him as the embodiment of this activity may lay claim to the salvation that the Kingdom of God offers. Since it, and only it, can grant life, it follows that the Law can no longer play its traditional role at the judgment.

These examples shed light on the limitation of the Law in the so-called violence saying of Matt 11:12–13 = Luke 16:16. They are also indications that the Kingdom of God and its new standards take precedence even when it is obvious that it is contrapuntal to the Law. There is no better expression of Jesus' own authority and the priority of the Kingdom of God than the fact that Jesus' offer of salvation tolerates no interference from the Law.

Such a statement, however, does not totally describe Jesus' understanding of the Law. Not only does the Kingdom of God set norms on its own authority, and not only is it willing, when necessary, to oppose the Torah, it also intensifies the requirements of the Law with a concentration on Jesus' social ethic. One must acknowledge all three points of view before one can claim to describe Jesus' understanding of the Law in its entirety. We have dealt with the first point already (§§5.2.2–5.2.4). We turn now to a discussion of the last one (§5.3.3). We will conclude with the explosive problem of the conflicts over the Law, especially (but not only) when they deal with the cultic Torah (§5.3.4).

5.3.3   The Heightened Demand in Jesus' Social Ethic

The Kingdom of God involves an uncompromising discipleship that has no regard for life's diversity and ambiguity. The norms that we have thus far considered were based on God's perfection, and they did not lead to an ethic of moderation that was careful not to place unreasonable demands on people and that left room for exceptions and appeals to fair play. Jesus confronted his hearers not with a pragmatic description of what was possible, but with the absolute will of God, who demands everything and who will be satisfied with nothing less. This sharply formulated will of God thus first of all opened the setting in which people should learn to see themselves before God, and it challenged them to take an active role in structuring their lives in terms of the insights they thereby gained.

The claims thus laid on people are not of an individual-ethical nature. They are, e.g., not told to control their desires, or to strive for inner harmony, or to submit to reason. They are directed instead to the relationships in which they already live. It is clear that life on the interpersonal level as it is conditioned by the Kingdom of God is at the center of attention in an especially urgent form. Individuals are challenged to give an unconditional yes to discipleship, but not in order to become hermits as Bannus had done (Josephus, *Life* 7–12). Instead, they are to enter the new community.

That is not to say, however, that Jesus lays down a community order that establishes structures, describes legal and social procedures, or regulates how one is to relate to outsiders. He does not even consider producing a covenant book such as Exod 20–23 or a community rule such as 1QS, since he is not interested in a community that is going to have a history. His is a community of the end-time, which is just beginning to gather itself, which conceivably might someday include all Israel, and whose existence and structure are guaranteed by the Kingdom of God itself. His ethic is focused on the social dimension of the Kingdom of God, even though it is only the individual whom he summons to enter it. The Kingdom of God will prepare and guarantee everything else, much as it relieves people, e.g., of the anxiety about food (cf. §4.3.2).

Within this general understanding Jesus is able to make use of various Old Testament norms. They are chosen in such a way that, in terms of the outline that we have laid out, they focus on behaviors that are destructive of community and turn them around so that the individual moves toward what is good. What is good, of course, is what the Kingdom of God aspires to become as a community of the end-time.

This understanding of the demand placed on human beings played an important role in our discussion of the command to love one's enemy (§5.2.3). Since in this case a Torah requirement provides the background and then is interpreted in such a way that a total and extreme demand is placed on the individual on behalf of the community, it is appropriate that we discuss it here, remembering what we said earlier. We are not dealing, however, with an individual case. Our discussion of the additional material begins with the two antitheses of Matthew's Sermon on the Mount (Matt 5:21–22, 27–28) that deal specifically with regulations from the Torah.

The earliest form of the double antithesis may have been something like:

1a   You have heard that it was said to the ancients:
b   "You shall not kill;
c   but whoever kills shall be liable to judgment."
2a   But I say to you: [5:22b]
b   "Whoever says 'Raka' to his brother shall be liable to the Sanhedrin.
c   Whoever says 'you fool' shall be liable to Gehenna [. . .]." [Matt 5:23–26]

3a   You have heard that it was said:
b   "You shall not commit adultery.*"*
4a   But I say to you:
b   "Every one who looks at a woman with desire
c   has already committed adultery with her [. . .]." [5:28–29]

Within the framework set by Matt 5:17–20, 48, Matthew offers six antitheses of which the third, the fifth, and the sixth have Lukan parallels that are not in antithetical form. It is safe to assume, therefore, that in these three cases it was Matthew who put the material into antithetical form. The question is whether it was Matthew who created the antithetical form in the first place.[89] It is unlikely that he did, since he uses the form of the antithesis nowhere else. He neither uses 1a or 3a elsewhere to introduce a quotation from scripture nor does he use 2a and 4a alone in this form. There are no signs of Matthew's vocabulary in 1a, 2a, 3a, 4a. The term *the ancients* appears elsewhere, e.g., only in the fourth antithesis (5:33), where it is taken over from 5:21. The first and second antitheses, on the other hand, are similar both in form and content. It is hardly accidental that they follow the order of the decalogue (Exod 20:13–14 = Deut 5:17–18), and both are prohibitions that stand under the sanction of the death penalty (Matt 5:21b; Exod 21:12; Lev 24:17; *Tg. Onq. Gen.* 9:6; Deut 22:13–30; John 8:5). Both are formulated from the perspective of the man, i.e., in terms of his relation to other men and to women. The two antitheses constitute an entire world, therefore, and it is the world of adults. Can it be accidental that they curb the two basic human drives of aggression and sex? They are, furthermore, not the sort of prohibitions that require either expansion or separation from each other. Among the six antitheses, these two are formally the most similar. One finds paired examples frequently in the early Jesus material (§§3.2.2; 3.2.3), and the unlimited expansion of what adultery means appears again in the prohibition of divorce in Luke 16:18 par. (see below).

Matthew also used these two antitheses, both of which come from his special material, as models for the others. In so doing he added Matt 5:23–24, 25–26, and 5:29–30 to the antitheses as commentaries. These lines change the original sense of the antitheses. In two of the cases the synoptic parallels reveal that they are independent traditions. Matthew also altered the text of the first antithesis. As a rule one either treats the antithesis as a unit or regards the last two lines as an addition.[90] There are problems, however, with regarding it as a unit, since the last two lines in Matt 5:22 neither in form nor in content parallel the statement: "Every one who is angry with his brother shall be liable to judgment." The problem is not the development from the Sanhedrin (the highest early court in Early Judaism) to the divine judgment (Gehenna; the fire motif is Matthew's addition; cf. Matt 18:9; 25:41); it is that the general term *judgment* in 5:22b does not fit. The sequence anger–raka–fool is also awkward, because the first item is so general. One could, of course, argue that the two final sentences with their concrete epithets and institutions were later added to a more general statement except for the fact that *judgment* in 5:21 is a wholesale term designed to combine the various condemnations in the sense of Exod 21:12, etc., while in 5:22 the word must parallel the other two courts and refer to an institution of judgment for which there is no semantic evidence. Thus the two references to *judgment* vary markedly in the way they are used. Still, the wording shows that the statement in 5:22 intentionally is based on 5:21. Our suggestion, therefore, is that Matthew himself created the first, more general line of 5:22 by assimilating it to the language of 5:28 (as he does also in 5:32). He is aware of the traditional connection between killing and anger (see below), and he repeats the wording of the last line of 5:21. Also in the case of the clumsy repetition of *his brother*, it was Matthew who added the first use of the term. This explanation has the advantage over the other option (viz., that the last two lines are later additions), since it attributes to Matthew the normal parenetic material and attributes the material that is unusual for Matthew to the earlier tradition. The last two lines, by the way, are formally, and probably intentionally, patterned after the final line of Matt 5:21 (=1c; "whoever . . . shall be liable").

Matthew understands anger in its traditional sense as an emotion (cf. Matt 9:4). His intention in the first antithesis, therefore, is to move from the outward act of killing to the inner attitude. The reference in the second antithesis to adultery in one's *heart* (Matt 5:28) indicates the same concern. For Matthew it is not simply the outward act of adultery that is forbidden; it is the inclination of the heart. We may conclude, therefore, that the reference to the heart in 5:28 also comes from Matthew, especially since it also appears elsewhere in Matthew (5:8; 13:19; 18:35). Without this addition the antithesis is sharper. Desire is not only criticized as a thought; it is identical with the act of adultery. The actual act in 5:28 (=4c) also better corresponds to that of 5:27 (=3b) and is then exactly parallel to the form of the first antithesis.

Understanding the two antitheses as pre-Matthean then opens the way for the question of whether the material can be attributed to Jesus. The answer is yes. The statement's uncompromising harshness speaks for its authenticity as does its unexplainable distinctiveness in spite of its obvious roots in Early Jewish tradition.

We begin our interpretation of this double antithesis with the observation that neither Early Judaism nor Primitive Christianity offers anything like the form of the antitheses. In the Early Jewish schools one interpretation could be contrasted with another with statements such as "but I say to you," but no one ever, not even indirectly, created an antithesis to the Torah.[91] It should be further noted that the introductory formula is not "God said in the Torah . . . , but I say to you . . . "[92] The dialogue is, rather, between Jesus and his hearers (*you*). It is their norm that is to be understood anew—a norm that has come to them by means of the tradition that they have heard in the synagogue. To be sure, the *ancients* are the members of the Sinai generation and subsequent generations, and the passive (*it was said*) implies that God is the subject. Every single hearer of Jesus also knew that both prohibitions go back to the will of God that was revealed in the Torah. The statement of the traditional norm is offered not as a literal quote, but as an accurate and unquestioned description of what, according to Jesus' opinion, the current standard is in Early Judaism and what can claim agreement with the Torah. In both cases the first line of the antithesis quotes not a controversial Halacha recognized by one particular group, but a unity of Torah and Halacha whose content was generally accepted.

Our interpretation must furthermore distinguish between the situation implied by the dialogue on the one hand and, on the other hand, the comparison between Jesus' position and analogous Early Jewish statements in general. With regard to the first point, the antitheses begin with the generally accepted opinion that it is appropriate to place limits on human behavior. Anyone who has committed murder or has had sexual intercourse with the wife (or betrothed) of a Jewish man deserves to die. The saying is not concerned with whether or how one carried out the death penalty in Jesus' day.[93] It is simply accepted that crimes of murder and acts of adultery are deserving of death. Both cases are dealing with offenses of individual members of the Early Jewish community against other members of the community. The issue here is not killing in the context of jurisprudence or military action.

Jesus' answer understands this consensus to mean that the norm creates an area in which anything that does not cross the boundary is not yet deserving of death. As long as one is in this area, one's life is not yet in danger. This free space, which to a degree cannot be regulated and which therefore is not subject to the sanctions of a human community, is for Jesus without exception every bit as serious as are murder and adultery. Every dimension of interpersonal relationships, whether large or small, is before God a life-and-death issue, since every life-forming act in a human community is an expression of one's relationship to God.

Beginning with a legal axiom, Jesus thus moves into a completely different dimension. From the legal determination of facts and their sanctions he turns to the hearers' fundamental existential conditions. They who must hear the words *you shall not* and thus already face the reality of their failures with others should not think that whatever does not reach the level of murder and adultery is less serious. When the first antithesis pairs minor examples of abusive language with the highest possible judgment, it is clear what is at stake. Or, instead of exaggerating the distance between the offense and its sanctions, one can achieve essentially the same result by focusing on the facts of the case. In the words of the second antithesis, the initial expression of desire is already full-blown adultery. Human responsibility, which has always carried the burden of human guilt, is therefore all-encompassing.

It is true, of course, that similar statements appear in Early Judaism— instructions designed to counter the attitude that one need not take seriously behaviors that fall short of murder and adultery. Such statements contain high ethical standards,[94] and they reveal that, at least in terms of their ethical content, Jesus says nothing new. Wherein then does his contribution lie? Three observations help us answer that question.

Jesus' pronouncement emphatically avoids practical concerns. It offers no Halacha, since he simply leaves it as a universal assertion with all of its blunt absoluteness. He gives neither instructions for living in community nor individual advice on how to deal with anger and with lust. The Early Jewish exhortation is clearly strong here. That Jesus avoids practical advice is due to his understanding of reality based on the Kingdom of God. Since for him the present activity of the Kingdom of God determines the new community and guarantees whatever is necessary, the time is past for negative behavior in the community.

The two antitheses do not negate the Torah, since obviously murder and adultery continue to be forbidden. They do, however, move in a different direction from the Halacha of Early Judaism, which in this case is not only formally identical with the Torah, but also agrees with it in content, and which at the beginning is quoted as the unity of Torah and Halacha. The words introduced by "but I say to you . . . " are not merely an expansion. It is not a simple statement of a Torah-norm. Instead, it marks a break. It does not simply say that by internalizing the Torah one learns to control anger and desire (cf. *T. 12 Patr.* and *'Abot*, etc.). Nor does it say that for the sake of community one can replace the Torah's death penalty with the following substitute penalties. Nor does it say that there are degrees of adultery and that one should as much as possible distinguish among them and establish different penalties. The expression "but I say to you . . . ," which does not exist either in Early Jewish Halacha or in early rabbinic debates on the Law, points to the same distinction made in Matt 11:12–13 par. and Matt 8:21 par. (cf. §4.2.2) between the time of the Torah and the present in which the Kingdom of God is at work. Since Jesus himself is involved in this process, he is able to proclaim emphatically "but I say to you. . . . " He does so as one who speaks on behalf of the claims of the impending Kingdom of God, which sets the conditions for life in the present, including the entire future.

Finally, we should consider the antitheses, along with all of Jesus' statements on ethics that we are dealing with in this section, alongside the cultic regulations that Jesus so strongly discredited. An examination of Jesus' total proclamation makes clear that he consistently intensifies social norms, while he shows little or no interest in cultic norms. He is thus, on the one hand, part of a dialogue in Early Judaism on the relative importance of cultic Torah and general Torah (§5.3.1). On the other hand, he is detached from this debate, since his convictions about the Kingdom of God lead to other interests, among which is a new way of looking at the Torah.

Alongside the antithesis in Matt 5:27–28 other relevant sayings from the Jesus material are Matt 5:31–32 = Luke 16:18 (probably from Q) and Mark 10:1–12 = Matt 19:1–12.[95] In Mark the latter text consists of an original controversy story (10:2–9), which originated in a Hellenistic-Jewish church,[96] and of a separate unit in vv. 11–12, which comes out of the same tradition as Matt 5:31–32. The variety among the four versions makes it difficult to determine what the original form of the tradition was, but it may have been:

1a   *Whoever* divorces his wife *commits adultery.*
  b   *Whoever* marries a divorced woman *commits adultery.*

Matt 5:31–32 offers a special version of the material that can be attributed to pre-Matthean or Matthean redaction. This editorial work is responsible not only for the form of the antithesis (v. 31 makes free use of Deut 24:1 under the influence of Mark 10:2–9) and for the unchastity exception, but also probably for the expression *makes her an adulteress* instead of *commits adultery.* The formulation makes it possible for the innocent husband who divorces his adulterous wife to marry again, although she may not. (He, of course, may not marry a divorced woman.) Matt 19:9 is then an abbreviated correction from Mark 10:11–12 in terms of Matt 5:32. It was necessary, because Matthew did not recognize the woman's right to divorce (Mark 10:12). As a non-Jewish right it could not be tolerated in Matthew's Jewish-Christian church.

It is at the same time clear that the two-sentence parallelism that appears in three texts is early, and that Matt 19:9 offers an abbreviation here as well. Likewise Matt 5:32 and Luke 16:18, contrary to Mark, secure the position of the husband as the subject of both lines. Matt 5:32a speaks only of divorcing one's wife; Luke 16:18c speaks of divorce and remarriage. Luke may have been influenced by Mark 10:11 here, since it disturbs the parallelism and is probably a softening of the harsh rule that completely prohibits divorce. The meaning for (Mark and) Luke is then that one should not divorce, but separation is possible if one does not remarry (cf. 1 Cor 7:9, 11, 15).

In their present form the four versions of this tradition are church rules on marriage, unlike our reconstructed original, which grandly ignores all the legal fine points on practical matters that are so important to the four texts (e.g., sanctions for adultery, separation without remarriage; cf. in even more detail *Herm. Man.* 29:1–11; 32:1–4). Since the present synoptic texts struggle to maintain the severity of their source while at the same time adapting it to the practical problems of church life, the earliest stage of the tradition must come from Jesus. What is here offered is neither a Law nor a rule, but a statement of the uncompromising will of God without any consideration for human frailties. In addressing only the husband the statement remains within the bounds of Early Judaism, since according to Deut 24:1–4 only he has the right to divorce his wife. This possibility is now eliminated. Marriage with one partner is for life; its dissolution is adultery.[97] Such a claim is for Jewish ears an intolerably negative judgment, which exceeds what the Torah says. It is equally true that a single man sins if he marries a divorced woman.

Jesus' statement is similar to the marriage laws of the Essenes to the degree that they also permitted only one marriage (CD 4:20–5:2).[98] Of course, unlike CD 4:20ff. Jesus does not base his description of the will of God on the Torah; he simply declares it on his own authority. Nor does he think in terms of a cultic ideal of purity as do the Essenes. Still, their regulations demonstrate that Jesus' pronouncement, harsh as it was, within the possibilities given by Early Judaism need not be seen as a rejection of the Torah. Deut 24 simply accepts that people write certificates of divorce; refusing to do so is not a violation of a Torah commandment or prohibition. Forbidding divorce does, of course, border on the intolerable in that day, and its difference from the rest of Judaism justifies attributing it to Jesus.[99] His preaching is similarly harsh in the antitheses when he says that the lustful look is not simply a prelude to adultery; it is adultery itself (Matt 5:27–28).

What is Jesus trying to accomplish, when he presents God's will in such a radical form? We must first of all remember how indifferent Jesus is to practical questions. He does not discuss, e.g., whether a widower may remarry or whether a widow who had been divorced may enter a second marriage. The Essenes prohibited such second marriages; in the rest of Early Judaism they were permitted (*Qidd.* 1:1; *Sabb.* 30a; cf. Rom 7:2; *Herm. Man.* 32:1–3). Jesus does not argue with his contemporaries, therefore, about Halachic regulations for all possible cases. Instead, he selects two extreme cases to illustrate what his fundamental view of marriage is. In both cases he is trying to say the same thing. If it is adultery for a man to terminate his marriage, then a divorced woman is not really divorced. The marriage still exists, and a divorced woman cannot be taken as the wife of a second husband. From Jesus' perspective the reason for all this is that in both cases the hard work of reconciliation in a difficult marriage is terminated (cf. §5.2.3). When a man rejects his wife in that culture, normally he has no more contact with her, and a divorced woman, once she has remarried, as a rule cannot return to her first husband. A man who takes either of these irreversible steps thus shuts himself off from the possibility of forgiveness, reconciliation, and love (cf. *Herm. Man.* 29:4–8). He returns to the old world, which is in the process of being overcome by God's unconditional acceptance. One should act even as God acts.

Whether the statement improves the position of women is a question that should be answered only in connection with Matt 5:27–28 and Luke 16:18. Since the man is the subject in both statements, neither considers the possibility that the husband might be the offender so that the wife is in the position of the forgiving partner.[100] It is also clear that the prohibition of divorce for the woman, given her weak position in the institution of marriage in those days, could have uncertain consequences. In any case, Jesus shows no interest in the casuistry that would be based on such a prohibition. The man, on the other hand, receives in the antithesis the full force of the harshness of the divine will. Given the binding nature of this will, depriving the husband of the right to divorce his wife must be seen as a reduction of male privilege. In the context of the cultural restraints of the day such a reduction in a sense intentionally challenges the special status of the husband in the marriage.[101] At the same time, the statements have no direct interest in the emancipation of women. Their purpose is rather to use concrete examples to confront people with their absolute and irre-

ducible responsibility before God and to their fellow human beings in view of
the dawning Kingdom of God.

The prohibition of swearing in Matt 5:33–37, with its close parallels in Jas
5:12, also belongs to the discussion of Jesus' heightened social demands. The
probable earliest form of the text, which is quite similar to James, is:

> *1* *[vv. 33, 34a] Do not swear [. . .]!*
> *2a Neither by heaven, [v. 34c]*
> *b   nor by the earth, [v. 35b]*
> *c   nor any other oath! [vv. 35d, 36]*
> *3a Instead, let your yes be yes*
> *b   and your no no,*
> *c   . . .*

The form of the antithesis in Matthew is secondary, since neither the vocabulary nor
the substance of 5:33 appears in 5:34–37, and the shift from the second person singular to
the plural reveals the existence of a seam. The parallel in Jas 5:12, which comes from the
same tradition and which reinforces the original second-person plural, confirms this observation. Furthermore, Matt 5:36 (which changes the number from plural back to singular)
repeats neither the vocabulary nor the substance of the three items of 5:34–35. For his part
James offers no parallel material and thereby reveals the extent of his earliest form. The
conclusion of Matt 5:37b (*anything more than these is of evil*) is also probably Matthean
(cf. 13:19, 38 and 5:47). The eschatological conclusion in Jas 5:12 (*lest you fall under
[the] judgment*, i.e., be declared guilty in the final judgment) fits well, but it is unlikely that
Matthew would have omitted it had he been aware of it (cf. Matt 5:26, 30). Or had the
material already taken a different shape before he received it? In any case, Matthew and
James show that some sort of original statement appeared here.

Before we proceed with the analysis, we should examine the structure of Matthew and
James closely. They have in common (1) the prohibition of swearing; (2) three examples
introduced with *nor by* and the sequence *heaven* and *earth* in the first two cases; (3) the
introduction of the appropriate speech by *but let it be* followed by the double *yes, yes* and
no, no or the predicate formulation of the second yes and no; (4) a concluding line. In view
of this similarity, any attempt to decompose the structure further would require weighty
arguments. In any case, the prohibition and the three examples are not mutually exclusive.
By delineating all possible forms of oath-taking, the examples show concretely that it is
impossible to avoid the prohibition. Those who would attribute the prohibition of swearing
and the call to truthfulness to separate traditions must explain how such short statements
would have been preserved and passed on. The only thing that we can be sure of is that
Matthew (or his tradition) filled out the three examples of 5:34–35 with the help of Isa
66:1 and Ps 48:3 and that James offers the more straightforward form of the call to
truthfulness. That is not to say that Matthew did not want to say the same thing. It would
be difficult to see how he could have directly contradicted his earlier prohibition against
swearing of any kind.

The debate over the authenticity of the saying is mixed. It is possible that Jesus material
can become anonymous and thus move from the Matthew tradition to James, just as it is
possible that early Christian traditions can become words of Jesus and thus Matthew can
have attributed the material to Jesus. To deny the prohibition against swearing to Jesus
simply because it found no resonance in Primitive Christianity is not only an argument
from silence; it would also have consequences for several other traditions that are likely

authentic. In the final analysis our understanding of the content of the material leads us to attribute it to Jesus.

The decisive question is whether the text speaks of a fundamental or a limited prohibition of swearing. For his part, Matthew shows Jesus swearing at his trial (Matt 26:63–64) and also in Matt 23:16–22; 26:72, 74, does not presuppose an absolute prohibition of swearing. The Essenes abstain from personal swearing, but give oaths in their induction ceremony and before a court of law (Josephus, *J.W.* 2.135, 139, 141–42; 1QS v 8–11; CD 9:8–12; 15:3–4; 16:7ff.). Against this background the general observations make sense, which describe the early Christians as regulating their relationships among themselves and their personal lifestyle, but, e.g., as having no interest in governmental functions such as legal proceedings (the oath of a witness), war (oath of allegiance), or general business proceedings (contractual swearing). This same basic attitude is also implied in the first antithesis in Matt 5:21–22. It is focused not on legal punishments or on the military profession, but on the individual's attitude to the neighbor, and it ignores all other killing. It makes sense, therefore, that Jesus, if he is the one speaking in the antithesis, is prohibiting swearing in a limited sense, i.e., that he is thinking of the realm of interpersonal relationships.

Matthew, and most likely James as well, taught the prohibition of swearing as a rule for life within the church. The church's members should deal so honestly with one another that they do not need the reassurance of oaths that would put them in danger of misusing God's authority. Jesus is not interested in legal regulations for a church. It makes much more sense to assume that, in view of the approaching Kingdom of God in which untruthfulness simply cannot exist, he expects that his followers will already recognize that the general practice of oath-taking as a way of supporting one's statement is a sign of the old world that is passing away. In this old order God was brought into the situation with the help of direct or indirect theophorus forms whenever one wanted to escape the gray area between the truth and a lie. Jesus' somewhat casually formulated, categorical prohibition of oath-taking is by implication focused on the relationship between individuals and their neighbors. Its purpose is not primarily to get people to avoid swearing; it is to get them to tell the absolute truth before God and before their neighbors, since only this kind of truth-telling is appropriate to the Kingdom of God. The holy God of the Kingdom of God (Matt 6:9–10 = Luke 11:2) does not want to be continually responsible for correcting the fundamental human ambivalence between truthfulness and deception. He wants to create relationships in which people live truthfully with one another because they are always in God's presence and not only occasionally in a presence artificially created by taking an oath.

That this interpretation makes sense in terms of Jesus' message does not yet mean that it is historically accurate. We have described what Jesus may have meant, but to claim a greater degree of certainty we need to compare the saying with the debate over oath-taking in Antiquity. The Old Testament presupposes the use of oaths, but it criticizes perjury and frivolous swearing (e.g., Lev 19:12; Num 5:11–31; 30:3; Deut 6:13; Isa 48:1; Jer 5:2, etc.). Early Judaism and the rabbis continued this approach (e.g., Sir 23:9–15; 27:15). We mentioned earlier the stricter regulations of the Essenes according to which they avoided oaths in personal conversations among themselves. Of course, they did not understand this practice as contrary to the Torah. Refusing to do something that the Torah permits is not a violation of the Torah. The Hellenistic-Roman world is also familiar with warnings against hasty and false swearing (Epictetus, *Ench.* 33.5; Iamblichus, *Vit. Pyth.* 28.144). Philo combines the Hellenistic and Early Jewish emphases when he states that it would be best if words could simply be true without oaths, accepts as the next best possibility that swearing and the truth should go together, but above all when he understands the issue of oath-taking in terms of God's holiness (*De Decal.* 84–86). In its discussion of swearing, therefore, Antiquity prepared the way for the basic view of Matt 5:34–37 and Jas 5:12, but it was only the Essenes who prohibited oath-taking in a limited sense. A critical discussion of the issue of swearing is missing in Primitive Christianity. It is clear that Matthew follows the Essene point of view, but it is Matthew's macrotext that offers that clarity; it is not yet there in the earlier material.

This earlier material is no longer aware of any positive value in oath-taking. Even if it is thinking only indirectly of swearing in a particular situation, it underscores in general terms how oath-taking is no longer appropriate. Since the Essene approach has nothing like this kind of sharp prohibition, the scales tip in favor of attributing the material to Jesus. This conclusion makes all the more sense when we are able to understand the material in the context of Jesus' rigorous social ethic. When the prohibition against swearing totally ignores all practical problems and is not even willing to acknowledge that an oath can serve a useful purpose in this kind of world, we are even more inclined to understand it in terms of the Kingdom of God, which, according to Jesus, will provide all such things.

We have discussed the traditions that demonstrate how uncompromisingly Jesus sharpens statements of the Torah dealing with interpersonal relationships. Neither historical diversity nor human ambivalence is allowed to compromise these intensified requirements. They are simply apodictically proclaimed. The apodictic stance for its part comes from Jesus' relationship to the Kingdom of God.

5.3.4 *The Devaluation of the Cultic Torah*

When Tacitus, as an outsider, speaks of what is special about the Jewish people, he emphasizes those things that struck non-Jews in general about Israel: the strict monotheism with its central cult, circumcision, the Sabbath, and the special purity laws (*Hist.* 5.4–5). While Jews at the time of Early Judaism might have offered more detail and made minor corrections, they would not have claimed that Tacitus had not touched on the elements that stood at the center of their self-understanding as Jews. Jesus had nothing to say on the subject of God and the gods.[102] Nor did he speak about circumcision, since he accepted it without question as a given.[103] On both issues he reveals his inner-Jewish perspective. While it is true that geographically the Hellenistic cities lay nearby, Jesus is rooted in the Galilean villages where neither question is an issue (§2). The gospels inform us, however, that things are different with the Sabbath and the laws of purity. The potential for conflict that they portray is in both cases explosive.

Judaism understood the Sabbath as a divinely ordained regulation that was grounded in both election and creation (Gen 2:2–3; Deut 5:15; *Jub.* 2:17–20). God had in a special way sanctified and blessed the seven-day week. Indeed, he himself celebrated the day (Gen 2:7–8; *Jub.* 2:1), and all the inhabitants of heaven and earth should celebrate it forever (*Jub.* 2:16–33; *Mas. Shir. Shabb.* 1:8–2:26). This day thus has from God its own special honor; it is, indeed, the day of the holy kingdom (*Jub.* 50:9–10) on which God's kingly rule is especially near to human beings (cf. the Sabbath hymns from Qumran). People are not permitted to structure the Sabbath for their own convenience. As early as Exod 31:14 (cf. *Jub.* 2:25) anyone who violates the sacred law of the Sabbath is subject to the death penalty (cf. also Mark 3:6, following 2:23–28 and 3:1–5, and John 5:16). The Jew keeps the Sabbath holy *to the Lord* (Exod 31:15) by resting from all work as God does, by sharing this rest with slaves, foreigners, and animals (Exod 23:12), by praising and honoring God, and by eating and drinking (*Jub.* 2:31). The Sabbath is a day that approaches final perfection, and the final perfection for its part will have the character of the Sabbath rest (*Jos. As.* 8:9; 22:13; *m. Tamid* 7:4; *'Abot R. Nat.* 1 [1c]; *Ber. Rab.* 17 [12a], etc.). This connection reveals why the Sabbath commandment was so highly regarded (*Ber.* 1 [3c 14–15]). Historically, of course, the intense feelings about the Sabbath were related to the outcome of the Maccabean revolt. Its importance must have been enormously enhanced when the Maccabees successfully rebelled against the Hellenistic prohibition against keeping the Sabbath (1 Macc 1:41, 43–44; 2 Macc 6:6) and subsequently the Syrian rulers recognized this Jewish distinctiveness (1 Macc 10:34–35).[104]

Defining what it meant to keep the Sabbath turned out to be less of a problem. The Torah itself distinguishes between work that is permitted on the Sabbath and work that is forbidden. *Jubilees*, the *Damascus Document*, and *Sabbat* all place their emphasis there. The concern is probably based on Gen 2:2, which claims that God rested from all work on the Sabbath. In general, everything was forbidden on the Sabbath that could be done at some other time. A situation in which one's life is in acute danger (usually) justifies violating the Sabbath rest (*m. Yoma* 8:6). There is thus a reverse side to the institution of the Sabbath. The perpetual covenant (Exod 31:16) can be profaned (Isa 56:1–8). The various Halachic regulations prohibiting work ensure that there is an understanding about what it means legally to profane the Sabbath, even if the individual Jewish groups did not totally agree with one another and occasionally went their separate ways.

It is not atypical that all of the Sabbath conflicts in the gospels deal with this prohibition of work. In each case there is no argument about the prohibition of work itself. The only question is whether and how, in spite of the rule, *work* is to be justified. No one claims, therefore, that it is not possible to violate the Sabbath or that the accusations of profaning the Sabbath are based on the special Halacha of one particular group such as, e.g., the Pharisees. In the controversies all parties agree that the acts involved violate the Sabbath according to what is generally accepted in Early Judaism and that they cannot be reconciled with the Torah and the general Halacha, which together are regarded as a unity (§5.3.1).

There is an astonishingly broad range of material on Jesus' Sabbath-conflicts. It has often been observed that, in contrast to the silence about Sabbath-conflicts in the Primitive Church, there are references to Jesus' conflicts in all four gospels and in the sources on which they drew. Moreover, the material is widely distributed chronologically, geographically, and with reference to the various streams of Primitive Christianity that speak about it. At the same time it is obviously concentrated on one theme, viz., healings on the Sabbath. (The exception is Mark 2:23–28 parr.) This combination of factors (a concentration on Jesus' healings, a widely distributed tradition, and the absence of any indication of a Sabbath controversy in the early church) can only be explained by recognizing that, behind all of the admittedly later changes in the material, there is a core that preserves a historical memory about Jesus' activity. An attempt to eliminate Sabbath-conflicts from Jesus' activity and to claim that all of the traditions originated in later problems of the post-Easter church founders on the fact that it can only speculate about what experiences occasioned such a development. By contrast, when circumcision was discontinued in Primitive Christianity (Acts 15; Gal 2), vigorous debate broke out that was not quickly or easily resolved (cf. the opponents in Galatians). One would expect similar controversy had there been an attempt in the early church to change the Sabbath observance, yet all the traditions not only concede that Jesus violated the Sabbath, but also defend his actions.

When we look for the oldest elements in the gospel narratives dealing with violations of the Sabbath, it is clear that, as is generally acknowledged, the Sabbath theme is a late addition to Mark 1:21–31 parr.; Luke 13:10–17; 14:1–6; John 5:1–18; 9:1–41. There remain two sayings, however, that are presently embedded in scenes of conflict over the Sabbath whose authenticity can be confirmed, viz., Mark 2:27 and 3:4 parr.[105] Since we can best get to the heart of Jesus' understanding of the Sabbath by dealing with them together, we begin by offering the earliest form of the two traditions.

Mark 2:27 reads:

1a *The* Sabbath *came into being for the sake of the* human person,
  b *and not the* human person *for the sake of the* Sabbath.

Mark 2:23–28 is a controversy story in which a setting (vv. 23–24) is followed by a threefold answer (vv. 25–26, 27, 28). The setting is formed from the perspective of the church. The disciples violate the Sabbath by harvesting grain. The church, which calls on Jesus' authority to justify its own freedom with regard to the Sabbath, sees itself in the disciples. The first answer is a scribal argument that is both complicated and not very convincing. The second answer not only has a new introduction that is superfluous; it is self-contained, and it is connected to the setting and to the first answer only by means of the catchword *Sabbath*. The third answer draws a conclusion that has nothing to do with v. 27, but is more appropriate to vv. 25–26. It could well come from the same editorial activity as Mark 2:10.

Verse 27 presupposes a controversy for which the sentence offers an authoritative solution. It redefines the relationship between Sabbath holiness and human beings. The formulation with *for the sake of* is polemical and suggestive, for the two realities cannot be forced into that easy a relationship. The superficial solution has the advantage of being able to resolve the general conflict over the Sabbath. One does not have to deal with the question about healing on the Sabbath, since the general rule is: Human well-being always takes precedence over the Sabbath.

The only Jewish parallel is an early rabbinic statement. Rabbi Simeon ben Menasya (ca. 180) is said to have commented on Exod 31: "The Sabbath is delivered to you, but you are not delivered to the Sabbath." (*Mek. Exod.* 31:12 [109b]). The point is that the Sabbath commandment can be broken if one is in acute danger. Mark 2:27, on the other hand, is a more general principle, which ignores the casuistic debate. That the fundamental scope of the saying was difficult for Primitive Christianity is clear from the two other answers. Mark 2:25–26 treats the Sabbath conflict as an exception for which the Old Testament provides adequate justification, while Mark 2:28 is compelled to handle the controversial theme in christological terms. Matthew and Luke probably omitted Mark 2:27, because they preferred the christological justification to the general saying. Everything speaks, therefore, for attributing v. 27 to Jesus.

The early material from Mark 3:4 appears as follows:

1a *Is it permitted to do* good *on the Sabbath or to do* evil,
  b *to* save *life or to* kill?

Following hard on the heels of 2:23–28, Mark 3:1–6 is created on the principle in Early Judaism that in the case of violations of the Torah such as breaking the Sabbath, which is a capital offense (3:6), first a solemn warning is given (2:23–28). A second offense of the same kind is then regarded as a deliberate act that can no longer be excused.[106] In order to preserve this scenario, a miracle story (3:1b, 5c) is made over into a controversy story about the Sabbath. The Pharisees from 2:24 become the actors who want to trap and convict Jesus, and even Jesus himself is described as provoking a confrontation.

Restructuring the narrative as a controversy story about the Sabbath required an appropriate answer from Jesus. For this purpose a separate saying was chosen, which now appears in Mark 3:4. It is an independent, rhetorical double question that, like Mark 2:27, reacts polemically and suggestively, obviously to accusations the contents of which are reflected in Jesus' question. The noncasuistic, nonchristological nature of the material is further reminiscent of Mark 2:27. Here also the issue is the relation of human beings to the Sabbath. It is inconceivable that a Jew of that time would have accepted such a line of reasoning, since it disregards the Sabbath's special status. We are able, therefore, to attribute the material to Jesus.

The two statements of Jesus about the Sabbath are not, as is often claimed, to be understood as emancipation proclamations. It is not Jesus' intention to do away with an institution that limits individual freedom—not in the sense of the freedom to love all humanity (cf. Mark 3:4), and certainly not in the sense of the freedom of self-expression (cf. Mark 2:27). Apart from the fact that Mark 2:27 is to be understood in terms of Mark 3:4—i.e., in terms of the relationship to one's neighbor—the statements themselves do not eliminate the special status of the Sabbath as an institution. They are not designed to replace the Sabbath with one's personal inner conviction so that people base their lives not on outward regulations that are foreign to them, but on their consciences or individual insights. In no sense does the assertion say: Down with the Sabbath! It says rather that in the end-time that is beginning the existing institution of the Sabbath is to be evaluated differently. Within the debate in Early Judaism, Jesus' position is that he does not in general abrogate a given commandment of the Torah. He says, rather, that in the creation of salvation in the present, which is also the end-time, God's will must take precedence over Sabbath regulations. In individual cases the Sabbath cannot stop his activity.

This new attitude of Jesus toward the Sabbath, of course, is not based on Gen 1, in the sense that since human beings were created before the Sabbath they are for all time superior to the Sabbath, and the Sabbath must conform to their needs.[107] Mark 2:27, in other words, is not an exegesis of Gen 1 that Jesus introduces into the debate. It is true that Early Judaism and Early Christianity are both familiar with the line of argument that claims that the earlier of two realities is superior to the other,[108] but to find that argument in Mark 2:27 we would first have to put it in the text. Mark 2:27, as is the case with Mark 3:4 parr., presupposes the Sabbath's present validity and significance. The scripture (e.g., Gen 1) is not consulted, nor is there any interest in the origins of the Sabbath and of human beings.

The statement "the Sabbath came into being for the sake of the human person" says that God determined (not only originally, but) continuously—i.e., for today and always—what the Sabbath is to be (cf. the observations on Matt 5:21, 27 in §5.3.3). A typical example of that kind of pronouncement in Early Judaism is found in *Jub.* 2:32: "And the Creator of all things blessed this day which he had created for blessing and holiness and glory above all days." Since God granted this blessing to Israel (*Jub.* 2:31), there is a close relationship between the Sabbath and human beings. Yet, the Sabbath is not limited to this relationship. It is also a cosmic institution that encompasses all of heaven and earth (*Jub.* 2:16–

33; 4Q 403, etc.). Jesus reduces this general, Early Jewish consensus to an anthropological perspective: The Sabbath exists for the sake of human beings. The limited perspective comes from his own situation. At the heart of the controversy are his healings of sick people on the Sabbath, and it is to this controversy that he speaks with the two sayings that have been preserved. They are repeatable, polemical statements, which he himself probably repeated and which therefore were preserved in the memories of his hearers.

For Jesus, healings represented God's end-time appearance (Luke 11:20; cf. §4.2.2). God's activity is always irresistible. Healings are eschatological blessings for human beings—events that no one may withstand—events that in all seriousness no one *can* withstand. When people receive God's eschatological blessing, the divine purpose is realized for the Sabbath, which is a *day of the holy kingdom*, whose blessing is a foretaste and image of the coming perfection. Are not Jesus' end-time and the awaited end-time Sabbath identical in the sense that they both are days of blessing for human beings? The institution of the Sabbath, therefore, cannot take precedence over Jesus' Sabbath healings. The opposite must be the case. God's desire to draw near to human beings supersedes all the claims of the Sabbath. Jesus did not go out of his way to break the Sabbath, but he had the freedom to do so when he believed that it was appropriate. As the second line of the saying makes explicit, such an attitude naturally is provocative. The Sabbath is essentially both a blessing and an obligation for Israel. The Torah regulates such obligations, but Jesus violates them with his healing activity on the Sabbath, regardless of how often he does it. God's will in the Torah is clear. When Jesus speaks as he does, his new understanding of God's will is in conflict with the Torah, and it is simply not acceptable for Early Judaism, for whoever ignores the Sabbath's obligations forfeits the Sabbath's blessing.

From this beginning we can understand Mark 3:4 parr. as well. The alternatives that Jesus poses take up formally the basic choice that characterized Judaism's debate over the Sabbath: to rest or to work. With very few exceptions the decision is made in favor of resting on the Sabbath, since the Torah permits no other choice. Since Jesus proceeds on the understanding that his activity on behalf of the eschatological Kingdom of God takes precedence over everything else, he recasts the Early Jewish options. The Kingdom of God that is intruding into the present is concerned for human well-being; in the face of threatening judgment it grants life. *To do good* and *to save life* thus are identical and they represent *to rest*. The new negative choices, *to do evil* and *to kill*, which of course no one wants, take the place of *to work*. Thus stated, the alternatives imply that one must agree with Jesus, but that agreement is not possible for anyone who has not first agreed with Jesus' understanding of his own activity. The double question also subtly strikes a second blow. With the limitations imposed by Sabbath regulations the Torah is naturally on the side of doing good and saving life, but Jesus makes the Sabbath identical with the other days of the week. He does so not by profaning the Sabbath, but by indirectly making all the days of the week part of the end-time Sabbath. The eyes that are trained by the Torah to recognize violations of the Sabbath see things only externally; it is the internal understanding that matters.

Now that we have discussed the central issue of Jesus' attitude toward the Sabbath, we can consider the scene of the disciples plucking grain (Mark 2:23). The scene is not a historical report, and it reflects the church's situation. At the same time, one can ask why a church would be concerned about such an unusual activity as plucking grain, which appears nowhere else in the tradition. The mainstream of the narrative is focused on miracles that provoke controversy over the Sabbath. Is it possible that the scene preserves a memory of a situation in the life of Jesus? The meaning would be that since in the end-time God provides for all human needs (cf. §4.3.2), plucking grain for Jesus would be simply an act of accepting the divine gift. Such thankful acceptance even on the Sabbath would thus also reflect the end-time situation and would explain why the prohibition of harvesting grain on the Sabbath no longer applies to Jesus.

After the institution of the Sabbath, the Torah's cultic laws of ritual cleanliness provide the second sticking point for frequent conflict over the Law. Early Judaism also places a heavy emphasis on this area. The Old Testament commandment "You shall distinguish between the holy and the profane, between the unclean and the clean" (Lev 10:10) scarcely left room for misunderstanding. Initially and above all, of course, it applied to the priests and then to the participants in the cult. Beyond that, however, in varying degrees it demanded that all Israel observe many purity regulations. The degrees of observance may have been defined differently from time to time and from group to group, but no Israelite was ever totally excused from the laws of purity. The life of each Israelite was fundamentally and continuously defined in terms of such regulations in a way that is hardly conceivable today.

Here also the Maccabean movement served to solidify an already existing tradition. At the very latest, once the Maccabeans in light of the threat to the Jewish religion from Hellenistic polytheism were willing to die rather than to violate such regulations as the Torah's food laws (1 Macc 1–2; 2 Macc 5:27; 6:7, 18–19; cf. also Josephus, *J.W.* 2.152), the Levitical purity laws become a politically charged sign of Israel's election. Keeping the regulations becomes a self-defining, confessional act for all of Early Judaism (e.g., *Ep. Arist.* 139). The evidence comes not merely from the Essenes, who, of course, emphasized the highest level of priestly purity for their community.[109] Nor are we dependent on the currently widely accepted hypothesis that the Pharisees contemporary with Jesus had taken it as their goal to disseminate the Levitical Law of purity among all the people.[110] How seriously Judaism as a whole took the Law of purity is clear not only from the sporadic appearances of the subject in the texts (e.g., Dan 1:7–21; Tob 3:15; *Jub.* 22:16; 33:20; *T. Benj.* 8:1–3; Jdt 10:5; 12:7–9, etc.); it is also clear from the fact that, wherever Jews lived in a Hellenistic environment, they never questioned the need to keep these laws in the most literal and detailed way, even when they made use of Hellenistic methods of interpretation such as allegory in interpreting the cultic Torah (cf. *Jos. As.*; *Ep. Arist.* 139ff.; 182ff.; Philo, *Quaest. Gen.* 4.5, 60; *De Spec. Leg.* 1.206–7; 3.208–9; 4.100–18). These laws indeed served to protect Israel as it lived as a holy people among the other nations (*Ep. Arist.* 128–29). Nowhere during this period was there any talk of minimizing or liberalizing this part of the Torah.[111] That is true even for Galilee, whose inhabitants had the reputation of dealing more casually with questions of purity. As an outsider Tacitus confirms this picture when he writes: "For the Jews everything is unholy that is holy for us, while they are permitted to do things that we (Romans) regard as an abomination" (*Hist.* 5.4).

Now it is safe to assume that the highly sensitive question of eating pork (Lev 11:7; Deut 14:8; Isa 65:4; 1 Macc 1:47; 4 Macc 5:2–3) or meat from other unclean animals was not an issue in the Galilean villages that Jesus visited. The same is probably true of eating Gentile food in general (Tob 1:11–12), or meat that had been improperly slaughtered, or meat from Gentile sacrifices (1 Cor 8). Given the circumstances, conflict over such fundamental Early Jewish questions of purity was not even a possibility. Jesus did not have to decide, therefore, to what degree blood as the bearer of life belonged solely to God, or whether and how the cult of the God of Israel could exist alongside the cults of foreign gods. These problem areas, which were related to God's existence as the only God, simply were not on the agenda.

There are, however, other kinds of purity questions. Foodstuffs from which the tithe has not been paid (cf. Luke 18:12), e.g., were regarded as unclean (thus Johanan ben Zakkai, *t. Kelim. B. Mes.* 7:9). Purity regulations were by no means limited to eating and drinking; they dealt with a broad range of issues related to *touching, hearing, and seeing* (*Ep. Arist.* 142) and, of course, to sexual relations (*Ep. Arist.* 152; Lev 12, 15, etc.). Illnesses such as skin diseases rendered a person unclean (Lev 13–14; Mark 1:40–44). Corpses were associated with an especially high level of impurity (Num 9:6; 19:11; Lev 11:24–25; Tob 2:5, 9). The areas of the sacred and the profane, the pure and the impure, thus dominated the lives of Jesus' contemporaries. Avoiding impurity was every bit as important and as much a constantly present obligation as was avoiding sin. Laypersons on a pilgrimage to the temple would have had to pay special attention to their own purity, but even Galilee with its relative distance from the temple was not free of the daily observance of purity regulations, since unholiness was a constant threat (Hag 2:10–13). It was not only those who tried to live their daily lives as if they were priests during the time of temple service who faced such questions. In one way or another the questions were always present, not only in issues related to the cult, but also in the area of social contacts.

Someone who like Jesus was not afraid of touching sick people (§4.3.3) and who accepted tax collectors and sinners into his table-fellowship (§4.3.2) could not avoid being drawn into the struggle between sacred and profane (§5.3.2), even when he dealt only with fellow-Jews, and eating with Gentiles was not a live issue for him.[112] When he was acting on behalf of the Kingdom of God, which was all about accepting the lost, he had, of course, at the same time to accept those who were unclean. All too often one could not occur without the other. Anyone who wants to live a life that is holy according to the Torah must avoid what is unholy. Whoever, on the other hand, is interested in inclusion rather than exclusion will of necessity come into situations in which it is neither desirable nor possible to avoid sinners and unclean persons. The return of the younger son in Luke 15:11–32, to which we referred earlier (§5.3.2), shows clearly that it is as a sinner that the son is accepted. Although it is not explicitly mentioned, he is at the same time unclean. When he is accepted into his father's house with a banquet, the issue of his impurity has obviously become irrelevant. According to Luke 10:8 Jesus sends out the disciples with the instructions to eat whatever is set before them. The statement could well reflect Jesus' attitude, since it appears in a Jewish Christian context. Jewish Christians would hardly have spoken that way without Jesus' authority. Would Jesus not have exhibited the same attitude in his table-fellowship? How can someone accept unclean persons and then avoid unclean food? Similarly we may ask whether the carelessness about hand-washing in Mark 7:2, 5 does not reflect historically Jesus' same basic attitude.[113]

Now there is a word of Jesus that explicitly speaks to the purity issue.[114] It appears in Mark 7:15 parr., and in its probable earliest form it reads:

1a   There is nothing that entering a person from the outside
b   can defile.
2a   But what comes out *of a person—that is*
b   what defiles the person.

Major problems are involved in an analysis of Mark 7:1–23. Fortunately, however, it is generally agreed that 7:15 is self-contained and has a broader focus than the introductory issue of hand-washing with the discussion that follows (7:1–13). The explanations in 7:17–23, which serve as a commentary on 7:15, also reveal that the verse is early and that it once existed independently, since they temper somewhat the sharpness of v. 15 and use it as the basis for moralizing. The vocabulary of 7:15 is pre-Markan.[115]

Verses 7:17–23 are not uniform. Verses 14, 17, and 18a come from the Markan redaction (cf. 4:10–11, 13). Verses 18b–19b and 20–21 contain an interpretation of v. 15 that builds on the distinction between heart and stomach or thoughts and food and that structurally repeats 15a and 15b in sequence, each time with explanations. In vv. 19c, 21b, 22, 23 we are dealing with a second level. Verses 19c, 21b are syntactically secondary, while the catalogue of vices in vv. 21b, 22 is traditional. Characteristic of this level are the neuter plurals in vv. 19c, 23, which are probably influenced by the catalogue of vices and which do not correspond to the neuter singulars in vv. 18b, 20.

Of course, the tension between singular (15a) and plural (15b) neuters that is present in 7:15 has often been cited as justification for dividing the verse. A more plausible explanation, however, is that the earlier commentary is based on a version of v. 15 that has the neuter singular in both halves of the verse. Then at the next stage of the tradition the neuter plurals were introduced and 7:15b was changed. If the singular form was original in both parts of 7:15, there is no reason to divide the verse, since it is the tension between outer and inner cleanliness that is the point of the saying.[116]

Some have claimed that this word could not have come from Jesus, since it seriously challenges Torah-faithfulness, which they assume for both Jesus and Jewish Christianity. They have cited the controversy that broke out over the table-fellowship between Jewish and Gentile Christians (Gal 2:11–14) and have alleged that it never could have happened had Mark 7:15 been known as an authoritative pronouncement of Jesus. They also have called attention to the fact that the sayings source contains no criticism of the Law and that it is Mark who first deals with the subject.[117] For a number of scholars, therefore, the history of early Christianity speaks against attributing the saying to Jesus.

There are, however, counterarguments. The existence of a monolithic Jewish Christianity that was faithful to the Torah is not supported by the sources. The Jewish-Christian circle around Stephen attacks the boundaries of Israel almost immediately after Jesus' death. That criticism of the Law was a factor in their behavior (Acts 6:8–15) is confirmed by Paul's persecution of the Hellenistic mission in Damascus.[118] It is further noteworthy that the primitive church in Jerusalem gathered around the apostles was spared the persecution that was directed at Stephen's followers.

The events at the Apostolic Council are also instructive, when the legitimacy of the Gentile-Christian church in Antioch is vigorously debated (Acts 15; Gal 2:1–10). The majority that accepts the developments in Antioch follows the lead of the *pillars*, Peter, James, and John. Had they been consistent in their faithfulness to the Torah, they would have had to refuse to recognize the church in Antioch. Instead, they acknowledged that Jewish Christians and Gentile Christians lived together on Gentile Christian terms and that, therefore, the walls that the ceremonial Law had constructed to protect Israel from Gentile contamination had now been torn down. That a Jew such as the Christian, Peter, immediately and without any problems ate in Antioch with Gentiles, i.e., with his non-Jewish brothers and sisters in Christian faith (Gal 2:12), suggests that the participants at the Apostolic Council were well aware of the consequences of their decision to recognize Gentile Christian churches, even if as individuals they reacted differently to the decision.[119] It also raises the question why Peter, unlike James and his followers (Gal 2:12), felt justified in taking what since the Maccabees had become such a highly sensitive step (§5.3.1). The Jewish point of view was explicit, and is stated in 4 Macc 5:19–21: "Do not think then that eating unclean food is for us a petty sin, for small and large transgressions are equally serious, since in either case the Law is equally despised." Our safest assumption is still that the position of the Hellenists around Stephen, of the *pillars* at the Council, and of Peter in Antioch, who soon after the so-called lapse in Antioch obviously reverts to his Gentile-Christian orientation, is based on the authority of Jesus.[120] For our purposes here we can leave open the details of how that happened.

There is a breadth to Jewish Christianity that reaches from the Judaizers of Galatians through James (Gal 2:12) to those who from the Jewish point of view would have been called assimilation-Jews, i.e., Jewish Christians who lived as did Gentile Christians (Barnabas, Prisca and Aquila, Apollos, Paul, the mission-aries of 2 Cor, etc.). In all probability such extreme diversity is to be explained only by the fact that Jesus himself worked within Judaism while criticizing the Law. In this way all of them were able to claim that they were legitimate heirs of his view.

No one knows whether anyone cited Mark 7:15 in the controversy in Antioch (Gal 2:11–14). The argument that Paul would have had to quote Mark 7:15 in Gal 2:11–14 and that, since he did not, he and the others must not yet have known it, is specious. It simply does not follow that an individual who does not use a saying is not aware of it, and such silence certainly has nothing to say about whether a community knew it. With such logic we would have to conclude that the entire miracle tradition of Jesus originated after Paul, since he otherwise would have used it in Rom 15:19 and 2 Cor 12:12, or that the parables unique to Luke had to have originated after Mark and after the sayings source. The entire issue of Paul's use of Jesus material is, furthermore, such a complex question[121] that we must avoid all such quick and easy conclusions. Finally, we should note that Mark 7:15 neither speaks directly of eating nor deals with the explosive issue of eating with Gentiles (including Gentile Christians). Anyone who would bring Mark 7:15 into the debate surrounding Gal 2:11–14 must recognize that, when all is said and done, this word of Jesus does not offer any direct help.

We should finally note that, however Mark 7:15 is to be understood and applied to the situation of Gal 2:11–14 in terms of one of the parties in the controversy, there are numerous examples of how uncomfortable words of Jesus were softened, limited, or reinterpreted. Matthew, e.g., does that with Mark 7:15. There is the phenomenon of a Judaizing reworking and sifting of Jesus material such as one finds, e.g., in the sayings source. That it does not contain the kind of Jesus material critical of the Law that one finds in Mark 2:1–3:6; 7:1–23 does not mean that the sayings source did not yet know such material and that Mark was the first to be aware of it. Such an argument presupposes the conclusion and suggests, on the one hand, that there was a straight-line development from the sayings source to Mark and that, on the other hand, there was no exceedingly complex process of selection both for the sayings source and for Mark.[122] There are, furthermore, remnants of the debate over the Law in the sayings source (Matt 8:21–22 par.; 11:19 par.; Luke 16:16 par.; Matt 23:4, 23, 25–26 par.[123]). In view of the impending judgment, Q is more interested in the call to repentance and the offer of salvation, and does not want controversial material such as issues over the Law to distract from this message.[124] Did not Jesus himself emphasize judgment and salvation so that questions of purity and other issues did not constitute his main theme?

If, then, the history of Primitive Christianity and its sources do not require that we deny Mark 7:15 to Jesus,[125] the way is clear to test its authenticity.[126] Jesus' meal-fellowships and miracle activity offer permanent situations in which the conflict presupposed by Mark 7:15 could have broken out. Solving the problem by making an authoritative statement is in keeping with the way he elsewhere deals authoritatively with problems of the Law. Jesus' description of Israel's lost condition solely in terms of its status as sinners (§3.2.5) and not in terms of ritual impurity is in keeping with the fundamental alternative in Mark 7:15, as is the monotone straightforwardness with which he expressed himself in the area of human responsibility in discipleship (§5.2) and in the social area (§5.3.3). Finally, Jesus solves the problem, just as he does elsewhere in his dealings with the Torah, by defining a fundamental perspective without offering any instructions on how to behave in a given situation. He simply offers a principle that avoids the whole casuistic and pragmatic debate over the Law. These considerations are all good reasons for understanding this decree in the context of the preaching of Jesus.

The authoritative decree is given in the form of antithetical parallelism with the emphasis on the final, positive statement.[127] Its sense is that true uncleanness is the result of living according to one's own plan for life—a plan for which people are themselves responsible, because it is centered in themselves. Here everyone must be careful. Here everyone is challenged, completely and without exception. With a play on words the saying speaks first of the impurity that infects people and then juxtaposes it to the impurity that they themselves produce. The distinction between *outside* and *inside* does not refer to body and soul in the sense of a Hellenistic understanding of the person; the context is rather a unified anthropology. What comes from the outside overwhelms the whole person. What comes from the inside—from people themselves as willing, thinking, planning human beings—reveals the whole person. (It is different then in Mark 7:19–23). The statement corresponds to the Old Testament–Jewish tradition that can speak in the same sense of *impurity* as an expression of sin and that regards this impurity as of greater importance than cultic uncleanness (cf. Isa 1:10–17; 6:1–13; Ps 51; Prov 20:9; *Jub.* 22:14–15; *As. Mos.* 7:3–10, etc.).

The opening line, which speaks of cultic contamination, is thinking not specifically of eating, but of the totality of the uncleanness that from a divided creation threatened every contemporary of Jesus. The absolute *nothing* with which the sentence begins is important. It is not only the case that the first sentence is subordinate to the second sentence in the sense: Cultic purity is less important, or: Levitical purity does not play such an important role in Galilean daily life. The two sentences also stand opposed to each other as alternatives. Jesus says yes to the second sentence and no to the first.

Now questions of sin and of purity determine whether one can approach God and whether, e.g., God will accept a sacrifice. At issue, therefore, is one's relationship to God. In view of the impending judgment, prior to the coming of the Kingdom of God this relationship is practically nonexistent (§§3.1; 3.2). Israel's righteousness and purity have long since been squandered. Yet, from the standpoint of the Kingdom of God there is a changed situation. Just as the Kingdom of God eliminates the lost condition of human beings, it also eliminates the division

between clean and unclean, both with persons and in creation (cf. Matt 6:9 and
§5.2.4). Wherever God establishes his end-time salvation, God also makes everything clean (cf. *Jub.* 1:23, 28; *Ps. Sol.* 17:26, 30c; *T. Lev.* 17:11; *Bib. Ant.*
3:10i).[128] Since the gifts that he makes available in the meal are his gifts, they are
pure (§§4.2.3; 4.3.2). When the diseases that are associated with uncleanness are
healed, they and the impurity are gone. In the presence of a Kingdom of God that
not only forgives human sin but also bestows gifts from creation, people should
give up their anxiety about being contaminated yet give serious attention to living
in a way that is appropriate to the Kingdom of God. In this way even Jesus
himself is able to accept those who are lost without being concerned about
questions of purity.

It is clear that there was no corresponding attitude anywhere in ancient Judaism.[129] Our interpretation, however, does not necessarily lead to a discussion of
the irrelevance of the ritual and the sole importance of the ethical. Mark 7:15
does not say that external impurity does not exist; it says that in Jesus' end-time
situation such impurity can no longer hurt anyone. Jesus does not say with Paul
that nothing is unclean in itself but that things are unclean only for those who
think they are unclean (Rom 14:14), and Jesus certainly does not eliminate the
presuppositions for the existence of the cult in Antiquity.[130] Instead, in the end-
time situation there is for him no nonhuman creature that can keep God and
human beings from coming together. Jesus' attitude is thus Jewish; yet at the
same time, because of the nearness of the Kingdom of God in his miracles and
table-fellowship, he reevaluates the Torah's purity regulations and the consequences for violations of the Torah. There is, therefore, a different picture with
regard to the cultic Law than there is in Jesus' social ethic, where he was more
concerned to intensify the Torah.

5.4 THE OPEN FAMILY OF GOD

Betz, H.-D. *Nachfolge und Nachahmung Jesu Christi im Neuen Testament.* Tübingen:
  J.C.B. Mohr (Paul Siebeck), 1967.
Hahn, F. "Die Nachfolge in vorösterlicher Zeit," in: *Die Anfänge der Kirche im Neuen
  Testament. EvFo* 8 (1967) 7–36.
Hoffmann, P. *Studien zur Frühgeschichte der Jesusbewegung.* SBAB 17. Stuttgart: KBW,
  1994, 139–70.
Jeremias, J. *Jesus' Promise to the Nations.* Philadelphia: Fortress, 1982.
Lohfink, G. *Jesus and Community: The Social Dimensions of Christian Faith.* Phila-
  delphia: Fortress; New York: Paulist, 1984.
Müller, Kh. (ed.) *Die Aktion Jesu und die Re-Aktion der Kirche.* Würzburg: Echter Verlag,
  1972.
Oberlinner, L. *Historische Überlieferung und christologische Aussage.* fzb 19. Würzburg:
  Echter Verlag, 1975.

Roloff, J. *Die Kirche im Neuen Testament*. GNT 10. Göttingen: Vandenhoeck & Ruprecht, 1993, 15–46.

Schroeder, H.-H. *Eltern und Kinder in der Verkündigung Jesu*. ThF 53. Hamburg-Bergstedt: Evangelischer Verlag, 1972.

Schulz, A. *Nachfolgen und Nachahmen*. Munich: Kösel, 1962.

Schürmann, H. "Der Jüngerkreis Jesu als Zeichen für Israel," in: idem, *Ursprung und Gestalt*. Düsseldorf: Patmos, 1970, 45–60.

Trilling, W. "Zur Entstehung des Zwölferkreises," in: *Die Kirche des Anfangs*. Festschrift H. Schürmann. R. Schnackenburg, ed. Freiburg/Basel/Vienna: Herder, 1978, 201–22.

As early as the previous century a trend developed in scholarship that was based on the accurate observation that Jesus was committed to realizing the Kingdom of God, but that he was not interested in a structured organization in the sense of a church. The references to the church in Matt 16:17–19 and 18:15–17 are special Matthean material that originated after Easter. None of the other gospels even uses the word *church*. From this statistical evidence, supplemented with other observations, one then concluded that Jesus only called individuals to a life of discipleship. Based on this correct assumption, one then looked no further for signs of an organizing structure in the Kingdom of God. We need to take a closer look at this issue, however. That Jesus left everything vague and open in this area is highly improbable, since his broad association of the Kingdom of God with the Zion tradition (§4.1), even though he did not actualize it, offered massive, structural descriptions, as texts such as Tob 13 or *Ps. Sol.* 17 quickly demonstrate.

In describing Jesus' point of view, the best place to begin is with the unusual connection between criticism of the family and the new family of God in the earliest Jesus material. It has long since been observed that Jesus distanced himself from his own family and that he demanded that the disciples in his inner circle separate themselves temporarily from their families (cf. §2). This phenomenon, however, is not simply of biographical or sociohistorical interest; it is the first step in a theological evaluation of the family. At least three traditions are relevant here, one of which is Matt 10:37 = Luke 14:26:

> *Whoever does not hate father and mother*
> *cannot be my disciple.*

Since, unfortunately, both the syntax and the vocabulary of the Q-tradition differ widely between Matthew and Luke,[131] a reconstruction of the earliest stage of the material remains hypothetical. Still, in view of Luke 9:59–60 (cf. §4.2.2) the content of this harsh saying can hardly be denied to Jesus. There is value, therefore, in attempting a reconstruction.

Luke will have adapted the beginning of the saying to the setting of 14:25. It was probably also he or his source who expanded the list to three pairs of relationships. The self-hatred with which the list comes to a climax is also best understood as an expression of the church's parenetic interest. Matthew clearly preserved the sentence structure better than did Luke. Of course, it was probably Matthew who was responsible for doubling the saying, since the sequence is unusual. (There is no reference to one's wife.) Matthew thus ends with a group of three (10:37–38), each of which ends with the refrain: "who is not worthy of me." With this formulation he emphasizes passing the test of discipleship, while Luke ("he cannot be my disciple"), as in Luke 9:60, is thinking of the act of becoming a disciple. The latter will be more original as is Luke's harsh *hate*, which Matthew replaces with a more agreeable formulation that grants Jesus the preeminence while not challenging the family's fundamental right.

Hating one's parents is not to be understood psychologically, in spite of its provocative description of the relationship. It is a Semitic way of describing the act of distancing one's self from one's parents. Luke 9:59–60 offers a possible concrete example, viz., not caring about burying one's dead father. If Luke 9:59–60 presupposes an understanding of discipleship that regards the Kingdom of God as the sole factor for determining life in the present, as opposed to which the structures of the past (such as the commandment to honor one's parents; §4.2.2) no longer have authority, then we must understand Matt 10:37 = Luke 14:26 in terms of the same basic attitude toward the family. Given this understanding, the character of discipleship is to be determined by the Kingdom of God, which is being realized in the present. This sole standard for a present that is understood as the end-time relegates other norms and structures to the time before the coming of the Kingdom of God. Indirectly the view is expressed that separating humanity into families, such as was taken for granted in all of Antiquity, loses its meaning in the Kingdom of God. Thus the family structure that for every Jew was given by creation (Gen 1:27–28; 2:23–24; 3:16) no longer determines the end-time.

That this concept is part of a comprehensive point of view is clear from Mark 3:31–35 parr.:

> 1a [v. 31] And a crowd was sitting around him.
> b And they said to him:
> c "Look, your mother and your brothers and your sisters outside are looking for you."
> 2a And he answered them and said: [v. 34]
> b "Whoever does the will of God,
> c this one is my brother, and sister, and mother."

The unusual sequence in 2c (first the siblings, then the mother) is best understood— indeed, probably only to be understood—as a chiastic reformation of the items of 1c. It follows then that the setting and the saying belonged together from the beginning. Those who (as is often done) want to understand v. 35 as an isolated saying must explain why the mother appears at the end of the list. That Jesus' followers are called brothers is documented elsewhere (John 20:17; Heb 2:11–18), but the reference to parents in such a context is unusual. The possible earliest form, therefore, was an apophthegm that Mark expanded at the beginning (v. 31) and in the middle (v. 34). The vocabulary of v. 34 clearly points to Mark.[132] Verse 31, with its shortened list of relatives, is an expansion that is obviously based on v. 32.

Only here does Mark speak of the will of God. In Judaism one can say that at the end God will so cleanse the Israelites that they will keep his commandments; he will be their *father*, and they will be his *children* (*Jub.* 1:23–25; cf. *Ps. Sol.* 17:26–27). Mark 3:35 says, however, that those who do God's will have a special kinship to him (cf. §4.3.3). If the church had created this saying, it would hardly have included the mother. The apophthegm thus effectively captures the reality of Jesus.

Jesus calls Israel together for the Kingdom of God, which, effective immediately, is being made real in his activity. One result of this activity is that he is estranged from his natural family (Mark 6:1–6 parr.; cf. §2). According to Mark 3:31–35 the members of his family confront him once again in the midst of his activity as the eschatological prophet of the Kingdom of God. He uses the event as an occasion for transferring the meaning of family from one set of relationships to another. Those who do the will of God by responding to the call to enter the Kingdom of God are family members with the one who proclaims God's present, end-time assumption of kingly power. The eschatological community that Jesus gathers is thus God's family.

Mark 3:31–35 is reminiscent of 1QH ix.35–36, where a member of the Essene community of salvation prays:

> For my father does not know me,
> and my mother has abandoned me to thee.
> For you are a father to all [sons] of your truth,
> and you rejoice over them like a mother over her child,[133]
> and like a nurse you feed all your creatures in your bosom.[134]

Because he has lost his own parents, the petitioner turns to God, who cares for all his creatures as a father. As father he has a special relationship of motherly affection with the members of the Essene community (*sons of truth*). The metaphors are similar to those of Mark 3, although, as we will demonstrate, Jesus has a different emphasis.

Before we turn our attention to that discussion, however, we note other texts on the theme, including a text that continues the theme of Mark 3:31–35 without the contrast with the natural family. The text is Mark 10:15 parr.:

> Truly I say to you:
> Whoever does not become like a child
> will not (be able to) enter the Kingdom of God.

That the saying at one time existed independently is established by the different contexts in which it appears in Matthew and Mark as well as by John 3:3, 5 and Justin, *Apol.* i.61.4. Its widespread tradition also speaks for its age. Even the statement's introduction is old (cf. John 3:3, 5!). As is often the case with sayings, Mark exhibits the most awkward syntax. It may have originated in an effort to smooth the transition from Mark 10:14. In any case, independently of each other Matthew and John preserve the early syntactic formulation. Of course, Matthew is responsible for the parenetic you-style, which he takes over from the introductory statement. By contrast, the descriptive style of Mark and John is less influenced by the context and thus is older.

Since the statement fits well the theme of the family of God, there is no reason not to attribute it to Jesus. The later church related the statement to baptism and thus read into the text a concern that it did not originally have.

The catchword *child* has been the occasion for a number of modern associations that have been read into the text. We can avoid the problem by remembering two Jesus traditions that point the way to a reliable understanding. In Matt 6:25–34 par. (cf. §4.2.3) one is called to abandon all anxiety about one's livelihood, because God with his kingly rule will, as father, provide everything that is needed. If we look at the statement from the perspective of the recipient rather than from the perspective of the giver, the opposite of the father is the child. To be a child thus means to behave according to the description given in Matt 6:25–34 par. The prayer of Jesus (Matt 6:9–13 par.; cf. §5.2.4) confirms this interpretation. It is directed to the *father*, from whom everything is expected. Mark 10:15 thus offers a glimpse into the make-up of the end-time community of salvation. Its father is God, and it is his family. To be more precise, the members of the community of salvation are children or, as Matt 5:44–45 par. (§5.2.3) says, "sons (i.e., brothers and sisters) of God."

In this context perhaps we should call attention to the antithesis from Matt 12:30 = Luke 11:23, which describes human behavior in the style of a wisdom saying. It reads:

> Whoever is not with me is against me.
> Whoever does not gather with me scatters.

Unfortunately, the issue of the saying's authenticity is complicated. On the one hand, there is no christological or ecclesiological evidence to suggest that it originated in the early church. On the other hand, there are no compelling reasons to attribute it to Jesus. Since, however, the saying is compatible with the other Jesus material in this section, we will tentatively claim it on behalf of Jesus. The saying is self-contained, and it appears in almost identical form in Matthew and Luke.

It is no accident that the distinction between gathering and scattering is reminiscent of texts such as Ezek 28:25; 29:13 or of God's promise to Israel to gather the chosen people from among the nations at the end of time. In the days of Jesus this expectation was a standard part of the eschatological hope within the Zion tradition (cf. §4.1.4). Yet, just as Jesus ignored the Zion elements of this hope in his word about the banquet of salvation in Matt 8:11–12 par. (cf. §3.2.4), it is possible that he ignored them also in the case of Matt 12:30 par. Jesus gathers Israel to live in community in the Kingdom of God. This community is no longer determined by the Zion tradition; it is the family of God grounded in creation. Those who are active with Jesus on behalf of this family share his work of gathering Israel into the end-time community. Those who are against Jesus are opposed to this goal. They scatter the eschatological community, which is beginning to coalesce under the impending Kingdom of God.

Now this new community within the Kingdom of God has three special emphases. The first is to be seen in terms of the relationships within the family of God. We find in a number of synoptic variants a tradition that poses the paradox that leadership in the community is determined by a reciprocal subordination among the members (Mark 9:35 = Luke 9:48d; Mark 10:43–44 parr.; Matt 18:4; 23:11). The Gospel of John also makes a contribution to the same theme (John 13:13–15). Paul offers his own rich and independent formulation (e.g., Rom 15:2, 7–8; Gal 5:13; Phil 2:3). While the references outside the synoptics document the theme's general importance throughout early Christianity, they have nothing to contribute to our understanding of the history of the synoptic tradition. What makes that understanding so difficult is the overwhelming variety among the synoptic sources. Along with the Johannine and Pauline material, this variety reveals how important the theme was for the churches. Of course, this wealth of material in no way proves that the tradition goes back to Jesus. Perhaps Mark 10:43–44 best approximates the tradition's beginning:[135]

> *Whoever would be great among you shall be your servant.*
> *Whoever would be first among you shall be the slave of all.*

The double saying bases greatness and preeminence in the community on serving and subordination in it. Thus out of a horizontally structured power pyramid, which in those days characterized every community, including the family, is made a vertically leveled equality of all the members in mutual service. The standard exercise of power is not criticized (although it is in the context; Mark 10:42 parr.), but the definition of *ruling* which the new form of community requires presupposes that it is the opposite of the way power is usually exercised. Indirectly, therefore, the saying is a criticism of power.

The saying probably envisages an extended family to which servants and slaves also belong. According to this opinion, in God's community of brothers and sisters, under God as the father, not only should equality rule, but all traditional expressions of power should be replaced by their opposites. The principle is reminiscent of the call to grateful sharing of the forgiveness that one has received (§5.2.3) and the behavior that is appropriate to it.

Old Testament prophecy is already familiar with tendencies to criticize the use of power. According to Isa 2:17 at the end of time only the God of Israel will be exalted (cf. also Zech 14:9). According to Jer 31:34 and Joel 3:1–2 the eschatological renewal of humanity will lead to the suspension of the advantage that the old have over the young and of the subordination of servants to their masters, because in that day all will have the same knowledge of God. Apocalypticism is also often critical of power structures (Daniel; *1 Enoch*). The final judgment will involve the destruction of all worldly authority (*1 Enoch* 38:4–6; 46:4–6; 48:8–9; 62:1–12; 63). This model of the end-time involves a wholesale rejection of the legitimacy of this authority, since the rulers do not acknowledge that they are God's vassals (46:5). God will totally eliminate such authority, and only he and his Son of Man will rule. All the righteous will participate in the end-time gifts of salvation in equal measure. There are no longer degrees of authority in the community of salvation (*1 Enoch* 5:7–9; 45:4–5; 48:1; 50:1, 5; 58:2–6; 62:13–16).[136]

That Jesus stands within this tradition should be beyond any doubt, but he takes it to another level. Instead of focusing on the external authorities from whom power will be taken,[137] he requires of his hearers that they abstain from power and that they practice subordination. This change also includes a rejection of the fundamental principle that governs *1 Enoch* (as well as other works), viz., that a reversal of relationships will take place in the last days. Those who now rule will then be tormented, and those who are now oppressed will then be triumphant (*1 Enoch* 37; 45:5–6; 46–47; 62–63). Jesus is not interested in that kind of equalizing reversal of fortunes, because it has no room for accepting those who are lost (§4.2.4).

We can summarize the second emphasis with the observation that it was Jesus' purpose not to gather a holy remnant of Israel,[138] but to get all Israel to accept his message. The totality of Israel, which is lost (§3.2), has the possibility of entering the Kingdom of God. When individuals follow Jesus, they realize the social dimension of the Kingdom of God,[139] because they participate in his table-fellowship (§4.3.2), just as they hope to be present at the final, eternal banquet of salvation (Matt 8:11–12 par.). In the same way the prayer of Jesus is a commu-nity prayer, not an individual prayer (cf. §5.2.4). The recipients of the beatitudes in Matt 5:3–5 par. (cf. §4.3.2) do not contradict this picture, since the poor are understood as a demonstration of the suffering of all Israel. At the same time, Jesus was no longer able to describe Israel's relationship to God in terms of the covenant-God and his covenant-people (§4.2.3). The one element that remains from that concept is the symbolic number twelve of the inner circle. It indicates that Jesus was addressing all Israel (cf. §2).

Anyone in Early Judaism who spoke of Israel's final salvation could hardly omit the subject of Israel and the nations. This theme raises the third emphasis in Jesus' concept of a family of God. It is beyond dispute that Jesus regards himself as sent to all Israel and that he therefore addresses only his fellow Israelites and is active only in Israel's territory (§2). He thus does not speak specifically of the nations in his preaching. He has absolutely no interest in winning proselytes or in a mission to the nations. In the history of Christianity, the Gentile mission is a post-Easter phenomenon that is connected with the history of the church in Antioch and, of course, with the missionary activity of the Apostle Paul. Mark (Mark 13:10), Matthew (Matt 28:16–20), and Luke (Acts 2; 10; 15) in their own way indicate that the mission to the Gentiles was a post-Easter phenomenon.[140]

Yet, anyone who relegates the theology of election and the covenant theology to the background at least indirectly opens the way for a fresh debate over Israel's special status. Anyone who dealt with the cultic Torah as Jesus did (cf. §5.3.4) at the very least relativizes Israel's exclusivity vis-à-vis the nations. To emphasize Israel's lost condition as much as Jesus did (cf. §3.2.2) is to eliminate much of the difference between Israel and the Gentile world. Unlike the two themes discussed previously, here we come across direct references to non-Jews in the earliest Jesus material (§3.2.4). Can anyone who so emphatically put the God of creation and his creation in the center of his message as Jesus did (§4.2.3) limit himself exclusively to an inner-Jewish point of view?

Without oversimplifying the situation too much, we can say that there were in Early Judaism four possible ways of picturing the role of the Gentiles in the final salvation for which Israel hoped. The harshest approach categorically rejected any participation. The nations simply would be destroyed (Sir 36:1–17; 1QM; *T. Sim.* 6:3–7). It was probably the Essenes and the Zealots who most took this approach. Other texts claim that the proselytes or a select few from the nations will, along with Israel, be excluded from judgment (*Jub.* 2:28; *T. Naph.* 8:2–3; Eighteen Benedictions 13; *4 Ezra* 3:36; *2 Apoc. Bar.* 42:5). This approach could have represented the Pharisaic point of view (cf. Matt 23:15). The third possibility is that the present power relationships under which Israel suffers will be reversed. Most of the Gentiles will be annihilated, but a remnant will celebrate the Feast of Tabernacles with Israel (Zech 14). A variation of this view is that the nations, or those of them that remain at the end, will have to serve Israel (*Ps. Sol.* 17:21, 28–31, 36, 45). Finally, there are statements that suggest a wide variety of ways the nations could participate equally in the final salvation, some by implication, others more explicitly. This approach begins with Deutero-Isaiah (Isa 42:1, 4, 6; 45:23; 49:6) and continues in Isa 2:2–5; 11:6–10; 56:7; 66:23; Mic 5:1–5; Zeph 2:11; Zech 2:15; 9:9–10, etc. Tob 14:6–7 calls the nations to repent so that God will have mercy on them.[141] Especially impressive are the formulations in *1 Enoch*: "And all the children of men shall become righteous, and all nations shall offer adoration and shall praise me, and all shall worship me" (*1 Enoch* 10:21). Echoing Deutero-Isaiah, the Son of Man is portrayed as the one who is *the light of the nations* in such a way that all inhabitants of the world shall some day worship God together (*1 Enoch* 48:4–5; cf. also 90:33–36; 105:1). Here there is no separation or unequal relationship between Israel and the nations. All the earth's inhabitants are gathered under one God. In worshipping this God they are all equal, and they all share equally in his final salvation.

Jesus' preaching was a variation of this last approach. In Matt 8:11–12 par (§3.2.4) he explicitly states that the nations will come together into the Kingdom of God. Admittedly, their gathering will not result from missionary activity; God himself will bring it about (cf. Isa 66:18–22, also 56:3–8). It is noteworthy that nowhere does Jesus say that at the end of time God will suspend Israel's servitude to the nations as well as the scattering of the Jews among the nations in order to punish the foreign rulers. There is not a single negative word about the nations that contributed to Israel's suffering in Jesus' day, unless one sees an implied criticism in such marginal statements as Matt 6:32 (cf. §4.2.3). In fact, in the pronouncements of judgment on Israel the Gentiles are frequently cited in a way that is designed to provoke Israel to accept Jesus' message.[142] Jesus shows no interest at all in the hated Roman forces of occupation.[143] It is impossible to miss this obvious silence as opposed to the zeal of a person like Phinehas (Num 25), who had been a popular role model since the days of the Maccabees, and we must conclude that it was intentional. We should also note that it is the Samaritan, not the priest or the Levite, who acts in Luke 10:30–35 (§5.2.3) in an exemplary manner. The great king of Matt 18:23–34 (cf. §3.2.4), who forgives a debt that for the people of Galilee was unimaginably large and thus reveals the fundamental law of the Kingdom of God, is also a non-Jew. Against this background it is not surprising that among the narratives from the miracle tradition an occasional Gentile request for healing is granted (Matt 8:5–13 par.; Mark 7:24–30 parr.; cf. §4.3.3). These witnesses clearly reveal that Jesus' mission to Israel was not understood in an exclusive sense. It was but the first stage in the final drama that began with Jesus. God would continue the drama by gathering the nations himself. This hope implies that Jesus already had an open attitude on the subject of Israel and the nations, and it helps explain why so soon after Easter the Stephen circle and the church in Antioch in different ways expanded the scope of their missionary activity.

NOTES

1. Thus H.-D. Wendland, *Eschatology*, 108 and H. Windisch, *Bergpredigt*, 20–21.
2. Thus R. Bultmann, *Jesus*, 51–52.
3. Thus, E. Fuchs, *Frage*, 200–1; E. Jüngel, *Paulus*, 212–13.
4. H. Merklein is especially compelling in arguing this case (*Gottesherrschaft*). Cf. also Becker, "Ethos," 38. When G. Deutzenberg ("Eigenart," 162–67) rejects this approach in his treatment of texts (such as Mark 2:27, 3:4, 7:15) that deal with the Law, but then claims, without any basis in the text, that Mark 14:58 is to be understood in terms of the Kingdom of God, his very inconsistency reveals the necessity of our approach.
5. On this point cf. once again especially H. Merklein, *Gottesherrschaft*, 37ff.
6. A. Schweitzer was the major figure in initiating this question (*Geschichte*, 580ff.; 620ff.). [The author refers here to material in later editions of Schweitzer's classic work, which was not included in the English translation, *Quest*. Tr.]
7. W. Schrage, *Ethics*, 31.
8. Cf. H. Merklein, *Gottesherrschaft*, 37; W. Schrage, *Ethics*, 31–32.
9. The question was inspired in large part by G. Theissen, *Palestinian*, 17–23.
10. The statement cannot be harmonized with the special tradition in John 12:6 and 13:29. Yet, the synoptic material so clearly shows that the harsh demand was softened that the requirement of Luke 10:4 has the historical priority over John.

11. The reference here is to discipleship in the general sense rather than to the discipleship of the inner circle.

12. Interpreting Matt 8:20d as a reference to Jesus' death (thus K. Löning, "Füchse") is too hypothetical.

13. Cf. the summary of the debate in W. Schrage, *Ethics*, 51; also Gnilka, *Jesus*, 172–73.

14. Cf. J. D. M. Derrett and R. Knüttel.

15. On the material cf. J. Jeremias, *Parables*, 200 and K. Berger, "Materialien," 2–9.

16. The theme of taking advantage of the last possible chance is worked out in the parable of Luke 16:1–8 from the perspective of a life-threatening situation, i.e., under precisely the opposite circumstances (cf. §3.2.2).

17. There is thus far no evidence in Early Judaism for the expression "to enter the Kingdom of God." It appears to be unique to the preaching of Jesus.

18. The connection appears to be totally missing in Qumran.

19. C. Hezser has collected the evidence (*Lohnmetaphorik*, 157–236).

20. The social relationships that the parable presupposes are typical for the period (cf. most recently C. Hezser, *Lohnmetaphorik*, 50–97). Without any commentary they are simply assumed as a reality of which everyone is aware, so that they can be used in the service of a new level of meaning.

21. C. Hezser argues differently, interpreting the parable from Matt 20 so thoroughly in terms of the Jewish materials that he even identifies the metaphor *work* with keeping the commandments of the Torah (*Lohnmetaphorik*, 237–50, esp. 241).

22. W. Harnisch, *Gleichniserzählungen*, 179.

23. Cf. H. C. Schnur, *Fabeln*, 43–44: "the house master called to his young son: 'Come and look,' he said, 'the grain is already ripe, and we need some help. Tomorrow, as soon as it gets light, go tell our friends to come and lend a hand.'"

24. There is no analogy in any comparable tradition.

25. As is the case with some of the rabbinic sources that C. Hezser has collected (*Lohnmetaphorik*, 157–236).

26. On this point G. Bornkamm's interpretation continues to point in the right direction ("Lohngedanke," 82).

27. For which L. Schottroff and C. Hezser (249) plead.

28. A. von Harnack, *Mission*, 148–49.

29. Since the conclusion of Luke 7:48–50 contradicts the intention of 7:44–47, it should be attributed to Luke.

30. P. Hoffmann calls attention to the new attitude of the aggressor (*Frühgeschichte*, 131–32). Jesus' statements are formulated, however, so that the hearers will see themselves in the situation of the victim who reacts in an unexpected way. The aggressors simply cause the difficult situation; they are not the focus of an attempt to create a new attitude.

31. Cf. by way of example D. Lührmann; P. Hoffmann; and J. Sauer, "Erwägungen"; and H.-W. Kuhn, "Liebesgebot," 223–24.

32. J. Sauer's attempt ("Erwägungen," and *Rückkehr*, 219ff.) to explain Rom 12:14–21 as a precursor to Luke 6:27–36 with Matt 5:44–45 then as a later addition from the church cannot explain why an early Christianity for which this material was so difficult would add it to the text.

33. Cf. H.-W. Kuhn, "Liebesgebot," 196–97.

34. Matt 5:43a takes this reference directly into the protasis of the antithesis.

35. Cf. K. Berger, *Gesetzesauslegung*, 92ff.

36. This basic meaning appears to have been universal in Palestinian Judaism. Only in the Diaspora, where one had to come to terms with the reality of a non-Jewish environment, did Early Judaism learn to define the neighbor in general human terms. Cf. K. Berger, *Gesetzesauslegung*, 112ff., 123ff.; J. Becker, *Untersuchungen*, 396ff.

37. Cf. M. Pohlenz, *Stoa*, 111ff.

38. Illustrating various aspects of the Early Jewish attitude are the texts Ps 35:13–14; Prov 25:21–22; *Ep. Arist.* 227; *Jos. As.* 22–29; *T. Jos.*, and *T. Benj.* Cf. on the subject J. Becker, *Untersuchungen*, 377ff.; H.-W. Kuhn, "Liebesgebot," 199–204; 224–26. Jesus is not alone, therefore, in moving from the love of neighbor to the love of the enemy.

39. Three other traditions must be eliminated from consideration as early Jesus material. The Golden Rule (Luke 6:31 = Matt 7:12) was known in Antiquity in a number of forms (see A. Dihle). In the context of the preaching of Jesus it is so vague that it is of no value in a discussion of his views. The double commandment of love in Mark 12:28–34 parr. is also part of the post-Jesus interpretation of the love commandment, even though many exegetes would like to include it in a discussion of Jesus (cf. Ch. Burchard, "Liebesgebot"; M. Ebersohn, *Nächstenliebegebot*, 214; U. Mell, *Winzer*, 312–53). Finally, the great Matthean allegory of judgment in Matt 25:31–46, with its summons to acts of mercy toward suffering people (limited, to be sure, to personal benevolence), is a christologically focused variation of the general and early Christian demand for mercy (cf. Luke 6:36; Gal 6:10, etc.). For many reasons, however, it cannot be regarded as authentic Jesus material (cf. Brandenburger, *Weltenrichter*, and the discussion in A. Wouters, *Willen*, 142–49).

40. Against G. Sellin ("Lukas") W. Harnisch (*Gleichniserzählungen*, 271ff.) has correctly emphasized once again the narrative unity of the parable and its tension with the Lukan context.

41. On the bandit phenomenon cf. Crossan, *Jesus*, 168–206. From the ancient sources note especially Josephus, *J.W.* 1.307; *Ant.* 14.417, and Paul's statement in 2 Cor 11:26.

42. See F. Hauck and W. F. Kasch, *TDNT* 6 (1968) 325–27; Hengel, *Property*, 12–22.

43. H. Stegemann, *Essener*, 245–64.

44. On the question of authenticity, cf. J. Sauer, *Rückkehr*, 322.

45. Cf., e.g., J. Sauer, *Rückkehr*, 316.

46. Cf. D. Zeller, *Mahnsprüche*, 128–30.

47. The issue is even more difficult for Mark 10:15 parr. While the saying about receiving the Kingdom of God as a child is well documented outside the Synoptics (John 3:3, 5; Justin, *Apol.* 1.61.4), the unusual expression *receiving the Kingdom of God* is too reminiscent of the vocabulary of the early Christian mission about *receiving* the gospel or the word (of God) to be free of its influence (Mark 4:16, 20; Acts 8:14; 11:1; 1 Thess 1:6; Jas 1:21, etc.). The relationship is also unclear between *receiving* and *entering* the Kingdom of God.

48. Luke 18:7, which has a striking parallel in Bar 4:25, for Luke is to be understood in terms of 17:20–37. When the judgment of the Son of Man comes, the *elect* (cf. Mark

13:20, 26–27), i.e., the church, will be vindicated (cf. Luke 17:22). Such an understanding of judgment and election cannot be documented for Jesus.

49. Thus most recently U. Mell, "Vater-Unser," 180.

50. Thus E. Grässer, who assumes such a strong, Jewish-Christian reworking of the prayer that an original, assumed to come from Jesus, can no longer be reconstructed (*Parusieverzögerung*, 96, 112).

51. R. Deichgräber surveys the titles for God in Early Judaism. His list needs to be supplemented with the texts that have become available since his dissertation appeared (*Gotteshymnus*, 87–105).

52. From this observation J. Jeremias draws far-reaching conclusions about Jesus' unique use of *abba* (*Prayers*, 15–67).

53. Treated thoroughly by A. Strotmann, *Vater*.

54. In looking for comparable prayers, therefore, we eliminate portions of a larger liturgy such as the doxological benediction that is known as the Kaddish (see below). They represent only a portion of a larger unit; they do not offer a coherent view of their own.

55. Thus U. Mell, "Vater-Unser," 175.

56. As K. G. Kuhn (*Achtzehngebet*, 40ff.) does with great success.

57. Cf. D. de Sola Pool, *Kaddish*, 26.

58. Selected examples are Exod 15:17–18; Isa 43:14–15; 44:6; Ps 68:6, 25; Dan 3:53–56 (LXX); *Jub.* 50:9; *1 Enoch* 25:3–7; 4Q 403 1i 31, etc.

59. Thus U. Mell, "Vater-Unser," 169–73.

60. From the language of hymns and prayers cf. Luke 1:49–50; John 17:11.

61. The term *debts* originates in the laws about work, trade, and taxes (Matt 18:23–35; Luke 7:41; 16:5, 7; Rom 4:4; 13:7). Its root, however, comes to be used for failure in a personal relationship (Rom 1:14; 13:8; 15:1, 27). According to Luke 13:2, 4 (§3.2.2) Jesus also used the root in this sense, i.e., he regarded *debtors* and *sinners* as synonymous terms. We should not cite the term, therefore, to support the claim that the prayer did not come from Jesus (thus U. Mell, "Vater-Unser," 178).

62. Examples given in J. Becker, "Ethos," 1; J.-W. Taeger, 15–16. Cf. also W. G. Kümmel, *Jahre*, 212–13.

63. Cf. M. Hengel, *Judaism*, 267–77.

64. The editors of *'Abot* clearly reflect this goal.

65. It is likely that such statements as Matt 6:1, 5, 16; 23:5–6, 15, presuppose this competition. Matthew's Jewish Christian church and the Pharisees were rivals within Early Judaism in a way that was typical for that period.

66. Cf., e.g., 1 Macc 2:23–26; 3 Macc 7:10–16; 1QpH; 4QpNah; 4QpPs 37; Josephus, *J.W.* 1.648–55; 2.4–13, 408–24; 4.169–70, 259, 263; 5.4, 402; *Ant.* 13.297–98; 18.16–17, 401–2, 410; Acts 23:6–9; *Yad* 4:6–8; *Sabb.* 14b–15a, 17a; *Sota* 3:4; 4:7a.

67. Cf. also the way the Pharisee Paul persecuted Jewish Christians (1 Cor 15:9; Gal 1:13; Phil 3:6).

68. The former Pharisee Paul may well have also understood it this way (cf. Phil 3:5–6 with Gal 1:13–14). The beginning of *'Abot* also shares this point of view.

69. When Kh. Müller ("Beobachtungen," 132–33) moves in this direction, he is confusing the question of the Halacha's presentation with the question of its self-understanding as it is often expressed in concrete-material ways.

70. Cf. the material in Kh. Müller, "Gesetz," and idem, "Beobachtungen."

71. For example, in the Essene criticism of Judaism, or in the question, debated since the days of the Maccabees, whether one could defend one's self on the Sabbath against hostile attacks (cf. the difference between 1 Macc 2:32–41 and *Jub.* 50:12), or also in the synoptic texts like Mark 7; 10:1–12; Matt 23.

72. One can find examples of this kind of polemical situation in Qumran's teacher-hymns as well as in the pesharim or in Paul (cf. Becker, *Paul*, 163–70).

73. Cf., e.g., E. Käsemann, *Essays*, 37–38; M. Hengel, *Nachfolge* 74–79; "Jesus," 170–71; P. Stuhlmacher, *Theologie*, 102–3.

74. Cf. M. Karrer, *Gesalbte*, 324.

75. Cf. P. Schäfer, "Torah."

76. Cf. H. Stegemann, "Jesus," 5ff.; G. Sauer, *Rückkehr*, 523ff.

77. See J. Becker, "Ethos," 6–7.

78. A line of argument such as one finds in CD 4:20–21, which cites Gen 1:27 to justify monogamy, cannot be the basis of the fundamental position attributed to Jesus, since CD 5:1ff. shows that the argument from primal history is only one among many possibilities.

79. Thus, e.g., Fiedler, "Tora," 74; F. Vouga, *Geschichte*, 47, and many others. Cf. the discussion in J.-W. Taeger, "Unterschied," esp. 28–29.

80. Frequently Luke 9:59–60 par. is attributed to this remnant (§4.2.2).

81. A number of people have observed this relationship; J. Blank , e.g., offers an especially good description ("Lernprozesse," 168–75). It is frequently pushed into the background, however, by the attempt to describe Jesus' concept of the Torah as a normal Early Jewish understanding. On the attempt to attribute to Halacha a relative independence in Early Judaism in order to minimize Jesus' own authority, see §5.3.1.

82. Cf. the language in Sir 6:24–25 and 51:34 about the yoke of wisdom that one should bear.

83. Cf. H. Donner, "Jesaja," 165ff.

84. K. Berger, *Gesetzesauslegung*, 219.

85. J.-W. Taeger, "Unterschied," 22.

86. To be sure, we cannot use Mark 7:9–13 to support Jesus' affirmation of the commandment about parents, since the text hardly goes back to Jesus. The use of the Septuagint in v. 10, the first reference in the early church to *the word of God,* and the nature of the polemic all speak against its authenticity. We should note, however, Matt 10:37 = Luke 14:26 (cf. §5.4).

87. In Matt 12:1–8 a Jewish Christian demonstrates how a typical argument would be conducted in Early Judaism in similar cases. It is assumed that plucking grain is a kind of work and is therefore forbidden on the Sabbath. This violation of the Torah and of Halacha is emphasized first as an exception (since hunger creates a special situation) and then, with the help of 1 Sam 21:1–10 and (probably) Num 28:9–10, as an exception that is permissible. The result conforms with the Torah. For Jesus, on the other hand, the case of Matt 8:21–22 does not pose an exception—it is normal behavior in light of the Kingdom of God—nor is he at all interested in what the Torah says.

88. The narrative world of the miracles of Jesus is admittedly the creation of the church (cf. §4.3.3), but we are justified in asking whether the lack of concern about

questions of purity in the stories does not preserve an element of reality from the life of Jesus. On Mark 5:25–34, a conspicuous example of this attitude, see P. Trummer in: I. Broer, ed. *Gesetz*, 52ff.

89.　A claim made by M. J. Suggs and I Broer, *Freiheit*.

90.　J. Sauer's suggestion about the history of the tradition is too complicated (*Rückkehr*, 228ff.).

91.　Cf. E. Lohse, "Ich aber sage euch," 75ff.

92.　Cf. most recently on the subject H.-W. Kuhn, "Liebesgebot," 213–17.

93.　In any case it is clear that the death penalty was no longer applied in such cases. Sir 23:22–27 and *T.12 Patr.* no longer mention it at all.

94.　Cf. by way of example the commentaries from U. Luz and J. Gnilka, that offer examples which equate hate with the spilling of blood or the lustful look with sexual intercourse.

95.　We cannot regard Mark 12:18–27 parr. and Matt 19:10–12 as authentic Jesus material. On the former text cf. U. Mell, *Winzer*, 267–311; on the latter G. Sauer, *Rückkehr*, 131–35.

96.　That the account originated in a post-Easter setting is generally recognized. At issue, however, is whether v. 9 was at one time independent (G. Sauer, *Rückkehr*, 97ff.). 1 Cor 7:10–11 is not relevant here, since the texts are too different in form and vocabulary. The subject in Mark 10:9b comes from v. 7, and v. 9a summarizes v. 8. Apart from the context it is unclear whether v. 9 is even speaking about marriage. Since the verse's sole purpose is to justify the results of Mark 10:2–8, it is not an independent saying.

97.　Cf. P. Hoffmann, V. Eid, *Jesus*, 110ff.

98.　Cf. H. Stegemann, *Essener*, 267–74.

99.　Cf. J. Sauer, *Rückkehr*, 124–25.

100.　This possibility is later considered by *Herm. Man.* 29:8–9.

101.　It is too much to say, however, as P. Hoffmann and V. Eid do (*Jesus*, 119), that the wife thus legally becomes an equal partner in the marriage.

102.　This reality is immediately changed, however, with the beginning of the post-Easter mission to the Gentiles for which 1 Thess 1:9 is probably the earliest evidence.

103.　Cf. Gen 17:10–11; Sir 44:21; *Jub.* 15:6–32; 1QM xiii 7–8, etc. The subject became acute in the history of the early Christian mission as soon as one crossed the borders of Israel. Cf. J. Becker, *Paul*, 63–66.

104.　The attitude of Hellenistic Judaism on the subject will hardly have been different from that of the Jews in Palestine. Cf. Philo, *Vit. Mos.* 3.27–28; *Spec. Leg.* 2.6–7; *Decal.* 20–21.

105.　Matt 12:11–12 par. might arguably be part of the discussion, but its argument was part of the Halacha debate at the time of Jesus (cf., e.g., Josephus, *J.W.* 2.147; CD 11:13–14; *b. Sabb.* 128b; *m. Bek.* 3:4).

106.　Cf. J. Jeremias, *Theology*, 279, n. 1.

107.　Thus, among others, E. Lohse, "Jesu Worte über den Sabbat," 68 (in: idem, *Einheit*); H. Stegemann, *Essener*, 346.

108.　Cf. *Sif. Deut.* 37 on Deut 11:10: "That which is more valuable precedes the other." Cf. also 1 Cor 11:7–10 and 1 Tim 2:11–13. That the view is common in Antiquity is illustrated by the deference to age. Cf. by way of example Plato, *Resp.* 412c.

109. Cf. H. Stegemann, *Essener*, 227–78.

110. Cf. J. Neusner (*Judentum*, 74ff.), whose thesis has widespread acceptance. It is based, however, on a more or less random statistical analysis of statements on the theme from much later texts.

111. That wisdom had long been able to praise God by singing the glory of a creation that was good (cf. Pss 104; 145; Sir 1:1–10, etc., and §4.1.7), without referring to the difference between clean and unclean in creation, does not mean that wisdom was not aware of the distinction (cf. Sir 7:29–31; 45:10, 15–16, 23–24; 50:1ff.; Eccl 9:2; *Ep. Arist.* 139ff., etc.). In a similar way wisdom can describe human greatness (e.g., Ps 8) without speaking of sin, even though it says a great deal about it elsewhere (e.g., Sir 2:12–15; 4:20–22; 7:1–2, etc.).

112. Cf. especially Dan 1:8–12; Tob 1:10–12; *Jos. As.* 7:1; 8:5; 3 Macc 3:4, 7. For early Christianity cf. Gal. 2:11–21.

113. There is evidence that hand-washing was not only an Essene and Pharisaic practice; at the time of Jesus it may well have been a general custom. Cf. Tob 2:5.

114. Were we to try to claim Matt 23 par. for Jesus, we would face insurmountable problems, since the text and the traditions lying behind it are filled with typical, early Christian polemics. Any reconstruction of early material would be too hypothetical.

115. Cf. W. G. Kümmel, "Reinheit," 121–22; J. Sauer, *Rückkehr*, 477.

116. *Contra* J. Sauer, *Rückkehr*, 476f. On other decompositions of Mark 7:15, cf. R. P. Booth, *Jesus*, 46–47, 67–68 and J. Sauer, *Rückkehr*, 477.

117. On K. Berger's line of reasoning (*Gesetzesauslegung*, 461ff.) cf. R. P. Booth, *Jesus*, 83–90.

118. On the entire subject cf. J. Becker, *Paul*, 63–69. This claim has been contested recently by E. Rau, *Jesus*, 79ff. A missionary activity, however, that was faithful to the Law while accepting uncircumcised Gentiles into a Jewish Christianity would pose within the context of Early Judaism a dilemma that E. Rau cannot explain.

119. Nevertheless, at the Council circumcision was not required of the Gentile Christian, Titus, nor were the so-called apostates (in the Jewish sense), Barnabas and Paul, excluded from fellowship.

120. In Acts 6:14 Luke explicitly makes this claim for Stephen.

121. Cf. J. Becker, *Paul*, 112–24.

122. One can study a similar phenomenon, e.g., in the Baptist material (cf. §3.1.1).

123. If we attribute Matt 12:11 = Luke 14:5 to the sayings source, we have another example.

124. It is probably safe to say that early Christianity in general was concerned to maintain relationships with the outside world that were as free of conflict as possible (cf., by way of example, Rom 12–13; 1 Cor 10:32; 1 Pet 2:11–25).

125. U. B. Müller does a good job of describing the complexity of the history of the Jerusalem church prior to Q and Mark ("Rezeption"). This opinion holds true even if one does not share all of Müller's conclusions.

126. On the following interpretation cf. H. Merklein, *Botschaft*, 96–100; J. Becker, "Ethos," 11–14; J.-W. Taeger, "Unterschied," 26–28.

127. On the types of interpretation cf. W. G. Kümmel, "Reinheit," 117–22; H. Merkel, "Markus," 341–50; J.-W. Taeger, "Unterschied," 13ff.

128.   Zech 14:20–21 probably alludes to an elimination of the distinction between clean and unclean in the end-time.

129.   Cf. J. Sauer, *Rückkehr*, 504–5. Often quoted in this context is Johanen ben Zakkai (*Pes.* 406): "a corpse does not render a person unclean, nor does water make a person clean, but it is an ordinance of the King of Kings. God has said, 'I have established a statute . . . no one has the right to violate my decree.'" The statement makes a concession to Hellenistic enlightenment, but then appeals to the authority of the Torah. Neither attitude is typical of Jesus.

130.   Thus E. Käsemann, *Essays*, 38–39. In agreement are, e.g., H. Merkel, *Gottesherrschaft*, 156–57 and W. Schrage, *Ethics*, 66.

131.   Attributing the saying to Q is frequently contested. Cf., however, J. Sauer, *Rückkehr*, 179–80.

132.   Cf. J. Sauer, *Rückkehr*, 153–54.

133.   Reminiscent of Isa 49:14–15.

134.   Cf. Num 11:12; Ruth 4:16.

135.   For a detailed analysis cf. P. Hoffmann, *Frühgeschichte*, 139–47.

136.   Cf. also *As. Mos.* 10:8–10; *Sib. Or. Pro.* 76–86.

137.   He is capable, however, of speaking disrespectfully of his ruling prince (Luke 13:32).

138.   Cf. Isa 7:2–9; Mic 4:7. In the time of Jesus the Essenes especially emphasize a remnant of Israel (CD 1:4–5; 2:6; 1QH vi 8; 1QM xiii 8; xiv 8–9).

139.   Cf. P. Pokorný, *Entstehung*, 28–29.

140.   The Fourth Gospel describes the situation somewhat differently. With the mission in Samaria (John 4) and the desire of the Greeks to talk to Jesus (John 12:20–22) the move beyond the limits of Israel is for the evangelist a pre-Easter phenomenon.

141.   In view of Jonah 3:9; 4:1; *Bib. Ant.* 30:4! and similar formulations the statement is to be understood in a positive sense.

142.   Cf. in §3.2.4 the texts Luke 4:25–27; 10:13–14 par.; Matt 8:11–12 par.

143.   Mark 12:14–17 hardly contains authentic material from the preaching of Jesus. Cf. U. Mell, *Winzer*, 205ff.

6

The Last Days in Jerusalem and Jesus' Crucifixion

Arai, S. "Zum 'Tempelwort' Jesu in Apg 6,14," *NTS* 34 (1988) 397–410.

Bajsic, A. "Pilatus, Jesus und Barabbas," *Bib* 48 (1967) 7–28.

Bammel, E. *Judaica*. WUNT 37. Tübingen: J.C.B. Mohr (Paul Siebeck), 1986, 59–72.

———. (ed.) *The Trial of Jesus*. Festschrift C. F. D. Moule. SBT II 13. London: SCM, 1970.

Becker, J. "Die neutestamentliche Rede vom Sühnetod Jesu," in: idem, *Annäherungen*, 334–54.

Betz, O. "Probleme des Prozesses Jesu," *ANRW*. Berlin/New York: de Gruyter, 1982, II 25.1, 565–647.

Blinzler, J. *The Trial of Jesus*. Westminster, MD: Neuman, 1959.

Bösen, W. *Der letzte Tag des Jesus von Nazaret*. 2d ed. Freiburg: Herder, 1994.

Brandenburger, E. "Stauros, Kreuzigung Jesu und Kreuzestheologie," in: idem, *Studien zur Geschichte und Theologie des Urchristentums*. SBAB 15. Stuttgart: KBW, 1993, 154–84.

———. *Markus 13 und die Apokalyptik*. FRLANT 134. Göttingen: Vandenhoeck & Ruprecht, 1984.

Büchler, A. *Das Synedrium in Jerusalem*. Vienna: Alfred Holder, 1902.

Busink, Th. A. *Der Tempel von Jerusalem*. 2 vols. SFSMD 3. Leiden: Brill, 1970, 1980.

Catchpole, D. R. *The Trial of Jesus*. SPB 18. Leiden: Brill, 1971.

Cohn, H. *The Trial and Death of Jesus*. New York: Harper & Row, 1971.

Dautzenberg, G. "Der Prozeß Jesu und seine Hintergründe," *BiKi* 48 (1993) 147–53.

Davies, P. E. "Did Jesus Die as a Martyr-Prophet?" *BR* 19 (1974) 37–42.

Delling, G. "Abendmahl II," *TRE* 1 (1977) 47–58.

Dibelius, M. "Das historische Problem der Leidensgeschichte," in: idem, *Botschaft und Geschichte*, Vol. 1. Tübingen: J.C.B. Mohr (Paul Siebeck), 1953, 248–57.

Dormeyer, D. "Die Passion Jesu als Ergebnis seines Konflikts mit führenden Kreisen des Judentums," in: *Gottesverächter und Menschenfeinde?* H. Goldstein, ed. Düsseldorf: Patmos, 1979, 211–38.

Finegan, J. *Die Überlieferung der Leidens-und Auferstehungsgeschichte Jesu*. BZNW 15. Gießen: Töpelmann, 1934.

Fitzmyer, J. A. *To Advance the Gospel*. New York: Crossroad, 1981, 125–46.

Flusser, D. *Die letzten Tage Jesu in Jerusalem*. Stuttgart: Calwer, 1982.

Gaston, L. *No Stone on Another*. NT.S 23. Leiden: Brill, 1970.

Gnilka, J. "Der Prozeß Jesu," in: *Der Prozeß gegen Jesus*. K. Kertelge, ed. QD 112. Freiburg/Basel/Vienna: Herder, 1988, 11–40.

———. "Wie urteilte Jesus über seinen Tod?" in: *Der Tod Jesu*. K. Kertelge, ed. QD 74. Freiburg/Basel/Vienna: 1976, 13–50.

Grant, R. M. "The Trial of Jesus in the Light of History," *Judaism* 20 (1971) 37–42.

Gubler, M.-L. *Die frühesten Deutungen des Todes Jesu.* OBO 15. Göttingen: Vandenhoeck & Ruprecht, 1977.

Hahn, F. "Zum Stand der Erforschung des urchristlichen Herrenmahls," in: idem, *Exegetische Beiträge zum ökumenischen Gespräch.* Göttingen: Vandenhoeck & Ruprecht, 1986, 242–52.

Haufe, G. "Der Prozeß Jesu im Lichte der gegenwärtigen Forschung," *ZdZ* 22 (1968) 93–101.

Kleinknecht, K. Th. *Der leidende Gerechtfertigte.* WUNT 2/13. 2d ed. Tübingen: J.C.B. Mohr (Paul Siebeck), 1988.

Kuhn, H.-W. "Kreuz II," *TRE* 19 (1990) 713–25.

———. "Die Kreuzesstrafe während der frühen Kaiserzeit," *ANRW.* Berlin/New York: de Gruyter, 1982, II 25.1, 648–793.

Kunkel, W. "Prinzipien des römischen Strafverfahrens," in: idem, *Kleine Schriften.* Weimar: H. Bohlaus Nachfolger, 1974, 11–31.

Lietzmann, M. *Der Prozeß Jesu.* Berlin: de Gruyter, 1931.

Maier, J. "Beobachtungen zum Konfliktpotential in neutestamentlichen Aussagen über den Tempel," in: *Jesus und das jüdische Gesetz.* I. Broer, ed. Stuttgart: Kohlhammer, 1992, 173–213.

McGing, B. C. "Pontius Pilate and the Sources," *CBQ* 53 (1991) 416–38.

Mommsen, Th. *Römisches Strafrecht.* Leipzig: S. Hirzel, 1899.

Müller, Kh. "Möglichkeit und Vollzug jüdischer Kapitalgerichtsbarkeit im Prozeß gegen Jesus von Nazaret," in: *Der Prozeß gegen Jesus.* K. Kertelge, ed. QD 112. Freiburg/Basel/Vienna: Herder, 1988, 41–83.

Myllykosky, M. *Die letzten Tage Jesu.* 2 vols. Helsinki: Suomalainen Tiedeakatemie, 1991, 1994.

Oberlinner, L. *Todeserwartung und Todesgewißheit Jesu.* SBB 10. Stuttgart: KBW, 1980.

Otte, G. "Neues zum Prozeß gegen Jesus?" *NJW* (1992) Heft 16, 1019–26.

Patsch, H. *Abendmahl und historischer Jesus,* CThM 1. Stuttgart: Calwer, 1972.

———. "Der Einzug Jesu in Jerusalem," *Zthk* 68 (1971) 1–26.

Puech, E. "A-t-on redécouvert le tombeau du grand-prêtre Caiphe?" *MB* 80 (1993) 42–47.

Reinbold, W. *Der älteste Bericht über den Tod Jesu.* BZNW 69. Berlin/New York: de Gruyter, 1994.

Riesner, R. "Golgata und die Archäologie," *BiKi* 40 (1985) 21–26.

Safrai, S. *Die Wallfahrt im Zeitalter des Zweiten Tempels.* FJCD 3. Neukirchen-Vluyn: Neukirchener Verlag, 1981.

Schenk, W. "Leidensgeschichte Jesu," *TRE* 20 (1990) 714–21.

Schlosser, J. "La Parole de Jésus sur la fin du Temple," *NTS* 36 (1990) 398–414.

Schreiber, J. *Die Markuspassion.* BZNW 68. Berlin/New York: de Gruyter, 1993.

Schürmann, H. *Gottes Reich—Jesu Geschick.* Freiburg: Herder, 1983.

———. *Jesu ureigener Tod.* Freiburg: Herder, 1975.

Schwier, H. *Tempel und Tempelzerstörung.* NTOA 11. Göttingen: Vandenhoeck & Ruprecht, 1989.

Söding, Th. "Die Tempelaktion Jesu," *Tthz* 101 (1992) 36–64.

Sommer, U. *Die Passionsgeschichte des Markusevangeliums.* WUNT 2/58. Tübingen: J.C.B. Mohr (Paul Siebeck), 1993.

Steck, O. H. *Israel und das gewaltsame Geschick der Propheten.* WANT 23. Neukirchen-Vluyn: Verlag des Erziehungsvereins, 1967.

Strobel, A. *Die Stunde der Wahrheit.* WUNT 21. Tübingen: J.C.B. Mohr (Paul Siebeck), 1980.

Stuhlmacher, P. "Warum mußte Jesus sterben?" *ThBeitr* 16 (1985) 273–85.

Theissen, G. "Jesus' Temple Prophecy," in: idem, *Social Reality*, 94–114.

Trautmann, M. *Zeichenhafte Handlungen.*

Untergassmair, F. G. *Kreuzweg und Kreuzigung Jesu.* PaThSt 10. Munich: Schöningh, 1980.

Vogler, W. *Judas Iskarioth.* ThA 42. Berlin: Evangelische Verlagsanstalt, 1983.

Vögtle, A. "Grundfragen der Diskussion um das heilsmittlerische Todesverständnis Jesu," in: idem, *Offenbarungsgeschehen und Wirkungsgeschichte.* Freiburg: Herder, 1985, 141–67.

————. "Todesankündigungen und Todesverständnis Jesu," in: *Der Tod Jesu.* K. Kertelge, ed. QD 74. Freiburg/Basel/Vienna: Herder, 1976, 51–113.

Walter, N. "Tempelzerstörung und synoptische Apokalypse," *ZNW* 57 (1966) 38–49.

Wilson, W. R. *The Execution of Jesus: A Judicial, Literary and Historical Investigation.* New York: Scribners, 1970.

Winter, P. *On the Trial of Jesus.* SJ 1. 2d ed. Berlin: de Gruyter, 1974.

————. "Marginal Notes on the Trial of Jesus," *ZNW* 50 (1959) 14–33.

6.1   JESUS' PROCLAMATION AND CONDUCT AS THE CAUSE OF HIS DEATH

In view of the current debate on this issue we need to make two preliminary observations. The purpose of the following discussion is to help clarify what a historian, based on the sources, might say on the subject, not to enter the debate over who bears the guilt for the death of Jesus. The question of guilt and an examination of historical causes are two different things. The historian's task is not to judge history, but to identify interconnectedness, contingency, and possible motives to the degree that such things are still discernible. Historians ask: What are the forces that came together to bring about a certain event? They do not ask: Who is guilty, and who must bear the consequences?

Before substantively debating the questions surrounding the death of Jesus, we must also remember that our sources make a historical debate very difficult. The main source is still the passion narrative of the gospels (cf. §6.3). No Jewish group, no Roman official says a word on the subject. Even those who with good reason see hints of an earlier, oral passion narrative behind the gospels never arrive at a historical report that can claim to be based on anything like a historical protocol, to be interested in trial law, or to describe the roles that the various persons play. From the very beginning, the passion narrative was designed to be part of the preaching about the suffering Christ and to strengthen the faith of the churches. That purpose does not in and of itself make the narrative unhistorical; no one would seriously claim that preaching and historical recollection are mutually exclusive. For preaching, however, history made contemporary is something quite different from the minutes of a meeting of the Sanhedrin. For this reason it is understandable that some people believe that Jesus' last days in Jerusalem are lost to history except for a few key terms: the pilgrimage to a Passover feast, a farewell meal, Judas' betrayal, the capture, the flight of the disciples, the judgment from Pilate, and Jesus' crucifixion and subsequent burial. This outline is not insignificant, but we probably need not be that skeptical. The question, of course, is: How much more can we wring from the sources? All of us, including those who think they know precisely what happened, are dealing with degrees of probability. One thing that is certain is that we know more about Jesus' activity in Galilee than we do about his last days in the City of David.

If we want to identify what Jesus might have done to cause his execution, we must first decide who his opponents were. Since the best assumption is that he was arrested by Jews and that it was Jews (whoever they might have been individually) who were his accusers before Pilate (cf. §6.3), then we must consider those aspects of Jesus' activity that in the competition among the various Jewish groups would have been offensive enough to occasion a charge before Pilate. The accusation before the Romans may have been political; it need not have revealed the real reasons. It is possible that we should also distinguish between an immediate occasion and a running controversy related to Jesus' appearance and preaching. The two possibilities are not mutually exclusive; indeed, they could well reinforce each other. An event in Jerusalem—e.g., the cleansing of the temple and/or a negative statement about the temple such as Mark 13:2 parr. or Mark 14:58 par.—could in theory have been sufficient reason for arresting Jesus, but it may also have been the last offense in a growing controversy. Of course, it is possible that nothing happened in Jerusalem to occasion Jesus' death. Only an analysis of the individual sources in detail will enable us to choose one of these options.

In Mark's portrayal of Jesus' hearing before the Sanhedrin (Mark 14:55–64) Jesus is condemned because of his claims regarding the Messiah and the Son of Man (vv. 61–64). It is clear, however, that the statements reflect the faith of the post-Easter church (cf. §§4.4.2; 4.4.3; 6.3). Furthermore, messianic claims did not constitute a capital offense for Jews. Prior to 70 CE the Romans probably pursued eschatological prophets who made messianic claims, but Jews did not.[1] Even Rabbi Akiba, who proclaimed Bar Cochba as the Messiah, was not executed for the offense.[2]

Of course, prior to Jesus' messianic statement, Mark refers to the witnesses who did not agree among themselves about a statement that Jesus allegedly had made against the temple (Mark 14:57–59). Even if it does not fit in with Mark's late reconstruction, it may well be that in a general sense Jesus' critical attitude toward the temple contributed partially to his death. What is the evidence for such a conclusion? Relevant statements of Jesus that represent independent tradi-tions[3] are found in Mark 13:1–2 parr. and Mark 14:58 par.; 15:29 parr.; John 2:19 (cf. Acts 6:14).[4] Relevant also is the provocative action in the temple from Mark 11:15–18 parr. and John 2:14–16, which have their own vocabulary and their own intention.

Mark 14:58b reads:

a   I will destroy this temple that is made with hands,
b   and in three days I will build another, not made with hands.

Only the variant of the saying in John 2:19, which has the following wording, is independent enough to be considered alongside Mark 14:58.[5]

a   Destroy this temple,
b   then in three days I will raise it again.

There are major differences in both the wording and the syntax of the two versions. In its form and vocabulary Mark's version is probably secondary. At the very least, the expressions "made with hands" and "not made with hands" must be regarded as Hellenistic-Jewish language. Not only are the words missing in John; they also disturb the symmetry of the sentences in Mark. If, in addition, the reference to three days is intended as an allusion to the events of Easter (1 Cor 15:4), it would be a clear indication of a christological signal from the primitive church. The second line, however, need not be read christologically. The Fourth Evangelist, who gives the saying a christological interpreta-tion, certainly assumed that it originally referred to the Jerusalem temple.[6]

Difficult also is a judgment about the widely diverging first lines. Of course, Mark's "I will destroy" appears only as the testimony of false witnesses.[7] Mark wants his readers to remember Mark 13:2 and thus to know that even the I-form, understood as an active and immediate threat to the temple, is a false charge. These considerations all support the conclusion that the Johannine version is original. It is, moreover, a typical ironic impera-tive such as is common elsewhere in prophetic speech (Amos 4:4; Isa 8:9–10). We might paraphrase it as: "You need only fulfill the condition of destroying this temple, and I will keep my word and rebuild it."[8] In opposition to Mark's version, which could never have been accepted by Christians, John offers a version that poses no problems for Christians. There is no basis, therefore, for the frequently made argument that Mark 14:58 could not have been formed from John 2:19, since that would mean that Christians put Jesus in a situation that was difficult both in cultic and in political terms and was also dangerous for them—that Mark 14:58 must therefore be original. On the contrary, Christians are quite comfortable with statements such as Mark 13:2 and John 2:19, and it is precisely Mark 14:58 that they reject. John 2:19 was not created to avoid the difficulty of Mark 14:58; it is, instead, the origin of a tradition that non-Christians later changed in order to put the Christians in a bad light. The Christian rejects the accusation. The situation in Mark 14:57–59 is every bit as apologetic as is Matt 28:11–15, so that Mark 14:58 functions in the same way as does Matt 28:13.

It is clear from *1 Enoch* 90:28–29 and 11QT xxix 8–10 that within Judaism there was the expectation that the temple would be destroyed and that it then would be rebuilt in the end-time.[9] If we claim, therefore, that Jesus said the temple word as it appears in John 2:19, we are faced with the fact that such a statement would not have been reason enough to kill him, as long as he did not actively do anything against the existing temple. Even if the temple word was spoken in connection with the cleansing of the temple, it still would not have led to Jesus' death. Of course, such association is purely speculative. The saying, whether in the Markan or the Johannine version, is textually near to the event in the temple only in John 2, and even here it is after the event, in the conversation about the demand for a sign, that the word appears about the destruction of the temple.

It is true that a conversation about authority similar to that of the Johannine demand for a sign immediately followed the temple action prior to Mark, since it was probably Mark himself who disrupted the connection between 11:15–18 and 11:28–33 by inserting 11:19–27. In the Markan pericope on authority, however, there is no saying corresponding to John 2:19. The sequence from temple action leading to a temple saying in the context of a subsequent controversy is an old tradition, but it is of no historical value, since both forms of the pericope on authority are composed from the perspective of the church. In Mark it has no connection with the action in the temple; in John it is only superficially related. Mark 11:27–33 and John 2:14–16 furthermore have in common against Mark 14:58 and John 2:19 that the temple pericope and the temple saying use different words for the temple—a clear indication that they were originally independent. Mark indirectly confirms this independence. He expects his readers, when they read the account of the hearing before the Sanhedrin, to think not of the temple pericope but of Mark 13:1–4. Regardless of what one may decide about the authenticity of John 2:19, therefore, it does not help us understand why Jesus died.

The arguments in favor of the saying's authenticity are quite weak. It was hardly accidental that Jesus excluded the covenant and Zion tradition from his message of the Kingdom of God (§§3.2; 4.2). Why then should he have looked toward a restoration of the temple in the end-time, especially since his image for the future salvation is an eschatological banquet (Matt 8:11–12 par.; §3.2.4) and not the everlasting worship of God? For Jesus, furthermore, bringing about the Kingdom of God is always something that God does. There is no parallel in Jesus' preaching for a final activity of Jesus like the rebuilding of the temple that is envisioned by the temple saying.[10] Both of these arguments would apply even if Mark 14:58 were the original form of the tradition. In that case one would have to ask additionally whether Jesus could actually have announced the active destruction of the temple, since such a violent stance is hardly in keeping with Jesus' attitude elsewhere.[11] We could cite other problems as well, but these should suffice to demonstrate that the temple saying does not belong to the authentic Jesus-material.

What, then, about Mark 13:2b? There it is said:

Not one stone will be left on another that will not be destroyed.

Since the saying has no clear object, it is not capable of existing as an independent tradition. In Mark's setting in 13:1–2, therefore, we can at the very least claim the catchword *temple* and probably also the cry: "Look, what great stones and what great buildings!" as the remnants of an apophthegmatic introduction.

Herod had expanded the temple area with unusually large, hewn stones, as indeed he had increased the splendor of the temple and the temple structure. In later years one could say that the temple had never been more magnificent than it was after his building project (Josephus, *J.W.* 5.184ff.; *Ant.* 15.416; Philo, *Leg. Gai.* 191). The memory of this magnificence probably lies behind the exclamation in 13:1. The splendor of Herod's temple is contrasted with the desolation of its predicted downfall.

According to Josephus (*J.W.* 6.250–66; 7.1–3), the temple was burned in the summer of 70, then shortly thereafter it was razed.[12] After the destruction, the temple area will have appeared much as it is described in Mark 13:2. The suspicion is unavoidable, therefore, that the prediction of the destruction was first given its theological significance after the event.[13] What we have is one of the earliest Christian interpretations of the destruction of Jerusalem that connects Jerusalem's fate with Jesus. Jesus predicts that God, who is the indirect subject of the two verbs, will destroy the temple. The tacit understanding is that just as Herod enlarged the temple (i.e., had it renovated), so God will have the temple destroyed. Every reader after 70 CE knows that, just as Isa 41:1–5, 25–29 sees Cyrus as the instrument of God's activity, the text is speaking of the Romans.

It is true, of course, that Jesus pronounced judgment on places and people (§3.2.4), but he did so because they were offended by his activity and had rejected him. That kind of explanation is missing here.[14] Mark 13:2b no longer needs to be explained, because the past event speaks for itself. In addition, Jesus' words are consistently related to the final judgment. Mark 13:2, on the other hand, is not focused on the end-time; it is precisely not said that God will act in such a manner at the end of time. Of course, one reason for the absence of an end-time focus is that the church that formulates Mark 13:2 knows that the temple was destroyed without the eschaton having come. Furthermore, none of Jesus' many pronouncements of judgment (§3.2) is as explicit as is Mark 13:2b. They all speak of the fate of persons even when they name places such as Chorazin and Bethsaida. Nowhere else is there an interest in the destruction of buildings. It is clear, therefore, that the pronouncement of the destruction cannot have come from Jesus.

Those who still would attribute the statement to Jesus are faced with the difficulty of explaining how it could have occasioned Jesus' death. Pronouncements about the destruction of Zion and Jerusalem as an act of judgment with God as the implied subject are common in the prophetic tradition (cf. e.g., Jer 26:6, 9, 18; Mic 3:12; also *T. Lev.* 15:1; *1 Enoch* 90:28; *Tg. Neof.* Lev 26:19, etc.). They are not by themselves a clear reason for executing the speaker. The attempt to have Jeshua ben Ananias executed for his pronouncement of judgment on Jerusalem and the temple (§3.1.2) is not successful. When he is turned over to the Romans, they merely scourge him and then release him. The Jews accept this turn of events, even in the highly explosive situation shortly before the outbreak of the war, when an ideological defeat was especially difficult for them.

If, then, Jesus' negative words about the temple were not the reason for his execution, is the situation any better with regard to his temple action, the so-called cleansing of the temple, in Mark 11:15–18 parr. and John 2:14–16? Even an answer in the affirmative leaves us with major problems. Fortunately, we need not decide whether Mark 11:15–18 was part of the pre-Markan passion narrative or at one time was an independent tradition (cf. John 2:14–16) that Mark incorporated into his portrayal of Jesus' passion.[15] Anyone who has decided that Jesus was probably in Jerusalem only once (cf. §2) will of necessity assign all Jerusalem traditions, and not only the passion narrative, to the last days of Jesus.

It is clear, of course, that Mark himself provided the immediate Markan context for the pericope, including especially Mark 11:18, the verse that identifies Jesus' act in the temple as the immediate cause of his death.[16] If, however, this comment comes from the evangelist's editorial work, there is neither in the Synoptics nor in John any other indication that Jesus' action in the temple had anything to do with his death. No matter which version of the passion narrative one may prefer, the temple action is an episode without consequences. The action itself, in whichever narrative form, nowhere indicates that it was the basis of an accusation and that it led to Jesus' execution. Those who would see in the temple action one of the causes, or even the only cause, for Jesus' death must come to terms with this reality. Relating Jesus' temple action to his death may be a popular thing to do today, but that connection is nowhere indicated by the sources. This lack of evidence in the sources is especially true for the oft-made supposition that Jesus went to Jerusalem with the express purpose of provoking a confrontation in the temple. The idea that the temple action was Jesus' way of forcing a confrontation with Judaism is a modern fiction.

The question remains, of course, what the action as portrayed may have meant and whether its inner sense may have provided the occasion for Jesus' death even without being identified as such. Determining that meaning is especially difficult, since the mixed scripture quotation from Isa 56:7 and Jer 7:11, which is put in Jesus' mouth after the action as a way of interpreting the scene, comes from Mark rather than from his source. Both the language of the transition in Mark 11:17a and the use of the Septuagint confirm this judgment. We are forced, therefore, to elicit from the uninterpreted portrayal of the event its own self-understanding. What is available to us prior to Mark is only Mark 11:15b–16:

> [. . .] *And he drove out those who sold and bought in the temple.*
> *And he overturned the tables of the money-changers and the seats of those who sold doves.*
> *And he did not permit anyone to carry a vessel through the temple.*

The contents of the first two sentences (Mark 11:15b, c) fit well together, and they offer a stylistically well-rounded picture. People are described performing two typical functions, and two typical sets of objects are included. The third sentence takes a new approach and fits less well (11:16). The tense of the verb changes, and John offers no parallel. Our interpretation of the scene will thus concentrate on 11:15.

The scene obviously takes place in the temple's outer Court of the Gentiles. The reference to *in the temple* in the first line clearly describes the area from which the sellers and buyers are driven out. Every knowledgeable reader must recognize that buying and selling on the Mount of Olives and on the temple mount are not included in Jesus' action. Nor does Jesus disturb the sacrificial cult and the priests in their service. He in no way appears, therefore, as someone who intends to disrupt the sacrificial cult and the cultic law.[17] Indeed, the opposite is the case. The purity and holiness of the Holy of Holies, extending outward in various degrees throughout the temple areas, are expanded to include the outer court. That area is now so holy that the activities that over the course of time had grown up in its precincts are no longer permitted. This position is entirely appropriate as a contribution to the debate[18] in Early Judaism over the holiness of the temple.[19]

Now that we have clarified the possible meaning of the action, we can ask whether Jesus actually would have done such a thing. It certainly would make more sense to attribute that kind of concern for the Jerusalem cult to a Jewish-Christian group[20] than to attribute it to Jesus, who in questions of purity acted exactly the opposite (§5.3.4). The scene itself also raises questions. Jesus' attack on persons and things is hardly in keeping with the image of him presented elsewhere. And are we to believe that by himself (there is no mention of the disciples), in an area some four times as large as the Acropolis in Athens, which at the time of the Passover festival was bound to have been crowded, he was able to drive out buyers and sellers without being apprehended by the temple police? Even the Roman troops stationed in the Tower of Antonia (Josephus, *Ant.* 20.106–7; *J.W.* 2.224–25; Acts 21:27–36), who during the Passover would have been on heightened alert, made no move. The attempt is often made to circumvent this problem by accusing the gospels of exaggerating and by claiming that Jesus engaged in only a small, symbolic action that attracted hardly any attention. How can one justify such a claim methodologically? In a manner reminiscent of the rationalistic method of explaining away the miracles of Jesus, one is simply boiling the text down until it reaches the level of what is historically possible. It is methodologically preferable to leave the scene as implausible as it is described. Such a conclusion means, however, once we have examined the various arguments, that Jesus did not engage in the action in the temple and that it cannot have been the cause of his final fate.

Reducing the action to a minor event in an effort to save its historicity would not alter this conclusion. How could such a minor action result in a person's death? Who in Judaism would have regarded enthusiasm for the holiness of the temple as a capital offense? No matter how we might twist the so-called cleansing of the temple, there is no reason to regard it as the reason, or even a reason, for Jesus' death. With the exception of the author of Mark 11:18, no one in early Christianity even thought of attributing Jesus' death to the temple action.

As a preliminary conclusion we can state that there is no evidence that Jesus was in opposition to the Jerusalem temple. The few traditional elements that the evangelists offer about Jesus' time in Jerusalem do not go back to Jesus. This conclusion is not only in harmony with what we know about his activity in Galilee; it also fits with the history of the primitive church in Jerusalem. If Jesus had predicted the destruction of the temple or had pronounced God's judgment on Jerusalem, the earliest post-Easter church would probably have established itself in Galilee rather than in Jerusalem. Yet, the church settled in Jerusalem as if that were the natural thing to do. It is more likely that criticism of the temple and Jerusalem along with words of judgment over them come from the history of Jewish Christianity, which looks back on Jesus' fate in Jerusalem and struggles to come to terms with its own increasingly difficult situation leading up to the revolt against Rome.

Once we have eliminated particular criticisms of the temple and the action in the temple as reasons for his death, the way is clear for asking whether Jesus' attitude in general was the underlying reason for getting rid of him. It is clear that many of his Jewish contemporaries were offended and irritated by Jesus' words and deeds. We could cite numerous examples, from his message of judgment, through his proclamation of a Kingdom of God that is already being realized, to his ethic and his attitude toward the Torah.

Jesus' preaching of judgment was especially offensive for all Jewish groups, since it was associated with his claim that Israel's salvation history had been squandered (§3.2). The Kingdom of God that Jesus understood to be already in the process of being realized not only involved a break with Israel's previous history (§4.2.2); it also ignored the Zion tradition in order to focus explicitly on all creation (§4.2.3). The manner in which Jesus understood the impending Kingdom of God as the salvation of the lost (§4.2.4) was especially offensive. This concept became visible in a special way when in the villages of Galilee Jesus ate with tax collectors and sinners (§4.3.2). To outsiders these meals must have looked like a mixing of sinners and righteous that clearly violated the Law. Of course, no one could object when sick people became well, but could it be acceptable when Jesus understood his miracle activity in such an irritating way as the realization of the Kingdom of God (§4.3.3)?

Nor could the authority that Jesus claimed for himself from the Kingdom of God have found general acceptance (§4.4.1). At the very latest the problem would have been clear to everyone when Jesus interpreted the will of God in such a way that on his own authority he declared what in view of the present Kingdom of God the commandment of the hour would be (§5.2). Then when he arbitrarily interpreted the Torah and, in the case of the Sabbath commandment and the purity regulations, actually violated the Torah (§5.3), he was bound to offend all Early Jewish groups. Jesus' total activity in Galilee, therefore, and not simply a solitary life-style, was reason enough for an explosive situation. Some aspects of that activity would not only have set Jesus apart from others; in the context of the group rivalries of the day they would have been enough to have invited an open attack. Jesus' lack of respect for the Torah and his concrete and notorious violations of some of its requirements would have been enough, had one been looking for such a justification, to have subjected Jesus to the same fate that John the Baptist had experienced.

This understanding of the underlying reasons and motives for Jesus' fate not only has the support of the gospels themselves;[21] it also has on its side the observations made about Jesus in Galilee that were related to hostility, opposition, and rejection (§3.2.4). Finally, those who claim that Jesus' death was based on a misunderstanding or on a single offense must explain why the Christian community continued to be persecuted, first immediately after Easter in the person of Stephen and his followers (Acts 6–7; 11:19–26); then in the attack on the church at Damascus at the hands of the Pharisee, Paul (1 Cor 15:9; Gal 1:13; Phil 3:6) and in the persecution of Jewish churches (1 Thess 2:14–15).[22] We do not need to trace this phenomenon in all its details, but it is noteworthy that we can find evidence of the synagogue's persecution of Jewish Christian churches beginning with the sayings source and including all the gospels. Josephus (*Ant.* 20.200) notes that James the brother of Jesus was one of the Jewish Christian martyrs who was stoned by his own people. It should be mentioned that a number of them were killed for having violated the Law. Josephus, whom we have no reason to doubt here, specifically offers that explanation for the death of James. We can conclude, therefore, that Jesus and his followers and the post-Easter Jewish-Christian churches were caught up within the rivalries among early Jewish groups, which not infrequently turned violent (§5.3.1). That Jesus' death (not solely, but to a degree) was related to conflicts over the Law fits well in this general framework.

Thus far in our discussion of the background for Jesus' death we have focused on his activity, which, of course, is where the discussion must begin. However, we cannot ignore a special problem related to Jesus' death. Jesus is arrested by Jews and charged before the Roman, Pilate. The Jewish accusers must have arrived at a consensus among themselves, therefore, and then have made a public charge before Pilate that would have some chance of success. Naturally, we know nothing about these internal Jewish conversations.

Nevertheless, we might note that a tactical-political reason for Jesus' death is suggested in the opening scene of the Johannine passion narrative, which the Fourth Evangelist has admittedly created. According to John 11:47–49[23] the members of the Sanhedrin are in agreement that they cannot ignore Jesus, since the Romans might take away "the place and the people" from the ruling class. The high priest then advises: "Do you not know . . . that it is better for you that one man should die for the people and not that the whole nation should be destroyed?" We can hardly make direct use of the scene historically, but it may well preserve an authentic element in the web of causes and motives.

This scene, along with the parallel scene in Mark 14:1–2 parr., also presupposes that there was something of a Jewish consensus about Jesus and about the desired execution. Since no one knows how it may have been formulated, the terrain is wide open for speculation. There is, however, an obvious hypothesis. According to Josephus (*Ant.* 18.116–19) Herod Antipas had already arrested John the Baptist, because the monarch feared that this disturbing prophet would stir up the people. Now in Deut 13:1–6 and 18:9–22 the Torah gives relevant instructions as to how one should deal with false prophets who lead the people astray.[24] They are to be killed.[25] In general, one could bring that charge against Jesus. Tactically, this approach would have two advantages: It would enable every Jewish group to include in the charge its own particular complaint about Jesus, and, given a political twist, it could be the complaint that would appeal to Pilate. The advantage of this suggestion for our historical work is that we are able to bring together all of the offensive dimensions of the activity of Jesus that we have been able to discover into the category of false prophecy.

6.2   JESUS' VIEW OF HIS OWN FUTURE

The earliest evangelist not only states that Jesus' Galilean opponents early on make plans for Jesus' death (Mark 3:6), which then for no apparent reason go unfulfilled until the Passover at which he dies; he also describes how Jesus himself during his Galilean activity repeatedly tells his disciples of his future death and resurrection (Mark 8:31; 9:31; 10:32–34). Indeed, he pictures Jesus as explicitly planning his journey to Jerusalem as the way that would lead to his death (10:32–34). According to this same Mark, Jesus explains to the disciples the saving significance of his death (Mark 10:45; 14:22–24) and calls them to follow him on the way to the cross (Mark 8:34–38).

It can hardly be disputed that this entire concept is a christological interpretation of Jesus of Nazareth, that its individual elements have a long history in early Christianity, and that it was Mark who blended them into a new whole. Nowhere else has the drive to reinterpret christologically the fate of Jesus left such lasting traces. From the perspective of the church this reinterpretation makes sense, since the fate of Jesus was the saving basis of its faith. All of the other gospels, therefore, have followed this christological path as a matter of course even to the degree that the Johannine Christ proclaims his preexistence and exaltation even as he as the Earthly One identifies himself with resurrection and eternal life (John 3:12–16; 11:25–26; 13:31–32).

Once we have come to terms with the inner consistency of this insight, we must recognize that its very agreement with the christology of the post-Easter church makes it impossible to attribute it uncritically to Jesus. At the same time we cannot automatically assume that none of the individual elements go back to Jesus. Unfortunately, striking a middle way between these two choices and examining each element for itself has led to a wide range of positions. Some claim that Jesus early on recognized that his activity would lead to his death and that he therefore accepted his death and gave it a saving significance. For others, Jesus' death surprised him as much as it did anyone else so that, faced with the sudden failure of his mission, he died in despair. In the one case, Jesus' activity and the fate that he intentionally planned blend into a unity. In the other case, his last days are unexpected, and they call into question his message. Neither extreme is convincing. One position cannot avoid the charge that it is willing to surrender the post-Easter image of Christ only when it is absolutely necessary. The other position transforms the picture of the gospels into its exact opposite and cannot avoid the charge that it is pure hypothesis.

The initial question is whether Jesus could have reckoned with his violent and premature death. Only those who think that he did so can begin to ask how Jesus would have understood that death. Those who describe Jesus' Galilean activity as essentially free of conflict will of necessity conclude that Jesus at the most anticipated his death during the final days in Jerusalem—indeed, that he may even have provoked it. This view ignores the fact that Jesus' itinerant life in Galilee was provocative if for no other reason than that it was not part of the normal life of the village (cf. §2). His life-style and that of his disciples was not only strange; it early on led to his expulsion from his family and from his hometown (Mark 6:1–6). That sort of news spreads quickly in a culture that is characterized by a clan mentality and by family relationships. One thinks of the typical scene in Tob 5, where Tobit refuses to accept the stranger until he has satisfactorily explained his tribal and family background.

In addition to this strange life-style, which was subject to all kinds of criticism, we must add Jesus' activity in word and deed. In the preceding discussion we have had frequent occasion to note that this combination was theologically (Matt 11:6 par.) as well as personally offensive (cf. the summary in §6:1). Jesus himself responded to uncompromising rejection and hostility with pronouncements of judgment (§3.2.4). Such statements not only reveal the depth of the conflict; they also show that his life was as much in danger as was that of John the Baptist or Jeshua ben Ananias (§3.1). When we then consider the violations of the Sabbath and the lack of respect for the purity regulations (§5.3.4), we cannot avoid the conclusion that Jesus must have known that he was in danger. His exposed position among the competing groups confirms this assumption (§5.3.1). Everyone knew that in an emergency you have to act quickly to eliminate a troublesome competitor. Jesus had seen it happen to the person who had given him his theological beginnings (§3.1). Judas' betrayal (§6.3) suggests that even Jesus' disciples knew as much, since it is likely that Judas was able to make the decision to betray Jesus only because he knew that Jesus was already in danger, and it was simply a matter of finding a way to deliver him to his enemies. If, therefore, Jesus must have been aware that he might face a premature death, we can then ask whether he himself saw meaning in his death.

There is in Luke's special material (Luke 13:31–33) a unit that, while admittedly shaped by Luke in its present form, may have some claim to authenticity. Luke, who is the only one of the evangelists who is able to describe Jesus' relationship with the Pharisees in a somewhat positive light (7:36–50; 14:1–24), here portrays the Pharisees as coming to Jesus to warn him of the treachery of Herod Antipas. In an initial reaction Jesus responds:

> *Go and tell this fox:*
> a   *"Behold, I drive out demons*
> b   *and perform healings today and tomorrow,*
> c   *but (not until) the third day am I perfected."*

Luke 13:33 offers a second answer that reinterprets the temporal statements of v. 32 and introduces the special Lukan catchword *Jerusalem* as the location of Jesus' death. The verse thus serves as a transition to the lament over Jerusalem (Luke 13:34–35) par. In Luke's outline it also serves both geographically (22:37; 23:5) and theologically to prepare the way for Jesus' journey to Jerusalem to suffer and die, since in v. 33 the reference to the prophet (cf. Luke 1:76; 4:24; 7:16; 24:19) introduces the topos of the prophet's violent fate.[26] If with Luke 13:33 Luke complements and interprets v. 32, then v. 32 is pre-Lukan material.

Of course, v. 32 presupposes some sort of introduction that would indicate who the fox is and who is to be the messenger. In Luke's presentation, however, we can only designate the metaphorical recipient of the saying and recognize in the situation described in v. 31b a remnant of the apophthegm's earlier introduction.

A number of considerations justify regarding Jesus' answer in v. 32 as historically reliable. The disrespectful metaphor[27] and the sovereign attitude that permeates the saying both fit well with what we know of Jesus. That Jesus' miracles (§4.3.3) were not subject to the wishes of the ruling prince is also clear elsewhere. The Kingdom of God that is being realized in the healings has its own rules for determining how and when it appears. These rules thus also determine how long Jesus will be active in Galilee. He will be at work *today and tomorrow*; i.e., he will be undeterred for the immediate future. In spite of the general knowledge, therefore, about Herod's treatment of John the Baptist (Josephus, *Ant.* 18.116–19; Mark 6:17–29 par.), Herod will have no control over Jesus' death.

The saying's claim to authenticity is strengthened by the fact that it leaves open questions about when, how, and where Jesus will die. His death is presented simply as the conclusion of his activity, but not as a death with saving significance. Nor is there any reference to a resurrection. There is no reason to deny Luke 13:32 to Jesus. By contrast, the Markan texts (8:31; 9:31; 10:32–34) not only offer a complete summary of the passion; they also contain a prediction of the resurrection and an explicit christology associated with the Son of Man title. Clearly they are part of the post-Easter understanding of Jesus' fate and his person.[28]

If, then, as early as his work in Galilee Jesus reckoned with the possibility of his violent death, we must ask whether he might have gone to Jerusalem to provoke a crisis. It is clear that Luke 13:32 has nothing to say on the subject. Nor does the journey to Jerusalem for the Passover festival necessarily imply such a plan. Going to Jerusalem for the festivals was a natural thing to do "as it is prescribed for all Israel by an everlasting decree" (Tob 1:6–7). Since we have found neither a saying nor an action of Jesus in Jerusalem, or specifically in the temple, that indicated that he was trying to force a final decision (cf. §6.1), there is no support there either for such an assumption. We conclude, therefore, that Jesus' decision to travel to Jerusalem in order to die was a Markan christological construct—a construct that admittedly has had a great influence, not only in the nineteenth century life of Jesus research, but also to a degree lasting into the present.

Luke 13:32 is also the beginning point for a further consideration that leads in another direction. Did Jesus attribute a special meaning to his possible death? The question leads to two Markan texts: the word about serving in Mark 10:45 (=Matt 20:28), which also says that Jesus came to give his life for many, and the tradition about Jesus' last supper from Mark 14:22–25 (parr.; 1 Cor 11:23–26; John 6:51c–58). Both texts are in prominent positions in Mark's gospel. After Jesus has announced his coming fate three times with almost the same words (8:31; 9:31; 10:32–34) and has set out for Jerusalem (Mark 10:32a, 46a; 11:1), for the first time he offers a soteriological interpretation of his death. He repeats this interpretation with special emphasis when he celebrates the last supper with his disciples. Mark thus lets his readers know that on two occasions prior to his arrest Jesus unmistakably attributed a saving meaning to his death. Of course, Mark's portrayal need not reflect Jesus' own view.

Mark 10:45 is the conclusion of a parenesis on discipleship, which requires of Jesus' followers a life of service and which then identifies the person of the Son of Man as the saving figure who saves precisely through serving and who thus provides a model for the life of discipleship as a life of service. This kind of two-part parenesis, consisting of exhortation and christological motivation, appears frequently in early Christian parenesis, even to a soteriological description of the way Jesus serves as the motivation (cf. by way of example Rom 15:1–3, 7; 2 Cor 8:7–9; Phil 2:1–11; 1 Pet 2:20–24; 3:17–22). This typical structure of the section raises serious questions about attributing it to Jesus. Statements about the suffering Son of Man are, furthermore, hardly to be included in the earliest group of Son of Man sayings (§4.4.2). The image of Jesus as a servant appears nowhere else in the Jesus tradition, but he consistently appears in the other parenetic texts as the one who accepts humiliation on behalf of those who belong to him. We cannot claim Mark 10:45, therefore, on behalf of Jesus. Since the text preserves the church's image of Christ, and especially since v. 45 shows the influence of Isa 53:10–11 (cf. the catchwords *serve, life, for many*), it is part of the church's tradition. The Lord's Supper tradition (Mark 14:25: *for many*) may also have played a role in the formation of the text, and this observation brings us to the second text that is important in this context.

All of the texts that deal with the last supper of Jesus reflect the liturgical concerns of the meal celebrations of the various churches. No text reports the historical event. The purpose of each text is, rather, to justify why the church celebrates the Lord's Supper as it does. Analyzing the history of the tradition behind liturgical texts is especially difficult, and with justification we have avoided trying to determine an original form of the tradition. We will have to be satisfied with analyzing its contours and individual motifs while leaving open a number of historical questions.

Mark 14:22–25 did not originally belong to the passion narrative. As Paul (1 Cor 11:23–26) and the Fourth Evangelist (John 6:51c–58) reveal, the text of the words of institution was at one time an independent cult etiology. The original passion narrative is aware of a final meal (Mark 14:18; John 13:2), but it uses it only as the setting for the statement about Judas' betrayal and the prediction of Peter's denial. Mark and John, as well as their sources, used the material in different ways: one of them for the foot-washing (John 13:1–20), another for the words of institution and the pericope about the preparation for the Passover (Mark 14:12–16).

It is clear from these observations that it was Mark who first put the words of institution in the setting of a Passover meal. Neither Paul, nor John, nor the words of institution themselves in Mark 14:22–25 have an unequivocal reference to a Passover meal. Mark 14:22a, 25 and 1 Cor 11:23 do indicate, however, that the Lord's Supper tradition understands itself in terms of a farewell meal of Jesus. In the case of John 6 and *Did.* 9–10, 14 this element has been lost. According to Mark 14:22–25, therefore, Jesus' meal was not a Passover feast, but it was probably a farewell meal.

Now Mark 14:22–25 is by no means a homogeneous unit. Verse 25 (=Luke 22:18) is especially to be separated from vv. 22–24. The only thing they have in common is the word *drink*. While the words of institution regard Jesus as the giver of bread and wine and trace the movement of the gifts from Jesus to the disciples, 14:25 speaks only of Jesus and his drinking. This will be his last occasion to drink wine before the final banquet of salvation in the Kingdom of God. While the words of institution speak of the *cup*, 14:25 speaks of *the fruit of the vine*. From this difference one might conclude that 14:25 was a later addition to the words of institution. Such a judgment would be premature, however, since the eschatological orientation of Mark 14:25 is firmly fixed in Paul's Lord's Supper tradition, although admittedly in a post-Easter form (1 Cor 11:26). We can also probably assume that the early Christian cry *Marana-tha* (*our Lord, come!* cf. 1 Cor 16:22; Rev 22:20) with its expectation of an imminent end was part of the Lord's Supper liturgy. Given these conditions, therefore, we should draw the opposite conclusion. It was the words of institution in 14:22–24 that were created for the liturgy, and it is they that in form and diction differ from

14:25. It is probable, therefore, that Mark 14:25 is the earlier interpretation of the meal and that in its essence it is an authentic saying of Jesus.

Admittedly, a comparison of Mark 14:25 with Luke 22:18 reveals that it is next to impossible to reconstruct the earliest form of the saying. What is certain is that the saying from the beginning reveals Jesus' certainty that he is going to die. It thus serves alongside Luke 13:32 to confirm that reality. Nor can we eliminate the connection between Jesus' fate and the Kingdom of God without opening ourselves to the charge that we make arbitrary judgments. Since all of Jesus' activity was dedicated to the Kingdom of God, it would make sense that he saw his anticipated death as having some relation to that kingdom. Given the nature of the evidence, however, we can only suggest how Jesus might have connected his death with the Kingdom of God, yet it is precisely in this regard that the two evangelists strongly differ. Both of them changed the text based on their view of the future. Did Jesus hope that in spite of his death he would be able to participate in the final banquet in the Kingdom of God, even as the long-dead patriarchs would (Matt 8:11 par.)?[29] The suggestion is appealing and is worth considering. In any case, the tradition demonstrates that Jesus did not believe that his death in any way jeopardized the realization of the Kingdom of God. He did not understand his anticipated death, therefore, as invalidating his message and his hope. Since it is God himself who is at work, Jesus' death will not keep the eschatological Kingdom of God from continuing to be realized.

The words of institution in the narrower sense (Mark 14:22–24) contain two ideas that must be considered briefly: the covenant concept and the idea of substitution. In speaking about covenant renewal, Mark alludes to Exod 24:8, while Paul makes use of Jer 31:31. The motif is missing in John 6. The post-Easter church quickly made use of the covenant concept (Rom 3:25; 2 Cor 3:7–11; Gal 4:21–31), although it was not part of the proclamation of Jesus, influenced as the latter was by the preaching of the Baptist (Matt 3:9 par.). Jesus' view of the Kingdom of God nowhere shows the influence of the covenant idea. The Kingdom of God is God's graciousness toward those lost persons who have abandoned the covenant. We will not claim for Jesus himself, therefore, this theological motif of the words of institution.

In Paul's version the expression *for you/for many* is attached to the statement about the bread, but it is precisely here that Paul most reveals the influence of the liturgical style and the Greek language. Luke's awkward text is probably a compromise between the Pauline and Markan versions. As in Mark, therefore, the expression *for many* originally was part of the statement about the cup. It is reminiscent of Isa 53:12, but Jesus cannot have spoken that way. Any suggestion of the drinking of blood would have been intolerable for Jewish ears. Furthermore, the idea of an individual's vicarious death on behalf of an entire group can be documented with any certainty only for Hellenistic Judaism.[30] When we examine Jesus' message elsewhere, we find nowhere the suggestion that God's gracious acceptance of the lost was dependent in any way on the sacrifice of

Jesus' own life. God is and remains the one who saves in the end-time simply because of his own sovereign will. Mark 14:25 says in essence the same thing without attributing a special saving significance to the death of Jesus. Jesus was able to release his life's work on behalf of the Kingdom of God, so to speak, into the hands of God, whose kingship will continue to be victorious even if Jesus dies. The hope expressed in Mark 14:25 adequately covered his own fate, since it assured that he would not be excluded from the final fulfillment of the Kingdom of God.

This description of Jesus' understanding of his death shows a consistent inner resolve, and at the same time it is independent of the post-Easter church's interpretation of Jesus' death. It anticipates nothing of the church's later christology—not even the idea of vicarious suffering—and it fits well in the context of Jesus' central concept of the Kingdom of God. It not only stands out in bold relief from the christological interpretations of the death of Jesus after Easter; it also avoids the view that is popular in the life of Jesus research that Jesus died in despair and in the belief that his work had been a failure. It is true, of course, that Jesus' enemies will have claimed that his execution as a criminal proved that he had failed, but Jesus himself, even when facing his own death, never abandoned his confidence in the Kingdom of God that was being realized.

6.3   THE FINAL EVENTS AND THE DEATH OF JESUS

The evangelists describe Jesus' Galilean activity by bringing together self-contained individual units into a coherent sequence of events that they themselves have created. The passion narrative that Mark puts at the end of his gospel, on the other hand, is from the very beginning a protracted series of events that are bound together by a unity of persons, time, and place. Of course, this narrative world with its dramatic developments is by no means identical with the world of the events themselves. As soon as we raise questions about what really happened in Jerusalem we are faced with fundamental problems of interpretation.

The main source for the last days of Jesus, therefore, is the passion narrative as Mark presents it. Matthew and Luke are both based on Mark. There is no reason to assume that Luke had an independent source that was as old and as important as the passion narrative that Mark used. Luke's differences are due to developments in the tradition and to editorial changes; they have no claim to originality. A separate problem is posed by the passion narrative in the Fourth Gospel. Nowhere is the Fourth Gospel closer to the Synoptics in vocabulary and in the order of the pericopes. The view that John used a passion narrative that goes back to the passion narrative that Mark used and that, before it was incorporated into the Gospel of John, had its own history remains the most plausible theory.[31] If we want to trace the outline of the earliest passion narrative and to inquire about the historical reality that lies behind it, we will need to pay particular attention to what Mark and John have in common.[32]

While the pre-Markan passion narrative is the decisive—indeed, for many matters the only—source for historical questions, there are scattered references in the early Christian literature that are not completely without historical value.[33] Among them, of course, are references to Jesus' death (e.g., 1 Thess 4:14; 5:9–10 as the oldest literary reference), to his death and burial (1 Cor 15:3b–5 as an early tradition), to his crucifixion (1 Cor 1:17–18, 23; 2:2; 2 Cor 13:4; Phil 2:7–8, etc.) or to his suffering on the *tree* (1 Pet 2:21–24). Heb 5:7–10 may even have preserved an independent tradition about the Gethsemane pericope, and in 1 Cor 11:23–26 we read about Jesus' last meal with his disciples. 1 Thess 2:15, Acts 2:23, 3:14–15, 4:10 refer to the participation of Jews in the death of Jesus. We must reckon, therefore, with the existence in early Christianity of knowledge about the last days of Jesus that was independent of the passion narrative, even though these traditions without exception preserve—at the most—isolated elements of the story and even though their historical value is tempered by the kerygmatic and liturgical forms in which they are preserved.

For understanding Jesus' days in Jerusalem a crucial question is what the form of the passion narrative was when the Markan and Johannine variants went their separate ways. It is probable that an initial decision to kill Jesus (Mark 14:1–2; John 11:47–57) was followed by the anointing in Bethany (Mark 14:3–9; John 12:2–11), the entry into Jerusalem (Mark 11:1–10; John 12:12–19), and the last supper with the predictions of betrayal and denial (Mark 14:17–31; John 13:1–30). There then followed the scene in Gethsemane and the arrest (Mark 14:32–42, 43–52; John 12:23, 27; 18:1–11), the hearing before the high priest and Peter's denial (Mark 14:53–72; John 18:12–27), the trial before Pilate (Mark 15:1–20a; John 18:28–19:3), and the crucifixion and burial (Mark 15:20b–47; John 19:16b–42). The narrative then ended with the discovery of the empty tomb (Mark 16:1–8; John 20:1–18).

Missing from this list is the so-called temple cleansing with the accompanying demand for authorization or a sign (Mark 11:15–17, 27–33; John 2:13–17, 18–22; cf. above, §6.1). It is by no means clear that it was part of the passion account, since in the Fourth Gospel it is located outside the context of the passion (John 2:13–22), and there is no other reference to it in Mark's narrative. If it was already part of the material when the Markan and Johannine passion narratives went their separate ways, it must have been one of the pericopes that circulated independently before they became part of the passion narrative. The anointing in Bethany and the Gethsemane pericope also belong to this category. That the latter theme had its own independent tradition is clear from Heb 5:7–10. If, moreover, remnants of this tradition are preserved in John 12:23, 27; 14:30–31; 18:11, then it is probable that the pericope was part of an original form of the passion narrative before it separated into Markan and Johannine branches.[34]

Another frequently debated issue is whether the passion narrative at one time

ended with the burial or whether prior to Mark it included the discovery of
the empty tomb in Mark 16:1–8.[35] The reasons for including the empty tomb in
the early form of the narrative are convincing. Of them the most important are:
The early formulaic material in 1 Cor 15:3b–5 is structured the same way. The
typology of the Old Testament theme of the suffering righteous person, which has
left its mark on the passion narrative, ends with God's acceptance of the sufferer
(e.g., Ps 22:23–26; 69:31–36; *Ps. Sol.* 2:16–20). Although independent in its
present form, John 20:1–18 presupposes the essence of the empty-tomb tradition
from Mark 16. It confirms, therefore, that this legend already formed the conclusion of the passion narrative when the Johannine version began to go its
own way.

We can add a further observation. It is generally recognized that the angel in
the tomb expressly connects the empty tomb with the church's reformulated early
Easter confession (Mark 16:6 and Rom 4:24; 8:11; 10:9; Gal 1:1, etc.). Without
exception, however, the latter speaks of Jesus as *died* or *dead* rather than as
crucified. In his gospel Mark also speaks of the cross on only one occasion
outside the passion narrative, viz., in Mark 8:34 in a figurative sense. Yet, in
Mark 16:6, in a modification of the early confessional language and in harmony
with the passion narrative (Mark 15:13–32), Mark refers to Jesus as crucified.
The vocabulary of the cross reveals, therefore, that the heart of the empty-tomb
tradition in Mark 16:6 was part of the passion narrative prior to Mark. This
linguistic connection can hardly be accidental.

This early account of the passion is a snapshot from the time when the Markan
and Johannine accounts began to go their separate ways. It was at that time
already a well-developed composition, yet in order to avoid unnecessary speculation we will begin our discussion of the historical questions with this text. Of
special importance is the question of the text's intention, since without an understanding of its theological purpose our discussion of the historical issues will be
purely speculative. An examination of the passion narrative's theological concept
reveals in each of its sections a post-Easter, Christian point of view. Two fundamental concerns appear throughout the narrative: the christological development
of the individual scenes and the (admittedly varied) partisan descriptions of the
Jewish and Roman roles.[36] The two options, always present in the narrative
pattern, impose value judgments on the story that oversimplify the historical
complexity, take clear stands on good and evil, and thus confirm the church's
present belief-system. Of course, every historical reconstruction is an attempt to
use history for one's own purposes, and we should not for that reason alone
immediately reject the passion narrative's construct. Only as we keep that reality
in mind, however, will we be able to use the passion narrative as a source of
historical information.

When we begin our historical evaluation with Jesus and his followers, the
relentless honesty with which the narrative portrays the failure of all the disciples
and the presence of only a faithful few at the cross (cf. §2) permits the following

conclusions. Jesus journeyed with his disciples and a few women to Jerusalem for the Passover festival. Judas, who went over to the enemy, demonstrates that Jewish representatives were especially interested in arresting Jesus, because Judas dealt with his Jewish brothers, not with the Romans.[37] That kind of conspiracy would not have been necessary had Jesus' action in the temple taken place (cf. §6.1), since in that case one could have arrested Jesus *in flagranti*.[38] Judas' behavior thus supports the conclusion that the temple action was not historical.

Another unusual element in the passion narrative at the beginning of the events in Jerusalem is Jesus' triumphal entry into the city (Mark 11:1–10 par.; John 12:12–19). In its present form the account is heavily christological. If it preserves any historical recollection at all, it might be that Jesus was so well known among the pilgrims from Galilee that they surrounded him wherever he appeared. If historically we cannot make use of the triumphal entry and the temple action as the beginning events of Jesus' days in Jerusalem, then we may understand Peter's failure and the flight of the disciples at the arrest as evidence that the disciples in no way were prepared for the possibility that Jesus intended to provoke a crisis in Jerusalem. It is much more plausible that, like all the other pilgrims, Jesus and his followers went to the city of Zion simply to take part in the festival. We have further support for that view if the image of the weak Jesus in Gethsemane preserves a kernel of historical reality. The picture of Jesus in the Gethsemane pericope is clearly different from, e.g., the way Luke describes in Acts the way of the martyr Paul.[39] This difference may well confirm that this image of Jesus is not simply a narrative invention.

As a provisional conclusion we can state, therefore: According to the passion narrative it is probable that there were early tensions between Jewish circles and Jesus, since Judas operates in that kind of milieu. However, Jesus and his followers do nothing to provoke the situation; they are normal pilgrims. Of course, Jesus probably soon realizes that he might be facing arrest and his possible execution. He thus celebrates (assuming the Johannine date of his death; cf. §2) a farewell meal with his disciples before the actual Passover (§6.2) in which he expresses the conviction that his fate will not alter the dynamic of the Kingdom of God and that he himself will participate in the final banquet of salvation.

At the beginning of the passion narrative one reads that the antagonists of Jesus and the disciples are the chief priests and the scribes (Mark 14:1; John 11:47). The typical and generalizing reference to *the Jews* is thus not historical (cf. 1 Thess 2:14–15; Acts 2:22–23; John 18:12, 14, 31, 36; 19:7, 12). Unhistorical also is the supposition that only Romans, but no Jews, were involved in Jesus' death. It is clear that in the passion narrative the priestly aristocracy takes the initiative in arresting Jesus and accusing him before Pilate (Mark 14:1, 43, 53, 60; 15:11). On the other hand, references to the Pharisees as a distinct group appear only infrequently in the passion narrative and are obviously secondary (Matt 27:62; John 18:3). It would be premature, of course, to conclude from that evidence that they were not in opposition to Jesus. The Galilean witnesses about

Jesus' activity clearly suggest that they were (§3.2.4). We can conclude, there-fore, that the Jewish priestly aristocracy led by the ruling high priest were Pilate's official counterpart as well as the dominant power group in Jerusalem. It is natural, therefore, that they were Jesus' actual opponents in the City of David.

In the narrative world a decision to kill Jesus is, of course, an effective way of leading into the drama that is to follow, yet historically no one on the Christian side would have had such secret knowledge. Mark 14:1–2 does not preserve information, therefore, about the accusers and their concerns. At the arrest Jesus and his disciples come into direct contact with the servants of the chief priests. Judas, about whose motives we can only speculate, arranges for this meeting to take place at night. The people who arrest Jesus are the servants of Jewish officials. It is John (18:12) who later adds that Roman soldiers were present at the arrest. John 18:1 locates the event in a garden on the opposite bank of the Kidron, while Mark 14:26, 32 speaks of Gethsemane on the Mount of Olives.[40]

The hearing in the house of the high priest follows immediately. Mark and Luke nowhere mention his name (Mark 14:53–72; John 18:12–27); Matthew identifies him as Caiaphas (Matt 26:57).[41] The Fourth Evangelist mentions two hearings, one before Annas (the high priest in 6–15 CE) and one before Caiaphas (high priest 18–37 CE; Annas's son-in-law). Changes in the text have been made here, however, in the course of the history of the Johannine passion narrative.[42] The early passion narrative did not mention the name of the high priest, but it obviously meant the one who was currently in office. Matthew later correctly added the name Caiaphas. The legal figure to deal with Jesus from the Jewish side was Caiaphas, therefore, who was the official spokesperson for dealing with the Roman prefect, Pilate. From the very beginning we are dealing not with a lynching by a mob, as in the case of Stephen (Acts 7:57–58; cf. also Acts 14:19; 2 Cor 11:25), but with an institutionally legal process.

What happened in Caiaphas' house? Was it a hearing in order to formulate an accusation to bring before Pilate, or was it a regular trial before the Sanhedrin? The interpreters of the passion narrative have long wrestled with this problem. It is such a difficult issue, because the scene in Mark 14:53, 55–65 is one of the key scenes in the passion narrative, and it has attracted a great deal of attention in the process of transmitting and editing the narrative. It is clear that the impression that we are dealing with a trial before the Sanhedrin comes from 14:53b ("And all the chief priests, and elders, and scribes came together"), from v. 55 ("The chief priests and the entire Sanhedrin sought testimony to justify executing him, but found none"), and from v. 64b ("And they all condemned him that he was deserving of death"). Yet, as such Markan statements as Mark 10:33; 11:27; 14:43 reveal, these statements probably all come from Mark himself, a judgment that is confirmed by John, who knows nothing of this scenario.

Those who do not accept this conclusion and who claim to see elements of the earliest tradition in these statements are faced with the well-known legal prob-lems posed by such a meeting of the Sanhedrin. They are, among other things, that the Sanhedrin could not meet in the house of the high priest (Mark 14:53–54 claims otherwise), that the Mishna prohibits trials on days leading up to festivals,[43] that criminal cases were to be heard by day and not at night (against Mark 14:17, 26, 32, 43, 53–54), and that a day must go by between the presentation of evidence and the passing of judgment (Mark 14:64 claims otherwise). (Cf. on all these issues *Sanh.* 4:1h. On the next-to-last point, cf. also Acts 4:3, 5.) However we might deal with these legal questions, a major problem remains, viz., whether the Sanhedrin was even competent to try capital cases in Pilate's day. John 18:31 is quite clear in denying that right to a Jewish authority. Other reports from that period give no reason to challenge John on this point.[44] Any time a court is not able to impose sentence, its very competence is called in question. We have a good example of how the authorities proceeded in another case, viz., the case of Jeshua ben Ananias (Josephus, *J.W.* 6.300–9). Instead of conducting their own trial, the Jewish officials brought the accused directly before the Roman governor, Albinus.

What took place in the house of the high priest, therefore, was a hearing designed to formulate the accusation and to question Jesus and the witnesses. If that is the case, we can then ask what the early passion narrative suggests happened during the hearing. If we ignore for a moment the material about Peter's denial, which of course in its essence was always connected with the scene in the house of the high priest, the text may at one time have read as follows (Mark 14:53a, 56, 60, 61a, 65):

1   *And they led Jesus to the high priest [vv. 53–55]. (And) many testified falsely against him, but the testimonies did not agree [vv. 57–59]. The high priest then stood up, went into their midst, and asked Jesus: "Do you have no answer to what these men testify against you?" But he was silent and said nothing [vv. 62b–64].*

2   *And some began to spit on him, and to cover his face, and to mistreat him, and to say to him: "Prophesy (who did that to you)!" And the attendants beat him.*

Since the Johannine parallel goes its own way, it serves only to confirm that there was a hearing before the high priest and that from the beginning it ended with the mocking of Jesus (Mark 14:65; John 18:22–23); it does not help clarify what was at one time in the scene. For neither of the two substantial sections of the hearing (Mark 14:57–59 or Mark 14:61b–64a) does John contribute anything. We can read such a statement as Mark 15:2 = John 18:33, therefore, without presupposing Mark 14:61–64, since the church that receives this material already is aware that Jesus is the Messiah.[45] In any case, *the Christ, the Son of the Blessed* and *the King of the Jews* are different titles. We furthermore have no way of testing the claim that texts such as John 7:50–51; 10:33, etc., show that the theme of Jesus' messiahship must have been mentioned in John 18:12–24.

Our analysis is limited, therefore, to Mark 14:53–65. In its present form the hearing contains four elements. There is a general declaration about false witnesses and a basic declaration about Jesus' silence. Each of these statements is then followed by a substantive unit: the false testimony about Jesus' statement about the temple, and Jesus' affirmation of his messiahship and his position as Son of Man. We may understand the two substantive units as later additions designed to fill out the general statements. That christological formulations were added is more plausible than that someone added the silence motif in v. 61 in clear contradiction of Jesus' speech in v. 62 or that someone created the general statement in v. 56 after the concrete statements of vv. 57–59 already existed. It is much more likely that someone felt the need to expand vv. 56 and 61–62, since by themselves they were inadequate. The early passion narrative thus contained neither the saying about the temple nor Jesus' confession, which in all probability was formulated by Mark.

This scene is so filled with motifs about the suffering righteous person (cf. Ps 35:11; Sus 51–59; Ps 38:14–16; Isa 50:6; 53:5–7) that it has no historical value. That observation makes even more compelling the argument that no one in the early church could have known what happened in the hearing. The historian can only say that servants of the high priest captured Jesus and brought him into Caiaphas's house where preparations were made for an accusation before Pilate. During the course of the evening Peter denied his lord.

Early the next morning (Mark 15:1; John 18:28)—i.e., at the normal time (Seneca, *De Ira* 2:7)—the chief priests (Mark 15:3, 11; John 18:35; 19:6, 15) bring charges against Jesus before Pilate,[46] the Roman prefect of Judea (26–36/37 CE). His residence was in Caesarea, but as a rule he came to Jerusalem for the major Jewish festivals in order to guarantee political stability. In all probability he used as his Jerusalem residence the palace of Herod in the western quarter of the city (cf. Mark 15:16 and Josephus, *J.W.* 2.301; 15.328; Philo *Leg. Gai.* 38 [299]; 39 [306]).[47] It stands to reason that he dealt with legal matters during his stay in Jerusalem. The two men who were crucified along with Jesus and the figure of Barabbas, who was released, suggest that on the morning before the Passover festival Pilate sat in judgment not merely on Jesus; he dealt with several cases.

A Roman judicial process differed significantly from a Jewish trial. The latter was based on the testimony of witnesses (an example is Sus 28–64); the former, like that of the Greeks, was based on the accusation and the ability of the accused to speak in his own defense (a famous example is the apology of Socrates). In addition, a prefect (like every governing Roman official in a province) had the right to circumvent the Roman legal process when dealing with provincials who did not have the right of Roman citizenship (*peregrini*)—to conduct a hearing according to his own best judgment (*cognitio extra ordinem*) and then to render a judgment.[48] Only he could pass the death sentence in the provinces. The roles in the trial are thus clear. The chief priests are the accusers, Jesus is the accused, Pilate is the judge. Since the accusers make a special effort to appear before Pilate who has the power of life and death for everyone in the province, they will have brought a charge that could result in the death penalty. For synagogue discipline such as a whipping (2 Cor 11:24) they would not have needed the Roman governor. They had to make use of him, because they did not have the right of capital punishment. The Jewish accusers thus had to come up with an accusation that would last long enough before Pilate to give them a good chance of achieving their goal of getting rid of Jesus once and for all.

The various elements of Mark's portrayal of the scene before Pilate (Mark 15:1–15 parr.; John 18:28–19:16a) are intentionally balanced against each other. The scene opens with the chief priests delivering Jesus bound to Pilate (the core element is Mark 15:1); it ends with Pilate turning Jesus over to his soldiers to be scourged and crucified (15:15b). Two scenes appear in this framework: a hearing (15:2–5) and the Barabbas episode (15:6–15a). The Fourth Evangelist, who had a similar source, created seven scenes, which, because of their dramatic effect, are among the most impressive sequences in the entire Fourth Gospel. It is noteworthy, however, that motifs and key words from Mark's framework and the two scenes that it encloses appear also in John. The Johannine passion narrative, which John knew from his own church's tradition and which had its own history even before him, thus confirms that Mark's narrative structure is quite old.

However one imagines that the details of the text took shape within this Markan structure, it appears that the intention from the very beginning was to cast Pilate in a good light. He does not pronounce the judgment that one would expect after 15:2. He gives Jesus ample opportunity to respond to the charges brought by his accusers (15:4). In the Barabbas scene he argues unsuccessfully for Jesus' release, so that at the end he no longer appears to be in charge of the situation (15:12). According to the same portrayal, the Jewish leaders and the people consistently and without exception are hostile to Jesus. Jesus himself is portrayed as innocent, and once again Jesus' fate is described in terms of the typology of the suffering righteous person (on 15:1 cf. Ps 26:12 [LXX]; Isa 53:6, 12; on 15:3 cf. Ps 109:3; on Mark 15:5 cf. Ps 14:61; Isa 53:7; on Mark 15:6–13 cf. Isa 53:5, 12). From this point on the motif of the *King of the Jews* runs through the story of the passion down to the inscription on the cross.

Achieving this theological configuration is the primary goal of the narrative, but in doing so it accepts some historical impossibilities. Jesus' response to the question whether he was the king of the Jews should have resulted immediately in his conviction. After the Romans had taken over the administration in 6 CE,[49] to claim in Jerusalem to be the king of the Jews (or even to act suspicious in that regard) is in the eyes of the Romans to engage in political rebellion and to be deserving of death (cf. Josephus, *Ant.* 17.272–85).[50] Legally, the wholesale accusations of Mark 15:3 are an absurdity. A ruling prefect who permits himself to be manipulated by a mob (Mark 15:11, 13–14) undermines the reputation of Rome, and Pilate would hardly have permitted that to happen. He certainly would not have forgotten to pronounce the judgment that should have come before 15:14. (Something like: "I sentence you to be crucified.") It is clear that these historical problems are all caused by the value judgments placed on the various characters. They are the result of the narrative's theological intention.

Only in general terms, therefore, are we able to answer the historical questions surrounding the trial before Pilate. The result of the trial is clear. Jesus was condemned to die by means of the Roman punishment of crucifixion (as an expression of Roman *coercitio*). A trial did take place before Pilate, therefore, who was probably the only judge, and the trial ended in an appropriate judgment. We cannot be certain about any of the details of the trial, especially about the reason for the judgment and about the alleged custom of releasing a prisoner at the Passover.[51]

This custom is documented nowhere else. It cannot have been a question of an amnesty after the sentencing, since Pilate, the judge, cannot also have been the official who suspended the sentence. Furthermore, provincial governors did not have the authority to grant amnesty; that right is documented only for the emperor. It is true that releasing a prisoner who had not yet been sentenced (*abolitio* or *venia*) would not have been illegal (cf. Josephus, *Ant.* 17.295), but it appears in none of the sources as a custom associated with the Passover festival (Mark 15:6, 8). On the other hand, it is unlikely that the name of Barabbas was a pure invention, even though the scene serves the purpose running through the entire narrative of making the Jews look bad and Pilate look good. It is a safe assumption, therefore, that Barabbas was imprisoned and that he was released on the same morning on which Jesus was sentenced.[52]

Since the punishment was crucifixion, we can assume that the charge on which Jesus was sentenced was political insurrection or *seditio*. We might narrow the charge to treason (*perduellio*) or to injuring the dignity of the Roman people (*crimen maiestatis populi Romani*), but the sources give us no basis for such distinctions. Now Jesus was certainly no anti-Roman revolutionary along the lines of the Zealots, yet part of the rich tradition associated with the term *Kingdom of God* was God's sole rule in the end-time and his judgment on all previous rule (§4.1). Such a view would imply a relativizing—indeed, a dissolution—of the existing *pax Romana*, even if Jesus did not say anything openly against Rome. Jesus may have removed all political implications connected with the eschatological rule of Israel's God and replaced them with statements about the created order, but the kingdom that he had in mind tacitly ignored Rome's present claims as world ruler. His attitude, therefore, would automatically have been regarded as insubordination toward the emperor and, in political terms, as rebellion against Rome. One can well imagine how the Sadducean aristocracy, which was highly suspicious of Jesus' religious activity but which certainly never expected him to pledge allegiance to Rome, would have described Jesus' message in political terms. If the high priest accused his own fellow countryman of *seditio* before the Roman prefect, Pilate certainly did not need to conduct an extensive investigation in Galilee to find out what those charges meant. When dealing with *seditio* one did not think twice. It was the job of the representative of Roman order to put out the fire immediately. An accusation in this area thus had a good chance of succeeding. It was not necessary to make the more specific charge that Jesus had claimed to be the (anti-Roman) Messiah. Whether he actually did so is a subject that we will take up in our discussion of the inscription on the cross.

The execution of Pilate's sentence, preceded by a scourging (cf. Josephus, *J.W.* 2.305–8), is presented in a major section (Mark 15:16–41 parr.; John 19:1– 3, 16b–37) that consists in part of loosely connected individual scenes and that gives evidence of having evolved gradually. At the same time, it offers a structure that in all probability follows an early outline. This early narrative may have been something like:

1a   But the soldiers led him away into the court [. . .] And they call
    together the entire cohort. And they dress him in a purple robe and
    put on him a woven crown of thorns. And they began to salute him:
    "Hail, King of the Jews!" [v. 19a] And they kneeled and worshipped
    him. And after they had mocked him, they took off the purple robe and
    put on his clothes.

2   And they led him out (of the city) in order to crucify him. And they
    forced a passerby, Simon the Cyrenian, who was coming in from the
    field—(he is) the father of Alexander and Rufus—to carry his cross.

3   And they bring him to the place, Golgatha [vv. 22b–23]. And they
    crucify him. And they divide his clothes, casting lots to see what each
    should take [v. 25]. And the inscription of his charge was written:
    "The King of the Jews." And they crucify two robbers with him, one
    on his right and one on his left [vv. 29–32].

4   And when the sixth hour came, darkness came over the whole land
    until the ninth hour [v. 34–35]. And someone ran and filled a sponge
    with vinegar, put it on a stick and gave it to him to drink [v. 36b]. But
    Jesus cried a loud cry and gave up (his) spirit [vv. 38–39]. But there
    were also women there watching from a distance. Among them was
    Mary Magdalene and Mary, the mother of James the little, and Mary,
    the mother of Joses, and Salome [v. 41].

In the first section (paragraphs 1–3 = Mark 15:16–32) three similarly formed opening sentences delineate a well-structured narrative (vv. 16, 20b, 22). In each case the soldiers are the subjects, while Jesus is the object of their action. In each case the action moves to a different location (into the courtyard, out of the city, to Golgatha). At all three locations there are additional activities. In the first paragraph the soldiers mock Jesus (v. 19a interrupts the action of paying homage to Jesus and also does not fit the motif of mocking).[53] In the second paragraph Simon is forced to carry the crossbeam. In the third paragraph Jesus is crucified, then three additional circumstances follow: the division of his garments, the inscription on the cross, and the crucifixion of the two robbers. (V. 23 is a doublet that parallels v. 36.) The first and third scenes carry approximately the same weight and use the term *King of the Jews* to provide balance. On two occasions (vv. 16, 22) explanations are given for topographical references, presumably for Greek readers and not for the earliest hearers of the passion narratives.

In all probability Mark 15:29–32 was formed in its entirety by Mark. The first scoffers, i.e., the ones who are passing by, are described in typically Markan language (cf. Mark

2:23, 9:30, etc.). The chief priests and scribes appear elsewhere in Mark in 8:31; 10:33; 11:18; 14:1, 43, 53. The two who were crucified with Jesus are carried over from 15:27, and Mark found the first verb for *mock* in 15:20. What is decisive, however, is that the abuses in vv. 29 and 32, both in their sequence and in their themes, come from the hearing before the Sanhedrin as Mark structured the scene. Within the context of the Markan redaction the Roman centurion in Mark 15:39 becomes then the counterpart of the Jewish scoffers.

In Mark 15:27 the soldiers carried out their assignment to crucify Jesus. The second section, 15:33–41 then portrays the hour of Jesus' death. In both vocabulary and substance much has changed from 15:16–32. Jesus, e.g., is not only named; he now appears as the subject of actions. About halfway through the section Jesus gives up his life (v. 37). Prior to his death the numinous (not apocalyptic) darkness[54] appears for three hours, which was the later occasion for dividing the text by hours (v. 25 with the doubling in vv. 24a and 34), and someone offers him a drink (v. 36a; cf. John 19:29). After the death, reference is made to the women who witnessed the event (v. 40). Verses 34, 36b (=Ps 22:2) are in tension with v. 37 and are probably a pre-Markan addition to which then v. 35 was added somewhat awkwardly. The tearing of the temple curtain (v. 38) interrupts the scene in terms of the unity of its location and is typical of Mark (11:15–19; 14:58; 15:29) as is the added explanation about the women (v. 41: Galilee!) who were probably four in number rather than three. A decision about the statement of the centurion is more difficult. It has no certain place either here or in 15:44–45. The statement also sounds less like an acclamation ("Truly, this man is God's Son!") than like a reflection ("Truly, this man was a son of God."). For Mark's christology it is less specific and therefore is probably a pre-Markan addition that is not related to the motif of the King of the Jews.

This analysis of the early form of the text is supported by the Johannine text. It is especially noteworthy that John offers no parallels to those elements in Mark 15:29–32, 38, 39, 41 that we have recognized as later additions. It is likely that John omitted Simon's carrying the cross and the darkness of three-hours' duration (Mark 15:21, 33). The Jesus who acts in the Johannine passion narrative in such a sovereign manner does not need help from another human being, and it is difficult to imagine the victorious "It is finished" (John 19:30) being spoken in darkness (cf. 12:35). The darkness is much more appropriate for Judas (13:30).

The text's orientation is consistently focused on the meaning that Jesus had for the church. It is mentioned only once in passing (Mark 15:27) that three persons are crucified. It is probable, therefore, that Pilate had sentenced three defendants in the same court session and that the three of them went directly from the courtroom to Golgatha. All three of them suffer the same fate, but the narrator is interested in only one of the three. Once again the typology of the suffering righteous person determines the character of the narrative (cf. by way of example Mark 15:24 with Ps 22:19, Mark 15:36a with Ps 69:22, and Mark 15:40 with Ps 38:12). The theological perspective involved is so important that neither is the dying Jesus portrayed in heroic terms nor are his sufferings described in detail (contrary to a work like 4 Macc).

As was the case in the scene before Pilate, the catchword *King of the Jews* is added to the motifs of the suffering righteous. How are we to understand this connection? The answer must begin with the recognition that the inscription on the cross is the core of the King of the Jews tradition. There was no established custom of hanging a poster from the neck of a condemned person identifying the charges or, in the case of a crucifixion, nailing such a poster to the cross. Not only is the evidence for such a practice not solid; it is geographically and temporally removed from our event.[55] Should we then conclude that the title was a later narrative invention of the Christians designed to communicate the idea of Jesus' (eschatological) kingship? How then would the narrator have come up with such an unusual connection? There is, e.g., no evidence of a prediction that could have inspired such a thought. If we deny its historicity because it is so unusual, we simply shift the difficulty of explaining it to another level. We can just as easily argue that it preserves a historical recollection about Jesus precisely because such inscriptions were not normal. Such an argument would be valid even for the inscription's content.

If we assume its historicity, the inscription makes sense. In the early Christian tradition available to us the expression *King of the Jews* appears frequently in the passion narrative of all the evangelists, yet outside the passion narrative it appears only in Matt 2:2. Nowhere in the early Christian christology is there any indication that the term in any way was a creative factor in a christological concept. It is the term that a non-Jew would have used to describe a Jewish pretender for a position of authority. (Jews would have said: *King of Israel*.) Tacitus (*Hist.* 5.9) is instructive: "After Herod's death a certain Simon claimed . . . the title of king. He was punished . . . by Quintilius Varus." We must assume that the punishment was crucifixion. (For a parallel see, e.g., Josephus, *Ant.* 20.102.) In the Roman emperor's sphere of influence anyone who lets it be known that he claims power is an enemy of the emperor.

This Roman view is identical with the Jewish understanding. Josephus (*Ant.* 17.285) gives a number of examples of anti-Roman revolutionary groups in Early Judaism that referred to their leader as *king* (cf. above, §4.4.1). Clearly there was also in Judaism the conceptual context in which hostility toward Rome and the leadership of a group by a king who contested Rome's rule of the Jews went hand in hand. Given this agreement between Roman and Jewish sources, the designation of Jesus as king of the Jews is appropriate, if we assume that Jesus stood accused of political activity against Rome. There is no reason to assume in addition hidden messianic connotations for the title, since even the anti-Roman revolutionaries hardly had messianic ambitions (cf. §4.4.1), and for Pilate the title would more than likely have evoked a shrug of the shoulders. It was the rebellion against Rome that interested him. It did not matter to him how it described itself.

Once we have understood the title this way, it is easy to understand why Christian narrators later used this motif as the basis for the entire passion narrative. They could use it to show how in a deeper, theological sense Jesus really was the king of Israel. Furthermore, would it not have been dangerous and counterproductive for the Christians in their desire to put Pilate in a good light and to describe his relationship to Jesus as relatively intact to invent the fiction that the Romans had crucified Jesus on a charge that for Roman ears would have sounded so dangerous, viz., that Jesus was a royal competitor of the Roman emperor? Would it not make more sense to regard the title as (unfortunately for the early Christians) a historical fact that then forced the Christians to work intensively to minimize its danger by, e.g., putting a statement about Jesus' innocence in Pilate's mouth? The arguments for the historicity of the inscription on the cross are much more compelling than are the arguments against. This judgment is compatible with our earlier rejection (§6.1) of the view that Jesus was arrested because of his action and words against the temple. The inscription on the cross points to a political negation of Roman rule and does not suggest in any way a cultic dimension.

In no other synoptic tradition do so many otherwise unknown names appear: Simon of Cyrene and his two sons, the four women, and a little later Joseph of Arimathea (Mark 15:43). In the case of the women it is probable that after Easter they were part of the Jewish Christian church. Simon is identified as a North African and thus as a Hellenistic Jew. Since his sons were expressly named to identify their father, even though they were not involved in carrying the cross, they would have been well-known in the church. It is likely, therefore, that they became Christians soon after Easter. It is less likely that the father was a believer. In the case of Joseph it is stated that he was a Jewish sympathizer, but not a member of the church.[56] Jesus' death is thus well documented. He was the recipient of help and concern, but not necessarily from those from whom one would have expected it. Without exception those who should have been there to help Jesus, the disciples, have completely disappeared. In all probability they felt that they were in danger of meeting the same fate as Jesus, or at least of being seriously punished. Peter's behavior suggests as much, when initially, after the disciples had fled, he dared to follow Jesus, but then denied who he was and disappeared.

Jesus' crucifixion and subsequent death by suffocation and exhaustion are described simply in the gospels. From the passion narrative we cannot even be sure of the external course of events. That it was preceded by scourging appears to have been a frequent practice. Carrying the crossbeam (*patibulum*), which then at the place of execution was attached to a perpendicular post, also is well documented. Beyond that, there are no fixed forms for the cross or for the post or for nailing or fastening one's hands and feet. It is Luke (Luke 24:39), rather than Mark and his passion narrative, who first states that Jesus' feet and hands were nailed (cf. John 20:25, 27; Col 2:14). The legs of the other crucified men are broken and Jesus' side is pierced with a spear only in John's special material (John 19:31–34). That according to Mark 15:44 Pilate is surprised that Jesus has died so quickly reflects the general knowledge that crucified persons take a long time to die. Indeed, it was the length of the torment that made it such a severe punishment. Since it was so gruesome, it was used primarily for slaves and for provincials without Roman citizenship who rebelled against Rome. Josephus states that it is the most wretched of all forms of death (*J.W.* 7.203).

The Romans did not invent crucifixion as a form of execution. They took it over from the Carthaginians in connection with the Punic wars. The Persians also were familiar with it and practiced it. As a possible Jewish punishment it has thus far been documented only once from pre-Maccabean times (11Q xix 64.6–13). Later, however, ca. 90 BCE, Alexander Jannaeus crucified eight hundred Pharisees (Josephus, *J.W.* 1.97–98; *Ant.* 13.380–83)—an act that resulted in severe Jewish protests (4QpNah i 7–8; Josephus, *J.W.* 5.450–51; 7.202). From the time of Roman rule in Palestine (beginning in 63 BCE) we have only evidence that Romans used it against Jewish rebels. In particular, between the death of Herod (4 BCE) and the first revolt against Rome, the Roman governors were quick to use this sanction to restore order. It is probably no accident that the evidence from Josephus[57] indicates that almost always a large number of Jews were crucified simultaneously (an exception is *J.W.* 3.321). On one occasion 2,000 were crucified at one time (*J.W.* 2.75; *Ant.* 17.295). Given the scarcity of evidence, comparisons with Roman policy in other provinces are not reliable.[58]

The location of Jesus' crucifixion is designated as Golgatha (Mark 15:22 parr.; John 19:17), which, probably accurately, was translated as *Place of the Skull* and was in the shape of a free-standing, rounded hill. The place is mentioned only in the New Testament and only as a chance rather than a traditional place of execution. It was north of Jerusalem and in those days, of course (cf. Lev 24:14; Num 15:35), outside the city walls (cf. Mark 15:20b: *led him out*; John 19:17, 20; Heb 13:12). It was not far outside Josephus's so-called *second wall*. These admittedly vague geographical references are thus far in agreement with the present location of the Church of the Holy Sepulcher. Of course, identifying the place of the crucifixion with a nearby tomb and the present Church of the Holy Sepulcher is not without problems, if not actually impossible, since Jerusalem was totally destroyed in 70 CE. Even if prior to that date the Jewish Christian community had known of a local tradition, it would not have survived, since the church fled Jerusalem at the beginning of the war. The entire landscape of the northern part of the city was further altered when under Hadrian the Roman settlement of the *Aelia Capitolina* was built after the Jews had once again been defeated by Rome in the Bar Cochba revolt. Centuries later Eusebius is surprised that the emperor Constantine locates Golgatha at its present traditional site (Eusebius, *Vit. Const.* 3.28). In view of the scarce and general nature of the geographical references, we will have to accept the reality that we can no longer locate the site with anything like reasonable certainty. Of course, other suggestions (such as, e.g., the Mount of Olives) are no more than vague guesses based on ambiguous evidence. They are, therefore, even more improbable.

Usually the corpse of a person crucified by the Romans was left hanging on the instrument of agony, since the Roman soldiers were responsible for, among

356 The Last Days in Jerusalem and Jesus' Crucifixion

other things, ensuring that the corpse was not secretly stolen and buried. In this way the executed person was dishonored even beyond death. An unburied corpse was always a problem for Jews (Deut 21:23; Tob 1:17–18; 2:3–8; Josephus, *J.W.* 3.377–78; 4.360–61).[59] Josephus's comment in *J.W.* 4.317 is relevant: "the Jews are so concerned about the burial of the dead that they even take down those who are condemned and crucified and bury them before sundown." If in spite of this concern burial did not take place and dishonor occurred, the corpses decomposed in plain view and were eaten by the birds.

Jesus did not have to suffer this fate. Joseph of Arimathea was able to get permission from Pilate to take possession of the corpse and to bury it (Mark 15:42–47 parr.; John 19:38–42).[60] Pilate, who as the presiding judge had sole authority in such cases, probably released the corpse because of the Passover festival out of consideration for the religious sensitivities of the Jews. Joseph of Arimathea was also probably most concerned about the sanctity of the Sabbath. He acted as a Jew, therefore, rather than as a (secret) follower of Jesus. It may well have been that the two who were crucified with Jesus are ignored in the text only because of the narrative's interest in Jesus. Given the Jewish feelings about burying the dead (Deut 21:23; Tob 1:17–18; 2:3–8) and the approach of the festival, it would make sense to assume that all three corpses were treated the same way.

According to the description in Mark 15:46, which is plausible, Jesus receives a simple burial involving only what is absolutely essential. He is wrapped in a linen cloth and laid in a nearby tomb that had been carved out of rock with a stone rolled against the opening. The usual washing of the corpse is omitted (cf. Acts 9:37). Spices are not used in the burial (cf. Josephus, *J.W.* 1.673).[61] Matt 27:60, Luke 23:53, and John 19:41 quickly turn the tomb into a previously unused tomb. John even includes an elaborate embalming in the burial (John 19:39–40), which may be intended to be reminiscent of a royal burial (cf. John 12:3).

NOTES

1. Cf. Josephus, *Ant.* 20.97–98; 169–70; *J.W.* 2.261ff.; 7.438ff.
2. Cf. P. Schäfer, *History*, 148–51.
3. Since Matt 23:37–39 par. is equally independent (cf. n. 4), one should not be too quick to look for combinations among the texts.
4. One will remember (§3.2.4, n. 47) that Matt 23:37–39 = Luke 13:34–35, the lament over Jerusalem, cannot be included among the authentic Jesus material.
5. To suggest, as does E. Rau (*Jesus*, 22–23), that the tradition begins with Acts 6:14 is to depend on hypotheses that one can no longer test.
6. Cf. J. Becker, *Evangelium*, 148–49.
7. An observation made once again by W. Reinbold (*Bericht*, 114).

8. If we follow the imperative form from John 2:19, the I-form of the apodosis is original. An advantage of this reading is that it fits with Mark 14:58. Those who postulate the third person for both clauses in the original form of Mark 14:58 have no way of explaining how the second clause was changed in the tradition.

9. Cf. E. P. Sanders, *Judaism*, 77–86.

10. Cf. Sauer, *Rückkehr*, 453.

11. The cursing of the fig tree (Mark 11:13–14, 20–21) does not serve as an analogy.

12. Cf. H. Schwier, *Tempel*, 36–40. The formulation in Mark 13:2 sounds like the advice of Hushai in 2 Sam 17:13: "We shall drag this city into the valley, so that not even a pebble will remain." There is no basis for concluding, however, that the text influenced Mark 13:2.

13. Cf. N. Walter, "Tempelzerstörung," 41–42.

14. It is a methodological error when one finds such a justification in Luke 13:34–35 and then uses it for Mark 13:2. The histories of the two traditions are independent, and they should not be confused (contra E. Rau, *Jesus*, 26).

15. On the current discussion cf. J. Becker, *Evangelium*, 144ff. and W. Reinbold, *Bericht*, 112ff.

16. Mark 11:18 is thoroughly Markan. Cf. Mark 1:22; 6:2; 3:6; 12:12; 14:1–2.

17. Thus, e.g., M. Trautmann, *Handlungen*, 108, and many others. Given this assumption, the interpretations of H. Merklein ("Jesus," 148) and Th. Söding ("Tempelaktion," 59–62) are especially impressive.

18. Cf. J. Becker, *Evangelium*, 147; H. Schwier, *Tempel*, 55–74.

19. Then whoever added Mark 11:16 expanded the scope of 11:15 to say that the temple area should not be used as a shortcut when transporting objects between the western quarter of the city and the Mount of Olives. The verse, however, is not unambiguous. Those who see in it a reference to cultic objects will conclude that Jesus was disrupting the cult. Cf. Th. Söding, "Tempelaktion," 46.

20. Cf., e.g., the cleanliness issue with regard to the reception of the Pauline collection in Jerusalem (J. Becker, *Paul*, 455–57).

21. Of course, they describe these conflicts in terms of their own experience of persecution.

22. On the text cf. J. Becker, *Paul*, 460–62.

23. Cf. J. Becker, *Evangelium*, 427ff.

24. These Torah texts were the subject of frequent discussion in Early Judaism and in the rabbinic schools (e.g., 11Q xix 54–56, 64; CD 12:2–3). Cf. A. Strobel, *Stunde*, 83–85.

25. The gospels and other Christian texts cite examples of false prophets misleading the people (Matt 27:63; Luke 23:5; John 7:11–12, 47; Acts 5:37; Justin, *Dial.* 108.1; *T. Lev.* 16:3–4). Of course, these texts simply reveal how later churches pictured Jesus' judgment.

26. O. H. Steck, *Israel*, 40ff.

27. Formal analogies, e.g., are Amos 4:1; Isa 1:10, 23; 1QH ii 31–32; 5:27–28; Matt 3:7 par.

28. Luke 11:49–51 par.; 13:34–35 par. are also the product of the early church. Cf. O. H. Steck, *Israel*, 45–58.

29. Such a view would fit with the view in Early Judaism and Primitive Christianity

that martyrs after their suffering will receive a special reward. Cf., e.g., Wis 3:1–3, 7–10; 2 Macc 7; 4 Macc 6:29; 9:8; 18:10–24; Acts 7:56–59; Rev 6:9–11; 7:9–17; *1 Clem.* 5:7.

30. Cf. the overview given by M.-L. Gubler, *Deutungen*, 206–335.

31. Cf. J. Becker, *Evangelium*, 632ff.

32. Cf. W. Reinbold, *Bericht*, 79ff.

33. Note the brief comment of Tacitus (*Annals*, 15.44.3), who confirms that Pontius Pilate was Jesus' judge.

34. Cf. the interpretation of the texts in J. Becker, *Evangelium*. W. Reinbold (*Bericht*, 87ff.) judges differently; he does not give enough weight to the agreements among the texts.

35. On the discussion cf. W. Reinbold, *Bericht*, 97ff.

36. This last concern also dominates Luke's presentation, which describes Paul in terms of the tension between Jerusalem and Rome (cf. J. Becker, *Paul*, 451–53).

37. Judas's kiss is in all probability the result of a formulaic description (cf. 2 Sam 20:9; Prov 27:6, etc.).

38. Mark 11:18 is a feeble attempt to come to terms with this problem.

39. Cf. J. Becker, *Paul*, 451–57. Ignatius's statements in his letters about his journey to Rome as the way of martyrdom show the same contrast to Jesus in Gethsemane.

40. On the discussion cf. W. Reinbold, *Bericht*, 139.

41. The claim that the grave of Caiaphas has been found, however, is an error. Cf. E. Peuch, "tombeau."

42. J. Becker, *Evangelium*, 652f.

43. One must keep in mind that the Jewish day began in the evening.

44. Cf. the material in Strobel, *Stunde*, 21ff. and Kh. Müller, "Möglichkeit," 66ff.

45. The following argument contradicts F. Hahn, *Der Prozeß Jesu nach dem Johannesevangelium* (EKK 2. Zürich: Benzinger; Neukirchen: Neukirchener, 1970) 52ff.

46. That Mark 15:1a is a Markan summary of 14:53–65 is clear from the vocabulary. Thus Mark, who produced 14:53b, 55, 64b, does not intend to indicate a second trial.

47. On the location of the hearing cf. the thorough discussion in W. Bösen, 205–13.

48. Th. Mommsen, *Strafrecht*, 229ff.; 142ff.; 340f.; G. Otte, "Prozeß," 1024.

49. In 6 CE Augustus exiled Archelaus to Gaul and added his ethnarchy and Judea, Samaria, and Idumea to the Roman province of Syria. In the process Judea achieved the status of an imperial province, third class.

50. We cannot avoid this conclusion by claiming that Pilate was free not to believe Jesus' confession (thus G. Otte, "Prozeß," 1025). For one thing, the text nowhere suggests that Pilate doubted Jesus; for another, the narrative expects the reader as a matter of course to recognize the truth of Jesus' confession.

51. We need to read with some reservations the negative image of Pilate that Philo even more than others presents (*Legat.* 38–39 §§299–310). To cite this source in a description of Pilate's behavior in the trial of Jesus is methodologically very questionable.

52. If they are historical, the statements about Barabbas in Mark 15:7 are so serious that it is unlikely that he was released. John 18:40 states that Barabbas was a *robber*, which does not necessarily mean that he was a political revolutionary (cf. on the contrary John 10:1, 8). One wonders whether Matthew changed the Markan text because of this problem (Matt 27:16: "a notorious prisoner").

53. Because of John 19:3, however, it is likely that v. 19a is older than Mark.

54. There are also other instances of a miraculous darkness at death of a famous man (J. Gnilka, *Evangelium*, 321).

55. Cf. H.-W. Kuhn, "Kreuzesstrafe," 733ff., but also J. Gnilka, *Jesus*, 305.

56. Matt 27:57 later makes him a disciple; cf. John 19:38.

57. H.-W. Kuhn, *TRE* 19, 714–15; Kh. Müller, *Möglichkeit*, 62–65.

58. H.-W. Kuhn, "Kreuzesstrafe," 682–723.

59. Exceptions are 2 Kgdms 4:10; 2 Macc 5:10.

60. There is absolutely no basis in the sources for the assumption that Jesus only appeared to be dead. Since D. F. Strauss it has been a product of modern fantasy and is an attempt to give a *natural* explanation for Jesus' resurrection.

61. Both the narrative and the reality of the situation require that in Mark 16:2 the women make up for this deficiency.

7

Easter Faith

For the one who dies, death brings an end to toil and pain, while the survivors under ordinary circumstances are left with the task of coming to terms with their loss in such a way that the life that has ended is fixed in their memories. Primitive Christianity reacted differently to the death of Jesus. It refused to engage in the usual kind of mourning, and it did not act with Jesus as Plato's pupils had with Plato, when they believed that it was their task to continue to develop their Platonic inheritance under conditions that Plato's philosophy had laid down. Instead, Primitive Christianity preserved the historical traces of Jesus of Nazareth in the basic assumption that they were making contemporary "the story of one who is alive."[1] From the very beginning Jesus' ongoing influence was identified with the special circumstances associated with the experience of Easter.

Were we to describe this Easter experience in an effort to make it accessible to the modern mind we would have to follow this portrayal of Jesus with a second volume.[2] As desirable as such an undertaking might be from a theological per-spective, for practical reasons we must reserve it for another time. What is essential at this point is to examine how Easter influenced the reception of the Jesus material. The foundation for that reception was laid in the earliest reflection on the Easter event, and it is available to the modern observer in a one-line resurrection formula, which we find in three versions: in the form of a participial declaration about God, in the form of a statement about God's act, and in the form of a firmly attached relative clause. These three expressions of the earliest Easter faith are: "(God), who[3] raised Jesus/him from the dead" (Rom 4:24; 8:11; Gal 1:1, etc.); or: "God raised him from the dead" (Rom 10:9; 1 Cor 6:14; 15:15, etc.); and, finally: "(through Jesus Christ) whom he (=God) raised from the dead" (1 Thess 1:10; Acts 3:15, etc.). There are good reasons for regarding the first form, i.e., the participial expression, as the earliest form of this structured formula.

Linguistically, Israel's tradition was familiar with such participial declarations about God, and Jews who were also Christians would have been able to praise God after Easter with their new creedal assertion as the one who in a unique situation unexpectedly did what only he could have done, viz., save Jesus and thus lay the foundation for their new life. However, from all of the participial constructions in Israel and Early Judaism that describe God's activity, the only one that parallels the content of the Easter formula is the classic statement that

"God brought Israel out of Egypt" (Deut 8:14; Jer 16:14, etc.). With this confessional formula Israel and Early Judaism identify which divine saving act defines Israel for all time as God's people. It is noteworthy that Jesus himself did not formulate any new creedal statements. Nor did the Jewish contemporaries of Jesus and of Primitive Christianity create a new confession. Indeed, it would have been impossible for them to be interested in such a formulation, since Early Judaism justified its existence by appealing to God's previous activity, which had been laid down in the Torah. In this sense the Easter confession of the early Christians is an innovation within Judaism that reveals that they regarded the Easter experience qualitatively as on the same level as God's classical act, the Exodus of Israel from Egypt.

Now when we compare Israel's Exodus formula with the resurrection formula of the primitive church as Jewish Christians formulated it, we must begin with Jer 16:14-15 and 23:7 (cf. also Isa 43:19-20; 48:6; 65:17). Here the prophet proclaims that in a future that is going to be qualitatively different Israel's credo and defining principle will no longer be the Exodus formula; it will instead be a new event of confessional stature that contains a new and foundational act of the God of Israel on behalf of his people. Old Testament prophecy is thus aware of the possibility that its God will create a totally new relationship with Israel by means of an unexpected and fundamental act. When then the primitive church formulates its new confession, it stands within this prophetic tradition and claims that immediately and with finality the basis of its new relationship with God is the event in which God has transformed Jesus' fate into a positive reality.

Jesus had acted to establish the end-time Kingdom of God, and it was as a consequence of that activity that he was executed. When God creatively and unexpectedly overcame this hopeless situation by not leaving Jesus in death, it was clear that Jesus had not died in vain, and it was obvious that the cause for which he had worked was not lost. God's eschatological saving work that had begun with Jesus had not ended. Easter could thus be seen as God's approval of the content of Jesus' work to establish the Kingdom of God, and at the same time it could function as the beginning of the continuing final fulfillment. On the one hand, Jesus was the suffering righteous person on behalf of whom God had intervened. On the other hand, his fate had become part of the final drama that he himself had proclaimed and had already initiated. He was, therefore, not just another righteous person in the course of history; he had a special relationship to the Kingdom of God that was being realized in the end-time. His fate took on eschatological significance. His death and his resurrection at the hands of God thus became the foundational event of the end-time and a beginning that would determine in a decisive way the continuing course of the end-time.

This special character of his fate as an eschatological foundational event fits well with the content of Jesus' message. Jesus had worked to establish the end-time Kingdom of God, which with finality saved the lost and whose aim was to transform a failed relationship with God into an eternally new and saving relationship. In the process Jesus himself became a lost and wretched figure, yet it was precisely this figure that God affirmed in the Easter event. God thus transformed the fate of the lost Jesus by openly and finally acting out in the person of Jesus the image of God that Jesus had espoused. Jesus' fate became the divine stamp of approval on Jesus' understanding of God. The Easter experience thus made the disciples aware that God wanted to be understood as the God who had graciously drawn near to the lost—as the God who now wanted to establish his salvation with finality.

This understanding provided the context for preserving the knowledge of Jesus' words and deeds as a living tradition. The importance of Jesus was not that especially pointed or memorable elements of his teaching were selected and passed on as had been done with Israel's sages whose pronouncements were collected in the sayings of the Fathers (*'Abot*). Nor was he remembered as an example of a way of life to be imitated. While in a limited way he may have served as an example for the Jewish Christian missionaries, in general the figure of Jesus was not preserved as a model to be imitated. Instead, the decisive continuum within which Jesus remained present for the church was his image of God, which represented an entire understanding of reality and which defined his activity and his fate. Within this continuity then—often by means of a reformulation of this basic insight—one could preserve individual sayings of Jesus and limited biographical data from the life of Jesus as a way of making him contemporary.

The essence of the message of Jesus and the sum of what the Easter faith has to offer thus complement each other; they both express God's final relationship to his lost creatures. This insight should also determine the way we appropriate the Jesus material today. Jesus is relevant today, because in a special way he confronted people with the question of God and offered a specific answer to that question.

Of course, the interpretation of the Easter experience did not end with the formulation of this declaration about God. This newly won perspective immediately became the basis for christological reflection on the person of Jesus. There is no early Christian tradition that is not thoroughly characterized by this development. The turbulent and multifaceted evolution of the early Christian christology was a consequence of the fundamental assertion that Jesus' fate was God's *yes* to Jesus' activity on behalf of the Kingdom of God. Christology was thus the way Christian faith explained the special relationship between God and Jesus. It changed the God of the Kingdom of God into the father of Jesus Christ, and it made of Jesus of Nazareth, who initiated the realization of the Kingdom of God, the personification of salvation—i.e., the object of faith. Jesus became the earthly figure who has now been transformed into the exalted Christ.

We can no more take the time to trace the intricate path of early Christian christology than we can describe and interpret the Easter events. We must remember, however, that the synoptic tradition was thoroughly conditioned by this process of christological reflection (cf. Chapter 1). This reflection was based on the conviction that the new faith understanding that came with Easter opened one's eyes for a deeper insight into Jesus' activity, which made it possible to understand the phenomenon of Jesus accurately and completely.

Interpreting a historical figure in retrospect this way is not a hermeneutical anomaly; it is the way people always appropriate the history that has preceded them. Contemporaries may experience history with more immediacy than do those who come later. They may be more familiar with and do a better job of experiencing the complexity of history's details. However, those who live later are not necessarily at a disadvantage, because they know what the contemporaries cannot know, viz., how history has progressed. As a result they are in a better position to evaluate the significance of what has happened and to distinguish between what is important and what is not important. Knowing history is never merely a matter of accumulating pure facts; it involves understanding history. That Goethe is the essence of German classicism and is (thus far) the greatest German poet is something we know in retrospect. Coming from his contemporaries such a judgment would have sounded presumptuous. Similarly, we cannot simply dismiss the christological form in which the Jesus material comes to us as a distortion of history, even though the historian must analyze and form judgments about the process in which the material took shape. For this reason in the preceding chapters we have described Jesus as much as possible without the later christological interpretation. Examining the history of the early Christian effort to solve the christological problem posed by Easter and thus by implication to interpret Jesus of Nazareth is a separate task. It must not be approached negatively, however, in the assumption that christology is a perversion of the so-called simple teaching of Jesus. On the contrary, when we examine the earliest Easter confessional formula alongside its subsequent christological development, we will understand that the God of the Kingdom of God and the father of Jesus Christ are one and the same.

NOTES

1.   This is the striking subtitle [in German] of E. Schillebeeckx's *Jesus*.

2.   Cf. J. Becker, *Epoche*, 29ff.

3.   We can translate the Greek or Semitic participle into German or English only as a relative clause.

General Bibliography

The following bibliography lists the works that I have consulted frequently. Those works that deal with special themes are cited at the beginning of each section. When articles from collected works and festschrifts are involved, I cite the entire work here, under the name of the editor, and then list the article at the beginning of the relevant section. The literature is cited in abbreviated form in the notes.

I have not tried to collect all of the literature. Instead, I have tried to strike a balance between a totally representative and a completely subjective selection, opting for a more narrow choice. Thus I have listed only the commentaries from which I quoted. In dealing with synoptic texts, however, I always consulted the commentaries in the series *Evangelisch-katholischer Kommentar zum Neuen Testament, Herders theologischer Kommentar zum Neuen Testament, Kritisch-exegetischer Kommentar über das Neue Testament (Meyer), Ökumenischer Taschenbuch Kommentar,* and *Theologischer Handkommentar zum Neuen Testament.* Finally, I was able to use only the literature that was available to me through 1994.

The abbreviations follow the usual custom and for the most part conform to S. Schwertner, *Internationales Abkürzungsverzeichnis für Theologie und Grenzgebiete* (2d ed. Berlin/New York: de Gruyter, 1992). Where they differ from IATG², their identification will be clear.

Anderson, Ch. C. *Critical Quests of Jesus.* Grand Rapids, MI: Eerdmans, 1969.

Baumbach, G. *Jesus von Nazareth im Lichte der jüdischen Gruppenbildung.* Berlin: Evangelische Verlagsanstalt, 1971.

Beasley-Murray, G. R. *Jesus and the Kingdom of God.* Grand Rapids, MI: Eerdmans, 1986.

Becker, J. *Annäherungen.* U. Mell, ed. BZNW 76. Berlin: de Gruyter, 1995.

———. *Paul: Apostle to the Gentiles.* Louisville, KY: Westminster/John Knox, 1993.

———. *Das Urchristentum als gegliederte Epoche.* SBS 155. Stuttgart: KBW, 1993.

———. *Das Evangelium nach Johannes.* ÖTK 4/1 and 4/2. 3d ed. Gütersloh: Mohn, 1991.

———. *Auferstehung der Toten im Urchristentum.* SBS 82. Stuttgart: KBW, 1976.

———. *Johannes der Täufer und Jesus von Nazareth.* BSt 63. Neukirchen-Vluyn: Neukirchener Verlag, 1972.

Ben-Chorin, Sch. *Bruder Jesus.* Munich: Paul List, 1977.

Berger, K. "Jesus als Pharisäer und frühe Christen als Pharisäer," *NT* 30 (1988) 231–62.

———. *Formgeschichte des Neuen Testaments*. Heidelberg: Quelle und Mayer, 1984.

———. *Die Gesetzesauslegung Jesu. Teil I*. WMANT 40. Neukirchen-Vluyn: Neukirchener Verlag, 1972.

———. *Die Amen-Worte Jesu*. BZNW 39. Berlin: de Gruyter, 1970.

Billerbeck, P. and H. L. Strack. *Kommentar zum Neuen Testament aus Talmud und Midrasch*. 4 vols. 2d ed. Munich: C. H. Beck'sche Verlagsbuchhandlung, 1956.

Blank, J. "Frauen in den Jesusüberlieferung," in: *Die Frau im Urchristentum*. G. Dautzenberg et al., eds. QD 95. Freiburg/Basel/Vienna: Herder, 1983, 9–91.

———. *Jesus von Nazareth*. 2d ed. Freiburg/Basel/Vienna: Herder, 1973.

Blinzler, J. *The Trial of Jesus*. Westminster, MD: Neuman, 1959.

Bornkamm, G. *Jesus of Nazareth*. New York: Harper & Row, 1960.

Bousset, W. and H. Gressmann. *Die Religion des Judentums im späthellenistischen Zeitalter*. HNT 21. 4th ed. Tübingen: J.C.B. Mohr (Paul Siebeck), 1966.

Bovon, F. *Das Evangelium nach Lukas*. EKK III/1. Zurich/Einsiedeln/Cologne: Benziger Verlag. Neukirchen-Vluyn: Neukirchener Verlag, 1989.

Brandenburger, E. *Markus 13 und die Apokalyptik*. FRLANT 134. Göttingen: Vandenhoeck & Ruprecht, 1984.

Braun, H. *Jesus of Nazareth: The Man and His Time*. Philadelphia: Fortress, 1979.

Bruce, F. F. *Dies ist eine harte Rede*. Wuppertal: Breckhaus, 1985.

———. *The Hard Sayings of Jesus*. Downers Grove, IL: InterVarsity, 1983.

Bultmann, R. *The History of the Synoptic Tradition*. 2d ed. New York: Harper & Row, 1968.

———. *Jesus and the Word*. New York: Scribners, 1958.

———. *Theology of the New Testament*. 2 vols. London: SCM, 1952.

Burchard, Chr. "Jesus," in: *KP*. Stuttgart: Alfred Druckenmuller, 1967, 2.1344–54.

Charles, R. H. *The Apocrypha and Pseudepigrapha of the Old Testament in English*. 2 vols. Oxford: Clarendon, 1913.

Charlesworth, J. H. (ed.) *Jesus and the Dead Sea Scrolls*. New York: Doubleday, 1992.

———. (ed.) *The Messiah*. Minneapolis: Fortress, 1992.

———. *Jesus within Judaism*. New York: Doubleday, 1988.

———. *The Old Testament Pseudepigrapha and the New Testament*. SNTS MS 54. Cambridge: Cambridge University Press, 1985.

———. (ed.) *The Old Testament Pseudepigrapha*. 2 vols. Garden City, NY: Doubleday, 1983, 1985.

———. "The Historical Jesus in Light of Writings Contemporaneous with Him," in: *ANRW*. W. Haase and H. Temporini, eds. Berlin/New York: de Gruyter, 1982, II 25.1, 451–76.

Conzelmann, H. "Jesus Christus," in: *Religion in Geschichte und Gegenwart* Volume 3. 3rd ed. Tübingen: J.C.B. Mohr (Paul Siebeck), 1959, 619–53.

Crossan, J. D. *The Historical Jesus: The Life of a Mediterranean Jewish Peasant*. San Francisco: Harper, 1991.

———. *In Fragments: The Aphorisms of Jesus*. San Francisco: Harper & Row, 1983.

Dalman, G. *Die Worte Jesu*. 2d ed. Leipzig: J. C. Hinrichs, 1930. Reprinted Darmstadt: Wissenschaftliche Buchgesellschaft, 1965.

Dibelius, M. *Jesus*. SG 1130. 2d ed. Berlin: de Gruyter, 1949.

Dodd, C. H. *The Founder of Christianity*. New York: Macmillan, 1970.

Donner, H. *Aufsätze zum Alten Testament*. BZAW 224. Berlin: de Gruyter, 1994.

Ebertz, M. N. *Das Charisma des Gekreuzigten.* WUNT 45. Tübingen: J.C.B. Mohr (Paul Siebeck), 1987.

Edwards, R. A. *A Theology of Q: Eschatology, Prophecy, and Wisdom.* Philadelphia: Fortress, 1976.

Elbogen, J. *Der jüdische Gottesdienst in seiner geschichtlichen Entwicklung.* 4th ed. Hildesheim: Georg Olms Verlagsbuchhandlung, 1962.

Evans, C. A. *Life of Jesus Research: An Annotated Bibliography.* NTTS 13. Leiden: Brill, 1989.

Falk, H. *Jesus the Pharisee.* New York: Paulist, 1985.

Farmer, W. R. *Jesus and the Gospel.* Philadelphia: Fortress, 1982.

Fiedler, P. *Jesus und die Sünder.* BET 3. Frankfurt: Peter Lang, 1976.

Flusser, D. *Jesus.* New York: Herder & Herder, 1969.

Fuchs, E. *Zur Frage nach dem Historischen Jesus.* Gesammelte Aufsätze 2. Tübingen: J.C.B. Mohr (Paul Siebeck), 1960.

Gemünden, P. von. *Vegetationsmetaphorik im Neuen Testament und seiner Umwelt.* NTOA 18. Göttingen: Vandenhoeck & Ruprecht, 1993.

Gnilka, J. Jesus von Nazareth: Botschaft und Geschichte. Rev. ed. HThK Supplementband 3. Freiburg/Basel/Vienna: Herder, 1993).

———. *Das Evangelium nach Markus.* EKK II/1, 2. 2d ed. Zurich/Einsiedeln/Cologne: Benziger Verlag; Neukirchen-Vluyn: Neukirchener Verlag, 1986.

Goppelt, L. *Theology of the New Testament* Volume I. Grand Rapids, MI: Eerdmans, 1981.

Grant, M. *Jesus: An Historian's Review of the Gospels.* New York: Scribners, 1981.

Grässer, E. Das Problem der Parusieverzögerung in den synoptischen Evangelien und in der Apostelgeschichte. BZNW 22. 3rd ed. Berlin: Alfred Töpelmann, 1977.

———. *Die Naherwartung Jesu.* SBS 61. Stuttgart: KBW, 1973.

Grimm, W. *Weil ich dich liebe.* ANTJ 1. Frankfurt: Peter Lang, 1976.

Grundmann, W. *Das Evangelium nach Lukas.* ThHNT 3. 10th ed. Berlin: Evangelische Verlagsanstalt, 1984.

———. *Das Evangelium nach Matthäus.* ThHNT 1. 6th ed. Berlin: Evangelische Verlagsanstalt, 1986.

Haenchen, E. *Der Weg Jesu.* 2d ed. Berlin: Töpelmann, 1968.

Hahn, F. *The Titles of Jesus in Christology.* London: Lutterworth, 1969.

Harnisch, W. *Die Gleichniserzählungen Jesu.* UTB 1343 2d ed. Göttingen: Vandenhoeck & Ruprecht, 1990.

Heiligenthal, R. *Der Lebensweg Jesu von Nazareth.* Stuttgart: Kohlhammer, 1994.

Hengel, M. *Judaism and Hellenism: Studies in Their Encounter in Palestine during the Early Hellenistic Period.* Philadelphia: Fortress, 1974.

———. *Nachfolge und Charisma: Eine exegetisch-religionsgeschichtliche Studie zu Mt 8,21f. und Jesu Ruf in die Nachfolge.* BZNW 34. Berlin: Töpelmann, 1968.

Hengel, M. and A. M. Schwemer. (eds.) *Königsherrschaft Gottes und himmlischer Kult im Judentum, im Urchristentum und in der hellenistischen Welt.* WUNT 55. Tübingen: J.C.B. Mohr (Paul Siebeck), 1991.

Hiers, R. H. *The Historical Jesus and the Kingdom of God: Present and Future in the Message and Ministry of Jesus.* Gainesville, FL: University of Florida Press, 1973.

Hoffmann, P. *Studien zur Frühgeschichte der Jesus-Bewegung.* SBAB 17. Stuttgart: KBW, 1994.

————. *Studien zur Theologie der Logienquelle*. NTA NF 8. 3d ed. Münster: Aschendorf, 1981.

Horn, F. W. *Glaube und Handeln in der Theologie des Lukas*. GTA 26. 2d ed. Göttingen: Vandenhoeck & Ruprecht, 1986.

Hurt, E. *Von der Evangelienparaphrase zum historischen Jesusroman*. EHS 1/1377. Frankfurt/Bern: Lang, 1993.

Jeremias, G. *Der Lehrer der Gerechtigkeit*. StUNT 2. Göttingen: Vandenhoeck & Ruprecht, 1963.

Jeremias, J. *New Testament Theology. Part One: The Proclamation of Jesus*. London: SCM; New York: Scribners, 1971.

————. *Jerusalem in the Time of Jesus*. Philadelphia: Fortress, 1969.

————. *The Prayers of Jesus*. SBT Second Series 6. Naperville, IL: Allenson, 1967.

————. *The Parables of Jesus*. Rev. ed. New York: Scribners, 1963.

————. *The Eucharistic Words of Jesus*. Oxford: Blackwell, 1955.

Jülicher, A. *Die Gleichnisreden Jesu*. 2 vols. Tübingen: J.C.B. Mohr (Paul Siebeck), 1888, 1889 (2d ed. of vol. 2, 1910). Reprinted, Darmstadt: Wissenschaftliche Buchgesellschaft, 1976.

Jüngel, E. *Paulus und Jesus*. HUTh 2. 4th ed. Tübingen: J.C.B. Mohr (Paul Siebeck), 1972.

Käsemann, E. *New Testament Questions of Today*. London: SCM, 1969.

————. *Essays on New Testament Themes*. SBT 41. London: SCM, 1964.

Kautzsch, E. (ed.) *Die Apokryphen und Pseudepigraphen des Alten Testaments*. 2 vols. Tübingen: J.C.B. Mohr (Paul Siebeck), 1900.

Kertelge, K. (ed.) *Das Gesetz im Neuen Testament*. QD 108. Freiburg/Basel/Vienna: Herder, 1986.

Klausner, J. *Jesus of Nazareth*. New York: Macmillan, 1925; Boston: Beacon, 1964.

Kloppenborg, J. S. *Q Parallels: Synopsis, Critical Notes, and Concordance*. Sonoma, CA: Polebridge, 1988.

————. *The Formation of Q: Trajectories in Ancient Wisdom Collections*. Philadelphia: Fortress, 1987.

Kraft, R. A. and W. E. Nickelsburg (eds.) *Early Judaism and Its Modern Interpreters*. Atlanta: Scholars Press, 1986.

Küchler, M. *Frühjüdische Weisheitstraditionen*. OBO 26. Göttingen: Vandenhoeck & Ruprecht, 1979.

Kümmel, W. G. *Vierzig Jahre Jesusforschung (1950–1990)*. 2d ed. Weinheim: Betz Altenäum, 1994.

Kümmel, W. G. P. Feine and J. Behm. *The Theology of the New Testament According to its Major Witnesses: Jesus–Paul–John*. New York/Nashville: Abingdon, 1973.

————. *Introduction to the New Testament*. New York/ Nashville: Abingdon, 1966.

Kuschel, K.-J. *Jesus in der deutschsprachigen Gegenwartsliteratur*. ÖTh 1. 3d ed. Gütersloh: Mohn, 1980.

Lapide, P. *Jesus—ein gekreuzigter Pharisäer?* GTB 1427. 2d ed. Gütersloh: Mohn, 1991.

————. *Wer war schuld am Tod Jesu?* GTB 1419. 2d ed. Gütersloh: Mohn, 1989.

————. *Ist das nicht Josephs Sohn?* GTB 1408. 3d ed. Gütersloh: Mohn, 1988.

Leroy, H. *Jesus*. EdF 95. 2d ed. Darmstadt: Wissenschaftliche Buchgesellschaft, 1989.

Lichtenberger, H. *Studien zum Menschenbild in Texten der Qumrangemeinde*. StUNT 15. Göttingen: Vandenhoeck & Ruprecht, 1980.

Lindeskog, G. *Die Jesusfrage im neuzeitlichen Judentum.* Darmstadt: Wissenschaftliche Buchgesellschaft, 1973.

Lüdemann, G. *Paul, Apostle to the Gentiles: Studies in Chronology.* Philadelphia: Fortress, 1984.

Lührmann, D. *Das Markusevangelium.* HNT 3. Tübingen: J.C.B. Mohr (Paul Siebeck), 1987.

————. *Die Redaktion der Logienquelle.* WMANT 33. Neukirchen-Vluyn: Neukirchener Verlag, 1969.

Lundström, G. *The Kingdom of God in the Teaching of Jesus: A History of Interpretation from the Last Decades of the Nineteenth Century to the Present Day.* Edinburgh/London: Oliver and Boyd, 1963.

Luz, U. *Matthew 1–7: A Commentary.* Minneapolis: Augsburg, 1989. On the rest of Matthew cf. *Das Evangelium nach Matthäus.* EKK I/2. Zurich/Einsiedeln/Cologne: Benziger Verlag; Neukirchen-Vluyn: Neukirchener Verlag, 1990.

Maier, J. *Geschichte der jüdischen Religion.* Herder Spektrum 4116. Freiburg: Herder, 1992.

————. *Das Judentum.* 2d ed. Munich: Kindler, 1988.

————. *Jesus von Nazareth in der talmudischen Überlieferung.* EdF 82. Darmstadt: Wissenschaftliche Buchgesellschaft, 1978.

Manson, T. W. *The Servant-Messiah.* Cambridge: Cambridge University Press, 1980.

————. *The Sayings of Jesus.* London: SCM, 1949.

Meier, J. P. *A Marginal Jew: Rethinking the Historical Jesus.* 2 vols. New York: Doubleday, 1991, 1994.

Mell, U. *Die "anderen" Winzer.* WUNT 77. Tübingen: J.C.B. Mohr (Paul Siebeck), 1994.

————. *Neue Schöpfung.* BZNW 56. Berlin: de Gruyter, 1989.

Merklein, H. *Jesu Botschaft von der Gottesherrschaft.* SBS 111. Stuttgart: KBW, 1989.

————. "Jesus, Künder des Reiches Gottes," in: idem, *Studien zu Jesus und Paulus.* WUNT 43. Tübingen: J.C.B. Mohr (Paul Siebeck), 1987, 127–56.

————. *Die Gottesherrschaft als Handlungsprinzip.* fzb 34. 3d ed. Würzburg: Echter Verlag, 1984.

Morgenthaler, R. *Statistische Synopse.* Stuttgart: Gotthelf, 1971.

Neusner, J. *Judaism in the Beginning of Christianity.* Philadelphia: Fortress, 1984.

————. *Das pharisäische und talmudische Judentum.* Tübingen: J.C.B. Mohr (Paul Siebeck), 1984.

————. *First Century Judaism in Crisis.* Nashville/New York: Abingdon, 1975.

Percy, E. *Die Botschaft Jesu.* Lund: C.W.K. Gleerup, 1953.

Perrin, N. *Rediscovering the Teaching of Jesus.* New York: Harper & Row; London: SCM, 1967.

————. *The Kingdom of God in the Teaching of Jesus.* Philadelphia: Westminster; London: SCM, 1963.

Pesch, R. *Das Markusevangelium.* 2 vols. HThK 2/1, 2. Freiburg/Basel/Vienna: Herder, 1989 (5th ed.), 1991 (2d ed.).

————. "Christliche und jüdische Jesusforschung," in: *Symposion: Jesus in den Evangelien.* SBS 45. Stuttgart: KBW, 1970, 10–37.

Pokorný, P. *The Genesis of Christology.* Edinburgh: T. & T. Clark, 1987.

Polag, A. *Die Christologie der Logienquelle.* WMANT 45. Neukirchen-Vluyn: Neukirchener Verlag, 1977.

Rau, E. *Von Jesus zu Paulus*. Stuttgart: Kohlhammer, 1994.

Reinbold, W. *Der älteste Bericht über den Tod Jesu*. BZNW 69. Berlin: de Gruyter, 1994.

Reiser, M. *Die Gerichtspredigt Jesu*. NTA NF 23. Münster: Aschendorff, 1990.

Riches, J. *Jesus and the Transformation of Judaism*. London: Darton, Longman & Todd, 1980.

Riessler, P. *Altjüdisches Schrifttum außerhalb der Bibel*. Freiburg/Heidelberg: F. U. Kerle, 1928.

Roloff, J. *Das Kerygma und der irdische Jesus*. 2d ed. Göttingen: Vandenhoeck & Ruprecht, 1973.

Sanders, E. P. *The Historical Figure of Jesus*. London: SCM, 1993.

———. *Jesus and Judaism*. 3d ed. Philadelphia: Fortress, 1991.

Sandmel, S. *We Jews and Jesus*. New York: Oxford University Press, 1965.

Sato, M. *Q und Prophetie: Studien zur Gattungs- und Traditionsgeschichte der Quelle Q*. WUNT 2/29. Tübingen: J.C.B. Mohr (Paul Siebeck), 1988.

Sauer, J. *Rückkehr und Vollendung des Heils*. Theorie und Forschung 133. Regensburg: Roderer, 1991.

Schäfer, P. *The History of the Jews in Antiquity: The Jews of Palestine from Alexander the Great to the Arab Conquest*. Australia–United States: Harwood Academic Publishers, 1995.

Schenke, L. *Die Urgemeinde*. Stuttgart: Kohlhammer, 1990.

Schillebeeckx, E. *Jesus: An Experiment in Christology*. New York: Seabury, 1979.

Schlosser, J. *Le Régne de Dieu dans les Dits de Jesus*. 2 vols. Paris: Gabalda, 1980.

Schmeller, T. *Brechungen*. SBS 136. Stuttgart: KBW, 1989.

Schmidt, K. L. *Der Rahmen der Geschichte Jesu*. Berlin: Trowitzsch & Sohn, 1919. Repr. 1964.

Schmidt, W.-R. *Der Mann aus Galiläa*. GTB 1426. 2d. ed. Gütersloh: Mohn, 1991.

Schnackenburg, R. *God's Rule and Kingdom*. New York: Herder & Herder, 1963.

Schneemelcher, W. (ed.) *New Testament Apocrypha*. 2 vols. Rev. ed. R. Mcl. Wilson, Engl. ed. Cambridge: James Clarke; Louisville, Ky.: Westminster/John Knox, 1991, 1992.

Schneider, G. *Das Evangelium nach Lukas*. 2 vols. ÖTK 3/1, 2. 2d ed. Gütersloh: Mohn, 1984.

Schottroff, L. and W. Stegemann. *Jesus and the Hope of the Poor*. Maryknoll, NY: Orbis, 1986.

Schürer, E. *The History of the Jewish People in the Age of Jesus Christ*. 3 vols. Rev. ed. G. Vermes, F. Millar, and M. Black, eds. vols 1, 2. G. Vermes, F. Millar, M. Goodman, eds. vol 3. Edinburgh: T & T Clark, 1973, 1979, 1986.

Schürmann, H. *Jesus, Gestalt und Geheimnis: Gesammelte Beiträge*. K. Scholtissek, ed. Paderborn: Bonifatius, 1994.

———. *Reich Gottes—Jesu Geschick*. Freiburg: Herder, 1983.

———. *Das Lukasevangelium*. HThK 3. Freiburg/Basel/Vienna: Herder, 1969.

Schweitzer, A. *The Quest of the Historical Jesus*. New York: Macmillan, 1910. Repr. 1968. Original German: *Von Reimarus zu Wrede*. Tübingen: J.C.B. Mohr (Paul Siebeck), 1906. Since 1913 it has born the title *Geschichte der Leben-Jesu-Forschung*.

Steck, O. H. *Israel und das gewaltsame Geschick der Propheten*. WMANT 23. Neukirchen-Vluyn: Neukirchener Verlag, 1967.

Stegemann, H. *Die Essener, Qumran, Johannes der Täufer und Jesus.* Herder Spektrum 4249. Freiburg: Herder, 1993.

―――. "Der lehrende Jesus," *NZSTh* 24 (1982) 3–20.

Stein, R. H. *Difficult Sayings in the Gospels.* Grand Rapids, MI: Baker Book House, 1985.

Steinhauser, M. G. *Doppelbildworte in den synoptischen Evangelien.* FzB 44. Stuttgart: KBW, 1982.

Stemberger, G. *Geschichte der jüdischen Literatur.* Munich: C. H. Beck'sche Verlagsanstalt, 1977.

Strobel, A. *Wer war Jesus? Wer ist Jesus?* CwH 127. Stuttgart: Calwer Verlag, 1973.

Strotmann, A. *"Mein Vater bist Du."* FTS 39. Frankfurt: Josef Knecht, 1991.

Stuhlmacher, P. *Biblische Theologie des Neuen Testaments* Volume I. Stuttgart: Kohlhammer, 1992.

Theissen, G. *Social Reality and the Early Christians: Theology, Ethics and the World of the New Testament.* Minneapolis: Fortress, 1992.

―――. *The Gospels in Context: Social and Political History in the Synoptic Tradition.* Minneapolis: Fortress, 1991.

―――. *Sociology of Early Palestinian Christianity.* Philadelphia: Fortress, 1978.

Trautmann, M. *Zeichenhafte Handlungen Jesu.* fzb 37. Würzburg: Echter Verlag, 1980.

Trepp, L. *Der jüdische Gottesdienst.* Stuttgart: Kohlhammer, 1992.

Trilling, W. *Die Botschaft Jesu.* Freiburg: Herder, 1978.

Uhlig, S. *Das äthiopische Henochbuch.* ISHRZ V 6. Gütersloh: Mohn, 1984.

Vermes, G. *Jesus and the World of Judaism.* Philadelphia: Fortress, 1984.

―――. *Jesus the Jew: A Historian's Reading of the Gospels.* New York: Macmillan, 1974.

Vögtle, A. "Jesus von Nazareth," in: *Ökumenische Kirchengeschichte.* Volume 1. R. Kottje and B. Möller, eds. Munich: Kaiser, 1970, 3–24.

Vouga, F. *Geschichte des frühen Christentums.* UTB 1733. Tübingen/Basel: Franke, 1994.

Weder, H. *Die Gleichnisse Jesu als Metaphern.* FRLANT 120. 3d ed. Göttingen: Vandenhoeck & Ruprecht, 1984.

Weiser, A. *Die Knechtsgleichnisse der synoptischen Evangelien.* StANT 29. Munich: Kösel, 1971.

Wendland, H.-D. *Die Eschatologie des Reiches Gottes bei Jesus.* Gütersloh: C. Bertelsmann, 1931.

Wilson, E. *The Dead Sea Scrolls 1947–1969.* New York: Oxford University Press, 1969.

Witherington, B. *Women in the Ministry of Jesus.* MSSNTS 51. Cambridge: Cambridge University Press, 1984.

Yadin, Y. *The Temple Scroll.* Jerusalem: Israel Exploration Society, 1983.

Zeller, D. *Die weisheitlichen Mahnsprüche bei den Synoptikern.* fzb 17. Würzburg: Echter, 1977.

Index of Biblical and Early Jewish Writings

Boldface represents pages on which cited text is quoted.

Name and Subject Index

Sepphoris, 25
Septuagint, 202
Septuagint texts, 21–22
Sermon on the Mount, 5–6, 11, 226, 288
Sermon on the Plain, 5–6
Shem, 97
Sickness, 178–179
Sidon, 65
Simeon ben Yoahi, Rabbi, 249, 267
Similitudes, 148–150
Simon, 98, 353
Simon Magus (Samaritan), 175
Simon of Cyrene, 354
Simon the Pharisee, 249
Sinai Torah, 227, 279–280
Sirach, 227
Sodom, 57, 206
Solomon, 65–66, 92, 99, 126–127, 129
Son-of-David issue, 186–197
Son of Man
  coming of, 47
  Early Judaism and, 46–47, 201, 203
  Jesus and, 196–211
  judgment of Jesus as, 183
  Kingdom of God and, 93–96
  as light of nations, 315
  in Mark, Gospel of, 196–197, 338–339
  Zion tradition and, 190–192
Sons of the bridechamber, 120
Stephen, 200, 305, 335
Stoicism, 175, 256
Strabo, 181
Suetonius, 9
Swearing, prohibition of, 294–296
Synagogue scene, 29–30
Synoptic material (*see also specific gospels*)
  Acts and, 28
  authenticity of, 12–15

evolution of sources of, 9–11
forces at work in receiving and transforming, 11–12
Synoptic tradition, 11–12, 15, 21
Systematic ethics, 226

Table-fellowship
  in Antiquity, 161
  Early Judaism and, 160–161
  end-time and, 120
  in Galilean villages, 21, 130
  between Jewish and Gentile Christians, 305
  Kingdom of God and, 130, 155–169, 286
  public appearance of Jesus and, 21
  salvation and, 285–286
Tacitus, 9, 175, 296–297, 353
Temple cult, 43–44, 88
Temple Scroll, 177
Theudas, 213
Thomas, Gospel of, 9, 143
Tiberias, 25
Titus, 275
Tobiads, 274
Tobit, 40, 337
Torah
  devaluation of cultic, 296–308
  false prophets and, 336
  food laws and, 302–304
  Halacha and, 227
  Jesus' attitude toward, 232, 273
  Jesus' criticism of, 11
  Jesus' interpretation of, 73, 215, 273–280, 279, 334–335
  Kingdom of God and, 281–287
  loving one's enemy and, 254–255
  obedience to, 77, 242
  Sabbath and, 297–298, 302
  Sinai, 227, 279–280
  violations of, 163, 228, 302
  wilderness time and, 103
  will of God and, 271–308